P9-BHS-513

THE LETTERS OF

ROBERT FROST

VOLUME I

THE LETTERS OF
ROBERT FROST

VOLUME I · 1886–1920

LIBRARY OF
CONGRESS
SURPLUS
DUPLICATE

EDITED BY
Donald Sheehy
Mark Richardson
Robert Faggen

THE BELKNAP PRESS OF HARVARD UNIVERSITY PRESS
Cambridge, Massachusetts
London, England
2014

Copyright © 2014 by the Estate of Robert Lee Frost

Certain letters contained in this volume have previously been published in *Selected Letters of Robert Frost,* copyright © 1964 by Lawrence Thompson, Holt, Rinehart and Winston, Inc. and the Estate of Robert Lee Frost, and *The Letters of Robert Frost to Louis Untermeyer,* copyright © 1963 by Louis Untermeyer and the Estate of Robert Lee Frost.

All rights reserved
Printed in the United States of America

Library of Congress Cataloging-in-Publication Data
Frost, Robert, 1874–1963.
[Correspondence]
The letters of Robert Frost / edited by Donald Sheehy, Mark Richardson, and Robert Faggen.
v. cm
Includes bibliographical references and indexes.
Contents: Volume 1. 1886–1920
ISBN 978-0-674-05760-9 (v. 1)
1. Frost, Robert, 1874–1963—Correspondence. 2. Poets, American—20th century—Correspondence. I. Sheehy, Donald Gerard. II. Richardson, Mark, 1963– III. Faggen, Robert. IV. Title.
PS3511.R94Z48 2014
811'.52—dc23
[B]

2013015203

Contents

Preface

Fifty years have passed between the appearance in 1964 of the *Selected Letters of Robert Frost* and the publication of this first volume of a four-volume scholarly edition of the *Letters of Robert Frost*. Following upon the publication of Harvard University Press scholarly editions of Frost's *Collected Prose* (2007) and his *Notebooks* (2006), and in anticipation of a scholarly edition of the complete poems, the *Letters of Robert Frost* advances significantly the process of bringing all Frost primary material into accessible print. A complete scholarly edition of an author's oeuvre is, of course, more than a welcome convenience; it is a confirmation of sorts, of realized stature and lasting influence, of continuing relevance. Such acknowledgment of Robert Frost has long been overdue.

In the half-century since his death in January of 1963, Frost's critical reputation—though not his popular appeal—has fluctuated, falling precipitously during the 1970s and 1980s under the weight of his unfashionably formal poetics and his perceived social conservatism. Derided for the "simplicity" of his language, his use of traditional forms, and his rural/pastoral subject matter, he was characterized as a latter-day "fireside poet" and largely ignored by academic critics and theorists. Fewer than a dozen scholarly books on Frost were published between 1965 and 1990, but among them were a few—by Frank Lentricchia (1975), Richard Poirier (1977), and John C. Kemp (1979)[1]—that would, through their treatment of Frost as a distinctly modern and philosophically sophisticated poet, lay the groundwork for a renewal of Frost scholarship in the decades that followed. Today, academic study of Frost flourishes, a revival of formal poetry has brought new attention to his poetics, and his claim to prominence in the canons of modern poetry and American literature is undisputed.

For reasons different, but not unrelated, Frost biography has followed a similar trajectory. In his last years, Frost had become an American icon, the

1. Lentricchia, *Robert Frost: Modern Poetics and the Landscapes of Self* (Durham: Duke University Press, 1975); Poirier, *Robert Frost: The Work of Knowing* (New York: Oxford University Press, 1977); Kemp, *Robert Frost and New England: The Poet as Regionalist* (Princeton: Princeton University Press, 1979).

wise and witty New England bard, the beloved figure of the poet as ordinary man. As accolades, honors, and magazine covers accumulated, his name became synonymous with "poet" for millions of Americans whose acquaintance with poetry outside of school was occasional and ceremonial at most, but who could nonetheless summon "Stopping by Woods," "The Road Not Taken," or "Birches" as evidence that "real" poetry still existed. Through countless newspaper features, interviews, and reminiscences, a popular hagiography had taken shape and was reinforced by the subtler idealizations of such works as Sidney Cox's character portrait, *A Swinger of Birches* (1957), and Elizabeth Sergeant's biography, *The Trial by Existence* (1960).[2]

In September 1964, as part of their "Junior Research" series, Prentice-Hall issued Doris Faber's *Robert Frost: America's Poet*, but the exemplary life outlined there for students had already been debunked and discredited. A month earlier, Henry Holt and Company had published Lawrance Thompson's edition of the *Selected Letters*, in the introduction to which Thompson had lodged his brief against Frost in the court of public opinion.[3] Even at this remove, the indictment is startling:

> Those who knew the poet largely from his poetry and his public appearances—and who take pleasure in remembering the evidence of his affirmations, encouragements, cherishings, tenderness, humor, wit, playfulness, and joviality—may not be prepared to see how often his private correspondence reveals periods of gloom, jealousies, obsessive resentments, sulking, displays of temper, nervous rages, and vindictive retaliations. Partly because he lacked confidence in himself, he suspected the presence of enemies everywhere, and he frequently indulged his passion for hurting even those he loved. (*SL*, viii–ix)

In *Robert Frost: The Early Years* (1966) and *Robert Frost: The Years of Triumph* (1970), the two volumes of the official biography that he lived to complete, Thompson deployed an enormous body of documentary evidence gathered over twenty-five years of research in the service of an interpretive agenda

2. Sidney Cox, *A Swinger of Birches: A Portrait of Robert Frost* (New York: New York University Press, 1957); Elizabeth S. Sergeant, *Robert Frost: The Trial by Existence* (New York: Holt, Rinehart and Winston, 1960).

3. Robert Frost and Lawrance Thompson, *Selected Letters of Robert Frost* (New York: Holt, Rinehart and Winston, 1964).

that the evidence simply does not support. The biography thus combines an invaluable record of events and circumstances in Frost's life with a thoroughly unreliable assessment of its inner workings. Unfortunately, though perhaps inevitably, the sheer accumulation of information lent weight and credibility to the psychoanalytic speculations imposed upon it. If one adds to this the "official" status of the biographer—his friendship with, and many years of privileged access to, his subject—it is not hard to see why many reviewers and readers found Thompson's portrayal as persuasive as it was disheartening. As is always the case with belated revelations of private defects in admirable public lives, the worst was assumed to be necessarily true and all shortcomings were magnified by virtue of having been deceptively "masked." Thus, the figure of Frost as ordinary man was displaced by Frost as extraordinary "monster."[4] Over time, even in the awareness of those who had no specific knowledge of Thompson's biography, the perception of Frost came to be shadowed always by this dark doppelgänger.

In 1984, with the publication of William Pritchard's eloquently sensible reconsideration of the poet's literary life, efforts to revisit and revise Thompson's version of Frost gathered momentum. Memoirs attesting to their authors' diverse experiences of Frost continued to appear.[5] In *Robert Frost Himself* (1986), Stanley Burnshaw recalled his years at Holt and his friendship with Frost in order to dispute Thompson directly, while others, such as John Evangelist Walsh (1988) and Lesley Lee Francis (1994), offered reassessments focused on particular periods in Frost's life.[6] Two new full-length biographies

---

4. In a review of *Robert Frost: The Years of Triumph,* Helen Vendler famously called Frost a "monster of egotism" who left "behind him a wake of destroyed human lives." See her "Robert Frost: A Disastrous Life," *New York Times Book Review* (August 9, 1970).

5. William H. Pritchard, *Frost: A Literary Life Reconsidered* (New York: Oxford University Press, 1984). A non-exhaustive list of memoirs would include those by Henry Dierkes, Robert Francis, Jack W. C. Hagstrom, Louis Mertins, Kathleen Morrison, Helen Muir, Victor Reichart, J. A. Robbins, Hugo Saglio, Daniel Smythe, Peter Stanlis, Wade Van Dore, and Louis Untermeyer.

6. Stanley Burnshaw, *Robert Frost Himself* (New York: G. Braziller, 1986); Lesley L. Francis, *The Frost Family's Adventure in Poetry: Sheer Morning Gladness at the Brim* (Columbia: University of Missouri Press, 1994); John E. Walsh, *Into My Own: The English Years of Robert Frost, 1912–1915* (New York: Grove Press, 1988). See also, Donald G. Sheehy, "(Re)Figuring Love: Robert Frost in Crisis," *The New England Quarterly* 63, no. 2 (June 1990): 179–231; and "The Poet as Neurotic: The Official Biography of Robert Frost," *American Literature* 58, no. 3 (October 1986): 393–410.

appeared, though of distinctly different character.[7] In *Robert Frost: A Biography* (1996), Jeffrey Meyers attempted to outdo, rather than undo, Thompson. Basing much of his narrative on portions of Thompson's unpublished notes and supplementing them with questionable conclusions drawn from his own interviews with members of the poet's family, he focused particular attention on Frost's relationship in later life with Mrs. Kathleen Morrison. Blending popular biography with celebrity exposé, Meyers adds a frisky and self-deluded "bad boy" to Thompson's spiteful and neurotic "bad man."

Begun well before the publication of Meyers's biography, Jay Parini's *Robert Frost: A Life* (1999) restored both a seriousness of purpose and a judiciousness of interpretation to an examination of Frost's life and character. It also devoted substantial and enlightening attention to the poems, reading them in the context of the poet's experience without reducing them to biographical data. Despite these cardinal virtues, however, even the more appealing Frost of Parini's *Life* remains in the shadow of Thompson's, as will every new biographer's as long as Thompson's version of the structure of the life—its key events, relationships, priorities, and motivations—remains intact. Thompson's fingerprints are all over the evidence; he framed it. No matter how assiduously the deck is shuffled and dealt, we are still playing with Thompson's cards.

Another category of Frost scholarship, therefore, merits more serious consideration: the discovery and/or publication of additional primary documents. A rising generation of Frost scholars now enjoys ready access to a wealth of archival materials through the ongoing digitalization not only of manuscripts, rare printed matter, photographs, and audiovisual media, but also of library catalogs, collection inventories, and finding aids. New editions of Frost's lectures and readings continue to offer additional insight into the style and substance of his public engagement, and publication of his notebooks allows a closer look into his habits of thought, revealing at times the germination and development of ideas that would find expression as poems, lectures, essays.[8] Most valuable as resources for a renewed exploration of the poet's life, however, are his letters. When Arnold Grade's edition of the *Family Letters of*

---

7. Jeffrey Meyers, *Robert Frost: A Biography* (Boston: Houghton Mifflin, 1996); Jay Parini, *Robert Frost: A Life* (New York: Henry Holt, 1999).

8. *Robert Frost Speaking on Campus: Excerpts from His Talks, 1949–1962*, ed. Edward C. Lathem (New York: W.W. Norton and Co., 2009); *The Notebooks of Robert Frost*, ed. Robert Faggen (Cambridge: Harvard University Press, 2006).

Robert and Elinor Frost was published in 1972,[9] attentive readers had sufficient reason to reconsider the depiction of Frost's parenting in the official biography. Because Frost's letters to his children were published in a separate edition, however, as were his letters to Louis Untermeyer and others, only the most determined of readers could gather a sense of the totality of the available correspondence. With the publication of the *Letters of Robert Frost,* all the published letters and hundreds of letters previously unpublished are available to be read in the order they were written, in the context they provide for each other, and in the further contexts supplied by thorough annotation.

What the *Letters of Robert Frost* does not provide, and deliberately so, is an interpretive or evaluative framework. As he introduced his hastily assembled and un-annotated *Selected Letters,* Thompson offered an invitation to readers. "One purpose of the editor is to invite any thoughtful and imaginative reader to 'roll his own' biography of Robert Frost from these 'makings' prior to the appearance of any formal biographies of the poet, including one in preparation by the editor." To assist in that process, he included the following entries under "Frost, Robert Lee" in the index: "Badness," "Cowardice," "Enemies," "Fears," "Gossip," "Insanity," "Masks and Masking," "Profanity," "Resentments," and "Self-Indulgence." Absent are entries for goodness, bravery, friends, hopes, discretion, sanity, honesty, genuineness, gratitude, generosity, and restraint. Frost was to be "rolled," it was clear, in more ways than one. The editors of the *Letters of Robert Frost* have no biography of Frost in preparation, but we trust that the availability of the correspondence in its entirety will represent both an occasion and a means to come to know Robert Frost anew.

---

9. *Family Letters of Robert and Elinor Frost,* ed. Arnold E. Grade (Albany: State University of New York Press, 1972).

Abbreviations

ABW: *A Boy's Will*, Robert Frost (London: David Nutt, 1913).

ACL: Amherst College Library, Amherst, Massachusetts.

ALS: Autograph letter, signed.

Arkansas: University of Arkansas, Fayetteville, Arkansas.

Bates: Bates College, Edmund Muskie Archives and Special Collections.

Bowdoin: Bowdoin College, George. J. Mitchell Depart of Special Collections and Archives.

Brown: John Hay Library, Special Collections, Brown University, Providence, Rhode Island.

BU: Boston University, Howard Gotlieb Archival Research Center.

Cardiff: Cardiff University Library Archive, Cardiff, Wales.

Chicago: University of Chicago, Special Collections Research Center, Chicago, Illinois.

Columbia: Columbia University Libraries, New York.

CPPP: *Robert Frost: Collected Poetry, Prose and Plays*, ed. Richard Poirier and Mark Richardson. New York: Library of America, 1995.

CPRF: *The Collected Prose of Robert Frost*, ed. Mark Richardson. Cambridge, MA: Harvard University Press, 2007.

DCL: Dartmouth College Library, Hanover, New Hampshire.

EY: *Robert Frost: The Early Years, 1874–1915*, Lawrance Thompson. New York: Holt, Rinehart and Winston, 1970.

FL: *The Family Letters of Robert and Elinor Frost*, ed. Arnold Grade. Albany: State University of New York Press, 1972.

Gloucester: Gloucester Archives, United Kingdom.

Harvard: Harvard University Archives and Special Collections, Cambridge, Massachusetts.

Hopkins: Johns Hopkins University, Special Collections and Archives, Baltimore, Maryland.

HRC: Harry Ransom Center, University of Texas at Austin.

Huntington: Huntington Library, Pasadena, California.

Indiana: Indiana University, Ruth Lilly Special Collections and Archives, Bloomington, Indiana.

Jones: Jones Library, Amherst, Massachusetts.

LoC: Library of Congress, Washington, DC.

LY: Robert Frost: The Later Years, 1938–1963, Lawrance Thompson and R. H. Winnick. New York: Holt, Rinehart and Winston, 1966.

Mass. Hist.: Massachusetts Historical Society, Boston.

MI: Mountain Interval, Robert Frost. New York: Henry Holt, 1917.

Miami, Ohio: Miami University, Walter Havighurst Special Collections, Oxford, Ohio.

Middlebury: Middlebury College Libraries, Middlebury, Vermont.

Minnesota: University of Minnesota Archives, Elmer L. Andersen Library, Minneapolis, Minnesota.

NB: North of Boston, Robert Frost. London: David Nutt, 1914.

NBRF: The Notebooks of Robert Frost, ed. Robert Faggen. Cambridge: Harvard University Press, 2006.

Newberry: The Newberry Library, Chicago, Illinois.

NH: New Hampshire, Robert Frost. New York: Henry Holt, 1923.

NYPL: New York Public Library, New York.

NYU: Fales Library and Special Collections, New York University.

Penn: University of Pennsylvania, Rare Book and Manuscript Library, Philadelphia, Pennsylvania.

Plymouth: Plymouth State University, Lamson Library, Plymouth, New Hampshire.

Princeton: Princeton University, Firestone Library, Princeton, New Jersey.

RFJB: Robert Frost and John Bartlett: The Record of a Friendship, Margaret Bartlett Anderson. New York: Holt, Rinehart and Winston, 1963.

RFLU: *The Letters of Robert Frost to Louis Untermeyer*, ed. Louis Untermeyer. New York: Holt, Rinehart and Winston, 1963.

RFSC: *Robert Frost and Sidney Cox: Forty Years of Friendship*, ed. William R. Evans. Hanover, NH: University Press of New England, 1981.

Rollins: Rollins College, Olin Library, Winter Park, Florida.

SC Hist.: South Carolina Historical Society, Charleston, South Carolina.

SL: *Selected Letters of Robert Frost*, ed. Lawrance Thompson. New York: Henry Holt, 1964.

SLU: St. Louis University, Special Collections and Archives, St. Louis, Missouri.

Southern California: University of Southern California, Special Collections Department, Doheny Memorial Library, Los Angeles, California.

TG: Telegram.

TL: Typed letter.

TLS: Typed letter, signed.

Trinity: Trinity College, Watkinson Library, Hartford, Connecticut.

Tulsa: University of Tulsa, Special Collections and Archives, McFarlin Library, Tulsa, Oklahoma.

UFL: University of Florida, George A. Smathers Libraries, Gainesville.

UM: University of Michigan Library, Ann Arbor.

UNH: University of New Hampshire, Douglas and Helena Milne Special Collections & Archives, Durham, New Hampshire.

UVA: University of Virginia Library, Charlottesville.

Vassar: Vassar College, Catherine Pelton Durrell Archives and Special Collections Library, Poughkeepsie, New York.

Wellesley: Wellesley College, Special Collections, Margaret Clap Library, Wellesley, Massachusetts.

Wisc. Hist.: Wisconsin Historical Society, Madison.

Yale: Yale University, Beinecke Library, New Haven, Connecticut.

YT: *Robert Frost: The Years of Triumph, 1915–1938*, Lawrance Thompson. New York: Holt, Rinehart and Winston, 1970.

Editorial Principles

The Letters of Robert Frost, of which this volume is the first of four, is without precedent. Lawrance Thompson's *Selected Letters of Robert Frost* (1964) is what its name implies, or perhaps somewhat less than what its name implies, given how highly selective it is. *The Letters of Robert Frost to Louis Untermeyer* (1963) is complete insofar as letters to its recipient are concerned. Untermeyer, a friend of the poet from 1915 until his death in 1963, elicited some of the most remarkable letters Frost ever wrote. But Untermeyer edited them inconsistently, bowdlerized a few (out of concern for his friend's reputation), allowed scores of transcription errors into the volume, and neglected to supply an index. Better edited by far are William R. Evans's *Robert Frost and Sidney Cox: Forty Years of Friendship* and Arnold Grade's *The Family Letters of Robert and Elinor Frost.* And yet there, too, we find Frost in only two or three of the many epistolary positions and postures he would adopt, which varied with each recipient. Margaret Bartlett Anderson's *Robert Frost and John Bartlett: The Record of a Friendship* is indispensable. But the letters therein are often reproduced only in part, woven, as they are, into the record spoken of in the title.

All of these books have long since been out of print. The best a reader could do, until now, has been to open the five volumes just named on a desktop, moving from one to the other as the weeks, months, and years roll on, at least if he or she wanted a consecutive and relatively unbroken record of one of the most beguiling men of letters in American literature. And such perseverance would still leave a reader wanting because, indeed, hundreds of letters have never seen the light of day, even as they've lain in wait, most of them anyway, in the great archives of Frost's papers held at Dartmouth College, Amherst College, the University of Virginia, the Library of Congress, Boston University, and elsewhere.

The Letters of Robert Frost redresses these problems. As has been pointed out in the preface, all of the poet's letters of which we have a record—including 282 letters gathered here for the first time—are now presented in a single, uniform edition, consistently and fully annotated, and all with due fidelity to the manuscripts and typescripts from which they derive. The present volume alone is considerably more extensive than Thompson's *Selected*

Letters. Yet it ends with a letter written in early February 1920, forty-three years before Robert Frost died, having dictated his last letter to his secretary and amanuensis, Kathleen Morrison, from a bed at Peter Bent Brigham Hospital in Boston.[1]

In this edition we provide carefully verified transcripts of the letters, grounded in extensive work in archives of his literary manuscripts. The vast majority of Frost's hand-written letters, and nearly all of his typed ones, exist in a form more or less conventional to letter-writing of the period: date and location of writing in the upper-right corner of the first page; salutation below and flush left; body of the letter following in conventionally paragraphed form, with lineation determined by the size of the paper, and with text flowing from sheet to sheet, or, on pre-folded stationary, from first page to second page, and then to the back of the first page, and so on; and with a signature following the whole with a customary valediction ("Ever yours," etc.). When Frost adds a post-script he does that, too, in the usual way—that is, below the signature (though sometimes in the margins, if he has run out of space). In other words, the disposition of the text on the pages of Frost's manuscript and typescript letters is never a significant feature of their meaning. In view of this, we have produced not type facsimiles but clean transcripts of the let-

---

1. Thompson reprints a number of letters written by persons other than Frost (his mother, father, and sister; college and university administrators; and so on). We have decided not to print incoming correspondence, or letters written by anyone other than Frost himself (though on occasion we quote from such letters in annotations). The reason is practical. Were we to reprint even a sampling of incoming correspondence, the edition, already slated for four volumes, would swell to unmanageable proportions. For similar reasons we have chosen not to reprint enclosures, when these are not integral to a given letter (though we usually describe them). For example, we do not reproduce the annotated copy of *Poetry and Drama* that Frost sent in an envelope to John Bartlett in December 1913. Readers interested in Frost's annotations will find them reprinted as "letter" sixty-nine in Thompson (*SL*, 103–106). Their intrinsic interest notwithstanding, the annotations do not, for our purposes, constitute a letter. Of course, what constitutes a "letter" is not always easy to determine, given (to take only one example) Frost's habit of inscribing books in quasi-epistolary ways. We take, again, a practical approach: the letters here reprinted are, almost without exception, conventionally "epistolary" in nature, just as we have said. One thing more bears mentioning. Publication of the present edition may bring additional letters (not held in archives) to light. We intend to provide an appendix in volume four for any letters that come to our attention subsequent to the publication of volume one.

ters. We concentrate entirely on the *intended* content of the original. When Frost makes a correction in a letter, he typically does so by striking out a word and continuing, or by striking out a word or phrase and inserting a correction interlinearly. Our practice (unless special circumstances apply) is to produce the single text that any corrections present in the document plainly require. In other words, when Frost inserts, say, the conjunction "that" interlinearly, we simply produce the sentence as he intended it to read without the special markings (carets or arrows, for example) that he employed to make it read that way.

We have, within tightly defined limits, adopted a policy of silent correction. When Frost has unintentionally repeated a word (for example, when he carries a sentence over from one sheet to the next, or from the front of a sheet to the back), we have omitted the repetition. The manuscript of Frost's May 16, 1915 letter to Louis Untermeyer reads, in part: "Call your attention to the fact that the author of A Tuft of Flowers forestalled the cynic by having the mower mow the the reeds which are worse forage than the butterfly weed: item that it is the country custom to mow everything—the weeds to keep them from seeding." Rather than render this "having the mower mow the the [*sic*] reeds," we simply omit the second "the." When Frost opens a quotation and forgets to close it, we have supplied the necessary punctuation; we do the same when a parenthesis is opened but not closed, and when a period has inadvertently been dropped. On those rare occasions when Frost mistakenly writes "to" for "too," we also make a correction (this error is by no means characteristic of him). Frost very often omits commas in a series; we respect this as characteristic of the prose. However, in a few cases we supply a comma when its omission is not a consistent feature of Frost's writing. In a March 24, 1919, letter, he explains why he declined to serve as judge in a contest in which his daughter Lesley had entered a poem: "People would say it takes two Frosts, father and daughter to win one prize—that is if we won it." We supply a comma after "daughter."

Frost uses apostrophes inconsistently and haphazardly, often within a single sentence (where one may find both "don't" and "couldnt"). Editors of Frost's letters have long respected these inconsistencies and we do so here. We have also left untouched misspellings of words and proper names, supplying an explanatory note where the misspelling in question might lead to confusion. In addition, we have left unamended instances where Frost uses spaces where one might expect to find a comma, chiefly in dates. He prefers "May 16 1916" to "May 16, 1916," and we respect the preference.

Any time Frost's phrasing is unusual enough to occasion difficulty, or to allow for a doubt as to the fidelity of the transcription, we insert the marker "[*sic*]" to assure readers that the manuscript reads exactly as we have rendered it. For example, in a November 1, 1915, letter to Untermeyer, Frost writes: "I must know certain things to a certainty before I go me [*sic*] into the world next week to preach the gospel of sound, which is as you remember Take care of the sound and the sense will take care of itself." The "*sic*" here indicates that the reading is correct and involves an unusual deployment of a reflexive construction. In a December 19, 1915, letter to Harold Rugg we find "Potes [*sic*] as *are* Poets are what they are," where the sense is: "Potes [such] as *are* [really] Poets are what they are." "*Sic*" here signals not merely that the transcription is correct—"Potes" is no slip of the pen—but that the reader should be aware that Frost may (or may not) have fetched in an archaic word (in this case, perhaps, a word from Scottish dialect: "pote" for poker, or for a kick or a shove). We do not specify, in this case, what joke, if any, Frost may be making (indeed, it likely concerns nothing but pronunciation). But we want the reader to know that, the transcription being correct, she may draw what conclusions seem apt. Another example should suffice to explain our practices. The poet adds a postscript to a January 15, 1916, letter to Helena T. Goessman—an instructor in English at the Massachusetts Agricultural College (now the University of Massachusetts, Amherst)—written from Methuen, Massachusetts: "When you write about your success with the poems use my Franconia [*sic*]. I mean to get back there in time to freeze to death this winter." Here Frost is elliptical, meaning "use my Franconia address" rather than the address at the head of the letter (Methuen).

Another sort of editorial intervention proceeds as follows. On those few occasions when an accidentally omitted word might better be added as a marked correction, as against a silent one, we use brackets to indicate that we have made it. The following example illustrates the practice. In a February 10, 1912, letter to Susan Hayes Ward, Frost writes: "The Marion C. Smith you were talking of when I was with you I was very certain I had heard of somewhere, but I didn't know where. It must have [been] here. Heard of her? Yes it is almost as if I had met her in the pages of the Companion."[2] We sup-

2. Marion Couthouy Smith (1853–1931) was the author of, among other works, *The Electric Spirit and Other Poems* (Boston: R. G. Badger, 1906). Just before mentioning Smith,

ply "been" in brackets to ease readers through the sentence while keeping them aware that a change has been made.

Headnotes to the letters identify the recipient, and provide such information as the reader may need in order to understand the occasion for the letter (when the text of the letter doesn't make this clear). Headnotes also indicate, with an abbreviation, whether the letter is an autograph letter signed (ALS), or a typed letter signed (TLS), and so on, and then give the location of the archive now holding the manuscript (or the person, in the case of private collectors). A table provides a key to all abbreviations used in this edition, in addition to the ones just mentioned. When a letter has been dictated by Frost to someone else (to his daughter Lesley, for example), this, too, is indicated in the headnote. For the most part, we rely on footnotes to identify—when identification proved possible: in some cases it did not—persons, poems, and events alluded to or mentioned in the letters. Our purpose is to provide on each page, right alongside the letter, all information about it that a reader may want to know. Sometimes we repeat footnotes concerning persons already identified, when enough pages have passed since the last notation such that a reader might wish to have a reminder. Finally, we have provided a biographical glossary of all recipients, for ease of reference, and a detailed chronology covering Frost's life from his birth to the date of the last letter included in this volume.

The general aim is to produce a book that is readable consecutively. As various persons become involved in Frost's life as a writer of letters, either as the recipient or the subject of a letter, the reader will be made acquainted with them, so that at any given point in the volume, if a reader has been moving through it consecutively, he or she will have in mind everything required to read the letters with satisfaction and comprehension.

Of course, some readers will not read the volume from beginning to end. They will instead consult it looking for letters to specific persons, references to specific writers or events, or for discussion of particular topics (say, Frost's theory of "the sound of sense," his great contribution to twentieth-century poetics). Readers using the volume in this way will find a comprehensive index that will direct them not simply to names of recipients but also to important recurrent themes in the letters, to references made in the letters

---

Frost refers to a poem "in print," which he had enclosed with the letter. This is most likely "Ghost House," published in *The Youth's Companion* for March 15, 1906. Hence Frost's remark: "it must have [been] here" (i.e., in the pages of *The Companion*).

to other writers and historical figures, and to information contained within the headnotes and footnotes. The aforementioned biographical glossary of recipients, located at the back of the book, serves as a handy reminder for readers who dip in to the book at some point after a correspondent has been introduced.

THE LETTERS OF

ROBERT FROST

VOLUME 1

Robert Frost in 1916 at his desk in Franconia, New Hampshire, by Huntington of *The Boston Post*.

Courtesy Plymouth State University Library.

Introduction

If you grant me the friendly letter as end and aim it is all I ask: you grant me everything.

—Robert Frost (*NBRF*, 84)

On February 26, 1913, in an access of delight at seeing his first book, *A Boy's Will*, in proofs, Robert Frost wrote to John Bartlett. Bartlett had been his favorite student at Pinkerton Academy only four years earlier, where Bartlett was also captain of the football team Frost goaded on and cheered, and editor of the school's literary magazine, the *Pinkerton Critic*.[1] Frost wrote from the house he and his family had rented in Beaconsfield, a suburb of London, and which he inevitably (with due affection) called "the Bung Hole," short for "bungalow." "About now you are in receipt of my coverless book," Frost began. "Now you are reading it upside down in your excitement. What's the matter? You look pale. I see it all as true to life as in a melodrama. Your wife gathers around the table. The dog gets stepped on—the Indian Runner Dog. And Ruksh the dog utters a fearful cry. No canine cry is that, etc. It curdles the Annie Frazier River. A chair goes over":

"Wait," you say.
"Wait a minute!"
"Hold on!"
"Give me time!"

1. Bartlett also played Mephistopheles when RF staged Christopher Marlowe's *Faustus* at Pinkerton (along with Milton's *Comus*, Sheridan's *Rivals*, and two plays by William Butler Yeats). See *EY*, 360–363, and *CPRF*, 75–77.

"I tell you I can understand this if you give me time and don't hurry me!"

"In fact it isnt that I cant understand it."

"I can understand it all right"

"But I cant believe it."

"It is what I may call the startlingness of the intelligence."

"Suppose I were to telegraph you from Raymond or some other center where things happen and news is manufactured that Sir Peg a Ramsey had demonstrated on the zylophone that there was more radium than neon and helium than yes than in no."

"You would be excited, wouldn't you?"

"Come own up. Of course you'd be."

"It would make all the difference in the world."

"You'd feature it—you'd call attention to it in a leader."

"Well it's like that—only—what shall I say?"

"Only more serious, more momentous."

"So unlike poetry—except Masefield's."[2]

"If a man has anything he wants to break to us let him use prose—prose is his vehicle."

"Listen to this—it comes with too great a shock in verse."

"Get ready!"

"eurt saw thguoht I lla fo erus erom ylnO"

"It is too, too much."

And so you run on till Mrs Margaret interposes with a woman's good sense:

"Perhaps if you read it right side up it wouldn't mean so much."

"It might not mean anything."

Still I think you will treat the book kindly for my sake. It comes pretty near being the story of five years of my life. In the first poem I went away from people; in the one called A Tuft of Flowers I came back to them actually as well as verbally for I wrote that poem to get my job in Pinkerton as little Tommy Tucker sang for

2. English poet John Edward Masefield (1878–1967), whom RF met in London. RF likely has in mind Masefield's poem "Dauber," which concerns (to speak generally) the travails of the artist and the scorn he often endures before, at last, realizing his aspirations. We thank Mark Scott for the suggestion.

> his supper and Brer Merriam read it for me at a Men's League Banquet in Derry Village because I was too timid to read it myself.[3]

What was it like on the receiving end of this epistolary Roman candle, part narrative, part farce in miniature (with its scene-setting and dialogue), and all jeu d'esprit? Doubtless Bartlett got the joke about the "Indian Runner Dog." The Indian Runner is, in fact, a breed of duck, notable for walking upright, and at the quick step, instead of waddling. But can we assume he understood why Ruksh the dog's yelp is "no canine cry"?—assume, that is, that Bartlett recognizes Ruksh as a horse in Matthew Arnold's "Sohrab and Rustum"?

> *Then Sohrab with his sword smote Rustum's helm,*
> *Nor clove its steel quite through; but all the crest*
> *He shore away, and that proud horsehair plume,*
> *Never till now defiled, sank to the dust;*
> *And Rustum bow'd his head; but then the gloom*
> *Grew blacker, thunder rumbled in the air,*
> *And lightnings rent the cloud; and Ruksh, the horse,*
> *Who stood at hand, utter'd a dreadful cry;—*
> *No horse's cry was that, most like the roar*
> *Of some pain'd desert-lion, who all day*
> *Hath trail'd the hunter's javelin in his side,*
> *And comes at night to die upon the sand.*

Indeed, Bartlett did know the poem, or anyway ought to have. Frost assigned "Sohrab and Rustum" in his English classes at Pinkerton, along with Macaulay's "Horatius at the Bridge" (*CPRF*, 77), and the easy allusion to it here may tell us something about how he taught the poem to Bartlett. Had he singled out this passage in the 892-line narrative Arnold drew from an ancient Persian epic?[4] Whatever the case, Frost crosses up, in the letter, anatidaen, canine,

---

3. Charles L. Merriam (1855–1914), a Congregational minister in Derry, invited RF to read "The Tuft of Flowers" at the banquet mentioned, but the poet, in a bout of stage fright, asked Merriam to read it in his stead; the event was instrumental in securing RF a teaching position at Pinkerton Academy.

4. As a study in blank verse, say—a matter of considerable interest to RF when he taught at Pinkerton: he was already at work on several narratives in blank verse that would go into his second book, *North of Boston* (1914). Of course, as RF well knew, Arnold treats blank verse at length in *On Translating Homer*, in terms as apt to "Sohrab and

and equine categories—and confuses notionally real dogs with literary horses that sound like pained desert lions.

And he "curdles the Annie Frazier River." Bartlett knew the Fraser well, of course. The longest river in British Columbia, it flows into the Pacific at Vancouver, where John and his wife Margaret (duly given her role in the letter) then lived. Bartlett, like Frost's own father, had gone west to launch a career in journalism. So fond of the young man was Frost that, in 1912, he briefly considered joining the Bartletts rather than moving to London. But the *Annie Frazier* River? Turns out Bartlett knew that one well, too, though it runs east, not west, and would have carried him and Margaret back to Pinkerton again, in Derry, New Hampshire—likely to some familiar bit of gossip unavailable to anyone else (the letter is intimate in its play): Ann Frasier had been a student at the academy, two years Bartlett's junior, Class of 1911. She may also have been something of a character, as the allusion to her here suggests.[5]

But best of all is the joke that awaited Bartlett in this squib, playfully attributed to him: "Suppose I were to telegraph you from Raymond or some other center where things happen and news is manufactured that Sir Peg a Ramsey had demonstrated on the zylophone that there was more radium than neon and helium than yes than in no." Raymond, New Hampshire, population 1,203 in 1910, was hardly a "center where things happen," as Bartlett understood (it was his hometown). But did he recall that in *Twelfth Night* (2.iii) Sir Toby Belch declares (in a fit of bawdy) "My lady's a Cataian, we are politicians, Malvolio's a Peg-a-Ramsey, and 'Three merry men be we' "?[6] Prob-

---

Rustum" as to *The Odyssey* (also on Frost's syllabus at Pinkerton). Arnold refers us, for example, to "the most rapid passages of Shakespeare's plays—a blank verse which does not dovetail its lines into one another, and which habitually ends its lines with monosyllables" (London: Longman, Green, 1861): 75. For RF's remarks about his own experiments in blank verse, see his July 8, 1914, letter to John Cournos.

5. Ann Frasier Norton died in the influenza pandemic of 1918, a Yeowoman First Class, attached to the Naval Shipyard in Portsmouth, New Hampshire. She was the first woman accorded full military honors by the Armed Forces of the United States.

6. "Cataian," *archaic:* a native of Cathay; also, a scoundrel. "Peg-a-Ramsey" (aka "Peggy Ramsey") figured in a lewd song current in the 1590s. See also Burns's "Bonie Peg-a-Ramsay," probably derived from the same (which RF likely knew): "Ne'er sae murky blew the night / That drifted o'er the hill, / But bonie Peg-a-Ramsay / Gat grist to her mill." George Gebbie explains, in *The Complete Works of Robert Burns: Self-Interpreting* (Philadelphia, 1886): "The title of this snatch of song is very ancient, as we may infer

ably, given what he read with Frost at Pinkerton. Bartlett also would have known Sir *William* Ramsay, the Scottish chemist who discovered the so-called "noble gases" (among them neon and helium), for which discovery he was awarded the Nobel Prize in Chemistry in 1904. Maybe Frost dropped Ramsay's name in conversation at Pinkerton, and not simply because he had a lively interest in science: by 1908 *The Youth's Companion*, in which Frost placed four poems (two while teaching at Pinkerton), had published five of Ramsay's essays, including "Radium and Its Products"—all collected in Ramsay's *Essays Biographical and Chemical* (New York: E.P. Dutton, 1909).[7] As for "zylophone": who knows but that Frost bore in mind how Ramsay derived the names of the six "noble gases"—in addition to the two named already: argon, krypton, xenon, and radon—from Greek, which also gives us "xylo-phone"?

Anyway, Frost *himself* plays the xylophone in this letter, running up and down his scales: "eurt saw thguoht I lla fo erus erom ylnO," he writes, reversing the last line of the first poem in *A Boy's Will,* a sonnet titled "Into My Own." And with *A Boy's Will* he certainly had come into his own.

One of my wishes is that those dark trees,
So old and firm they scarcely show the breeze,
Were not, as 'twere, the merest mask of gloom,
But stretched away unto the edge of doom.
I should not be withheld but that some day
Into their vastness I should steal away,
Fearless of ever finding open land,
Or highway where the slow wheel pours the sand.

---

from its being quoted in *Twelfth Night*. Tom D'Urfey in his [*Wit and Mirth, or, Pills to Purge Melancholy* (1719–1720)], gives a rude version of the old song, in which we can scarcely find one verse that is decent enough to quote. The following may furnish some idea of it: 'Some do call her Peggy, and some do call her Jane, / And some do call her "Cross-ma-loof," but they are a' mistaen; / For Peggy is a sonsie lass that thrives by her mill; / And she is fullest occupied, when men are standing still. / With a hey trolodel, hey trolodel, merry goes the mill'" (vol. 6: 57).

7. RF had read *The Youth's Companion* since 1890, when, in response to an advertisement in the magazine, he sold subscriptions in a successful bid to win a telescope. See *EY*, 92. When RF was at Pinkerton *The Companion* had more than half a million subscribers; William Cullen Bryant, Mark Twain, William James, William Dean Howells, Thomas Huxley, Jack London, Booker T. Washington, and Emily Dickinson (among others) had all appeared in its pages.

I do not see why I should e'er turn back,
Or those should not set forth upon my track
To overtake me, who should miss me here
And long to know if still I held them dear.
They would not find me changed from him they knew—
Only more sure of all I thought was true.

Any close reader of the poem sees the play here. We needn't recall Frost's mischievous quotation of it in a wild letter to John Bartlett to be reminded of that. Of course the woods do *not* stretch away "unto" the Shakespearean "edge of doom" (Frost borrows the phrase from sonnet 116). These woods are the "merest mask" of a gloomy "vastness" evoked by a "youth" speaking from the pages of a book called *A Boy's Will.* (Frost so designates the speaker of the poems in glosses attached to the table of contents in the first edition of the book, the one John Bartlett held in his hands as the chair turned over and the dog whinnied like a desert lion.) Easy enough, too, to speak of stealing away, "fearless of ever finding open land," when all one does is speak of it. Self-congratulation for a deed not done, or for a deed "done" only in (highly literary) prospect, borders on the risible. Frost's claim that poems are words become deeds is only partly true (he knew better).[8]

Anyhow, we have to do with "a *boy's* will." We mustn't hear these lines as spoken in propria persona. What pride-stung boy hasn't told us how much we'll miss him when he's gone? Really, the poem "holds dear" what it doesn't ever forsake. Forsaking those he holds dear is only "*one* of [the] wishes" this willful boy entertains anyway. No one need "overtake" him to make some pledge of undying allegiance, precisely because he never leaves. His extravagance is pretty well contained. Extravagance always is with Frost, who knew how, in singing, not to sing. He brackets off this youthful cri de couer (if that's what "Into My Own" is) with wit, and with narrative fancy. We must bear in mind (again) the qualifying fact that a "youth" speaks in "Into My Own," not the thirty-nine-year-old father of four who collected it in a slim volume published in London, and who now appropriates his own poem for epistolary purposes that include instruction in how *A Boy's Will* is to be read:

8. "Sometimes I have my doubts of words altogether, and I ask myself what is the place of them. They are worse than nothing unless they do something; unless they amount to deeds, as in ultimatums or battle-cries. They must be flat and final like the show-down in poker, from which there is no appeal. My definition of poetry (if I were forced to give one) would be this: words that have become deeds" (*CPPP*, 701).

"It comes pretty near being the story of five years of my life. In the first poem I went away from people; in the one called A Tuft of Flowers I came back to them actually as well as verbally."

But what extravagance, what vagaries, we find in the letter to Bartlett, who had gone west to come into *his* own. Frost sets the quarterback-turned-journalist to reading backward, the better to say to him: *Actually, yes, you bet I'm only more sure of all I thought was true, even as long ago as 1894.* On the occasion of his first publication in a professional journal, the *Independent* (in New York), Frost made a startling confession to Susan Hayes Ward, literary editor of the journal, in a letter dated April 22, 1894: "Such an one am I that even in my failures I find all the promise I require to justify the astonishing magnitude of my ambition." This on the strength of one poem, "My Butterfly: An Elegy," and the fifteen dollars it earned him. Bartlett would find the poem again in the pages of *A Boy's Will* Frost sent for his perusal. That's a nice rounding out. Nearly twenty years had passed since Frost first lodged in print something of what would become the book that gave him entrée into the literary scene in London that makes up so much of the matter of the letters he would send to Bartlett as 1913 unfolded. Read it right to left, as in the letter to Bartlett, and "Into My Own" is exactly what it appears *not* to be when read left to right: the promise of a deed duly undertaken and fulfilled.

This letter is all sorts of fun, in its sheer wherewithal, but not only fun. Something of the tender regard Frost had for John Bartlett shows in it. Whom should he send unbound sheets of his first book to but a man barely out of high school and by no means established in his trade? Bartlett could hardly "feature" the new book yet, or "call attention to it in a leader," though he would, at the poet's instigation, pen articles on Frost for dispatch to local papers back in New Hampshire.[9] With Bartlett Frost could allow his pleasure free rein, tickle the xylophone, and trust that whatever he neglected to say might go without saying. True, the note of importunity one sometimes hears in the letters to his younger friend makes one wonder, occasionally, how fully Bartlett requited Frost's affection. But that the affection was

9. RF would later regret having asked Bartlett to do this. "Never you let that silly business of remembering me to my Derry friends put any strain on your feeling for me," he wrote in early November 1913. "I keep not hearing from you; and I begin to be afraid I have asked you to do more than you could do or wanted to do. Very likely you didn't like the idea of stirring 'em up in our old haunts. I don't know that I blame you. It was just my impulse."

deep and ingenuous is beyond dispute. Scores of letters gathered here—to Bartlett, to Jack Haines, to Edward Thomas, to Louis Untermeyer, to George Whicher, to Charles Lowell Young, to Susan Hayes Ward, to Sidney Hayes Cox, to Morris Tilley, to Harriet Moody and others—show how various and important his friendships were. Nearly every one of these letters is striking, touched by startling intelligence, and, as often as not, by the highest sort of play—play that transcends itself. Frost was, as he liked to say, never more serious than when fooling.

Frost may have sent one of the earliest review copies of *A Boy's Will* to the former star of the football team at a small New England prep school, but he also set about quickly enough to place his book where it mattered, as the letters collected here attest. Frost didn't miss a trick. Whatever else his letters are, they are a means to secure not just an audience, but the right *kind* of audience. Nothing came easier to Frost than telling people how, and how not, to read him. He does as much, as we have seen, in the letter to Bartlett: *A Boy's Will*, Frost says, "comes pretty near being the story of five years of my life," and so on. Bartlett would have been able to place those years precisely: from 1900, when Frost started farming in Derry, New Hampshire, through about 1906, when, indeed, he gave up farming and joined the faculty at Pinkerton Academy—and of course met John Bartlett, who now had in hand a "story" in lyric poetry as to how it all came about.

Heading up a letter "Fourth-of-July 1913," Frost declared his literary independence, again to Bartlett—and again with intimations as to how he *ought* to be read:

> To be perfectly frank with you I am one of the most notable craftsmen of my time. That will transpire presently [i.e., when *North of Boston* appears]. I am possibly the only person going who works on any but a worn out theory of versification. You see the great successes in recent poetry have been made on the assumption that the music of words was a matter of harmonized vowels and consonants. Both Swinburne and Tennyson aimed largely at effects in assonation. But they were on the wrong track or at any rate on a short track. They went the length of it. Anyone else who goes that way must go after them. And that's where most are going. I alone of English writers have consciously set myself to make music out of what I may call the sound of sense.

Friendship allows for liberties. Bragging isn't really "bragging" when it's so manifestly a *performed* thing. There's a twinkle in the letter, forgivable in a poet who waited two decades to make his mark. But the astonishing sense of ambition realized, and of confidence more than warranted, is certainly there to be found in letters to friends and acquaintances in England, and to established literary figures back in the United States.

In July 1914 Frost wrote to his friend Jack Haines, a barrister who lived near him in Gloucester, about a recent review of *North of Boston:*

> Thank you for the review—Abercrombie's work as your wife thought. I liked it very well. The discussion of my technique wouldn't have been what it was if Abercrombie had had nothing to go on but the book. He took advantage of certain conversations in which I gave him the key to my method and most of his catchwords. "Method" is the wrong word to call it: I simply use certain principles on which I accept or reject my own work. It was a generous review to consider me in all ways so seriously and as I say I liked it.

Lascelles Abercrombie's work—just as Haines's wife had thought. Only not entirely Abercrombie's work: he "took advantage" of "certain conversations" in which Frost gave him "the key" to his method and "most of his catchwords." Took *advantage* of certain conversations? His *catchwords* aren't even his own? The letter has about it a certain hauteur. Another sort of writer (say, Thornton Wilder) might have said: "Abercrombie's discussion of my technique, truth be told, might not have been what it is if he, like most readers, had to rely on the book alone. I may as well confess I coached him." But then, why would Frost point the fact out in the first place? He might have let the credit lie right there with Abercrombie. It is as if Frost would steal the thunder with which a friend was booming his own book. Wouldn't it have been best to allow Haines (and anyone he might be talking to) to assume that Abercrombie had arrived at his assessment of Frost's second book from its pages and nowhere else? Frost may have lived with the Georgian poets. But he also remained literarily aloof, keeping his extrication.

If the poet seems a bit petty here, we should bear in mind how much of an "interest" (in every sense of the word) he took in ordering his collections of poems; in when and how they were published; in the little groups of poems he placed in periodicals to herald their advent; in who would illustrate them (if they were to be illustrated); and even—as his relationship to his American publisher, Henry Holt and Company, matured—in who would design the special "limited editions" that accompanied regular trade editions of his books. Letters gathered here to Alfred Harcourt, Lincoln MacVeagh, and other men and women associated with Henry Holt and Company show how Frost had a hand not simply in shaping critical opinion but in fashioning the very look of his books.

A great many letters in the present volume reveal yet another side of his enterprise in poetry: the creation, cultivation, and expansion of his audience by means of the lecture platform, where he would talk about poetics and read his poetry, largely before audiences at colleges and universities (but before civic clubs of one sort or another, too). At first he was paid $50 a night for his presence, but pretty soon he was getting $75 to $100. By September 1921, eighteen months after writing the last letter herein, we find Frost taking up what was, at the time, almost unheard of: a position as Fellow in the Creative Arts, with a stipend of $5,000, at the University of Michigan.[10] Readers interested in the business side of books will also find, in subsequent volumes, letters written in Frost's capacity as a paid consultant to Henry Holt and Company (from late 1920 on).

Let the letter to Haines strike readers now as it may, but there is this to be said of it (and of a good many others dating from the same period): Frost was as careful to distinguish his enterprise in poetry as any writer then going. He knew what he was up to, and wanted to win readers (and book buyers) who knew it too. And why not? It was (and still is) easy enough to miss the subtle genius of his first two books. Frost says as much in a July 17, 1913, letter to the American publisher and bibliophile Thomas Mosher, who had wanted *A Boy's Will* for his own Lyric Garland series:

> I am made too self-conscious by the comment on my first book to think of showing another like it for some time. If I write more lyrics it must be with no thought of publication. What I *can* do next is bring out a volume of blank verse that I have already well in hand and won't have to feel I am writing to order. I had some character strokes I had to get in somewhere and I chose a sort of eclogue form for them. Rather I dropped into that form. And I dropped to an everyday level of diction that even Wordsworth kept above.

10. The equivalent, now, of some $65,000.

> I trust I don't terrify you. I think I have made poetry. The language is appropriate to the virtues I celebrate. At least I am sure I can count on you to give me credit for knowing what I am about. You are not going to make the mistake that Pound makes of assuming that my simplicity is that of the untutored child. I am not undesigning.

The great desiderata: never write to order and always be self-aware. Successful books bring audiences about, and an audience can spoil a poet if he lets it get out in front of him in the wrong way. Many of the letters Frost wrote from 1913 through 1916 are meant to keep that fate from befalling him. Not that he always succeeded. As the 1920s unfolded, his sheer popularity, and the stage persona he had developed in scores of readings and talks, earned him condescension from certain quarters, where Pound and Eliot were held in awe, and where Frost was routinely mistaken in his "simplicity" (as he phrases it in the letter to Mosher).

Once Eliot published *The Waste Land* in 1922, the problem may well have been that Frost *didn't* terrify most of his readers—at least until Lionel Trilling gave him his modernist imprimatur in 1959.[11] Uncanny that Frost should have anticipated such difficulties from the get-go in 1913, when no one knew what a "modernist" was. As the letter to Mosher indicates, he took the "old-fashioned way to be new" (as he would later phrase it in an introduction to E. A. Robinson's 1935 volume *King Jasper* [*CPRF*, 116]). Modern he certainly was, and hardly "undesigning." Every poet worth his salt had "designs" on the art in 1913: imagists, vorticists, Georgians (Frost had his encounters with them all, while in England). But Frost un-anxiously took up where Wordsworth left off. He attached no special merit, as Pound did, to breaking the pentameter line. Instead, he "made poetry" not incompatible with what he found in Arthur Quiller-Couch's two great anthologies, *The Oxford Book of English Verse* and *The Oxford Book of Victorian Verse;* but poetry not altogether like what he found there either. The letters collected here show us a poet perfectly at ease with tradition and perfectly aware of what, with his "individual talent," as Eliot would say, he had set about to do to tradition.

Frost wrote to John Cournos on July 27, 1914, shortly after *North of Boston* appeared:

---

11. For an account of Trilling's speech, delivered at the poet's eighty-fifth birthday dinner, see *LY*, 267–278.

> I have got you the book and I meant to have before this copies of the Bookman and Pell Mell [*Pall Mall Gazette*] reviews. I will send them along as soon as they come. You have The Outlook. If not, say so, and I will send it. Here are The Times and Nation reviews with passages marked as of interest to me.
>
> One thing to notice is that but one poem in the book will intone and that is "After Apple Picking." The rest talk.

No, Frost didn't mind telling people what to "notice" (or sending them reviews—a few of which he had cultivated, so to speak—to help them to it). In a March 22, 1915, letter, written six weeks after his return to America, he schools the literary editor of the *Boston Evening Transcript* (William Stanley Braithwaite) in how to take him:

> Ive got as far as finding you the copy of Book I I promised you. Perhaps as a busy man you wont resent my telling you what to read in it if you are going to read at all. It is the list I always give to friends I wish the minimum of suffering: pages 1, 2, 4, 7, 9, 14, 20, 22, 23, 25, 26, 34, 41, 42 (once printed in The Transcript) 45, 46 (8–18 line [*sic*]—first poetry I ever wrote that I could call my own—year 1892) and 49. Don't read those unless you have to, but don't read the others on any account.
>
> The book is an expression of my life for the ten years from eighteen on when I thought I greatly preferred stocks and stones to people. The poems were written as I lived the life quite at the mercy of myself and not always happy. The arrangement in a book came much later when I could look back on the past with something like understanding.
>
> I kept farm, so to speak for nearly ten years, but less as a farmer than as a fugitive from the world that seemed to me to "disallow" me. It was all instinctive, but I can see now that I went away to save myself and fix myself before I measured my strength against all creation. I was never really out of the world for good and all. I liked people even when I believed I detested them.
>
> It would seem absurd to say it (and you mustn't quote me as saying it) but I suppose the fact is that my conscious interest in people was at first no more than an almost technical interest in their speech—in what I used to call their sentence sounds—the sound

of sense. Whatever these sounds are or aren't (they are certainly not of the vowels and consonants of words nor even of the words themselves but something the words are chiefly a kind of notation for indicating and fastening to the printed page) whatever they are, I say, I began to hang on them very young. I was under twenty when I deliberately put it to myself one night after good conversation that there are moments when we actually touch in talk what the best writing can only come near. The curse of our book language is not so much that it keeps forever to the same set phrases (though Heaven knows those are bad enough) but that it sounds forever with the same reading tones. We must go out into the vernacular for tones that havent been brought to book. We must write with the ear on the speaking voice. We must imagine the speaking voice.

I say all this biographically to lead up to Book II (North of Boston). There came a day about ten years ago when I made the discovery that though sequestered I wasnt living without reference to other people. Right on top of that I made the discovery in doing The Death of the Hired Man that I was interested in neighbors for more than merely their tones of speech—and always had been. I remember about when I began to suspect myself of liking their gossip for its own sake. I justified myself by the example of Napoleon as recently I have had to justify myself in seasickness by the example of Nelson.

I like the actuality of gossip, the intimacy of it. Say what you will effects of actuality and intimacy are the greatest aim an artist can have. The sense of intimacy gives the thrill of sincerity. A story must always release a meaning more readily to those who read than life itself as it goes ever releases meaning. Meaning is a great consideration. But a story must never seem to be told primarily for meaning. Anything, an inspired irrelevancy even to make it sound as if told the way it is chiefly because it happened that way.

I have run on unpardonably. I couldnt write a whole biography; so I just had to plunge into the middle of things. I have pretty well jumbled the story of how I see my own development and some of my theories of art. You are not going to use anything directly, I take it. You will be sure to veil what is too personal. This isn't quite

> the same as an interview. I have met you and now we are getting further in getting acquainted.
>
> Ask me for anything I don't think to supply for your newspaper article.[12]

Reading this letter one cannot help but recall Frost's indignation on learning that Ezra Pound had assisted Frank S. Flint in a review published in Harold Monro's *Poetry and Drama,* as here, in a letter written on June 24, 1913:

> Worse and more of it. He had a finger in the writing of his own review, did he? Damn his eyes! An arrivist from the word go.[13] He has something to show us there. But I'm blessed if I came all the way to London to be coached in art by the likes of him. He can't teach me anything I really care to know.

Whether Flint's reply set Frost back on his heels isn't clear: "We mustn't be too hard on E.P. I *asked* him to help me write that review (1) because I didn't know what to say about the book and (2) because I thought he had been treated badly by the *Poetry Review* and that this might be some measure of reparation!"[14]

Frost's letter to Braithwaite more than fulfills condition (1), as laid out by Flint: the literary editor of the *Boston Evening Transcript* would not find himself at a loss as to what to say about *A Boy's Will* and *North of Boston.* But, as Richard Poirier pointed out some decades ago, when Frost undertakes to have a hand (so to speak) in his own reviews, or when he rates himself and his career to people in a position to speak for him in venues where things matter, he almost invariably strikes a tone that signals (or forthrightly

---

12. Braithwaite's "A Poet of New England: Robert Frost, A New Exponent of Life" appeared in the *Boston Evening Transcript* on April 28, 1915 (part 3: page 4).

13. In a June 23 letter to RF, Flint had written: "I think over all we said yesterday. I am very angry about E.P. [Pound]. Somehow or other words have not been so obedient to me of late as they were of yore; but my ability to feel and understand is fresh as ever; and there is much that I feel and understand in the E.P. case that sickens. I admit now and avow now that I had always lurking doubts about E.P. You will find evidence thereof (all my writings betray me) in what I have said about his books in the *New Age* and *The Poetry Review.* Not in the review in *Poetry & Drama,* for the reason that Pound and I wrote that together. (This is a secret!) But I have always hated and loathed insincerity hypocrisy and *arrivisme*" (letter held now at DCL).

14. This letter is held now at DCL.

points out) that he is well aware of his own calculations.[15] As here, in a May 6, 1916, letter to the anthologist, poet, and critic Louis Untermeyer (a champion and lifelong friend of Frost):

> I am going to tell you something I never but once let out of the bag before and that was just after I reached London and before I had begun to value myself for what I was worth.* It is a very damaging secret and you may not thank me for taking you into it when I tell you that I have often wished I could be sure that the other sharer of it had perished in the war. It is this. The poet in me died nearly ten years ago. Fortunately he had run through several phases, four to be exact, all well-defined, before he went. The calf I was in the nineties I merely take to market. I am become my own salesman. Two of my phases you have been so what shall I say as to like. Take care that you don't get your mouth set to declare the other two (as I release them) a falling off of power, for that is what they cant be whatever else they may be, since they were almost inextricably mixed with the first two in the writing and only my sagacity has separated or sorted them in the afterthought for putting on the market. Did you ever hear of quite such a case of Scotch-Yankee calculation?
>
> *Toop [i.e., tuppence]

Well, it certainly *would* be hard to come up with a better case of Scotch-Yankee calculation than the letter to Braithwaite just quoted above. The most striking thing about it is not the aplomb with which Frost engages in occasional self-deprecation but the idea that he thought he could bring such a thing off to begin with—that Braithwaite and everyone else wouldn't "see him coming," as he phrases it in another letter to Mosher. The sense of self-mastery is utterly unabashed and so (a bit paradoxically) quite winning: "Perhaps as a busy man you wont resent my telling you what to read in it if you are going to read at all. It is the list I always give to friends I wish the minimum of suffering: pages 1, 2, 4, 7, 9, 14, 20, 22, 23, 25, 26, 34, 41, 42 (once printed in The Transcript) 45, 46 (8–18 line [*sic*]—first poetry I ever wrote that I could call my own—year 1892) and 49. Don't read those unless you have to, but

15. See Poirier, *Robert Frost: The Work of Knowing* (New York: Oxford University Press, 1977): 50.

don't read the others on any account." Frost herewith enlists Braithwaite into a kind of co-conspiracy: *You see the flattery and self-deprecation I indulge in here for what they are. We're both in on the joke.* The result is that a letter that seems condescending may not condescend at all.[16] *You're a busy man—we both are; and the poetry business is a business like any other. There's always the market to worry about. We know that, don't we?* Typical that Frost should tell Braithwaite flat out what he is up to, and what he has just done with and in this letter; typical that he should point out also what Braithwaite should—no, *will*—do with it: "I have run on unpardonably. I couldnt write a whole biography; so I just had to plunge into the middle of things. I have pretty well jumbled the story of how I see my own development and some of my theories of art. You are not going to use anything directly, I take it. You will be sure to veil what is too personal. This isn't quite the same as an interview. I have met you and now we are getting further in getting acquainted. Ask me for anything I don't think to supply for your newspaper article." Which newspaper article duly appeared, following the outlines Frost laid out as well as a poet might have hoped. "He had a finger in the writing of his own review, did he? Damn his eyes! An arrivist from the word go." But, no. Frost was never an arriviste. He had waited twenty years to "arrive" and he did it only when, as he whimsically suggests to Untermeyer, he was quite ready to stand and unfold himself in "four" "well-defined" "phases." As he mock-exclaims later in the same letter: "Great effect of strength and mastery!" Frost may *say* that the "strength" and "mastery" are only "effects," but he also intimates that they are, perhaps, quite real. He usually hedges the larger claims he makes for himself and his art with wit and irony.

But what of the following remarks in that remarkable letter to Braithwaite?

> I say all this biographically to lead up to Book II (North of Boston). There came a day about ten years ago when I made the discovery that though sequestered I wasn't living without reference to other people. Right on top of that I made the discovery in doing The Death of the Hired Man that I was interested in neighbors for

16. One must bear in mind, however, that in letters to Louis Untermeyer and others, RF is, on more than one occasion, much worse than condescending in remarks made about Braithwaite. Indeed, about Braithwaite RF could be insulting in the extreme.

> more than merely their tones of speech—and always had been. I remember about when I began to suspect myself of liking their gossip for its own sake. I justified myself by the example of Napoleon as recently I have had to justify myself in seasickness by the example of Nelson. I like the actuality of gossip, the intimacy of it. Say what you will effects of actuality and intimacy are the greatest aim an artist can have.

The allusion to Napoleon is cunning in the way Frost's allusions often are in the letters, given how playfully he mocks his own youthful pose of misanthropy, given the merely instrumental relation he purports to have entertained to his neighbors as a literary artist, and given his Napoleonic ambition to "measure his strength," as he says in the letter, "against all creation." Frost likely has in mind Emerson's essay on Napoleon in *Representative Men,* and we would do well to take a brief look at it here, if only because the essay associates Napoleon's interest in gossip with all sorts of behaviors (manipulative, ambitious, secretive) that Frost comically adopts in the letter to Braithwaite—and winks at even as he adopts them. "Bonaparte was singularly destitute of generous sentiments," Emerson says. "He is a boundless liar. The official paper, his 'Moniteurs,' and all his bulletins, are proverbs for saying what he wished to be believed." In addition to everything else he is attempting to do in the letter before us here, Frost enlists the literary pages of the *Boston Evening Transcript* to propagate what he "wished to be believed" about him and his first two volumes of poetry. If ever a poet wrote with the "theatrical éclat" Emerson ascribes to Napoleon, Frost does in the letter to Braithwaite—and does so precisely with a roguishly charming allusion to Napoleon.

But there is still more of interest in that essay from *Representative Men:* "[Napoleon] has a passion for stage effect," Emerson says.

> Every action that breathes of generosity is poisoned by this calculation. He was thoroughly unscrupulous. He would steal, slander, assassinate, drown, and poison, as his interest dictated. He had no generosity; but mere vulgar hatred; he was intensely selfish; he was perfidious; he cheated at cards; he was a prodigious gossip; and opened letters; and delighted in his infamous police; and rubbed his hands with joy when he had intercepted some morsel of intelligence concerning the men and women about him, boasting that 'he knew everything.'

"In short," Emerson concludes, "when you have penetrated through all the circles of power and splendor, you were not dealing with a gentleman, at last; but with an impostor and a rogue; and he fully deserves the epithet of Jupiter Scapin, or a sort of Scamp Jupiter" (the epithet was first applied to Napoleon by his secretary Abbé de Pradt, who borrowed it from the name bestowed on the scampy valet in Molière's comedy *Les Fourberies de Scapin*).

We have no way of knowing what Braithwaite made of Frost's allusion to Napoleon. But anyone not innocent of Lawrance Thompson's biography of Frost can see where the poet's talk of "justifying" himself "by the example" of Napoleon might lead an ungenerous (and tone-deaf) reader like Thompson. Letters of the kind we are reading here are precisely what led him to paint a portrait of the poet as Scamp Jupiter in volume two of his perniciously iconoclastic three-volume biography. Thompson calls the letter to Braithwaite "a thoroughly successful campaign strategy," and that is, to be sure, all he sees in it. The biographer thought he found the poison of calculation tainting all the letters Frost addressed to editors, anthologists, and critics on his return to the United States in 1915. But, as Richard Poirier understood, Thompson misses the point entirely. Frost's "calculations" are almost always aboveboard, and most often very winning. Letters such as the one to Braithwaite invite their recipients—Braithwaite, Louis Untermeyer, Sidney Cox, John Bartlett, and many others—into complicity in what is, after all, not simply a "campaign" to advance one poet's career, but a happy parody of the "campaigns" poets are forever on to advance their careers. I doubt Braithwaite felt he was being used, or that Frost was attempting to do in the pages of the *Transcript* what Napoleon did in the pages of the *Moniteurs*. There's absolutely no reason to suspect Braithwaite of being so dull a reader as not to the see the mischief in a poet who "justified" himself, in a single sentence, with reference both to Napoleon and to Nelson (the admiral who defeated Napoleon's fleet at Trafalgar).

And yet there is guile in the letter, though of a "theoretical" sort. The narrative it lays out is not what it appears to be—and this fact, perhaps, Braithwaite did not discern. How much does an interest in gossip "for its own sake"—that is, for the sake of what is said—really differ from a "technical" interest in gossip for the "tones of speech" it "somehow entangles" in its "syntax, idiom, and meaning"? The question is the more intriguing, given that Frost's Napoleonic interest in poetry is not, in fact, an interest in "gossip" per se, but rather in "effects" approximating the "actuality" of gossip. (The letters are everywhere animated by these motives.) We arrive at the point, here, where theme and technique merge—at the point where the "subject" and the "enterprise" of poetry merge; the point where what the poem is about and how the poem works amount to the same thing; the point where the "subject matter" of a poem becomes merely one more resource for making it sound as different from every other poem as is possible (to borrow Frost's way of putting it in "The Figure a Poem Makes" [*CPRF*, 131]); and at the point where Scotch-Yankee calculation calls itself exactly what it is (as when theatrical pickpockets, in their patter, apprise the audience of what they're up to, detail how they'll achieve it, and then get away scot-free—hiding in plain sight).

In May 1915 Frost spoke to the boys at the Browne and Nichols School in Cambridge about what he (still) called "the sound of sense." George Browne, cofounder of the school, took notes on the talk and mailed them to Frost for amendment and expansion (the result is a short talk called "The Imagining Ear" [*CPPP*, 687–689]). In a June 1, 1915, letter to Browne, Frost writes: "Will you give me a little longer with those notes? I want to do them for you: I see an object in it—look out for me." That's right: *look out.* And Frost continues, hinting at another element in the "astonishing magnitude" of his "ambition" (namely, his lively interest in pedagogy): "The further I read in the pamphlets you loaded me with the surer I am that we did not meet for nothing: there was some fatality in the meeting. I see now that I could have gone a good deal deeper in my talk to the boys on images of sound and you would have had no quarrel with me. I can see a small text-book based on images of sound particularly of the kind I call vocal postures or vocal idioms that would revolutionize the teaching of English all the way up through our schools." Scotch-Yankee calculation or "fatality"? Connivance or serendipity? Sheer genius or plain dumb luck? All of the above, actually. To read the letters dating from 1913 to 1916 is to see a career in poetry unlike any other before it—or any other since—realize itself.

To read them also is to feel the (usually happy) "animus," as Frost would call it, that both occasions and is occasioned by this or that letter. Talking about poetry with Richard Poirier for the *Paris Review,* Frost has this to say, in winding things up: "And what is it that guides us—what is it? Young people wonder about that, don't they? But I tell them it's just the same as when you feel a joke coming. You see somebody coming down the street that you're accustomed to abuse, and you feel it rising in you, something to say as you pass each other. Coming over him the same way. And where do these thoughts come from? Where does a thought? Something does it to you. It's him coming toward you that gives you the animus, you know. When they want to know about inspiration, I tell them it's mostly animus" (*CPPP,* 893). Consider what a query from the Boy Scouts of America gave rise to when Frost saw it coming out of his mailbox in June 1915:

> Dear Sirs:
>
> Please don't count on me for the kind of poem you would like for your Boy Scouts' Song Book. If I happen to write one, I shall be happy to let you have it. I am pleased to be asked to write for the boys. Who wouldnt be when he considers the immortality they can confer?
>
> Faithfully yours
> Robert Frost

One wonders whether the authors of the *Boy Scout Handbook,* for their part, saw that last remark coming. Is it sarcastic? Not entirely. The boys can confer a certain kind of "immortality," though not really the kind Frost sought. But if not altogether sarcastic, the remark's not altogether innocent. The request got a rise out of Frost. His reply has in it a characteristic "animus," which holds people off while keeping them charmed, or at any rate somewhat baffled. *Faithfully yours.* Moments like this abound in the letters. Whatever else one may say about Frost as a "man of letters," one has to say first that he was game.

Robert Frost circa 1892 in Lawrence, Massachusetts.

Courtesy of the Dartmouth College Library.

The Early Years

September 1886–July 1912

Such an one am I that even in my failures I find all the promise I require to justify the astonishing magnitude of my ambition.

—Robert Frost to Susan Hayes Ward, April 22, 1894

[To Sabra Peabody (1876–193?), RF's childhood sweetheart. Sabra was the daughter of Ephraim Peabody, whose son, Charles, was a playmate of the young RF (Lawrance Thompson reports that Charlie taught the San Francisco–born RF to "swing" birches). The Peabody family lived along the rail line connecting Lawrence, Massachusetts, to Salem Depot, where the poet's mother taught school. As Thompson reports, the letters to Sabra, the earliest we now have by RF, were found by their recipient, some decades after their composition, in the "secret compartment" of a pencil box. We've let RF's misspellings and solecisms stand in the letters to Sabra, unflagged by the insertion of [sic]*; the latter would diminish the charm of these boyhood epistles "offaly." ALS. Jones.]*

[September 1886]

Dear Sabe,

I read your letter with great pleasure and will try and answer it in a very few lines. I liked those leavs you gave me and put them in my speller to press. I have got read a composition after recess and I hate to offaly.

I have got to stop now so as to learn my Geography.

From your loving
Rob.

[To Sabra Peabody. ALS. Jones.]

[Fall 1886]
Don't show this.

love

Dear Sabe,

I enjoyed reading your letter very much. You need not excuse yourself about writing for mine is as bad. Those nuts I gave you were not as good as I expected but I am glad you liked them.

As usual I cant think of much to write. I wish you were at the supper last night but we did not have much fun because their were not enough there. I suppose Eva hasnt gotten back yet.[1] Are you going to the Hall tomorrow night. I must stop now and remember and write soon. From your loving Rob

[To Sabra Peabody. ALS. Jones.]

[Fall 1886]

Dear Sabe,

I read your loving letter with great pleasure as I alway do. As you could not think of much to say neither can I. I hope you will have a good time to-night and I guess you will and I would like to go if I didnt have to go some where else.

Ever your faithful lover. Rob

[To Sabra Peabody. ALS. Jones.]

[Fall 1886]

love write soon

Dear Sabe,

I will answer your letter to let you know that I am well and hope you are the same. About me liking Lida better than you you are all wrong because I like you twice as much as I do her and always have thought more of you than any other girl I know of. I thought you were going to the entertainment the other night but I didnt see you there I saw Eva Hattie and your mother there.

---

1. Eva was Sabra's sister.

There is no fun in getting mad every so lets see if we cant keep friends I'm sure I am willing. I know I have not treated you as I ought to sometimes and sometimes I dont know wheather you are mad or not and we have gotten mad and then we would get friends again ever since Westons party when I first came here. There are not many girls I like but when I like them I fall dead in love with them and there are not many I like just because I can have some fun with them like I can Lida but I like you because I cant help myself and when I get mad at you I feel mad at myself to.[2]

From your loveing
Rob

[To William Hayes Ward (1835–1916), an American clergyman, editor, and Orientalist. He joined the editorial staff of the New York Independent *in 1868 and was editor in chief from 1896 until 1913. ALS. Huntington.]*

Lawrence Mass.,
March 28 [1894]

Editor of The Independent.
Dear Sir:—

The memory of your note will be a fresh pleasure to me when I waken for a good many mornings to come; which may as well confirm you in the belief that I am still young. I am. The poem you have is the first of mine that any publication has accepted.[3] At about the same time however that I sent you this, I disposed of three others in a similar way in other quarters. As yet they are not returned. As for submitting more of my work, you may imagine I shall be only too glad to avail myself of your kindly interest. Nevertheless since I have but recently discovered my powers, I have, of course, no great amount of verses in store and furthermore, being still inexperienced of myself, I cannot easily tell when I will have. But I shall not forget my obligations.

If you mean what might be called the legitimate education I have received when you speak of "training" and "line of study," I hope that the quality of my poem would seem to account for far more of this than I have really had. I

2. Thompson identifies the rival as Lida Storer, but she may be Lila Storer, one year RF's junior (the 1900 census has her living in Middlesex County, Massachusetts).

3. RF refers to "My Butterfly: An Elegy," which had been accepted for publication in the New York *Independent*.

am only graduated of a public high-school. Besides this, a while ago, I was at Dartmouth College for a few months until recalled by necessity. But this inflexible ambition trains us best, and to love poetry is to study it. Specifically speaking, the few rules I know in this art are my own afterthoughts, or else directly formulated from the masterpieces I reread.

I sincerely hope I have done nothing to make you over-estimate me. It cannot be, though, for rather than equal what I have written and be satisfied, I will idle away an age accumulating a greater inspiration.

There is no objection to using my name with the poem.

Yours
Robert Lee Frost.
Tremont St.
Lawrence, Mass.

[To Susan Hayes Ward (1828–1924), sister of William Hayes Ward, and poetry editor of the Independent. *In its November 8, 1894, issue, the magazine printed the first poem RF ever placed as a paid poet, "My Butterfly: An Elegy" (collected two decades later in* ABW*). ALS. Huntington.]*

Lawrence Mass.
Apr 22, 1894

Dear Miss Ward

It is just such a letter as you wrote me that I have been awaiting for two years. Hitherto all the praise I have received has been ill-advised and unintelligent; all the criticism, this general one upon the rueful fact that I, once the friend of so-and-so, should have at last turned poetaster. So that something definite and discriminating is very welcome. My thanks unlimited! Yet this consideration is hardly due me. Take my word for it that poem exaggerates my ability. You must spare my feelings when you come to read these others, for I haven't the courage to be a disappointment to anyone.[4] Do not think this artifice or excess of modesty though, for, to betray myself utterly, such an one am I that even in my failures I find all the promise I require to justify the astonishing magnitude of my ambition.

---

4. We cannot be sure which poems RF enclosed, but over the next three years "The Birds Do Thus," "Caesar's Lost Transport Ships," and "Warning" would also appear in the *Independent* (*CPPP*, 500–503).

You ask to know more of me. This is certainly very tempting. It might well throw one into a talking trance which nothing could dispel but a reversal of the charm. I am inclined to think, too, that I have several attributes akin to those of that Franco-Russian introspectionist (whose name[5] I dare not attempt in writing.) But whatever the inducements to the contrary I must promise to content myself with but a slight sketch.

When I am well I read a great deal and like a nearsighted person follow the text closely. I read novels in the hope of strengthening my executive faculties. The Polish triology,[6] "With Fire and Sword," "The Deluge," and "Pan Michael" are engaging me at present.[7] Thomas Hardy has taught me the good use of a few words and, refering [*sic*] still to me, "struck the simple solemn."[8] And as opposed to this man, Scott and Stevenson inspire me, by their prose, with the thought that we Scotchmen are bound to be romanticists—poets.[9] Then as for poems my favorites are and have been these: Keats' "Hyperion," Shelley's "Prometheus," Tenneson's [*sic*] "Morte D'Arthur," and Browning's "Saul"—all of them about the giants. Besides these I am fond of the whole collection of Palgrave's.[10] So far everything looks auspicious. But it

---

5. RF writes "Franco-Russian," but perhaps the reference is to Henri-René-Albert-Guy de Maupassant (1850–1893), whose short stories, many of them set during the Franco-Prussian war (in which he had served), were widely read in the 1880s and 1890s. (We thank Mark Scott for the suggestion.) Maupassant took so keen an interest in the new disciplines of psychology and psychiatry (hence, possibly, "introspectionist") as to have been associated with them. Nietzsche writes, in *Ecce Homo:* "I can think of absolutely no century in history, in which a netful of more inquisitive and at the same time more subtle psychologists could be drawn up together than in the Paris of the present day," whereupon he instances Maupassant, among others (from the Ludovici translation).

6. This alternate spelling of "trilogy" fell out of use in the late nineteenth century.

7. RF refers to three historical novels published between 1884 and 1888 by Polish author Henryk Sienkiewicz.

8. RF borrows the phrase from "Rabbi ben Karshook's Wisdom" (1856) by Robert Browning:

Thus Karshook, the Hiram's-Hammer,
The Right-hand Temple-column,
Taught babes in grace their grammar,
And struck the simple, solemn.

9. RF's mother, née Isabelle Moodie, was born in Alloa, Scotland, near Edinburgh.

10. The first reference RF makes to Francis Turner Palgrave's *The Golden Treasury of Songs and Lyrics*; he would often speak of it, and "Waiting: Afield at Dusk," collected in *ABW*, specifically alludes to it ("the worn book of old-golden song" [*CPPP*, 24]). While a student

is necessary to admit that I teach "orthography" in a district school:[11] and that in the fitness of things, the association of Eugene Aram with children in this capacity seems no more incongruous than my own.[12] In fact so wholly uncongenial is the work that it has become for me a mere test of physical endurance. For several weeks now when not teaching I have spent my time lying around either consciously sleeping or unconsciously waking and in both cases irresponsibly irratable [*sic*] to the last degree. It is due to my nerves—they are so susceptible to sound. Consequently the prospect is not bright—for the immediate future at least. When in this condition I can neither read nor write: nevertheless I find a few hours for study and, as I say, I always entertain great hopes.

I have never read Lanier's poetry nor the volume of his you mention. I have read no technical works.[13] The extent of my studying now is a little Greek and, for relaxation, French. Of course I have a great desire to master the former for reasons that would be commonly given. Homer is very difficult for me as yet, though, and I am often entirely discouraged. But I assure you, sometime, money or no money, I shall prove myself able to do everything but spell.

I have not succeeded in revising the poem[14] as you requested. That Aztec consonant syllable of mine, "l," spoils a word I am very sorry to dispense

---

at Dartmouth in the fall of 1892, RF had been introduced to Palgrave's anthology by Charles Francis Richardson (1851–1913), Professor of Natural Philosophy at Dartmouth College and a pioneering historian of American literature; see also RF's October 29, 1906, letter to Susan Hayes Ward.

11. Possibly an echo of Benedick's remarks about Claudio in *Much Ado about Nothing* (3.iii): "He was wont to speak plain and to the purpose, like an honest man and a soldier, and now is he turned orthography; his words are a very fantastical banquet, just so many strange dishes. May I be so converted and see with these eyes? I cannot tell; I think not."

12. Eugene Aram (1704–1759) was an English philologist and schoolmaster, but also infamous as the murderer in Thomas Hood's ballad, "The Dream of Eugene Aram" (1831).

13. RF refers to *The Science of English Verse* (New York: Scribner's, 1880), by Sidney Lanier (1842–1881).

14. "My Butterfly: An Elegy," the first draft of which contained some of the phrases RF cites, as for example in its fifth verse-paragraph:

These were the unlearned things.
It seemed God let thee flutter from his gentle clasp,
Then, fearful he had let thee win
Too far beyond him to be gathered in
Snatched thee, o'er-eager, with ungentle grasp,
Jealous of immortality.

Lawrence Mass., Apr. 22, 1894.

Dear Miss Ward,—

It is just such a letter as you wrote me that I have been awaiting for two years. Hitherto all the praise I have received has been ill-advised and unintelligent; all the criticism, this general one upon the rueful fact that I, once the friend of so-and-so, should have at last turned poetaster. So that something definite and discriminating is very welcome. My thanks unlimited! Yet this consideration is hardly due me. Take my word for it that poem exaggerates my ability. You must spare my feelings when you come to read these others, for I haven't the courage to be a disappointment to anyone. Do not think this artifice or excess of modesty, though,—for to betray myself utterly, such an one am I that even in my failures I find all the promise I require to justify the astonishing magnitude of my ambition.

You ask to know more of me. This is certainly very tempting. It might well throw one into a talking trance which nothing could dispell but a reversal of the charm. I am inclined to think, too, that I have several attributes akin to those of that Franco-Russian introspectionist (whose name

This letter to Susan Hayes Ward on April 22, 1894 illustrates the formality of Frost's early epistolary style and the elegance of his early penmanship.

Courtesy Huntington Library (San Marino, California).

with. The only one I think of to substitute for it is "eddying" which of course weakens the impression—although I am not sure but that it merely changes

---

See Robert Newdick, "Some Early Verse of Robert Frost and Some of His Revisions," *American Literature* 7 (May 1935): 181–187. Reprinted in William A. Sutton, ed., *Newdick's Season of Frost: An Interrupted Biography of Robert Frost* (Albany: State University of New York Press, 1976), 397–403.

it. The would-be cadence howe'er may be incorrect also, but I did not suspect it at the time. It is used in the same sense as "at any rate" would be in that case. But I cannot sustain the usage by any example I have in mind: and when once I doubt an idiom my ear hesitates to vouch for it thereafter. The line, "These were the unlearned things," is wretched. It refers directly to the two lines preceeding [*sic*] and indirectly to the answer inevitable to that question "And did you think etc," which answer would be, God did nevertheless! Yet the line is manifestly redundant as well as retruse and I must invent one to supplant it.[15] I shall prefer to hear from you again, if it is not asking too much, before I return the copy, not only so that I may gain time but also that I may have the benefit of your further advice.

Yours by right of discovery
R. L. Frost

Two of these are the returned poems and the other is no better.

[To Susan Hayes Ward. ALS. Huntington.]

Lawrence Mass
June 10 1894

Dear Miss Ward:

It is clear this letter must be in the nature of a defence. Since last I wrote I hope I have aged enough not to seem so callow and distasteful as I used: at any rate I have been thoroughly overhauled in search of affectations.

Yet even as I am, my inclination would be to give thanks immoderately for that volume of Lanier's poems. As you expected I have been very much interested in the memorial; and I have been enthused over what I conceive to be Lanier's theories of art.[16] I wish I had the Elizabethan knack of expressing gratitude.

---

15. Abstruse (from Latin *retrusus,* concealed).

16. Susan Hayes Ward's brother, William Hayes Ward, wrote the critical-biographical introduction to *Poems of Sidney Lanier,* edited by the poet's wife, Mary D. Lanier, and issued by Scribner's in 1891. As for Lanier's "theories of art": RF refers, again, to *The Science of English Verse.* The book includes a chapter ("Of Tune in Speech: Its Nature and Office") that anticipates RF's theories about "the sounds of sense," as laid out in letters dating from 1913 to 1916. Lanier writes: "In point of fact, (1) tunes—melodies, distinctly formulated patterns of tones varying in pitch—exist not only in poetic readings, but in all the

Will you allow me to correct several wrong impressions I seem to have given you? My pride sees nothing degrading in teaching. We provincials affect Bohemianism—experience, give us experience! I have sold newspapers "on the streets of" San Francisco and worked in the mills and on the farms of New England. My pride is peculiar.

And my friends! how have I betrayed my friends! True they have not encouraged me much as a poet: but if I were so accomplished as to be able to improvise a few heroic metres for them by the campfire next summer, be sure they would appreciate me. Written poetry is rather ineffectual after all, unless artists are the readers of it.

It has been painful for me trying to induce a passion like the one that is the spirit of my poem. I am afraid I cannot revise the thing. I am greatly dissatisfied with it now. Do you not think it would be well to suppress it. If I am not overworked this summer I promise to write you something better by far. Nevertheless I have cancelled one line, altered two, and now the whole is at your disposal.

Explain my cancelled line[17] this way. I close the idea, jealous of immortality. (tentative period) Then there is an afterthought. In a way everything is immortal that outlives me. Things I don't care for will do this. You have not—you were fair.

(Then repeat) Jealous of immortality—
(And add) In one so fair at any rate.

Really
Robert L. Frost

---

most commonplace communications between man and man by means of words. (2) Further: every affirmation, every question, has its own peculiar tune; every emotion, every shade of emotion, has its tune; and such tunes are not mere accidents but are absolutely essential elements in fixing the precise signification of words and phrases. (3) Further still: these tunes not only affect the signification of different words, but they greatly modify the meaning of the same words, so that a phrase uttered according to one tune means one thing, according to another tune another thing" (252–254). For further discussion of Lanier and RF, see *CPRF*, 299–301.

17. Another reference to the text of "My Butterfly: An Elegy," which RF was revising for publication.

[To Susan Hayes Ward. ALS. Huntington.]

Boston Mass.
Aug 22, '94

Dear Miss Ward:—

Surely you have not received my last letter. I shall be sorry if it is too late to arrange to meet you. Write to me at least.

For I perceive that my childishness in regard to poem (said poem) may have become wearisome. It is very trying to be noticed, you know. But give me another chance: I may have disqualified myself for a political career by one foolish act but I cannot have for a literary one:—all the cannonized [*sic*] afford me consolation.

I am learning to spell.

I am writing better poetry.

It is only a matter of time now when I shall throw off the mark and declare for literateur mean it poverty or riches.[18]

You are amid real poetry, I presume: and I can imagine that a conventional verse or stanza and the familiar see-saw of phrases in antithesis, would distemper you.

Sincerely
Robert L. Frost

Boston, Mass.
35 Cambridge St.[19]

[To Susan Hayes Ward. ALS. Huntington.]

Lawrence, Mass,
Dec. 4, 1894

Dear Miss Ward,—

Now that you have ceased expecting to is the time you hear from me. The occasion is, or was, the appearance in print under your supervision of my first poem. I am going to thank you. Four weeks ago and until Friday last I

18. RF misspells "littérature": the literary life, life as a man of letters, etc.

19. During the spring and summer of 1894, RF worked at a number of odd jobs in and around Boston (but did not maintain a residence there).

was in Virginia, North Carolina, and Maryland, very liberally and without address, so that I have not been aware of my own doings as expressed in the phrase "I published a poem."[20] That is the point or points:—I thank you tardily because I for my part have been out of time a little while, and thank you because you and not I published a poem, a work that certainly requires qualities I lack. And the poem does look well—don't you think it does?

Before proceeding further I perceive I must assume an attitude, or else endanger the coherency of my remarks, for my natural attitude is one of enthusiasm verging on egotism and thus I always confuse myself trying to be modest. It is my rule to be despondent to be dignified (or coherent) and I might be cynical for the same purpose, but really unless it be enthusiastically I am at a loss to know how to comport myself on the present occasion. You see I am just returned from experiences so desperately absorbing that I am nothing morbid now and can enjoy the poem as freshly as if it were but lately written and I had not since wasted eight months in ineffectual aspiration.

Yes, I think sound is an element of poetry, one but for which imagination would become reason. I justify the use of dialect in this way; it contributes to the illusion (perhaps) and gives the artist the courage of his imaginings. Kipling says nearly all he says under the influence of sound. I am so fond of sound that I was wishing the other day he would write some more poetry. Listen to that!—when we generally read poetry because we are in the business and it is written.

I have one or two poems to send you when I find time to revise them.

Sincerely
Robert Frost

20. In the fall of 1894, RF had two copies of his first "collection" of verse, *Twilight*, printed in Lawrence, Massachusetts, one for himself and one for Elinor Miriam White (whom he would marry in 1895). After presenting Elinor with a copy at her dormitory at St. Lawrence University, and mistaking her reserve for rejection, RF briefly returned home to Lawrence, Massachusetts, before intemperately decamping, on November 6, for the Dismal Swamp, along the Virginia-North Carolina line. A party of boatmen picked him up, took him to Elizabeth City, North Carolina, from which point he began the long trek back to Massachusetts, hopping freight cars up to Baltimore before wiring his mother for fare money to Lawrence, where he arrived on November 30.

[To Susan Hayes Ward. ALS. Huntington.]

Lawrence Mass.
Dec. 28, '94

Dear Miss Ward,—

It is no use: I must let you know now. At the thought of visiting you, so many things to talk with you about filled my mind, seeming to urge as necessary my visiting you, that I was long in realizing the unaltered, patient fact that I could not. I want to find some good friend of mine whom I can satisfactorily authorize to admit for them the incapacity of my enemies. I will not repeat what they say. But did not you say the line Its two banks etc. was intelligible?[21] O I had many things to talk about, and I am very very sorry that, as you express it, it will be unwise for me to reach New York.

There is no need to introduce these verses. I have reason to hope that you will discover their purpose unaided. But do not be too hard on the untitled American one, because I like it and it is not American.[22]

With thanks, regrets, and best wishes,

Rob't L. Frost

[To Susan Hayes Ward. ALS. Huntington.]

Lawrence Mass.
Jan 6 1895

Dear Miss Ward—

I trust that circumstances favored your return to New York as early as you hoped. Your postal came on New Year's morning, too late for one of my limited resources to undertake the proposed expedition.

I thank you again for your thoughtfulness: but you are really too kind: a little more and I shall begin to question my right to trouble you with manuscript, friends, you know, having an old grievance on this head relative to which there is a jest current painful to the sensitive mind.

Fortunately (it seems)
Robert L. Frost

---

21. See line nine of "My Butterfly: An Elegy" (RF dropped the sub-title when he collected the poem in *ABW*).

22. It is not clear which poem RF has in mind; he sent a number to Ward in the mid-1890s.

[To Susan Hayes Ward. ALS. Huntington.]

Lawrence [MA]
Jan. 30 '95

Dear Miss Ward,

You are not to pardon my remissness: but it is the truth that you have wished me well to such a good purpose that I have been busy night and day for two weeks. I am a reporter on a local newspaper![23]

You will guess what I have been thinking about all this time—especially just after waking. There are those they can harm with impunity, but in my case they will make a martyr. I am endorsed now by a professional critic.[24]

If it is seriously I must speak, I undertake a future. I cannot believe that poem was merely a chance. I will surpass it. Maurice Thompson will not hope to discourage me by praising me surely? I would tell him that he is not so inscrutable as he might be when he does so inconsistently.

I needed your good words and as you see they have not been in vain. You give me a new courage: at last I feel as if I could afford to be modest.

My newspaper work requires a brave effort. They assure me I have much to learn particularly in the way of writing: but what care I: I have done the best I can with what I know and if I know everything I have reached my limit. Let them teach me.

I am saving you one or two unpretentious poems—concerning which I have my doubts.

Yours sincerely
Robert L. Frost

---

23. In the winter and spring of 1895, RF worked briefly for the Lawrence *Daily American* and (also briefly) for the Lawrence *Sentinel*. See *CPRF*, 246–249.

24. James Maurice Thompson (1844–1901) was an American novelist. Having received from William Hayes Ward a copy of the *Independent* containing RF's "My Butterfly," Thompson wrote Ward praising the poem but advising that the poet learn a trade in order to avoid poverty.

[To Susan Hayes Ward. ALS. Huntington.]

Lawrence Mass
Jan 25 '96

Dear Miss Ward,

Perhaps you had better not wait any longer. I have done my level best, in the time that has elapsed since last you heard from me, to make good my promise as a poet. But I fear I am not a poet, or but a very incomprehensible one.

The enclosed are an excuse for writing to you, nothing more.[25] You will not find what you want in them, although it is not for me to say anything against them, who have learned to be thankful for little things.

Do not think but what I would have been glad to hear from you any time these six months, but of course I could not expect to. Possibly I may now when you come to understand the good and sufficient reasons for my long silence.

Robert Lee Frost

Address: Central Bldg.

[To Susan Hayes Ward. ALS. Huntington.]

Lawrence Mass
July 8 '96

Dear Miss Ward,

You are to hear from me now only because school is closed and I am quite rested having slept more or less soundly for a whole week night and day. Well I did what I tried to do so that the future is not so uncertain though it is not with success as it is with failure which is final, while success to a coward is only suspense, the most awful of tortures.

You sent me a poem by John Bennett.[26] You didn't say what you thought of it but if you will kindly do so to Mrs Smith, for <u>me.</u>[27] There could hardly be

---

25. The enclosures were separated from the letter and cannot now be identified.

26. John Bennett (1865–1956), born in Chillicothe, Ohio, was an important literary figure in his adopted city of Charleston, South Carolina. He was a poet, illustrator, and the author of children's books; his "Magnificat of the Hills" had appeared in the *Independent* in 1892. The *Chap-Book*, a semimonthly illustrated magazine, was published in Chicago.

27. Marion Couthouy Smith (1853–1931), author of, among other works, *The Electric Spirit and Other Poems* (Boston: R. G. Badger, 1906). Her work appeared in a number of magazines, including *Harper's*, *Outlook*, and *The Youth's Companion*.

two opinions with regard to it. Tell Mrs Smith, very nice. O say—Yes I am right. Upon inquiry I find that it is a John Bennett who designed the cover of the current Chap-Book. Why he's somebody already.

I fear me my idiom is greatly confused tonight and I shall not write very much. O these Yorkshiremen.[28] One would do well to avoid them when he can and as for walking abroad with them all day and seeing things through their eyes, it is unpardonable. I verily believe there is such a thing as not knowing whether you have opened your lips or not. Speech is a strange thing and however little thought preceeds [*sic*] it, it is still distinct from thought and the proof is that the one may be utterly at variance with the other and the thought be no less definite.[29]

But to the point. If it is not too late I am anxious to avail myself of your kindness and publish one more poem before I die. It is ten to one however that you are off on a vacation and this will not come to your notice for some time. Whatever happens is for the best. You are not obliged to change your plans out of consideration for me. I know you wouldn't. I offer you my suggestion for the closing line of the poem nevertheless in case you are still at liberty to use it.

And overhead the petrel, wafted wide.[30]

This is tedious and I know it and I would fain curb myself but I cannot. There is one thing I can do. I can make an end; which I hereby do, with rememberences [*sic*] for all in particular,

R. L. Frost

---

28. Perhaps RF had been browsing through such books as William Andrews's *Modern Yorkshire Poets* (1885) and *North Country Poets: Poems and Biographies of Natives or Residents of Northumberland, Cumberland, Westmoreland, Durham, Lancashire and Yorkshire* (1888). Or he might have been reading, again, Kipling, who took satisfaction in his father's Yorkshire origins and temperament, in whose work Yorkshiremen occasionally figure (sometimes marked by force and bluntness, even to the point of arrogance), and whose mastery of "sound" RF admired; see RF's December 4, 1894, letter to Susan Hayes Ward.

29. An anticipation of RF's theories regarding the "sound of sense" or "sentence sounds," as developed in letters dating from 1913–1916.

30. The line closes RF's early and uncollected poem "Caesar's Lost Transport Ships," published first in the *Independent*, January 14, 1897 (*CPPP*, 501–502).

[To Susan Hayes Ward. ALS. Huntington.]

Lawrence Mass
Aug 15 '96

Dear Miss Ward,

You were very considerate in the matter of the title. I presume the other poem as emended was not satisfactory.[31] Will you let me know?

There are other things I would like to know. Write me if you are not too busy.

We are about to move down town again to open school.[32] I am becoming dangerously interested in that concern, to the exclusion I fear of things more lofty. (Don't believe him)

Miss Ward has been enjoying the warm weather? Now what has my friend to say about life in the city. There is much to be done for the poor isn't there if Bryan were only the man to do it.[33]

But I must hear from you directly before I continue. I have lost touch with mankind and must approach the individual circumspectly.

Remember me to Miss Hetta please.[34] Tell her that I am botanizing will I nill I. You make the laws and an enthusiast here is found to enforce them. I am overwhelmed with books on the subject. Mrs W. S. Dana and I don't know who all![35]

Be sure to write.
R. L. Frost

---

31. Three poems by RF appeared in the *Independent* in 1896–1897: "The Birds Do Thus" on August 20, 1896, "Caesar's Lost Transport Ships" on January 14, 1897, and "Warning" on September 9, 1897. It is not clear which RF refers to here.

32. The Frost family moved to a house on Haverhill Street in Lawrence, to which address the poet's mother had relocated the school she then taught; RF and his new wife Elinor occupied the second floor of the house.

33. William Jennings Bryan (1860–1925), who had, in July, been nominated for president at the Democratic National Convention in Chicago.

34. Hetta Lord Ward (1842–1921) was Susan's sister.

35. Frances Theodora Parsons (1861–1952), usually writing as Mrs. William Starr Dana, was an American botanist and author of *How to Know the Wild Flowers* (1893), the first field guide published covering North American wildflowers.

[To Susan Hayes Ward. As Frost playfully suggests, the closing and signature are in another hand, most likely that of Elinor Frost. ALS. Huntington.]

Lawrence Mass
Dec 27 '96

Dear Miss Ward:—

Don't think because I haven't written I haven't once thought of you all this time. I have thought of you often and as often tried to write to you but in vain. It is just possible you do not understand this: all I can say is I do, though to no purpose. I wish I were reporting again and writing so much a day under compulsion. Then you would get the letters!

The last I heard of you you were on your way to Bath Me. not to see Mr Sewell [*sic*]. You were opening the campaign so to speak in the Republican interest. Since then how many calamitous things have not happened to the disappointment of how many people, particularly in the state of Colorado.[36]

As nothing that happens matters much and as most of my thoughts are about myself I am always at a loss for likely subject matter. I am the father of a son if that is anything.[37] What would William Canton[38] say under such circumstances. My soul what wouldn't he say!

It has dawned upon me that those were proofs you sent me and should have been corrected and returned.[39] They were all right as they were. Many thanks.

And a Happy New Year! May you discover an immortal genius and enter into your earthly reward. If I ever improve beyond recognition I will let you discover me over in part payment for all you have done. You think I couldn't disguise my handwriting?

Sincerely yours,
Robert L. Frost

---

36. A wealthy shipbuilder and Maine industrialist, Arthur Sewall (1835–1900) was the Democratic vice-presidential candidate in 1896. The defeat of the "Silverite" ticket of William Jennings Bryan and Sewall dealt a blow to the mining economy of Colorado.

37. Robert and Elinor Frost's first son, Elliot, was born on September 25, 1896; he died of cholera on July 8, 1900.

38. William Canton (1845–1926), British author best known for his children's books.

39. Proofs of RF's poem "Caesar's Lost Transport Ships," published in the *Independent* a month later (January 14, 1897).

[To LeBaron Russell Briggs (1855–1934), dean of men at Harvard University, and later, dean of faculty. ALS. Harvard.]

Lawrence Mass Sept 11 [1897]

Dear Sir,

You are the one it seems for me to submit my case to if you will be so kind as to consider it. You will discover the propriety as I proceed.

I desire to enter Harvard this fall, if possible a candidate for a degree from the outset. It came to me as a surprise only the other day that I might reasonably hope to do so consequently I find myself somewhat unprepared for examination. This is the great difficulty. I graduated from the Lawrence High School as many as five years ago (having in 1891 passed examinations for admission to Harvard occupying seven hours for which I hold a certificate.) It is true that since that time I have been teaching school and tutoring more or less in Latin Algebra and Geometry. Still my studies are all at loose ends. In particular I have neglected my Greek. If proficiency in English were any consideration, I make no doubt I could pass an examination in that. You will find verses of my inditing in the current number of the Independent[40] and others better in back numbers. I might possibly pass in French also and in Physics and Astronomy for that matter but in Greek I fear not. You'll say it doesn't sound very encouraging.

Another embarrassing circumstance is the fact that once upon a time I left Dartmouth without having applied to the proper authorities of that paternalism for an honorable dismissal. I stood not upon the order of my going[41] but went incontinently—for reasons I am free to explain. I assure you the matter will bear looking into.

This is the whole case not very clearly or succinctly stated. The question is what will you advise me to do. Let me say that if I enter college it must be this year or never. It will be hard if a fellow of my age and general intelligence (!) must be debarred from an education for want of technical knowl-

40. "Warning," published in the *Independent* for September 9, 1897; RF never collected it.

41. RF echoes *Macbeth* (3.iv), where Lady Macbeth urges the guests at the banquet to

speak not; [the King] grows worse and worse;
Question enrages him. At once, good-night:
Stand not upon the order of your going,
But go at once.

edge representing less than two months work. All I ask is to be admitted. I don't care how many conditions you encumber me with. I will take the examinations if you say so, or I will enter as a special.[42]

I am anxious to hear from you soon. Rev. John Hayes of Salem or Rev. W. Wolcott of this city will answer questions with regard to me.[43]

Respectfully
Robert L. Frost

[To LeBaron Russell Briggs. ALS. Harvard.]

Lawrence Mass
Sept 18 1897

Dear Sir,

About the "Dartmouth affair." When I left college I thought I knew best whether or not it was advisable for me to do so and I didn't care to discuss the matter with anyone. The fact was I was in financial straits and I wasn't the kind that could serve for hire his own classmates in a menial capacity. An education wasn't worth it. But I don't think that I left college in debt or else I should have heard of it as my name with my address appeared several times in the Dartmouth[44] during the following year.

I shall take the examinations as you advise. Thank you for your letter.

Respectfully
Robert L Frost

42. RF did in fact take examinations in Greek, Latin, English, French, ancient history, and physical science. He was admitted as a freshman (not as a "special student") in fall 1897.

43. John A. Hayes (1858–?), a Swedenborgian pastor, had married RF and Elinor in the Essex Street office building of the poet's mother on December 19, 1895. William E. Wolcott (1852–1911), pastor of the First Congregational Church in Lawrence, was a friend of Hayes and of William Prescott Frost, Sr., RF's grandfather.

44. The student newspaper.

[To Susan Hayes Ward. ALS. Huntington.]

West Derry N.H.
Jan 15 '01

Dear Miss Ward

Perhaps you will care to know how authorship progresses. I send you this selection from the poems I have been writing with a view to a volume some day.[45] If you can use it I shall be glad to have you.

Sincerely
R. L. Frost

L. Box 140[46]

[Frost published two letters to the editor in Farm-Poultry *(in which journal a number of his short stories and articles had appeared [see* CPRF, *35–73]), one under his own name, one under the name of his friend John Hall. The occasion was RF's error in his article "Three Phases of the Poultry Industry." In the third section of that article, "A Typical Small Breeder," RF describes Hall's poultry farm in Atkinson, New Hampshire, mentioning in passing Hall's flock of geese: "Mr. Hall's geese roost in the trees even in winter. Such a toughening process would be too drastic for hens, but these have to take it according to their strength" (*CPRF, *61).* Farm-Poultry *printed a letter from an H. R. White on January 15, 1904: "Will you kindly inform me through your next issue what kind of geese Mr. Hall has that Mr. R. L. Frost speaks of in your issue of Dec. 15th? According to Mr. Frost these geese roost in trees even in the winter time. Now I am 45 years old and have been among geese all my life time, and I can never remember seeing a goose in a tree. I thought if I could get a breed of that kind I could dispense with the coops. Doylestown, Mass. H. R. White." The editor added a note: "Letting Mr. Frost's statement pass is one 'on' us. The writer's attention was called to the evident error before the paper was mailed, but too late to make correction. Then we thought we'd wait and see how many would notice it. Mr. Frost will have to explain." Mr. Frost's temporizing explanation appeared in the February 15 number of* Farm-Poultry, *from which the letter here is transcribed. Incidentally, the editor added a note to the letter: "Mr. Frost seems not to be aware of the fact that geese generally*

45. These might be any of a number of poems that now reside at the Huntington Library, together with the letters to Ward. However, after this date only "The Quest of the Orchis" and "The Trial by Existence" appeared in the *Independent* (the former on June 27, 1901, the latter on October 11, 1906).

46. "Lock Box 140": RF's postal address in West Derry. He got his mail there, though the farm the family inhabited lay some three miles south of Derry Village proper. See *SL*, 33.

remain out of doors by choice practically all the time. The same thing may be said of ducks. My Indian runner ducks (now deceased) would stay out in a snow storm from daylight to dark rather than go into a comfortable shed where they were sheltered and amply provided with bedding." The matter did not rest here. Edward Connery Lathem and Lawrance Thompson explain in Robert Frost: Farm-Poultryman *(Hanover, New Hampshire: Dartmouth Publications, 1963): "Before his own letter (with this unexpected editorial comment and correction) appeared, Frost had decided it might be well to protect himself further by having John Hall write a letter in his defense. But . . . John Hall had had little schooling, and his talents did not include epistolary abilities. The best he could do was to enter into collusion with his friend by giving approval to a letter actually composed by Frost" (19–20).]*

[Derry, NH]
[circa February 15, 1904]

Editor FARM-POULTRY:—

In reply to Mr. White's (and yours) of recent date in regard to the error in the article on Mr. Hall's place, there is this to say:—Geese would sleep out, or float out, let us say, where hens would roost in the trees. To be sure. But what more natural, in speaking of geese in close connection with hens, than to speak of them as if they <u>were</u> hens? "Roost in the trees," has here simply suffered what the grammarians would call attraction from the subject with which it should be in agreement to the one uppermost in the mind. That is all. But the idea will have to stand, viz., that Mr. Hall's geese winter out,—and that is the essential thing. Mr. White is not after geese that roost in the trees, but geese that don't need coops. Well, Mr. Hall has them that prefer not to use coops, whether they need them or not. My impression is that he has them in several varieties, and I'll risk my impression. But Mr. Hall is a good fellow and will be glad to tell Mr. White about his geese himself—doubtless, also, to do business with him.

R.L.F.

[To the editor of Farm-Poultry. *RF confessed his authorship of this letter much later, in a 1913 letter to John Bartlett: "I wrote up one or two poultrymen . . . filling in the gaps in my knowledge with dream material. I think I managed fairly well except for the time I spoke of John Hall's geese roosting in the trees. I should have let geese severely alone. It took an artistic letter from John Hall himself (I wrote it for the douce man) to save me from the scandal that started." See the headnote to RF's letter to the same journal (above) as published in its February 15, 1904, number for further information about this exchange. Transcribed from the text as published in the number for March 15, 1904.]*

[Derry, NH]
[circa March 15, 1904]

Editor FARM-POULTRY:—

I noticed Mr. H. R. White's letter in your paper asking about the kind of geese I kept that sleep out in the winter. They are Toulouse, Embden, and Buff. They don't roost in trees. I don't know how Mr. Frost made that mistake, for of course he knows better.

We have often talked about the way they take to the water at night, a favorite place for them to hang up being on a stone just under water. A good many nights in winter, as well as in summer, I have no idea where they are; and I think they are better every way out doors as long as there is any water not frozen over. But speaking of geese in trees, I don't suppose Mr. White has ever seen a duck in a tree. I have. And I once had a duck that laid her eggs in a tree high enough to be out of reach from the ground, and brought off twenty-two ducklings. These were Brazilians, and I don't know what they won't do.

It has always seemed strange to me how people succeed in keeping geese shut up. If I shut mine up they begin to be restless right away, and go off in looks, especially plumage. Mr. White needn't think because I let my geese run wild I think any less of them than other folks. They are good ones,—as they ought to be with the advantages I give them. They win, too, where they are shown.

The records in your paper ought to show what they did in Lawrence this year; but I notice they don't. So Mr. Frost was pretty near right about my geese; and if Mr. White wants some good ones that a little rather than not sleep out, I've got them.

John A. Hall

[To William Hayes Ward. Across the top of the letter in another hand is written "The poems sent were uncommonly good[.] W." We do not know which poems Ward refers to or whether they survived. ALS. Huntington.]

West Derry NH.
Feb. 24, '06

Dear Dr Ward:

I trust I do not presume too much on former kindness in addressing these verses to you personally. Sending MS to the Independent can never be quite like sending it anywhere else for me.

I often think of you and your sister in my work. I believe Miss Ward left the staff of the Independent some years ago to write books.[47] Please remember me to her either formally or by showing her any of my verses—whether you can use them or not.

Sincerely yours,
Robert Frost

[To Susan Hayes Ward. ALS. Huntington.]

W. Derry N H
July 17 '06

My dear Miss Ward,

My wife will be visiting at Pocantico Hills[48] next week, and that is so near you I thought I should like to have her call on you, if you happened not to have gone away for your summer vacation. Would there be any afternoon of the week after July Twenty-fourth when it would be convenient for you to see her?

Very truly yours
Robert Frost

---

47. Susan Hayes Ward authored a number of books. RF may have in mind her most recent, at the time this letter was written: *George H. Hepworth: Preacher, Journalist, Friend of the People* (New York: E.P. Dutton, 1903).

48. Near Sleepy Hollow and Tarrytown, New York.

[To Susan Hayes Ward. ALS. Huntington.]

W. Derry N.H.
Oct 29 '06

My Dear Miss Ward,—

I suspect from the fact that I saw no proof that I was rushed into print perhaps a little ahead of my turn by favor. Well I am not the one to complain of that, even though as a result I am made to look as if I intended to rhyme life with life and lived in Derby (where the ram lived.)[49] The great thing is to get out where one can be read. That I was read this time I have tangible evidence in a letter from the Vice-Something of a pencil company who liked my idea well enough to want to see it restated in honest prose. The Vice-Something, mind you. His motives for so much flattery would have been less liable to misconstruction had his letter head and envelope been freer from advertisement of his own goods.

Eversince [*sic*] Elinor came back from New York breathing inspiration, I have been ambitious to get some of my larger thoughts into shape for you; but it seems they wont be driven—not at least by a sick man. There's one about the Demiurge's Laugh[50] (good title?) which if I can take it by surprise someday ought to be made to mean something. Meanwhile there are these. Believe me, it is not from anything like neglect that I have not sent them sooner. Since the ragweed dusted, I have done nothing and written nothing—except my own epitaph provisionally like this:

There was a poor mortal believer
Who gave way to a thought of hay fever:
He coughed like a cold
Till over he rolled,
And went into the hands of a receiver.

A very false gallop of verses which I achieved in despite of my invention and which I insert here with some hesitation, it having met with no especial success in the family. But to my poems. My fear is that you will feel overwhelmed

49. RF refers to "The Trial by Existence," which appeared in the *Independent* for October 11, 1906. The magazine mistakenly printed "life" for "strife" in line fifty, and gave RF's address as "Derby" rather than "Derry." "The Derby Ram" (or "As I Was Going to Derby") is a traditional English folk song, dating at least to the eighteenth century.

50. "The Demiurge's Laugh" did not see print until RF collected it in *ABW.*

by the number. You need read of them only so long as your patience holds out. Too bad that they are still a little timid. Daring is with me a plant of slow growth—or say health is. But I shall get the right tone yet, give me time.

Last week's Independent came with its only poem a reprint of one that appeared in the Oct. 27th issue. It does seem too bad to waste good space in that way. These things were not thus in the old days when I read your editorial accompanying Hovey's Elegy on the Death of Parsons, and then and there gave you my allegiance whether you had need of it or not.[51] I call it your editorial—I think likely you wrote it. It was in the fall of 1892 and I was at Dartmouth then with C. F. Richardson neglecting my studies for Palgrave, which I had just got hold of.*[52] I remember your generosity to Hovey very well: you likened the exaltation of his close to Milton's sunken daystar that yet anon repairs his drooping head.[53] It seems to me like yesterday. And only last spring the Independent took a whole page to declare itself the immemorial friend of poets. But if it expects the slighted poets to believe its protestations, it must not get into the habit of stopping a gap twice with the same poem. Now must it?

Elinor joins me in sending love and wishing you joy of the Winter Town.

Sincerely
Robert Frost

* Halcyon days!

---

51. American poet Richard Hovey (1864–1900) published *Seaward: An Elegy on the Death of Thomas William Parsons* in a single volume in 1893; it had previously appeared in the *Independent* on November 17, 1892, when RF encountered it at Dartmouth.

52. Charles Francis Richardson (1851–1913) was professor of natural philosophy at Dartmouth College.

53. See lines 168–169 of Milton's "Lycidas."

[To Susan Hayes Ward. The situation RF describes resulted from the publication of "The Trial by Existence" in the Independent *and the editorial substitution of "Derby" for "Derry," where he resided. The letter for which RF apologizes was written on October 29, 1906. ALS. Huntington.]*

West Derry N.H.
Dec. 26, '06

My dear Miss Ward,

If the hero as poet has been saying something to give offense, won't you vouchsafe a line to say whether it is about poetry and the Independent, and won't you forgive it if satisfactorily explained? Really there was provocation that you could know nothing about. I had just begun teaching at Pinkerton Academy when my poem about the heretofore turned up in the school library. Its effect was startling. From the moment of its appearance, all the teachers abruptly broke off all but the most diplomatic relations with me. Put to it for a reason, I thought at first my poem had led them to question my orthodoxy (if not my sanity.) Then I thought that a flock of teachers would be more apt to loathe me for misspelling Derry than for grafting Schopenhauer upon Christianity. Mr Merriam says that I was twice wrong.[54] I had made myself unpopular by the simple act of neglecting to give Pinkerton the credit for harboring the poet that wrote the poem. It was too funny. But while it lasted and I was still guessing, I was rather miserable. Then it was that I wrote the letter which I ask you to forgive, but which I know you can't. It seems as if I took these things more seriously than I used to before I was twenty. You must remember, too, that life doesn't look the same away off here as it does in N.Y.

Sincerely
Robert Frost

---

54. Charles L. Merriam (1855–1914), a Congregational minister in Derry who admired RF's poetry, had been instrumental in securing him a teaching position at Pinkerton Academy.

[To Susan Hayes Ward. ALS. Huntington.]

W. Derry N.H.
Jan 12 '07

My dear Miss Ward,

So I was not to be pacified until I had gotten a sick friend propped up on pillows to write me a reassuring letter. I am duly ashamed now that I have read the reassuring letter. I might have known that it would be because you were busy or ill if you were silent. But don't for a moment believe that it was anxiety about my poems that made me so blindly inconsiderate.

We have all been miserably sick with grippe, too, so that we know how to sympathize with you on that score—if we are not quite so clear in our own provincialism as to what it might mean to miss an oratorio. We humbly trust that you may be able to make it up to yourself for missing that by attending (when you are well and about again) a few selected operas at one house or the other.

Sincerely
Robert Frost

The poems enclosed are not for review.[55]

[To Susan Hayes Ward. Only the closing page of this letter survives. Thompson dates the letter to July 1907 on the basis of RF's reference to Elinor's health and his own. In the spring of 1907, RF had suffered a serious bout of pneumonia; in June, Elinor's difficult pregnancy had ended in the birth and subsequent death of Elinor Bettina Frost. ALS. Huntington.]

[Derry, NH]
[circa July 1907]

[. . .] poem, though I say it who am not an editor and was not intended to be. I am half afraid they do not appreciate its unusual blend of humor with vague beauty over on Fulton St. or it could not have gathered dust as long as it has.[56] However I forgive them, and only wish my muse were as much to

55. The enclosures were separated from the letter and are now unidentifiable.

56. The editorial offices of the *Independent* were at 130 Fulton Street, New York. The reference may be to "What Thing a Bird Would Love" (*CPPP*, 510), written in 1905 (it must

their high purpose as they once found that of the author of The Cry of the Children.[57]

Yes we are both the merest convalescents for the present (Mrs Frost will write and tell you all about it sometime), barely equal to wishing you one good wish of health and happiness between us.

Sincerely
Robert Frost

A daimen icker in a thrave's a sma' request[58]

[To Susan Hayes Ward. ALS. Huntington.]

W. Derry NH
Aug 6 '07

Dear Miss Ward:—

I must add my word to urge the visit Mrs Frost proposes in her letter. It would be so very pleasant to see you again and there would be so many things to talk about, that here we are accustomed to keep locked in the bosom of the family from one year's end to another. I sent the inoffensive poem to the unoffending editor and soon, I expect, I shall be enough richer to buy

---

have gathered some dust at this date) and touched by the wry humor and complexity of understatement typical of RF's mature work.

57. Elizabeth Barrett Browning's "The Cry of the Children" (1842) is a powerful, if sentimental, indictment of the cruelty of child labor in industrial England. The *Independent* published a number of Browning's poems in the early 1860s.

58. RF's postscript is taken from the third stanza of Robert Burns' "To a Mouse" (1786):

I doubt na, whyles, but thou may thieve;
What then? poor beastie, thou maun live!
A daimen-icker in a thrave
'S a sma' request:
I'll get a blessin wi' the lave,
An' never miss't!

The speaker does not begrudge the mouse its theft of an occasional [daimen] ear of corn [icker] from twenty-four sheaves [thrave], for he will get by with the remainder [lave]. RF's allusion may be to the children starved by greed in Barrett Browning's poem, to the modesty of his hope that the editors would take one poem of the sheaf he submitted, or to some issue raised elsewhere in the letter.

a few more books—Meredith, Dobell, Yeats, and one or two others I shall have to think up.[59] (Have you anything to suggest?) So that you would find us right in the middle of five or six new enthusiasms. That would not bore you too much, I hope. But of course if you are going to plead poverty and stay at home, I have nothing to say. We too have tasted poverty (and all but death)—at the hands of the general practitioner if not the specialist. It is too bad that we are not where we could see you more easily. Sometime we intend to be nearer New York than we are, if it can come about in the right way. But that is one of the dreams. Poetry, I am afraid, will be less likely to bring us there than prose.

Sincerely
Robert Frost

(Another infliction on the next page.)[60]

[To Susan Hayes Ward. ALS. Huntington.]

Bethlehem N.H.
Sept 8 1907

My dear Miss Ward,

I have carried a wrong impression from your last letter. As that left it, I thought, we were to expect you at such a time in mid-September as you should later fix, and nothing remained for us but to wait to hear from you again. Our plans remain unchanged except that we must leave here a few days earlier than we intended—on the twenty fourth of this month instead of the first of next—which I trust will make no material difference to you. It would be the greatest disappointment not to have you come so you must not fail us. You are really not very far from us over across the mountains as the light flies in the morning. People here go down to the surf at Old Orchard and

59. In addition to George Meredith (1828–1909) and William Butler Yeats (1865–1939), RF refers to the British poet Sydney Thompson Dobell (1824–1874).

60. Accompanying the letter were fair copy manuscripts of two poems: "Choice of Society" (an early version of the sonnet "The Vantage Point") and "A Dream Pang," to which RF appended a "Comment": "I shall master the sonnet form in time." As to the mastery already achieved in "A Vantage Point," see Paul Fussell's remarks in *Poetic Meter and Poetic From* (McGraw-Hill, 1977): 102–103.

return the same day like Freedom rejoicing in each of the two mighty voices, one of the Sea, one of the Mountains.[61]

Rather strangely I have a letter from your brother dated identically with yours Sept 4. In it he accuses me of false grammar—justly, justly, if we are to look at it in the right way instead of in the way I tried hard to look at it to eke out a triple rhyme.[62] As a teacher I am behind both my hands with mortification.

You will write again then and tell me what train you take from Portland so I will know when to meet you at Bethlehem. There will be a drive for you at this end of the journey, but not of fifteen miles—only three. We are higher up in the world than Bethlehem even. I am glad to think you will enjoy the mountain air.

Sincerely yours
Robert Frost

Bethlehem N.H.
c/o John Lynch[63]

[To Susan Hayes Ward. The Frost family had just returned from Bethlehem, New Hampshire. ALS. Huntington.]

Derry N.H.
Nov 4 1907

My dear Miss Ward,—

We have been at home for some time, but this is the first opportunity I have had to say so in so many words. I know you will forgive my not writing sooner when I tell you that my little capacities have been taxed to the utmost

---

61. See Wordsworth's "Thoughts of a Briton on the Subjugation of Switzerland": "Two voices are there; one is of the sea, / One of the mountains; each a mighty voice." Old Orchard Beach fronts the Saco Bay on the Maine coast, near Biddeford.

62. See stanza two of "What Thing a Bird Would Love," the manuscript of which is now at the Huntington (*CPPP*, 510):

I paused to rest and turned,
And if I had not turned,
I had not seen the west
Behind, how it burned.

63. John and Mary Lynch owned a farm in Bethlehem, New Hampshire, at which the Frost family stayed during hay fever season.

in getting our English department to rights at school. On top of everything else I have been asked to prepare a historical article on the Academy—in prose.[64] Naturally I consume some part of every day merely dreading to undertake that. But written it will have to be, if I am to save any reputation as a poet (upon which everything hangs.) I am beginning to commence to think about casting about for my material. Elinor has been wanting to write to you, but I have claimed precedence, and she, too, has been unco[65] busy.

I am moved to melancholy reflexion by the news that comes to us that you have been buying potatoes in Bethlehem. When you were an editor, do I think for a moment that you ever went that far out of your way for a poem? Did you ever send to Derry for a poem? No, the poetry sought you, not you the poetry—else you got along famously on prose. And what are potatoes, pray? Starch. You may ask the man who writes the advertisements for grape-nuts [sic(k)].[66] I cannot help but think. One of my apple trees, standing stock still and rooted, earns more money in a year than I can earn with all my locomotion and artistic detachment. The moral seems to be that I must write more and better poetry if I hope to compete in the market with things to eat.

How long ago and far away Bethlehem is already. Our summer was one of the pleasantest we have had for years. But it is almost hard for me to believe in the reality of it now. I have been that way from boyhood. The feeling of time and space is perennially strange to me. I used to lie awake at night imagining the places I had traversed in the day and doubting in simple wonderment that I who was here could possibly have been there and there. I can't look at my little slope of field here with leaves in the half dead grass, or at the bare trees the birds have left us with, and fully believe there were ever such things as the snug downhill churning room with the view over five ranges of mountains, our talks under the hanging lamp and over the fat blue book,[67]

---

64. See *CPRF*, 74–75.

65. Scottish dialect: strangely, remarkably, unusually, etc.

66. The "sic" / "sick" joke is RF's, exactly as rendered here. Advertisements for C. W. Post's "Grape Nuts" current in the summer of 1907 claimed that the processes unique to Post allowed for starch to be transformed into "glittering specks" of grape sugar, just as "the sap of the hickory or maple tree will frequently show in the shape of white sugar on the sawed off ends of logs."

67. Likely Arthur Quiller-Couch's *Oxford Book of English Verse*, published first in 1900. RF would, in later years, always have a copy on hand (as letters sent from England in 1913 attest). Indeed, the book had dark blue board covers. RF would have known the anthology by 1907, if not earlier—and not only because a woman then resident in Derry, Sarah

the tea-inspired Mrs Lynch, baseball, and the blue black Lafayette.[68] There is a pang there that makes poetry. I rather like to gloat over it.

Sincerely yours
Robert Frost

[To Susan Hayes Ward. Only the closing page of the letter survives. Thompson dates the letter to January 1908; we follow his precedent here. ALS. Huntington.]

[Derry, NH]
[circa January 1908]

[. . .] he hadn't. We resolved then and there not to lie about where we had been for fear of being doubted whether we lied or not. We went right to work to make our observations on the sun moon and Orion just as scientific and non-committal as possible. So you can rely on everything I have said in this letter.

You say you are coming to live over back here in So. Berwick.[69] Why then we'll be neighbors. You'll be less than a stone's throw from us. Indeed we regularly play football with a team that regularly plays with the So. Berwick boys.[70] I have been half way to So Berwick on foot. We Frosts claim the whole region thereabout by right of having settled it and fought Indians in it. So I'd really be more at home in it than you will be. I must send you sometime some Whitmanish of mine on my bad ancestor the Indian Killer who sleeps under a bowlder [*sic*] in Eliot Me.[71] But that won't be till you lend me the po-

---

H. Couch, claimed kinship with Quiller-Couch (a matter about which RF jokes in a December 25, 1912, letter to John Bartlett). We thank Mark Scott for the suggestion.

68. Mt. Lafayette, in the White Mountain range; the Frosts would later settle there in 1915, almost in the shadow of the mountain, on a farm in Franconia.

69. The Ward family would soon retire to a residence in South Berwick, which RF did, on occasion, visit.

70. A reference to the Pinkerton Academy football team.

71. In the 1630s, Nicholas Frost acquired substantial acreage near what is now Eliot, Maine. In 1650 his wife and daughter were captured and killed by Native American raiders. In "Genealogical," RF recounts the history of Nicholas Frost's son, Major Charles Frost, a colonial militia leader during King Philip's War who was ambushed and killed near Eliot on July 4, 1697. Seeking revenge on Major Frost for his role in the capture and execution of Native American warriors twenty years earlier, his assailants removed his body from the grave and displayed it. When he was again buried, a massive stone was used to protect the grave. RF's description of "Genealogical" as "Whitmanish" refers to

ems by the Sweet Singer of Mich. which you promised me once.[72] Meanwhile we are all from Margery[73] up and from me down

Very truly yours,
Robert Frost

[To Susan Hayes Ward. ALS. Huntington.]

Plymouth New Hampshire
Dec 19 1911

Dear Miss Ward:—

I don't know where you are, nor how you are, nor how you are at present disposed toward minor poets. And I have been such a laggard in letter writing that I don't believe I deserve to know. Well then take this book of manuscript verse as a peace offering.[74] I thought it might be nearer right in the circumstances than anything I could buy in the book mart. It represents, needless to tell <u>you,</u> not the long deferred forward movement you are living in wait for, but only the grim stand it was necessary for me to make until I should gather myself together. The forward movement is to begin next year. Luckily I am not George B. McClellan to have to fear being removed from command by the politicians just on the eve of accomplishment.[75] So it is still mañana, you see. But don't think to laugh with impunity at my boast as you may have laughed at the boasts of so many before. In my case you would find yourself mistaken. Elinor will tell you so. I should so very much like to see

---

its unrhymed and nonmetrical lines of variable length. He eventually sent Ward a copy. See RF to Ward, December 19, 1911.

72. Julia Ann Moore (1847–1920), the "Sweet Singer of Michigan," was an American poetaster of the sentimental "obituary" school. Her popularity was greatest in the 1870s, and she is thought to be Twain's inspiration for the character of Emmeline Grangerford in *Huckleberry Finn*.

73. Marjorie Frost was the youngest child in the family (born in 1905); RF spells her name inconsistently in letters. The other children were Irma (born in 1903), Carol (born in 1902), and Lesley (born in 1899).

74. RF had made a booklet of seventeen poems as a Christmas token. All of these materials are in the Huntington Library collection.

75. In November of 1862, Abraham Lincoln ordered General McClellan to be relieved of command of the Union Army because he had not pursued Lee following the Confederate loss at Antietam in September.

you for a talk on such vanities that I should be quite inclined to run down to New York for a two days' visit toward the end of next week (or some other time) if you asked me. You are to think of me now as a dweller in Plymouth in the White Mountains where I teach psychology in the State Normal School.[76] I am sending along as collateral that authentic bit of family history I once promised you. I sha'n't apologize for the Whitmanesque.[77] To these things let me add Christmas greetings for the season, but more especially friendly greetings for all the year round.

Sincerely yours
Robert Frost

[To Susan Hayes Ward. ALS. Huntington.]

Plymouth N.H.
Dec 28 1911

Dear Miss Ward:

I so burned four or five of my fingers on merry Christmas morning that I have been afraid I ought to give up the idea of visiting you this week. It was not so much the pain, which I walked off in a few hours, as the disfigurement that troubled me. I was almost sure I shouldn't be fit to be seen for a while. But two days have made a great improvement in me and at this writing I haven't very much left to show for my meddling with the hot steam-pipes and by tomorrow should have less. And though getting along in years like other folks, I still find myself young enough to hate and abhor giving up what I have once really set my heart on. So I am coming to have a spoken word with you, if no more than a word. And this as of obligation; for how are we going to continue to read each other's letters satisfactorily unless we renew in memory from time to time the image of the living voice that informs the sentences.[78] I shall start from here Friday and should reach you early

---

76. In fall 1911, RF accepted Ernest L. Silver's invitation to join the faculty at Plymouth State Normal School (Silver had previously been headmaster at Pinkerton Academy, where RF taught from 1906 until leaving for Plymouth).

77. "Genealogical" (*CPPP*, 514–516).

78. Another early intimation of what RF would later call, variously, "sentence sounds" and "the sounds of sense."

Saturday. I can have till Monday afternoon with you, I think, provided I can get leave to omit a lecture or two on Tuesday morning. Till I see you then.

Sincerely yours,
Robert Frost

[To Susan Hayes Ward. ALS. Huntington.]

Plymouth N.H.
Circa Jan 15 1912

Dear Miss Ward:

It wasn't to be expected that I would get back to business the minute my train arrived; and I didn't. And that was not because I can't move as fast as a train when I am on a train, but because it is so much further from the literary to the psychophysical than it is from little New York to Plymouth. I have been a constant sufferer since my visit with you from that Where-was-I-when-I-left-off or What-did-I-say-last feeling as I should have made complaint before if I had felt constrained to write you before I got safely and thoroughly home. I must tell you that one day—I couldn't for the life of me say how afterwards—I actually turned a recitation in the History of Education into a recitation of irrelevant verse. But there's no harm done, perhaps even some good. At any rate Elinor and I think so. It will never be counted against you with us that you have encouraged my poor Muse with interest when you couldn't with praise.

If this doesn't look like a very long letter to be writing to a friend and benefactor (by actual count of words it will prove longer than it looks), please remember who it was that Luther thought the proper target to throw ink at by the bottleful.[79] Not the friend and benefactor of anyone in particular was it?

Sincerely yours
Robert Frost

Sonnet on the next page for my Moth and Butterfly book.[80]

---

79. While completing the first translation of the New Testament into German, Martin Luther claimed to have fought the Devil on a daily basis. Legend has it that he flung an inkwell at the Devil, a misunderstanding that likely grew out of his wry comment that he had "driven the devil away with ink" (i.e., with his translation of the Bible).

80. Accompanying the letter is a manuscript fair copy of a sonnet entitled "In White," an early version of "Design." "Moth and Butterfly book": perhaps a reference to the fact

[To Susan Hayes Ward. ALS. Huntington.]

Plymouth N.H.
Feb 10 1912

Dear Miss Ward:

You should receive almost simultaneously with this your long-lost Sweet Singer.[81] I ought to say that I don't think I laughed at her as much as I should have if I had been a hearty normal person and not something of a sweet singer myself. She is only a little more self-deceived than I am. That she was not altogether self-deceived I conclude from the lines in which she declares it her delight to compose on a sentimental subject when it comes into her mind just right. There speaks something authentic anyway.

Two lonely cross-roads that themselves cross each other I have walked several times this winter without meeting or overtaking so much as a single person on foot or on runners. The practically unbroken condition of both for several days after a snow or a blow proves that neither is much travelled.[82] Judge then how surprised I was the other evening to see a man, who to my own unfamiliar eyes and in the dusk looked for all the world like myself, coming down the other, his approach to the point where our paths must intersect being so timed that unless one of us pulled up we must inevitably collide. I felt as if I was going to meet my own image in a slanting mirror. Or say I felt as we slowly converged on the same point with the same noisless [*sic*] yet laborious stride as if we were two images about to float together with the uncrossing of someone's eyes. I verily expected to take up or absorb this other self and feel the stronger by the addition for the three-mile journey home. But I didn't go forward to the touch. I stood still in wonderment and let him pass by; and that, too, with the fatal omission of not trying to find out by a comparison of lives and immediate and remote interests what could have brought us by crossing paths to the same point in a wilderness at the

---

that a funereal moth figures into "In White," while the first poem RF sent to the Wards was "My Butterfly: An Elegy."

81. Julia Moore. See RF's January 1908 letter to Ward (which survives as only a fragment) and notes.

82. This and several other phrases in the paragraph seem to anticipate what would later become "The Road Not Taken" ("neither is much travelled," etc.) (*CPPP*, 103), and, perhaps, also "Design" ("what could have brought us by crossing paths to the same point in a wilderness at the same moment of nightfall. Some purpose I doubt not, if we could but have made it out") (*CPPP*, 275).

same moment of nightfall. Some purpose I doubt not, if we could but have made it out. I like a coincidence almost as well as an incongruity. Enclosed is another in print. The Marion C. Smith you were talking of when I was with you I was very certain I had heard of somewhere, but I didn't know where. It must have [been] here. Heard of her? Yes it is almost as if I had met her in the pages of the Companion.[83]

Nonsensically yours
Robert Frost

[To Thomas Bird Mosher (1852–1923), an American publisher and bibliophile. Mosher published a magazine entitled the Bibelot, *and specialized in small, ornate editions; his first publication was George Meredith's* Modern Love *(1891). ALS. UVA.]*

State Normal School
Plymouth, N.H.
Feb 19, 1912

My dear Mr Mosher:

I was just saying of my poetry that it didn't seem to make head as fast as I could wish with the public, when the letter came in which you said almost the identical thing of your Bibelot. But you could add of your own motion that you were getting, you supposed, all that was coming to you. Not to be outdone by you in philosophy (which is my subject of instruction) I made myself say it after you for a discipline: I suppose that I am getting all that is coming to me. (These are harder words for me to pronounce than they ever could be for you—for reasons.) And then see how soon I had my reward. The very next day what should my poetry bring me but a check for twenty-five dollars, which is more than it ever brought before at one time. Some part of this belongs to you in simple poetic justice. Five dollars say. You wouldn't tempt me to spend forty dollars on the Bibelot or anything else if you knew the ambitious schemes I have at heart, imposing habits of the strictest economy for the next ten years. But I can, and herewith do, send five dollars for books; and without impropriety, I trust, to satisfy my sense of the fitness of

83. Marion Couthouy Smith (1853–1931). Her work had indeed appeared in *The Youth's Companion*. The poem RF enclosed "in print" was therefore probably "Ghost House," published in *The Youth's Companion* for March 15, 1906.

things, I copy on the inside of this sheet the poem[84] by which I earned it, glad of the chance to show poems of mine to one whose life is so conspicuously devoted to the cause of poetry.

Very truly yours,
Robert Frost
(over)

[To Thomas Bird Mosher. ALS. UVA.]

Plymouth N.H.
March 4 1912

My dear Mr. Mosher:

You must have my whole story of the poem Reluctance. It was The Atlantic that had returned it and left me in that dejection your letter lifted me out of. I am not for the High Seas (or should I say the High Cs) yet it seems; and you must not think it of me. The Companion took the poem. Following hard upon that piece of good luck The Forum took another poem which I call My November Guest.[85] I suppose both poems were accepted with Reluctance as I was assured by The Atlantic that the first was rejected with Reluctance, more than the usual Reluctance. I do not say that either of them heralds a new force in literature.[86] Indeed I think I have others still under cover that more nearly represent what I am going to be. They are a beginning—that is all, and in print, with the chance of making friends, should encourage me to make more.

If it is anything for you to know it, both your letters have been a help in the work I have set my hand to. What that work is I know full well and what it entails. I expect nothing. Even the small mercies you speak of I have schooled myself to think of as too large for me. My great difficulty is going to be to get a hearing with the crowd-deafened editors. And there are other difficulties. I

84. "Reluctance," a fair copy of which RF inscribed on the reverse side of the letter. The poem, later collected in *ABW,* would appear in *The Youth's Companion* for November 7, 1912.

85. Published in *The Forum* for November 1912 and, with "Reluctance," collected in *ABW.*

86. A year later RF would, however, make the claim that the poems collected in *NB,* his second volume, *did* herald a new force in literature. See his July 4, 1913, letter to Bartlett, written while he was assembling *NB*: "To be perfectly frank with you I am one of the most notable craftsmen of my time. That will transpire presently."

think I have considered them all and for the most part face them with serenity. Only there are impatient moments when I need the good word of a sympathizer to recall me to a sense of my philosophy.

Sincerely yours
Robert Frost

[To Ernest Leroy Silver (1878–1949). Silver was head of the Plymouth (New Hampshire) Normal School, where RF taught psychology (among other things) from 1911 to 1912. Littleton, New Hampshire, lies some ten miles from Franconia. ALS. DCL.]

Franconia N.H.
June 13 1912

Dear Silver:

Your friendly invitation came altogether too late for us. It takes a letter directed to us at Littleton a whole day extra to reach us and then it only reaches our box in the post office where it may lie another day before we go after it. We got yours when the show was about over at Plymouth.[87] I made a futile effort to get you on the telephone and thank you and ask you to leave a key with Hardy or someone else so that if the truck comes for me to go after the furniture I can get at it all right. It's the truck I have been waiting for. The man who offers to go to Plymouth for me will do it for fifteen dollars a trip when his truck is repaired. There's some part of it he is waiting for from the manufacturer.

I should rather get down when you are in Plymouth and perhaps I can manage to put off the business, though we begin to need the furniture.

Things have hung fire fearfully since I spoke you [*sic*] in passing. I am living on a small farm that I expect to buy if the vicegerent[88] of my grandfather on earth doesnt fail me. I am going to farm a little. I have had two cows come in this week, so that we are swimming in milk already—if you call that farming. At the same time there are great uncertainties.

87. The "show" was almost certainly the New Hampshire Summer Institute and School of Science, convened yearly under the auspices of the State Superintendent of Education.

88. Wilbur Rowell, executor of RF's paternal grandfather's estate, from which the poet received an annuity. RF did eventually buy a farm in Franconia, but not until the spring of 1915. The present letter suggests that, even as late as June 1912, RF had not yet decided to leave for England, as he would two months later in August.

Can't you run up here once in a while this summer? You won't mind our camping ways. You would be interested in telling us what to do with our cheap little farm. We have some woodland to look over and some barns that want condemning.

We were sorry not to be able to be with you especially at the feeding event. Of course everything went off well as everything always does go off when you manage it without seeming to manage it.

With best regards.

Sincerely yours
Robert Frost.

[To Wilbur Rowell (1862–1946), executor of RF's paternal grandfather's estate. The letter is written on the letterhead of Plymouth Normal School. ALS. UVA.]

Plymouth N.H.
June 25, 1912

Dear Mr. Rowell:

I must be letting you know that I shall be here (and no longer at Derry) when the time comes round to make the annual award. I felt almost sorry to be so far from Lawrence when the syndicalist strike was on. How much Lawrence has and has not changed since I left the town twelve years ago! The Letts and the Portuguese and the Greeks and the Syrians are all quite new. But at the same time they appear not to have altogether displaced the older population. I never heard of the Syrian dentist who was for dying a martyr to the cause at the hands of the militia. But I was going to say I knew all the other people the papers mentioned from Clark Carter to John Breen.[89] I went

89. RF refers to a textile strike under the leadership of the Industrial Workers of the World in Lawrence during January–March 1912. The strike, often called the "Bread and Roses strike," lasted ten weeks and involved some 30,000 workers, more than half of them women and children. John Breen, a local undertaker and a member of the Lawrence school board, was arrested and charged with planting explosives in a plot to discredit the workers. The Reverend Clark Carter, who did missionary work among the poor in Lawrence, and city postmaster Louis Sherburne Cox (party to the militia assembled to maintain order in the city), both gave testimony inimical to the strikers when Congress investigated the incident. Daniel "Danny" James Murphy, a Harvard alumnus, was Solicitor of Lawrence from 1906 to 1908 and again from 1910 to 1916. The "Syrian dentist" is named, in a *New York Times* account of the strike, as a Doctor "Hazyar." One of

to one college with Danny Murphy, to another with Louis Cox. I went to the Hampshire St. school with John Breen. I am proudest to have known John—as you may suppose.

Very truly yours,
Robert Frost

[To Wilbur Rowell. The letter is written on the letterhead of Plymouth Normal School. ALS. UVA.]

[Plymouth, NH]
July 16 1912

Dear Mr Rowell:

I dont know just what to say about the things Mr Abbott[90] has in keeping. It is kind and thoughtful for you to have troubled yourself with them at all, and I am unwilling to trouble you further. Perhaps if you could give me Mr Abbott's address, I could write to him for some idea of what there is and so make up my mind whether the case calls for a trip to Lawrence. I should suppose not. No books my uncle collected are likely to be of any value. Possibly there may be photographs I should like to keep in the family; but those it might not be too much to ask Mr. Abbott to have bundled and sent to me.

Thank you for the check.

Very truly yours,
Robert Frost

---

the two people killed by the militia was a fifteen-year-old Syrian boy named John Rami. As RF indicates in the letter, he and Cox were at Dartmouth College at the same time (that is, in fall 1892: Cox graduated with the class of 1896), and Murphy was at Harvard when RF matriculated there in 1897.

90. Lawrance Thompson identifies Abbott as the executor of the estate of RF's uncle, Elihu Colcord. See *SL*, 48.

Robert Frost in 1915 in Littleton, New Hampshire. Taken by Eaton's Studio, this photograph was used in Holt publicity with the caption, "New England's New Poet."

Courtesy Dartmouth College Library.

“England in the Grip of Frost”

Beaconsfield, September 1912–March 1914

Here we are between high hedges of laurel and red-osier dogwood, within a mile or two of where Milton finished Paradise Lost on the one hand and a mile or two of where Grey lies buried on the other and within as many rods or furlongs of the house where Chesterton tries truth to see if it wont prove as true upside down as it does right side up. To London town what is it but a run?

—Robert Frost to Susan Hayes Ward, September 5, 1912

[To Susan Hayes Ward. On August 23, 1912, the Frosts boarded a ship to sail from Boston to England, where they settled in the London suburb of Beaconsfield. RF would soon head his letters playfully, and variously, "The Bung," or "The Bung-hole," or "The Bung, Beaks, Bucks." ALS. Huntington.]

The Bungalow
Beaconsfield
Buckingham
England
September 15 1912

Dear Miss Ward:

Perhaps I ought not to conceal from you, as one of the very few mortals I feel in any sense answerable to, that I am in the mood called aberrant. Psychology holds me no longer. What have I taught for, anyway, but to confute my well-wishers who believed I was not enough of the earth earthy to be above a fool? And now that I have proved myself as a teacher in two departments of learning without benefit of college, my soul inclines to go apart by itself again and devise poetry. Heaven send that I go not too late in life for the emotions I expect to work in. But in any case I should not stay, if only for scorn of scorn—scorn of the scorn that leaves me still unnoticed among the least of the versifiers that stop a gap in the magazines. The Forum gives me space for one poem this year; the Companion for two.[1] The Independent,

1. "My November Guest" appeared in *The Forum* in November 1912, "October" in *The Youth's Companion* for October 3, 1912, and "Reluctance" in the same magazine for November 7. "Of the earth, earthy" (earlier in the letter): see 1 Corinthians: 15:47.

longest my friend, has held one of my poems unprinted now these three years. So slight is my consideration. I may be too old to write the song that once I dreamed about ("The tender touching thing"[2])—at least I can achieve something solid enough to sandbag editors with.

Here we are between high hedges of laurel and red-osier dogwood, within a mile or two of where Milton finished Paradise Lost on the one hand and a mile or two of where Grey[3] lies buried on the other and within as many rods or furlongs of the house where Chesterton tries truth to see if it wont prove as true upside down as it does right side up.[4] To London town what is it but a run? Indeed when I leave writing this and go into the front yard for a last look at earth and sky before I go to sleep, I shall be able to see the not very distant lights of London flaring like a dreary dawn. If there is any virtue in location—but don't think I think there is. I know where the poetry must come from if it comes.

Sincerely yours always
Robert Frost

[To Ernest L. Silver. RF refers in the first sentence to the playwright George Bernard Shaw. Dating suggests late September 1912, as the Frosts arrived in London on September 2 and stayed there for a week, during which they saw a performance of Fanny's First Play. *ALS. DCL.]*

The Bungalow
Beaconsfield
Bucks
England
[circa late September 1912]

Dear Mr Silver:—

The first thing I really saw on arriving here was not, as you may have been lead [*sic*] to suppose, the hoe whereof I wrote, but Fanny's First Play by the

---

2. A line from stanza one of "After Many Years" by the Australian poet Henry Kendall (1839–1882); the poem was first collected in Kendall's *Songs from the Mountains* (Sydney, 1880).

3. Thomas Gray (1716–1771), English poet, was buried in the churchyard at Stoke Poges in South Buckinghamshire.

4. G. K. Chesterton (1874–1936), the English philosopher, poet and playwright, lived in Beaconsfield.

author of Candida and Mrs. Warren's Profession. The hoe, however, when I did see it, made me forget everything else for the time being. It was made yesterday, so to speak, by men living to-day. We bought it brand new at the ironmonger's. But it carried me back in time further than any building I have seen in the Gothic style, further than anything I have seen except a little fossil shell I broke from the side of a chalk cliff, which you think I am inventing for literary purposes but which I should send you if I could be sure of getting it through the customs. The fossil carried me back two hundred thousand years (I'll leave it to the Rev Smith if it didn't); the hoe to the transition period between the Paleolithic and the Neolithic ages.[5] To me it looked like the implement the caveman took in hand when he went courting, just as now no well-dressed Englishman but carries his cane, for you know the former was always violent in love as the latter is sometimes violently in love—though not in Fanny's First Play (565th performance.)

And so I might continue indefinitely in the approved manner of the diverting correspondent.

But speaking of Fanny's First Play (which I can't seem to get away from), you may say I have come a long distance for what I might have had in Boston or New York next winter. Yes, and just so I have come a long distance to be what I could have been quite as well on a New Hampshire farm and that is myself. How charming is divine philosophy when she wants to be disagreeable.

Well, then, what have I found in Albion that I couldn't have found nearer home.[6] Perhaps you would like it in the form of statistics. So best you will know you are getting it. I have found:—

No ragweed
No ice (and no need of any)
No lack of manners (especially in public servants)
No mosquitoes
No flies (to speak of. Total population of six at last census)
No screens (and no need of any)
No difference in cost of living (Hay is £6 a ton)

---

5. Gilbert N. Smith (1796–1877), amateur geologist and archaeologist, and rector of Gumfreston in South Wales; he unearthed fossils of extinct species at North Caldey Island.

6. Oldest known name of the island of Britain.

No railroad wrecks (let them tell it)
No real warmth (Climate that of a ship at sea)
No cellars. No stoves
No American news (unless you count the birth children of international marriages)
No dry goods (drapery, and less of that in some quarters than you would expect in this clime.)
No sun

But I desist, reminded by the last item that Tom Hood has listed the Noes of these parts quite exhaustively in a poem called November.[7] Get Miss Bird to recite it to you.[8]

I must have troubled you a great deal leaving things the way I did when I came away (Mrs Frost adjures me to lay this on pretty thick making abject apology and I will later when I can devote a whole letter to the business); I am to trouble you further by asking you to have my mail (excepting newspapers and The Independent) forwarded to me at The Bungalow as above.

I sigh for something to teach psychology to.

Sincerely yours
Robert Frost

---

7. Thomas Hood (1799–1845), British poet and humorist (and father of Tom Hood [1835–1874], a playwright, humorist, and editor of the magazine *Fun*). "November" reads:

No sun—no moon!
No morn—no noon—
No dawn—no dusk—no proper time of day.
No warmth, no cheerfulness, no healthful ease,
No comfortable feel in any member—
No shade, no shine, no butterflies, no bees,
No fruits, no flowers, no leaves, no birds!—
November!

8. Grace E. Bird, who then taught at Plymouth State Normal School.

[To Thomas Bird Mosher. TLS. DCL.]

The Bungalow,
Beaconsfield, Bucks,
England.
Nov. 19, 1912.

Mr. Thomas B. Mosher,
Portland, Me., U.S.A.

Dear Mr. Mosher:

One has some bad luck, but one has some good luck, too. The Amphora is beautiful luck, not unqualified, I must confess, by the intelligence that my poem just missed a place in it.[9] Your offer to print a volume of mine is the same kind of mixed pleasure. The Dea knows[10] I should like nothing better than to see my first book, "A Boy's Will," in your Lyric Garland Series. It even crossed my mind to submit it to you. But under the circumstances I couldn't, lest you should think I was going to come on you as the poor old man comes on the town. I brought it to England in the bottom of my trunk, more afraid of it, probably, than the Macnamara of what he carried in his.[11] I came here to write rather than to publish. I have three other books of verse somewhere near completion, "Melanism," "Villagers," and "The Sense of Wrong," and I wanted to be alone with them for a while. If I ever published anything, I fully expected it would be through some American publisher. But see how little I knew myself. Wholly on impulse one day I took my MS. of A Boy's Will to London and left it with the publisher whose imprint was the first I had noticed in a volume of minor verse on arriving in England,

---

9. The *Amphora* (1912) was a collection of excerpts of prose and verse, edited by Mosher.

10. RF uses an archaic expression he favored, as in his 1948 essay "A Romantic Chasm": "The Dea knows (as we still say in New England) I would go to any length short of idolatry to keep Great Britain within speaking, or at least shouting, distance of America in the trying times seen ahead" (*CPRF*, 158). The *Oxford English Dictionary* bears RF out: "Dea, deac, n. U.S. colloq. abbrevs. of deacon." All instances cited in the *OED* are from New England sources.

11. Radical labor activist James McNamara was convicted, along with his brother John, of dynamiting the *Los Angeles Times* building in October 1910. Clarence Darrow mounted their unsuccessful defense.

viz., David Nutt.[12] I suppose I did it to see what would happen, as once on a time I short-circuited a dynamo with a two-foot length of wire held between the brushes. What happened pleased me at first—in the case of the MS., I mean. I am not so sure how I feel about it now. David Nutt made me a proposal on a royalty basis. I have signed no contract as yet, but after what has passed, I suppose I am bound to sign, if pressed, almost anything that doesn't seem too one-sided. I expect the publisher will drive a hard bargain with me: who am I that he shouldn't have a right to? One thing that disconcerts me, however, is the eleventh-hour claim he makes on my next three or four books, verse or prose. I wish I knew what you would say to that. I suppose I ought to be proud to be so much in demand: the embarrassment is so novel in my experience. But wont it seem traitorously un-American to have all my first work come out over here? And how about you in whose hands I should feel so much happier and safer. And then there is Richard Badger of Boston who has asked to see material for a book.[13] Why couldn't you have spoken two weeks sooner and saved me all this perplexity? It seems to me you owe me something in the way of helpful advice for not speaking. Perhaps I can stave off that contract till I can get an answer from you. Have I made a serious mistake in going to David Nutt? Do you know anything about him (or her, if I may drop the business fiction)? Am I too far committed to draw back? I am nearly the worst person in the world in a muddle like this.

---

12. As John Evangelist Walsh notes (in *Into My Own: The English Years of Robert Frost* [37]), the poet in question was William Ernest Henley (1845–1903). David Nutt published several books by him, including, in 1898, his *Poems*. That book went through ten printings, down to 1907, and the following remarks, in the preface Henley wrote for the first edition, may have moved RF to consult David Nutt: "My friend and publisher, Mr. Alfred Nutt, asks me to introduce this re-issue of old work in a new shape. The work of revision has reminded me that, small as is this book of mine, it is all in the matter of verse that I have to show for the years between 1872 and 1897. A principal reason is that, after spending the better part of my life in the pursuit of poetry, I found myself (about 1877) so utterly unmarketable that I had to own myself beaten in art, and to addict myself to journalism for the next ten years. Came the production by my old friend, Mr. H. B. Donkin, in his little collection of 'Voluntaries' (1888), compiled for that East-End Hospital to which he has devoted so much time and energy and skill, of those unrhyming rhythms in which I had tried to quintessentialize, as (I believe) one scarce can do in rhyme, my impressions of the Old Edinburgh Infirmary. They had long since been rejected by every editor of standing in London—I had well-nigh said in the world; but as soon as Mr. Nutt had read them, he entreated me to look for more. I did as I was told."

13. Richard G. Badger of the Gorham Press in Boston.

Once again let me say how much I think of the book—the books—I have had time to look at but one yet. I am going to have you send two or three books to a young friend in Vancouver,[14] but I leave the order for another letter, when I shall have had leisure to pick and choose.

Very truly yours,
Robert Frost

You will notice my corrected address.

[To Ernest L. Silver. ALS. DCL.]

The Bung. Hole
Beaconsfield Bucks Eng.
Dec 25 1912

Dear Mr. Silver:

The way you keep calling for a literary letter, just as if I hadn't given you one in that laconic monograph on the Neanderthal hoe.[15] I might follow it up with another on the Boadicean chariot with the scythes left off the axles in which the milkmen deliver their milk.[16] But if the first was too archaeological to be literary, possibly the second would be too historical or military. I have what you want. You have heard of the land of Tir-nan-Og, "Where you may buy joy for a penny."[17] Well, this is It. One can buy anything here for a penny that he can buy in the States for a cent or without money and without

14. John T. Bartlett, a student of RF's at Pinkerton Academy, had moved with his wife Margaret to British Columbia to launch a career in journalism.

15. In a November 18, 1912, letter to RF (largely discussing the recent presidential election and affairs at the Plymouth Normal School), Silver had asked, in closing, that RF "write something literary to enjoy" (the letter is held at DCL). For the "hoe," see RF to Silver September 1912.

16. "Boadicean": having to do with Queen Boudicca of the Brittonic Iceni tribe of modern day East Anglia who, according to Tacitus, led an uprising in CE 60 or 61 against the Roman governor Gaius Suetonius Paulinus. Boudicca—whose name, derived from the Gaelic *bouda*, means victory—became an important symbol for citizens of the United Kingdom, with Queen Victoria portrayed as her namesake. A statue near Westminster Pier commissioned by Prince Albert and completed by Thomas Thornycroft in 1905 shows Boudicca in a chariot with scythes extending horizontally out from its axles.

17. Tir na nÓg ("Land of the Young"), from an Old Irish mythical story in which every seven years any man can compete for the king's throne. RF quotes a line from a poem by

price—such as a glass of water on his travels. And please to remember a penny is two cents.[18] It is a just inference that we have crossed the ocean to double the cost of living. Yet if that is the case, I don't make out how it is that more than half the men in this kingdom manage to "Come it brave and meek on thirty bob a week"—and even less.[19] The best-paid London Bobby in all his glory earns from five to six dollars a week and found [*sic*] only when he gets lost in a fog. Farm hands earn ten and twelve shillings and find themselves. I speak but the sober (and sobering) truth. Their young of school age help out by howling and rattling tins all day in the winter wheat and rye to keep the crows off. I begin to get some idea of how it would feel to be "not worth a breakfast in the cheapest country under the cope."[20] But here I go running into economics when my forte is supposed to be literature.

In a last mad attempt to be literary (before I actually am literary) let me ask you to reread Lorna Doone from start to finish and see if you don't say it gives the impression that we have real winters here.[21] By we I mean me and the king and Lord Burnham and the rest of the English. Recess of five minutes during which you comply with my request. All right, you have reread Lorna. What do you say? We have real winters? Well, we haven't. Yon book is the damnedest piece of unrealism. I saw it praised the other day for moderation. But—, what dont we get praised for! To date I personally haven't seen a flake of snow. There are three feet of mud on the level—I mean I speak on the level. A douce farmer-man backs up his dump-cart to his mangel wurtzel pile to get a load.[22] He has previously cut the ground up a good

---

Katharine Tynan Hinkson (1861–1931) that begins: "You may buy joy for a penny yonder in Tir na nÓg." Thomas Bird Mosher had published the poem in his *Bibelot* in 1903.

18. Archaic phrasing. "Please to remember" was commonly used in the eighteenth century, but largely fell out of use by the end of the nineteenth.

19. RF quotes a line from "Thirty Bob a Week" by the Scottish poet John Davidson (1857–1909).

20. See Shakespeare, *Pericles* (5.vi): "If your peevish chastity, which is not worth a breakfast in the cheapest country under the cope, shall undo a whole household, let me be gelded like a spaniel."

21. *Lorna Doone: A Romance of Exmoor* (1869), by R. D. Blackmore (1825–1900), where chapters 41–45 describe the Great Winter of 1683–1684.

22. "Douce," as RF uses it, is carried over from Scottish and Northumbrian dialects, perhaps as heard in the speech of his mother, who was born in the Scottish lowland town of Alloa. RF often uses dialect peculiar to the region (even as he quotes, elsewhere in the present letter, a Scottish poet and an old Scottish song). See the *Oxford English Dictionary*:

deal and to-day he incontinently goes in to the hubs of his wheels and the knees of his horse. He loses his temper and goes home to dinner without his horse. Maybe he comes back in the afternoon with a shovel to rescue the poor beast and maybe he doesn't come back till next week after he has heard the Sunday sermon on the immanence of the spirit. He knows the horse is perfectly safe all the time. No one can steal it without taking more trouble than its worth. It can sink in just so far and then something, an old Roman pavement I venture to say, will stop it. And meanwhile the horse patiently stands through several rains the very type and image of the English lower class taught to know and accept its place. We have had ice a few times on the rain barrel if that constitutes winter. And one morning early in December, the papers were out with scare heads like this:

ENGLAND IN THE GRIP OF FROST

I accept the omen, says I, I accept the omen. Better so than that Frost should be in the grip of England. And yet when all is said the season is far from balmy. There's a slant of wind we get that's daggers in the pulmonary lung. And when you scrape your face the stubble on your razor blade looks greyer than before you came down with seasickness, but it's owing to mould, nothing but mould. I set out to be literary and only succeed in being meteorological and pathological, you see.

Between you and me, though, I know what would be literary and highly literary. To talk about myself. I have been keeping this back for effect. You have doubtless heard through my friend Concubar[23] that I am publishing the first book and that is the good news you refer to in your Christmas postal. I signed articles a week or two ago for my first five books prose or verse (should I ever live to write so many). I'm not likely to live, what with this climate and the way I am burning the candle at both ends. Intemperance is my curse. There is nothing I do or don't do that I don't over do. Last summer it was ten-

---

"douce, *adj.* 2. Quiet, sober, steady, gently sedate; not light, flighty, or frivolous. *Sc.* and *north. dial.*" The "mangel-wurzel" is a type of beet.

23. According to Lawrance Thompson, a humorous reference to RF's wife, Elinor, but certainly he is mistaken. RF refers instead to Daniel P. Connor (1870–1953) of Manchester, New Hampshire. Connor was a real estate agent and the author of a number of local color sketches and histories of the White Mountain region of New Hampshire; Connor used the pen name "Concubar" (the name of a legendary Gaelic king). This letter suggests that RF knew Connor and wrote to him; however, efforts to track down his papers have proved fruitless.

nis till the family trembled for my reason. Since I reached Beaconsfield it has been verse "like a pawing horse let go"[24] (I was almost forgetting to ring in quotations). When I ask myself in the words of the song "Oh why left I my home, Why did I cross the deep,"[25] I have to confess it was to write prose and earn an honest living. Poetry is not a living. It is not even a reputation to-day. It is at best a reputation next year or the year after. And yet I always feel as if I was justified in writing poetry when the fit is on me—as it was last January. Very little of what I have done lately goes to swell the first book, just one or two things to round out the idea. You may look for a slender thing with a slender psychological interest to eke out the lyrical. Call it a study in a certain kind of waywardness. My publisher is David Nutt of London and Paris, a friend as it turns out of Bergsons.[26]

I got some of the news from the Prospect but not enough.[27] I am homesick at times.

Sincerely yours
Robert Frost

[To John Bartlett (1892–1941), a student of Frost's at Pinkerton Academy and thereafter a lifelong friend. ALS. UVA.]

The Bung. Hole
Beaconsfield Bucks Eng
Dec 25 1912

Dear John:—

I worry about you when I don't get one letter from you in a month. You never say anything about Alec any more. The new press must be in: has it made no difference in your arrangement with him?[28] It is such matters as that that I am interested in. Is there nothing in the wind? I suppose I am lead [*sic*] to expect kaleidoscopic changes in your fortunes from the way things

24. The line occurs in Coleridge's *The Rime of the Ancient Mariner,* part five.

25. From the Scottish song, "Oh! Why Left I My Home" (words by Robert Gilfillan).

26. French philosopher Henri Bergson (1859–1941), whose *Creative Evolution* (1907) RF read in 1911.

27. Campus newspaper at Plymouth State Normal School.

28. James Alexander ("Alec") Paton, publisher of the *Point Grey Gazette* in Vancouver. Bartlett had loaned Paton six hundred dollars, the Bartlett family's entire savings, to purchase a new printing press for the newspaper; the investment later failed to pay off.

went when you first struck pay dirt. Not that I want to see you earning any more money—or even as much. I hoped that you would settle down, domesticate, so to speak, on one or other of your two papers and be satisfied with one salary. I infer that you are working at all hours. That may do for a short time. It can't last forever. No matter if it isnt hurting you—and I should like assurance on that head—it is leaving you small leisure for self-improvement (to put it in that ugly utilitarian way). It leaves you small leisure for the good old reading—that's the way I like better to say it. I don't say you must get on. I won't say it. But I do say you must invite you [*sic*] soul. Write something for me, something for someone better than your Vancouver reading public. I venture a hat that you wouldn't have to try very long if you set your John-T. wits to it, to make a place for some of your stuff in some of the weeklies here like T.P.'s or the new Everyman's.[29] Shape it short. Give it a touch of the color of the far west where the Frazer goes out.[30] Emphasize the social values. Give it a pain, a laugh, a thrill. And there you are. I am at you again as I was in the beginning. I haven't forgotten your Hindu boy.[31] Nothing ever came of him. A pity. But theres better fish you know—The question is who's characters out there? Whom do you run across that you could give a Londoner the feeling of? To the devil with this kind of preaching though unless you are going to take some stock in it. I have half a mind to go to writing up Vancouver myself.

It is altogether painful to me not to hear from you. The long letter Mrs Frost had from Margaret[32] was some consolation. But we must hear more and more definitely about your health and your satisfaction in your work. Gifts of God is it? Well dont let that scare you into redoubling your efforts to

29. *T.P.'s Weekly* was founded by Thomas P. O'Connor (1848–1929), Irish nationalist and member of Parliament. *Everyman,* a literary magazine, was first published in London in October 1912 by Joseph Malby Dent (1849–1926); Dent had started the Everyman's Library series in 1906.

30. The Fraser River has its mouth in Vancouver.

31. Apparently a reference to an article on which Bartlett had been at work. In 1908, Canada enacted legislation to limit Indian immigration, for which Vancouver was a major port of entry. The tensions over exclusionary practices flared most notably in the turning away of Sikh, Hindu, and Muslim passengers (all British subjects) aboard the Japanese steamer *Komagata Maru,* which sailed into Vancouver from the Punjab, via Hong Kong, Shanghai, and Yokohama, on May 23, 1914. Although most Indians in Vancouver were Sikh, they were indiscriminately labeled as Hindus.

32. John Bartlett's wife; both had been students of RF's at Pinkerton Academy.

make money when you are working double shifts as it is. Take care of yourself. I'm fond of you in my blundering way. Im glad your mother doesnt know how fond I am or she might make it a ground for disliking me. One advantage of being so far off is the freedom it confers of saying things in writing I couldn't say to your face. I never had more than one real row with you and that was about Pamir.[33] I was reminded of that to-day when I was browsing over Asia with Carol.[34] You were the best pupil I ever had and Margaret was the next best. So dont you do a single thing that I don't want you to.

I am not expected to say much about the Gifts of God I hope. All I say is dont let them influence you or divert you from your chosen way. Dont let them reduce you to the ranks. Only then will they live and grow up to thank you. Don't you fall into any error about the value of more than enough money at this stage of the game.

I should defy even Sarah Couch (wasn't that her name?) to make anything out of what I have written if she should open my letter for reasons of state or motives of curiosity.[35]

Sahrahh's distant relative Quiller-Couch[36] (I can recall the assumed modesty of the squint and curtsy with which she claimed him through the bars of the P. O. window) is very great shucks in these parts. Great on anthologies.

R F

---

33. The Pamir Mountains (Persian for "roof of the world") in Central Asia. RF probably refers not so much to the mountains as to certain passages in Matthew Arnold's "Sohrab and Rustum" in which they figure; he assigned the poem to his English class at Pinkerton. See also RF's February 26, 1913, letter to Bartlett for an allusion to the poem (the two men had apparently discussed it in detail).

34. Carol Frost, RF's only surviving son, then ten years old.

35. Town directories place Sarah H. Couch (occupation listed as "clerk") in Derry Village during the time RF taught at Pinkerton; her residence is given as Hildreth Hall, a building owned by the academy. She served as postmistress in Derry.

36. Arthur Quiller Couch (1863–1944) was an English author, poet, and literary critic, best known now as editor of *The Oxford Book of English Verse* (1900) and *The Oxford Book of Victorian Verse* (1912), both of which RF cherished. He bought the latter anthology on his arrival in England. For a possible allusion to the former, see RF's November 4, 1907, letter to Susan Hayes Ward and notes.

[To Sidney Cox (1889–1952), whom RF met in 1911 when Cox was teaching high school English in Plymouth, New Hampshire. Cox later enjoyed a long and distinguished teaching career at Dartmouth College, and the friendship between the two men lasted until Cox's death. Enclosed with the letter is a poem RF never collected. Cox apparently shared the letter with someone; in the left margin of the first sheet he writes: "I want to save this. Please send it back. S." In the early stages of the correspondence, RF misspelled Cox's first name as Sydney. ALS. DCL.]

The Bung. Hole
Beaconsfield Bucks Eng.
Dec 26 1912

Dear Sydney Cox:

I fully intended to write you some word that should reach you somewhere near Christmas time. You might need it to help you over the vacation and you might not. I knew you wouldn't be going down East this year. At any rate you would have time to read it if you didn't have time to answer it. But you have no idea of the way I mismanage myself since I broke loose and ceased to keep hours. It seems as if I did nothing but write and write and everything else I planned to do went where the Scotchman's saxpence went when he went to London. If you don't know that story you can ask me about it next time you see me.[37]

You will accept I suppose a note that shall be no more than promissory of more to come. I write chiefly to assure you of our pleasure in your good letter as I should have written the minute I received the characteristic postal that came posting on its heels. It needed no apology. You were enthusiastic about your studies, matter-of-fact about your menial duties, a happy combination that strikes me as peculiarly American.[38] What more could anyone ask in one off-hand letter? But if the letter was good enough for us, the postal was better. That rises to heights almost universal in that it voices the complaint of everyone who writes anything, viz., that nothing he writes quite represents his thought or his feeling. It is as hard to fill a vacuum with nothing as it is to fill a poem (for instance) with something. The best one can hope for is an approximation. Wilfred Meynell calls his latest volume of poetry

---

37. A common joke, as in this form, derived from *Punch,* in which a Scotsman says, on his return from London: "I had na been there an hour when bang! went saxpence!"

38. Cox was then a graduate student at the University of Illinois.

Verses and Reverses and owns in a preface that they are mostly reverses.[39] There you have it. The veteran learns to value what he writes as little for graces of style as for spelling. What counts is the amount of the original intention that isnt turned back and lost in execution. Symonds says Dowson (the sad sinner) for once says everything in Cynara.[40] I wonder what Dowson would say if he were alive as he might have been with a little less liquor and a little more of the water one sees so seldom over here—never a drop of it in lunch rooms, railroad stations, or streets.

There that's all I can give you now.

Of course Miss Howard[41] must make us a visit if she is coming to England. Tell us more about her plans when you write next time. Mrs Frost says she will join me in my next letter.

R.F.

IN ENGLAND

Alone in rain I sat today
On top of a gate beside the way,
And a bird came near with muted bill,
And a watery breeze keep [sic] *blowing chill*
From over the hill behind me.

I could not tell what in me stirred
To hill and gate and rain and bird,
Till lifting hair and bathing brow
The watery breeze came fresher now
From over the hill to remind me.

---

39. British poet Wilfrid Meynell (1852–1948) published *Verses and Reverses* first in 1900; a second edition followed in 1910, and a third in 1912.

40. John Addington Symonds (1840–1893), British poet and literary critic, supplied a preface for *The Poems of Ernest Dowson*—who died in 1900 at the young age of thirty-three—in which he said: "In the lyric in which he has epitomized himself and his whole life, a lyric which is certainly one of the greatest lyrical poems of our time, 'Non sum qualis eram bonae sub regno Cynaræ,' he has for once said everything, and he has said it to an intoxicating and perhaps immortal music." The title of Dowson's poem derives from Horace's Ode 4.i.: "I am not what I once was when Cynara ruled."

41. Evans explains in *RFSC*: "[Cox] had fallen in love with Beth Howard [a fellow student], who refused to marry him because he 'lacked self-confidence' " (18).

The bird was the kind that follows a ship,
The rain was salt upon my lip,
The hill was an undergoing wave,
And the gate on which I balanced brave
Was a great ships [sic] *iron railing.*

For the breeze was a watery English breeze
Always fresh from one of the seas,
And the country life the English lead
In beechen wood and clover mead
Is never far from sailing.

R.F.

[To the editor of The Youth's Companion *(at the time, Mark Antony DeWolfe Howe [1864–1960]). ALS. BU.]*

The Bungalow
Beaconsfield Bucks
England
[Winter 1912–13]

The Editor of The Companion
Boston, Mass., U.S.A.

Dear Sir:

Again I have to ask your permission to use verse of mine that has appeared in The Companion. This time it is the three poems "Reluctance," "October," and "Ghost House" for my forthcoming slip of a book "A Boy's Will" (David Nutt, London). "Occult, withheld,"[42] impersonal as you have been in dealing with me, I can't believe you are above a human interest in the fortunes of one you helped through lean years. I want you to know about my book. It is a series of lyrics standing in some such loose relation to each other as a ring of children who have just stopped dancing and let go hands. The psychologist in me ached to call it "The Record of a Phase of Post-adolescence."

42. RF borrows the phrase "Occult, withheld" from "The Blessed Damozel," by Dante Gabriel Rossetti.

Wouldn't that have edified Stanley Hall?[43] The book was lucky enough to find a publisher to assume all risks in the first house I left it with. I don't know how that happened unless it was because I didn't know enough to be afraid it wouldn't happen.

One of the poems I enclose is the riddling kind that I thought might do for a children's page.

Sincerely yours,
Robert Frost

[To Harry Alvin Brown (1869–1949), district superintendent of schools, Colebrook, New Hampshire, and director of the Bureau of Research of the New Hampshire Department of Public Instruction. ALS. Middlebury.]

The Bungalow
Beaconsfield
Bucks
England
Jan 7 1913

Dear Mr Brown:—

I have sent for your departmental ditty on the Colebrook High—more for the sake of having it than anything else.[44] I am in no immediate need of rereading it. I was on the point of asking for half a dozen copies to distribute among the educational acquaintances I am likely to make once I set seriously about visiting schools. I am glad the bulletin was so generally noticed. It was a good stroke for you, Mr Morrison, and the state.[45]

---

43. G. Stanley Hall (1844–1924) was author of, among other works, *Adolescence: Its Psychology and Its Relations to Physiology, Anthropology, Sociology, Sex, Crime, Religion and Education* (New York: D. Appleton & Company, 1904).

44. Harry Alvin Brown, *The Readjustment of a Rural High School to the Needs of the Community* (Washington, DC: U.S. Government Printing Office, 1912). The pamphlet concerns Colebrook Academy, in Colebrook, New Hampshire. As for "departmental ditty": see Rudyard Kipling's *Departmental Ditties and Other Verses,* published first in Lahore in 1886, and subsequently widely reprinted (sometimes in expanded editions, or with *Barrack-room Ballads*).

45. Henry C. Morrison (1871–1945) was superintendent of the New Hampshire Department of Public Instruction; after visiting RF's classroom at Pinkerton in 1909, he was so

Thus far I have visited but one English school. My reception was cordial enough after the ice was broken. But the fact that there was any ice to break showed a difference between schools here and in America. I made up my mind that I shouldn't really go visiting schools till I got around to ask Mr Morrison or some of you fellows for an introduction to the honorable board of education whose headquarters are in London. Time enough for that when I get my first book off my hands and two or three more off my mind.

(This pen works like respiration.)

My book wont be much larger than yours—fifty or sixty pages I figure it. It should be out some time in February. Its safe mediocrity is attested by the good luck it has had to start with. I had to show it to but one publisher, and he takes it entirely at his own risk, a thing, they tell me, that doesn't happen to anybody's first book over here. It never happened to any of George Meredith's books (of verse) as long as he lived.[46] It must have happened to mine because, as I say, it was so very ordinary and because I didn't know enough to be afraid it wouldn't happen. So far, so good.

I seem to forget just what event I had brought myself down to in my last letter. I think I had reached England, if you mean by reaching England—well, what do you mean by reaching England? What do I mean? I have been asking myself. Did I reach England when I went on board ship? Of course the ship was English—all ships are—and I could have been arrested there by English officers for any crime done in England (such as writing a bad poem). Legally I was on English ground. Or did I reach it when I got outside the three mile limit on the American coast and onto the high seas? It is well known that England owns the oceans now-a-days and those that dig canals between them only dig for her.[47] Or did I reach it when I first saw the coast of Galway which, peaceful though it looked through the haze, is where the wild and fascinating Irishman still snipes the deputies of the absentee landlord?[48] Or did I reach it when I nearly got myself thrown overboard by a

---

impressed that he invited the teacher-poet to speak before a small convention of educators in Exeter, New Hampshire (see *EY*, 348–349).

46. George Meredith (1832–1909), Victorian novelist and poet, published his first collection of verse, *Poems* (1851), at his own expense. The book attracted scant attention. Meredith never recouped the costs he incurred.

47. At the time, the Panama Canal was nearing completion; it opened in 1914.

48. RF alludes to the so-called "Land War," a period of agrarian rebellion in rural Ireland in the late nineteenth century. In February 1870, Prime Minister William Gladstone introduced the Landlord and Tenant Act, which sought to redistribute land from

Scotchman for innocently calling the fleet I saw off the Mull of Cantire English instead of British?[49] (I was finding out that if Ireland loves England in one way Scotland loves her in another.) Or did I reach it when I set foot in "Glasgie mud and dirt"? Or when we picnicked, the six of us by ourselves, in the snug compartment of the toy train for eight hours on end straight across the counties to Euston station in London? Or when I paid thrippence thruppence or six cents for my first London Times sometimes called in New York The Thunderer for the Jovian majesty of its pronouncements? Or when I heard G. B. Shaw tease the Suffragettes at one of their own meetings till they didnt know whether he had come to help (as advertised) or hinder them?[50] Or when I got my card of admission to the Library of the British Museum? Or when I came here to Beaconsfield to live behind a fifteen-foot hedge of American laurel more flourishing than any I ever saw in America? Or, being a teacher, wasn't it until I entered my first English school?

A word or two about that school. It was a rambling brick structure nowhere more than a storey high and covering a good deal of ground. I walked right into it from the earth of the yard to the tile floor of the room of the highest grade. There was no step up or down. There was a large open fireplace more for ventilation than warmth. The desks were for all the world like what you may see in one or two of the oldest halls at Harvard, one long backless bench of three inch stuff for the haunches, one long ditto a little higher for the elbows, books, and papers. The lighting was generous. I saw two or three battered old Broadwood pianos about and heard them too. The

---

absentee landlords, who were predominantly Protestant, to tenants, who were predominantly Catholic. The rebellion, spearheaded by the Irish National Land League, led to a prolonged period of (often violent) civil discord, lasting well into the 1890s. We thank Robert Bernard Hass for clarifying this allusion (in addition to several others in the present letter).

49. The Mull of Kintyre (formerly Cantyre) is the southwestern most tip of the Kintyre Peninsula in southwestern Scotland.

50. An active member of the Fabian Society, George Bernard Shaw had spoken in Hyde Park on February 9, 1907, before a meeting of the National Union of Women's Suffrage Societies: "I deny that any social problem will ever be satisfactorily solved unless women have their due share in getting it solved," he declared. "Let us get this obstacle of the political slavery of women out of the way and then we shall see all set to work on the problems—both sexes together with a will." Though devoted to women's suffrage, Shaw irritated many by arguing (somewhat impractically) for a "coupled vote," in which every ballot cast would be for paired male and female candidates, the idea being to secure an elected body equal parts women and men.

lads in broad white collars sang "Odds, bobs, hammers and tongs" for me.[51] That was all good. Text books were scarce and I will not say antiquated, for that is a fault we Americans are too apt to find, but unpedagogical. Beaconsfield is a fairish-sized town fifteen miles from the largest city in the world. It has no library for child or man. So much the more need for a working library in the school. What I was shown interested me. I heard its history. Lord Burnham, the school patron, keeps it up by occasional gifts of books that come to his newspaper office for review.[52] It is what Lord Burnham didn't want and what none of his office assistants wanted—leavings. There are perhaps 200 volumes in all, absolutely non-literary and non-educational, as dead wood as so many volumes of eighteenth century sermons. So much for equipment.

I saw too little of the teaching to judge it justly. I liked the teachers and I liked their looks. Two of the seven or eight I met were men. I should have said that the school takes care of all the poor children of the town for as many years as any of them go to school, say five or six at most. The teachers have classes of about forty apiece. The two men made two rooms of one by drawing a green baize curtain between them. I had some talk with the principal and have meant to see him again.[53] He is a gentle body, well read in a different way from most of our men. He knows the literary names better than the educational. He had not heard of Montessori. Neither for that matter had his teacher of the kindergarten. I did not allow myself to be surprised. Some people save themselves a lot of trouble by not hearing of new things too soon. You can see how. I counted it more to Mr Baker's discredit that he was proud of his school library than that he hadn't heard of Montessori. He had the common scepticism about the value of psychology to teachers. He put it to me straight if I thought the stuff was worth very much. "It's deep, I know" he wound up by way of voluntary concession.

---

51. "Odds, bobs, hammer and tongs": Captain Hook's favorite expletive in J. M. Barrie's *Peter Pan*. The phrase derives from a refrain in one of Royal Navy officer and novelist Frederick Marryat's sea ballads. See his *Snarleyyow, or The Dog Fiend* (1837): "Odds, bobs, hammer and tongs, long as I've been to sea, / I've fought 'gainst every odds—and I've gained the victory."

52. The title of Baron Burnham was created in 1903 for the influential owner of the *Daily Telegraph,* Sir Edward Levy-Lawson, thereafter Lord Edward Levy-Lawson, First Baron Burnham.

53. Arthur Baker (b. in Eton, Buckinghamshire, ca. 1856), headmaster (at the time) of a school in Beaconsfield, where RF lived; his daughter Edith (age twenty-three at the time) was a teacher there.

I have said a good deal already or I should like to tell you about the children. They were well enough when one considers what they were. One would have to go to the slums of the city for their like in face and form in America. I did not see the sprinkling of bright eyes I should look for in the New England villages you and I grew up in. They were clean enough—the school sees to that. But some of them were pitiful little kids. Mr Baker stood them on their seats for me to inspect like slaves in the market—cases of malformation and malnutrition. Too many of these in proportion, I thought. But you have to remember that no one here sends his children to the government schools if he can possibly send them elsewhere.

We heard from Miss Murphy about the result at Durham.[54] And afterward Mr Silver wrote about it in accents so sincerely sorry that I am left in doubt whether I did the man an injustice or not last summer. I wish I knew.

I want you to keep that road broken through the Notch.[55]

Regards from all of us to both of you.

Lesley is going to make out for you a schedule of studies such as obtains in the kind of dame's school she is attending.

It is now two o'clock in the morning in Beaconsfield and eleven o'clock at night in Colebrook—time to go to bed in either place.

Sincerely yours
Robert Frost

---

54. Likely Alice E. Murphy (b. 1875), a teacher in Strafford, New Hampshire, not far from Durham. For the "results" at Durham (as they pertain to Henry Morrison), see RF to Silver, July 10, 1913.

55. Franconia Notch, familiar to the Frost family from when they summered in northern New Hampshire during ragweed season.

[To F. S. Flint (1885–1960), British poet and translator. The occasion to which RF refers in the following letter is the opening of Harold Monro's Poetry Bookshop, Devonshire Street, London, January 8, 1913. It was here that RF first met F. S. Flint, whose 1910 volume, In the Net of the Stars *(London: Elkin Matthews), RF discusses in the letter. The house RF rented in Beaconsfield, a suburb of London, was called the Bungalow. "Bucks" is Buckinghamshire. ALS. HRC.]*

The Bungalow
Beaconsfield
Bucks
Jan 21 1913

Dear Mr. Flint:

I trust there was nothing ambiguous in my rather frank enjoyment of an unusual situation the other night. Considering certain gentle gibes you dealt me, I am not quite sure in the retrospect that you didn't think I was laughing at someone or something, as the American newspapers laughed (some of them) at Yeats. You will take my word for it that there was nothing in my sleeve: I showed just what I felt. I was only too childishly happy in being allowed to make one for a moment in a company in which I hadn't to be ashamed of having written verse. Perhaps it will help you understand my state of mind if I tell you that I have lived for the most part in villages where it were better that a millstone were hanged about your neck than that you should own yourself a minor poet.

About your book. Promise not to suspect me of reviewing it, as of obligation, because I bought it so ostentatiously under your eyes, and I will tell you in a word what I think of it. Poet-like you are going to resent my praising what I want to praise in it, when it comes to details. But you wont mind my saying in general that the best of it is where it came from. And the next best is the beautiful sad figure of the title, which recurring in the body of the book, and, if I recollect aright, in the poem in the English Review, gives to the whole significance. We are in the net of the stars to our sorrow as inexorably as the Olympian pair were in another net to their shame.[56] I don't know what theory you may be committed or dedicated to as an affiliated poet of Devonshire St., but for my part give me an out-and-out metaphor. If that is old-fashioned, make the most of it. And give me a generous sprinkling of

56. Venus and Mars, whom Vulcan, in a fit of jealousy, trapped in a net laid for them in Venus's bed; he thus exposed the pair to the ridicule of the gods.

words like "brindled" for the bees, "gauze" for the sea-haze, "wafer" for the moon, "silver streak" for the swans mirrored neck and "tarnished copper" for her beak.[57] (And by the way wasn't streak with beak a fruitful rhyme?) I am disposed to think that the image finds its word and phrase with you more nearly than it finds its cadence. That is not to say that I am not taken with the sound of what you write.

"The winds that leave to-night in peace."[58]

There it is the cadence that does it. So also is it the cadence in the first fourteen lines of "Simplicity," and in a different way in the five-word line

"No more? But no less."[59]

Something akin to that effect is what I go reading book after book of new poetry for—if you understand what I mean.

In closing I will name you my selection for the anthologies. Mrs Frost says "Once in Autumn"; I say "Evening" or your "Foreword." Now you have something to go on if you are determined "to have me in the number of the enemy"—the expression is that of an earlier invader of your country, in fact the earliest whose name has come down to us.[60]

All this is uncalled for I know. The more reason, from my point of view, for saying it. I had your book, I had your card, I had the impression of your prevailing mood, I was impelled to write, and I have written. You make me long to ask you a question that your book only makes a lovely pretense of answering. When the life of the streets perplexed me a long time ago I at-

57. RF refers to several poems in Flint's *In the Net of the Stars* (Elkin Matthews, 1909). The "brindled" bees and the sea-hazy "gauze" appear in "From a Garden Song"; "He Advises Her" describes the moon as a "wafer"; the descriptive details pertaining to the swan are from "A Swan Song."

58. Last line of "He Sings a Song in the Garden of Night."

59. From "He Tells of the Eternal Wistfulness."

60. Julius Caesar, whose expeditions into Britain in 55–54 BCE antedated the Roman conquest under Claudius. RF has the following passage in mind, from chapter 6, book 6 of Caesar's *Gallic Wars:* "Caesar, having divided his forces with C. Fabius, his lieutenant, and M. Crassus his questor, and having hastily constructed some bridges, enters their country in three divisions, burns their houses and villages, and gets possession of a large number of cattle and men. Constrained by these circumstances the Menapii send embassadors to him for the purpose of suing for peace. He, after receiving hostages, assures them that he will consider them in the number of his enemies if they shall receive within their territories either Ambiorix or his embassadors" (*Caesar's Commentaries: Gallic and Civil Wars,* trans. W. A. McDevitte and W. S. Bohn [New York: Harper and Brothers, 1872]).

tempted to find an answer to it for myself by going literally into the wilderness, where I was so lost to friends and everyone that not five people crossed my threshold in as many years. I came back to do my days work in its day none the wiser.

Sincerely yours,
Robert Frost

[To Harriet Monroe (1860–1936), American editor, publisher, critic, and poet. The letter is undated but has been stamped as received on February 27, 1913. Given the speed of transatlantic mail, the letter was likely composed in late January 1913. ALS. HRC.]

The Bungalow,
Beaconsfield, Bucks,
England.
[late January 1913]

Miss Harriet Monroe,
Editor of Poetry,
Chicago; Illinois, U.S.A.

Dear Madam:—

A thing like the enclosed group of Ruralia needs no bush or you don't want it.[61] It is not a preface nor a prospectus that I am going to take your time for, but just a word about myself to say that I am an American and not an Englishman, for fear being the latter might be a bar to your consideration. I am not advised as to whether you invite contributions from over sea [*sic*]. To be on the safe side I enclose my card to prove citizenship.

Very truly yours,
Robert Frost

---

61. See the epilogue to *As You Like It*, where Rosalind speaks: "If it be true that good wine needs no bush, 'tis true that a good play needs no epilogue." It is not clear which poems RF enclosed, but they were ("ruralia") undoubtedly among those he would collect in *NB* in 1914; hence the allusion here to *As You Like It*, a "pastoral" of another kind. The first poem RF placed in *Poetry* (February 1914) was "The Code—Heroics" (the subtitle was dropped for *NB*).

[To F. S. Flint. RF's suggestion that he might send Flint's book to Thomas Mosher, together with his concession that he as yet lacks "the literary authority to put it through," perhaps dates this letter from February 1913, shortly after RF met Flint but before his own first volume appeared. ALS. HRC.]

The Bung
Beak
Bucks
[early February 1913]

Dear Flint

You make me want to shake you and perhaps I shall shake you before you are very much older. You will have to be gotten out of your present mood somehow.[62] But perhaps it is not as bad as I am disposed to believe, and even while I talk this way and you talk that other way you are cunning by planning and executing your magnum. Lets hope so.

Anyway I can do one thing. It isn't much because I lack as yet the literary authority to put it through. I want to try it just the same unless you refuse me your consent. I am going to send my new-found friend Mosher a copy of your Net of the Stars with the request that he will like this dreaming. 'You, sir, are on the look out for poetry for your Bibelot and your Lyric Garland, etc.' I shall say very little: the less said the better. Forbid me not. I wish I felt sure that I could get away with it. You may prefer that I should say nothing—just let the book speak for itself. Tell me.

Yours
R.F.

---

62. Flint had written, in a January 30 letter thanking RF for his remarks on *In the Net of the Stars:* "Tonight my head is so wooden and dull that I cannot find the right words to say. Why did you not ask the question my book is only a pretense of answering? Why be so timid in these things? . . . I wish I could say something more now than the few banal words I have put down here; but I am clean exhausted, and a lively conscience has pricked me on just at this moment to answer your very kind and very thoughtful letter" (letter held at DCL). Incidentally, it was in this January 30, 1913, letter that Flint again referred RF to Ezra Pound, enclosing the latter's calling card and listing his books to date by title.

[To F. S. Flint. Precise dating uncertain. ALS. HRC.]

The Bungalow
Beaconsfield
Bucks
[February 1913]

Dear Flint

I have been so full of a number of things that I haven't realized how far along in the week we were. Will you have time to let me know where and when on Saturday you will see me? Here's hoping this finds you as full.

Yours
R.F.

[To John Bartlett. The coverless book is a proof copy of ABW *(1913). ALS. UVA]*

The Bung. Hole
Feb 26 1913

Dear John:—

About now you are in receipt of my coverless book. Now you are reading it upside down in your excitement. What's the matter? You look pale. I see it all as true to life as in a melodrama. Your wife gathers around the table. The dog gets stepped on—the Indian Runner Dog. And Ruksh the dog utters a fearful cry. No canine cry is that, etc. It curdles the Annie Frazier River.[63] A chair goes over.

"Wait," you say.

"Wait a minute!"

"Hold on!"

"Give me time!"

"I tell you I can understand this if you give me time and don't hurry me!"

"In fact it isnt that I cant understand it."

---

63. The Indian Runner is a breed of duck, and Ruksh the name of a horse in Matthew Arnold's "Sohrab and Rustum" ("Ruksh, the horse, / Who stood at hand, utter'd a dreadful cry;— / No horse's cry was that, most like the roar / Of some pain'd desert-lion"). The Fraser River flows through British Columbia to Vancouver, where John and Margaret Bartlett had settled, and where John pursued a career in journalism. Ann Frasier had been a student at Pinkerton Academy, two years Bartlett's junior, Class of 1911.

"I can understand it all right"

"But I cant believe it."

"It is what I may call the startlingness of the intelligence."

"Suppose I were to telegraph you from Raymond or some other center where things happen and news is manufactured that Sir Peg a Ramsey had demonstrated on the zylophone that there was more radium than neon and helium than yes than in no."[64]

"You would be excited, wouldn't you?"

"Come own up. Of course you'd be."

"It would make all the difference in the world."

"You'd feature it—you'd call attention to it in a leader."

"Well it's like that—only—what shall I say?"

"Only more serious, more momentous."

"So unlike poetry—except Masefield's."[65]

"If a man has anything he wants to break to us let him use prose—prose is his vehicle."

"Listen to this—it comes with too great a shock in verse."

"Get ready!"

"eurt saw thguoht I lla fo erus erom ylnO"[66]

---

64. The joke here is threefold. Raymond, New Hampshire (John Bartlett's hometown), with a population of 1,203 in 1910, was hardly a "center where things happen." In *Twelfth Night* (2.3), Sir Toby Belch declares: "My lady's a Cataian, we are politicians, Malvolio's a Peg-a-Ramsey, and 'Three merry men be we.' Am not I consanguineous? Am I not of her blood? Tillyvally. Lady! [*Sings*] 'There dwelt a man in Babylon, lady, lady!' " Finally, RF refers to Sir William Ramsay (1852–1916), the Scottish chemist who discovered the so-called noble gases, among them neon and helium (for which discovery he was awarded the Nobel Prize in Chemistry in 1904). As for "zylophone," RF may have in mind that Ramsay derived the names of the six "noble gases" (in addition to neon and helium: argon, krypton, xenon, and radon) from Greek, which gives us "xylophone." Also worth noting: in 1903, at University College London, Ramsay and British radio chemist Frederick Soddy (1877–1956) verified that radium, when it decays, produces helium. RF's—and Bartlett's—familiarity with Ramsay could only have been enhanced by the fact that a number of his essays (including "Radium and Its Products") appeared in *The Youth's Companion*, in which RF placed two poems while at Pinkerton.

65. English poet John Edward Masefield (1878–1967), whom RF met in London. RF likely has in mind Masefield's poem "Dauber," which concerns (to speak generally) the travails of the artist and the scorn he often endures before, at last, realizing his aspirations. We thank Mark Scott for the suggestion.

66. Last line of the first poem in *ABW*, "Into My Own," spelled backward.

"It is too, too much."

And so you run on till Mrs Margaret interposes with a woman's good sense:

"Perhaps if you read it right side up it wouldn't mean so much."

"It might not mean anything."

Still I think you will treat the book kindly for my sake. It comes pretty near being the story of five years of my life. In the first poem I went away from people*; in the one called A Tuft of Flowers I came back to them actually as well as verbally for I wrote that poem to get my job in Pinkerton as little Tommy Tucker sang for his supper and Brer Merriam read it for me at a Men's League Banquet in Derry Village because I was too timid to read it myself.[67]

Elinor will be writing to Margaret soon. She has been prevented from doing anything extra by various cares and anxieties of late. Lesley has resprained an ankle she sprained in Derry once and it makes a very bad case. She may be two months off her feet. The specialist in London was grave about it. That is hard on a mother. Lesley had a chance to see her own bones in the x-rays.

R.F.

* and college[68]

[To John Bartlett. In recounting his adventures in literary London, RF names a roster of notable contemporaries, starting with William Butler Yeats. The letter is undated but accompanied by a postmarked envelope, from which the dating given here is derived. ALS. UVA.]

[The Bungalow,
Beaconsfield,
Buckinghamshire]
[March 11, 1913]

Dear John,—

I have nothing to write about except our anxieties for you and Margaret and my anxieties for the success of my book which are two so incommensurable things that they ought not of right to be brought together in one letter.

67. Charles L. Merriam (1855–1914), a Congregational minister in Derry, New Hampshire, invited RF to read "The Tuft of Flowers" at the banquet mentioned, but the poet, suffering a bout of stage fright, asked Merriam to read it in his stead; the event was instrumental in securing RF a teaching position at Pinkerton Academy.

68. RF left Dartmouth College after a mere three months, in the fall of 1892.

However one must write something, for you will be wanting to hear. A letter now and then even if it seems an answer to nothing in particular can't come amiss. I know I could bear to get one from you oftener than I do. I have no regular correspondent on the other side either in Derry or in Plymouth. I cut myself off from the Derry crowd in disgust when John C. gave the Academy to that Roman-Anglican-Catholic Congregationalist son of the man that did such things at the Plymouth Normal School.[69] I rather deliberately queered myself with Silver and the Plymouth crowd by laying it on pretty thick, though with studied modesty, about my little achievements here in answer to their clamor for something literary from the neighborhood of Westminster Abbey. You see I could talk about myself on that for a joke and call it highly literary. Instead of lingering over the tombs and busts in the Abbey (where I have never been) I talked in simple truth about my book. I had it in for them. Silver asked three times for something literary. Then he got it. He hasn't yipped since. The Lord do so to me and more also if I could help it. And I was artful enough to leave something untold that I could send around and make sure of his getting as if by accident by way of Mrs Frost and some of the ladies. He's an awfully mild master, is Silver, when he has you where he can pay you what he wants to. But he's jealous to a fault. I know where he lives. The story when pieced together amounted to just this—I don't know whether I have bothered you with it before. I found a publisher for my book in the first office I walked into. The firm pays all expenses of publication which is a very unusual thing in the case of a first book. I am under contract to let the same firm have my next four books if I ever write any more. I had hardly signed this contract when I had requests for a book from two American publishers, one a most flattering thing from Mosher of Portland whose letter press is considered perhaps the most beautiful in the States.[70] I seem to have found a friend in Mosher. Sometime when you are happy and feeling flush I wish you

---

69. John C. Chase, a civil engineer, and president of the Benjamin Chase Company, was secretary of the Pinkerton Academy board of trustees and chairman of its executive committee. (Chase resided at the academy's Hildreth Hall.) The Reverend George Washington Bingham ("that Roman-Anglican-Catholic Congregationalist") served as principal, replaced, in 1910, by Ernest L. Silver, who, a year later, would take RF with him when he assumed the presidency of Plymouth Normal School.

70. The second publisher who'd expressed interest in RF was Richard G. Badger of the Gorham Press, Boston.

would send him a dollar for a year of his little magazine of reprints call The Bibelot. His address is Portland, Maine. You will like the magazine.

I have got off the track a little bit. But I think I have told you about the whole story as Silver had it. Where the anxieties come in? Bless you, all that hit my Plymouth friends so hard is just the beginning of a book's career. I am in mortal fear now lest the reviewers should fail to take any notice of it. Such a work isn't sold in the bookstores but through the notices in the papers entirely. It is going the rounds now and it remains to be seen whether it will fall flat or not. Something however it has already done for me in ways too mysterious to go into. It has brought me several interesting friendships which I can tell you about without exciting any jealousy in your breast because you know that I care more for you and your opinion of me (formed when I was fifteenth in command at Pinkerton) than for the opinion of all the rest of them put together. Yeats has asked me to make one of his circle at his Monday nights when he is in London (and not in Dublin). And he told my dazzling friend Ezra Pound that my book was the best thing that has come out of America for some time. Of course we needn't believe that. I spent the evening with Yeats in his dark-curtained candlelit room last week. We talked about The Land of Heart's Desire[71] among other things. He is the big man here in poetry of course, though his activity is largely dramatic in late years. I have met Maurice Hewlett within a day or two, Hewlett not very intimately. You know him for his novels. He himself cares only for his poetry. And then there is May Sinclair the author of The Divine Fire etc etc. I took tea with her yesterday and expect to go there again shortly. She professes to see something unusual in my book. I like that of course because she is known as an expert in new poetry. She is the lady who made the reputation of Vaugn [*sic*] Moody, Torrence and Edwin Arnold [*sic*] Robinson by naming them as the principal poets in the States.[72] And Ezra Pound, the stormy petrel, I must tell you more about him when I have more time. He has found me and sent a

71. Bartlett knew the play well. RF had staged it with his students at Pinkerton Academy, along with Marlowe's *Faustus* (in which Bartlett played Mephistopheles), Milton's *Comus*, and Sheridan's *Rivals*. See *CPRF*, 75–77.

72. May Sinclair was the pen name of Mary Amelia St. Clair (1863–1946), British novelist and poet; her novel *The Divine Fire* first appeared in 1904; several short letters from Sinclair to RF (concerning appointments to meet) are held now at DCL, all dating from the spring of 1913. RF refers to William Vaughan Moody (1869–1910), whose widow the Frosts later befriended, and two other writers whom RF would meet on his return to America, Ridgley Torrence (1874–1950) and Edwin Arlington Robinson (1869–1935). See

fierce article to Chicago denouncing a country that neglects fellows like me. I am afraid he over did it and it may be a mercy all round if it isn't printed. It is likely to be though as he always seems to have his way with the magazine it has gone to.[73] All this ought to be enough to satisfy me for the time being you would think. But dear dear. The boom is not started yet. And then there is the money question. I am going to run short and have to go to the American Consulate for assisted passage home. There is little money ahead. Hewlett was boasting that he had three pounds, his first royalty on a book of poems published four years ago. Gosh.

I hope this letter will pass two or three coming the other way and bringing good news of Margaret and of you.

Affectionately,
R. F.

[To John Bartlett. The letter is undated but internal evidence suggests 1913. Thompson places it circa March 18, 1913; we follow his lead. ALS. UVA.]

[The Bungalow,
Beaconsfield,
Buckinghamshire]
[circa March 18, 1913]

My dear dear John:—

Your last letter rather piles on the agony. But we are not going to let it worry us too much. You will be writing in a day or two that Margaret is better or has gone through the operation all right and that Gerry has ceased to press you for further copy on the critters of your imagination.[74]

Sinclair's essay, "Three American Poets of Today," *The Atlantic Monthly* 98 (September 1906): 429–434. Maurice Henry Hewlett (1861–1923) was a British novelist, poet, and critic.

73. The reference is to *Poetry;* Pound's "fierce article" was not, in fact, published, at least as RF describes it here.

74. Bartlett, who was paid by the line, needed to raise money for his wife Margaret's pending appendectomy (as it happened, she never underwent it). He satisfied his editor ("Gerry") by fabricating several articles in the pages of the *Vancouver Sun* in 1912. RF's admonition, later in the letter, as to "faking articles" is a response to Bartlett's confession to a journalistic sin of which the poet himself had once been guilty. We have been unable to identify "Gerry."

But you are terribly overwrought. I see you in a vision as you appeared the day Doe hit you in the eye.[75] If you don't look as wild as that, you feel enough worse to more than make up for it. And yes, I repent that I didn't get out there where I could perhaps do or say or be a little something to help you over a bad place.

You mustn't fake articles any more. Not even in details. Them's orders. I'll tell you why. It's taking an unfair advantage. Of whom? Of the public? Little I care for them. They would deceive themselves were there no one else to deceive them. Of your fellow journalists then? I suspect that they can hold up their end. No it is taking an unfair advantage of the gentlemen who profess fiction. I used to think of it when I faked in a small way for another paper named the Sun which was published in Lawrence Mass.[76] All I had to do was to claim for my yarns the virtue of fact and I had story writers of twice my art and invention skun a mile. I thought of it again when partly for the fun and partly for the lucre I tried my hand at poultry journalism. I wrote up one or two poultrymen as you did Biblical Smith filling in the gaps in my knowledge with dream material. I think I managed fairly well except for the time I spoke of John Hall's geese roosting in the trees. I should have let geese severely alone. It took an artistic letter from John Hall himself (I wrote it for the douce man) to save me from the scandal that started.[77] I had a little right on my side. As a matter of fact John Hall had among others a few Brazilians that sometimes roosted on a pollared willow and even on the chimney and he could honestly say so (if someone would write the letter for him, for he was without clerkly learning.) But I was uncomfortable all the time until I settled back to write out-and-out stories. It had occurred to me previously that some fiction not purporting to be true otherwise than as fiction is true, true to the life of the farm and especially the poultry farm, wouldn't derogate

---

75. Duffy Doe, a member of the Sanborn Seminary football team—Pinkerton Academy's rival—once intentionally punched Bartlett, captain and quarterback of the Pinkerton team. The very next play, his eye bloody and nearly swollen shut, Bartlett scored the winning touchdown. In celebration, RF penned the following ditty, which he wrote on the blackboard in class: "In the days of Captain John, / Sanford Sem had nothing on / Pinker-ton, Pinker-ton." See *RFJB*, 21–22.

76. The Lawrence *Sun-American,* for which RF worked briefly in 1895. See *CPRF,* 246–250.

77. See RF's letters of February 15 and March 15, 1904. The articles and short stories RF wrote for *The Eastern Poultryman* and *Farm-Poultry* are reprinted in *CPRF,* 35–73; see also *CPRF,* 251–256.

from the serious not to say solemn interest of a poultry journal. I succeeded in creating a limited demand for it and was making a very little money when I decided I could make more in Pinkerton. I tell you all this to show you. A little faking in our salad days is none so sinful—a novice naturally takes it as a lark—he can't feel that he has tasted the full flavor of the world the flesh and his grown-up-mans job if he hasn't tried it. But you will soon sicken of it, if you havent sickened already. Give us a rest about the money you need. I don't want you to get rich too fast.

I speak lightly enough. All the same I shall feel mightily relieved when you write that the danger of your being found out in the Manuel-and-His-Little-Shell game (Conchita must mean shell) is safely past.[78] What I fear is that someone on the Sea Island will rise up to question your authenticity—or the Spanish Consul if there is such a thing on the coast.[79] I should be scared blue if I were in your predicament. No harm in my saying as much at this distance since by the time you hear me you will either have come through safely or have been ridden on a rail out of the Sun office. We will laugh at all these worries someday when we are collaborating on a brisk novel of Vancouver in the days of the land speculation.

Our love to Margaret. Both of you are young and brave and fine and the best stuff ever. Write 'em as short as you please but write oftener. And we like to see the paper once in a while.

R. F.

---

78. Among the stories Bartlett fabricated was one about "Biblical Smith, an itinerant preacher of sorts, with a capacity for raising funds, and then disappearing quietly," and another about Manuel, a "crafty Spaniard with sly eyes and shifty fingers," who ran a shell game. Bartlett also fabricated stories about "bones discovered in the Vancouver dump, 'thought to be of prehistoric man!'" and a romance entitled "The Nouvelle Evangeline" ("star-crossed lovers searching for each other half-way around the world to meet again—in Vancouver—but, alas too late; death had snatched the loved one across the final barrier"). Some of the fake stories were picked up by the syndicated press; hence Bartlett's apprehensions. Subsequently, Bartlett heeded RF's advice. For details see *RFJB*, 40.

79. "Sea Island" lies across from Vancouver proper, in an estuary of the Fraser River, close to the Bartlett residence on Lulu Island.

[To John Bartlett. The letter is undated but accompanied by a postmarked envelope, from which the dating supplied here is derived. ALS. UVA.]

The Bung
Beck. Buck
Eng.
[April 5, 1913]

Dear John:

I have to be chary of my favors to get anything out of you. The book goes with this as per your kick of recent date. You are now supposed to order of your own motion and without undue pressure from me not less than fifteen nor more than twenty copies at forty cents (inclusive of post.) the copy. You must do this of the publisher and not of me so as to make it look as if I had taken hold in the far west (why, God only knows). Then you must get me a notice in the most literary of the Vancouver dailies or weeklies. Make it personal if you like, a sort of news item. Like this: Jaunty Bart., the popular and ever censorious fakeer of the Sun staff is in receipt of etc etc till you get to "allow me to sell you a couple" (quoting from Alice).[80] You know the sort of thing. Be sure to say, This is hot stuff. A few choice copies left. Call it a farm product without fear of contradiction. It is inevitable (that's the word) as inevitable as a cabbage or a cucumber (if the cut worms don't get it). Funny how you and I both go in for farming. I am looked on as someone who has got the poetry of the farm. Can't you ring me into one of your columns in the Montreal Star?[81] In a word do your dambdest and hang the consequences.

I am mes enfants

Living in you more than
you can imagine.
R. F.

---

80. See "Advice from a Caterpillar," in chapter five of *Alice in Wonderland:*

"In my youth," said the sage, as he shook his grey locks,
"I kept all my limbs very supple
By the use of this ointment—one shilling the box—
Allow me to sell you a couple?"

81. In 1913 Bartlett obtained a position as British Columbia Editorial Representative for the Montreal *Weekly Star.*

[To Sidney Cox. ALS. DCL.]

The Bung Hole
Beaconsfield
Bucks
May 2 1913

Dear Sydney Cox:—

It grows a long time since we heard from you and I begin to wonder whether or not you can have gone over to the enemy. There is the other possibility that you have been addressing letters as above and that the Eng. postman has failed to see the Am. joke. This, you must bear in mind, is The Bungalow. It is only The Bung for short and Hole by discourtesy. You are not on terms to be calling it that. We who love it call it any thing we please like the affectionate father in H G Wells' story who called his favorite daughter Maggots.[82] We are pretty much at home here by now. You ought to see us, theoretically up to our eyes in the flowers of an English spring. I could say actually if we were as our neighbors amateurs of gardening. I like that about the English—they all have time to dig in the ground for the un-utilitarian flower. I mean the men. It marks the great difference between them and our men. I like flowers you know but I like em wild, and I am rather the exception than the rule in an American village. Far as I have walked in pursuit of the Cypripedium, I have never met another in the woods on the same quest.[83] Americans will dig for peas and beans and such like utilities but not if they know it for posies. I knew a man who was a byword in five townships for the flowers he tended with his own hand. Neighbors kept hens and let them run loose just to annoy him. I feel as if my education in useless things had been neglected when I see the way the front yards blossom down this road. But never mind; I have certain useless accomplishments to my credit. No one will charge me with having an eye single to the main chance.[84] So I can afford perhaps to yield a little to others for one spring in the cultivation of one form of the beautiful. Next year I go in for daffodils.

---

82. In H. G. Wells's 1912 novel *Marriage*.

83. The *Cypripedium reginae*, an orchid more commonly known as the "showy lady's slipper," and quite rare in New Hampshire. The flower figures in RF's poem "The Self-Seeker," collected first in *NB*.

84. See Matthew 6:22: "The light of the body is the eye: if therefore thine eye be single, thy whole body shall be full of light."

I think I understood Yeats to say the other night that Tagore whose poetry is the latest big thing here, has been visiting your college at Urbana.[85] I meant to ask Yeats more about it. I wonder if you met Tagore. Very likely I shall run across him before he goes back to Bengal. I was to have met him at Ernest Rhys' Sunday but decided in the end to take some other day for my call when I could have Rhys more to myself.[86] Tagore comes to Yeats here as the greatest English poet. How slowly but surely Yeats has eclipsed Kipling. I have seen it all happen with my own eyes. You would expect to see Tagore seeking Kipling for his Indian sympathies and interests. But no, he is drawn to Maeterlink[87] [*sic*] on the continent and to Yeats on these islands.

Sincerely yours
Robert Frost.

85. The Bengali poet Rabindranath Tagore (1861–1941) visited England in 1912; William Butler Yeats had written the introduction to the 1912 British edition of Tagore's *The Gitanjali; or Song Offerings*. Cox was, at the time, a graduate student at the University of Illinois, to which, in 1906, Tagore had sent his son Rathindranth. The latter received a B.S. in Agriculture at Illinois in 1909 and was a graduate student there from 1909 until 1913. Tagore himself visited Urbana in November 1912, giving his first address in the United States at the Unitarian Church there (now called the Channing-Murray Foundation). In 1961, RF would give a talk before the Asia Society in New York on the occasion of Tagore's centenary: "When you think of it, one of the differences between the East and West is that the East is maybe more ineffable than the West. But let me tell you about that. I talked with [Tagore] about it once, years ago [i.e., in London]. Many people think meditation is the same thing as contemplation. That's because they haven't thought enough. We made the distinction: the West is more meditative; the East is more contemplative . . . 'meditation' is meditating something to do; and 'contemplation' is something to be lost in; to lose yourself in, so as to find yourself. It's a spiritual difference." See RF, "Remarks on the Occasion of the Tagore Centenary." John Frederick Nims transcribed RF's talk from a tape recording and published it in *Poetry* (November 1961): 106–119. RF did not assist in preparing the published text.

86. Ernest Percival Rhys (1859–1946), English poet and editor.

87. Maurice Maeterlinck (1862–1949), Belgian playwright, poet, and essayist, and winner of the Nobel Prize in Literature for 1911.

[To Ernest L. Silver. ALS. Plymouth.]

The Bungalow
Beaconsfield
Buck, England
May 7 1913

Dear Mr Silver:

I am not sending you the book with the certainty that it will give you pleasure. Some like it and some don't over here and when they don't they are freer to say so than anywhere else in the world except in Paris. Of course those who do like it are apt to be much more nearly right than those who don't, though the Lord knows those who like it for the wrong reasons are bad enough.

Spring will have struck you hard by the time you get this. If any one starts to tell you about the charm of spring in England don't you bother to lift your eyes from the little ledger Foster gave you.[88] There is some grass and yes there are some cherry trees—rather more of the latter than you would see in New England. But I can't forgive this place the mud. It is enough to give one spring halt, the sudden and unexpected way one's feet come away from the ground when they do come away. My original theory was that mud here took the place of snow at home. It is worse than that. Mud here takes the place of everything at home. Three hours without rain constitutes a drought. We had three hours sunshine last week a thing so remarkable that it set the ladies cooing over their tea, "Don't you think the English is a much maligned climate?" It is in our household. We have heard the coocoo sing (and blushed); we have seen the lark do his stunt which is to mount singing almost straight up to about the height of the Singer Bld (N.Y.) <u>not</u> "to the last point of vision and beyond"[89] as the poet hath it, sing a little on the top of the rise, and then descend singing to the grass—round trip five minutes; but nothing can compensate for this weather. I wish you would tell Mrs Hodge[90] about it so she won't be imagining all sorts of things about us that aren't true. Her letters are too romantic.

---

88. Unidentified.

89. First line of stanza two from "To the Skylark," by William Wordsworth (1770–1850). The poem appears in Francis Palgrave's anthology *The Golden Treasury,* a favorite of RF's since he first bought it as a student at Dartmouth in 1892.

90. Marie A. Hodge was a residence hall preceptress at the New Hampshire Normal School, Plymouth, New Hampshire (now Plymouth State University).

I suppose the amount of it is that I am homesick, and so not disposed to like anything foreign. Twenty-five years in New England have made very much of a damned Yankee of me. I foresaw it would turn out that way. I did not expect to like the ordinary Englishman though you may be sure he is much more endurable in his own country than when met in isolated cases in the States. But his schools! I have meant to have Lesley make out a schedule for you of the work done in the school she has attended. I would swear if I was sure I would remember to enclose this in three envelopes when I got through. My friend Ezra Pound has a blasphemy I must try to get through the customs for you when I go back. But speaking of the schools—there are good ones here if you can only take time to find out where they are before you settle down—and if you can only pay the price. The free schools are well enough taught as schools go, but they are given up and abandoned to a class of children lower than any we have outside the big cities. Class-distinction everywhere. I wish you could rub elbows with it.

The best you can say for the country is that it contains London but that is another story. If I stay on another year it will be because of the friends I have made down in the city. One has only to write a little insignificant book like mine to be brought in contact with people who have done all sorts of things—literary men almost greater than any we have had in America. I must write you a long letter some day about the interesting people I have met. I suppose I enjoyed most Yeats, the man who wrote the play I read to the 1913 girls in the parlor last winter. His candle-lit room is more like a shrine than a room; his manner is like that of a man in some dream he cant shake off. It is not a pose with him. He has to take himself that way. So different from Maurice Hewlett for instance. Hewlett talks and acts like a man of the world which is doubtless the sensible thing to do even when you are a poet. Nevertheless Yeats is much the greater man by common consent. I haven't met Chesterton yet.[91] That seems to be coming. I haven't wanted to seek him tourist-fashion. But several friends have said they wanted me to know him. You know how I feel toward Chesterton. And then there is my particular friend Ezra Pound the dazzling youth who translates poetry from six languages. Someone says he looks altogether too much like a poet to be a poet. He lives in Bohemia from hand to mouth but he goes simply everywhere in great society. A lot of daffy duchesses patronise him and buy tickets to expensive little lecture courses he gets up when he has to raise the wind. It sounds peculiar, but he's

91. G. K. Chesterton lived in Beaconsfield. Also mentioned, again: English novelist and poet Maurice Henry Hewlett.

really great sport and a yank, an expatriate. I fell in with him by a series of accidents I mustn't detail here.

Thus a letter runs into pages. I was only going to depreciate the book and ask you about the furniture—whether it would be too much in the way if we decided to hang on another year. Really I can't afford to stay and really I don't want to except for the allurements of the London literary crowd. I'm not doing as I promised myself to do. I have let myself be entirely diverted to writing poetry and every day I don't write prose brings me so much nearer the day when I will have to go to work again for this family. But Hell! Lets talk of something else for a change. I'll have a smoke talk with you. If on May 20 (by which time you will be sure to have got this letter) you will go to your upstairs front (if that is where you still camp) and light up in honor of the Normal School Class of 1913 at precisely seven o'clock P.M. Plymouth time I will do the same here at precisely ten o'clock P.M. Beaconsfield time so that we shall be smoking together. And let's talk politics. Did you get your gym? Who's who in Concord and who's going to be in the immediate future? How about the call to Chicago? And how about tennis? That's what Lesley wants to know. Poor youngster, she has been two months confined to a chair with an injured foot. She doesn't look the athletic girl she did last summer.

Sincerely yours,
Robert Frost.

Mind, I'm not saying we are not coming home

[To Susan Hayes Ward. ALS. Huntington.]

The Bungalow
Beaconsfield
Bucks
England
May 13 1913

Dear Miss Ward:—

I must have displeased you with my last letter else I should have heard from you in reply before this.[92] I am trying to think what I said that was so bad. I remember that I was tragical (and that is an offense against taste) but it

92. See RF to Ward, September 15, 1912.

was in a vein that wasn't meant to be taken too seriously. I must have been tragical with you before in similar circumstances. It seems to be my "awful way of doing business."[93] Still it is just possible the reason I haven't heard from you is because you felt you had nothing to say until you saw how my rash adventure was going to turn out. To date it has turned out the book I am sending, which is a good book in spots. I don't need to tell you. The beauty of such things as Into My Own, My November Guest, A Dream Pang, Mowing, and Reluctance is that they are not just post-graduate work, nor post-post-graduate work, but the unforced expression of a life I was forced to live. That seemed not to matter to anyone at home. Already it has attracted the attention of Yeats, Newbolt, Rhys, Pound and Miss Sinclair over here.[94] Maybe I was hasty in coming away before showing my verse to any American publisher in book form. I don't feel sure. As it turned out Mosher of Portland would have taken it. He wrote of his own motion to ask for a book for his Lyric Garland Series when it was too late and I had made an arrangement with David Nutt. I showed my manuscript to the one firm. It was as simple as that. I had nothing to pay. I shall have royalties. And I am under some sort of contract to let David Nutt have my next book and the next after. I seem in a fair way to become an Englishman.

And yet we are very very homesick in this English mud. We can't hope to be happy long out of New England. I never knew how much of a Yankee I was till I had been out of New Hampshire a few months. I suppose the life in such towns as Plymouth and Derry and South Berwick is the best on earth.

Elinor and I pool our regards.

Sincerely yours
Robert Frost

---

93. See Rudyard Kipling's 1897 poem, "Pharaoh and the Sergeant":

There were years that no one talked of; there were times of horrid doubt—
There was faith and hope and whacking and despair—
While the Sergeant gave the Cautions and he combed old Pharaoh out,
And England didn't seem to know nor care.
That is England's awful way o' doing business—
She would serve her God (or Gordon) just the same—
For she thinks her Empire still is the Strand and Holborn Hill,
And she didn't think of Sergeant Whatisname.

94. Sir Henry Newbolt (1862–1938), Ernest Rhys, and May Sinclair, British poets and critics.

This picture will give you some idea of the size of the children as compared with that of the house they live in.

R.F.

[To Wilbur Rowell, executor of RF's grandfather's will. A note in Rowell's hand indicates that the remittance here requested was made on July 1 in the amount of $750.00. ALS. UVA.]

The Bungalow
Reynolds Road
Beaconsfield
Bucks
England
June 6 1913

Dear Mr Rowell:—

Would it be possible for you to send me the money in some sort of cashier's check, made in duplicate, on some London bank? The ordinary check would have to go back to the States before I could get it cashed and I haven't the time to lose waiting for it. Indeed I almost feel like asking you to mail the check a few days earlier than usual if it would not be too irregular a proceeding. It would be ten days on the way, so that if it isn't sent till July 12 I shall have to wait for it till well toward the end of the month and my wish was to get away to France with friends by July 15. It would be harder for me to handle it in France than here where I am known. I have published a book here and expect to publish another before Christmas. Will you kindly drop me a line to let me know what to expect?

Sincerely yours,
Robert Frost

[To F. S. Flint. Other letters allow for a dating of mid-June; see RF to Flint, June 17, 1913. ALS. HRC.]

The Bungalow
Beaconsfield
Bucks
Dunnow date
[mid-June 1913]

Dear Flint:

You are hereby reminded that you are coming out here for a long day Sunday—unless you don't want to. And you are going to fetch along the lot of free poems that you have thus far failed to send.[95] I have been looking for them now these two weeks. And I have been looking for something like the same length of time for some word from Hulme.[96] I begin to think he may have sent my manuscript through the mail with a wrong address. Dont say anything to make me seem impatient. But if you could find out from him about it. Lord, lord I live in a state of suspense when I have manuscript out.

Sincerely yours
R.F.

[To Thomas Bird Mosher. ALS. Tulsa.]

The Bungalow,
Beaconsfield,
Bucks,
England.
June 15 1913

Dear Mr Mosher:

I am sending you the book in question. You will be glad to hear that it has done things for me over here. Since about the time I won your recognition everything has seemed to be going right with me. Perhaps you have seen some of the reviews. Ezra Pound acclaimed me publicly. Yeats has said in

95. Flint did in fact soon send RF a poem, enclosed with a June 24 letter apologizing in advance for its shortcomings (held at DCL). The manuscript of the poem (title unknown) was separated from the letter at some point.

96. T. E. Hulme (1883–1917), poet, critic, and philosopher of aesthetics. RF met him on more than one occasion to discuss poetry and poetics.

private that the book is the best thing American for some time. May Sinclair has been showing it to people. Don't ask me how they ever found it in the confusion of all sorts of stuff that comes from the press. It must be my good luck. A little of the success I have waited for so long won't hurt me. I rather think I deserve it. And I don't want you to think I don't deserve it. And I don't want you to think that I have had so much of it that I wont thank you for anything you will do to help me in the States—and elsewhere.

Sincerely yours
Robert Frost.

*[To John Bartlett. The letter is undated, but circumstances indicate early summer of 1913. Thompson dates the letter circa June 16 (*SL*, 75). ALS. UVA.]*

The Bungs
Beaks
Bucks
[circa June 16, 1913]

Dear John:

What do you say if we cook up something to bother the enemies we left behind in Derry? It won't take much cooking, but what it does will come on you. You have two of my reviews now. If you haven't I will see that you have others to take their place. One is good for one reason: the other for another. Pound's is a little too personal. I don't mind his calling me raw.[97] He is reckoned raw himself and at the same time perhaps the most prominent of the younger poets here. I object chiefly to what he says about the great American editors. Not that I have any love for the two or three he has in mind. But they are better ignored—at any rate they are better not offended. We may want to use them sometime. The other I value chiefly for its source, The English Review, the magazine that found Maesfield [*sic*] and Conrad.[98] The editor himself wrote that particular notice.[99]

---

97. See Pound's review of *ABW* in *Poetry* (May 1913): "Mr. Frost's book is a little raw, and it has in it a number of infelicities; underneath them it has the tang of the New Hampshire woods, and it has just this utter sincerity" (72).

98. English poet John Masefield, whom RF met in London, and Polish-born English novelist Joseph Conrad (1857–1924).

99. Austin Harrison (1873–1928) was editor of *The English Review* from 1910 until 1923, but the article on RF was written by Norman Douglas (1868–1952), a British novelist who worked for *The Review* from 1912 to 1914.

I am sending you one more review which you can hold on to for a while. One more still and we shall have the ingredients of our Bouillabaise (sp.) assembled. If nothing slips up we will get that in the August number of The Bookman (English).[100] The editor has asked me for my photograph and a personal note to accompany the review. I suppose everything depends on whether I look young enough in my photograph to grace the ballet. Why did you wear me out teaching you things you knew already?

Well then in August, say, as soon as you get The Bookman you can begin a little article for Morse—back of The News and Enterprise[101] like this: Former pupils of R.F. at Pink may be interested to learn of the success of his first book published in London. A recent number of The Bookman (Eng.) contains etc.—You are not to get the least bit enthusiastic—I know you my child. Keep strictly to the manner of the disinterested reporter. Make the article out of the reviews almost entirely. In mentioning The English Review you might mention the fact that it is a leading literary monthly here.

All this is if you have time and inclination. It will necessitate some typewriting. I would copy Ezra Pound's article so as to get rid of the break about the editors. Leave in any derogatory remarks. We like those. I fancy I should leave out the quotation from "My November Guest" which only mangles a poem that needs to be taken as a whole and then quote it as a whole in the Poetry and Drama review I am enclosing. You see the scheme is to make The Bookman affair the occasion for your article and then drag the rest in by the ears. Say simply "The following is taken from"—Or if you see some other way to go about it, all right. You might do it in the form of a letter to The News, beginning "I thought former pupils of RF at Pink etc" and sign yourself J.T.B. Anything to make Mrs Superior Sheppard and Lil 'Art' Reynolds unhappy.[102] (You put these people into my head.) But I suppose I care less about teasing my out-and-out enemies than my half friends like John C.

100. English poet and novelist Arthur St. John Adcock (1864–1930) reviewed *ABW* in the *Bookman* (August 1913).

101. William F. Morse edited the *Derry News and Enterprise,* a Derry, New Hampshire newspaper.

102. Annie Bartlett Shepard (1861–1944), formerly a teacher at the Derry Village School, was a voice for conservatism in the civic, cultural, and religious life of the town; she led the local Anti-Suffrage Society. Her husband, Frederick Shephard, served on Pinkerton Academy's Board of Trustees. (Their grandson, incidentally, was the astronaut Alan Shepard.) Arthur W. Reynolds, Harvard '98, became superintendent of Derry schools in 1910.

Chase.[103] I told you how I charged John C. forty dollars for the catalogue and when he winced told him that I didn't get it often but when I did I got about that much for my poetry. He never quite got over that. He clipped a cheap joke on poets a day and sent it to me by Miss Bartley so that she would share in my discomfiture.[104] I only stood it tolerably well. I didn't mind it at first so much. I got tired of it.

Affectionately, mes enfants
R.F.

[Frost appended to his letter a longhand, and annotated, copy of portions of the Poetry and Drama *review, reprinted here:]*

From Poetry and Drama 2s.6d.
(Quarterly) June 1913
London Devonshire St,
Theobalds Road.

"xxxx Be it said, however, that Mr Frost has escaped from America and that his first book has found an English publisher. So much information extrinsic to the poems is necessary. Their intrinsic merits are great, despite faults of diction here and there, occasional inversions, and lapses where he has not been strong enough to bear his own simplicity of utterance. It is this simplicity which is the great charm of the book and it is a simplicity that proceeds from a candid heart:

My November Guest
(Quoted in full)

Other poems almost or quite as perfect as the one above are: A Late Walk, To the Thawing Wind, Mowing, Going for Water, Reluctance. Each poem is the complete expression of one mood, one emotion, one idea. I have tried to find in these poems what is most characteristic of Mr Frosts poetry; and I think it is this: direct observation of the object and immediate correlation

---

103. John C. Chase, secretary of the Pinkerton Academy board of trustees and chairman of its executive committee; for the article he paid RF forty dollars to write; see *CPRF*, 74–76.

104. Susan D. Bartley taught at Pinkerton during RF's time there.

with the emotion—spontaneity, subtlety in the evocation of moods, humour, an ear for silences. But behind all is the heart and life of a man [xxxx]"

The first and last sentences are too personal for my taste. I am not bothered so much by the fault finding. A little of that won't hurt me.

There was a favorable but unimportant review in T. P.'s Weekly a month or so ago. I have lost track of it. I think it quoted the first poem in the book and mentioned In a Vale.[105] Maybe you have seen it.

You might say that A Late Walk was published in The Pinkerton Critic.

I have become acquainted with the author of this.[106]

[To Marie Hodge (1856–1944), a residence hall preceptress at the Plymouth Normal School and a Frost family friend. Dating derived from internal evidence. ALS. BU.]

The Bungalow
Beaconsfield
Bucks
(Not Buckingham)
England.
[June 1913]

My Dear Mrs Hodge:

This is growing into a business between us—I mean in regard to the books. I feel as if you deserved a commission.

As I can't possibly get the books to you before school closes, how would it do for me to hold them until you send me the girls home addresses? Then I can send them to them severally from David Nutt's office. I wish if you haven't sent the money you would have the money order made payable to David Nutt Publisher, London. That is the way to help me with my publisher by making him see that my book is selling. You see the first edition is of a thousand copies and only five of them belong to me.

Do you mean that the teachers and girls in your list would like my signature in the books they are buying? I can easily arrange that. But I feel some-

---

105. The review, published in *T.P.'s Weekly* on May 30, 1913, reads, in part: "[*A Boy's Will*] is a book of verse afield. There is a fragrance here, and now and then a little touch of quiet humour, like a sudden ruffle of the breeze on still water. 'In a Vale' could not have been written by any but a close companion of flowers and night and mist."

106. F. S. Flint wrote the review for *Poetry and Drama* (June 1913).

what shamefaced not to be rich enough to give them all a copy. Do you think I ought to? At least I can give Miss McClean Miss Dougan and Miss Allen copies in addition to the ones they buy.[107] I will afford that. Books for one thing are cheap here.

I am putting in a note I had today from Ezra Pound for the idea it may give you of the mildly literary life we lead, having ceased to be a teacher. Ezra Pound is London representative of two American magazines and the author of Personae, Exultations, Canzoni, and Ripostes (Small, Maynard) besides some notable translation. The Hulme mentioned is a translator of Bergson.[108] The Farm Hand mentioned is a long thing of mine which is going to one of Pound's magazines.[109]

It is only fair to this English weather to say that it has done well and very well by us lately. It took a wholly unexpected turn for the better in the middle of May.

I find it hard to realize that you people are up to your eyes in graduation. Well, you've a long rest coming. I hope you'll all enjoy it.

Sincerely yours
Robert Frost

[To F. S. Flint. ALS. HRC.]

The Bungalow
Beaconsfield
Bucks
June 17 1913

Dear Flint:—

Let it be Sunday the twenty-second if you can. Bring something of your own to read. And you will be able to tell me what all this talk of a post-Georgean [*sic*] anthology means.[110] There is a train from Paddington at 9.18;

---

107. Unidentified.

108. T. E. Hulme translated Henri Bergson's *Introduction to Metaphysics* (New York: G. P. Putnam's Sons, 1912).

109. "The Death of the Hired Man," which Pound was attempting to place in either *Poetry* or the *Smart Set* as of June 1913.

110. In speaking, to Flint, of a "post-Georgean anthology," RF likely refers to what would become *Des Imagistes* (London: Poetry Bookshop, 1914). The origins of what came

one from Marylebone at 10.30. Come on either or both. I shall be at the station for both only in case I don't find you on the first.

Sincerely yours
Robert Frost

[To F. S. Flint. In the following letter (which bears no salutation), RF refers to Pound's reviews of ABW, *one of which appeared in* The English Review *in June, the other of which appeared in May in* Poetry; *he mentions as well Flint's review of the book in the June number of Harold Monro's* Poetry and Drama. *The poet "with a finger in the writing of his own review" is, again, Pound, whose help Flint had solicited in writing a review of Pound's* Ripostes. *Precise dating derived from internal and contextual evidence. ALS. HRC.]*

[The Bungalow,
Beaconsfield,
Buckinghamshire]
Tuesday [June 24, 1913]

Thanks for all the information of your letter of this morning.[111] We have to consider such things. Very thoughtful of you and your wife.

We enjoyed having you here so much that I hate to have you say you can't come again. We could manage better another time. We should have sent you

---

to be called "imagism," a school that would rival the Georgians (for which see note 205 in the present chapter), lay in the friendship Flint formed with T. E. Hulme in 1909, when the two poets, both conversant with French *vers libre* and with French symbolism, made common cause to reform modern poetry in English. Pound joined them, ultimately bringing with him H. D.—Hilda Doolittle, whom he had once courted—and her new English husband Richard Aldington (both spoofed by RF in his Poundian parody, "Poets Are Born Not Made" [see page 159]). The movement took shape, informed not only by French *vers libre,* but by Japanese poetry (partly through the influence of Laurence Binyon). To his 1912 volume *Ripostes,* Pound mischievously appended "The Complete Poetical Works of T. E. Hulme," which amounted to five brief lyrics. The provocation was accompanied by a prefatory note, which introduced the term "imagiste" to the literary world, associating it with "the school of 1909." When, in the March 1913 number of *Poetry* (Chicago), Flint published a note on imagism, and Pound his "A Few Don'ts by an Imagiste," the "school" had its manifestoes. *Des Imagistes* provided a body of work to match them.

111. In a letter dated June 23, Flint had passed along his wife's suggestion that RF join the Civil Service Supply Association and avail himself and his family of its commissary, for groceries and other goods.

off earlier and on a train that starts from nearby and hasn't the same chance to be late. We hope Ianthe came up smiling for the next day.[112]

Worse and more of it. He had a finger in the writing of his own review, did he? Damn his eyes! An arrivist from the word go.[113] He has something to show us there. But I'm blessed if I came all the way to London to be coached in art by the likes of him. He can't teach me anything I really care to know.

But I shouldn't take his unmasking too much to heart. The thing to do is to write something. Be a poet—be a scholar. You don't need his sanction. And whatever you do don't judge him too hardly on my authority. See his new protégé's poems before you condemn them.[114] I am not quite a fool in the matter of poetry, but I may make preposterous mistakes, as Ezra Pound manifestly made a mistake when he thought he knew how to praise my poetry for the right thing. What he saw in them isnt there and what is there he couldn't have seen or he wouldn't have liked them. I have to thank you for the word "subtlety" in your review. The poems are open. I am not so sure that the best of them are simple. If they are they are subtle too. I thank you, too, for seeing the humour. Pound would never in his life see the humour of "In a Vale." But who cares? And if I am not so very impatient of success why should you be, who have the advantage of me by ten years in the race?

RF.

---

112. Flint's daughter.

113. In his June 23 letter to RF, Flint had written: "I think over all we said yesterday. I am very angry about E.P. [Pound]. Somehow or other words have not been so obedient to me of late as they were of yore; but my ability to feel and understand is fresh as ever; and there is much that I feel and understand in the E.P. case that sickens. I admit now and avow now that I had always lurking doubts about E.P. You will find evidence thereof (all my writings betray me) in what I have said about his books in the New Age and The Poetry Review. Not in the review in *Poetry & Drama,* for the reason that Pound and I wrote that together. (This is a secret!) But I have always hated and loathed insincerity hypocrisy and *arrivisme*" (letter held at DCL).

114. American poet Skipwith Cannell (1887–1957), whom Pound would publish in *Des Imagistes* (London: Poetry Bookshop, 1914).

[Frost never sent the following letter-in-verse to Pound, though he did pass along a copy to Flint sometime in June 1913. ALS. HRC.]

[The Bungalow,
Beaconsfield,
Buckinghamshire]
[June 1913]

I am a Mede and Persian
In my acceptance of harsh laws laid down for me
When you said I could not read
When you said I looked old
When you said I was slow of wit
I knew that you only meant
That you could read
That you looked young
That you were nimble of wit
But I took your words at their face value
I accepted your words like an encyclical letter
It did not matter
At worst they were good medicine
I made my stand elsewhere
I did not ask you to unsay them.
I was willing to take anything you said from you
If I might be permitted to hug the illusion
That you liked my poetry
And liked it for the right reason.

You reviewed me,
And I was not sure—
I was afraid it was not artis[ti]cally done.
I decided I couldnt use it to impress my friends
Much less my enemies.
But in as much [as] it was praise I was grateful
For praise I do love.

I suspected though that in praising me
You were not concerned so much with my desert
As with your power

That you praised me arbitrarily
And took credit to yourself
In demonstrating that you could thrust anything
upon the world
Were it never so humble
And bid your will avouch it[115]

And here we come close to what I demanded of you
I did not want the money that you were distributing
among your favorites
for two American editors.
Not that.
All I asked was that you should hold to one thing
That you considered me a poet.
That was [why] I clung to you
As one clings to a group of insincere friends
For fear they shall turn their thoughts against him
the moment he is out of hearing.
The truth is I was afraid of you

[To F. S. Flint. Dating derived from internal evidence. ALS. HRC.]

The Bung
Beak
Bucks
[June 25, 1913]

Dear Flint

It occurs to me that I may have caused you anxiety. Be sure that I wouldn't drag you into any quarrel of mine. Nor would I betray a confidence.

It occurs to me also that you may have thought my feelings about your poem rather mixed and my way of manifesting them of doubtful propriety. Let me say again I liked the poem.

R.F.

I have copied you two of mine but I can't enclose them in a post card.

---

115. RF borrows the phrase from *Macbeth* (3.i), where Macbeth orders the murder of Banquo.

Things are always occurring to me

Do you suppose you could get Hulme to listen with you some night to my theory of what would be pure form in poetry?[116] I don't want to talk to a salon, but to a couple of clear-heads who will listen and give my idea its due. I will be greatly helped in what is before me by a little honest criticism. You would advise as metrical expert and he as philosopher. Do I ask too much.

R. Frost

Be sure not to force Hulme. I wouldn't put him to sleep for the world.[117]

[To F. S. Flint. Flint had given RF a new poem of his to look over; RF apparently returned it with the following letter. The reference to Monro acknowledges Flint's intercession on RF's behalf with the editor of Poetry and Drama. *In this letter RF also responds to Flint's reception of the letter-in-verse to Pound. See note 117 (below). ALS. HRC.]*

The Bungalow
Beaconsfield
Bucks
June 26 1913

Dear Flint

I have mauled your poem this way from an old habit of school criticism. I wanted to see how it would sound with certain things left out. My presumption shows worst in wanting to try it with certain things put in. I think it is

116. For the idea of "pure form in poetry," see RF's July 4, 1913, letter to John Bartlett.

117. Flint replied with a postcard on June 26: "We mustn't be too hard on E.P. I *asked* him to help me write that review (1) because I didn't know what to say about the book and (2) because I thought he had been treated badly by the Poetry Review and that this might be some measure of reparation! Your 'poem' [i.e., the one addressed to Pound: 'I am a Mede and Persian'] is very amusing! I think it might annoy him! We were together at 67 Frith St. on Tuesday evening. He was very talkative! You know I think his bark is much worse than his bite; and that much that seems offensive to us externally is merely external and a kind of defense—a mask." Flint continued: "I am seeing T. E. Hulme tomorrow, and I will ask him when he could meet us both as you suggest. I deny that I am a metrical expert: Hulme is always interested in ideas, and always gives something in return." Flint then asked: "Has my poem floored you?" At last, he added, by way of postscript (which explains RF's remark about Monro in the next letter): "I spoke to Monro about printing your new work. He was responsive" (letter held at DCL).

one of the best poems you ever wrote. But I want the sentimental touch just a little lighter than you would have it perhaps. If you could catch forty moments in life as momentous as that you would have an important book.

Thanks for urging me on Monroe [*sic*]. Perhaps we shall have something for him soon. I have been in such a fever of what-shall-I-call-it that I haven't had application enough to sit down to two hundred lines on the Blick.[118] But you shall have The Housekeeper before long.[119]

You take Ezra sadly and I angrily. But what is the use. We will hate the arrivist in him and like what there is left to like. He wants to be good to us all. And having fired myself off in about five pomes [*sic*] like the one I sent you I feel better toward him.[120] What goes against me though is the suspicion that he only likes my poetry for philanthropic reasons as he manifestly does the poetry of Canaille.[121] He likes it because I have four children to feed and it flatters his vanity to be in a position to sell me to American editors. Perish the thought. We will think of other matters. I wrote him—I may as well confess—a rather wild letter demanding my manuscript back for no assigned reason. He told me I was having a fit of nerves and refused to comply. The terms on which we are likely to meet next are problematic. I commend you to the Muse

Robert Frost.

118. The Blick Company manufactured portable typewriters.

119. Collected in *NB*.

120. Three of RF's parodies of Pound survive: "Poets Are Born Not Made" ("My nose is out of joint . . ."), enclosed with an autumn 1913 letter to Flint; "I am a Mede and Persian . . . ," sent to Flint in June 1913; and the body of RF's short August 4, 1919, letter to Untermeyer.

121. Another reference to American poet Skipwith Cannell (1887–1957), whose surname takes its accent on the second syllable. Pound was then promoting Cannell's work and would include him in the 1914 anthology *Des Imagistes* (likely the "post-Georgian" anthology RF mentions in his June 17, 1913, letter to Flint). RF (one assumes) deliberately misspells Cannell's name for a joke at his expense, which the Francophone Flint would have well understood. "Canaille" derives from the Latin *cane* (dog), and as a French epithet suggests bohemian countercultural poseurs, or, in other contexts, the proletariat and lumpenproletariat; the word is sometimes translated as "the rabble."

[To Marie Hodge. The date is written in another hand, perhaps by the Boston University archivist, by the original collector of the letter, or by Marie Hodge herself. ALS. BU.]

The Bungalow
Beaconsfield
Bucks
England
[July 3, 1913]

My dear Mrs Hodge:

I must thank you for liking my book. If it keeps for me a few old friends and gains a few new ones, that is as much as I can ask of it. It pleases me that some of the girls care enough to want to own it. And it's good of you to take the trouble to take their orders. Could you send me their names with their home addresses and forty cents apiece for the books and postage? Their school addresses will be out of date almost before you get this. If you should get it in time will you say the right thing from me to the class of 1913 about their graduation. I hope they will have as good a time teaching others as I had teaching them. I have thought of you and them and a few others in Plymouth a good many times this year. Some of you may feel an interest in the review I am enclosing.

Sincerely yours,
Robert Frost

[To John Bartlett. In a sequence of letters to Bartlett of which this is the first, RF provides an early and definitive statement of his poetics. Above the salutation, RF appended a note: "Maybe you'll keep this discourse on the sound of sense till I can say more on it." ALS. UVA.]

The Bungs
Beaks
Bucks
Fourth-of-July, 1913

Dear John:—

Those initials you quote from T. P.'s belong to a fellow named Buckley and the explanation of Buckley is this that he has recently issued a book with David Nutt, but at his own expense, whereas in my case David Nutt assumed the risks.[122] And those other people Buckley reviewed are his personal friends or friends of his friends or if not that simply examples of the kind of wrong horse most fools put their money on. You will be sorry to hear me say so but they are not even craftsmen. Of course there are two ways of using that word the good and the bad one. To be on the safe side it is best to call such dubs mechanics. To be perfectly frank with you I am one of the most notable craftsmen of my time. That will transpire presently. I am possibly the only person going who works on any but a worn out theory* of versification. You see the great successes in recent poetry have been made on the assumption that the music of words was a matter of harmonized vowels and consonants. Both Swinburne and Tennyson aimed largely at effects in assonation. But they were on the wrong track or at any rate on a short track. They went the length of it. Anyone else who goes that way must go after them. And that's where most are going. I alone of English writers have consciously set myself to make music out of what I may call the sound of sense. Now it is possible to have sense without the sound of sense (as in much prose that is supposed to pass muster but makes very dull reading) and the sound of sense without sense (as in Alice in Wonderland which makes anything but dull reading). The best place to get the abstract sound of sense is from voices behind a door that cuts off the words. Ask yourself how these sentences would sound without the words in which they are embodied:

You mean to tell me you can't read?
I said no such thing.
Well read then.
You're not my teacher.

He says it's too late.
Oh, say!
Damn an Ingersoll watch anyway.

One—two—three——go!

---

122. In 1912 David Nutt published Reginald R. Buckley's *St. Francis: A Troubadour of the Spirit*, comprised of two parts: an essay devoted to "The Franciscan Ideal," and a twenty-page poem titled "St. Francis of Assisi." Buckley also regularly published reviews and books of criticism.

No good! Come back—come back.
Haslam go down there and make those kids get out of the track.

Those sounds are summoned by the audile imagination and they must be positive, strong, and definitely and unmistakeably [*sic*] indicated by the context. The reader must be at no loss to give his voice the posture proper to the sentences. The simple declarative sentence used in making a plain statement is one sound. But Lord love ye it mustn't be worked to death. It is against the law of nature that whole poems should be written in it. If they are written they won't be read. The sound of sense, then. You get that. It is the abstract vitality of our speech. It is pure sound—pure form. One who concerns himself with it more than the subject is an artist. But remember we are still talking merely of the raw material of poetry. An ear and an appetite for these sounds of sense is the first qualification of a writer, be it of prose or verse. But if one is to be a poet he must learn to get cadences by skillfully breaking the sounds of sense with all their irregularity of accent across the regular beat of the metre. Verse in which there is nothing but the beat of the metre furnished by the accents of the pollysyllabic [*sic*] words we call doggerel. Verse is not that. Neither is it the sound of sense alone. It is a resultant from those two. There are only two or three metres that are worth anything. We depend for variety on the infinite play of accents in the sound of sense. The high possibility of emotional expression all lies in this mingling of sense-sound and word-accent. A curious thing. And all this has its bearing on your prose me boy. Never if you can help it write down a sentence in which the voice will not know how to posture specially.

That letterhead shows how far we have come since we left Pink. Editorial correspondent of the Montreal Star sounds to me [*sic*]. Gad, we get little mail from you.

Affectionately
R. F.

*Principle I had better say.

[To F. S. Flint. ALS. HRC.]

The Bungalow
Beaconsfield Bucks
July 6 1913

Dear Flint:

I am glad of your warning against monotony.[123] I must look to my lines. You may infer from a list of my subjects how I have tried to get variety in my material. I have the following poems in something like shape for my next book:

1. The Death of the Hired Man—an elegy
2. The Hundred Collars—a comedy
3. The Black Cottage—a monologue
4. The Housekeeper a tragedy
5. The Code—Heroics, a yarn
6. The Mountain, a description
7. Arrival Home, an idyl[124]
8. Blueberries, an eclogue

But variety of material will not excuse me for lack of it in treatment. I shall have to take care.

I am grateful for what I got out of you. I only wish there had been more. You may say some things that more than half persuade me you like the poems. Of course I want you to like them. I value your opinion. The only fault I find with you is that you speak with too much diffidence. You are afraid of yourself. I was impatient when you used that word "weakness" for your feeling about Pound's perfidy. You are in awe of that great intellect abloom in hair. You saw me first but you had to pass me over for him to discover. And yet compare the nice discrimination of his review of me with that of yours. Who will show me the correlation between anything I ever wrote and his quotation from the Irish, You may sit on a middan and dream stars. You may

123. Flint had written, on July 3: "I need not say to you that you must avoid monotony of treatment in a book full of pieces like the four I have seen. I do not mean that I have felt such monotony; but I wondered what the effect of—say—another dozen would be read right off on end" (letter held at DCL).

124. Almost certainly "The Generations of Men."

sit on a sofa and dream garters.[125] But I must not get libre again. But tell me I implore you what on earth is a middan if it isn't a midden and where the hell is the fitness of a word like that in connection with what I wrote on a not inexpensive farm.

One thing I'd like to ask: Did I reach you with the poems, did I get them over, as the saying is? Did I give you a feeling of and for the independent-dependence of the kind of people I write about. I am no propagandist of equality. But I enjoy above all things the contemplation of equality where it happily exists. I am no snob. I may be several other kinds of fool and rascal but I am not that. The John Kline who lost his housekeeper and went down like a felled ox was just the person I have described and I never knew a man I liked better—damn the world anyway.[126]

I don't know but that I have delivered the best of what I had to say on the sound of sense. What more there may be I will be on hand to talk over with you and Hulme at five, Tuesday. My ideas got just the rub they needed last week.[127]

Remember Mrs Frost and me to your wife. Next time you come out here we will have a vegetarian dish of the American Indian called succotash. Do you know it?

Sincerely yours,
Robert Frost

---

125. Pound's review of *ABW* appeared in *Poetry* in May 1913. It reads, in part: "I remember Joseph Campbell telling me of meeting a man on a desolate waste of bogs, and he said to him, 'It's rather dull here;' and the man said, 'Faith, ye can sit on a middan and dream stars.' And that is the essence of folk poetry with distinction between America and Ireland. And Frost's book reminded me of these things."

126. "John Kline" would become John Hall (a man RF indeed knew) in "The Housekeeper."

127. "Tuesday": July 8. For the previous meeting with Hulme, see RF's June 25, 1913, letter to Flint.

[To Sidney Cox, enclosing several poems.[128] *ALS. DCL.]*

The Bungalow
Beaconsfield
Bucks Eng
July 10 1913

Dear Cox:—

I get your story and I am sorry for you. The only thing I don't understand is the philosophical not to say meek way in which you take your luck. You attribute it to your lack of self confidence. What would that mean I wonder. Are you any less sure of yourself than are others of your age? And is it in religion or in business or in politics or in society or in love? One thing I know: you will not be any more sure for a while after an experience like this. I don't like it for you.

If you want my opinion, I think it all comes of your overhauling your character too much in the hearing of others. You give your case away as Tennyson did his when he confessed that wherever he wrote King Arthur he had in mind Prince Albert.[129] He spoiled the Idyls for the present generation (I mean our own) and perhaps for all generations to come. And yet the poems are neither better nor worse for the confession. You <u>must</u> <u>not</u> disillusion your admirers with the tale of your sources and processes. That is the gospel according to me. Not that I bother much to live up to it.

And if you want my opinion, there is one other thing that enhances your effect of extreme youth. You are too much given to being edified-benefited-improved by everybody that comes along, including me. You must learn to take other people less uncritically and yourself more uncritically. You are all eaten up by the inroads of your own conscience.

---

128. RF enclosed three poems with the letter: "A Misgiving," later collected in his fourth book, *NH,* with a few emendations; "Good Hours," collected in *NB,* with a few emendations; and "Bond and Free," collected in RF's third book, *MI,* again with emendations (RF indicated that he considered "Bond and Free" the best). All three poems, incidentally, are followed by the phrase "Plymouth N.H.," indicating that they were written during RF's brief tenure at the New Hampshire State Normal School there (1911–1912).

129. Prince Albert, husband of Queen Victoria and Alfred Lord Tennyson's patron. When William Wordsworth died in 1850, Albert helped secure Tennyson the position of poet laureate. After Prince Albert died in 1861, Tennyson dedicated his *Idylls of the King* to him.

To get back to your trouble.[130] I can't account for the calm you preserve except on the assumption that you hope there is still hope. Be frank about that. If it is anything to you, or can result in anything, for us to meet Miss Howard, Mrs Frost and I will be glad to have her out to see us in August. But if the affair is closed I am afraid I should only be awkward in meeting her. What should I say. I am not good at talking about everything but what is in the back of my mind. But you shall decide. Do you have something like a real wish that we should talk with her—for some secret reason that you may not want to own to even to yourself? Let me know soon. I will scold you more in my next letter.

Sincerely yours
Robert Frost.

[To Ernest L. Silver. ALS. DCL.]

The Bungalow
Beaconsfield
Bucks. Eng.
July 10 1913

Dear Mr. Silver:—

I was hungry for the kind of news your letter supplied. I don't know that I get quite clearly in mind where you are building the new dormitory. Didn't you do well to get it? What did Keene[131] get? The building operations will afford you the same kind of amusement—diversion—that the repairs at the cottage did when we first struck Plymouth. More fun than the goat climbing the beplastered temporary stairs walking the loose floor-boards. What's the use of talking—you like it better than pedagogy. (Even high school teachers over here know so much more of Greek than the art of teaching that never having heard that word, they ask me if it ought not to be pronounced with two hard g's.) (A woman who formerly taught in the University of London, whose husband is professor of archeology there[132] now, picked me up on the

130. As Evans explains in *RFSC*: "[Cox] had fallen in love with Beth Howard [a fellow student], who refused to marry him because he 'lacked self-confidence'" (18).

131. The Keene Normal School (now Keene State College) is in Keene, New Hampshire. It was founded in 1909 to train teachers.

132. Ernest Arthur Gardner (1862–1939) was professor of archaeology at University College London; at the invitation of Gardner and his family, the Frosts visited Scotland in late August 1913. See RF to Bartlett August 30, 1913.

word only the other day and started to determine speculatively how it should be pronounced—if there was going to be such a word.)

The die seems cast for another year's stay here. The climate is Hell, as are also the politics in a country where party division proves to be altogether on religious lines—there are no Liberals who are not non-conformists, chapel-goers as they are called, and no Tories who are not Episcopalians. I don't like that. I should never get the hang of it. But certain people in London are so friendly to the kind of thing I write that it would seem a pity to tear away from them till I have published one more volume of poetry and, if I can bring myself to it for the money, at least one volume of prose. I find their society mighty stimulating especially to the writing of verse.

So we will let the furniture rest where it is.[133] The carpet came with us and is under my feet as I write. English moths may get it—not American. There was that stair carpet that I thoughtlessly took up. I should have left it for you. I'm blessed if I know where it is, though. It would hardly pay for you to dig for it.

What seems to be the matter with the Hon Brown, I wonder. Has he grown so great that he won't work in his socket? I was to write to him and I wrote. I got a stilted answer from him, dictated. He would be most happy to have me order a copy of his bulletin on Colebrook High from the Educational Department at Washington. Morrison had lost Durham.[134] The bulletin had made a

---

133. With Silver himself, who had agreed to store the Frost family's furniture while they were abroad.

134. For more on Harry Alvin Brown, who worked under New Hampshire State Superintendent of Education Henry C. Morrison, see RF's January 7, 1913, letter to him (where Brown's "bulletin" on Colebrook High is also discussed). In October 1912, Morrison, though backed by Brown, lost his bid to become president of the University of New Hampshire at Durham (then called the New Hampshire College of Agricultural and Mechanical Arts). The position went instead to Edward Thomas Fairchild (1854–1917), formerly Superintendent of Public Instruction for the state of Kansas, at a salary of $5,000. The letter from Brown that RF here correctly characterizes is dated November 29, 1912, and reads, in part: "I received your very interesting letter sometime ago and I should have answered it long before this. Doubtless you realize many of the duties which fall to the lot of a district superintendent. . . . Colebrook Academy is going along about as usual; the bulletin is out and there is comment in practically all the educational magazines in the country, large and small. I shall be very glad to have you write for it" (letter held at DCL). The surviving correspondence between RF, Brown, and Silver suggests that the poet contemplated a return to work in public education in New Hampshire up until the date of his move back to America in February 1915. However, the success of *NB*

stir. That was all. But I didn't let it phase [*sic*] me. I assumed good intentions and wrote again. Maybe he didn't like the excitement I was laboring under during my first six months here. I suppose I was somewhat scared at my own temerity. I wrote some funny letters in those days. Anyway he failed to notice me. I may do him injustice in thinking he has swollen anywhere. It may be from modesty he hasn't written, lest he should have to tell me of his election to sit at the right hand of Grace[135] (in Concord.) It may be he is simply afraid to put himself on paper for me to criticize—I gave his little bulletin such a merciless going over. But I did that because I was asked. I'm not really a prig. Aint my own writing off-hand. Do you know I bring my suspicion down to this: the simple fellow is mad at me because I didn't say I was sorry enough to suit him about Morrison's defeat. He wanted me to sing his Lord's song. But how could I in a strange land? He ought to be more reasonable. Funny world! One says that oftener and oftener as he draws nearer forty.

I have grown to know London better than any other of the large cities I have lived in for any length of time—San Francisco Boston New York (I lived in New York three months once). London is a fine city to get around in with such a network of tubes under it. And of course the names of the old villages that merge to make it easily fix themselves in one's mind because one has heard them so often in books. I see lots of Americans as I go about with their box-toed boots:[136] but they are mostly of the personally conducted variety. I yearn toward them just the same. I'm a Yank from Yankville.

This letter is designed to deal with the matter of the carpet.[137] It is lacking in unity and some other things.

Sincerely yours
R Frost.

---

in its American editions (1915), and the substantial fees RF soon drew from talks and readings in 1915 and 1916, allowed him, for a while, to support the family almost entirely in his capacity as poet; he did not return to teaching until Amherst College offered him a professorship in 1917.

135. Perhaps Grace Episcopal Church, Concord, New Hampshire.

136. According to RF, when he asked how F. S. Flint knew he was an American, Flint pointed down and replied, "Shoes."

137. That is, with the disposition of furnishings the Frosts left behind when they moved to England.

[To F. S. Flint. ALS. HRC.]

The Bungalow
Beaconsfield
Bucks. Eng.
July 10 1913

Dear Flint:

This is not that letter, but just a little note of misgiving—a minor note by a minor poet.

Please don't show these poems to Hulme till you hear from me again if it is not till this month next year. I am suffering from uncertainty with regard both to the poems and to myself. Sometimes I despair of myself for several kinds of a fool. Never ask me why. But we will wait a while.

Lucky for you that you got in ahead of the Canaille. Now for the good vacation.[138]

I will tell what I think of Pound when I have seen him once or twice more. Just because I have no use for myself I see no reason why I should have any use for anyone else. Look out for that unexpected affirmative (new figure of speech not listed in the rhetorics).

Sincerely yours
Robert Frost.

---

138. Yet another reference to Skipwith Cannell (1887–1957), whose surname takes its accent on the second syllable, and whose "Nocturnes" would follow Flint's five poems in *Des Imagistes* (London: Poetry Bookshop, 1914). In any case, Flint replied with a card posted on July 15: "I got your poems all right; but I have been so taken up these last few days that I haven't had a minute of repose in which to read them." He continues, acknowledging RF's opening reference to a letter to come: "I shall be glad to see the letter you spoke of, because all your writing contains something intensely interesting (rotten phrase but a hurried postcard). My verses are in Poets. So Canaille hasn't shoved me out. The more I think of Canaille, the greater grows my wrath and resentment against [Pound]. And yet all the time I'm wishing to remain friends with him and I still cherish the belief that there is gold—good gold—beneath the mud" (letter held at DCL).

[To Wilbur Rowell. ALS. UVA.]

The Bungalow
Beaconsfield
Bucks Eng.
July 17 1913

Dear Mr Rowell:—

The money is here in good season and thank you very much.[139] You can send the remainder later when I get back. I shall not be away from England more than two or three weeks.[140] We are getting most out of the things we see and the people we meet right here in London. The book has done rather well. At any rate it has done this much: it has introduced me to other people who write. I shall be glad to send you a copy, though I am not too sure that you will care for my sort of stuff—so very personal in this first book. You might call it a farm product, written as practically all of it was five years ago on the farm in Derry. The next book, if it comes off, should be more objective and so perhaps more generally interesting.

Sincerely yours
Robert Frost

[To Thomas Bird Mosher. ALS. DCL.]

The Bungalow,
Beaconsfield,
Bucks, Eng.
July 17 1913

Dear Mr. Mosher:—

I like the decision with which you speak and am content to let you prefer Reluctance to anything else I have written. Nevertheless the book contains a dozen poems that are at least good in the same kind and for the same reason. In Mowing, for instance, I come so near what I long to get that I almost despair of coming nearer.

I am made too self-conscious by the comment on my first book to think of showing another like it for some time. If I write more lyrics it must be with

139. See RF's June 6, 1913, letter to Rowell, and the headnote.

140. The Frosts spent several weeks in Scotland in the late summer and early fall.

no thought of publication. What I can do next is bring out a volume of blank verse that I have already well in hand and won't have to feel I am writing to order. I had some character strokes I had to get in somewhere and I chose a sort of eclogue form for them. Rather I dropped into that form. And I dropped to an everyday level of diction that even Wordsworth kept above. I trust I don't terrify you. I think I have made poetry. The language is appropriate to the virtues I celebrate. At least I am sure I can count on you to give me credit for knowing what I am about. You are not going to make the mistake that Pound makes of assuming that my simplicity is that of the untutored child. I am not undesigning.

You will be amused to hear that Pound has taken to bullying me on the strength of what he did for me by his review in Poetry.[141] The fact that he discovered me gives him the right to see that I live up to his good opinion of me. He says I must write something much more like vers libre or he will let me perish of neglect. He really threatens. I suppose I am under obligations to him and I try to be grateful. But as for the review in Poetry (Chicago, May), if any but a great man had written it, I should have called it vulgar. It is much less to my taste than the shorter reviews in Poetry & Drama and in The English Review.[142] The more I think of it the less I like the connection he sees between me and the Irishman who could sit on a kitchen-midden and dream stars. It is so stupidly wide of the mark. And then his inaccuracies about my family affairs![143] Still I think he has meant to be generous.

I wish sometime if you know Robinson you could put me in the way of knowing him too—sometime, if it comes right. Not a month ago I was asking Miss Sinclair if she shouldn't have put him ahead of Moody and Torrence in her article of a few years back in the Atlantic.[144] She said that Robinson was the only one of the three she still cared for.

---

141. Pound's review of *ABW* appeared in *Poetry* in May 1913; see the notes to RF's July 6, 1913, letter to Flint.

142. F. S. Flint wrote the review for *Poetry and Drama* (June 1913), while Norman Douglas reviewed *ABW* in *The English Review* (also in June 1913).

143. In his review, Pound made the following remarks as to RF's "family affairs": "There is perhaps as much of Frost's personal tone in the following little catch ['In Neglect'], which is short enough to quote, as in anything else. It is to his wife, written when his grandfather and his uncle had disinherited him of a comfortable fortune and left him in poverty because he was a useless poet instead of a money-getter."

144. May Sinclair, "Three American Poets of Today," *Atlantic Monthly* 98 (September 1906): 429–434.

You know I want you to use my poem in your catalogue.

Sincerely yours
Robert Frost

About my book in America. I shall do nothing for the present. Seymour of Chicago was out here from London to talk about it.[145] Mrs Nutt is going to have to be very much consulted in the matter. These are things I don't know very much about.

R.F.

[To John Bartlett. The letter is undated, but internal evidence suggests it was written in August 1913. ALS. UVA.]

The Bung
Beak
Bucks
[August 1913]

Dear John:

I ceased to worry about you when you didn't get jailed for faking the Nouvelle Evangeline.[146] And I suppose I shall cease again when I hear that the money is all right that you have been investing in Paton.[147] You know best because you are on the spot: do you consider him a good investment? You are young and brave and bully and I wouldn't shake your confidence in anybody you trusted for the world. If you are sure of him, stay sure. I may say, stay sure anyway. There is no alternative under the circumstances. You have so little to gain and everything to lose by suspicion. I suppose I wouldn't be saying even this much if I knew Paton.

---

145. Ralph Fletcher Seymour (1876–1966), head of R. F. Seymour, a Chicago publishing house. Seymour was an acquaintance and correspondent of Ezra Pound, who submitted *Patria Mia* to him for consideration in 1913 (the firm did not publish it until 1950).

146. See RF's March 18, 1913, letter to Bartlett and notes.

147. James Alexander Paton, publisher of the *Point Grey Gazette* in Vancouver. Bartlett had loaned Paton six hundred dollars to purchase a new printing press for the newspaper; the investment later failed to pay off and Bartlett lost most of his money.

And if you lose everything you have and Vancouver itself goes bankrupt you can ask Gerry for a job and go to the Cronicle [*sic*] (the office of which I remember as a boy) in San Francisco.[148]

I always feel perfectly right for a whole day after I have had a letter from you. You and your tale of Aggy-papers! And do you remember Little Dickey Potter, Ben Bolt?[149] You despised him for a farmer once and now look at you writing rabbity poultry articles for a farm journal. We never know. You were studying Greek then; Potter is doubtless teaching it now. Turn, fortune, turn thy wheel and lower the proud.[150]

One of the curious fatalities in our lives is that without collusion we have simultaneously turned our minds to run on rusticity. You will gather from the Bookman article (which I sent yesterday) what my next book is to be like. I ought to send you some of it. I may decide to call it New England Eclogues. Which do you think from the following list of titles you would prefer to read? The Death of the Hired Man, The Housekeeper (or Slack Ties), The Wrong, A Servant to Servants, The Code (of Farm Service), Swinging Birches, Blueberries, The Mountain, A Hundred Collars, The Cellar Hole, The Black Cottage.[151] All are stories between one hundred and two hundred lines long.

---

148. The *San Francisco Chronicle* had been in operation since 1865, nine years before RF's birth in the city.

149. Potter had been a classmate of Bartlett's at Pinkerton. As for "Ben Bolt," RF refers to a popular poem of that name by Thomas Dunn English (1819–1902), American politician and poet; more particularly, see stanza five (given that RF had been schoolmaster to both boys):

And don't you remember the school, Ben Bolt,
With the master so cruel and grim,
And the shaded nook in the running brook
Where the children went to swim?
Grass grows on the master's grave, Ben Bolt,
The spring of the brook is dry,
And of all the boys who were schoolmates then
There are only you and I.

150. First line of Tennyson's "Idylls of the King: Song from the Marriage of Geraint."

151. RF refers to a number of poems that would appear in *NB*, his book of "New England Eclogues." "The Wrong," "The Cellar Hole," and "The Lantern" would become "The Self-Seeker," "The Generations of Men," and "The Fear," respectively. "Swinging Birches" is an early draft of "Birches," published in RF's third volume, *MI* (1916).

I have written one today that I may call The Lantern if Mrs Frost doesn't dissuade me: she doesn't think it a fit. None of the lot is a love affair except The Cellar Hole and I am not sure that that isn't least successful of all.

R

Be well, mes enfants.

[To John Bartlett. RF provides only the date and month; internal evidence dates the letter to 1913. ALS. UVA.]

The Bungalow
Beaconsfield
Bucks.
Aug 6 [1913]

Dear John:—

I have had no word out of you to encourage me to go on with the material for the article you were going to please John C. and Henry's Mother with.[152] You should have three reviews in hand, the one from Poetry, the one from The English Review and the one from Poetry and Drama. I am sending the personal notice from the August English Bookman.[153] You may use them or not in the way I suggested. I shan't care too much if you don't. I know you must be very busy. Consult your own inclination.

No one of the articles but should be used with some judgement. This Bookman piece for instance makes me out as able to earn a living on a farm with both hands in my Norfolk-jacket pocket. Rats. I should rather you would eliminate that. The word "stark" in it will do well enough, though it is wide enough of the mark. As things go here in criticism it passes for a term of praise. "Bizarre" is a way off for A Hundred Collars. But never mind it was kindly meant. And the editor only knew the poem by hearsay. On the whole

152. John C. Chase. Henry Bradford Shepard (Pinkerton Academy, class of 1911) lived in East Derry (see also RF to Bartlett, June 16, 1913).

153. Ezra Pound reviewed *ABW* in *Poetry* magazine (May 1913), Norman Douglas reviewed it in *The English Review* (June 1913), F. S. Flint in *Poetry and Drama* (June 1913), and Arthur St. John Adcock in the *Bookman* (August 1913). Relevant passages from the reviews follow in the notes below.

I think the Bookman article needs manipulation as little as any.[154] It is fairly discrete [*sic*].

Be sure to get rid of the slam at America in the English Review article; also in the "Poetry" and "Poetry and Drama" articles. The remark about the Great American Editors is not quite fair either to the editors or to me.[155] For the rest I leave it to you. Dont let the paragraph in T.P.'s worry you. This getting reviewed for poetry over here is all sorts of a game. The explanation of the T.P.'s reviewer is this. He is my rival for the affections of David Nutt and his own little volume of verse hasn't been reviewed at all.[156]

I don't know whether I am a craftsman or not in your sense of the word. Some day I will take time to explain to you in what sense of the word I am one of the few artists writing. I am one of the few who have a theory of their own upon which all their work down to the least accent is done. I expect to do something to the present state of literature in America. That is why I don't want any slaps at my friends at home.

Now don't you do a thing you aren't moved to. Perhaps for some reason you think poorly of the Derry News plan. Would it be better to do it for the Manchester Union?

---

154. The *Bookman* piece was less a review of *A Boy's Will* than an effort—at the behest of May Sinclair—to make amends for a brief and dismissive review of the book that had appeared earlier. Adcock, the editor and most likely the author of the article, met with RF and then offered the first published account of the poet's life, including the description of farm life that troubled RF: "After his marriage he cut himself off from all his other belongings, and for several years lived with his wife and four children on a lonely farm in a forest clearing; he was nothing much of a farmer, but contrived to make enough by it for the needs of himself and his family whilst he was giving his soul room and time to grow. . . ." RF had also used the interview on which the article in *The Bookman* was based to reveal a bit about the contents of a second volume he had ready for publication, then called "Farm Servants and Other People" (i.e., *NB*); thus the mention of "A Hundred Collars."

155. Douglas had written, in *The English Review*: "Nowhere on earth, we fancy, is there more outrageous nonsense printed under the name of poetry than in America; and our author, we are told, is an American." Pound had written, in the first paragraph of the review in *Poetry*: "David Nutt publishes at his own expense *A Boy's Will*, by Robert Frost, the latter having been long scorned by the 'Great American Editors.' It is the old story." Finally, Flint, in *Poetry and Drama*, suggested that the story of RF's life had been "a constant struggle against circumambient stupidity for the right of expression. Be it said, however, that Mr. Frost has escaped from America. . . ."

156. Reginald R. Buckley; in 1912 David Nutt published his *St. Francis: A Troubadour of the Spirit*.

I am very busy myself for a person whose temperament is so self-obstructive. The next book begins to look large. Though I cant be sure that I will be ready with it this fall. I should like to sell some of it to the magazines first. A few hundred dollars earned that way might save my neck.

No use saying that we wish we heard from both of you more often.

Affectionately
R.

[To John Bartlett. Ernest Arthur Gardner (1862–1939) was a distinguished professor of archaeology at University College London. RF repeatedly misspells Gardner as Gardiner. ALS. UVA.]

Kingsbarns
Fifeshire
Aug 30 1913

Dear John:

To relieve my feelings just a word from Scotland on the funny holiday we are having with the Professor Gardiners. They are a family I got entangled with at the opening of the Poetry Shop in High Holborn last winter.[157] It was not my fault at all. I want you to know one thing: I have thrust myself and book on no one here. I have made my way partly on my merits, mostly on my luck, but I have never forced my way one inch. These Gardiners are the kind that hunt lions and they picked me up cheap as a sort of bargain before I was as yet made. I ought not to draw them too unsympathetically, for they have meant to be kind and I count it to their credit that they have embraced the whole family in their attentions. But, but! There is a string to it all, I find. They are a one-hoss poet and artist themselves and at the present moment they are particularly keen on lions as creatures who may be put under obligations to

157. Harold Monro's Poetry Bookshop opened on January 8, 1913. It was located on 35 Devonshire Street (now Boswell Street), Theobalds Road, in the Bloomsbury District of London (not the adjacent High Holborn District). Among the poets present at the opening were Henry Newbolt (1862–1938), Chair of Poetry for the Royal Society of Literature, Edward Marsh (1872–1953), W. H. Davies (1871–1940), and Frank S. Flint (1885–1960). RF stumbled upon the opening by accident (it was an invitation-only event) and talked his way in. See Elizabeth Shepley Sergeant, *Robert Frost: The Trial by Existence* (Holt, Rinehart and Winston, 1960): 101.

review them in the papers. Sic ad astra itur in London town.[158] It would make you weep. The Missus Gardiner is the worst. Nothing would satisfy her but we must all pack up and come to Scotland (Firth of Tay) to be near them for two weeks. So we let ourselves be dragged. Now the question is what do we think of their book.[159] Well, I haul off and start to say what I don't think with appropriate sops to my conscience. But such integrity as I have is all literary. I make a poor liar where the worth of books is concerned. I flounder and am lost. Thus much in the historical present. The Gardners don't like me any more. They despise my judgement and resent my tactlessness. But here I am on their hands. They are a gentleman and must carry it off with manners. Himself being an archaeologist (London University) he proposes to entertain us of an afternoon by conducting us to a cave near St Andrews for a look at an elephant a horse and an ass done by paleolithic man on the walls. These are the first drawings (or cuttings) of cavemen discovered in the British Isles and as Gardner discovered them and the discovery is going to make a stir when it is announced presently naturally we were expected to feel the honour of being taken into what is as yet a profound secret. But, but! Same old hoodoo of my too critical mind. I wanted to see the animals and I saw them. There were many marks on the cave wall, some wavy grooves due to water, some sharp-edged depressions due to the flaking off of the sandstone strata. It would have been strange if some of the marks hadn't accidentally looked like something. The sandstone was so soft and moist that a little rubbing easily made them look more like something. Animals are always the better for rubbing. And think of it—tracery like that and in such a substance assumed to have lasted for ten–twenty thousand years.[160] Why I'd be willing to leave it to the cavemen as to whether they had anything to do with the elephant the horse or the ass. I'll bet the layer of sandstone they are on hasn't been uncovered five hundred years if it has been a hundred. I begin to think I must be some archaeologist myself, I doubted the authenticity of this prehistoric

158. RF paraphrases Virgil's *Aeneid* (IX, 641): *sic itur ad astra* ("thus you shall go to the stars"—that is, achieve immortality).

159. *Plain Themes: Verses,* by Mary and Phyllis Gardner (London: J. M. Dent and Sons, 1913).

160. Likely Constantine's Cave at Fife Ness, Scotland. Subsequent excavations (first conducted in June 1914) bore RF's skepticism out. Artifacts indicate that the cave's earliest inhabitants date from about the second century CE. As for the drawings of animals: these are of Pictish origin—similar to ones found in the Wemyess caves, to the south St. Andrews—and date from 800–1000 CE.

menagerie so easily. The beasts left me cold. I tried to rise to the moment, but the cave was clammy and there were other things, principally the literary literature. Still I have no doubt a rumpus will be raised over Gardner's discovery. Sic ad astra itur in highbrow circles. Let's see didnt you dig up a Neanderthal man in the Vancouver city dump?[161]

Not a word to your city editor about all this. I am betraying a confidence in consigning it to paper. But damn—

St Andrews is old enough anyway without the cave drawings. We stood in the town under a tower that has figured in history since the sixth century—St Regulus' Tower. All round us were the ruins of the great cathedral that John Knox preached his followers into setting on fire during the Reformation.[162] I haven't given you much of this sort of thing. Sounds very travelly.

Dont write to me here. We are only Fifing for a couple of weeks. Pretty little village Kingsbarns—where the king used to store his grain when his capital was at Dunfermline town and his Piraeus at Aberdour (read again the ballade of Sir Patrick Spens.) Right foreninst us is the Bell Rock Lighthouse which was the Inchcape Bell of Southey's poem.[163] The children like it. I suppose it wont hurt my New Hampshire impressions as I have always been afraid learning a new language might hurt my English style.

Affectionately
R.F.

---

161. See RF's March 18, 1913, letter to Bartlett and notes.

162. In 1559 John Knox preached a militant sermon in St. Andrews Cathedral, and the twelfth-century edifice was "cleansed" as a result. In 1561 it was abandoned, and the former headquarters of the Scottish Church was left to fall into ruin.

163. Dunfermline was a royal capital from the eleventh through the fifteenth century; RF suggests that Aberdour was port to Dunfermline as Piraeus was to Athens. Dunfermline and Aberdour both figure in "The Ballad of Sir Patrick Spens" (anon. seventeenth century). "Foreninst": Scottish dialect for "in front of," "opposite." "The Inchcape Rock" (1820) by Robert Southey tells the story of a fourteenth-century attempt to install a warning bell on the same dangerous reef on which the lighthouse would be built in 1810.

[To Sidney Cox. RF misspells "Yeats" throughout the letter. Dating from internal evidence. ALS. DCL.]

The Bungalow
Beaconsfield Bucks
[circa September 15, 1913]

Dear Cox:

Suppose I put off scolding you the rest till another time and allow myself the freedom in pencil of saying anything that comes into my head. I wonder if there is anything in particular you would like to know about how life goes over here and I wonder if I am mind-reader enough to guess what it would be.

There is Yates you spoke of as being rated by the departmental professor considerably below that good boy from Oxford, the sing-songing (as distinguished from song-singing) Alfie No-yes. Do you want to hear what I think of him? If you are where you can lay hands on the Oxford Book of Victorian Verse I can talk to you from that.[164] It gives Noyes plenty of space to show his paces. "When spring comes back to England" is a pleasant enough lilt—the children like it—very likely it is the best thing Noyes has done. But no one would say that it was stirring. The second poem with the tiresome "mon bel ami" refrain expects you to be moved at the thought that Venus has settled down to suckle John Bull's baby by an English hearth. The thought is not stirring: the note is not deep enough to be stirring. Swinging is not stirring, you know. Neither is swelling necessarily stirring. The poem in which he gets Frances Tompson's [*sic*] "purpureally enwound" swells, but who cares a pin. I wish I knew what you thought he had written that got below the surface of things. I believe he has preached a little—is preaching now on the subject of peace.[165] I recall a poem beginning, Beyond beyond and yet again

164. Alfred Noyes (1880–1958), English poet. The first three poems referred to here all appear in Arthur Quiller-Couch's *Oxford Book of Victorian Verse* (1912). "When Spring comes back to England" opens "The World's May Queen" (the first poem by Noyes in the anthology); *"N'oserez vous, mon bel ami?"* is the refrain in the second ("Our Lady of the Sea"), in which Venus, mourning Adonis, wanders north from Greece (through Italy, Spain and France) to make her home, at last, among the English (who draw her in "with a joyful cry / To the hearth where she sits with a babe on her knee"); the phrase "purpureally enwound" figures in "On the Death of Francis Thompson" (and is adapted from Thompson's own "The Hound of Heaven").

165. In 1913, Noyes published *The Wine Press: A Tale of War*, a book-length poem dedicated, caustically, "To those who believe that Peace is the corrupter of nations"; it was widely discussed in the press.

beyond! What went ye forth to seek oh foolish fond.[166] That strikes a note. ("Foolish fond" is rather awful.) I doubt if there is very much to him however. He is nothing for the American people to rage over. His attractive manners and his press agent have given you an exaggerated idea of his importance.

Yates' lines

"For the good are always the merry
Save by an evil chance,"

are worth all of Noyes put together.

"Who dreamed that beauty passes like a dream?"

That line fairly weeps defiance to the unideal, if you will understand what I mean by that.

The Rose of the World, The Fiddler of Dooney,[167] The Lake Isle of Innisfree, Down by the Sally Gardens, The Song of the Wandering Aengus, The Song of the Sad Shepherd[168]—those are all poems. One is sure of them. They make the sense of beauty ache.

"Then nowise worship dusty deeds."

Such an untamable spirit of poetry speaks there. You must really read Yates. He is not always good. Not many of his longer things are more than interesting. But the Land of Hearts Desire is lovely and so is On Shadowy Waters in poetry and Cathleen ni Hoolihan in prose.[169]

Someone the other day was deriving all the Masefield and Gibson sort of thing[170] from one line of Yates' Land of Hearts Desire,

"The butter's at your elbow, Father Hart."

Oh Yates has undoubtedly been the man of the last twenty years in English poetry. I won't say that he is quite great judged either by the way he

---

166. Noyes' "Art, the Herald," which begins: "Beyond; beyond; and yet again beyond! / What went ye out to seek, oh foolish-fond?"

167. From which two poems, respectively, the lines just quoted are drawn.

168. RF conflates two different poems, "The Sad Shepherd" and "The Song of the Happy Shepherd" (the latter of which he next quotes).

169. RF staged the plays *The Land of Heart's Desire* and *Cathleen ni Hoolihan* with his students at Pinkerton Academy in 1910.

170. John Masefield and Wilfrid Gibson were associated with the Georgian school, whose colloquial style RF has in mind in citing, as a model, the line from Yeats ("the butter's at your elbow . . ."). Gibson and RF would soon become friends.

takes himself as an artist or by the work he has done. I am afraid he has come just short of being. The thing you mention has been against him. I shouldn't care so much—I shouldn't care at all if it hadn't touched and tainted his poetry. Let him be as affected as he pleases if he will only write well. But you can't be affected and write entirely well.

You'll be thinking this is an essay on something. Lets be personal for a change.

I had a chance to see and hear the other night how perilously near Yates comes to believing in fairies. He told with the strangest accent of wishful half belief of the leppercaun (spell it) two old folks he visited had had in a cage on the wall. The little fellow was fine and sleek when they trapped him but he pined in captivity until they had to let him go. All the time they had him another leppercaun hung about the house morning [*sic*] (in silence) for him. And when the old folks out of pity let him go the two fairies hurried off hand in hand down the glen. Yates I could see was in a state of mind to resent being asked point blank what he thought of such a story. And it wouldn't have been best for anyone to go on the assumption that he told it to be amusing. My Catholic friend Liebich[171] tells me he for his part didn't know but that everybody had some sort of belief in fairies. He said it was something like the belief in the communion of saints.

There's a good story I had pretty directly from Mrs Sharp about how she was out with her husband (Fiona Macleod[172]) walking somewhat ahead of him in an English lane one day when she saw something childlike with a goat's legs scuttle into the woods. She stood still with astonishment. Her husband came up, "William, what do you think?—a faun! I saw him!"

"It's nothing," said William without coming to a standstill, "such creatures are all about this part of the country."

We are just back from a two weeks' journey in Scotland. We went up the coast to Dundee by boat and from there by train to Kingsbarns a little old town close to St Andrews. We saw some sights inevitably though we were not out sight-seeing. The best of the adventure was the time in Kingsbarns where tourists and summer boarders never come. The common people in the south of England I don't like to have around me. They don't know how to

171. Franz Liebich, Frost family friend and a pianist of some repute in London.

172. Fiona Macleod is the pseudonym of William Sharp (1855–1905), Scottish poet and literary biographer. Sharp was associated with Yeats in the Celtic revival of the 1890s. His wife was Elizabeth Amelia Sharp.

meet you man to man. The people in the north are more like Americans. I wonder whether they made Burns' poems or Burns' poems made them. And there are stone walls (dry stane[173] dykes) in the north: I liked those. My mother was from Edinburgh. I used to hear her speak of the Castle and Arthur's Seat, more when I was young than in later years.[174] I had some interest in seeing those places. The children saw the Black Watch march into the Castle with a band of bagpipes.[175]

The trouble with this sort of composition is that one could go on with it forever. I have told you enough to show you what we are doing with ourselves. If I haven't—well today we walked to Jordans and stood between Penn's grave and the graves of his five little children.[176] It is not far to go we have done the walk before. We mean to get down to church there some day. The meeting home is much as it was in Penn's day. Only the money-changers have got a foothold in it—I mean the sellers of picture postal cards to the fugitive American. I dont know who is to blame for this, the Englishman or the American. People here blame the latter. Etc etc etc etc.

You may do anything you can to give the boys of Poland a better chance for all I care.[177] I am not always a doubter. Have me in mind five or six years from now when results begin to show. You must work off your enthusiasm in any way you can.

Tell us about the new job. You will soon be drowning your cares in unlimited theme-correcting. Mortify the flesh, old man. Suffer. My soul, how you like it.

Sincerely yours
Robert Frost

---

173. Scottish spelling for "stone."

174. "Arthur's Seat" is a peak in central Edinburgh, about one mile east of Edinburgh castle; it affords a panoramic view of the city.

175. The Black Watch (Royal Highlanders), an infantry battalion in the Royal Regiment of Scotland, is often deployed for ceremonial purposes.

176. Jordans Quaker meetinghouse, near Chalfront, St. Giles, Buckinghamshire, England, where William Penn is buried.

177. Cox then taught in Poland, New York.

[To F. S. Flint. In the following letter occurs the first reference in RF's correspondence to Edward Thomas (1878–1917), critic, journalist, and poet, who was to become RF's closest friend in England. He was later killed in combat in France. ALS. HRC.]

The Bungalow
Beaconsfield
Bucks England
October 10 1913

Dear Flint:

Would you think it too disloyal to the man "through whom alone you have a market for your poetry" (I quote) to meet with me some afternoon or evening a person who loves Pound as little as the critic Edward Thomas?[178] Figure that out at your leisure and give me an answer in the spirit in which it is meant.[179] Thomas was remembering your book the other day and I saw from the way he spoke he would like to know you.

Yours
R.F.

[To Marie Hodge. ALS. BU.]

The Bungalow
Beaconsfield
Buck Eng
Oct 10 1913

Dear Mrs Hodge:

I have to thank you for the additional book order and for Miss Darling's letter which I think was meant to be entirely nice in spite of the repeated use

---

178. Thomas, Flint, and RF met in London on Monday, December 22, as a December 17, 1913, note from Thomas to RF held at DCL indicates. A letter from the poet Ralph Hodgson (1871–1862), dating from late September or early October 1913, speaks of Thomas to RF, and may have occasioned their first acquaintance: "Shall you by chance be in Town on Tuesday? If so you might turn up at St Georges Res[t] next to the Coliseum in St Martin's lane close by Trafalgar Square—at about 4. Edward Thomas will be up and I think you'd both like to know each other" (letter held at DCL). This dates RF's first meeting with Thomas to early October.

179. Flint did not figure it out. In an October 14 reply he writes: "I should like very much to meet E.T. What does your sarcasm (?) about E.P. and the 'only market' mean? Have I used these words? Quarter me if I have—seriously" (letter held at DCL).

of that dubious word "verses." Perhaps I shall meet Miss Darling if I ever get back to the States. Thank her for me.[180]

You are all so made over by this time that I shouldnt know where I was if I fell out of the sky in the neighborhood of Plymouth. There's not a pupil left that I knew and perhaps you are all living in the new building. I might find some of the old teachers still teaching one thing or another but not myself teaching psychology.

I'm busy for me. Of course I can't write poetry on time every day as I would go to a recitation, but there is copying to do and there are people to see and what with this and that I seem on the go most of the time. If you happen to know Quiller-Couch's Oxford Book of Victorian Verse—well I was looking that over the other evening to see how many of the poets represented in it I had met and I found it was most of them under fifty and I seem in a fair way to meet the rest. Ezra Pound, my fellow countryman, is one of the most describable of them. He is six inches taller for his hair and hides his lower jaw in a delicate gold filagree of almost masculine beard. His coat is of heavy black velvet. He lives in Grub Street, rich one day and poor the next. His friends are the duchesses. And he swears like a pirate and he writes what is known as vers libre and he translates from French, Provençal, Latin, and Italian. He and I have tried to be friends because he was one of the first to review me well, but we don't hit it off very well together. I get on better with fellows like Gibson who are less concerned to dress the part of poet. Gibson is a much greater poet too. Well I musnt tire you with these people.

We have had a gracious summer and I take back much of what I said about the English climate.

When you are not too busy—any news you may have—

Mrs Frost wishes to be remembered. She says she will be writing to you.

Sincerely yours,
Robert Frost.

180. Unidentified.

[To Harold Monro (1879–1932), a British poet, publisher, editor, and bookseller. As proprietor of the Poetry Bookshop in Devonshire and as editor of Poetry and Drama, *he was an influential figure in early modern poetry. ALS. Trinity.]*

The Bungalow
Beaconsfield
Bucks
Oct 12 [1913]

Dear Monro:

I regretted not being able to join you in Frith St.[181] I was away on a long tramp when your card came yesterday and did not get in till late. Perhaps next meeting—if you have decided to have another meeting. Thanks for thinking of me.

Of course I very much want you to print something of mine. At the same time I doubt if the poem you have chosen is as representative as the Hundred Collars. You may say that it will bear printing alone better than the Hundred Collars; and that, to be sure, is a consideration. I have felt from the first that it was too much to ask you to use two poems at once.

You can tell me more about it when I am with you to consider your exceptions to The Fear.[182]

Sincerely yours
Robert Frost

181. T. E. Hulme hosted a salon at 67 Frith Street, the home of his close friend Ethel Kibblewhite. In the heart of London, the lavish house had at one time served as the Venetian embassy. See RF's letter to Flint, early December 1913.

182. Monro published both "The Fear" and "A Hundred Collars" in *Poetry and Drama* in December 1913.

[To F. S. Flint. ALS. HRC.]

The Bungalow
Beaconsfield
Bucks
Oct 12 [1913]

Dear Flint:

How have you time during work or energy after work to be torturing jokes out of my sacred name? I should think I would have been safe from you.[183]

Yes, since you ask me, I have melted (with ruth for all mankind).[184] But I have not evaporated. In this climate at this time of year, nothing evaporates, not even the water in the clothes on the line—you ask your wife.

And yet there is an American sense in which I have evaporated: I have dried up. Which is to say I have shut up. Which is to say I am not saying. I have said all I am going to say for a while.

I make haste to add that that won't preclude my writing now and then to a friend—when I have any thing better than your post card laconics to write in answer to. You will have to say something to start me off. Come on.

I'll tell you what I will remark gratis, however, and that is, what a pretty romance in the Poetry Shop, and I trust you have not been behind-hand with felicitations.[185] You don't feel as poor Monro does, I trust, that the whole thing is a conspiracy to rob him of a contributory poet and confidential secretary at one and the same fell stroke.

I mean to see you soon. Doubtless you were at Monro's party in Frith St. last night. I should have seen you there, if I had been able to get in. I must arrange with Thomas for the meeting I spoke of. I'll let you know.

Blessins.
R.

---

183. That is, as many puns might be made on the surname "Flint" as on "Frost."

184. See Milton's "Lycidas": "Look homeward Angel now, and melt with ruth."

185. The "romance in the Poetry Shop" was between Wilfrid Gibson, who had moved into one of the bed-sits above the shop in November 1912, and Monro's secretary, Geraldine Townshend. The couple married in December 1913. See also RF's March 26, 1914, letter to Sidney Cox.

[To Gertrude McQuesten (1864–1931), a teacher at the Emerson College of Oratory in Boston. RF met McQuesten in 1911 when she gave a reading at Pinkerton Academy, where he then taught. Her family lived in Plymouth, and the Frost family became friends with her mother Louella after relocating there when RF took a position at the Plymouth Normal School. In opening the letter, RF refers to Mrs. McQuesten's recent death and to Gertrude's sister, Nettie. Dating derived from internal evidence. NB *did not appear in February 1914 but on May 15. ALS. BU.]*

The Bungalow
Beaconsfield
Bucks Eng
[circa October 20, 1913]

Dear Miss McQuesten:

We guessed what was keeping you silent so long.—I am glad we went to Plymouth in time to get acquainted with your mother and see you with her. She must have had some special story she told you on Sunday afternoons when you were you were young that made you and your sister such good daughters. It seems sad to think of the little house in the steep street without her.

Naturally you will turn to places other than Plymouth for your summers now. You may imagine how glad we shall be to see you over here as soon as ever you can come. We shall want you to spend a few days with us if we are not in too close quarters and if we are we can find you board close to us with some good English farmer. We may be in Gloucester by the time you get here.[186] There will be poets with us I know you will like to meet. Two of them are readers of their own poetry (which sounds funny.) They would read to you and you would read to us. I will tell you more about it when our colony down there is more of an assured thing. You simply must plan not to run about in England all the time. You must take the English country for a week sitting still if not in Gloucester, somewhere else. We'll hope it may be in Gloucester. We ought to be able to take care of you two somehow.

The bit of program you send bears familiar names. Two of the readers I have actually heard with my ears, you and Copeland.[187] Yours was an un-

---

186. In April 1914 RF and his family would move to Little Iddens, Leddington, Ledbury, in Gloucestershire.

187. George Copeland Jr., a musician who had once performed on a program (given by the Boston Symphony Orchestra) that included McQuesten's reading of scenes from Shakespeare's *Midsummer Night's Dream*. The play by Robert Browning is, presumably, *In*

usual selection, wasnt it? I have been rereading the play to see why you chose it. I should be afraid of some of those Browning tortuosities. But if you made it go beautifully that's all there was to ask. I gather that you feel you are still adding more to much in your art. I'm glad to see you coming to what is yours. Let's storm something high in the name of Hildreth Hall Derry N.H.[188] where you and I first talked poetry and the poets.

I may yet live to hear you read in public something from my own dramatic work. Poetry and Drama (London) will print two things of mine, "The Fear" and "The Hundred Collars" in December. If it's not easy for you to see it perhaps I'll send you a copy as a foretaste of the next book due in February. The two in Poetry and Drama are the editor's choice from several; there are others in the book that I should think might be more to your taste. You will say they are dramatic. The form is something I have partly devised for myself. The nearest thing to them is the eclogue. I want you to be interested in the book. I'm on the subject of people this time and I leave it to you if you don't go boldly up to some of them and take them by the noses. Laurence Binyon speaks of my muse in A Boy's Will as a shy muse.[189] It would be strange if she wasn't that, for I was a shy youngster when I went away by myself in to the Derry woods to write it. But shyness is a thing one can't keep if one wants to. Once I fled from everybody. But I find I am only a little abashed by the only human in my later days. At least I grow less and less afraid of imaginary people. The new book proves that.—I call it "North of Boston."

I wonder what notice of my first book Miss Grace McQuesten has been seeing.[190] Something English you say. It has done very well here. My pub-

---

A Balcony, also on the program for the 1909–1910 season of the Boston Symphony Orchestra.

188. Hildreth Hall stood on Pinkerton Academy's campus.

189. Robert Laurence Binyon (1869–1943), British poet, dramatist, and critic. At the suggestion of James Cruickshank Smith, he had written RF on October 8, 1913—on letterhead from the British Museum, where he worked in the Department of Prints and Drawings—inviting him to lunch, and speaking warmly of *ABW.* A second note from Binyon (dated October 14) indicates that the two met on Friday October 17, 1913. Robert Bridges (1844–1930), poet laureate from 1913 until his death, joined them. The two letters from Binyon are held at DCL; neither speaks of RF's "shy muse."

190. Grace McQuesten—born June 10, 1878, in Litchfield, New Hampshire, and unrelated to Gertrude—taught piano at Pinkerton Academy and subsequently had a successful career as a composer, collaborating with W. S. Braithwaite as lyricist. She was also active in Boston literary circles.

lisher (Mrs Nutt) sent but two copies for review to America. (The one to The Dial Chicago was well received.[191]) She doesn't seem to feel that there is any hurry about getting me home to my own people. I rather hope though to be read more in the States than in England before all is over. I find that nothing quite affects me like interest on the part of old friends. Remember me to Miss McQuesten when you see her again.

We are pretty quiet these days. We had a jaunt in Scotland in the summer that we could ill afford. But Scotland was my mother's country (she was born near Edinborough) and I felt as if we ought to get a glimpse of it. My mother used to sing a song that said she couldn't. "Oh I can't get a blink o' my ain countree."[192] We were some time near St Andrews where John Knox knocked and Golf took its rise.[193] We were with literary friends, but the best of it all was the new friends we made by chance on the beach. They were literary too—or at least one of them was—what he himself called a distinguished amateur of poetry—writes none but edits Shakespeare and Spencer [*sic*] and knows by heart all the great poetry in Greek Latin and English.[194] He has introduced me to an entirely new set of people and that looks like the beginning of more running to London. But I have to remember I am here primarily to write and not to see society.

We go to the theatre sometimes with someone and now and then I shall have to run into London, as on Tuesday, for a meeting of the younger poets.[195] We'll eat in Soho and then talk about what it is necessary not to know to be a poet. Of course the all important thing to know nothing about is metre. There are two ways out of it for the candidate: either he must never have known or he must have forgotten. Then there is a whole line of great poets he must profess not to have read or not to have read with attention. He must say he knows they are bad without having read them. I should like these fellows in or out of motley. Their worst fault is their devotion to method.

---

191. *The Dial* favorably reviewed *ABW* in its September 16, 1913, number.

192. A folk song: "Oh, why left I my hame? Why did I cross the deep? / Oh, why left I my hame where my forefathers sleep? / I sigh for Scotia's shore. And I gaze across the sea. / Bat I cannot get a blink o' my ain countree."

193. See RF's August 30, 1913, letter to Bartlett and notes. The friends RF mentions are Ernest and Mary Gardner.

194. James Cruickshank Smith (1867–1949), inspector of schools at Edinburgh, editor of *The Poetical Works of Edmund Spenser* (Oxford: Clarendon Press, 1910), and general editor of the Oxford series *Selected Plays of Shakespeare* (1912–1916).

195. At the salons T. E. Hulme hosted.

They are like so many teachers freshly graduated from a normal school. I should have thought to escape such nonsense in the capital of the world. It is not a question with them of how much native poetry there is in you or of how much you get down on paper, but of what method you have declared for. Your method must be their method or they won't accept you as a poet. You may be a very good fellow and all that, but on your own showing you can't write. They haven't read your book—didn't know you had written one etc etc etc. You can see that it wouldn't be by favor of them one would win to recognition. But they're nice fellows all the same and one wants to see something of them.

My real intimates are of another kind. Gibson is my best friend. Probably you know his work. He is much talked up in America at the present time. He's just one of the plain folks with none of the marks of the literary poseur about him—none of the wrongheadedness of the prosperous literary man. He will be of the Gloucester colony. Abercrombie is already living in Gloucester. Be sure you are up on the works of these two when you come to see us. Read Gibson's "Fires" and Abercrombies "Sale of St. Thomas" (Georgian Anthology).[196]

Let us hear from you as often as you have time for us.

Sincerely yours
Robert Frost.

[To Thomas Bird Mosher. ALS. DCL.]

The Bungalow,
Beaconsfield, Bucks,
England.
October 28 1913

Dear Mr Mosher:

I had your letter and the two copies of your catalogue with my poem where I am pleased to see it.[197] There is but one thing more you could do for me at present and possibly there are too great difficulties in the way of that. The

196. Extracts from Wilfrid Gibson's long poem "The Fires" appeared, together with Lascelles Abercrombie's "The Sale of St. Thomas," in *Georgian Poetry (1911–1912)* (London: Poetry Bookshop, 1912).

197. "Reluctance."

most insuperable would be your not wanting to do it. Then there is Mrs Nutt. Still I am very jealous of Bottomley, whom I expect to know shortly through Travelyan.[198] Perhaps I shouldnt equal myself to Bottomley, and I won't: but I give you fair warning I am going to have my moderate success in these islands. The signs are not wanting. The review you speak of is one of them. The kind of people the book is interesting is another. Binyon had me to lunch the other day with Bridges.[199] When I can get rid of this house I am to go to Gloucester to live, to be with Wilfrid Gibson and Abercrombie.[200] I am out with Pound pretty much altogether and so I don't see his friend Yeats as I did. I count myself well out however. Pound is an incredible ass and he hurts more than he helps the person he praises.

These Englishmen are very charming. I begin to think I shall stay with them till I'm deported. If I weren't so poor I should plan to stay five years anyway.

Dont take me as urging my book on you too seriously. I have made no move to urge it on anyone over there and am like to make none until people have had time to hear of it a little. I suppose that sort of thing will keep. I am an almost fatally patient person as a tale I could tell would show. At any rate I have no strength to batter out against the indifference of those who will meet me with a "Who are you?" or "Go get a reputation."

Parts of my next book should begin to appear here and there soon. Monro told me he would use A Hundred Collars and perhaps one other eclogue (or what you will) in the Dec. Poetry and Drama. Poetry (Chicago) has announced something—I don't know what—very likely The Black Cottage.[201] The book will not be named as Mrs Nutt had it but more likely "New Englanders" or "New England Hill Folk."[202] The name is about the only part not ready to go to press. The poems are rather too long for most magazines. I think I may offer one or two to Kennerley but I have little hope of his seeing them in the

198. Mosher had published several books by Gordon Bottomley in 1909 and 1910. Robert Calverley Trevelyan (1872–1951) was an English poet and translator.

199. On October 17.

200. RF made the move in April 1914.

201. Harold Monro indeed published "A Hundred Collars" in *Poetry and Drama* (December 1913). *Poetry* magazine (Chicago) published not "The Black Cottage" but "The Code" (with the subtitle "Heroics") in February 1914. Both were collected in RF's second volume, *NB*.

202. The 1913 catalogue published by David Nutt and Company advertised the title of the new RF book as *Farm Servants and Other People.*

ruck.[203] I think of him as more than usually overwhelmed with manuscript. Of course I should like any money I can get from the magazines. One has to live and eat.

Well well. This letter has run into lengths.

Sincerely yours
Robert Frost.

[To John Bartlett. The letter is undated, but the surviving envelope was postmarked as it passed through British Columbia on November 18, 1913. ALS. UVA.]

The Bung Hole, Still.
[early November 1913]

Dear John

Never you let that silly business of remembering me to my Derry friends put any strain on your feeling for me.[204] I keep not hearing from you; and I begin to be afraid I have asked you to do more than you could do or wanted to do. Very likely you didn't like the idea of stirring 'em up in our old haunts. I don't know that I blame you. It was just my impulse. You are quite free to beg off in the matter. I trust it is no worse than that. It occurs to me as possible that you may have tried to deliver the article on Birch Street and got a snub for your pains. It would have been through no fault of yours, but you may have been uncomfortable about it all this time. The whole thing is of no importance—utterly. I ought not to give way to thoughts of revenge in the first place. Still there were a few people in Derry who vexed me and one or two who did more than that and I am human enough to want to make them squirm a little before I forgive them.

You are about all I saved from the years I spent in Derry, you and Margaret, and the three children born to us on the farm, and the first book that was mostly written on the farm before I attended school at Pinkerton. I really care not a fig either way for or against anyone else I fell in with in my teaching days. I don't want you to grow cold in letter writing. You are to act always on the assumption that we are going to get together again across the meridians. Of course we are. I always think if you would take measures to

203. Mitchell Kennerley (1878–1950) British-born American publisher; he managed the New York offices of the London firm John Lane.

204. See RF's June 16, 1913, letter to Bartlett.

strike up a correspondence for one of these London papers you would sooner or later land here among the literary people, and with better prospects of staying than I have because you know how to make money. Think it over. I am reminded of you every time I see a special article from British Columbia.

You musn't take me too seriously if I now proceed to brag a bit about my exploits as a poet. There is one qualifying fact always to bear in mind: there is a kind of success called "of esteem" and it butters no parsnips. It means a success with the critical few who are supposed to know. But really to arrive where I can stand on my legs as a poet and nothing else I must get outside that circle to the general reader who buys books in their thousands. I may not be able to do that. I believe in doing it—dont you doubt me there. I want to be a poet for all sorts and kinds. I could never make a merit of being caviare to the crowd the way my quasi-friend Pound does. I want to reach out, and would if it were a thing I could do by taking thought. So much by way of depreciation before I begin. Now for it, a little of it.

I suppose I arrived in a sense the other day when Laurence Binyon asked me to lunch with Robert Bridges the Lauriat [*sic*]. It meant this much: Binyon had decided that my book was one of the few and he was good enough to want me to have my chance with the Chief. So I took it. That is the best sounding thing I have to tell. I don't know that it pleased me any more than to find Trevelyan, a man who is known as a patron of art, with my book in his pocket. He had bought it on the recommendation of somebody who is supposed to know all about poetry. I am sure that it pleased me less than the friendly attentions I have had from Wilfrid Gibson and Laselles [*sic*] Abercrombie. These fellows you can know if you can get hold of either Q's Oxford Book of Victorian Verse or The Georgian Anthology.[205] They are something more than my casual acquaintances. If or when we can get rid of this house I am going down into Gloucester to live near them. The second book is what

205. "Q" is Arthur Quiller-Couch. The *Georgian Anthology* for 1911–1912 announced in its preface (by Edward Marsh): "This volume is issued in the belief that English poetry is now once again putting on a new strength and beauty. Few readers have the leisure or the zeal to investigate each volume as it appears; and the process of recognition is often slow. This collection, drawn entirely from the publications of the past two years, may if it is fortunate help the lovers of poetry to realize that we are at the beginning of another 'Georgian period' which may take rank in due time with the several great poetic ages of the past." The anthology included poems by (among others) Lascelles Abercrombie, Rupert Brooke, William H. Davies, John Drinkwater, John Masefield, and Harold Monro—all of whom RF had already met or would soon meet.

has drawn them to me. Some of the manuscript has been passed around and they have seen it.

I think that's all except that Mrs Nutt in her devotion to my cause has already announced the second book without waiting for me to say the word. So the anxiety of finding a publisher is off my mind. As the boys say here, It is success enough if your first book does well enough to get you a publisher for the second. The book should be out in February. You shall have some of it before then if you write me a decent letter and give me your new address. Gone out of the rabbit business, hey?[206] Aint working the land? Easier to write about it? Think I don't understand?

You and Margaret ought to see how few pieces of furniture we keep house with. It is cosy enough, but it would be a lesson to you in plain living. I would give anything if you could drop in on us.

Affectionately
Rob.

[To Sidney Cox. Dating derived from the postmark. ALS. DCL.]

[November 8, 1913]
The bung-hole-still.

Dear Cox

You must send me these two reviews back if you will. Not that I want them to treasure; I am not given to laying up for myself treasures of that kind. But I may want them to impress one more person with before I get through. On second thought, I will consent to spare the one from The Academy on condition that you send it to the professor who found my quality so indefinable.[207] (Don't get mad: it has never entered my head but that he meant to be nice: thank you for showing him the book.)[208]

---

206. See RF's August 1913 letter to Bartlett ("now look at you writing rabbity poultry articles for a farm journal").

207. A laudatory (anonymous) review of *ABW* appeared in the *Academy: A Monthly Record of Literature, Learning, Science and Art* (London) on September 20, 1913.

208. The professor in question may be Stuart P. Sherman (1881–1926), who was a literary critic and English professor at the University of Illinois, where Cox earned his master's degree in English.

We have just had Guy Fawkes Gun Powder Plot Day which for squibs or fire crackers is to our Fourth-of-July as water is to wine or as poor damp pop-corn is to good pop-corn. I saw nobody hanged in effigy—not even Loyd [*sic*] George, though he must have been hanged many times over.[209]

Yours
R.F.

Have I sent you David Nutt's catalogue?

[To Harold Monro. ALS. UVA.]

The Bungalow
Beaconsfield
Bucks
Nov 25 1913

Dear Monro:

I shall have to get better, sha'n't I, with so much to encourage me. Ten pages seems a great deal of space for one little poet. I sha'n't forget these favors.

About the MS. The proof is beautifully clean. I agree with you that the line you stumble over ought to contain the word seemed. But

"Nothing." It seemed to come from far along the road,[210] is too long by a foot. The original M.S. read

"Nothing." It seemed to come from far away. What would you think of that?

"Nothing." It came from well along the road, I have thought of to keep certain solid words I like, but I object to "well." Without more ado, will you let me ask you to decide for me?

---

209. David Lloyd George, 1st Earl Lloyd-George of Dwyfor (1863–1945), British Liberal politician and statesman; at the time, Chancellor of the Exchequer, later prime minister (1916–1922). Guy Fawkes Day (November 5) commemorates the failure of the Gunpowder Plot of 1605 (an attempt to assassinate King James and install a Roman Catholic on the throne). During early observances of the holiday the Pope was often burned in effigy.

210. From "The Fear," collected in *NB*, where the line reads: " 'Nothing.' It came from well along the road."

We get a Sunday morning mail here. I shall see that you have The Hundred Collars right back.

I expect to be able to be with you Tuesday, thanks. I look forward to it.

Sincerely yours
Robert Frost

[To Sidney Cox. Dating derived from postmark. ALS. DCL.]

The Bungalow
Beaconsfield
Bucks Eng
[November 26, 1913]

Dear Cox:

The next thing to do is to get married and, as the hero of one of the eclogues in "North of Boston" says, "forget considerations."[211] Go out of yourself some fine morning and by way of celebration lick something if it is no more formidable than the Peace Movement. You do right to damn grammar: you might be excused if you damned rhetoric and in fact everything else in and out of books but the spirit, which is good because it is the only good that we can't talk or write or even think about. No don't damn the spirit.

You will be all right (Do the theme-children—Charles Lamb had dream-children[212]—do the theme-children still want to spell it alright?) You ought to be a tremendous force for something when the right touch releases you. A belief in fairies may be just the thing. What are they but the Irresponsibilities, and a precious source of inspiration midway between heaven and hell. We haven't always to be either good or bad you know. Or rather you don't know, but a lady has been sent to tell you. There are whole days when the fairies and a belief in them will justify you in being gay, nothing but gay.

---

211. The phrase appears nowhere in *NB* as published. In an August 1913 letter to Bartlett, however, RF lists "Swinging Birches" among the "eclogues" to be included in *NB*; perhaps an earlier version of "Birches" contained a line anticipating the familiar turn of the published version: "It's when I'm weary of considerations, / And life is too much like a pathless wood . . .

212. "Dream Children; a Reverie" appears in Charles Lamb's *Essays of Elia*.

I preach. But this is the last time. You will not need to be preached to any more. Not even by your own conscience! Give yourself a chance. The world is ourn.

Let's hear a little more about it at your leisure. I feel sort of half introduced to someone. Take your time. As it comes natural.

Mrs Frost and I were at a play on Saturday in which we were asked point blank to profess our faith not only in fairies, but in devils and black art as well. So I suppose I shall have to. Do I, then? I do, as they say in the marriage ceremony. Only I shall have to be allowed to define in what sense. But that is another story and a lifelong one.

I'm glad for you. So also is Mrs Frost. She wants me to tell you that specially from her. It is not the first time we have had to be glad for a friend in need lately. First there was John of Vancouver.[213] Then it was Wilfrid Gibson and now it is you. Well well. Be young, mes enfants.

Ever yours
Robert Frost.

I am writing this without having read your Japanese letter.[214]

[To F. S. Flint. Enclosed with the following letter to Flint is another satirical response in verse to Pound. The letter is undated, but RF's apparent reference, in the poem, to his book's having been out "not nine months" places it in the fall of 1913. ALS. HRC.]

The Bungalow
Beaconsfield
Bucks
[Autumn 1913]

Dear Flint:

I had a funny feeling in the region of my dorsal fin this afternoon and when I came to again I had written this debased Whitmanesque. I am impelled to show it to you. You may show it to Pound if you think it won't get me into any worse trouble than I deserve to get into. You could type it and show it to him for his opinion. Say a young fellow of whom you are beginning to have some hopes did it. Say the accents are made to go that way on

213. John Bartlett.

214. William Evans, in *RFSC*, suggests that "the letter may be from Cox's Japanese friend, Rio, whom Cox had met at Bates [College]" (34).

purpose just as soldiers are made to break step in crossing a bridge for fear too much rhythm will shake the bridge down. I have another poem I could write on the subject of "knowing my father" but I spare you.

Sincerely yours
Robert Frost.
{over}

POETS ARE BORN NOT MADE

My nose is out of joint
For my father-in-letters—
My father mind you—
Has been brought to bed of another poet,
And I not nine months old.
It is twins[215] *this time*
And they came into the world prodigiously
united in wedlock
(Don't try to visualize this.)
Already they have written their first poem in
vers libre
And sold it within twenty-four hours.
My father-in-letters was the affluent American
buyer—
There was no one to bid against him.
The merit of the poem is the new convention
That definitely locates an emotion in the belly,
Instead of scientifically in the viscera at large,
Or mid-Victorianly in the heart.
It voices a desire to grin
With the grin of a beast more scared than frightened
For why?
Because it is a cinch that twins so well born will be able to sell almost
anything they write.

R.F.

215. The "twins" are likely H. D. and her husband, Richard Aldington, at the time two protégés of Pound.

[To F. S. Flint. Dating derived from internal evidence. ALS. HRC.]

The Bung
Beak
Buck
[early December 1913]

Dear Flint

What must you think of me out gadding as at that affair in Kensington yesterday. My excuse must be that I didnt go for to do it; also that I trusted that you wouldn't find me out. For it is to your very self and no one else on earth that I have forsworn the full stream. And I meant it; and I mean it some more. Not that it isn't all very pleasant when you get there among nice people with whom you have everything in common (including Ezra and excepting money.) But godfrey mighty, it's sheer extravagance at my age. The thing of it was we were taken unawares one afternoon at the theatre and were committed before we knew it. The Liebichs are good and they made us enjoy ourselves. I almost overtook something elusive about rhythm that I am after when Liebich played Debuyssy [*sic*].[216] I have to thank the day for that. But I am done—at least after one or two more indulgences. I am going to Hulme's once more to take some daughter of a Scottish philosopher Hulme would have read—Adamson[217]—and I am going to St George's Resteraunt [*sic*] in St Martin's Lane (near Coliseum) on the Monday before Christmas to pull off a meeting between you and E. Thomas, gentle person.[218] I like him awfully, as another gentle person hath it. Four would be the time of day if you could manage it. If not let me know now and I will be arranging another place and time.

---

216. Franz Liebich, Frost family friend, was a pianist of some repute in London. His wife Louise Shirley Liebich published *Claude-Achille Debussy* in 1908 (London: John Lane), and translated several volumes about Mozart and other composers. In 1911–1912, T. E. Hulme delivered a series of lectures about Henri Bergson at the Liebich home. The Liebichs were known for presenting a number of "recital-lectures," in which she offered commentary about a composer and he performed illustrations. G. B. Shaw rather caustically, if hilariously, reviewed one such event (on Chopin) in 1893. See Eric Bentley, ed., *Shaw on Music* (New York: Doubleday, 1955).

217. Scottish-born philosopher Robert Adamson (1852–1902) held posts at Owens College, Manchester University, the University of Aberdeen, and the University of Glasgow.

218. The three met on December 23.

Once we showed each other some poetry in manuscript; since when silence on both sides. I was to see more of your poetry, but I approved myself unworthy of the confidence by the way I messed criticism in handing down an opinion of what I had seen. I erred on the side of particularity. Or was it that I liked the wrong poem and was not born out [*sic*] in my judgement by the arbiter of Church Walk or that other of Devonshire St?[219] I took that risk. Out of my showing you poetry comes my appearance in bulk in Poetry and Drama this month. Of course I am not sorry. Don't you hear me thanking you? But ten pages![220] It rather loosens the hinges of my knees like standing in the wings waiting for my cue to go on with my clothes off: so that if at the present moment anything sudden should come upon me, if Monro should overpay me, why the family doctor says he wouldn't be answerable for the consequences. I'm all tired out anyway, what with all I have written to keep (sixteen pieces) and all I have written to throw away. I do make such hard work of it all. The Hundred Collars is most for an ague to me. (One's idiom!)

Well now we'll have to do some prose for diversion. How about that book on Meter Cadence and Rhythm we were going to collaborate on? We won't pay each other a shilling a thousand for correcting each other's spelling but we'll link names on the title page.

Let's write a What Though poem for this Happy Christmas Tide.[221]

No post cards sent or received. Any mere card from you the postman stuffs through my door I shall stuff back at him. Damned if I dont.

I say it in all tenderness.

Robert F.

---

219. The "arbiter of Church Walk" is Pound, who had an apartment there; the arbiter of Devonshire Street is presumably Harold Monro, owner of the Poetry Bookshop, where RF first met Flint.

220. The "ten pages" RF had in *Poetry and Drama* comprised "The Fear" and "A Hundred Collars"; they appeared in the December 1913 number.

221. RF may refer to a popular Christmas carol by Annie Matheson (1853–1924):

What though the snow be on the hill
And winter in the weather,
With love and hope and sweet goodwill
We keep the feast together:
Let heart with heart in joy accord
On this, the birthday of the Lord.

[To John Bartlett. ALS. VA.]

The Bungalow
Beaconsfield
Bucks Eng
Dec 8 [1913]

Dear John:

It was the greatest relief when Margaret's letter came and set my mind at rest. I write so hard when I do write that in the intervals of excitement I simply slump an easy prey to doubts and fears. I knew Alex would get you, but I don't expect to rank as a prophet on that account, for the reason that that was only one of the bad things I knew would happen and the rest of them haven't come off—and probably never will. And even Alex might be worse. You are lucky to save sixty percent out of him.[222] I trust he didn't add rankling insult to injury as is the way with the injurious to make it right with their consciences.

In the same mail with Margaret's letter came a copy of The Plymouth Normal School Prospect with a reproduction of the whole of what you did for me in The News.[223] You exercised the proper discretion. If I have a fault to find it is with the rosy picture you painted of our life in the pretty London suburb inextricably involved in the literary society of the great. But the exaggeration does your heart credit and it wont hurt me as much as it will some people in Derry (Christ forgive me the sin of vengefulness: from this hour forth I will have no more of it. Perhaps I only say so because for the moment I am sated.) We could go among the great (in our humble way—we are far from important yet) but at the same time we can't. Our means forbid. Wander not from the point I keep making that we are playing a rather desperate game with our little wealth. The poets here are of three kinds the poor rats in one room and a suit of clothes with no family to take care of and much too cunning to be caught in that trap, the gentlemanly minors with a graceful weakness for verse and by common consent quite rich enough to indulge it and the few like Masefield who arrive at one jump. I am like none of these. I must make my way very slowly: such is my doom I am afraid. There will be little money return directly from my poetry—at least for the present. Indirectly if I am clever enough and strong enough I may get some part of a liv-

222. Late in 1912, Bartlett had loaned James Alexander Paton (publisher of the *Point Grey Gazette* in Vancouver) six hundred dollars to purchase a new printing press.

223. The *Prospect* was the student newspaper at Plymouth Normal School; the *Derry News and Enterprise* was published in Derry, New Hampshire.

ing out of it by following it up with commercial prose. Mrs Nutt looks for that. The paralyzing thought is that I was always a poor hand to do what I had to do: I write bad stuff under pressure. So you see I am no stranger to worry. All is not beer and skittles that wears the look at six thousand miles.

I think Silver may have written the few words of introduction to your article in The Prospect. He spoke of you as a "distinguished journalist of Vancouver" and formerly a pupil of mine at Derry. Very nice of him all round. I didn't know how he would relish my glorification. I never know how to take him, as friend or enemy. I used to notice he believed what I said about people. I stood in with him that much. I never said you were even better than you showed in school without seeing sooner or later its effect on him. Now it is working the other way. I helped establish your reputation with him and now you are increasing mine with him. We must both walk up and simultaneously ask a big favor of him when he gets to be king of New Hampshire.

I don't know how much of the new book to send at once. It will be more fun to throw it to you in pieces. Here are four or five to start with. Poetry and Drama for this month will have two more: Poetry at an early date one and perhaps two.[224] I'll see that you get those. Poetry and Drama, a quarterly, costs so much it will have to be my Christmas present to you this year. I am literally and disgustingly busted. The book will be called "North of Boston."

The loveliest stroke you did for me was telling Hamilton Mabie about the other book.[225] I am only afraid he may have too much trouble in getting hold of it. I haven't gone looking for a publisher in America yet. Mrs Nutt sent but two copies over there for review. We got a rise out of one of them, The Dial, in Chicago.[226]

I'll be writing again soon; and Elinor will be writing to Margaret. Both write as often as you can: you have no idea how much we look for your letters.

Affectionately
Rob.

In "North of Boston" you are to see me performing in a language absolutely unliterary. What I would like is to get so I would never use a word or

---

224. In addition to the "ten pages" devoted to RF in *Poetry and Drama* (already mentioned), "The Code—Heroics" appeared in the February 1914 number of *Poetry* (RF dropped the subtitle when he collected the poem in *NB*).

225. Hamilton Wright Mabie (1846–1916) was an American essayist and critic, and editor of the *Outlook*.

226. *The Dial* reviewed *ABW* in its September 16, 1913, issue.

combination of words that I hadnt heard used in running speech. I bar words and expressions I have merely seen. You do it on your ear. Of course I allow expressions I make myself. War on clichés.

[To Ernest L. Silver. ALS. DCL.]

The Bungalow
Beaconsfield
Bucks Eng
Dec 8 1913

Dear Mr Silver

I suppose I am to take that complimentary copy of The Prospect; complimentary in more ways than one, as a letter from you. The handwriting on the envelope would seem to be yours and anyway the advertising I am given in the magazine is your work. So thank you. I can stand it. I have about come to the conclusion that a man can stand being overpraised better than underpraised. Strange, ain't it? If John lays it on a little thick anywhere, you have to remember John was a favorite pupil and never disliked anything I said or did. The only trouble is that he must make it sound to an American ear as if my poetry had made my fortune. Of course my royalties on a forty-cent book have done no such thing. At most poetry can pave the way for prose and prose may or may not make money. I have still the battle all before me and with not much stomach for the money-making part of it. I am less inclined to prose than I thought I was when I looked into the future out of a normal school window in Plymouth. I was always that way: Two or three days on end I would write prose, first having resolved it was the thing for a man with a family to do. But just when I thought I bade fair to produce a novel, right in the middle of chapter three or four I would bring up in another inconsequential poem.[227] Sort of incorrigible I am. Once I actually did write some half dozen short stories I sold to Farm Poultry (Boston) for ten dollars apiece.[228] That was about as far as I ever got.

No it remains to be seen whether I shall take hold and earn a living as a writer. I find writing hard work. I have been a harder boss on myself than ever you were on me. I am clean shucked out by this last book—(North of

227. No drafts of a novel by RF survive.

228. See *CPRF*, 35–73. RF also published fiction in *The Eastern Poultryman*.

Boston, I have decided to call it). There's some hope that I may die again. If I were sure, I'd try to take out some more insurance. This is the side of the picture John didn't give you—the funny side.

Gertrude McQuesten writes that she is coming over here to see the country and will have a look in on us. You bet we'll be glad to see someone from home. Of course no amount of success can keep us here more than another year after this. My dream would be to get the thing started in London and then do the rest of it from a farm in New England where I could live cheap and get Yankier and Yankier. We may decide to go home this year. I wish I knew how you were fixed at the cottage—on account of the furniture. Is the state going to build you a parsonage? Or shall you live on where you are or were?

Good old Wilson.[229] I suppose some of the papers are against him. Odd how all the party controversy dies to nothing at this distance. So far as we are concerned there is a dead hush over American politics. Just as well that way for a while. It gives one a new sense of values. From the little American news one gets in the papers here one would think the President was without critics.

Homesickness makes us news-hungry. Every time the postman bangs the letter-slot-door our mouths go open and our eyes shut like birds' in a nest and we can't move for a moment. The Prospect mentions some names we know—none too many. That was good as far as it went. I seem to live more in Plymouth than in Derry.

Remember me to everybody.

Sincerely yours
Robert Frost

229. RF likely refers to Wilson's battle to secure passage of the Federal Reserve Act of 1913. After some nine months of often hotly partisan debate, the president would sign it into law on December 23.

[To F. S. Flint. RF met Edward Thomas (mentioned in paragraph two) in October 1913, not long after returning from Scotland. He arranged a meeting between Thomas and Flint on December 23, the Monday before Christmas in 1913, which dates this letter December 13. ALS. HRC.]

Saturday Night
[December 13, 1913]

Dear Flint

I am sorry; and I promise not to laugh at any thing whatsoever while it is going on. All the world hates a bureaucrat qua bureaucrat. But you mustn't blame Muir, the man.[230] I wish you could meet him. I wonder if he would be large enough to distrust the system you are a victim of. Give me any day a nation of adventurers (like me) who have got in by hook or crook in preference to one of examinees. There'll soon be no one left alive but those who can't be outfaced by a point-blank question. The ultimate unnatural selection: selection by quiz. How many feet across is equal to three feet sideways? I-dunnow-oh-Radamanthus.[231] How then shalt thou be entrusted with spade and pickaxe to dig in the street if you will not answer the simplest question that has nothing to do with the job? Outer darkness for yours.

But you must tell me that you will meet Thomas on Monday week either at four or some hour you like better. I know he wants to see you and I think he blames me a little that I haven't brought you together before. Just a word, so that I may let him know. I will accept a card under the circumstances.

You dont mean that you have actually to pass an examination to hold the job you have?[232] There's some advancement you are looking for.

Affectionately
R.F.

---

230. Scottish-born poet Edwin Muir (1887–1959) later supplied a preface to the English edition of RF's *Selected Poems* (London: Heinemann, 1923).

231. Rhadamanthus, son of Zeus and Europa, appears variously in Greek mythology as a wise king, as inhabiting the Elysian Fields (*Odyssey*, IV, 564), and as judge and punisher of the dead in the underworld.

232. Flint worked as a typist and stenographer for the British postal service.

[To Sidney Cox. ALS. DCL.]

The Bungalow
Beaconsfield
Bucks
Jan 19 1914

Dear Cox

Absolve me of trying to make you think of me as hobnobbing with the great over here and I am ready to begin my <u>very</u> short talks based on Quiller Couch.[233] I'm far from important enough for the likes of the Poet Laureate to have sought me out. I'm simply going to tell you about him because I happen to have eaten at the same table with him by an accident. I was visiting Laurence Binyon (see anthology) when Bridges turned up.[234] I have a right to tell you how the King looked to the cat that looked at him.[235]

He's a fine old boy with the highest opinion—of his poetry you thought I was going to say—perhaps of his poetry, but much more particularly of his opinions. He rides two hobbies tandem, his theory that syllables in English have fixed quantity that cannot be disregarded in reading verse and his theory that with forty or fifty or sixty characters he can capture and hold for all time the sound of speech. One theory is as bad as the other and I think owing to much the same fallacy. The living part of a poem is the intonation entangled somehow in the syntax idiom and meaning of a sentence. It is only there for those who have heard it previously in conversation. It is not for us in any Greek or Latin poem because our ears have not been filled with the tones of Greek and Roman talk. It is the most volatile and at the same time important part of poetry. It goes and the language becomes a dead language the poetry dead poetry. With it go the accents the stresses the delays that are not the property of vowels and syllables but that are shifted at will with the sense. Vowels have length there is no denying. But the accent of sense supersedes all other accent overrides and sweeps it away. I will find you the word "come" variously used in various passages as a whole, half, third, fourth, fifth, and sixth note. It is as long as the sense makes it. When men no longer know the intonations on which we string our words they will fall back on what I may call the absolute length of our syllables which is the length we would give them in passages that meant

233. That is, on Arthur Quiller-Couch's anthologies, *The Oxford Book of Victorian Verse* (1912) and *The Oxford Book of English Verse* (1900).

234. Robert Bridges was poet laureate from 1913 until his death in 1930.

235. A reference to the Mother Goose tale "Puss in Boots" (aka "The Master Cat").

nothing. The psychologist can actually measure this with a what-do-you-call-it. English poetry would then be read as Latin poetry is now read and as of course Latin poetry was never read by Romans. Bridges would like it read so now for the sake of scientific exactness. Because our poetry must sometime be as dead as our language must Bridges would like it treated as if it were dead already. I say you cant read a single good sentence with the salt in it unless you have previously heard it spoken. Neither can you with the help of all the characters and diacritical marks pronounce a single word unless you have previously heard it actually pronounced. Words exist in the mouth not in books. You can't fix them and you dont want to fix them. You want them to adapt their sounds to persons and places and times. You want them to change and be different. I shall be sorry when everybody is so public-schooled that nobody will dare to say Haow for What. It pleases me to contemplate the words Sosieti that the reformers sport on their door plate in a street in London. The two i's are bad enough. But the o is what I love. Which o is that if we must be exact.

Bridges wants to fix the vocables here and now because he sees signs of their deteriorating. He thinks they exist in print for people. He thinks they are of the eye. Foolish old man is all I say. How much better that he should write good poetry if he hasn't passed his time. He has been a real poet, though you never would judge it from a thing in the Dec Poetry and Drama in which he takes the unsentimental view of teachers that they cram us with dead dry stuff like the dead flies on the window sill.[236]

You will have to import your own books I'm afraid, unless Sherman French & Co of Boston would get them for you.[237] Books and postage in the awful quantity you mention would cost you four American dollars. You mustn't get one book more than you honestly feel that you can dispose of. No silly promises are binding.

Yours
R Frost

Make you a present of all the words I have misspelled in this letter. They'll do you good if they correct a little your tendency to think as a teacher that everything must be correct.

---

236. Bridges' poem "Flycatchers" appeared in the December 1913 number of *Poetry and Drama;* the poem speaks of a schoolteacher feeding his pupils "with flies / Dead flies—such as litter the library south-window."

237. A Boston publishing firm.

[To Thomas Bird Mosher. ALS. UVA.]

The Bungalow
Beaconsfield
Bucks
Eng
Jan 20 1914

Dear Mr Mosher:

All that Richard says and more also.[238] It seems to me you must lead the pleasantest life north of Boston.

North of Boston by the way is the name of my forthcoming book which at your suggestion I am offering to Sherman-French. Here again I have to thank you—and Bill Reedy too—whether anything comes of it all or not.[239] Do you think I ought to send Reedy a copy of my book—first book? I have hardly been noticed in America. Mrs Nutt sent but two copies over for review, one to The Dial and one to some newspaper. The whole continent remains virgin soil to me.

You spoke once on a time of giving up The Bibelot after a volume or two more. You must think twice before you do it. I sometimes dream you may use it yet to foster something very American in literature. It isn't always the subsidized ventures that accomplish things. "Poetry" (Chicago) hasn't done anything but foster Pound and a few free-verse friends. I wonder if you noticed the comparison Hueffer instituted in it between De la Mare and F. S. Flint.[240] And I wonder what you thought of it. Do you know De la Mare's

---

238. Possibly British poet Richard Le Gallienne (1866–1947), who published a short tribute to Mosher in 1914: *Thomas Bird Mosher: An Appreciation* (privately printed). RF may have seen it prior to publication.

239. William Marion Reedy (1862–1920) had reprinted "Reluctance" in his journal *Reedy's Mirror,* published in St. Louis; the journal also promoted the work of Ezra Pound, Sara Teasdale, Theodore Dreiser, Carl Sandburg, Edgar Lee Masters, and other innovative writers.

240. The English novelist Ford Madox Ford (1873–1939), born Ford Hermann Hueffer (he changed his name in 1919). RF refers to Hueffer's "Impressionism—Some Speculations: II," published in *Poetry* in September 1913: "Mr. De la Mare and Mr. Flint are rather literary, Mr. Pound, as often as not, is so unacquainted with English idioms as to be nearly unintelligible" (224).

"Listeners"?[241] Beautiful book. I have a copy of Flints "In the Net of the Stars" if you haven't seen it. Flint belongs to Pound's clique. Hueffer patronizes it en bloc.

Sincerely yours
Robert Frost

Later. I met Mrs Nutt in London to-day and got politely rebuked for having entered into correspondence with Sherman-French about my book. I was told that I must write at once and refer Sherman-French to David Nutt; also that I must not think I had the right to publish so much as a poem in a magazine during the term of my contract with David Nutt. Dearie me! I feel quite upset, the more so as I have already sold to magazines some five of the sixteen poems in "North of Boston," rather I should say in honesty the more so as I haven't sold more than five of the sixteen poems. This must be "good crowner's quest law."[242]

[To Wilbur Rowell. ALS. UVA.]

The Bungalow
Reynolds Road
Beaconsfield
Bucks Eng
15 Feb, '14

Dear Mr Rowell

There is a matter of fifty dollars still due me which you haven't forgotten, but are probably holding till I tell you where and when I want it sent. Will you kindly send it here as soon as convenient. I shall be two or three months

---

241. *The Listeners and Other Poems* (London: Constable, 1912). Four years later, with RF's encouragement, Henry Holt and Company—RF's publisher from 1915 until his death—would issue an American edition.

242. See *Hamlet* (5.i), where the two clowns discuss Ophelia's drowning: "*First Clown:* Give me leave. Here lies the water; good: here stands the man; good; if the man go to this water, and drown himself, it is, will he, nill he, he goes,—mark you that; but if the water come to him and drown him, he drowns not himself: argal, he that is not guilty of his own death shortens not his own life. *Second Clown:* But is this law? *First Clown:* Ay, marry, is't; crowner's quest law."

longer in Beaconsfield, after which I go to Hereford to be with Wilfrid Gibson the English poet for a year. Two or three more books before I go home. One is going through the press now and another is ready when the publisher is ready.

Very truly yours
Robert Frost

Mr Wilbur E Rowell
The Bay State
Lawrence Mass U.S.A.

[To John Bartlett. ALS. UVA.]

Bung Beak Buck
Eng
22 Feb '14

Dear John:

I consent not to guess, but I insist on knowing. And I don't intend to wait too many "moons of Marriage" either.[243]

I feel as if I were losing track of you you write so seldom and so meagrely [*sic*] not to say mysteriously. The facts of your case as I have them at date are these: Some thing is going to happen to you in not more than nine months that you refuse to tell me about till it happens.

You have lost a lot of money by Alex Paton, but you expect to get 250 dollars out of him. I shall feel better when I hear that you have it.[244]

You are still earning something a week from The Sun and something a week from several other papers. At least you haven't told me that you aren't.

I'm not supposed to know it if you are not writing for an agricultural paper or two and one monthly magazine.

You have friends in that bad country, one of them a highly educated journalist who knows so much more about poetry than you that you let him tell you what is good poetry and what isn't.

---

243. The phrase appears early in W. B. Yeats's play *The Land of Heart's Desire,* which RF had staged with students while at Pinkerton Academy.

244. Another reference to the money Bartlett loaned James Alexander Paton, publisher of the *Point Grey Gazette* in Vancouver.

The District of Columbia is bad country in every way, physically socially and financially.

You dont mind making me tremble a little (as much as you can) for your security away off there at your age and with a wife to support.

You are dissatisfied with journalism as she is in Vanc. (I wonder if the Editor of The World that Marie Lloyd whipped isnt dissatisfied with it too?[245] Was he someone you wanted whipped?)

You dont like your own stuff. You are tired of it. It seems to you to come the same way all the time as it naturally would on the same monotonous subjects.

You are fairly well, though not perfectly free from asthma. You would probably be as sick as you used to be if you weren't so much happier than you used to be. I wonder if you think it would kill you to go back to New England. It wouldn't break your heart anyway would it?

Some of these informations I am indebted to Margaret for. I think I have set down all I know or am warranted in inferring.

I dont mind your being tired of your own stuff. Isis got tired of the millions of men and sought the millions of the gods but in the end she got tired of the millions of the gods and sought the millions of the spirit.[246] Much virtue in getting tired of your work if you are free enough in body or mind either to go away from it or to convert it into something different or better.

I set a good deal of store by the magazine work you are doing or going to do. That is your way out of bondage. You can—must write better for a magazine than there is any inducement to do for a daily.

My notion is that your work is coming on. Your style tightens up. What you will have to guard against is the lingo of the newspaper, words that no-

245. English music hall queen Marie Lloyd (1870–1922) made a brief and scandalous appearance in Vancouver in February 1914, outraging the guardians of public morality and antagonizing the local press. The *Vancouver Daily World* was founded in 1888; at the time, Sara Anne McLagan (widow of founder John McLagan) was its editor and president.

246. The legend of Ra and Isis is told in the Egyptian "Book of the Dead," which had been translated into English from the Papyrus of Ani (held in the British Museum) by E. A. Wallis Budge. The salient passage reads, in the 1895 edition of Budge's translation (published in London by the British Museum): "Now Isis was a woman who possessed words of power; her heart was wearied with the millions of men, and she chose the millions of the gods, but she esteemed more highly the millions of the khu's [spirits]" (xc–xci).

body but a journalist uses, and worse still, phrases. John Cournos who learned his trade on the Philadelphia Record, where he went by the nickname of Gorky, has come over here to write short stories.[247] He is thirty. His worst enemy is going to be his habit of saying cuticle for skin.

I really liked what you wrote about me. Your sentences go their distance straight and sure and they relay each other well. You always had ideas and apprehended ideas. You mustnt lose that merit. You must find some way to show people that you have initiative and judgement. You must "get up" new things as new even as a brand new department for some paper.

But as I was about to say, I am sure your style improves. Let me see some of the more important things you do. I'll traverse them line by line with a pencil if you will let me. Some of my criticism may be wrong but it will stir you up. It wont hurt you and you won't let it offend you.

You can know and you are going to know as much about poetry and any other form of literature as anybody. You know a good deal more now than you think you do, as would soon transpire if you and I were where we could protract talk.

I want to write down here two or three cardinal principles that I wish you would think over and turn over now and again till we can protract talk.

I give you a new definition of a sentence: A sentence is a sound in itself on which other sounds called words may be strung.

You may string words together without a sentence-sound to string them on just as you may tie clothes together by the sleeves and stretch them without a clothesline between two trees, but—it is bad for the clothes.

The number of words you may string on one sentence-sound is not fixed but there is always danger of overloading.

The sentence-sounds are very definite entities. (This is no literary mysticism I am preaching.) They are as definite as words. It is not impossible that they could be collected in a book [or] dictionary[248] though I dont at present see on what system they would be catalogued.

They are apprehended by the ear. They are gathered by the ear from the vernacular and brought into books. Many of them are already familiar to us in books. I think no writer invents them. The most original writer only catches them fresh from talk, where they grow spontaneously.

---

247. John Cournos (1881–1966), novelist, translator (from the Russian), and imagist poet.

248. RF writes the word "dictionary" under the word "book," while striking out neither.

A man is a writer if all his words are strung on definite recognizable sentence-sounds. The voice of the imagination, the speaking voice must know certainly how to behave how to posture in every sentence he offers.

A man is a marked writer if his words are largely strung on the more striking sentence sounds.

A word about recognition: In literature it is our business to give people the thing that will make them say, "Oh yes I know what you mean." It is never to tell them something they dont know, but something they know and hadnt thought of saying. It must be something they recognize.

A Patch of Old Snow

In the corner of the wall where the bushes haven't been trimmed, there is a patch of old snow like a blow-away newspaper that has come to rest there. And it is dirty as with the print and news of a day I have forgotten, if I ever read it.[249]

Now that is no good except for what I may call certain points of recognition in it: patch of old snow in a corner of the wall—you know what that is. You know what a blow-away newspaper is. You know the curious dirt on old snow and last of all you know how easily you forget what you read in papers.

Now for the sentence sounds. We will look for the marked ones because they are easiest to discuss. The first sentence sound will do but it is merely ordinary and bookish: it is entirely subordinate in interest to the meaning of the words strung on it. But half the effectiveness of the second sentence is in the very special tone with which you must say news of a day I have forgotten—if I ever read it. You must be able to say Oh yes one knows how that goes. (There is some adjective to describe the intonation or cadence, but I won't hunt for it.)

---

249. RF collected the poem in *MI*, where it takes this form:

There's a patch of old snow in a corner
That I should have guessed
Was a blow-away paper the rain
Had brought to rest.
It is speckled with grime as if
Small print overspread it,
The news of a day I've forgotten—
If I ever read it.

One of the least successful of the poems in my book is almost saved by a final striking sentence-sound (Asking for Roses.[250])

Not caring so very much what she supposes.

Take My November Guest. Did you know at once how we say such sentences as these when we talk?

She thinks I have no eye for these.

———

Not yesterday I learned etc.

———

But it were vain to tell her so.

———

Get away from the sing-song. You must hear and recognize in the last line the sentence sound that supports, No use in telling him so.

Lets have some examples pell-mell in prose and verse because I dont want you to think I am setting up as an authority on verse alone.

My father used to say—

You're a liar!

If a hen and a half lay an egg and a half etc.

A long long time ago—

Put it there, old man! (Offering your hand)

I ain't a going hurt you, so you neednt be scared.

Suppose Henry Horne says something offensive to a young lady named Rita when her brother Charles is by to protect her. Can you hear the two different tones in which she says their respective names, "Henry Horne! Charles!" I can hear it better than I can say it. And by oral practice I get further and further away from it.

Never you say a thing like that to a man!

And such they are and such they will be found[251]

Well I swan!

Unless I'm greatly mistaken—

Hence with denial vain and coy excuse[252]

A soldier and afraid! (afeared)

---

250. In *ABW*. RF later removed it when he brought the book into his *Collected Poems* (New York: Henry Holt and Company, 1930).

251. From Byron's *Don Juan*: Canto VIII, stanza V, line one.

252. From Milton's "Lycidas," line 18.

Come, child, come home.

The thing for me to do is to get right out of here while I am able.

No fool like an old fool.

It is so and not otherwise that we get the variety that makes it fun to write and read. The ear does it. The ear is the only true writer and the only true reader. I have known people who could read without hearing the sentence sounds and they were the fastest readers. Eye readers we call them. They can get the meaning by glances. But they are bad readers because they miss the best part of what a good writer puts into his work.

Remember that the sentence sound often says more than the words. It may even as in irony convey a meaning opposite to the words.

I wouldnt be writing all this if I didn't think it the most important thing I know. I write it partly for my own benefit, to clarify my ideas for an essay or two I am going to write some fine day (not far-distant.)

To judge a poem or piece of prose you go the same way to work—apply the one test—greatest test. You listen for the sentence sounds. If you find some of those not bookish, caught fresh from the mouths of people, some of them striking, all of them definite and recognizable so recognizable that with a little trouble you can place them and even name them you know you have found a writer.

Before I ring off you may want to hear the facts in the case of us.

We are still in Beaconsfield but trying hard to get rid of our house six months before our lease is out in order to get away into Gloucester with Wilfrid Gibson and Lasselles [*sic*] Abercrombie (see Victorian anthology for both of them.)

Book II, North of Boston, should be out now. The publisher is dilatory. I shall have another book done (out and out plays this time) before she gets Book II out. This is rough on me because I feel that now is the time to strike while there is a certain interest in me for what I have done.

I expect to be roasted more for Book III than for Book II—if for no other reason, because the fact is out that I am an American. That nasty review by Alford in the magazine I sent shows you how they feel toward us here. He begins by saying he cant get hold of enough books to find out whether we have any literature or not and then he proceeds to say we have none.[253] I am sure he will lay for me somewhere. And there are others who have me marked.

---

253. John Alford wrote the American Chronicle for Harold Monro's *Poetry and Drama*. He begins his December 1913 column: "This is not a Chronicle. One cannot write a

J. C. Smith (editor of an edition of Shakes. and several other classics for the Oxford Library) will give an evening to a new American poet named Me before an Edinburgh literary society in March.[254]

Poetry (Chicago) printed in Feb the thing I call The Code. Did I send it to you? If I didn't, you may want to look it up. It may be in the library.

No money comes in of course yet. I won't make much from poetry—I suppose you know that. I talk about prose but as long as I can put off writing pot boilers I shall. It seems to me as I look at it now I had much rather farm than write for money.

We plan to go home in September of 1915. I dont know where I shall settle. You may be coming back to New England sometime. Somehow we must plan to be together.

The children all keep well but as they have found the schools impossible here they come pretty heavily on Elinor. She has not been at all well this year. I may have to give up my wilder schemes and turn to money making for the family. Not that I am ever asked to. On the contrary.

I wonder if there is anything more you are as anxious to hear as I am anxious to hear more about you.

Our love to you both. And may God amend my spelling.

Affectionately
Rob.

Chronicle with only a dozen books published during the last eighteen months for data. Nor does an examination of these books, combined with more or less casual acquaintance with American literary journals, suggest that a periodic Chronicle would be of particular interest or value." Notably, Louis Untermeyer, with whom RF would strike up one of his most enduring friendships in 1915 on his return to America, wrote letters to the editor of *Poetry and Drama* complaining that Alford consistently did American poetry injustice.

254. James Cruickshank Smith (a Frost family friend) edited *The Poetical Works of Edmund Spenser* for Oxford in 1910 and was general editor of the Oxford series *Selected Plays of Shakespeare* (1912–1916).

[To Ernest L. Silver. RF adds a postscript at the head of the letter. ALS. DCL.]

You don't have to read all this. I got going.

Bung Beak Buck
Eng
23 Feb '14

Dear Mr Silver:

I may lose the last part of your letter, or sell it for the autograph, or give it away, but the exordium with its generous tribute to my modesty I shall keep as long as I am liable to want a job and have use for a testimonial.[255]

I'm really more modest than I look sometimes when resenting imaginary affronts to my dignity. But I'm not as modest as I ought to be—a thing I dont intend to worry over any more because it doesn't matter whether I am modest or not if I can get enough modest men to say I am modest.

I am grateful for your good opinion but you mustn't try to spur me on to do great deeds with the names of Brown and Marinan [*sic*].[256] It is too cruel. Suppose I should excel in the way I have always wanted to and should make one or two honestly good but unprofitable short poems, do you think Brown

---

255. At the start (not the close) of the January 11, 1914, letter to which RF here replies, Silver had written: "I will admit that I suggested copying John's article. You surely can be justified in being pleased—just a little, as becomes your modest temperament—at the recognition you have now. I rejoice for you and with you" (letter held at DCL). John Bartlett had written an article on RF for circulation in the papers in Plymouth and in Derry, New Hampshire.

256. Silver wrote: "You must hurry your prose to get ahead of your friends, Brown and Marrinan" (letter held at DCL). Harry Alvin Brown was author of *The Readjustment of a Rural High School to the Needs of the Community* (Washington, DC: U.S. Government Printing Office, 1912). See RF to Brown, January 7, 1913. John Joseph Marrinan (1884–1968), a graduate of Dartmouth, was principal at Pinkerton Academy at the time this letter was written. In 1913 he published an article titled "The Children and Religion" in *The Pedagogical Seminary* (20.2). RF's correspondence with Silver and Brown (incoming and outgoing), and also with other educators, provides an illuminating context in which to understand his many remarks in regard to writing a book about the pedagogical implications of what he called "the sound of sense" and "the vocal imagination." As in this December 1914, letter to Sidney Cox: "Thomas thinks he will write a book on what my new definition of the sentence means for literary criticism. If I didn't drop into poetry every time I sat down to write I should be tempted to do a book on what it means for education." Or in this June 1, 1915, letter to George Browne: "I can see a small text-book based on images of sound particularly of the kind I call vocal postures or vocal idioms that would revolutionize the teaching of English all the way up through our schools."

would estimate the achievement as anything above a badly written bulletin for Washington? No, I can't stack up against Brown. I have neither strength nor expectation of life.

What funny things I am talking about. Here I am ready to think the worst of Brown's conceit because he hasn't taken the trouble to write to me. If you'll testify to his modesty as you do to mine, it will be all off—I shall harbor nothing against him. I leave it to you to say whether his new job has stuck him out like a pouter pigeon and thrawn his neck about.[257]

I have really made the acquaintance of but one schoolman and of him entirely through my writing. He is a Scot in Edinburgh named J. C. Smith[258] who earns his living, I believe, as inspector of the five or six so-called teacher's training colleges in Scotland. With all the work he must have to do, he still finds time to edit Shakespeare for the Oxford press and then after everything new in English literature. Like all of them over here he reads in half a dozen languages and like all the educated ones I have met over here he is so utterly unassuming that you might look and not see him. He is in the civil service which may partly explain his comfortable unaggressive assurance. He doesnt have to think of holding his own against anyone. He doesn't have to think of getting on. Oxford too partly explains him. The saying is that a man who has been to the English universities always appears to know less than he knows a man who has been to the Scotch appears to know more than he knows. I don't mean that Smith's knowledge doesn't show when and where it should. The last time I saw him I don't know how many poems by all sorts of great poets he recited whole. He would say to me "How does that lyric of Shelley's go? 'Life of life thy lips enkindle—' You know it. Help me."[259] And when I didn't help him, he would proceed to reconstruct the poem him-

257. "Thrawn": Scottish dialect. As for the new job: Harry Alvin Brown had been given oversight of elementary and secondary schools in New Hampshire.

258. Scholar James Cruickshank Smith was inspector of schools at Edinburgh.

259. From scene five of *Prometheus Unbound,* by Percy Bysshe Shelley:

Life of Life, thy lips enkindle
With their love the breath between them;
And thy smiles before they dwindle
Make the cold air fire; then screen them
In those looks, where whoso gazes
Faints, entangled in their mazes . . .

Francis Turner Palgrave published the passage separately under the title "Hymn to the Spirit of Nature" in his *Golden Treasury,* of which RF had a copy.

self. Somewhat different from being a brow-beating school boss with nothing on the brain but statistics. Mind you I don't mean to imply that we haven't plenty of good men at home. Smith is no more than human. I wouldnt paint him so. I only mean you would like him. When you come over whether I am still here or not, he will be one person I shall want you to meet.—I suppose Whitcher is a fine sort. What he talks about represents so much genuine enthusiasm and not just desire to impress.[260]

While I am on the subject of people let me tell you about the Welshman Davies.[261] It has been a strange life over here more on account of the people I have seen than the places I have hardly been sight-seeing at all. I will send you a magazine for your own particular self with something by Davies and something of my own in it. I'm not afraid that what I write will hurt anyone, but what Davies sometimes writes the growing girl would as well not read.[262]

Davies is the kind of poet you read about. He has a pension from the British Govt. on his merits, so we won't question him as a poet. As a personality he is lovely. He said to me the other day "Didn't I see you at Monro's supper at Picorini's? I thought so. I was in pretty bad." I assured him I really hadn't noticed it until he began to talk about revisiting Baltimore for an oyster sandwich. "Well," he said, "it was worse after you went. I left the room to go to the lavatory and I got lost. I can't remember whether I went out for another drink. But I never got back." He ought to have been more ashamed than he was. He was late at supper anyway and those that stayed after I went did so out of respect for him.

Later I heard him talking in simple wonder at himself for never having been moved in the flesh by his landladies, two old maids who made his bed and fed him on the British plan for ordering the provisions and sending the bills to him to foot. "You know how I am," he said to Hodsdon[263] another frank poet who follows the prize ring. Then he wound up by denouncing them as thieves for living on the provisions they handled for him.

---

260. George H. Whitcher, a New Hampshire educator mentioned in the letter to which RF here replies. Whitcher had been given charge of practical arts courses and courses in commerce at Plymouth Normal School. In the January 1912 number of *The Elementary School Teacher*, he had published an essay on "Domestic Arts Courses in Public Schools."

261. William Henry (W. H.) Davies.

262. *Poetry and Drama* published RF's "The Fear" and "A Hundred Collars" in its December 1913 number, along with Davies' "The Bird of Paradise," which begins: "Here comes Kate Summers who, for gold, / Takes any man to bed."

263. RF misspells Ralph Hodgson's name.

Don't blush if I tell you a little more like this. Hulme is a hulking English squire of thirty who holds forth on philosophy. He is just home from Germany with the intelligence that people there are genuinely lamenting the decay of British coarseness. He tells it triumphantly as something he had noticed and set himself to arrest. He has a Tuesday evening at which he talks to mixed society about anything that comes into his head. Not long ago one evening it was how he was out here in Bucks somewhere at a Russian actress' country house and heard two very minor poets just down from Oxford addressing her in erotic verse of their own. Passion and emulation had sent both of them up tall trees. Alford (author of the stupid roast on American literature in the magazine I am sending) would shout to the wind "Come lie with me!" or words to that effect. Are they not written in a book by Alford recently published at his own expense? He spoke of her marmoreal legs. (It is in the book.)[264] All of which made Hulme laugh so that the Russian actress had to rebuke him for not knowing how to take a thing as it was meant. But the best was: The shouts of the arboreal poets had attracted a small crowd outside the paling that no one noticed till a boy cried out "Say, Mister, are you nesting?" Alford was not nesting as it turned out. The other fellow won the lady's favor or favors and is now her housemate outside the law.

You'll be afraid I am losing my innocence. Anyway you will realize how far it is possible to get from Plymouth and Derry for seventy five dollars.

It is necessary to make some distinctions in all the above. Hulme is not immoral in thought or action. Plain-speaking is part of the conservatism he affects and preaches. Davies may be bad enough, but he is what you would call naturally rough. He has a good heart and he is something of a marvel when you consider that he has come up from tramping and selling shoestrings on the street. Alford I rather loathe and Russian actresses.

There, I ought to have restricted myself to the weather and set myself to correct the bad impression I gave you of this climate last winter. It has not been half bad this winter. We have seen the sun for whole days and often several days in succession. All told we may have had three weeks of frost and two snow storms. Maximum thickness of ice less than two inches.

We are hoping to get down to Gloucester to be with friends next year. The difficulty is to find a house to live in. Under the higher rents there are few

---

264. For more on John Alford's "roast," see note 253 to RF's February 22, 1914, letter to John Bartlett. His *Poems* (London: Poetry Bookshop, 1913) bears the following note: the volume is "published for the author by the Poetry Bookshop." The phrase "marmoreal legs" does not appear in the book.

houses built in England and the old houses are not more than half enough to go around. So the papers and politicians all say and such is our observation as far as it goes.

The poor, I have made up my mind, have a hard hard time here, with no houses to live in and no wages to buy common food with. I heard a great man say that the English shilling would buy as much as the American dollar. He should have known better. In this town eggs have been sixty cents a dozen all winter, milk is eight cents a quart, apples are five cents a piece, corn is sixteen cents a can, tomatoes are twelve cents. Say, I will make out a list of provisions with prices some day and send it you to show Baily and ask him to affix American prices to.[265]

And there are thousands of people here, men I mean, who earn from 20 shillings down to 10 a week. I have seen and talked with people who have brought up families on less than 20. There are kinds of food they simply never taste. The children go to work the minute the law allows and help out with six pence a day. The old mothers whose usefulness is more or less past instead of puttering about the house and minding the baby go into the fields to work picking up stones at a shilling a day. I saw three of them at it in the rain. They gathered the flints (size of a fist or two) and carried them clear off the field in their aprons without the help of horse or cart.

But the worst of it is not this. These people are allowed to call only a small part of their soul their own. I musn't go into that. It will keep till I get home.

1915 will see us back in America, and in many ways glad to get back. The fortunate monopolize too much here. The fortunate are very delightful people to meet, they afford so many of the virtues and graces. But one can't help seeing the unfortunate who may afford a virtue or two but not one graces [*sic*] I'm afraid. I should want my children to grow up in America.

Sincerely yours
Robert Frost

If you really want to impress my publisher with the fact that I have a friend at home, you can send 40 cents for the book to David Nutt 6 Bloomsbury St London W.C. Eng. It is too much trouble to go to.

Thanks for the diagram[266]

---

265. Unidentified.

266. Silver had sketched out plans for a new building on the Plymouth Normal School campus that featured dormitory, gymnasium, and swimming pool.

[To Sidney Cox. Dating derived from postmark. ALS. DCL.]

The Bungalow
Beaconsfield
Bucks
[March 3, 1914]

Dear Cox

Would you or would you not lend me a matter of twenty-five or fifty dollars (if fifty is too much, twenty five) to help me out of a tight place? I am making a change which will cost a little and for various reasons it has to come just when I am out of money. I might have to keep you waiting till I get my allowance in July and then again if returns from certain things come in I may be able to repay you at once. I have several things out which will appear in magazines if they can be got in before my book appears.[267] If not I lose on them. Mrs Nutt is against me on the matter of my selling to the magazines. She seems jealous of my getting cold cash for anything that in book form is so unprofitable. She seems so I say. I dont know quite what to make of her. She is friendly enough except when we are on the subject of magazines and American publishers. She acts as if she thought I was up to something. Last time I saw her she told me frankly she thought I had no right under my contract to traffic in my poetry before I brought it to her. This is embarrassing.

Don't hesitate to refuse me the loan if you must: I had rather ask a favor like this of you and John than any one else.[268] I ought to be able to go to the trustees of my grandfather's estate, but they have always been chiefly trustees of his hostility to my poetry.

You will be amused to hear that the Edinburgh English Society will give a whole evening to a new American poet named Me this month.[269] Too bad my book isnt out to take advantage of the local interest that may stir up.

Now you be perfectly honest.
Yours ever and whether or no,
Robert Frost.

---

267. See RF to Harriet Monroe, March 26, 1914.

268. John Bartlett.

269. James Cruickshank Smith arranged it.

[To Harold Monro. RF refers to the publication of North of Boston. *ALS. Trinity.]*

The Bungalow
Beaconsfield
Bucks
March 11 1914

Dear Monro:

This is to ask your permission to use "The Fear" and "The Hundred Collars" in my forthcoming book. I am expecting the book in April or May (or November). You won't think that too soon after the appearance of the poems in Poetry and Drama?

Very truly yours
Robert Frost.

[To Wilbur Rowell. ALS. UVA.]

The Bungalow
Beaconsfield
Bucks Eng
March 26 1914

Dear Mr Rowell:

Thank you for the fifty dollars and for the hundred so close upon its heels. Thank you too for your friendly letters. Jean[270] was quite right: I find the money very convenient at this moment to help me make the move to Gloucester, where, as I think I told you, I am going to be with my friends Gibson and Abercrombie, the English poets.

My address there will be Iddens, Leadington [*sic*], Ledbury. I shall be very nearly on the line between Gloucestershire and Herefordshire.

With our best wishes.

Sincerely yours
Robert Frost.

Wilbur E Rowell Esq
Lawrence Mass
U.S.A.

---

270. Jeanie Florence Frost (1876–1929), the poet's sister.

[To Harriet Monroe. ALS. Chicago.]

The Bungalow
Beaconsfield
Bucks Eng
March 26 1914

Dear Miss Monroe

I have carelessly let this cheque lie only to discover, now when I could use it, that it is unsigned. So I shall have to trouble you with it.

While I am writing may I ask if you could publish my "Black Cottage" in May or June?[271] I should be very grateful. It will have to come soon to be ahead of my next book, North of Boston.

Sincerely yours
Robert Frost

Before your answer can reach me I shall be at
Iddens
Leadington [*sic*]
Ledbury Eng.[272]

271. "The Black Cottage" was not, in fact, published anywhere prior to its appearance in *NB*, which David Nutt issued on May 15.

272. The Frosts moved to the Dymock region of Gloucestershire in April 1914, taking up residence near Wilfrid Gibson and Lascelles Abercrombie. RF's move to Little Iddens saw him joining a group that came to be known as the Dymock poets (or, sometimes, the Georgian poets), including, in addition to Abercrombie and Gibson, Edward Thomas, John Drinkwater, and Rupert Brooke—all of whom regularly contributed to *Georgian Poetry*, an annual anthology edited by Edward Marsh (1872–1953) and published by Harold Monro, proprietor of the Poetry Book Shop in London (Monro also published *Poetry and Drama*).

[To Sidney Cox. ALS. DCL.]

The Bungalow
Beaconsfield
Bucks Eng
March 26 1914
(This being my birthday.)

Dear Sidney

(I think it should be first names between us by this when it is already first names between me and my later-found friends in England.)

I have no friend here like Wilfrid Gibson whom I am going to join in Glouscestershire [*sic*] next week. We bid a long farewell to London to be near him and Lasselles [*sic*] Abercrombie. The cottage is already found for us. Iddens it is called—in Ledington [*sic*] Ledbury. You must address us there from now on. I dont know, but I suppose we shall sleep under thatch. Those other poets do.

I was worried about the money to make the move, but we shall pull through all right. You shall have your suit of clothes and know at the same time that we are not in straights [*sic*].

We shall make a week of it in London before we drink silence and hide ourselves in cloud. I sold some poetry to Poetry and Drama and I propose to take it out in room rent in the upper floors of the Poetry Shop in Devonshire St Theobalds Road London W.C. if you know where that is. I may have told you about it. It sells nothing but poetry. The fellow that runs it and edits the quarterly I speak of is a poet and all about him are the poets my friends and enemies. Gibson had a room there for the year before he married the proprietor's secretary.[273] Epstein, the futurist sculptor, the New York Polish Jew, whose mind runs strangely on the subject of generation whose work is such a stumbling block to the staid and Victorianly but who in spite of all is reckoned one of the greatest living geniuses, will be across the hall from us.[274] All the poets will be in and out there. It will be something that Lesley of the children will be sure to remember.

We mean to do the city for the youngsters as much as I am capable of doing a city or anything else. There must be a great deal to see in London if one

273. See RF's October 12, 1913, letter to Flint.

274. Jacob Epstein (1880–1959), American-born British sculptor.

will look for it. There is the Tower and—well there simply must be something else. I must get a guide book.

I really do take an interest in the historical places. I didn't fail to notice that I passed the scenes of two battles Evesham and Worcester when I was traveling the other day.[275] But I dont know what I would have done if I had been set down in either of them. It thrilled me enough merely to see the names on the stations. I got as much out of seeing Dunfermline town[276] from the train as from straggling around Edinburgh Castle for a day. The best thing in Edinburgh Castle was the Black Watch on parade. Places are more to me in thought than in reality. People are the other way about. (Probably not so—I am just talking.)

I ought not to be talking. I have really too much else to do till we get away. I meant this to be but a short letter to make you easy on my score. I shall write you more at length when we are nearer the Severn Sea (see in Anthology the really good poem by Davidson. Poor Davidson.[277])

Yours ever
R.F.

---

275. Evesham is the town in Worcestershire near one of the two major battles of England's Second Barons' War in the thirteenth century. The battle took place August 4, 1265. Worcester was the site of the final battle, on September 3, 1651, of the English Civil War, in which Cromwell's New Model Army defeated King Charles II's forces.

276. In Fife, Scotland; birthplace of Charles I and Andrew Carnegie, and the home of the King in "The Ballad of Sir Patrick Spens."

277. "A Runnable Stag" by John Davidson (1857–1909), which Arthur Quiller-Couch reprinted in his *Oxford Book of Victorian Verse,* the anthology to which RF here alludes. The final stanza reads:

Three hundred gentleman, able to ride,
Three hundred horses as gallant and free,
Beheld him escape on the evening tide,
Far out till he sank in the Severn Sea,
Till he sank in the depths of the sea—
The stag, the buoyant stag, the stag
That slept at last in a jewell'd bed
Under the sheltering ocean spread,
The stag, the runnable stag.

Davidson disappeared March 23, 1909, and is believed to have drowned himself at Penzance, in Cornwall.

"This Quiet Corner of a Quiet Country"

Gloucestershire, May 1914–February 1915

The cottage is already found for us. Iddens it is called—in Ledington Ledbury. You must address us there from now on. I dont know, but I suppose we shall sleep under thatch. Those other poets do.

—Robert Frost to Sidney Cox, March 26, 1914

[To Sidney Cox. As he does consistently, RF misspells Leddington. ALS. DCL.]

Little Iddens
Ledington [*sic*]
Ledbury
May 18 1914

Dear Cox:

I have taken particular pains to write the address legibly and do you take notice. We are actually in Gloucestershire but near the line and our post office is at Ledbury in Herefordshire. This is a great change from Beaconsfield which was merely suburban. We are now in the country, the cider country, where we have to keep a barrel of cider for our visitors and our hired help or we will have no visitors nor hired help. So we are in the way of adding drink to cigarette smoking in the record of our sins. Even Elinor gets drawn in since the only kind of ladies we know over here are all smokers. I think the only house I visited where the cigarettes weren't passed around was Ernest Rhys'.[1] I never thought of that till this moment. I don't know why it was, probably because Rhys himself isn't a smoker. His son is though.

Lets see—you say be personal. I wish I knew what you meant by personal. I thought I was egotistically so in telling you of my encounter with the great-

---

1. Ernest Rhys (1859–1946), English poet and editor. Subsequently mentioned: Robert Bridges (1844–1930), the English poet who served as poet laureate from 1913 until his death; William Henry (W. H.) Davies (1871–1940), a Welsh poet; and *The Oxford Book of Victorian Verse* (1912), edited by Arthur Quiller-Couch (an anthology much favored by RF).

est poet (titular) in England. I believe I told you what I told Bridges about the science of verse, matter that is of the highest importance and not yet to be found in book form on earth.[2] The novelty if you didn't miss it was the definition of a sentence which is calculated to revolutionize the teaching of literary composition in the next twenty years.

My late encounter with the man who considers himself the second greatest poet in England and heir apparent to the Laureateship was of another description. He is the Davies (W.H.) of the Victorian Anthol. I saw something of him in London—once, as I think I told you, at a dinner in Soho where he made an exibition [*sic*] of himself. He is the unsophisticated nature poet of the day—absolutely uncritical untechnical untheoretical. He has the honor of having a pension from the British government. Society runs after him. He sells upward of 100£ worth of small poems in a year. His success seems to have hurt him a little and its not strange that it has when you consider his origin. Six years he tramped in America till he fell under a freight car and lost a leg. Then he came home and stumped about selling shoe strings and penny rhyme sheets. Then my friend Adcock discovered him and the rest has followed—recognition from Shaw Conrad and everyone else that counts.[3] The poems in the Anthol are a fair sample of what he can do. No one at the present time can get those flashes in a line as he can. His note is Elizabethan. No one doubts that he is a very considerable poet, in spite of several faults and flaws everywhere. But his conceit is enough to make you misjudge him—simply assinine [*sic*]. We have had a good deal of him at the house for the last week and the things he has said for us to remember him by! He entirely disgusted the Gibsons[4] with whom he was visiting. His is the kind of egotism another man's egotism can't put up with. He was going from here to be with Conrad. He said that would be pleasant because Conrad knew his work <u>thoroughly.</u> After waiting long enough to obscure the point we asked him if he knew Conrads work <u>thoroughly.</u> Oh no—was it good? We told him yes. He was glad we liked it. He set about encouraging Lesley to write about nature. It would be good practice for a child. He admitted that he had used it up as copy. Lesley is old enough to have to struggle to keep a

---

2. For more on RF's opinion of Bridges, see his January 19, 1914, letter to Cox.

3. Arthur St. John Adcock (1864–1930), English novelist and poet; George Bernard Shaw (1856–1950), Irish playwright; and Joseph Conrad (1857–1924), Polish-born English novelist.

4. The family of poet Wilfrid Gibson.

straight face in such circumstances. There now, he said, see that little bird, that little green one, I wonder what kind he is. Says Lesley It's a sparrow and it isnt green, is it? And Davies stumped into the house. He doesn't really know nature at all. He has lately been telling the British public that the American Robin isn't red breasted and it has no note that he ever heard.

I suppose he is the most naively wicked person that walks, or should I say limps? He always makes me think of Ferguson's Scorney Bwee (in The Vengence [*sic*] of the Welshmen of Tirawley)—he's that lewd and lame.[5] His private life is public property, so he makes no bones of speaking in any company of the women he spends his money on. They are cheaper than in America and I don't suppose his tastes are up to the most expensive ones here: the one of his fortnight before coming down to the country cost him thirty shillings. The strange thing is he is humanly fond of his creatures and takes their side against the respectable kind. I believe he has written a simple-hearted book about them in which they are rather finely discriminated—the golden girls he has met. He's a little weathered man with none of the personal charm of the lady-killer remember. Yet Bernard Shaw considers that he has made himself an authority on the ladies (daughters of Lilith) our society builds on, but prefers to know nothing about. I have no doubt he knows much more about them than about birds cows and flowers. He really cares little for nature except as most other people do in books. He asked me confidentially before he left why I had been so foolish as to get so far from London.

If this isn't being personal, let me try what I can say in a few words about where we are. The important thing to us is that we are near Gibson; we are far from any town. We are on a lane where no automobiles come. We can go almost anywhere we wish on wavering footpaths through the fields. The

---

5. Scorney Bwee figures in "The Welshmen of Tirawley" by Samuel Ferguson (1810–1886); RF encountered the poem in Quiller-Couch's *Oxford Book of Victorian Verse* (1912). In it, Bwee triggers a feud between two families, the Lynotts and Barretts. The poem begins as follows:

> *Scorney Bwee, the Barretts' bailiff, lewd and lame,*
> *To lift the Lynott's taxes when he came,*
> *Rudely drew a young maid to him!*
> *Then the Lynotts rose and slew him,*
> *And in Tubber-na-Scorney threw him*
> *Small your blame,*
> *Sons of Lynott!*
> *Sing the vengeance of the Welshmen of Tirawley.*

fields are so small and the trees so numerous along the hedges that, as my friend Thomas says in the lovliest [*sic*] book on spring in England, you might think from a little distance that the country was solid woods.[6]

You mustnt mind if I write and never look back. I write few such long letters to anyone as I write to you. I have to save myself for other things. Elinor and the children wish to be remembered. Lesley will hardly be one of the children much longer. She's as tall as her mother and reads a decent paragraph of Caesar off without looking up more than a couple of words. Sometimes too she does a paragraph of English writing I admire.

Here's hoping the best for you next year. Did you get the raise you asked for?

Yours ever,
R.F.

Later.

My book seems to be out, though I haven't seen it yet.[7] I have had these slips from the publisher. Perhaps you could send them where they would do some good.

We expect to see Miss Grace [*sic*] McQuesten of Plymouth N.H. and the Emerson School of Oratory over here in a week or two.[8] I don't suppose you knew her—she was in Plymouth so little while you were there. She lived on the slope street that ran down to Coffee's Ice Cream Soda Fountain. You and I are far from there.

---

6. RF refers to *In Pursuit of Spring* (1913) by Edward Thomas (1878–1917).

7. David Nutt published *NB* on May 15, 1914.

8. RF's error. The reference is to Gertrude McQuesten, not Grace. The Emerson College of Oratory was the name of Emerson College (Boston) when it was founded in 1880.

[To F. S. Flint. ALS. HRC.]

Little Iddens
Ledington
Ledbury
May 18 1914

Dear Flint:

I hope you liked what I liked in the review of your Anthology in the New Weekly.[9] Think of me still as a literary person with literary interests, though already up to my waist in peas and broad beans and holding up a hoe to mark the place of my disappearance. That last week in Arcady with Monro—I have that to remember—<u>and</u> the naked slum woman wailing for her disembowelled cat. Write something every day (pumice expolitum[10]), and as W. T. Stead is said to have said in the last message he has succeeded in getting across, follow the truth—as the French see it.[11] Never shall I forget my emotions (aestus se ab alto excitavit[12]), my esthetic emotions, as I stood with you before the plate glass window in Regent Street and looked in on that scene of insular domesticity done in furniture for sale. It was so Egyptian, especially in the stiff gesture of the wax husband. I say Egyptian, and if you don't believe me (and believe something that Hulme says) just run up to the Museum and have a glance at the industrial scenes the Egyptians did in wood. We were two husbands together, with homes to go to and yet—

And now farewell![13]
I am writing a whole lot,

---

9. Edward Thomas reviewed Ezra Pound's *Des Imagistes: An Anthology,* in which several of Flint's poems had appeared, in the *New Weekly* (then edited by Rolfe Arnold Scott-James [1878–1959]) for May 9, 1914.

10. RF borrows the phrase from Catullus (poem 1):

Cui dono lepidum novum libellum
arido modo pumice expolitum?

To whom do I dedicate my charming, new little book,
just polished with dry pumice?

We thank Yu Onuma for vetting the English translation.

11. British journalist William Thomas Stead (1849–1912) died aboard the *Titanic.*

12. "The fire drew itself down from on high."

13. Here RF breaks into an impromptu parody of the *vers-librist* style, drawing whimsically on Tennyson's *Idylls of the King.*

If indeed I write,
(For all my mind is clouded with a doubt)
From the island valley of Avillion
Where falls not hail or snow,
At this time of year,
Nor ever wind blows loudly.
But it lies
Deep meadowed
Fair with orchard lawns
And bowery hollows crowned.
But thou
Pray for my soul
More
Things
Are
Wrought
By
By prayer!
What are men?
Sheep or goats?
Blind life in the brain———
If having hands.

What I was trying to get to was that "swarthy webs" quotation that Thomas used in his review.[14] But something seems to be the matter. Perhaps I struck in at a place too far off, or worse still after instead of before what I was looking for. Certainly hands aren't webs.

I am always yours, old man, and do wish you could get down to see us this summer—you and your wife. At least you could plan your trip so as to take us in on your way and see us for a few days.

R.F.

14. The phrase "swarthy webs" appears in *Idylls of the King,* where it describes the feet of a swan. Thomas quoted Tennyson in the review to ridicule Skipwith Cannell's "Nocturnes" (printed in *Des Imagistes*), which has a swan's feet being white: "Thy feet are white / Upon the foam of the sea; / Hold me fast, thou bright Swan, / Lest I stumble."

[To Lascelles Abercrombie (1881–1938), British poet and literary critic. Undated. It is likely that RF enclosed a copy of NB*, published on May 15, 1914. Epistolary evidence available in John Evangelist Walsh's* Into My Own: The English Years of Robert Frost *indicates that Abercrombie was not in Gloucester at the time (169–170). Abercrombie would soon publish a glowing review of* NB *in* The Nation *(London) on June 13. ALS. UVA.]*

[Little Iddens,
Leddington,
Ledbury]
[circa mid-May 1914]

Dear Abercrombie

Wilfrid[15] said I could send you this—I needn't wait till you came home. It seems almost too bad to intrude on life and a holiday with books; but this is something more than books: this is friendship.

Sincerely yours
R.F.

[To Wilbur Rowell. ALS. UVA.]

Little Iddens
Ledington
Ledbury
May 20 1914

Dear Mr Rowell:

Will you let me take advantage of your offer to the extent of another twenty pounds? Or ten pounds would do—just which you find convenient. I shall greatly appreciate the favor.

We go to the reviewers with the second book this week.[16] We are as excited as you could expect us to be in this quiet corner of a quiet country.

Sincerely yours
Robert Frost

15. Wilfrid Gibson.

16. The letters that follow often refer to reviews of *NB*, which were almost invariably laudatory. We have cited these wherever possible.

[To Clarissa Hall (1891–1988), formerly a student of RF's at Pinkerton Academy and at the Plymouth State Normal School. Written on a postcard advertising the publication of NB, *the message is undated and unaddressed, indicating that it was enclosed in an envelope for mailing. Archival notes at the University of New Hampshire supply the date, but the physical evidence is no longer present. ALS. UNH.]*

[Little Iddens]
[Leddington]
[Ledbury]
[1 June 1914]

My dear Miss Hall:

We often wonder what school you have been teaching well this year—city or country. Well, you can be counted on to have a good time wherever you are. The school was never assembled that could make you miserable. Elinor means to write you a real letter one of these days.

Sincerely yours
Robert Frost

[To Laurence Binyon (1869–1943), English poet, dramatist, and scholar of art. ALS. British Library.]

Little Iddens
Ledington
Ledbury
June 1 1914

Dear Mr Binyon:

Thank you for taking so much trouble for me with the poem. I have to respect your opinion. I know very well what you have tried to do (I suppose you mean in the "London Voluntaries"[17]) and how well you have done it. No doubt I need to be cautioned in the way I am going. At the same time the lines you complain of are part of my venture. I am impatient if such accents of the practical cannot be made poetry. You will find me trying them over and over all through the book—possibly sometimes with an approach to success. I suppose I am in danger of thinking of a marked intonation, fresh-

17. RF apparently confuses the title of William Ernest Henley's *London Voluntaries; The Song of the Sword and Other Verses* (1893) with Binyon's *London Visions* (1908).

caught from the vernacular, almost as an ornament. I experience a curious satisfaction in having hit on "Oh just another kind of outdoor game" and on "But it's not elves exactly"[18] (narrowing the eyes) and elsewhere on "Come in: no one will care."[19] Each indicates such a definite posture for the voice. At least my "Oh" in the first example is neither of the stock oh's of poetry.[20] But very likely I am on the wrong track.

Will you take this book from me and not feel that it carries with it any obligation of sympathetic criticism? I shall be honored.

I hope by this time you are getting rested from your overwork.

Sincerely yours
Robert Frost

---

18. Phrases from the first poem in *NB*, "Mending Wall."

19. A line from "The Black Cottage," also in *NB*.

20. RF writes in one of his notebooks: "Take six interjectional Ohs and write them in a column. They all look alike but I want them all said differently. My best way my only way to get them said differently is to write them as of sentences. (In speaking I can get along very well with the Oh's alone)

> Oh / I see now what you mean.
> Oh / isn't he lovely.
> Oh / you sad fool why would you?
> Oh / I slipped. Let me try again.
> Oh / murder—help—murder!
> Oh / King live forever (This is commonest in poetry—too common)"
> (*NBRF*, 645–646).

[To John Wilton Haines (1875–1966), a solicitor and amateur botanist; he lived in the city of Gloucester, near Ledbury.[21] *ALS. Gloucester.]*

Little Iddens
Ledington
Ledbury
June 1914

Dear Mr Haines:

The address was right and the selection from the book was right—that is if your object in it was to please me.[22] I like "In a Vale" only a little less than "Mowing." It has been singled out once or twice by reviewers, but you should hear the tale of what it has suffered at the hands of American editors. Your praise atones for much.

---

21. Eighteen letters to Haines fall within the date range for the present volume. Of these, only this one survives in its original form, at the Gloucester Archives in England. Photostats of eighteen other manuscript letters to Haines are held now at DCL (in box 26, folder 92, of the Robert Frost Collection, General Correspondence). A number of these letters bear notes, obviously written by Haines, that indicate that he held on to the originals for a great many years. Possibly the DCL photostats were Lawrance Thompson's own, made for him by Haines, or by him with Haines's permission; no cataloging data at DCL indicate their provenance. Thompson reports four additional letters as being in Haines's hands (from the date range of the present volume) at the time he published *SL* in 1964: RF to Haines April 25, 1915: *SL*, 170–172; RF to Haines July 17, 1915: *SL*, 183–184; RF to Haines July 4, 1916: *SL*, 205–206; and RF to Haines April 27, 1917: *SL*, 216. These are not now among the DCL photostats. Why these four letters—included in *SL* and placed, by Thompson, in Haines's hands as of 1964—did not make it into this stack of photostats, and where their originals now reside, are facts unknown. However, typed copies of two of the letters just listed (July 4, 1916 and April 25, 1915), presumably made by Haines, are held in the Gloucester Archives; we have relied on these copies in preparing the present edition. For the other two letters, we have had to rely on Thompson's transcriptions (as noted where necessary). The DCL photostats of manuscript letters to Haines, and the Gloucester typescript copies, are so identified in this volume, where appropriate, to distinguish them from unique manuscripts.

22. RF writes in reply to Haines's May 31 letter, which refers, it would appear, to their first meeting (on May 30), and which opens on a note of confusion as to RF's address. The poems Haines had marked in his copy of *ABW* are: "Into My Own," "Ghost House," "My November Guest," "To the Thawing Wind," "Flower-Gathering," "Rose Pogonias," "Waiting," "In a Vale," "Mowing," "The Tuft of Flowers," "Pan with Us," "A Line-Storm Song," and "My Butterfly." Haines singled out "In a Vale": "One of these that neither of us referred to yesterday I think particularly beautiful, 'In a Vale'" (letter held at DCL).

Don't confuse "My Butterfly" with the other butterfly poem, "A Tuft of Flowers." It was the latter I sang for my supper.[23] "My Butterfly" dates back to 1893 and is among the first twenty things I wrote in verse. You could find it in the files of the New York "Independent" for 1894 or 5. However a part of it (the second paragraph) is as good as anything I have done. The speaking note I got there for the first time is mine: you will hear it in the other poems you like: those you don't hear it in I ought to have had courage enough to leave out of the book.

We must have that walk to May Hill[24] soon—not next week, which I shall have to keep open for a possible visitor from London, but the week after if you say the word.

We shall be sure to look you up in Gloucester some day—thanks for your invitation.

Our best regards.

Sincerely yours
Robert Frost

[To John W. Haines. ALS/Photostat. DCL.]

Little Iddens
Ledington
Ledbury
June 1914

Dear Mr Haines:

You leave me too much choice. Suppose I take the first thing you name and undertake to meet you at Newent.[25] I have my instructions as to the trains.

I look forward to seeing you. I have seen one or two flowers you must tell me about.

Till we meet.

---

23. In 1906, the Reverend Charles L. Merriam invited RF to read the poem before a banquet of the Men's League in Derry, New Hampshire; the poet demurred and asked that Merriam read it aloud for him; the event nonetheless led to RF's employment at Pinkerton Academy.

24. Several miles south of Ledbury; Haines had spoken of it in his May 31 letter.

25. Between Ledbury and Gloucester (where Haines made his home).

Yours ever
Robert Frost

[To John W. Haines. A note, in Haines's hand, indicates that this letter was received on June 16. ALS/Photostat. DCL.]

Little Iddens
Ledington
Ledbury
[circa June 15, 1914]

Dear Mr Haines:

I had just written you a letter, but what I had to say in it will keep till I see you.

I am sorry for your loss. It must be particularly hard for your father. Naturally he wants you with him to take things off his shoulders.[26]

Any time for the walk you say. From Wednesday week I shall be engaged for a few days.

Sincerely yours
Robert Frost.

[To Mary Wilson Gardner (?–1936), wife of Ernest Gardner, a professor of archaeology at University College London. The Gardners met RF at the Poetry Bookshop in London in January of 1913. The Frost family later visited the Gardners at their home in Scotland in August of that year. ALS. NYU.]

Little Iddens
Ledington
Ledbury
June 1914

My dear Mrs Gardner:

You havent kept your promise to come down here with the children; and you haven't written to tell us if it was because of the company we keep; and you haven't asked to be forgiven. Yet I am going to forgive you in the most demonstrative way I have at command, by sending you this book I care a

26. Haines's mother, Caroline Charlotte Haines, had died.

great deal for. You mustn't try to like it beyond your inclination. Let your thanks be personal rather than literary—as the gift is personal.

We wish you might camp down near us some time this summer. We have our own little hill from which we can see as much or as little of our vast neighbors as we choose. There's a farmer over the field that takes good care of our friends when they come.[27] An ex-color-sargent and minor hero, he has an arsenal of poisoned arrows from the West Coast and Dervish knives from Atbara and Obdurman to save your lives with (and from) and he only charges seventeen shillings a week.[28] July is the best time to come: he may have a houseful in August.

Our best regards to you all.

Sincerely yours
Robert Frost.

I have just got a very heavy pair of shoes I am very much interested in.

---

27. The farm is Oldfields, adjacent to Little Iddens, and owned by John and Mary Chandler. Edward Thomas and his family stayed at Oldfields when they visited RF later in the summer of 1914. In an August 8, 1914, letter to John Freeman, Edward Thomas describes "Mr. Chandler" as an "old soldier of 21 years service" who had just been "called up" at the outbreak of World War I.

28. RF refers to two battles in the Mahdist War (Anglo-Sudan War): the Battle of Atbara (April 8, 1898) and the Battle of Omdurman (September 2, 1898) in both of which the army of British general Sir Herbert Kitchener defeated the forces of 'abd Allāh Ibn Muhammed. The Sudanese rebels were variously called Mahdists, since they followed Mohammed Ahmed (the Mahdi), or dervishes. Though widely used in the Western press, the latter term was frequently misapplied, since dervishes were, strictly speaking, mendicant monks, members of a Muslim ascetic order. Poisoned arrows were a prominent feature of warfare on the west coast of sub-Saharan Africa.

[To Margaret Reynardson (1861–1930), wife of Aubrey H. Birch Reynardson, gentleman and solicitor at Gray's Inn. Their daughter Evelyn ("Evie"), born in 1900, was a year younger than Lesley Frost. Born Margaret Spring-Rice, Mrs. Reynardson was the sister of Sir Cecil Arthur Spring-Rice. ALS. BU.]

Little Iddens
Ledington
Ledbury
June 8 1914

My dear Mrs Reynardson:

Would there be room on the table by Keats and Shelley for another book of poems from New Hampshire?[29] I shouldn't like to crowd the first one off: I care too much for it for that. I shall always think lyrics more important—less slight, less trivial—than anything on earth except an act of Parliament.

When you have read enough of this to reach a decision (The Death of the Hired Man, say, and Blueberries and After Apple Picking), will you tell me if I may send a copy through you to the English Ambassador at Dublin New Hampshire?[30] That would be full circle—from New Hampshire back to New Hampshire.

Mrs Frost joins me in sending our best regards; and will you remember all the children to Evie? It would have been delightful if Leslie[31] and Irma could have studied with her as you planned. You must tell her they got so much Roundheaded English history out of her book last winter that I was afraid sometimes they wouldn't leave any between the covers for anyone else.[32]

Sincerely yours
Robert Frost

---

29. Again, *NB*, in which the poems subsequently mentioned appear.

30. Sir Cecil Arthur Spring-Rice served as British ambassador to the United States from 1912 to 1918; Dublin, New Hampshire, was a popular summer retreat for eminent Washingtonians and their foreign counterparts.

31. Lesley and Irma were RF's eldest daughters. Both RF and Elinor spelled their children's names variously (in this case Lesley as Leslie).

32. RF may refer to John George Edgar's *Cavaliers and Roundheads, or Stories of the Great Civil War* (1881), a popular boy's book that went through a number of printings, and which Evelyn Reynardson may have owned. Perhaps the Frost children borrowed a book or two from the family, *Cavaliers and Roundheads* among them.

[To the law firm of Wilbur Rowell and Paul R. Clay. ALS. UVA.]

Little Iddens
Ledington
Ledbury Eng
June 16 1914

Rowell & Clay
The Bay State
Lawrence Mass. U.S.A.

Dear Sirs:

Thank you for the cheque for one hundred dollars. I enclose my receipt. I hope Mr Rowell will look us up if he is in our neighborhood.[33]

Very truly yours
Robert Frost.

[To the law firm of Wilbur Rowell and Paul R. Clay. ALS. UVA.]

Little Iddens
Ledington
Ledbury Eng
June 28 1914

Rowell & Clay
The Bay State
Lawrence Mass

Dear Sirs:

Yes, if you will—send the money to this address: I expect to be here for some months.

Very truly yours
Robert Frost.

---

33. Wilbur Rowell, executor of RF's grandfather's estate, was apparently in England at the time (no record of a visit survives).

[To F. S. Flint. The first paragraph refers to "The Death of the Hired Man" in NB. *RF supplies only the month and year in dating the letter. ALS. HRC.]*

Little Iddens
Ledington
Ledbury
July 1914

Dear Flint:

No one's praise of the book weighs more with me than yours. Possibly you are a little partial to the book from friendship just as I am a little partial to your praise from the fact that you were the first poet I ever knew. Stand by me, wont you?—and I may do something yet. I shan't forget the day when I tried the Hired Man on you and you waxed prophetic. I hear I am getting some rather good reviews; I mean to see some of them: meanwhile I have your letter.

Pound can be cruel in the arbitrary attitudes he assumes toward one. It pleased him to treat me always as if I might be some kind of a poet but was not quite presentable—at least in London. Some of the things he said and others I imagined drove me half frantic. In your case I suppose his assumption is (for the moment) that you may be a poet, but you are no critic nor French scholar. It suits his convenience or whim to think that. He would need no arguments to support the theory. Well all I can say is—not that you are weak to stay and get what you can out of your natural associates—it is too foolish to put down to weakness what is only common sense—all I can say is that you must write another book. You must! Climb up out of harm's way.

When I last talked with Pound he was surer that you were the man to write the French Chronicle than that you were a poet.[34] I have heard the French Chronicle spoken of as far off as Ryton as the best thing in P&D.

I wish I had cut that article on Claudel from the Times.[35] I thought you must have seen it. A month or two ago it must have appeared.

I simply infer from the tenor of Wilfrid's poetry of parenthood that he will not long be kept from having children. He hasn't had to let his trousers out at

34. The "French Chronicle" was a section in *Poetry and Drama* ("P&D") devoted to literary developments in France; F. S. Flint often authored it.

35. Paul Claudel (1868–1955), French poet and dramatist; his older brother was the sculptor Camille Claudel.

the waist yet. But he has been doing some tall thinking—as you may judge from the poem Hoops (not hoop skirts) in the forthcoming New Numbers.[36] Plainly he expects to gain merit as a man by becoming a parent. It has been said that there is no thing so easy. I wish I could see you for a talk. I may have to go up to the city before long. If I do will you let me have a meal with you?

My plans are strangely vague. I almost ended my tenancy here this very morning by punching my own hand a number of times very close to my landlord's face to the accompaniment of words words words.[37] I haven't liked his ways and I am just Futurist enough to take my way of telling him I expected him to do better in the Future.

I shall probably go to France, southern France if it can be managed, where perhaps the winter will be less hard on my sideache. I need advice in the matter. You don't know where we would get most out of it? Of course the main thing is to write. I want to be warm in the winter.

I expect to go to Hell via America in the end.

Our best to you both and to Ianthe.[38]

Yours ever
R.F.

Spanish letters be damned.

---

36. Wilfrid Gibson's one-act play "Hoops" appeared in the first issue of *New Numbers* (pages 135–146). The periodical was to be a forum for the Dymock poets. The title page indicates that it was "published at Ryton, Dymock, Gloucester" in 1914; contributors to this first number include, in addition to Gibson, Lascelles Abercrombie, Rupert Brooke, and John Drinkwater. The war brought its existence to a close after four issues.

37. *Hamlet* (2.ii): "*Pol.* How say you by that? Still harping on my daughter: yet he knew me not at first; he said I was a Fishmonger: he is farre gone, farre gone . . . I'll speake to him againe. What do you read my Lord? *Ham.* Words, words, words."

38. Flint's daughter.

[To John Cournos (1881–1966), poet and novelist. Born in the Ukraine, Cournos emigrated to Britain, where he began his literary career in the 1910s (and, after 1917, a career also as an anti-Bolshevik and anti-Soviet propagandist); later he relocated to the United States. In 1914 he was associated with the Imagists. ALS. Trinity.]

Little Iddens
Ledington
Ledbury
July 8 1914

Dear Cournos:

Thanks for your good news. I have just read Hueffer's article and I like every word of it.[39] What more could anyone ask for a while?

My versification seems to bother people more than I should have expected—I suppose because I have been so long accustomed to thinking of it in my own private way. It is as simple as this: there are the very regular preestablished accent and measure of blank verse; and there are the very irregular accent and measure of speaking intonation. I am never more pleased than when I can get these into strained relation. I like to drag and break the intonation across the metre as waves first comb and then break stumbling on the shingle. That's all. But it's no mere figure of speech, though one can make figures enough about it.

I am down here farming on my own for economy this summer, where I should be glad to see you if you ever range so far. I shall be in London from the 20th on for a few days and will look you up then if I may.

You mustnt say such things about New York to a poor cuss who may have to go back there to live some time.

Sincerely yours
Robert Frost.

---

39. Ford Hermann Hueffer (later Ford Madox Ford) reviewed *NB* in the *Outlook* for June 27, 1914.

[To John W. Haines. Dating from internal evidence. ALS/Photostat. DCL.]

Little Iddens
Ledington
Ledbury
[circa July 20, 1914]

Dear Haines

Thank you for the review—Abercrombie's work as your wife thought.[40] I liked it very well. The discussion of my technique wouldn't have been what it was if Abercrombie had had nothing to go on but the book. He took advantage of certain conversations in which I gave him the key to my method and most of his catchwords. "Method" is the wrong word to call it: I simply use certain principles on which I accept or reject my own work. It was a generous review to consider me in all ways so seriously and as I say I liked it.

I don't believe I had one uneasy moment with you the other day from the moment when I saw you throw the car door open. I should think you were the kind of person I could ask over here to sprawl—not call. I object to callers more and more in my old age. In my wife's present state of health I have to do some of the meals (so to call them), but you won't mind that will you? And you will overlook some other things if we can laze and talk for a day. You must come on the early train and go on the late.

Thomas has been with us after being with Bottomley in the north.[41] We had a day on your mountain.[42] You are to meet him when he is here for the month of August—and a mighty fine fellow you'll say he is.

When are you going to ask me to Gloucester to meet your wife?

Sincerely yours
Frost.

---

40. Abercrombie's review of *NB*, "A New Voice," appeared in *The Nation* (London) for July 13, 1914.

41. English poets Edward Thomas and Gordon Bottomley (1874–1948).

42. May Hill, south of Ledbury.

[To John Cournos. ALS. DCL.]

Little Iddens
Ledington
Ledbury
July 27 1914

Dear Cournos:

Back to the woods again—or rather the fields. There are no trees but hedgerow elms for ten miles around here.

I have got you the book and I meant to have before this copies of the Bookman and Pell Mell reviews. I will send them along as soon as they come. You have The Outlook. If not, say so, and I will send it. Here are The Times and Nation reviews with passages marked as of interest to me.[43]

One thing to notice is that but one poem in the book will intone and that is "After Apple Picking." The rest talk. I spoke of a particular line I like in "The Fear":

"She pushed past him and got it for herself"

I also think well of those four "don'ts" in Home Burial. They would be good in prose and they gain something from the way they are placed in the verse. Then there is the threatening

"If—you—do!" (Last of Home Burial)

It is that particular kind of imagination that I cultivate rather than the kind that merely sees things, the hearing imagination rather than the seeing imagination though I should not want to be without the latter.

I am not bothered by the question whether anyone will be able to hear or say those three words ("If—you—do!") as I mean them to be said or heard. I should say that they were sufficiently self expressive. Some doubt that such tones can long survive on paper. They'll probably last as long as the finer meanings of words. And if they don't last more than a few hundred years that will be long enough for me—much longer than I can hope to be read.

---

43. Wilfrid Gibson reviewed *NB* in the *Bookman* for July 1914, under the title "Simplicity and Sophistication"; an unsigned review appeared in the *Times Literary Supplement* on May 28; another review appeared in the *Pall Mall Gazette* for June 20 ("Pell Mell").

I have ordered the picture from High Wycombe.[44]

I shall be glad to see your story when it is ready, and see you too if you can come down. We may be nearer London before winter. This is a good country but—

Sincerely yours
Robert Frost

[To Thomas Bird Mosher. ALS. UVA.]

Little Iddens
Ledington
Ledbury Eng
July 27 1914

Dear Mosher

I have thought of you in connection with my new book several times since its appearance. It has done so well here that I should almost venture to send you a copy in spite of your well-known predilection for the manner of the nineties. There have been long and remarkably favorable reviews from all quarters from some of which you may have gathered what I am about. The two and a half columns in The Nation put the case very well and so did the shorter article in The Times.[45] Hueffer's three columns in The Outlook rather bungled the technical question but on the whole I could not quarrel with it.[46] All these you are likely to have seen. I am sending one or two others you would probably miss. Please tell me if on consideration you have reason to think you would care for the book and I shall be only too happy to see that you have one from my hand. You were one of the first to see me coming—you are nearly the only one thus far in America—and I should like to know that I had not lost favor with you at the same time that I was gaining it with really a good many important people over here.

Sincerely yours
Robert Frost.

---

44. RF's first (and most famous) publicity photo, taken to promote *NB*, was made at High Wycombe, a town in Buckinghamshire, in June 1913; the picture had appeared in the London *Bookman* in August.

45. Lascelles Abercrombie reviewed *NB* in *The Nation* (London) for June 13 1914 and Jessie B. Rittenhouse in the *New York Times* for May 16, 1914.

46. See RF's July 8, 1914, letter to John Cournos for more on Hueffer's review.

[To John Cournos. Dating from internal evidence. ALS. Jones.]

Little Iddens
Ledington
Ledbury
[circa August 15, 1914]

Dear Cournos:

I've been thinking of you in these hot times. I don't suppose you are going to run away to America. I'm not. I am too much committed. But it's going to be poor picking for some of us before it's over. We ought to pull through better in the country than you in the city. I hope you see your way clear.

I find that there are no more Bookmans of July to be had.[47] The news agent has just sent me several copies of the Aug number in hopes I may make those do instead. It doesn't much matter unless you think Gibson's review might have special weight in America and especially with the Transcript which has been his chief boomer on the other side. I will make one more effort to get a copy or two. Perhaps Adcock will find them for me.[48]

I have just seen the notice in the August Eng Review—almost the best I have had, I should think. And I have just heard that The Transcript has been talking about my send-off in The Nation.[49]

Let me hear how things are with you.

Sincerely yours
Robert Frost

---

47. With Gibson's review in it.

48. Arthur St. John Adcock (1864–1930).

49. *The English Review* devoted a full page to *NB* in August 1914. RF alludes also to the *Boston Evening Transcript,* which had, in a regular column called The Listener, quoted liberally from Abercrombie's review of *NB* for *The Nation* (London) under the title "A New Voice" (June 13, 1914).

[To Sidney Cox. ALS. DCL.]

Little Iddens
Ledington
Ledbury Eng
Aug 20 1914

Dear Cox

You must think I have been and gone to war for the country that has made me a poet. My obligation is not quite as deep as that. If I were younger now and not the father of four—well all I say is, American or no American, I might decide that I ought to fight the Germans simply because I know I should be afraid to.

The war is an ill wind to me. It ends for the time being the thought of publishing any more books. Our game is up. There will really be genuine suffering among the younger writers. My friends have all been notified by the editors they live on that there will be no more space for special articles and reviews till the war is over. De La Mare (greatest of living poets) has just lost twelve or fifteen hundred a year by being dropped by the publisher he read MS. for.[50]

So we may be coming home if we can find the fare or a job to pay the fare after we get there.

I don't mean to complain. I like the war and the idea of abolishing Prussia, if there is any such thing.

The book was lucky in one respect. It may not have had time to sell much; at least it had made its mark with the reviewers. I give you a list of the chief articles about it in case you should care to look them up. No book of verse has had as much space given it for a good while.

Eng Nation	June 13	3 Cols
Outlook	June 27	3 Cols
Pell Mell Gazette[51]	June 20	
Egoist	July 1	Col
Times	July 2	
Bookman	July	Col
News & Leader	July 22	Col

50. Walter de la Mare (1873–1956), English poet and novelist.

51. Again, RF's whimsical spelling of the *Pall Mall Gazette*.

Eng Review	Aug	Page
New Weekly	Aug 8	Col

They have all been ridiculously favorable. The Times has talked of the book three times. I understand that there has been an article in the Boston Transcript based on the Nation article. And the Plymouth (N.H.) Public Library has bought me. And I have had a letter from Stowe Vermont which showed that the book had penetrated to that village behind a mountain.[52]

I will send you a book as soon as ever I can afford to and with it one or two of the reviews you might not be able to see easily. Will you be good enough to send them along to some professor of literary inclinations?

We are here or in this neighborhood till we sail for home. Probably that means for some time. We are going to share house with the Abercrombies for the winter to cut down expenses for both families. Abercrombie is a poet too. See your Anthology.[53] Our address then will be (you can write to me there in answer to this): The Gallows, Ryton, Dymock, Gloucestershire.

I have talked enough about myself for your purposes and mine. Lets hear about you.

Yours ever
Frost.

[To Ernest L. Silver. ALS. Plymouth.]

Little Iddens
Ledington
Ledbury
Eng
Aug 22 1914

Dear Silver

Sooner or later this war must drive us out of here and in a more or less crippled condition. There will be nothing doing from now on in the kind of odd jobs by which poor poets turn an honest penny and less than nothing in poetry itself. It may be hard for me to pack this crowd home if boat rates go

52. The letter was from Florence Taber Holt, wife of the publisher Henry Holt (1840–1926), who would, in 1915, bring out American editions of RF's first two books, inaugurating a relationship that would last throughout the poet's lifetime.

53. The last three poems in *The Oxford Book of Victorian Verse* (1912), edited by Arthur Quiller-Couch, are by Lascelles Abercrombie.

up. But assuming that we ever get home, I wonder if I can count on your friendship to help me to some place where I can recoup. You know the kind of thing I should like—something in the English department, if possible, where I should have some energy to spare for my poetry.

I can probably hang on another year if I have to, but there will be the more need in the end of my finding work because by that time I shall be in debt. I am prepared to be patient. I suppose I ought to register with some agency and await results. The reputation I have made here ought not to go for nothing.

We are just going to live with another poet Abercrombie, to cut rent in two and cut down other expenses for as long as we stay.[54] Abercrombie is worse off than I for the moment, having lost at one stroke all his hack work which he depended on for a living. The talk is, however, that he and his like (real Eng. poets) are to have something done for them by the government.

This row was exciting at first. But it has lost some of its interest for us. We begin to feel as much out of place in it as a casual caller in a house where one of the family has just come home full of news from a long absence. And I suspect the fear of what we would be in for if the Germans came makes us a little homesick for the furniture stored in your back attic.[55]

Not that I think the Germans will come. I bet one of my little amateur bets the other day that not one of them would set foot in England.

I am sending one or two of my reviews. I believe you had a copy of the book from me.

Sincerely yours
Robert Frost

[To Sidney Cox. Dating from internal evidence, following Evans's suggestion in RFSC. *ALS. DCL.]*

[Little Iddens]
[Leddington, Ledbury]
[circa August 25, 1914]

Dear Cox

I should take it kindly if you would pass these along. Anything you can do for me just at this time will be a double service. My only hope is that some

54. The Frosts soon joined Abercrombie and family at their house in Dymock.

55. Silver had agreed to store some of the Frost family furniture in his house when they departed for England in 1912.

interest will be taken in the book in America: here none can be from now on: people are too deeply concerned about the war. Did I ask you if you would try to find an article about this Nation article in The Boston Transcript.[56] It must have appeared in late June or early July. I should like to see a copy of it very much.

Luck to you in everyway.

R.F.

[To Gertrude McQuesten. ALS. BU.]

Ryton Dymock
Goucestershire [*sic*] Eng
Aug 30 1914

My dear Miss McQuesten:

We gathered from your last letter but one that you were off within a few days: otherwise we should surely have insisted on your coming the short distance out of your way you would have had to come for the entertainment we had arranged for you. It seems you were as near as Stratford and Oxford. Well no matter, I suppose we must forgive you, if by avoiding us you can say you booked a few more show cities to your satisfaction. What we could have given you was only an introduction to a few people not unknown to fame in America as well as England; which would be as nothing in the scale against a cathedral—especially as anything you got out of us you would have had as pay for reading aloud to the colony.

You mustnt count on finding us here when you come back in three years. The chances are better of your seeing us in America in as many months. You cant have realized how really desolated the country you went touring through already was. Some of my friends are among the first hard hit. Right here's the end of the particular art of peace that they practice. No more publishing of books for I dont know how long, perhaps till they have had time to be forgotten and have everything to do over. Several magazines have gone under; all newspapers have dispensed with their literary departments. For many literary men it means turning to the state for help. I dont so much matter because I can go home and get work to tide me over. That's what it will

56. Again, Abercrombie's June 13 review of *NB* in *The Nation* (London).

come to. Meanwhile I go to live with another poet with the idea of cutting down expenses for both families. It is romantic but—you see?

Today recruiting parties have been scouring the countryside for young men who haven't answered the call to arms. They have to speed the enlisting to keep ahead of the wastage at the front. Some of the young men have to be made to realize that it is a great war. No fear but the strong will want to fight when they see the need. A cartload of them swept out of this hamlet tonight—one a man who has a boy as old as Carol—a funny man who is said to have fallen out of fruit trees and off housetops with comparative abandon since Lloyd George's insurance came in.[57] The horse was going fast and they waved their hats with an intimacy advanced by the thought of their sacrifice. The place seems lonelier. The moon looks to me as if it tried to look the same as usual to hide something it knows (actually sees in France), but it looks as if it doesn't quite succeed.

Elinor joins me in sending regards.

Sincerely yours
Robert Frost

[To John W. Haines. Dating derived from internal evidence and from the letter Haines wrote by way of reply on September 15; RF provides only the month. ALS/Photostat. DCL.]

The Gallows
Ryton Dymock
September [circa 14, 1914]

Dear Haines:

You must look me up in a new place when you come. Our land-lord wanted the house on Ledington Hill for hired help and so we have come to the Abercrombies for the winter. I don't believe it will be for as long as the winter myself: there's some likelihood of my being called nearer London on business. While I'm not out for money, and indeed ran away from the filthy stuff when I crossed the deep, I begin to feel as if I ought to be earning a little again provided I can do so with dignity, that is, without asking for the chance.

57. In 1911, while still an MP, Lloyd George put through Parliament the National Insurance Act, providing financial support for those suffering sickness and invalidism; he followed this achievement with the Unemployment Insurance Act.

But I will tell you more about this when I know more myself. Nothing may come of it. Real money has always had a way of eluding my clutch at the last moment. The only way I ever catch it is by feigning dead—dead to it and everything else—till it comes up to smell me over and sort of poke into my pockets. Two or three times I let it go in and out of the pocket on the lower right hand side (we'll say) to give it confidence and then suddenly when it's clear in I clap my hand on it and—my wife is glad.

To think that you should have talked with G.B.S. without knowing him and probably without his knowing that you didnt know him.[58] That was an adventure for you. I hope you didn't "contrary" him on any point or in any way act as if you set up to be his equal. I hope you didn't beg leave to differ with him as to the path up or down the mountain which he may have enquired of you out of weakness only to be sorry for it the minute the words were out of his mouth.

The Gibsons are off in Ireland for a few weeks and I am going to Scotland for a week or so toward the end of next week.[59] I dont know whether I can get down to see you before I go. Would you like to have me? I believe I'll try to if you say you would. Or would you prefer to come here?

The children were pleased with the cards you sent from the north.

Wilfrid hates the war, Lascelles hates the Germans. I hate the Germans but I must say I dont hate the war. Am I a jingo?

Yours ever
R.F.

---

58. George Bernard Shaw. At the time, Shaw lived in Hertfordshire, though he also maintained a residence in London. In his September 15 reply, Haines writes: "You made a wonderfully correct guess of what actually did pass between G.B.S. & myself up on the mountain. I am sure he thought I knew who he was, but, as a matter of fact, I mistook him for a rather unusually well-dressed plutocrat of arrogant manners" (letter held at DCL). The mountain in question is May Hill (elevation 296 meters); Haines and RF speak of it several times in their correspondence.

59. RF traveled to Scotland in late September (with his daughter Lesley) to visit James Cruickshank Smith.

[To Ernest Jewell (1872–1938), a classmate of RF's at Lawrence (Massachusetts) High School.[60] *Date supplied by the owner of the letter before Boston University acquired it. What Jewell had taken amiss remains unknown, though RF had borrowed $675 from him in 1902 and never, so far as RF's biographers have determined, fully repaid the debt. RF's handwritten IOU is in the Barrett Collection at the University of Virginia. ALS. BU.]*

Ryton Dymock
Glos. Eng.
[circa September 15, 1914]

Dear Jewell

Sorry, old man, if you take it amiss. My attitude is the same always. I can't think you have ceased to care what becomes of me.

Yours ever
R.F.

[To Sidney Cox. Dating derived from postmark. ALS. DCL.]

Ryton
Dymock
Gloucestershire
Eng.
[September 17, 1914]

Dear Cox

You wont catch me complaining of any war—much less of a great war like this that we wage on both sides like mystics for a reason beyond reason. Some philosopher has spoken for the Germans: "The hour of obedience has come"—the hour of the triumph of German obedience, religious and secular,

---

60. RF later recalled him in an essay titled "The Way There" (*CPRF*, 195): "The birch of 'Wild Grapes' was one a girl swung in when she didn't weigh enough to bring it to earth. She told me about it eighty years later and asked me to write a poem about it for girls to match the other birch poem that she claimed was written for boys. She clenched her hands in memory of the pain of having had to hang on in the tree too long. I had to write the poem for her because she was the first editor ever to publish me. Her name was Susan Hayes Ward. The poem was the first thing in prose or verse I ever wrote to order. She was my first publisher unless I count the Senior in the Lawrence High School who published three years earlier in our high school paper the first thing in prose or verse I ever wrote at all. And his name was Ernest Jewell."

the hour for the rest of the world to learn to obey.[61] Just so we thought the Germans thought. Therefore we go out to kill them. I wish we might lose none of our own in the struggle but Norman Angell David Starr Jordan, Andrew Carnegie Alfred Noyes and the Peace-editor of the Independent.[62] No I love this war regardless of what it does to me personally. That, I fear, is going to be a good deal, though nothing of course in comparison with what it will do to thousands of Englishmen. It ends my little literary game—that's all. No more books from anybody for the present. And the fact seems to be that it needed just one more book to clinch my business. As it is I am caught betwixt and between. No need to go into it. Enough to say that if I spend money here another year, I spend it for nothing. I shall just have to try to get home and live to write another day. I have two fervent hopes. One is that the Germans may not sow the Western Ocean with mines before I cross with the family and the other is that I may find something to do to make up for lost money when I get across.

I havent read Lockhart and I dont think I should much care for him from what you say.[63] Not that I ask for analysis. I am in love with the kind of books that get along without it. But I have little interest in Scott—the Scott at least

61. RF may have formed his ideas about the philosophical underpinnings of German nationalism while at Harvard, where, in 1898, he enrolled in George Santayana's course on the history of philosophy. Santayana's views on the matter are vividly expressed in his 1915 volume *Egotism in German Philosophy* (New York: Charles Scribner and Sons): "So [Johann Gottlieb] Fichte gives us prophetic glimpses of an idealistic Germany conquering the world. The state does not aim at self-preservation, still less is it concerned to come to the aid of those members of the human family that lag behind the movement of the day. The dominion of unorganized physical force must be abolished by a force obedient to reason and spirit" (78–79). We thank Robert Bernard Hass for the suggestion.

62. Norman Angell (1872–1967), English journalist and member of Parliament for the Labour Party, knighted in 1931; he won the Nobel Peace Prize in 1933. David Starr Jordan (1851–1931), an ichthyologist who served as president of Indiana University (1885–1891) and as president of Stanford University (1891–1913), is best known now as a peace activist and strident opponent of U.S. intervention in World War I. Andrew Carnegie (1835–1919), industrialist and philanthropist, founded the Church Peace Union (CPU), a group of leaders in religion, academia, and politics. Hamilton Holt (1872–1951), on the editorial staff at the *Independent* (New York) from 1897 to 1921, was an outspoken advocate for international peace; he served on the executive committee of the League to Enforce Peace from its origin in 1915 until its dissolution in 1923. Also mentioned is British poet Alfred Noyes (1880–1958), whose *The Wine Press: A Tale of War* (1913) is dedicated, caustically, "To those who believe that Peace is the corrupter of nations"; it was widely discussed in the press.

63. John Gibson (J. G.) Lockhart (1794–1854), Scottish editor and author of the definitive biography of Sir Walter Scott.

that Lockhart seems to have seen, the gentleman the goodfellow the entertainer the knight (was it) of Abbottsford (I once lived for a year in a barn of a hotel of that name in San Francisco).[64]

There are many answers to old Bridges.[65] I dont know the one I had in mind when I wrote to you. I can always find something to say against anything my nature rises up against. And what my nature doesnt object to I dont try to find anything to say against. That's my rule. I never entertain arguments pro and con, or rather I do, but not on the same subject. I am not a lawyer. I may have all the arguments in favor of what I favor but it doesnt ever worry me because I dont know one argument on the other side. I am not a German: a German you know may be defined as a person who doesnt dare not to be thorough. Really arguments don't matter. The only thing that counts is what you can't help feeling.

Who wants to fix the present sounds of words? Who by any diacritic device could fix stress on paper if he wanted to? No one in God's world can pronounce a word that he hasn't heard. No one can pronounce a word unless he can pronounce the whole language to which it belongs.

The fellow I'm living with at present is the last poet in your Victorian Anthology. If you want to see him to better advantage you must look him up in the Georgian Anthology where he shows well in a long poem called "The Sale of St Thomas." Or if I can find it I will send you sometime the copy of New Numbers containing his "End of the World" a play about to be produced in several places—Birmingham next week, Bristol soon, and Chicago sometime this winter.[66] He is one of the four treated in an article in the Nineteenth Century lately[67]—Gibson, Masefield, Davies and Abercrombie. I've told you about Davies.[68] Did I tell you he was down here with us and one night the Gibsons limped him over on his wooden leg three miles in the rain from their house to Abercrombies? They hurried poor Davies till the sweat broke out all over him. It was partly out of spite. They had been having a bad

64. Located at the corner of Larkin and Broadway in San Francisco, Abbotsford House was where the Frost family lived intermittently in 1880.

65. Robert Bridges served as Poet Laureate from 1913 until his death; in what follows RF mocks his theory that English verse could be, and ought to be, quantitative.

66. Abercrombie, whose "The Sale of St. Thomas" appeared in *Georgian Poetry 1911–1912* (1912), edited by Edward Marsh. "The End of The World" (mentioned also) appeared in the second issue of *New Numbers*. For more on *New Numbers*, see the notes to RF's July 1914 letter to F. S. Flint.

67. *The Nineteenth Century* was inaugurated in London in 1914.

68. See RF's May 18, 1914, letter to Cox.

time together as rivals in poetry. To make it full and running over for Davies they told him he ought to be proud because he was going to see the greatest poet in England. "Huh," says Davies. When he arrives in the dooryard dead beat, "good thing it's the greatest poet in England." He said it bitterly, but the Gibsons taking him at his word hurried in to tell Abercrombie that by consent of Davies he was the greatest poet in England. But that's what Davies thinks he is himself. And that is what Gibson, or Gibsons wife, thinks Gibson is. (Gibson and Davies both make more out of their poetry than Abercrombie. Davies sells well here and Gibson in America.)

Abercrombie has written a good deal of prose for a living. You ought to be able to find something of his in your library—his "Thomas Hardy" his "Epic" or his "Speculative Dialogues."[69]

We are in another old house, this time under a very ancient thatch: the bottom layer of straw is rye—perhaps put on two or three hundred years ago. We are away in the country where you wouldnt think we would have any part in the excitement of war. But we haven't escaped being taken for spies. As writers we are a little mysterious to the peasant kind. They have had the police busy about us—about Abercrombie, too, in spite of the fact he is well connected in the "county." They confused me in some way with a Dutchman we had with us, a Van Doorn, with an accent and a long black beard.[70] They suspected Abercrombie because a year ago he entertained a strange artist lady who goes about the country on her hands and knees because she's paralyzed or thinks she is. Sometimes she rides in a pony cart. She has to be lifted in and out of that. She gets anybody to pick her up off the ground. She is all wasted to nothing. But as the country folk remember her she might well have been a German officer in disguise.

This is supplementary to that other letter with the reviews. I shall write again soon and send you if you will let me some of David Nutts folders advertising my book.

Elinor joins me in sending regards—best.

Yours ever
R.F.

69. Abercrombie's *Thomas Hardy: A Critical Study* was published in 1912; *The Epic* (1914) appeared in the Art and Craft of Letters series published by Martin Secker in London; his *Speculative Dialogues,* also published by Martin Secker, appeared in 1913.

70. Willem Van Doorn (1875–1959) was a Dutch critic known in England for his essays on Yeats, and also for an anthology he edited, *Golden Hours with English Poets* (Meulenhoff, 1910).

[To Carol Frost. Undated and with no salutation or signature, RF addressed this post-card to his son at Ryton, Dymock. RF and his daughter Lesley traveled to Edinburgh in late September 1914 to visit with the family of James Cruickshank Smith.[71] *The other children remained in Dymock with Mrs. Frost. The front of the card pictures the Forth Bridge in Edinburgh, a monumental structure completed in 1890 that spans the Firth of Forth between South Queensferry and North Queensferry. ALS. UVA.]*

[late September 1914]

I suppose the Germans would like to do something to this. I have seen a lot of fellows marching about here who will do something to the Germans.

[To John W. Haines. ALS/Photostat. DCL.]

20 Braid Avenue
Edinburgh Scotland
Sept 30 1914

Dear Haines

We had not too bad a time coming north, though we never had a compartment to ourselves. The way we managed was by turning that disadvantage to account and making friends with the people we had to sit with. They were right out of one of the dimmest places on earth, the Falkland Islands. I can't say that I had actually been looking for them, but I had a lot of things I wanted to pump out of them and I pumped a long time before I satisfied not my curiosity but my hanker to live in out of the way places.

We had the loveliest time with you in Gloucester and now I learn that you and your wife have been being good to all my family that I didn't bring away.

Here I am among professors and school inspectors chiefly. We talk about poetry to a certain extent, but more about the war. Bless that Emden![72]

---

71. John W. Haines made inquiries on RF's behalf as to the train fare to Edinburgh, apprising him of the result in a September 21 letter held at DCL—which letter incidentally suggests that RF and Lesley left Dymock for Scotland on Friday, September 25.

72. The SMS *Emden,* a light cruiser in Germany's Imperial Navy, commissioned in 1909, and named for the city in northwestern Germany that sponsored it. Operating in the Pacific and in the Indian Ocean during the early weeks and months of World War I, the *Emden* enjoyed (from the point of view of the Allies, anyway) infamous success, sinking, in September alone, some fifteen British ships. RF, deeply sympathetic to British fortunes in the war, had good reason to "bless" the *Emden* in the colloquial American sense of the word (as in "blesséd" for "cursed").

I haven't been very well for a few days and am shut in today, a little worse than I have been. Half-heated English houses are the trouble.

My best regards to you and your wife.

Sincerely yours
Robert Frost.

[To Sidney Cox. ALS. DCL.]

The Gallows
Ryton Dymock
Gloucestershire Eng
October 1914

Dear Cox

It warms me cockles to see you so enthusiastic over my book. Three or four more such friends and I should be a made man. You have done so much more than you ought already that you wont object to doing a good deal more for me. So I send you with the book certain circulars to scatter. To be most effective they should go to people who care especially for you or for me or for poetry. But if you like you may give them to some boy to distribute on the street corner when the mills are emptying at night. Or flutter them yourself from the tail end of an electric. Don't count on doing too much execution with them. Not everyone will find them persuasive and not everyone will like the book as well as you would like to have him. A good many simple souls, educated or uneducated, will miss the "poeticisms" by which they are accustomed to know poetry when they see it.

Sometime we must discuss that minister and his creed.[73] I make it a rule not to take any "character's" side in anything I write. So I am not bound to defend the minister you understand.

We grow more and more concerned for our future. The prose I sometimes talk of writing for bread and butter would simply bring me nothing now if I wrote it. I may have to go home soon. The difficulty there is that the expense of getting home would leave me under the necessity of getting a job for a while till I got on my feet again. I should awfully like a quiet job in a small college where I should be allowed to teach something a little new on

73. See "The Black Cottage," collected in *NB*.

the technique of writing and where I should have some honor* for what I suppose myself to have done in poetry. Well, but I mustnt dream.

Sincerely yours
Robert Frost

*just a little little bit

[To John W. Haines. ALS/Photostat. DCL.]

Ryton Dymock
October 1914

Dear Haines

What you proposed in your last letter wasn't necessary because what you guessed wasnt so. We were in Scotland for our pleasure—not to be out of the way of the oncoming baby.[74] It was thoughtful of you, just the same, to make the offer.

I should have accepted your invitation to stay over in Gloucester a train or two if my home-coming had not been rather in a hurry on a summons. The children were sick and my wife tired out.

I was under the doctor's care myself while I was in Edinburgh, but my visit was not altogether spoiled by the bad luck. I had a better time than I should have thought anyone had reason to give me.

I have just had my copies of his books from Gibson. I havent had time to look through them for what I haven't read in them. You know what I think of Gibson in this phase. He is rather below the form of "Fires."[75]

Our best regards to you and your wife.

Sincerely yours
Robert Frost

74. Ralph Abercrombie, born in December 1914 to Catherine and Lascelles Abercrombie, in whose house the Frosts were living.

75. Elkin Mathews (London) published Wilfrid Gibson's *Fires* in three volumes in 1912; the same firm published two more of his books in 1914: *Borderlands* and *Daily Bread* (RF has the latter two in mind in speaking of "this phase").

[To Thomas Bird Mosher. ALS. UVA.]

The Gallows
Ryton Dymock
Gloucestershire
October 1914

Dear Mr Mosher:

I am content to leave it that way. Anything you care to give—It is not for me to make terms with you. All I have in mind is to reach through you an American public. So long as you get me read I shall ask no questions about royalties. Mrs Nutt however is another matter. She would say that as one of her indentured poets I have no right to be corresponding with an American publisher even in friendship.[76] In fact she has just forbidden me to have anything to do with American publishers. I must refer them all to her. She will be the difficulty. Lately her mood has been especially bitter. You have heard perhaps of her attack on The Mirror because it quoted two verses from Henleys England.[77] She demanded five guineas for the breach of copyright. To my knowledge she has been asking St John Adcock fifty guineas for six of Henley's poems he wanted for an anthology.[78] She is a well-meaning but far from reasonable lady of business.

We are very quiet in spite of the war. An occasional hobnailed boot on the metalled lane is all that disturbs us—that and a certain fear we don't know what of. It wont be of Zeppelins at this distance from big towns and it wont be of invading armies—yet. I doubt if we are going to be invaded at all.

I hope the war may not make as much difference in your business as you feared.

Sincerely yours
Robert Frost

76. Widow of Alfred Nutt and head of the firm that published RF's first two books, David Nutt. Worries about the contract he signed with her dogged RF well into 1916.

77. William Ernest Henley (1849–1903) was an English poet, critic, and editor. His "Pro Rege Nostro"—with the memorable refrain "What have I done for you, England, my England?"—became popular during the First World War.

78. Arthur St. John Adcock (1864–1930).

[To Thomas Bird Mosher. ALS. DCL.]

Ryton Dymock
Gloucestershire Eng
November 1914

Dear Mr Mosher

It is lucky I warned you, if you mind trouble. Mrs Nutt bears you no good will as I found out when I tried to get her to look at some of your book work. Some people are best not stirred up.

You would have been too late for my book anyway. Some one else took it some time ago, I am informed.[79] I want to thank you for your interest just the same. I see you have begun reading De la Mare. And you find him not a "free verster." Some careless reviewer had let you in wrong as to his classification. I knew you would like him when you gave him a fair trial. The nineties produced no single poem to put beside his "Listeners."[80] Really the nineties had very little on these degenerate days when you consider. Yeats Jonson and Dowson they had, and that is about all.[81] De la Mare and Davies are the equal of any of them in lyric and Abercrombie (whom I mustn't praise too much for he is in the house with me) leaves them all behind in the sublime imaginative sort of thing. I wonder you haven't discovered Davies. He seems in your line.

This war mars all for the like of us, but it does so much worse for a million others that I don't feel justified in worrying let alone complaining.

Let me congratulate you on the completion of your Twenty Years' Bibelot. I wish you sales.

Sincerely yours
Robert Frost.

---

79. Henry Holt and Company.

80. Walter de la Mare published *The Listeners and Other Poems* in 1912 (London: Constable); at RF's encouragement, Henry Holt and Company would issue an American edition of the book in 1916.

81. Lionel Johnson (1867–1902), English poet and literary critic; Ernest Dowson (1867–1900), English poet and novelist.

[To Gertrude McQuesten. This letter, for the most part illegible owing to faded ink, was transcribed by collector Paul Richards before Boston University acquired it; we checked his transcription (also held at BU) against the manuscript, with the following result. ALS. BU.]

Ryton, Dymock
Gloucestershire, England
November 1, 1914

Dear Miss McQuesten:

You treated us so incredibly badly this summer that I think you will want to distribute these three little circulars for me as some slight atonement. The heinousness of your crime lay in your knocking all our plans for your galley-west. We were going to have you read to the assembled poets down here and I did want them to hear you at the Poetry Bookshop in Holborn in London.[82] There they have all sorts (though not many) in the British style of reading poetry. I wanted them to get an idea of the right American style. You were cruel and you meant to be. You were just out of Austria full of prejudice against the English and hostile to us because we live in England. I was cross with you and I may never quite get over it.

Nevertheless I hope you may prosper with your audiences this winter. I was always that way—wishing to have my friends succeed even though I had quarreled with them. Mrs Frost is more forgiving than I am and she goes so far as to send personal regards.

Sincerely yours
Robert Frost.

[To Sidney Cox. Dating from internal evidence. ALS. DCL.]

Ryton Dymock
Gloucestershire Eng.
[circa November 1, 1914]

Dear Cox

This is only to say that Henry Holt will supply the book in America. Will you write that on any circulars you have still to send out?

82. Harold Monro's shop.

They say the germans [*sic*] have made the whole Atlantic unsafe. This raises questions for me.

1) Do I dare to go home now?
2) Won't it be more dangerous to go every day we delay?
3) Won't it be impossible to get money across to live on pretty soon?
4) Do I dare to stay?

Perhaps you think I am joking. I am never so serious as when I am.

If you never hear from me again, write Henry Holt & Co Publishers New York, on the circulars and let it go at that.

Yours ever
Robert Frost.

You got the book I sent?

[To Harold Monro, undated and without address. As the next few letters show (see also RF's August 7, 1915, letter to Monro), RF and Monro had hopes of publishing a chapbook of Frost's poems through the Poetry Bookshop. Since ten poems making "something like a set" would be appropriate to such a venture, this letter can be provisionally dated to the fall of 1914 and thus from Dymock. ALS. Trinity.]

[Ryton, Dymock]
[Gloucestershire, England]
[Fall 1914]

Dear Monro

I have decided to let you see ten of these. They have enough in common to make something like a set whatever number you care to use. You must excuse my being so late: I always find something I want to do with MS at the last moment and it's the devil to make a selection. I could supply names for the pair in the eclogue if you thought I ought to.

Sincerely yours
Robert Frost

[To Harold Monro. ALS. Trinity.]

Ryton Dymock
November 1914

Dear Monro

I should like nothing better than to see these poems in chap-book form. I know they could be made to go so far in that way that I could well afford to wait your two years before publishing them in any other way. The idea of the chap book is attractive to me. I wonder if it wouldn't be to any poet.

I am sorry about P & D.[83] But I am sorry about a good many things lately as I hope you will believe though I haven't sent you any poetry to that effect.

The proof seems OK. My choice of the poems would very nearly coincide with yours. Not that that makes any difference to you. It does to me though, as something to check my judgement by.

Sincerely yours
Robert Frost

[To Harold Monro. Throughout, RF refers to poems in Children of Love, *a chapbook of his own work that Monro published through the Poetry Bookshop in 1914. ALS. Trinity.]*

Ryton Dymock
December 1914

Dear Monro

I have been enjoying the book you sent. I find I like something in most of the poems, though I like you best where you are least theological as in London Interior and Great City. In neither of these do you make me tremble for my peace of mind or my growing children or whatever it is you make me tremble for elsewhere. You turn life rather too terrible by the use of such words over a cat drinking milk as "creeping lust," "transfigured with love," "dim ecstasy," "Her world is an infinite shapeless white," "holy drop" and

83. In the December 1914 issue, Monro would announce that publication of *Poetry and Drama* would be suspended for a year; it was never resumed, though Monro did eventually launch a new journal, *The Chapbook* (*The Monthly Chapbook* for its first two issues), which ran from 1919 through 1925.

"lies defeated."[84] I suppose I ought not to shrink from seeing resemblances to our humanity on the lower side, but I feel as if they pulled me down or dizzied me—I dont know what. But I am writing nonsense. I quite go with you the length of "Children of Love." That wisdom is lovely and not dark. Of course it is sad that the two loves should have sometime met and yet not hit it off together.[85]

Think of me as engaged in a little war on my own down here with a bad gamekeeper who attacked me for going where he had allowed the Gibsons to go as gentry. Me he called a damned "cottager." Now who will have the better claim to the title of the People's Poet? Thomas says it is the best testimonial I have had and I must get my publisher to use the game-keeper in advertising me—that is if I survive my war with the brute—and even if I don't—[86]

Sometimes I wish I were in London.

Yours ever
Robert Frost

Next page

My wife's choice is Overheard in a Saltmarsh. I like that, too. But the two I have named, London Interior and Great City, are best. They are altogether fine.

R.F.

---

84. All quoted phrases are from "Milk for the Cat."

85. In the title poem to *Children of Love*, Cupid and Jesus meet:

Cupid at last
Draws his bow and softly lets fly a dart.
Smile for a moment, sad world!—
It has grazed the white skin and drawn blood from the sorrowful heart.
Now, for delight,
Cupid tosses his locks and goes wantonly near;
But the child that was born to the cross
Has let fall on his cheek, for the sadness of life, a compassionate tear.
Marvelous dream!
Cupid has offered his arrows for Jesus to try;
He has offered his bow for the game.
But Jesus went weeping away, and left him there wondering why.

86. For RF's dust-up with the gamekeeper, see *EY*, 467–468. See also the notes to RF's April 17, 1915, letter to Thomas.

*[To Harold Monro. For the "British Museum Story—in verse," see "The White-Tailed Hornet" (*CPPP*, 253). ALS. Trinity.]*

Ryton Dymock Glos
Dec 1914

Dear Monro

I can't believe I was the least bit sarcastic but if I seemed so it was just as bad and you deserve as much credit for forgiving me and placing me so well in such a good number of P & D[87] and offering me your spare rooms when I should come to London. I wish I could get in to see you and I may try to soon—before the rain of bombs begins. Meanwhile I am sending a friend of mine J. W. Haines a Gloucester lawyer to call. I should like to ask you to say a friendly word to him if he turns up at the Shop when you happen to be in. He reads and buys more poetry than anybody in the West Countree. He's a good judge of the stuff. I know he would be flattered to have the chance to tell you he likes your book and to expostulate with you for not going straight on with P & D.

Dont put your inclination to preach off on the parsons [sic] in you. Everybody has it. I know I have, and in me sea and land meet (as they do at the shore): I am a son of sailors (pure) on one side and farmers (pure) on the other.[88] And as Alford tells Amy Lowell—well, it is written in P & D.[89]

You take what I say about the Cat Drinking Milk too seriously.[90] The phrases I picked out were merely a dotted outline of an analogy or kind of

---

87. Monro published four of Frost's poems in the December 1914 issue of *Poetry and Drama:* "The Sound of Trees," "The Cow in Apple Time," "Putting in the Seed," and "The Smile."

88. Isabelle Moodie Frost (born near Edinburgh) was the daughter of a sailor; the poet's father, William Prescott Frost, descended from a family that had been in New England since the seventeenth century.

89. John Alford authored the American Chronicle column, a survey of contemporary American letters, in *Poetry and Drama.* RF refers to Alford's December review of Amy Lowell's 1914 volume *Sword Blades and Poppy Seeds*: "She has prefaced her new book, Sword Blades and Poppy Seed, with a little discourse on the business of poets and poetry. 'Poetry should not try to teach. . . . but many of us do not yet see that to write an obvious moral all over a work of art, picture, statue, or poem, is not only ridiculous, but timid and vulgar.' We have heard it all before, as recently as the publication of Mr [James Elroy] Flecker's last book. The business of poetry is to be poetry; if it likes to try and teach as well, I for one have no objection."

90. See previous letter to Monro.

analogy that scares me. Sometime I will tell you a story about "resemblances to our humanity on the lower side"—a British Museum story—in verse. It will have to be when nobody is listening, because I am not supposed to touch any but rural themes.

I understand that the Gibsons were pleased with your handling of their Twins.[91]

Yours ever
Robert Frost

[To Sidney Cox. ALS. DCL.]

Ryton Dymock Gloucestershire
England
Dec 1914

Dear Cox

I am glad you are going into it with me and one or two others. Thomas thinks he will write a book on what my new definition of the sentence means for literary criticism. If I didn't drop into poetry every time I sat down to write I should be tempted to do a book on what it means for education.[92] It may take some time to make people see—they are so accustomed to look at the sentence as a grammatical cluster of words. The question is where to begin the assault on their prejudice. For my part I have about decided to begin by demonstrating by examples that the sentence as a sound in itself apart from the word sounds is no mere figure of speech. I shall show the sentence sound saying all that the sentence conveys with little or no help from the meaning of the words. I shall show the sentence sound opposing the sense of the words as in irony. And so till I establish the distinction between the grammatical sentence and the vital sentence. The grammatical sentence is merely accessory to the other and chiefly valuable as furnishing a clue to the other. You recognize the sentence sound in this: You, you—! It is so strong that if you hear it as I do you have to

91. Monro reviewed Wilfrid Gibson's new books, *Borderlands* and *Thoroughfares*, under the heading "Mr. Gibson's Two Volumes": "Mr Gibson is a serious and diligent craftsman; there have been many changes and developments in his work: many are doubtless still to come. He has freed the vocabulary and widened the scope of poetry; he has the gratefulness of the English public" (*Poetry and Drama,* December 1914: 378–379).

92. See also RF's June 1, 1915, letter to Browne.

pronounce the two you's differently. Just so many sentence sounds belong to man as just so many vocal runs belong to one kind of bird. We come into the world with them and create none of them. What we feel as creation is only selection and grouping. We summon them from Heaven knows where under excitement with the audile imagination. And unless we are in an imaginative mood it is no use trying to make them, they will not rise. We can only write the dreary kind of grammatical prose known as professorial. Because that is to be seen at its worst in translations especially from the classics, Thomas thinks he will take up the theme apropos of somebody's scholarly translation of Horace or Catullus some day when such a book comes his way for review.

I throw all this out as it comes to me to show you where we are at present. Use anything you please. I am only too glad of your help. We will shake the old unity-emphasis-and-coherence Rhetoric to its foundations.

A word more. We value the seeing eye already. Time we said something about the hearing ear—the ear that calls up vivid sentence forms.

We write of things we see and we write in accents we hear. Thus we gather both our material and our technique with the imagination from life: and our technique becomes as much material as material itself.

All sorts of things must occur to you. Blaze away at them. But expect to have to be patient. There are a lot of completely educated people in this world and of course they will resent being asked to learn anything new.

You aren't influenced by that Beauty is Truth claptrap. In poetry and under emotion every word used is "moved" a little or much—moved from its old place, heightened, made, made new.[93] See what Keats did to the word "alien" in the ode.[94] But as he made it special in that place he made it his—

---

93. For more on this, see RF's talk "The Unmade Word; or Fetching and Far-Fetching" (*CPPP*, 694–697).

94. In the penultimate stanza of "Ode to a Nightingale":

Thou wast not born for death, immortal Bird!
No hungry generations tread thee down;
The voice I hear this passing night was heard
In ancient days by emperor and clown:
Perhaps the self-same song that found a path
Through the sad heart of Ruth, when, sick for home,
She stood in tears amid the alien corn;
The same that oft-times hath
Charm'd magic casements, opening on the foam
Of perilous seas, in faery lands forlorn.

and his only in that place. He could never have used it again with just that turn. It takes the little one horse poets to do that. I am probably the only Am poet who haven't [*sic*] used it after him. No if I want to deal with the word I must sink back to its common usage at Castle Garden.[95] I want the unmade words to work with not the familiar made ones that everybody exclaims Poetry! at. Of course the great fight of any poet is against the people who want him to write in a special language that has gradually separated from spoken language by this "making" process. His pleasure must always be to make his own words as he goes and never to depend for effect on words already made even if they be his own.

Enough of that. I don't blame your good friend. Nor do I blame the poor educated girl who thought the little book was difficult. The "contents" notes were a piece of fooling on my part. They were not necessary and not very good.[96]

I'd like to thank specially the fellow who picked out Mowing. I guess there is no doubt that is the best poem in Book I. We all think so over here. Thank Hatch for me too.[97] Don't forget.

And thank yourself for all you are doing for me. I need it in this game.

I should like a good talk or three with you. On the war if you chose. On anything. You are going to do a lot all round I know. Your opinions are worth listening to because you mean to put them into action—if for no other reason. But there is no other reason as important. What a man will put into effect at any cost of time money life or lives is what is sacred and what counts. As I get old I dont want to hear about much else.

I have nearly written myself tired for tonight.

Write often and keep my courage up.

Yours ever
R.F.

Get rid of that Mr. on my name next letter or take the consequences.

---

95. From 1855 to 1892, Castle Garden, at the southern tip of Manhattan, was the point of entry for immigrants into New York; hence the de-Keatsianizing play on the word "alien."

96. In the table of contents to *ABW*, RF appended glosses to the titles of most of the poems; he removed them when he brought the book into *Collected Poems* (1930). See *CPPP*, 968–969.

97. In *RFSC* Evans identifies him as "Clarence Hatch, a former student of Cox's" (56).

[To Ernest L. Silver. Text derived from SL, *143–144. When he prepared his edition in 1964, Thompson listed the manuscript of the letter as held at DCL; it is no longer there.]*

[The Gallows]
[December 23, 1914]

Dear Silver,

I ought not to have begun stirring up my friends so impulsively. The fact is the war took me by surprise and for a time I thought I had lost by it pretty much all I played for. I have lost some money, undoubtedly, but perhaps not so much that I can't hope still to go to a farm when I go home, as I originally intended. It may be necessary for me to teach a year or so somewhere to catch up and it may not. At any rate I shant sign on with Pease till I know my own mind better.[98]

No one quite knows what the war has done to him yet. We may be dead, the whole crowd of us, and not able to realize the fact. It is as hard to know how the war has affected us individually as it is to tell off hand what the war is all about, or to understand a modern battle.

I suspect a modern battle hasnt got to be and wont continue to be the futile thing it is. It remains a stand-off to date because no man big enough has had time enough to seize the tactical use of all the weapons science has dumped down on us since the last great war. No one is sure where so simple a thing as the Maxim should come in.[99] So both sides are fighting just not to lose. It was like that in naval warfare when Rodney and Nelson came on the scene.[100] It always takes time for the Nelsons to emerge from the brass-bound peace generals and win victories. The peace-trained men are good enough to hold the other peace-trained men. Both do it by the book. Each knows what the other knows. There can be no secrecy and no surprise. But all that is changed the minute a man appears with one fresh idea (big idea) of his own. No spy will find that out and no military critic either perhaps until years af-

98. Alvin F. Pease (1852–1939), together with William F. Jarvis, ran the Winship Teachers' Agency, located at 29A Beacon Street, Boston. "We have unequalled facilities for placing teachers in every part of the country," declared the agency's advertisement.

99. The Maxim Gun, invented by Sir Hiram Stevens Maxim in 1884, was the first self-powered machine gun.

100. George Brydges Rodney, 1st Baron Rodney (1718–1792), British naval officer celebrated for his victory over the French at the Battle of the Saintes in 1782 (as a part of the American Revolution). Horatio Nelson, 1st Viscount Nelson, 1st Duke of Bronté (1758–1805), was killed in action at the Battle of Trafalgar (which he won).

ter. They say Napoleon didn't know his own big idea to state it to the day of his death, and only acted on it when in top form and perfect health. It is in all the books now. I haven't the least doubt there are twenty decisive victories in succession for the right man in the telling use of rapid fire guns alone. I wonder which side will be the first to find the right man.

As for what it is all about: I heard an old cottage woman say this to the proposition that England was fighting for Belgium: "In a way we are—the same as we would fight for a wall we had put between ourselves and danger." No sentimental rot there.

In spite of all you may hear to the contrary from interested parties, Germans and English conscriptionists with an ax to grind, enlistment goes forward perfectly. There are soldiers swarming over everything. I have seen them by thousands in all stages of development—some of them veterans, already wounded, recovered and on their way to the front again. These last are the ones to pity.[101] I knew personally of one who had been wounded and temporarily blinded by a bursting shell. He was getting well enough to go back but his nerve was gone and he was crying every day at the prospect. A Colonel Gordon home with a paralyzed arm, showed a photograph of the officers of his regiment taken before the war and he said every one of them was wounded, dead, or in the madhouse.

English people assume that they have the sympathy of Americans, at least of New Englanders, and I suppose they are not wrong.

I may look in on you before many weeks for my furniture. Nothing is certain except that poetry is a drug here now and that I feel as if I ought to get the children out of any danger there is, however slight. We are always homesick. So that if I can see my way I may take passage in February or March.

With our regards

Sincerely yours
Robert Frost

---

101. See "Not to Keep," collected in *NH*.

[To Thomas Bird Mosher. ALS. Middlebury.]

Ryton Dymock
Gloucestershire Eng
December 27 1914

Dear Mosher

I meant to make it perfectly clear to you how sorry I was that I couldn't see my books named in your catalogue. I venture to say it would make less difference to me than to you if they didn't sell. My first care is that the poetry shall be right. For ten or fifteen years that was all I thought of. Lately I have begun to care a little about placing it where it will stand the least chance of being lost. I feel the responsibility for it that one does for a grown-up child: I want to give it a fair start in life.

You knew I was sorry you weren't going to print me and you just sent me that lovely book of Allen's to make me sorrier.[102] Thank you—for the book—not for your evil intentions.

Dont you worry about Pound's or Abercrombie's causing me any purturbation [*sic*] of the orbit. I happen to be living in Abercrombie's house at present, but I really know him no more intimately than I do Davies or Gibson or Hodgson or anyone of a dozen others.[103] This is a small England and especially so speaking literarily. There are only a few poets in even the greatest countries (America, for instance) and if you know one you know, or can know, them all. Pound and I fell out nearly a year ago. But I see he still reviews me in <u>Poetry</u> (Chicago.) Pound is the most generous of mortals.[104]

It turns out that my American publisher is Henry Holt. I have just learned the fact lately, and I dont know how it came about unless it was through someone of the name of Holt who wrote me an appreciative letter from

102. In 1914 Mosher published *The Last Christmas Tree: An Idyll of Immortality* by Kentucky writer James Lane Allen (1849–1925).

103. British poet Ralph Hodgson (1871–1962), whom RF met in England in 1913 (it was Hodgson who introduced RF to Edward Thomas). The other poets mentioned here (save Pound) formed part of the Georgian circle RF had come to know.

104. Under the title "Modern Georgics," Pound favorably reviewed *NB* in the December 1914 number of *Poetry* magazine, passing such judgments as these: "[*North of Boston*] is a contribution to American literature, the sort of sound work that will develop into very interesting literature if persevered in" (130).

Stowe Vermont in the summer. I think it is only North of Boston that is in question. The first book is to be forgotten.[105]

I see Billy Bryan and John Masefield are out in favor of Walt Mason of Kansas.[106] Yon's a poet for you. For me, give me De la Mare.

I wonder how the war looks to you. It isn't over yet, is it?

Sincerely yours
Robert Frost

[To Sidney Cox. ALS. DCL.]

Ryton Dymock
Gloucestershire Eng
Jan 2 1915

Dear Cox

Be sure to send your article as soon as you have it.[107] I see you really doing something in the next few years to break into the worst system of teaching that ever endangered a nations literature. You speak of Columbia. That reminds me of the article on American literature by a Columbian, George Woodbury, in the Encyclopedia Britannica.[108] I wish you would read it or the

---

105. Florence Taber Holt, wife of the publisher Henry Holt, had written RF from her summer home in Stowe, expressing interest in *NB*. Henry Holt and Company would not "forget" *ABW*: the American edition appeared in April 1915.

106. Walt Mason (1862–1939) was a popular poet and newspaper humorist based in Emporia, Kansas (he was born in Canada, but became a U.S. citizen). "Uncle Walt," as he was called, was declared by some to be "poet laureate of American democracy." William Jennings Bryan wrote a short preface to his *Rippling Rhymes to Suit the Times All Sorts of Themes Embracin'* (Chicago: A. C. McLurg, 1914): "I have shared the satisfaction that his increasing fame has brought him and have encouraged him to publish this collection that his readers, now numbering people of many lands, may have permanent companionship with him." The book featured blurbs from William Dean Howells, Sir Arthur Conan Doyle, James Whitcomb Riley, and Theodore Dreiser, among others. John Masefield had also given him favorable notice and appears in blurbs for other books by Mason.

107. A draft of Cox's "A Plea for a More Direct Method in Teaching English," which would appear in the *English Journal* in May 1915 (4.5): 302–305. See also RF to Cox, June 24, 1915.

108. RF misspells the name. George Edward Woodberry (1855–1930), American literary critic and poet, authored the entry on "America in Literature" in the celebrated elev-

last part of it just to see that we are not alone in thinking that nothing literary can come from the present ways of the professionally literary in American universities. It is much the same in the Scottish. Everything is research for the sake of erudition. No one is taught to value himself for nice perception and cultivated taste. Knowledge knowledge. Why literature is the next thing to religion in which as you know or believe an ounce of faith is worth all the theology ever written. Sight and insight, give us those. I like the good old English way of muddling along in these things that we cant reduce to a science any way such as literature love religion and friendship. People make their great strides in understanding literature at most unexpected times. I never caught another man's emotion in it more than when someone drew his finger over some seven lines of blank verse—beginning carefully and ending carefully—and said simply "From there to—there." He knew and I knew. We said no more. I don't see how you are going to teach the stuff except with some such light touch. And you cant afford to treat it all alike, I mean with equal German thoroughness and reverence if thoroughness is reverence. It is only a moment here and a moment there that the greatest writer has. Some cognizance of the fact must be taken in your teaching.

Well I didn't intend to be running on like this so soon again but somehow you set me off. I have my work to think of too—though I don't get on with it to speak of in these unsettled times. The war has been a terrible detriment to pleasant thinking[;] in spite of all I can do to approve of it philosophically I don't know whether I like it or not. I don't think I have any right to like it when I am not called on to die in it. At the same time it seems almost cowardly not to approve of it on general principles simply because it is not my funeral. It seems little minded. There we will leave it. I hate it for those whose hearts are not in it and I fear they must be many, though perhaps not so many as it is the fashion to make them out, nor so many as they were in Nelsons[109] navy for example where more than half the sailors, some say, were

---

enth edition of the *Encyclopedia Britannica*. From 1891 to 1904, Woodberry was professor of comparative literature at Columbia University. RF refers to the conclusion to Woodberry's survey: "Nor has anything been developed from within that is fertile in literature. . . . The universities have not, on the whole, been its sources or fosterers, and they are now filled with research, useful for learning but impotent for literature. The intellectual life is now rather to be found in social, political and natural science than elsewhere; the imaginative life is feeble, and when felt is crude; the poetic pulse is imperceptible."

109. Admiral Horatio Nelson (1758–1805).

"pressed" that is to say, kidnapped. One of the most earthly wise of our own time thinks the common soldiers do actually know what they are fighting for and he has said so in the only good war poem I have seen. (Thomas Hardy's my man.)[110] There are many possibilities. The soldier may not know. He may not know as in Southey's After Blenheim.[111] He may be at fault for not knowing, deficient in national imagination. He may be the larger for not knowing: he may have been a fool always when he thought he knew, playing into the hands of captains and kings. It may be as the Syndicalists hold that his interest is no longer in nations (never was in fact) but in the federation of industrial groups without masters. This must be a slippery piece of paper—I run to length so easily on it.

There are about half a dozen things I wanted to say to you before ringing off—business things.

The first is that you mustnt take me so seriously. You may be just as friendly as you like. I shall need your good opinion of my books in the fight that is ahead for them in my own country.

---

110. See Hardy's "Song of the Soldiers," published first in the *London Times* on September 9, 1914. It reads, in part:

Is it a purblind prank, O think you,
Friend with the musing eye
Who watch us stepping by,
With doubt and dolorous sigh?
Can much pondering so hoodwink you?
Is it a purblind prank, O think you,
Friend with the musing eye?
Nay. We see well what we are doing,
Though some may not see—
Dalliers as they be—
England's need are we . . .

111. Robert Southey (1774–1843), British poet and Poet Laureate (1813–1843). "After Blenheim" (1796) concerns the War of the Spanish Succession. In it, an old man whose farm lies on what had been the battlefield, speaks to his grandchildren:

"It was the English," Kaspar cried,
"Who put the French to rout;
But what they fought each other for
I could not well make out.
But everybody said," quoth he,
"That 'twas a famous victory."

That brings me to my second. I fear I am going to suffer a good deal at home by the support of Pound. This is a generous person who is doing his best to put me in the wrong light by his reviews of me: You will see the blow he has dealt me in Poetry (Chicago) for December, and yet it is with such good intention I suppose I shall have to thank him for it.[112] I don't know about that—I may when I get round to it. The harm he does lies in this: he made up his mind in the short time I was friends with him (We quarreled in six weeks) to add me to his party of American literary refugees in London. Nothing could be more unfair, nothing better calculated to make me an exile for life. Another such review as the one in Poetry and I shan't be admitted at Ellis Island. This is no joke. Since the article was published I have been insulted and snubbed by two American editors I counted on as good friends. I dont repine and I am willing to wait for justice. But I do want someone to know that I am not a refugee and I am not in any way disloyal. My publishing a book in England was as it happened. Several editors in America had treated me very well, particularly those of The Companion The Forum and The Independent.[113] It was not in anger that I came to England and there was no shaking of dust off my feet. Pound is trying to drag me into his ridiculous row with everybody over there. I feel sorry for him for by this time he has nearly every man's hand against him on both continents and I wouldn't want

---

112. Pound's "Modern Georgics," *Poetry* (December 1914): 127–130. RF has in mind Pound's opening salvo: "It is a sinister thing that so American, I might even say so parochial, a talent as that of Robert Frost should have to be exported before it can find due encouragement and recognition. Even Emerson had sufficient elasticity of mind to find something in the 'yawp.' One doesn't need to like a book or a poem or a picture in order to recognize artistic vigor. But the typical American editor of the last twenty years has resolutely shut his mind against serious American writing. I do not exaggerate, I quote exactly, when I say that these gentlemen deliberately write to authors that such and such a matter is 'too unfamiliar to our readers.' There was once an American editor who would even print me, so I showed him Frost's 'Death of the Hired Man.' He wouldn't have it; he had printed a weak pseudo-Masefieldian poem about a hired man two months before, one written in a stilted pseudo-literary language, with all sorts of floridities and worn-out ornaments."

113. Some poems in *ABW* first saw print in the *Independent* (edited by Susan Hayes Ward and William Hayes Ward, whom the Frost family befriended); in *The Youth's Companion* (while Mark Anthony DeWolfe Howe was editor); and in *The Forum* (edited, during the years RF placed poems in the journal, by Joseph Mayer Rice and Frederick Taber Cooper).

to hurt him. But I feel sorry for myself too. You can imagine the hot patriot I will have become by the time I get home. And then to be shut out! I dont see that it is possible to do anything publicly to dissociate myself from Pound but do you think it would be a discreet thing for you to say a word to Sherman[114] or perhaps (what do you think?) even write a short letter to The Sun or The Times or both saying that you have reason to know that I would have no pleasure in that part of Pound's article in Poetry that represented me as an American literary refugee in London with a grievance against Amer. editors. The article was very generous. Pound was a generous person who had gone out of his way to do me several favors for which you supposed me grateful. But you knew I had favors to thank American editors for too. A good deal of my first book (in fact one third) had been published in American magazines—the three I have named (you could name them.) My publishing over here was as it happened. I had come across to write rather than to publish. And it was too bad to use a tolerably good book in honest verse forms to grind axes on. Books have enough to contend against anyway.

You could say something like that to Sherman if you thought he would be likely to have been offended by the article in Poetry. Many have seen it and been offended. Do as you please. I leave The Sun and Times to your discretion. Sometimes it is better not to take arms against such misfortunes.

I am not quite heartbroken over the way it has gone in this matter. I have done what I have done and I believe I have made place enough for myself to be sure of a hearing for anything else I do. I ask no more. I should like now to go to a small college with the chance of teaching a few ideas or barring that I shall get me to a farm where between milking one cow and another I shall write Books III IV & V and perhaps draw a few people about me in time in a sort of summer literary camp. We will talk of this some day.[115]

Do you suppose it might be worth my while to sing myself to McCracken?[116] I am half inclined to try.

---

114. Stuart P. Sherman (1881–1926), professor of English at the University of Illinois, where Cox had studied; he published in *The Nation* and other important outlets.

115. RF would entertain ideas about a "summer literary camp" through 1915, as a number of letters show; see, e.g., his June 26, 1915, letter to Thomas, and his August 8, 1915, letter to Bartlett.

116. Henry Noble MacCracken (1880–1970), scholar of English literature and president of Vassar College from 1915 to 1946.

Write when you aren't too busy. I havent heard what proportion of good boys you have had to work with where you are.

Yours ever
R.F.

P.S.
We won't stir the Pound matter up I think. You can take what I have written as so much entertainment. If ever anyone gives you the chance in public or otherwhere—well you have the facts and you can use them. Pound sought me in every instance. He <u>asked</u> for the poem he speaks of and then failed to sell it. It was even worse than that. I had demanded the poem back when I learned the name of the magazine he was offering it to but he went ahead in spite of me. And then began our quarrel. I thought never to see him again. But when Book II came out he asked me for "copies" (plural) for reviews in such a way that I couldn't refuse to meet what looked like generosity half-way. It wouldnt do to go into this, but what I have written in the body of the letter you could use should I be attacked when Holt sends out copies for review. Of course it is quite possible that I exaggerate the importance of Pounds article. Let's hope so.

We think of home all the time.[117]

---

117. Following the letter are four pages from Ezra Pound's review of *ABW* in *Poetry*. RF singles out for comment these remarks on "In Neglect": "There is perhaps as much of Frost's personal tone in the following little catch, which is short enough to quote, as in anything else. It is to his wife, written when his grandfather and his uncle had disinherited him of a comfortable fortune and left him in poverty because he was a useless poet instead of a money-getter." RF strikes out the remarks about having been "disinherited" and adds a note: "I have scraped out some personalities (very private) which are not only in bad taste but also inaccurate." Highlighted also are two other passages: "David Nutt publishes at his own expense *A Boy's Will*, by Robert Frost, the latter having been long scorned by the 'great American editors,'" to which RF adds this note: "The author's surmise-inference from my sad look"; and "Mr. Frost's book is a little raw, and has in it a number of infelicities," to which, again, RF adds a note: "This is the superior person who objected to Trial by Existence."

[To John W. Haines, who supplied the year in a note on the manuscript. ALS/Photostat. DCL.]

Ryton Dymock
Jan 5 [1915]

Dear Haines

Good of you to ask me down, but I am afraid there is too much to think of at present. We are on the move at last after all the threats. Life is once more one grand uncertainty and I'd not be the one to lament the fact if I was sure I was well. But never mind—

I have got to make a flying visit north on business before I go home (if indeed I go, for all my mind is clouded with a doubt). Would you let me know at once if you can learn of any cheap fares this week to Edinburgh?—or if not this week not later than Tuesday next week.

It may be I can stay a day with you on my way back. I shan't be in Scotland more than a day or two.[118]

I will tell you more when I see you.

Till then I'm yours

R.F.

[To Edward Thomas (1878–1917), the English poet, essayist, biographer, and reviewer. This letter, together with two others to Thomas, were in the hands of the collector Howard George Schmitt, an acquaintance of RF's, when Thompson printed them in SL*. They have since gone missing; efforts to locate Schmitt's papers have been unsuccessful. The text given here is drawn from* SL*, 149–151. Dating from internal evidence (by February 2, RF had decided to sail on an American liner). It is not clear where RF was when he penned this letter, perhaps on his way back from Scotland.]*

[late January 1915]

Dear Thomas

Nothing but business this time. It's what I'm full of.

I wish you would ask one or two kinds of people before I see you if they think the American Liners much to be preferred for safety to any other in this crisis. My own idea is that there would be no special danger in sailing by

118. RF's purpose in making the trip was to see once again, before he left for America, his friend James Cruickshank Smith; the visit occurred sometime after January 22 (as letters from Smith to RF, held now at DCL, indicate).

a White Star Dominion Liner.[119] We should save money and get put down nearer where we wanted to. I'd not give the matter two thoughts if it wasnt for the children. Just throw out a feeler where you happen to.

Did I say that our day would be somewhere near the twentieth of February?[120] If you wrote Tuesday you should certainly have an answer by that time but with not many days to spare. As I understand it your best way will be to let me speak for a berth for Merfyn now.[121] You will have to put down a holding fee of two pounds and be prepared to lose it if Scott goes back on you. Authorise me to do it for you when I am in Gloucester seeing about our berths.

I have just stumbled onto a difficulty which, however, I think can be got over. If Merfyn were going with one of his parents he could be as young as he saw any object in being. Since he is sailing without either of them he should appear as sixteen years old in the manifest. So I am told. I dont know what there is in it. I will enquire further. You might see what you can find out by writing to the American Consulate in London. Say you are sending a son to —— Scott in America to be educated. Say who you are and who I am that he is going with. Ask if he would better have a passport. Say he may be staying a matter of a year or two and leave it to the consul to mention ages if he likes to. Hurry this up.

Can you hold off your visit till Saturday? We are not sure to be at Ledington till Friday late. Elinor is tired to begin with so I don't suppose we can hope to do our packing in less than several days. Let me know what train.

Great to see you again. There's a lot to say.

We had long talks with Miss Farjeon.[122] Seldom I have such a chance to expand. I should like to think I hadnt bored her with First Principles.—Oh and by the way let her know that Wilfrid has been here fondling me, but saying cruel things about Viola Meynell for having used my poem where it

---

119. The White Star-Dominion Line was British owned and based in Liverpool.

120. The Frosts sailed on February 13.

121. Accompanying the Frost family back to the United States was Thomas's fifteen-year-old son Mervyn, who would live, while in America, under the care of Russell Scott of Alstead, New Hampshire (a relative of Thomas's, mentioned here). As of this date Thomas himself was considering emigrating to America to live near RF, where the two planned to start a kind of writer's colony (a "summer literary camp," as RF speaks of it in a January 2, 1915, letter to Cox).

122. Eleanor Farjeon (1881–1965), English poet and author of children's books; she was close to Edward Thomas and his wife, Helen.

doesnt fit.[123] He happens to have her book for review. He will slate her. He spoke with peculiar animus that I had no right to understand yet thought I did understand. Bless it all.

Oh and one more thing. I figure it this way.

From Liverpool to Portland or Boston

(second class) 11 £

From London to Liverpool——

From Portland or Boston to Keene (direct) 12 S

Inci- and accidentals ! £

Yours ever
R.F.

[To John W. Haines. Dating from internal evidence, and from a note in Haines's hand: "rec'd Feb 3rd 1915." Oldfields is the farm owned by John and Mary Chandler (see RF's June 1914 letter to Mary Gardner). ALS/Photostat. DCL.]

Oldfields Ledington
Ledbury
[late January 1915]

Dear Haines

All is so good of you; but much as we should like to be near you for a few days before we go, we don't see how it is possible.[124] We are giving away furniture for our rent here and couldnt save anything by shortening our stay to make up the extra expense at Gloucester. Thirty shillings looks large compared to next to nothing. And then there would be etcets—extra fares and pay for service.

I cant help being glad I decided to use the protection of our flag.[125] I must see you somehow before I go. This is no letter. I will write more when I have things arranged more to my satisfaction.

Yours ever
Robert Frost.

---

123. "The Pasture." See RF to Cox, February 2, 1915.

124. Haines penciled in a note at the foot of the letter: "As a matter of fact he came and brought Lesley for a night or two."

125. RF had booked passage on the United States Mail Steamer *St. Paul*, operated by the Philadelphia-based American Line.

[To Sidney Cox. ALS. DCL.]

Herefordshire England
Feb 2 1915

Dear Cox

No more letters here please. We sail for home by the St Paul from Liverpool Feb 13. If you want to be first to welcome us you can drop us a line on that c/o the American Line New York. I should think it might reach us. Be sure to name the boat and her date of sailing. I shall inquire for a letter.

You and I wont believe that Gibson's is a better kind of poetry than mine. Solway Ford is one of his best.[126] It is a good poem. But it is oh terribly made up. You know very well that at most all he had to go on was some tale he had heard of a man who had gone mad from fear and another of a man who had been pinned and overtaken by the tide in Solway. I am even inclined to think he invented the latter. It hardly sounds plausible. The details of what he asks you to believe his hallucinations were all poetical, but not very convincing. And then look at the way the sentences run on. They are not sentences at all in my sense of the word. The sentence is everything—the sentence well imagined. See the beautiful sentences in a thing like Wordsworth's To Sleep or Herrick's To Daffodils.[127]

Remember, a certain fixed number of sentences (sentence sounds) belong to the human throat just as a certain fixed number of vocal runs belong to the throat of a given kind of bird. These are fixed I say. Imagination cannot create them. It can only call them up. It can only call them up for those who write with their ear on the speaking voice. We will prove it out of the Golden Treasury someday.

Current Opinion was kind. I have to thank you for so much notice in America. There was a grudging note that I suppose didnt escape you. Never

---

126. "Solway Ford" was first collected in Wilfrid Gibson's 1914 volume *Thoroughfares*.

127. See also RF's remarks in "The Constant Symbol" (1946): "The poet goes in like a rope skipper to make the most of his opportunities. If he trips himself he stops the rope. He is of our stock and has been brought up by ear to choice of two metres, strict iambic and loose iambic (not to count varieties of the latter). He may have any length of line up to six feet. He may use an assortment of line lengths for any shape of stanza, like Herrick in 'To Daffodils'" (*CPRF*, 149).

mind. The book is epoch making. I dont ask anyone to say so. All I ask now is to be allowed to live.[128]

You have been splendid. Poetry needs just the kind of help you are giving me.

I wish you and your friend could be in places near me next summer.

I do this in a hurry. Don't expect to hear again till I send you a card from the boat.

Bluffers are the curse. I sometimes have my doubts of all the High Schools together. Your German friend[129] is probably a sceptic as regards the higher education of the masses. I am not really with him: at the same time—

Yours ever
Frost

Words are only valuable in writing as they serve to indicate particular sentence sounds. I must say some things over and over. I must be a little extravagant too.

For goodbye The Nation named N.O.B. among the four best books of verse for 1914 and Viola Meynell used the Pasture poem to introduce her latest novel Columbine.[130] I wish Sheffauer [*sic*] might have seen N.O.B. It seems more in his line than Book I.[131]

---

128. The January 1915 number of *Current Opinion* printed a note on *NB:* "'North of Boston' is a unique and interesting piece of work; but we are not prepared to call it epoch-making. It is very simple narrative verse, for the most part unrhymed, dealing with rural scenes and characters in a most convincing way. Most of the poems are too long to reprint here. We must content ourselves with one of the shortest, but one which is included by *The English Review* in the list of what it calls 'masterpieces of deep and mysterious tenderness'" (54); whereupon follows the text of "The Woodpile."

129. Alex Bloch, a German schoolteacher then living in America.

130. Viola Meynell Dallyn (1885–1956), English novelist and poet. The London firm of Martin Secker published her *Columbine* in 1915 bearing, as epigraph, "The Pasture" (the poem that opens *NB*).

131. Robert Haven Schauffler (1879–1964), anthologist, critic, and (as Evans points out in *RFSC*) a correspondent of Cox's.

[To Ernest L. Silver. ALS. Plymouth.]

Herefordshire England
Feb 2 1915

Dear Silver

We <u>had</u> thought of going north of Plymouth to a hay feverless altitude and of going north west to be near new friends in Stowe Vermont and of going to South Berwick Maine to be near old friends who have lately gone there from New York to settle down in their old age.[132] But money is really going to be short and we must go where we can go with a reasonable chance of making ends meet. I may even have to look for a salary or a half salary somewhere as I told you. Still I should like to hear more of your plan for developing the farm at the Lake. I wish it were in the mountains and I wish it were nearer schools. We can talk it over when I see you. I oughtn't to commit myself to anything at this distance.

We sail by the St. Paul from Liverpool on Feb 13 the Kaiser permitting. We dont like that man's submarines we dont like his mines and we dont like what we can learn of the man himself. I shall feel easier when I am as far from him as 1000 miles west of Ireland. He hasnt troubled me till within the last few days except as a man troubles you with his ideas. That can be a great deal. I doubt if most Americans care as much as I do what philosophy Germans hold. I have always found their latter-day philosophy terribly provocative and more startling than anything they have done in the teeth of God and man in this war.[133] It prepared me for all this rather absurd "frightfulness" and discounted it in a way, if it didnt quite prepare me to find that all Germans were soldiers to the back bone. I couldn't realize that it had gone into the lives of a whole nation. It must be a great and profound philosophy to have done that. I have a kind of respect for it, but as an American (as an American mind you) I hate it and fear it and defy it.

So I might rail on. Shall I have to wear a muzzle when I get home to keep the peace with pro German Yankees? I gather that there are such things. I

---

132. The Henry Holt family (RF's new American publishers) had a home in Stowe, Vermont. William Hayes Ward and his sister, Susan, had retired to their family home in South Berwick, Maine, in 1914.

133. See RF's September 17, 1914, letter to Cox.

think of poor old Clade (of Derry). But he wasn't a pro-German Yankee so much as a prohibition German.[134]

Your politics fresh from Concord stir something in me that I must inherit from a politician father.[135] You doubtless wrote from the Eagle Hotel where politicians are made and unmade.[136] I hope you get your appropriation if you have to take it out of Fairchilds salary.[137] Mrs Master Adams ought to be in a book.[138] Someone told me the other day that the Plymouth Normal School was beating New England. It seems as if you ought not to be denied money to go on with.

I infer from your letter that you think you might harbor us somehow in Plymouth for a day or several days if you knew when we were coming. Will you drop me a line to say whether I infer aright? Dont address me here of course. I should think a letter to me as "on the St Paul sailing from Liverpool Feb 13 c/o The American Line New York City" might reach us.

Thanks for that missive from mine ancient enemy The Atlantic. It seems she has not relented, and it seems she remembers my American address.[139]

I knew Miss Griffin could. I told Brown he wanted her for Colebrook.[140]

Sincerely yours,
Frost

---

134. Frank C. Clade, born in Germany in 1864 but listed as a resident of Derry, New Hampshire, in the 1910 census.

135. William Prescott Frost (1850–1885), the poet's father, was active in Democratic Party politics in San Francisco until his death from tuberculosis. He was part of the California delegation to the National Democratic Convention in Cincinnati, which, in June 1880, nominated General Winfield Scott Hancock for president.

136. The Eagle Hotel, in Concord, New Hampshire, was built in 1827, and is now listed on the National Register of Historic Places.

137. Edward Thomson Fairchild (1854–1917), third president of the New Hampshire College of Agriculture and Mechanical Arts in Durham, New Hampshire, from 1912 to January 23, 1917, when he died in office. Silver had been out hunting up funds for the state Normal School.

138. We have been unable to identify this apparently memorable woman.

139. RF refers more particularly to Ellery Sedgwick, editor of *The Atlantic*. When RF submitted several poems to the magazine in 1914, Sedgwick replied with a terse note, "We are sorry that we have no place in the *Atlantic Monthly* for your vigorous verse" (*YT*, 12).

140. Harry Alvin Brown. See RF to Brown, January 7, 1913. Phila May Griffin (1892–1976) graduated from Plymouth Normal School in 1913. She joined the faculty in 1915 (see the *Plymouth Prospect* 10, no. 1, 23). After leaving Plymouth, she had a long career as a supervisor for the New Hampshire Bureau of Education.

[To Ernest Leroy Silver. Marie Hodge was a preceptress at the Normal School. ALS. DCL.]

England Feb 5 1915

Dear Silver

Elinor is afraid the prosal [*sic*] in your letter was to get the cottage ready for us to stay in for some time. You mustnt do that or in any way put yourself about. I took it that you had in mind some provision for us in the old dormitory where, as it isnt fire proof, you must have rooms to burn now that the other one is built. Less than two or three smoke-talks wont be enough to show you how well I have learned to smoke a cigarette in England. I shall be glad if you will invite us to stay a few days in Plymouth. In fact I can see that I shant feel as if I had come home unless you do. Afterward we can go on to Bethlehem where there has always been a refuge for us these ten years.[141] Generous of you to ask us to the cottage if that was your idea.

I wish I had this family safely across. Hope the best for us and tell Mrs Hodge to do the same.

Sincerely yours
Frost.

[To John W. Haines. Dating derived from internal evidence, and from a note in Haines's hand: "rec'd Feb 10 1915." Petersfield, where Edward Thomas resided, is some seventeen miles north of Portsmouth and sixty miles southwest of London on the railway. ALS/Photostat. DCL.]

Steep Petersfield
[circa February 9, 1915]

Dear Haines

I came down to London on business and thought I would run out here to see what Thomas would say to coming down for next week if we could get our boat changed and stay over till Feb 20.[142] All things considered though we doubt if it would be wise to put off the evil day. The Germans have only a little to do with our decision. I will tell you more about it when I see you.

141. The Frosts had often summered (while living in Derry) with the John and Margaret Lynch family in Bethlehem, New Hampshire.

142. See RF to Thomas, circa February 1, 1915; the visit he mentions here is first referred to there.

The only suggestion I now have to offer is that you might find a way to entertain us Thursday night and perhaps Friday. We may think it best to get to Liverpool Friday for fear of missing the boat by delays on the railroad. Excuse all this confusion in plans.

Thomas is sorry we couldnt have a few days all together: he asks to be remembered.

My best to you both.

Yours ever
R.F.

[To F. S. Flint. The letter wasn't posted; see RF to Flint, August 24, 1916. ALS. HRC.]

[February 13, 1915[143]]
U.S.M.S. "St Paul"

Dear Flint

I ought to know by the length of your silence that you dont want to write to me any more—cor silicis.[144] And if you don't I ought to have pride enough not to ask you to. But no matter: I must at least say goodbye to the man who opened England to me. You are good.

Sincerely yours
Frost

[To Harold Monro. The letter is undated, but "Feb 15th" is written in the upper left in another hand and "answered Feb 18th" in the lower left. ALS. Trinity.]

[Liverpool]
[circa February 13, 1915]

Dear Monro

This with my best goodbyes and thanks for everything. I had intended to see you before leaving. But at the last moment we go rather precipitately; so that I am scanting duties. Anyway I don't want too much made of my going

143. On this date the Frosts set sail from Liverpool, bound for New York.

144. *Cor silicis* is Latin for "heart of stone," or, as is more likely here, "flinty heart"; RF is making a cross-linguistic pun, as the noun inflection *silex* (we thank Yu Onuma for advice here) can mean, in Latin, "flint," as it does also in English.

or I should feel as if I were never coming back. I shall be back just as soon as I have earned a little more living. England has become half my native land—England the victorious. Good friends I've had here and hope to keep.

Yours ever
Robert Frost

Robert and Elinor Frost with their children (Lesley, Irma, Carol, and Marjorie, clockwise from upper left) at Bridgewater, New Hampshire, 1915.

Courtesy Plymouth State University.

Making It in America

February 1915–December 1917

Forgive me my nonsense as I also forgive the nonsense of those who think they talk sense. All I insist on is that nothing is quite honest that is not commercial. You must take that as said in character. Of course I dont mean by that that it isnt true.

—Robert Frost to Louis Untermeyer, July 8, 1915

[To Lesley, Carol, Irma, and Marjorie Frost. The letter is undated, but a note in the archive in Lesley Frost's hand indicates that it was written in "Feb. 1915—to the family in Bethlehem [New Hampshire]." Mervyn Thomas, the fifteen-year-old son of Edward and Helen Thomas, accompanied the Frosts to the United States, where he was to reside in New Hampshire. Complications in the immigration process, owing to his status as a minor, resulted in Mervyn's being held at Ellis Island until RF could provide evidence of suitable arrangements. ALS. UVA.]

[New York, NY]
[February 1915]

Dear Kids

This is where Merfyn suffered imprisonment for five days and got acquainted with the scum of the earth while I got acquainted with a poet who wrote a poem called Scum of the Earth.[1] Poor Merfyn had to be all alone most of the time and he was in the realist danger of being sent straight back in the boat he came by. There was one man down there who shot himself while we were there rather than be sent back. And there were mad people and sad people and bad people in the detention rooms. I don't know how I ever got Merfyn out of it. What a liar that American consul in London was to say Merfyn would come in all right. He came in all wrong.

Papa

---

1. While in New York, RF met Robert Haven Schauffler (1879–1964), who had published "Scum o' the Earth," a poem sympathetic to the plight of poor immigrants, in 1911.

[To Ernest Jewell, a former high school classmate of the poet's. In an unpublished chronology held now at UVA, Lawrance Thompson reports that on this date RF had lunch with Alfred Harcourt and the editors of The New Republic. *ALS (on Hotel Chelsea letterhead). UFL.]*

Feb 24 1915
[Hotel Chelsea, NY]

Dear Jewell

Here I be. And I shall be nearer still in a few days. I hope you want to see me as much as I look forward to seeing you. There are some new friends to be dealt with before I can leave New York and then for old friends and the region "North of Boston." I have come right in on them talking about my book and of course the temptation is too much not to stay and listen to my own praises (and dispraises). Amy Lowell starts the critical ball with three columns in The New Republic for Feb 20.[2] The Holts are doing all sorts of things for me. I seem to have made even a little stir. But never mind, it will be over by and by.

I had your letter with the distressing story of how you had been torn as a family. I thought as I was soon to talk with you in person, there was not much need of writing. I was sorry for you—and I understood.

I wonder if you can take care of me for a day or two when I get to Lawrence. I think I will chance it. There is hardly time for you to write to me here.

Sincerely yours
Robert Frost

[To Sidney Cox. ALS. DCL.]

March 2 1915

Dear Cox

Your letter was the first thing I read in America. In fact I read it before I was in America that's to say before I passed quarantine. You are always encouraging.

I wish I could afford to visit you at Scenectady [*sic*] and see you first and then anyone else you cared to bring along.

---

2. Amy Lowell, "North of Boston," *New Republic*, February 20, 1915, 81–82.

I ran spank on to your Shauffler[3] (pronounced Shoffler) in New York and made him a friend. I think we can like each other despite the irreconcilability of what we write. You must meet him.

You know that the Holts have my book out. Pretty cover. But the best of the Holts is that they are going to be a father to me.

Did you see what Amy Lowell had to say in the New Republic for Feb 20. She will pervert me a little to her theory, but never mind.[4]

I am on the way to Bethlehem New Hampshire. Write to me there in care of John Lynch.[5] I wish we might be near you in the summer somehow. More of my plans when I know more of them myself.

Allers yours
R.F.

[To Sidney Cox. ALS. DCL.]

Littleton NH
March 13 1915

Dear Cox

Write to me as soon as you can to say you got my letter from New York and understood my reasons for not going to Schnectady [*sic*]. I was aching to see you and almost hoped you would propose coming to us. You have a salary and can go and come as you please. When I got to Lawrence where I could ask for money[6] (and might or might not get it) I had less than fifty cents left in my pocket. You can read Browning's Up at the Villa for a

3. See RF's February 2, 1915, letter to Cox.

4. Such theories as Lowell set out in her (unsigned) preface to the 1915 anthology *Some Imagist Poets* (Boston: Houghton Mifflin), which would appear in April.

5. The Frost family had known John and Margaret Lynch since their Derry years, when they occasionally vacationed at the farm the Lynches owned near Bethlehem, New Hampshire.

6. From Wilbur E. Rowell, executor of his paternal grandfather's estate. Lawrance Thompson reports that RF received an advance on his $800 annuity in the amount of $200 (*YT*, 11).

proper statement of why a man of my means might live in the country.[7] As a matter of fact I like the country and might live there all the time of choice. At the present moment however I must live there of necessity. I am not rich enough to live even for a few weeks in the style you suggested in Schnectady [*sic*].

I didn't get through New York and Boston without more attention than you may think I deserve from my fellow countrymen. The Holts are splendid. If you want to see what happened in Boston, look me up in the Boston Herald for Tuesday March 9 under the heading Talk of the Town. A number of my old editorial enemies actually asked me for poems. Let us weep before it is too late.

Yours ever
R.F.

Address
R.F.D. No 5
c/o John Lynch
Littleton
NH

---

7. See Robert Browning, "Up at a Villa—Down in the City":

Had I but plenty of money, money enough and to spare,
The house for me, no doubt, were a house in the city-square;
Ah, such a life, such a life, as one leads at the window there!

Something to see, by Bacchus, something to hear, at least!
There, the whole day long, one's life is a perfect feast;
While up at a villa one lives, I maintain it, no more than a beast.

Well now, look at our villa! stuck like the horn of a bull
Just on a mountain-edge as bare as the creature's skull,
Save a mere shag of a bush with hardly a leaf to pull!
—I scratch my own, sometimes, to see if the hair's turned wool.

[To Albert Shaw (1857–1947), an American journalist, author of a number of works about international law and political institutions, and editor-in-chief of the American edition of Review of Reviews *from 1891 until 1937. RF refers to Sylvester Baxter, whose profile of him appeared in the April 1915 issue of the* Review of Reviews, *and who had requested that RF send a photograph to Shaw for use with the article. ALS. NYPL.]*

Littleton N.H.
March 15 [1915]

Dr Albert Shaw
Irving Place
New York

Dear Sir

My new-found friend Baxter wires me to hurry this forward to go with the personal notice you are so kindly giving me in The Review. I am greatly obliged to both of you for your interest in my work.

Sincerely yours
Robert Frost

[To Lascelles Abercrombie. ALS. Jones.]

Littleton New Hampshire
U.S.A.
R.F.D. No 5
March 15 [1915]

Dear Abercrombie

That was a good shove you gave us in going and it lasted us till we ran bang into an inspector at the gangway in Liverpool who was for keeping us in England till our greatness ripened a little more. Very well says I, maybe you know more about what's good for me than I do myself. I like England and I'm willing to stay if someone else will take the responsibility. But I give you fair warning: if I dont go now I wont go at all. I shall become a British subject and "run for" the Laureateship. That seemed to make him think. He let us go on board—muttering.

We withheld our speed and didnt sail till dark; and we had when we did sail two battleships with us all down the Irish Sea—to pick us up I suppose if we got into the water for any reason. But we didn't get undermined and we didnt get torpedoed—else you would have heard of it before this. We got kicked about a good deal for nine whole days and seasickened and discouraged from ever crossing again.

Then we came to New York and were hailed by one or two intelligent people as a poet and family. In the excitement of the moment I made two or three promises that I cant fulfill unless you send me two or three copies of the New Number containing The End of the World because I can't afford to buy them and I'm no longer living at The Gallows where I can steal them.[8]

If I forget England! My thanks for all you did to make her what she is to me. Now go ahead and win the war.

My love to you all and especially to the little boy I taught while he was young and there was yet time, a way to make a big splash with a small object and a small splash with a large object. Ask him if he remembers.

Let me know how your plans for coming over are coming on.

Yours ever
Robert Frost

[To William Stanley Braithwaite (1878–1962), poet, anthologist, and literary editor of the Boston Evening Transcript. *ALS. Middlebury.]*

Littleton N.H.
R.F.D No 5
March 22 [1915]

Dear Mr Braithwaite:

Ive got as far as finding you the copy of Book I I promised you. Perhaps as a busy man you wont resent my telling you what to read in it if you are going to read at all. It is the list I always give to friends I wish the minimum of suffering: pages 1, 2, 4, 7, 9, 14, 20, 22, 23, 25, 26, 34, 41, 42 (once printed in The Transcript) 45, 46 (8–18 line [*sic*]—first poetry I ever wrote that I could call my own—year 1892) and 49.[9] Don't read those unless you have to, but don't read the others on any account.

---

8. Abercrombie's play, "The End of the World," appeared in *New Numbers* in 1914. His house in Ledbury, at which the Frosts had stayed, was called The Gallows.

9. Given the pagination, RF had sent Braithwaite a copy of the first English edition of *ABW*. He identifies "Now Close the Windows" as having been printed in the *Transcript*

The book is an expression of my life for the ten years from eighteen on when I thought I greatly preferred stocks and stones to people. The poems were written as I lived the life quite at the mercy of myself and not always happy. The arrangement in a book came much later when I could look back on the past with something like understanding.

I kept farm, so to speak for nearly ten years, but less as a farmer than as a fugitive from the world that seemed to me to "disallow" me. It was all instinctive, but I can see now that I went away to save myself and fix myself before I measured my strength against all creation. I was never really out of the world for good and all. I liked people even when I believed I detested them.

It would seem absurd to say it (and you mustn't quote me as saying it) but I suppose the fact is that my conscious interest in people was at first no more than an almost technical interest in their speech—in what I used to call their sentence sounds—the sound of sense. Whatever these sounds are or aren't (they are certainly not of the vowels and consonants of words nor even of the words themselves but something the words are chiefly a kind of notation for indicating and fastening to the printed page) whatever they are, I say, I began to hang on them very young. I was under twenty when I deliberately put it to myself one night after good conversation that there are moments when we actually touch in talk what the best writing can only come near. The curse of our book language is not so much that it keeps forever to the same set phrases (though Heaven knows those are bad enough) but that it sounds forever with the same reading tones. We must go out into the vernacular for tones that havent been brought to book. We must write with the ear on the speaking voice. We must imagine the speaking voice.

I say all this biographically to lead up to Book II (North of Boston). There came a day about ten years ago when I made the discovery that though sequestered I wasnt living without reference to other people. Right on top of that I made the discovery in doing The Death of the Hired Man that I was interested in neighbors for more than merely their tones of speech—and always

---

and lines 8–18 of "My Butterfly" as the first poetry he could call his own. His recommendations for reading are: "Into My Own" (page 1), "Ghost House" (2), "My November Guest" (4), "A Late Walk" (7), "Storm Fear" (9), "Flower Gathering" (14), "In a Vale" (20), "A Dream Pang" (22), "In Neglect" (23), "Mowing" (25), "Going for Water" (26), "The Tuft of Flowers" (34), "The Demiurge's Laugh" (41), "Now Close the Windows" (42), "October" (45), "My Butterfly" (46), "Reluctance" (49).

had been. I remember about when I began to suspect myself of liking their gossip for its own sake. I justified myself by the example of Napoleon[10] as recently I have had to justify myself in seasickness by the example of Nelson.

I like the actuality of gossip, the intimacy of it. Say what you will effects of actuality and intimacy are the greatest aim an artist can have. The sense of intimacy gives the thrill of sincerity. A story must always release a meaning more readily to those who read than life itself as it goes ever releases meaning. Meaning is a great consideration. But a story must never seem to be told primarily for meaning. Anything, an inspired irrelevancy even to make it sound as if told the way it is chiefly because it happened that way.

I have run on unpardonably. I couldnt write a whole biography; so I just had to plunge into the middle of things. I have pretty well jumbled the story of how I see my own development and some of my theories of art. You are not going to use anything directly, I take it. You will be sure to veil what is too personal. This isn't quite the same as an interview. I have met you and now we are getting further in getting acquainted.[11]

Ask me for anything I don't think to supply for your newspaper article.[12] Probably you want a few dates and data.

I was born in San Francisco forty years ago.[13] My father was an editor out there. He died when I was young.

I went to the public schools in Lawrence Mass. I was married there.

My farm was in Derry, New Hampshire.

I taught literature at Pinkerton Academy, Derry, and psychology at the Normal School, Plymouth for the five years before I went to England.

In England I saw a good deal of two or three literary circles in London for a year or two and then went down into Gloucestershire and Herefordshire for another year. I never saw <u>New</u> England as clearly as when I was in Old England.

Just to show you that the interest in my work over there was partly on the technical side or where the material shades off into the technical I enclose a

10. RF may have in mind a passage from Emerson's essay on Napoleon in *Representative Men:* "He cheated at cards; he was a prodigious gossip and opened letters and delighted in his information police."

11. Nathan Haskell Dole introduced the two men on March 5, 1915, while RF was in Boston.

12. Braithwaite's "A Poet of New England: Robert Frost, a New Exponent of Life" appeared in the *Boston Evening Transcript*, April 28, 1915 (part 3), 4.

13. For many years RF believed that he had been born in 1875 rather than 1874.

circular my English publisher got out. The quotation from The Nation was used by The Listener in The Transcript (July 8)[14]

No more of this.

May I hope really to see something of you when I am in Boston again? I'd like to have a talk about poetry by ourselves alone.

Sincerely yours
Robert Frost.

[To Le Roy Phillips (1870–?), a Boston publisher, editor, critic and playwright. Frith Street, where T. E. Hulme often hosted the literary salon to which RF likely refers here, is in London. ALS. BU.]

Littleton NH
March 22 1915

Dear Mr Phillips

Someone tells me you have been remembering the night I met you in Frith St a long way from here. With no more pleasure I'm sure than I remember it with. "Hereafter in a better world than that"—how goes the quotation?[15]

Sincerely yours
Robert Frost

[To Thomas Bird Mosher. ALS. UVA.]

Littleton N.H.
March 22 1915

My dear Mosher:

Your letter finds me. I am back on our side again. To think that I should have been as near you as lunching at the same club at the same hour and not known it. And with the last letter I had from you at The Gallows, Ryton, Dymock, Gloucestershire, England in my pocket. About Pound!

You are often in Boston I suppose. I shall hope to get down around the first of April, but if I can't how about the first of May? I believe I am to read a

---

14. The Listener, a regular column in the *Boston Evening Transcript*, quoted at length from Lascelles Abercrombie's June 13, 1914, review of *NB* in *The Nation* (London).

15. RF adapts *As You Like It*: "Hereafter, in a better world than this, / I shall desire more love and knowledge of you" (1.ii.273–274).

poem to someone on the fifth of May.[16] And the someone will of course have to pay my fare. So that I can go with a clear conscience then.

This correspondence must not be allowed to proceed much further before we have met.

Sincerely yours
Robert Frost

[To Louis Untermeyer (1885–1977), American poet, anthologist, critic, and editor. ALS. LoC.]

Littleton N.H.
March 22 1915

Dear Mr Untermeyer:

What must you think of a silence as long as this to a letter as good as that? But let me tell you by way of what places the letter has just reached me: the office of The New Republic, the office of Henry Holt, South Fork Penna., Wildwood N.J. and Philadelphia. Such is the fact though I cant prove it by the envelope which has been travelling some of the time in other envelopes.

Your cordiality is especially warming. There's not a person in New York I should have had more pleasure in meeting than Louis Untermeyer. For I was already feeling a good deal acquainted with you from having heard your name so often mentioned under a certain thatch roof in Ryton Dymock Gloucestershire England.

You make me wonder if I hadn't better get back to New York in a month or two. I can just see and hear myself having a good time with you somewhere where there's not too much noise of the city. I could tell you a lot about Abercrombie.

You are all too good about "North of Boston."[17]

Sincerely yours,
Robert Frost

16. On May 5, 1915, RF addressed a luncheon meeting of the Boston Author's Club; later in the day he read before the Phi Beta Kappa Society at Tufts College, delivering three unpublished poems, "Birches," "The Road Not Taken," and "The Sound of Trees" (all of which were collected the next year in *MI*). He spent the night in Medford, Massachusetts, with Tufts Professor Charles E. Fay (see *CPRF*, 170).

17. Untermeyer would soon publish a review of the book in the *Chicago Evening Post* (April 23, 1915, 11).

You weren't thinking of coming to Boston in May, were you? I believe I am expected there somewhere round the fifth.[18]

R.F.

[To Sidney Cox. ALS. DCL.]

Littleton N.H.
R.F.D. No 5
March 22 1915

Dear Cox

Of course you wouldn't be anything so petty as miffed. But you might be honestly hurt or disappointed if you weren't given thoroughly to understand.

Dont worry too much about my money difficulties. Some time I will tell you exactly how it is I can be down to my last shilling and yet in no immediate danger of coming on the town. I am always more or less in trouble but it wont be for five years or so that I'll be in jail or the poor house. My only hope in those days will be my children or such of them as think well of me—don't judge me too hardly for having written poetry. There's Marj—she told Mrs Lynch,[19] I'm told, that I was a good one to write poetry and to bring up children. She's very likely wrong, but as long as she believes what she says—

And a word more to you my son. You are to dispense with further talk of disparity between us. I have never had such thoughts and I dislike having them thrust upon me.

Thus shamelessly I send you the Herald scrap.[20] If the fellow who wrote it seems to know more of my goings and comings than he could without complicity of mine, the reason is because he is a lovely old boy and quite took

18. See the notes to RF's March 22, 1915, letter to Mosher.

19. See the notes to RF's March 2, 1915, letter to Cox. "Marj" is RF's youngest daughter, Marjorie.

20. Nathan Haskell Dole (the fellow who "quite took possession" of RF) published an article on RF in the *Boston Herald* on March 9, 1915, in its Talk of the Town column that begins: "Boston's literary sensation of the day has been the homecoming of Robert Frost. Three years ago a young New Hampshire schoolmaster went over to England, lived in retirement for a while, and published a volume of poems which won him many friends in a quiet way. Some time ago another volume of verse went to the same publisher and one morning Robert Frost found himself famous. His work was hailed as a striking new note in modern poetry."

possession of me while I was in Boston. When he wasnt actually with me like Mary's lamb he was keeping track of me by telephone. I believe he is doing for me on principles. He's got me on his conscience. The Ellery Sedgwick of the piece is mine ancient enemy the editor of the Atlantic.[21]

Yours ever
Robert Frost.

[To Nathan Haskell Dole (1852–1935), a journalist and poet, descended from an illustrious New England family that included missionaries, abolitionists, painters, and clergymen. ALS. Harvard.]

Littleton N.H.
March 26 1915

Dear Dole

Do it some more in red ink. You write well in any ink or in pencil for anything I know to the contrary: but if this letter is a fair sample and if I am any judge you are at your best and truthfullest in red ink.

I am slow to recover from the awful dazing you gave me in Boston. I was afraid my special pertness was never coming back. I sat on the edge of the bed for days together rubbing my eyes and (yawning I was going to say but no) crying at intervals like Balaam mourning for her children, "The cuss is all gone out of me!"[22]

Possibly it is. I shall know better when I have made up the rest of my lost sleep. At my age a fellow forgets kindness and shakes off obligations with the greatest difficulty. Still it can't be I am going to let myself sink under benefactions at the age of forty. I shall yet manage to do something I owe it to my friends and relatives not to do.

Perhaps reading to the Phi Beta Kappa is the thing.[23] That should get me into sufficient trouble to make me feel at home. You know I can't read. Why would you put temptation in my way? For I suppose you did it.

---

21. See the notes to RF's February 2, 1915, letter to Silver.

22. See Numbers 24:10: "And Balak's anger was kindled against Balaam, and he smote his hands together: and Balak said unto Balaam, I called thee to curse mine enemies, and, behold, thou hast altogether blessed them these three times."

23. At Tufts College on May 5.

Another experience I cant seem to get over is Ellis Island. I dreamed last night that I had to pass a written examination in order to pass the inspection there. There were two questions set me.

1. Who in Hell do you think you are?
2. How much do one and one make?

Note. Candidates are advised to use influence in passing inspection. They are warned that if they think they are Christ or Napoleon or a poet they will do well not to say so if they dont want to be deported as of unsound unsounded and unfathomable mind. They are warned also against any levity in their answer to the second question. It will count heavily against them in the highest official circles if they try to get round the difficulty by answering that one and one if they are of opposite and conflicting sexes may produce a dozen.

When I dream at all, I always dream good sense.

Sometime I will read your Rose of the Kennebec and glad of the chance.[24]

We have these mountains pretty much to ourselves at this time of year.

In May I shall probably be seeing you again.

My wife is sure I will forget to thank you for the good coffee.

My best to all your household.

Yours ever
Robert Frost

This is my birthday.

[To Ernest LeRoy Silver. No year is given, but 1915 seems likely given the heading "Littleton, N.H." ALS. DCL.]

Littleton N.H.
March 26 [1915]

Dear Silver:

You gave me a good time in Plymouth and now you give me a flattering description of the little I gave in return. Double thanks.

24. Dole descended from a New England family that traced its roots back to the Kennebec Valley in Maine. No book by the name "Rose of the Kennebec" appears among Dole's scores of published works, nor does a poem by that name appear in his major collections of verse.

Hope you got your pedagogy renovated by the kid-glove contingent at the institute.

May you grow in proficiency at the billiard table!

Yours ever
Robert Frost

Letters addressed to Littleton get me sooner than Bethlehem.

[To John Bartlett. The letter is dated only "April" but internal evidence suggests April 1915. The manuscript is badly blotted, faded, and torn; speculative readings are enclosed in brackets. ALS. UVA.]

Littleton NH[25]
April [1915]

Dear John

There seems nothing to talk about on my side but the wearing subject of the fortunes of my book. Some day there will be an end of that. You cant wonder that it is a good deal on my mind with a review appearing every few days and letters coming in from all quarters. I wish I could describe the state I have been thrown into. I suppose you could call it one of pleasurable scorn when it is not one of scornful scorn. The thought that gets me is that at magazine rates there is about a thousand dollars worth of poetry in N.O.B.[26] that I might have had last winter if the people who love me now had loved me then. Never you doubt that I gave them the chance to love me. What, you ask, has come over them to change their opinion of me? And the answer is What?—Doubtless you saw me noble countenance[27] displayed in The Herald Saturday. The Transcript will deal with me next. The literary editor of The Chicago Post writes to say that I may look for two columns of loving

25. In an unpublished chronology held at UVA, Lawrance Thompson reports that from March 9 to May 3, 1915, RF was "in Bethlehem [New Hampshire] and environs, trying to buy a farm." Littleton, from which RF posted this letter, lies a few miles northwest of Bethlehem. The Frosts ultimately bought a farm in nearby Franconia.

26. Henry Holt and Company issued the first American edition of *NB* on February 20, 1915, some three days before the Frosts sailed into New York Harbor.

27. The word "phony" appears to have been inserted interlineally above "countenance."

kindness in The Post in a day or two.[28] It is not just naught—say what you will. One likes best to write poetry and one knows that one did that before one got one[29] reputation. Still one can't pretend not to like to win the game. One can't help thinking a little of Number One.

I couldn't or wouldn't go into all this with anyone else as I am inclined to go into it with you. I feel as if it couldnt hurt you (who are no fool) and may even do you some good. I want you to see young what a thing it is. Not that I'm on exhibition as a very terrible example—more as an amusing an edifying example. I don't say that anyone should actually be warned to avoid my mistakes. But there they are for anyone to avoid who likes to and knows how to.

You alone of my American friends havent wished me a pot of money out of my poetry. Is it because you are too wise or because you have too good taste or because you are too unworldly to have thought of it. And yet I need money even as I suspect you may yourself.

Are you saving your talk of plans for when I am South [along] in a week or two? Say any [tentative] thing that comes into your head without fear of being held to it by me—write it I mean. It will give me something to think of.

Affectionately
RF

[To George Herbert Palmer (1842–1933), who by this date had retired from the philosophy department at Harvard. Though the fact goes unmentioned here, RF admired Palmer's translation of the Odyssey *and read from it to his children. The meeting alluded to in this letter took place when RF was a student at Harvard in 1898. ALS. Wellesley.]*

Littleton, N.H.
April 2 1915

My dear Prof. Palmer:

This from you is great happiness. Any time these twenty years if I had been asked to name my own judges to judge me when I was ready I should

28. Llewellyn Jones was literary editor of the *Chicago Evening Post*. The reference here is to Untermeyer's article "Robert Frost's 'North of Boston'" and to an editorial on RF by Jones; the two items appeared together on page 11 of the *Post* on April 23, 1915. See RF's May 26, 1915, letter of thanks to Jones.

29. One expects "one's," but this is a bit of wordplay; the manuscript is clear.

have chosen you for one. You may wonder where I have come near you to have learned such respect for your judgement. It is not altogether in your writing; for I have sat with you in the room walled all on one side with poetry and heard you talk of Old Walt[30] and of the farmers' wives in Boxford[31] (I think) who liked to hear you read "The Ring and the Book."[32] So that when I call on you, as I shall hope to soon, it will not be for the first time in my life. Thank you for your kindness.

Sincerely yours,
Robert Frost

[To John W. Haines. ALS/Photostat. DCL.]

Littleton New Hampshire
U.S.A.
April 2 1915

Dear Haines:

Nothing yet from you to show that you have had anything from me.[33]

We are still in a good deal of snow, though the sap has begun climbing trees. Late spring here in the mountains always. You mustnt tell us too much of the coming of spring to England or the contrast will make us unhappy.

And you mustn't tell me a single thing about Gibson if you dont want to detract from the pleasure of your letters from fifty percent up. I shall have to be made aware of his existance [*sic*] upon earth now and then anyway. But do

30. Walt Whitman, about whom Palmer wrote in his 1904 book *The Nature of Goodness.*

31. A rural village situated some thirty miles north of Boston.

32. By English poet Robert Browning (1812–1889).

33. Haines had written a letter to RF on March 7: "Although we have not yet heard of your safe arrival I think we should have heard something if you hadn't" (DCL); RF's letter doubtless crossed this one in transit. In any case, an April 7 letter from Haines survives (at DCL); Haines's postscript explains the reference in the present letter to Gibson: "Your letter of April 2nd arrived five minutes ago just as I am posting this. I nearly tore it up on account of the reference to Gibson but have decided to risk it! I will write again at once & note as to papers" (for explanation of the last remark "as to papers," see RF's request later in the letter for news). Apparently, after reading RF's April 2 letter, Haines went back over the one here described (March 7) and, for RF's delectation, stamped (in purple ink) the word "Hyppocrit" above the reference to Gibson.

you not remind me of him unnecessarily. Come to think it all over I cant help looking on him as the worst snob I met in England and I cant help blaming the snob he is for the most unpleasant memory I carried away from England; I mean my humiliating fight with the gamekeeper.[34] Gibson is a coward and a snob not to have saved me from all that. I was tickled to hear on oh, excellent authority that his latest work had deceived no one over here not even the editor of The Atlantic.[35] And let that be the last space I ever give him in a letter to you. May I ask you, too, not to mention me to him or to tell him of the least of my successes over here if I have any lest I grow to suspect myself of tiring you with the object of reaching and impressing him. I saw enough of his hypocritical joy over my good reviews last summer.

As nearly as I can make out I am going to be noticed a little by my Americans. I am told that Ella Wheeler Wilcox[36] spoke with superior contempt of me in New York City the other night. I am told too that casual passengers on the street have been heard to mention my name. But cheer up, all may not be as bad as this sounds. One really good piece of news is that Madame Nutt has lost both books: both have been pirated and will be on the bookstands in an American edition some day this week. The thing was put through in a rush to be beforehand with someone else who was about to pirate them. Madame Nutt has herself to thank: it is no job I put up on her. The pirate had bought sheets of the book of her and sold them all out before the day of publication. He asked so quickly for more that she saw her opportunity and began haggling. I believe he offered her something for the American rights. He spent a month or so wiring and writing and then getting wind of what some rival was up to decided to take matters into his own hands. The pirate, I dont mind saying, is my very dear friend Alfred Harcourt the moving spirit in the firm of Henry Holt & Co.

You and Thomas can put the different things I tell you together and see what you make of them.[37] I've told him some of this. I don't know just how much.

Thomas sounds cheerful at this distance. He writes he may be going down to visit you.

---

34. For an account of the fight, see *EY*, 467–468. See also RF's April 17, 1915, letter to Thomas.

35. Ellery Sedgwick.

36. Ella Wheeler Wilcox (1850–1919), American poet.

37. Edward Thomas, who would enlist in the infantry in July 1915.

And you sound cheerful in your view of the war. You seem not to mind the toll of two ships a day. I suppose that is nothing and yet—well I am glad I am not on the two ships. Send me the front sheet of a newspaper with each letter will you so that I shall get some idea of how the war seems to you. Our experts sum March up thus: on land nothing done by France and England. The advance into the Dardanelles a failure.[38] They are disposed to extend the time for the war.

Practically everyone I know wants Germany beaten. But no one is as much against Germany as he is against the war. I believe most of us are such moralists that we are more rejoiced to see beer put down than we would be to see Germany put down.[39] I wonder if you follow the workings of our minds.

Be sure you'll get "Birches" and "The Exposed Nest"[40]—when I get the review you are doing.

Our best to you both.

Yours Ever
Robert Frost

---

38. The Allied advance on the Dardanelles (often called the Gallipoli Campaign) began with a series of naval barrages in March, to be followed by an invasion on April 25.

39. Such organizations as the Anti-Saloon League, by this date the most powerful temperance organization, exploited anti-German (and pro-nativist) sentiment in America after the war broke out.

40. "Birches" was due out in *The Atlantic* in August, together with "The Road Not Taken" and "The Sound of Trees"; later RF brought these and "The Exposed Nest" into his third book, *MI* (issued in November 1916).

[To Ernest Hocking (1873–1966), an American philosopher and Harvard professor, and his wife, Agnes. The manuscript of this letter was badly water damaged, as Hocking (or so it appears) explains, by a "roof-leak" that occurred on the morning of August 24, 1959. In March 1915, RF visited the Hockings, who gave him a copy of Ernest Hocking's The Meaning of God in Human Experience: A Philosophic Study of Religion *(Yale University Press, 1912), which he discusses below. ALS. Harvard.]*

Littleton N.H.
April 3 1915

Dear Mr. and Mrs. Hocking:

I can see that I am not going to get all I want out of this book in time for polite thanks. So let me say a little with thanks now and say the rest later—orally perhaps. (A good deal would naturally take the form of questions.)

And since such a book is first of all a feat of poetry (I know that because I read it the first time through in heat), let me say in Tennyson's poetry what it reminds me of. It is as if

"a ninth wave, gathering all the deep,
And full of voices, slowly rose and plunged
Roaring, and all the wave was in a flame:
And down the wave and in the flame was borne"—[41]

well, Something Incarnate. It is the humanity of it all—the insight.

What ministers to me most perhaps is your doctrine of freedom in necessity. I have poetry for that too: "The fact is the sweetest dream that labor knows."[42] The fact is not one thing and the dream another to be kept separate. We have learned to dream in the fact. Labor has taught us so to dream. The line is charged with pragmatism.

I must read deeper for your understanding of reason. I see reason "picking" my steps, as in a country road in mud-time, or over floating ice-cakes off the Grand Banks, and so giving me my direction for short or long stretches but never giving me my general direction. It uses things and the motion of things to get on by. But its weakness is for continuity. It can't help regretting sleep and forgetfulness and fragmentary knowledge, though it has been told not to regret them. It wants to ride on things the way they are going after their way ceases to be my way—like a man so pleased with the train he is in

41. Four lines from Tennyson's "The Holy Grail."
42. From RF's poem "Mowing," in *ABW.*

that he gets carried past his junction where he ought to change to another train. It is such a slave of logic and allegory that it would go off wrong in all directions if the will wasn't extricating it all the time by the scruff of the neck. Let us exalt the gift of extrication. Without it how should we strike straight across things, how should we ever swim or wade through anything either to a throne or a Hero waiting on the shore?

But you will tell me more of this sometime. The book has yet to yield me more.

Let me thank you for so much book. It has been pretty much all my reading since I came to these heights. You mustn't smile when you see the size of the book I am sending you in return.[43]

I address you both together as one philosopher. I trust that that is no more unconventional than you suspected me of being.

If I haven't said everywhere in this letter that I was very happy with you in Cambridge, then I won't try to say it in so many words here just at the end like a man who makes his peace with Heaven on his deathbed.

Sincerely yours
Robert Frost

[To Albert Shaw. ALS. NYPL.]

Littleton, N.H.
April 4 1915

My dear Mr Shaw:

Let me thank you for Baxter's good article; and for the review of the book, also, which was much to my liking—whoever wrote it.[44] I have had no better. The quoted passage about Thomas Jefferson is a favorite of mine and one I seem to like the looks of in a magazine of politics.[45]

---

43. The first American edition of *ABW*, a very slender volume, was issued in April; Hocking's *The Meaning of God* ran to some 586 pages.

44. An unsigned review of *NB* opened an omnibus review of "Recent Poetry" in the March 1915 *Review of Reviews*.

45. The reviewer quoted a passage from "The Black Cottage," which included the following lines:

Her giving somehow touched the principle
That all men are created free and equal.

But thanks most of all for your letter testifying to the truth of my New England. So you are a Yankee, too. I am supposed to have caught in my book the last moments of a dying race. Well for a dying race, it must be admitted that we are pretty liberally represented among the editors of magazines, with you and Colonel Harvey and Mr. Sedgwick in the seats of the mighty.[46] I wonder if we are not pretty much everywhere still—except in the wholesale and retail trade in New York City.

Sincerely yours,
Robert Frost

[To William Stanley Braithwaite. ALS. Jones.]

Littleton N.H.
April 4 1915

Dear Mr Braithwaite

I trust you got the small book.[47] I want to be sure to have that right. You bought the other in my presence with such a friendly little flourish.

Sincerely yours
Robert Frost

And to hear her quaint phrases—so removed
From the world's view to-day of all those things.
That's a hard mystery of Jefferson's . . .

46. George Brinton McClellan Harvey (1864–1928) was owner and editor of *Harper's Weekly* from 1901 until 1913; Ellery Sedgwick was owner and editor of *Atlantic Monthly* from 1909 until 1938.

47. *ABW*. Braithwaite had bought a copy of *NB* when he met RF in Boston in March 1915 (*YT*, 15).

[To Edward Thomas. This letter, together with two others to Thomas, was in the hands of the collector Howard George Schmitt, an acquaintance of RF's, when Lawrance Thompson printed them in SL (1964). They have since gone missing; efforts to locate Schmitt's papers have been unsuccessful. The text given here is drawn from SL, 164–166.]

[Bethlehem, NH]
April 17 1915

Dear Edward

The goodness is in Lob.[48] You are a poet or you are nothing. But you are not psychologist enough to know that no one not come at in just the right way will ever recognize you. <u>You</u> can't go to Garnett for yourself; <u>you</u> can't go to De la Mare.[49] I told you and I keep telling you. But as long as your courage holds out you may as well go right ahead making a fool of yourself. All brave men are fools.

I like the first half of Lob best: it offers something more like action with the different people coming in and giving the tones of speech. But the long paragraph is a feat. I never saw anything like you for English.

What you say of Taber I shan't fail to pass along to his sister.[50] I am going to Stowe tomorrow at her invitation to see if I can find a farm there.

We are still unsettled. Hopes grow in every way but one. I should say we seem to have hopes of everything except more money. If some of these editors who profess to love me now had only loved me in time to buy my poems when they were in MS. It's not in me to take hold and write them anything to catch them in the mood.

I shall have Merfyn come to see us as soon as ever we know where we are. Scott bores me too, though I never got nearer him than talking on the telephone at 400 miles distance. I don't so much mind his mesalliance as I do all his muddle headed compromises to avoid the single compromise of making it a marriage. I had to laugh when his sister-in-law told me he was ready to make it a common-law marriage if she would come into the game to save Merfyn. She was the lovely one—with a twinkle in her mind. But she wasnt messing up with Scott's troubles. And I couldn't blame her when I had seen and heard. Mind you, she's fond of Scott.

---

48. Thomas had sent the poem ("Lob") to RF for review.

49. English critic Edward Garnett and English poet Walter de la Mare.

50. Mildred Minturn Scott, sister of Taber Minturn, was married to Arthur Scott. Scott's brother Russell (of Alstead, New Hampshire) served as Mervyn's guardian in America.

You must be wrong about your Christian Science Transcript. There is a C.S. Monitor and there is a Boston Transcript. I should like to see that review. I have thought (but I wouldnt say anything to you about it) that you might pick up some work over here as you come along up to us through Boston and New York. By all the signs there should be a few people in both places I could introduce you to. Thats more than I could have said three months ago.

Jolly to think of you at the Duke of Marlborough. She that standeth in the shoes of the first Duchess is an American and if you pleased her might be able to introduce you to more people over here than I can.[51]

Will you have to visit the battlefields of Oudenarde Blenheim and Malplaquet?[52]

I have just had two letters from you at once. The mails continue to come safely through. I wonder when we shall get the first letter sunk.

Poor Haines will be sorry you couldnt get down to see him.[53]

You ought not to be left out of this: I have had one note from Wilfrid in which he says Ellery Sedgwick writes that he had a pleasant talk with me on English traits peculiarities idiocyncracies [*sic*] etc. Wilfrid wishes he could have heard that talk! I wish he could. It was all about Wilfrid's nice feeling for country society <u>and</u> the Albrights.[54] Amy Lowell says I have no sense of

---

51. Charles Richard John Spencer-Churchill, 9th Duke of Marlborough (1871–1934), British soldier and Conservative politician, married Consuelo Vanderbilt (1877–1964), American heiress to the Vanderbilt railroad fortune, in 1895; the couple divorced in 1921.

52. RF names battlefields where the English won victories during the War of Spanish Succession (1701–1713). Most of Queen Anne's English troops served under legendary commander John Churchill, 1st Duke of Marlborough.

53. John W. "Jack" Haines, a Gloucester barrister and friend of RF's and Thomas's.

54. George Stacey Albright (1855–1945), a wealthy industrialist, owned the private preserve where RF and Thomas had, in the fall of 1914, encountered a gamekeeper (named Bott) while on one of their long walks. The gamekeeper accused them of trespassing; a heated quarrel ensued; RF warned Bott never again to challenge his or his children's right to move freely about the countryside; whereupon (as RF later reported to Robert Newdick) Bott leveled a shotgun at the two poets. The local constable then served RF a summons, charging him with having physically threatened Bott. When RF turned to Wilfrid Gibson for help, Gibson refused (out of deference, RF discerned, to the local gentry). Eventually Lascelles Abercrombie appealed to John W. Haines to help resolve the dispute. Gibson's refusal to come to RF's aid permanently wounded their friendship. The incident has been much discussed by RF's—and, now, Thomas's—biographers.

humor, but sometimes I manage to be funny without that gift of the few.[55] Not often, you know. Ellery Sedgwick (ed of the Atlantic) wanted to let it all out, but didn't quite dare.

Did I tell you Sedgwick said Wilfrid rather invited himself over here—asked Sedgwick outright if he couldn't arrange him a tour. That is not as I had it from Wilfrid. He was under the delusion that he had been urged to come over and save the country.

Looked at a little farm yesterday right forninst Lafayette.[56]

We are with the Lynches.[57] Old Lynch hates England but entertains no nonsense as to what would happen if Germany won. Every Yankee in America (practically) wants England to win—England and France. They all think you will win, but perhaps not this year. But few consider the war any affair of ours. No one goes into a war on general grounds of humanity. We extend sympathy on general grounds of humanity. We fight only when our material interests are touched. Yours were when Belgium was invaded; ours weren't. Damn the Germans. Did I tell you of my friend Alice Brown the novelist who hung up a picture of the Kaiser in her barn and drove nails into the face like a damsel in Malory doing despite to a knights shield?[58]

Well I have run on. Let short and frequent letters be the rule.

Let me keep the poems. I suppose you want the woodsy letter from the parson. I believe I'll hold it over a while though to show to Ellery Sedgwick. I would not have him run off with the idea that because I poked a little fun at Wilfrid I am no lover of the English—when they're right.

Yours ever

R.F.

---

55. An allusion to certain remarks in Lowell's review of *NB* (*New Republic*, February 20, 1915, 81–82).

56. RF would soon buy the farm, with its splendid view of Mt. Lafayette. "Forninst": Scottish dialect for "in front of," "opposite."

57. That is, the John Lynch family, friends of the Frosts since their days in Derry.

58. Alice Brown (1856–1948), American novelist, poet, and playwright, was an early admirer of *NB*. As for Thomas Malory, see his *Le Morte d'Arthur*, Book IV, Chapter XVI: "Then was Sir Gawaine ware in a valley by a turret of twelve fair damosels, and two knights armed on great horses, and the damosels went to and fro by a tree. And then was Sir Gawaine ware how there hung a white shield on that tree, and ever as the damosels came by it they spit upon it, and some threw mire upon the shield."

[To Louis Untermeyer. Dating supplied by Untermeyer. Text derived from RFLU, *5. We have been unable to locate the original document, which is not among the Untermeyer papers at LoC, the Jones Library, or DCL.]*

[Littleton, NH]
[Spring 1915]

Dear Untermeyer—

Have this from me with my love. Your faith has made it yours.

I suppose it is good for a poet to be required to eat at the same table with Ella and even to listen for a moment to what she thinks. It is the sort of experience that can only come to him while he is on earth.[59]

Down with our enemies and down with the drinks (before Bryan[60] shuts off the supply of the latter and packs us off to The Hague with the former.)

I'll write again soon.

Yours ever
Robert Frost

[To Harold Goddard Rugg (1883–1957), librarian, historian, naturalist, and graduate of Dartmouth College (1906). When this letter was written, Rugg was executive assistant to the librarian at Dartmouth College; he was subsequently promoted to assistant librarian, a position he held until retiring in 1953. ALS. DCL.]

Littleton N.H.
April 20 1915

Dear Sir

You are correctly informed: I was some part of a year at Hanover with the class of 1896. I lived in Wentworth (top floor, rear, side next to Dartmouth) in a room with a door that had the advantage of opening outward and so of

---

59. Untermeyer explains: RF "liked to hear gossip of the literary circles in New York, and this I was glad to furnish. The reference to eating 'at the same table with Ella and even to listen for a moment to what she thinks' was prompted by such an item of gossip. The occasion was a dinner of the Poetry Society of America, and Ella was [the poet] Ella Wheeler Wilcox" (*RFLU*, 5). RF's suggestion that such a meeting with Wilcox "is the sort of experience that can only come to [a poet] while he is on earth" is a paradoxical joke: Wilcox had a keen interest in spiritualism, theosophy, the ouija board, and in the possibility of communication with the dead.

60. William Jennings Bryan (1860–1925), at the time Woodrow Wilson's secretary of state, opposed America's entry into the war and was a staunch prohibitionist.

being hard for marauding sophomores to force from the outside. I had to force it once myself from the inside when I was nailed and screwed in. My very dear friend was Preston Shirley (who was so individual that his memory should be still green with you) and he had a door opening inward that was forced so often that it became what you might call facile and opened if you looked at it. The only way to secure it against violation was to brace it from behind with the door off the coal closet. I made common cause with Shirley and sometimes helped him hold the fort in his room till we fell out over a wooden washtub bathtub that we owned in partnership but that I was inclined to keep for myself more than my share of the time. I may say that we made up afterward over kerosene. One of us ran out of oil after the stores were closed at night and so far sacrificed his pride as to ask to borrow of the other.

I'm afraid I wasn't much of a college man in your sense of the word. I was getting past the point when I could show any great interest in any task not self-imposed. Much of what I enjoyed at Dartmouth was acting like an Indian in a college founded for Indians.[61] I mean I liked the rushes a good deal, especially the one in which our class got the salting and afterwards fought it out with the sophomores across pews and everything (it was in the Old Chapel) with old cushions and even footstools for weapons—or rather fought it to a standstill with the dust of ages we raised.

For the rest I wrote a good deal and was off in such places as the Vale of Tempe and on the walk east of the town that I called the Five Mile Round. I wrote one of the poems I still care for at about that time. It is preserved in my first book, "A Boys Will." I wrote while the ashes accumulated on the floor in front of my stove door and would have gone on accumulating to the room door if my mother hadn't sent a friend a hundred miles to shovel up and clean house for me.

You are the third person I have found common interest with in Willoughby. There are never many people at the lake at any one time and yet there seem a good many who have been there. I too expect to get back there some summer—probably not this. Isn't Pisgah (otherwise Willoughby) your

---

61. Eleazar Wheelock, a Puritan pastor, founded Dartmouth College in 1755 as Moor's Indian Charity School in Lebanon, Connecticut, for the purpose of training Native American missionaries. Wheelock relocated the school to Hanover, New Hampshire, in 1769 under a charter from King George III providing "for the education and instruction of Youth of the Indian Tribes in this Land" and also for the "youth" of English settlers.

mountain for the ferns?[62] I have found some things on the Hor[63] side (chiefly Braun's Holly—and an orchid whose name I should know again if I saw it) but more on the other along the great cliff. Don't put me down for a botanist. I wonder if you ever met a farmer named Emerson who lives just above the dam on the Barton road.[64] He's a product of the flowers of the region. I think of him as the Calypso[65] man.

I am just this minute off for Stowe in your state. I believe I can see from this "side-hill" in the White Mts the tip of Camel's Hump in the Green Mts. I shall be somewhere in that neighborhood this evening.

Probably Holt would send you copies of my books if you will let me ask him to.

Very truly yours
Robert Frost

[To John W. Haines. Transcribed from a typescript copy of the original letter, presumably made by Haines. TL (copy, unsigned). Gloucester Archives.]

Littleton, N.H.
April 25. 1915.

Dear Haines,

I feel angry but it is an Englishman's anger that after all the talk of what Kichener's [*sic*] army was going to do in the spring you should have let the Germans be beforehand with you in opening the spring campaign.[66] Some part of me that doesn't fit too tight inside actually gets right up and starts to

62. In RF's poem "A Servant to Servants," the speaker's (unheard) interlocutor camps at Lake Willoughby (in northern Vermont), botanizing after ferns. RF had vacationed with his family at the lake in the summer of 1909. Shortly before he died Rugg was elected president of the American Fern Society, of which he had been a member since 1906.

63. Mt. Hor stands in what is now the Willoughby State Forest.

64. Possibly one Nathaniel W. Emerson, who lived in Hanover when RF was a student there in 1892; census records for 1900 list his occupation as "farmer."

65. A type of orchid (*Calypso bulbosa*), commonly known as the fairy slipper or Venus's slipper. See RF's poem "An Encounter," collected in *MI*: "Sometimes I wander out of beaten ways / Half looking for the orchid Calypso."

66. RF refers to the Second Battle of Ypres, begun on April 22 when the Germans launched an offensive, deploying more than 160 tons of chlorine gas. Field Marshal

go somewhere to do something about it. Rotten news. I'm sick of it. And so ARE MY CHILDREN. We threaten to have our paper stopped.

Every day I have said "Tomorrow the advance on Berlin will begin." Damned lucky if it isn't the advance on Paris.

What I long for is certainties where I have fixed my heart. I am not permitted to be certain of anything. It is the same with my own personal affairs as with the war. From over there I thought I saw what must be easy when I got home. I have been looking for a farm for three months and no nearer settled down now than I was on board the St. Paul.[67] The year will be lost as far as farming is concerned if I don't find what I want at a possible price before many days.

I am not altogether to blame for having failed thus far of my object in coming home. There have been distractions on distractions. If I was a man dazed by the reviews that happened to me last summer and the friendliness of the English what am I now? These people once my enemies in the editorial offices are trying to be my generous friends. Some of them are making hard work of it. Some are making very hard work. They can't help trying to explain away my success with the English critics. It must be due to my lack of polish. And I sit so scornful of the pack and yet so willing to get all the glory going and see my books sell that you would think I was in some dream. It has a curious effect on me. Twenty years I gave some of these people a chance. I wish I were rich and independent enough to tell them to go to Hell. You ought to have seen the lovely recollections I did (by request) of my life at Dartmouth College.[68] I ought to have kept a copy for you. You know me well enough to have read under the surface of it. Elinor said I simply mustn't gratify anybody by doing the usual thing about all I owed to my alma mater. And I didn't. I wasn't hypocrite enough for that. I had a little fun.

I weep inwardly over it all.

Remember there are good people against whom I harbour no resentment. There's Alice Brown and Sylvester Baxter and Louis Untermeyer and

---

Horatio Herbert Kitchener, 1st Earl Kitchener (1850–1916), was, at the time, secretary of state for war in the British cabinet.

67. In February, the Frost family had returned to New York from Liverpool aboard the U.S.M.S. *St. Paul*.

68. See RF to Rugg, April 20, 1915.

[Llewellyn][69] Jones and Amy Lowell and nearly the whole staff of The New Republic and Albert Shaw.[70] I'm glad of such friends in a country where I had not one three years ago.

While this excitement lasts you will see that it would be affectation for me to pretend not to be interested in it. It means nothing or next to nothing to my future poetry; it may even hurt that; but there is me personally to think of. It may save me from ruin and starvation. So I shall send you a good review now and then just as if I was as vain as you think I am. The one by Louis Untermeyer you might pass along to Abercrombie.[71] Untermeyer is a friend of his I have heard. All others keep to yourself.

I'll write you out a little poem about the brook on my old farm.[72] It always dried up in summer. The Hyla is a small frog that shouts like jingling bells in the marshes in spring.

Won't flirt with your cousins.

Get me credit with your wife for having said that.

Yours ever,
R. F.

Send along your review.[73]

---

69. In preparing a typed copy of the letter, Haines apparently could not make out RF's handwriting here; he left a black space. We have inserted Jones's first name.

70. Alice Brown, the American novelist mentioned above, admired *NB*. Sylvester Baxter (1850–1927) was a journalist (often writing for the *Boston Evening Transcript*), poet, and urban planner, in which latter capacity he helped design the Metropolitan Park System of Greater Boston. Albert Shaw (1857–1947), an American journalist, was the author of a number of works about international law and political institutions, and editor in chief of the American edition of *Review of Reviews* from 1891 until 1937.

71. Untermeyer's review of *NB* appeared in The Friday Literary Review in the *Chicago Evening Post*, which Llewellyn Jones edited, on April 23, 1915.

72. "Hyla Brook," collected in *MI*.

73. We have found no evidence of a review authored by Haines. He did, however, give several talks on the poet.

[To Albert Shaw. ALS. NYPL.]

Littleton NH
April 27 1915

Dear Dr Shaw:

I trust it wouldnt be taking unfair advantage of your offer if I asked you to have copies of The Review of Reviews for April sent to all these friends:[74]

A. St John Adcock esq
Editor of The Bookman
Warwick Square
London E. C.
England

J. W. Haines esq
Hillview Road
Hucclecote
Gloucester
England

J. C. Smith[75] esq
20 Braid Avenue
Edinburgh
Scotland

Mrs Chandler[76]
Oldfields
Leddington
Ledbury
England

---

74. See RF to Shaw, March 15, 1915.

75. James Cruickshank Smith, inspector of schools in Edinburgh and editor of (among other things) the Oxford series *Selected Plays of Shakespeare*. The Frosts vacationed with the Smiths in Scotland in late summer 1913.

76. Edward Thomas and his family rented rooms from John and Mary Chandler, who owned Oldfields, a farm just a few meadows away from where the Frosts had lived at Little Iddens.

Mrs Gardner[77]
Farm Corner
Tadworth
Surrey
England

Miss Jeanie Frost
40 North 19th St
Philadelphia

Daniel P. Connor esq[78]
Maple St
Manchester
New Hampshire

Nearly everybody else in the world seems to have seen Baxter's article. These people may have seen it too, but they have been backward in writing to say so.

Thank you for all your kindness.

Sincerely yours
Robert Frost.

[To Harry Gordon Jacobs (1880–1936), reporter, foreign correspondent, and editor at the Brooklyn Daily Eagle. *Jacobs published an article on RF in the* Daily Eagle, *April 24, 1915, section 2, 5. ALS. ACL.]*

Littleton N.H.
April 29 1915

Dear Sir:

We seem to like each other's writing: you say you like mine and I should have to be more than human not to like yours when you say it. I shan't forget what I owe you and some others for deciding to let me come home and

77. Mary Wilson Gardner, wife of Ernest Gardner, a professor of archaeology at University College London. The Gardners met RF at the Poetry Bookshop in London in January of 1913.

78. Writing as "Concubar," Daniel P. Connor published a number of volumes of local-color sketches and history of the White Mountains and Manchester, New Hampshire.

be a poet in my own country. I particularly like the terms on which you accept me.

You might have been a little kinder to my first book. It contains eight or ten really good lyrics. Of course you had to "say it as you saw it"; but you may live to see it differently and want to make the book amends.

I wish I might be permitted to look you up sometime when I am in New York and thank you personally for the Eagle article. And if you are in these mountains, will you try to find me? This gives you my address.

Sincerely yours
Robert Frost

[To Louis Untermeyer. ALS. Jones.]

Littleton N.H.
April 30 1915

Dear Untermeyer:

There are a dozen things in your article[79] that I should like to thank you for in detail, but I must stop for just one of them now. You make the point that there must be many poetical moods that haven't been reduced to poetry. Thanks most of all for seeing that and saying it in a review of book [*sic*] by me.

You see so well the necessity of our being generous to each other as fellow artists. I probably dont deserve all your praise, but you'll never be the poorer for having uttered it and trust my enemies to discount it where it needs discounting.

I am in your book almost as I write and full of the large spirit of it. You are the same in your letters in your reviewing and in your poetry. Really I knew you in England. I admire and envy you for knowing what you want to urge in prose and verse. I shall love your book.

All this is in haste. My chief object in writing is to get you word in time that I am to be at Sylvester Baxter's, 42 Murray Hill Road Malden Mass on April 4. On April 5 I shall be at Tufts College. On April 6 and on for several days at Baxter's again.[80] Will you look me up there?—or call me up? Baxter

---

79. "Robert Frost's North of Boston," published in the *Chicago Evening Post* on April 23 (page 11).

80. In his haste, while house hunting in and around Littleton, RF mistakes the dates: he stayed with Baxter on May 4 and read at Tufts on May 5.

would be glad to have you come to see us both. I did think, though, that I should like it if we could steal away somewhere by ourselves.

Yours ever
Robert Frost.

I must thank Jones.[81]

[To Nathan Haskell Dole. ALS. Harvard.]

Littleton N.H.
May 2 1915

Dear Dole:

Goose am I? Well here I come honking south again.

I hear that you are to be at Tufts College Wednesday night. If you see anyone that looks like me there, don't put it down for a case of mistaken identity: it may well be me, though I shouldn't advise you to take my word for it either one way or the other.

The article in The Bellman has begun to bring me friendly letters.[82] I have to thank you for all such things. I was glad you could make Mrs Spofford[83] think she liked the small book. You are not expected to go on with such work for the cause until you have a copy you can call your own.

This is just to tell you that I am coming. More when I see you.

Yours ever
R.F.

81. Llewellyn Jones; see RF's May 26, 1915, letter to him.

82. See Dole's "A Migration of Poets," *Bellman*, April 24, 1915, 532.

83. Harriet Elizabeth Prescott Spofford (1835–1921), American poet and novelist.

[To John Bartlett. The letter is undated, but "May 8, 1915" has been written at the head of the page in another hand. RF refers to the sinking of the Lusitania *by a German U-boat on May 7, 1915, which confirms the date. Only one page of the letter survives. AL (no signature). UVA.]*

42 Murray Hill Road
Malden Mass
[May 8, 1915]

Dear John:

I got through my Phi Beta Kappa and my speech before the Authors Club but what does it matter about me? I'm sick this morning with hate of England and America because they have let this happen and will do nothing to punish the Germans.[84] They can do nothing. I have no faith in any of them. Germany will somehow come out of this war if not completely victorious at least still formidable and needing only time to get wind for another round. Dammit.

I cant get away till some day[. . . .]

[To John W. Haines. ALS/Photostat. DCL.]

Littleton N.H.
May 15 1915

Dear Haines:

Your papers faced the setback at Ypres more honestly than ours. And there's an inference to be drawn from that my friend if you will but draw it, namely that we are deeply concerned that you shan't be beaten. We are sorry to have to admit that you have lost an inch.

But we are out of this fight to stay out. The quarrel is not enough ours as we see it. We are not materially touched as you were by the invasion of Belgium. Sentiment is one thing and sentiment merged with interest is another. No nation ever went to war from sentiment alone. I have said this before.

I was struck sad for Rupert.[85] But he chose the right way. Your letter telling of his death came right on the heels of another from Smith saying how

---

84. On April 22, during the Second Battle of Ypres, German forces launched the first major chlorine gas attack of the war. The attack opened a gap in the Allied lines, which two battalions of the Canadian Expeditionary Force filled and held at great cost.

85. The British poet Rupert Brooke, whom RF met while living in England, and who was associated with the Georgian poets, died at the age of twenty-eight on April 23, 1915,

much the war had done to make him a better poet.[86] The war saved him only to kill him.

I wonder if your papers made you realize that we are ready to fight over the Lusitania if Germany doesn't come to terms.[87] We don't quite see what good we could do by taking a hand in the war: in fact we think we can do more good by remaining a neutral source of military supplies because as things are all our manufactures go to you and France; but if Germany insists I suppose we cant disoblige her. Everybody is saying Throw Dernburg[88] into the Atlantic.

I say one thing and another with the idea of trying to give you what no paper can. Don't expect me to be consistent. Remember that I dont speak for myself. You know what my feelings are personally: I dont need to go over those. You are after the national feeling.

I wonder if you could get me a copy of my first book for a friend here who wants it with my signature in the first edition. Mrs Nutt won't let me have a copy for love or money.

We expect to have our farm before many days—in the Amanoosuc [*sic*] valley almost in the shadow of Lafayette.[89]

Our best to you all.

Yours ever
Robert Frost

I think one of my letters may have gone down with the Lusitania. I have been seeing a good deal of the sister of the Millet who discovered Broadway and drew so many Americans after him there. He was lost on the Titanic.[90]

---

while being treated for an infection aboard a French hospital ship moored off the Aegean island of Sykros; Brooke was to have taken part in the Gallipoli Campaign.

86. Almost certainly, again, James Cruickshank Smith.

87. The RMS *Lusitania,* a British ocean liner, sank on May 7, 1915, when a German U-boat torpedoed it; 1,198 passengers died in the attack, and American public opinion gradually began to favor the entrance of the United States in the war.

88. Bernhard Dernburg (1865–1937), German banker, politician, and former head of the German Imperial Colonial Office. In 1915, the Fatherland Corporation published his *Search-Lights on the War,* a pro-German propaganda pamphlet intended to influence American opinion. Dernburg (and his wife) had also authored a number of pro-German articles in such venues as the *New York Times.*

89. RF was then in negotiations to purchase a farm in Franconia, New Hampshire.

90. Francis David Millet (1846–1912), American writer, sculptor, and painter, died in the sinking of the *Titanic.* He had gathered about him a colony of American artists in the Cotswolds village of Broadway (in Worcestershire). His sister Lucia (wife of Frost family

[To Louis Untermeyer. ALS. LoC.]

Littleton N.H.
May 16 1915

Dear Untermeyer

I've just got home out of that.

Blow in with any breezy news you will. You know I see nothing here.

You needn't be afraid of being too romantic for me—you or your friends. I liked you all as I found you sprinkled through The Masses.[91] It's all sorts of a world.

Call your attention to the fact that the author of A Tuft of Flowers[92] forestalled the cynic by having the mower mow the reeds which are worse forage than the butterfly weed:[93] item that it is the country custom to mow everything—the weeds to keep them from seeding. The cynic attitude toward poetry is not as safe as it looks.

Call your attention to the fact that there are no signs that I coveted a British-made reputation. At thirty-seven I had pretty well despaired of a reputation of any make. I went to England to write and be poor without further scandal in the family.

Comfort me with apples.

You are a lot of fun as Owen Hatteras and something of a terror.[94] I'm glad you didn't bite me.

Contrary to what I thought was the understanding Ellery Sedgwick is still hanging on to Birches.[95]

---

friend Sylvester Baxter) had lived with her brother in Broadway and left, in letters home to American friends, a detailed record of life in the colony.

91. Left-wing magazine published in the United States from 1911 until 1917, when federal prosecutors shut it down under the auspices of the Espionage Act of 1917, vigorously enforced by then–Postmaster General Albert S. Burleson. *The Masses* regularly featured work by Max Eastman, John Reed, Floyd Dell, Dorothy Day, and others; Untermeyer occasionally contributed to it.

92. Collected in RF's first book, *ABW*.

93. *Asclepias tuberosa*, a species of milkweed; more commonly known as "butterfly weed" because its nectar attracts the insects. See, in addition to "The Tuft of Flowers" (*CPPP*, 30), RF's late poem "The Pod of the Milkweed" (*CPPP*, 425).

94. Owen Hatteras was a pen name chiefly used by H. L. Mencken and George Nathan, editors of the *Smart Set*. Untermeyer occasionally wrote under it.

95. Sedgwick would publish "Birches," together with "The Road Not Taken" and "The Sound of Trees," in the August 1915 number of *The Atlantic*.

You have seen me—well where you have seen me, and if you can still remain my friend, all I can say is that—well I remain yours.

R.F.

I ought to say dammit that the farm I was to have had for a thousand dollars has gone up a hundred or two owing to the owner's having seen my picture in the paper. You can see how that might be.

[To Sidney Cox. ALS. DCL.]

Littleton N.H.
May 16 1915

Dear Cox

Jessie B was all right.[96] I ask no more than temperate praise from any of them. Temperate praise in the long run will help me most. And do you remember that when you get your chance to write of me as you know me. Don't let your admiration run away with you. Consider appearances in public. Make the most of the advantage of having known me personally to correct any lies about me that may be current. But don't overdo the praise.

The only nastiness in Jessie B's article is the first part where she speaks of the English reviews as fulsome. There she speaks dishonestly out of complete ignorance—out of some sort of malice or envy I should infer. Her anthology with the silly name made a very bad miss in England.

She has no right to imply of course that I desired or sought a British-made reputation. You know that it simply came to me after I had nearly given up any reputation at all. That you may have a chance to tell 'em some day.

Jessie B has a right to think what she pleases of Book I. I know pretty well what she thinks and why she thinks it.

You mustnt judge of how things are going with me by the limited number of papers you see. Already I have had in America more notice than any American poet in many years. I mean public notice. Privately I have been

---

96. Jessie Belle Rittenhouse (1869–1948), anthologist, critic, and poet. RF refers to her article on *NB*, published (even as he penned this letter) in the *New York Times Book Review* on May 16, 1915 (page 89). It reads, in part: "Just why a made-in-England reputation is so coveted by the poets of this country is difficult to fathom, particularly as English poets look so anxiously to America for acceptance of their work." The "anthology with the silly name," mentioned later in the letter, is Rittenhouse's 1913 *Little Book of Modern Verse*.

overwhelmed with the friendship of Howells, George Palmer, Mrs Marks Alice Brown Basil King E. A. Robinson Mrs T. B. Aldrich[97] and any number of others you might or might not know. I tell you this to set your mind at rest. I dont like to see you so troubled about me when I am the envied of all my fellow craftsmen.

One of my best friends is young Louis Untermeyer. Shauffler didnt pan out very well.[98] He showed jealousy of my British made reputation. I suspect you didn't tell me all he said in his letter to you. I found him a treacherous second-rate mind.

So rest easy. Take life easy as the leaves grow on the tree. When you see your chance do what you can for me. There are several false impressions at large that I should like to see nailed.

Since you are not going to college next year perhaps you will feel that you can afford a visit to us in the summer. We hope to be settled on a farm of our own before long. We have found what we want in Franconia.[99]

The summer-camp scheme will have to wait a while.[100]

Be good.

R.F.

---

97. William Dean Howells (1837–1920), the so-called dean of American letters, would soon publish an article on RF in his Editor's Easy Chair column in *Harper's* (September 1915, 634–637). For George Palmer, see the headnote to RF's April 2, 1915, letter to him. Josephine Preston Peabody Marks (1874–1922) was an American poet and dramatist (and wife of Harvard professor Lionel Marks). Alice Brown (1856–1948) was an American novelist, poet, and playwright. William Benjamin Basil King (1859–1928) was a Canadian-born clergyman, novelist, and critic. RF met the poet E. A. Robinson (1869–1935) in Boston in early May 1915. Lillian Woodman Aldrich, wife of author Thomas Bailey Aldrich (1836–1907), would, in 1920, publish a memoir of the couple's literary life together (*Crowding Memories* [Boston: Houghton Mifflin]).

98. See the notes to RF's February 2, 1915, letter to Cox.

99. The Frosts moved to their new farm in Franconia in June 1915.

100. There is good evidence that RF once hoped to gather together, in New Hampshire, some of his English-poet friends, including Lascelles Abercrombie and Edward Thomas, to form a kind of writers' colony.

[To Ernst B. Filsinger (1880–1937), a successful exporter and an expert on foreign trade. In December 1914, he married Sara Teasdale (1884–1933), an American poet from St. Louis. In 1916 the couple moved to an apartment on the Upper West Side in Manhattan. Teasdale divorced Filsinger in 1929. ALS. UVA.]

Littleton N H
May 16 1915

Dear Mr Filsinger

I have had it in my heart for some time to thank you for your generous praise. But you know how it is: "we are selfish men";[101] the great thing is to get such a letter as yours; the answering it can be left to a less luxurious mood.

I know your wife's poetry and admire it. Only recently I have been talking of her with Louis Untermeyer.[102]

If someone will pave the way for me with chances to read and lecture, it is not impossible that I may some day get west to you in St. Louis, and I know we shall be friends.

Sincerely yours
Robert Frost

[To Harold Goddard Rugg. ALS. DCL.]

Littleton N.H.
May 16 1915

Dear Mr Rugg

A complimentary (very complimentary) copy of The Third Rail[103] has just arrived with your name in a corner of the wrapper to remind me that when I ran away to Boston two weeks ago I left a friendly letter of yours unanswered. I fully meant to do something about it before I got home but you may imagine how it was: what with lecturing and reading and seeing and being seen (to put it thus shamelessly) in all the two weeks I found not a quiet moment that I could call my own.

---

101. RF quotes from line six of Wordsworth's "London, 1802."

102. RF owned an inscribed copy of Teasdale's third collection of poetry, *Rivers to the Sea* (1915). He later recommended that she be awarded first prize in a contest he, Katharine Lee Bates, and John Livingston Lowes judged in March 1921.

103. A newspaper published by students at Dartmouth College.

But that is past now and I am myself again or shall be in a few days. And before long I hope to be settled on a farm of my own in Franconia, where I shall want you to visit me for a good talk when you will. Perhaps you will lead me to some flowers I havent met before and I can get some information out of you without effort and without price. The farm is already fixed upon. But there is a difficulty about moneys. The owner is going up on what he first asked when he thought I was a farmer and before he saw me depicted in the papers as a poet.

Will you thank Mr Griffith for his good article if you are in the way of seeing him?[104] Something he says in it puts it into my head that I could give you an interesting talk over there on "Technique and the Imagination." I should be glad of any chance you can get me to earn a little by lecturing or reading. I am booked for a lecture at Wellesley soon and at several other places next winter. I have several ideas on the bare art of writing that I must promulgate in self-defense. Braithwaite has been doing what he could with them in the last two Saturday Transcripts.[105]

Sincerely yours
Robert Frost

[To Claude Thaddeus Lloyd (1894–1968), a graduate of Simmons College (1917) in Abilene, Texas. Lloyd would later complete a PhD at Yale (1925). Apparently, Lloyd had written a letter in praise of NB, *the American edition of which had been published by Holt on February 20. ALS. Private collection.[106]]*

Littleton N.H.
May 20 1915

My Texas Friend:

Yours is a good spontaneous way of hailing a man from afar. I think what you want to thank me for is filling a place on the map with life and people that might otherwise have been blank. You meant to tell me too that you

104. William Griffith (1876–1936), American editor, author, and poet.

105. A reference to Braithwaite's "A Poet of New England: Robert Frost, a New Experiment of Life" (*Boston Evening Transcript*, April 28, 1915 [part 3], 4), and "Robert Frost, New American Poet: His Opinions and Practice—An Important Analysis of the Art of the Modern Bard" (*Boston Evening Transcript*, May 8, 1915 [part 3], 4).

106. The letter was previously printed in facsimile, together with an article honoring Lloyd, in the *bordertownNews* (Newburyport, Massachusetts) on July 11, 1973.

could do the same thing for the western part of Texas. You must go ahead and do it. I venture the guess however that when it is done, if it is well done there will be little recorded of six-shooters and such like properties because we have had our fill of them and they are no more true of western life than a lot of soberer things you could say. Isn't it true that you could write just exactly the same homely tale of the western men and women that I have written of the eastern?

Thanks for your good word.

Sincerely yours
Robert Frost

[To John Bartlett. The first page of the letter is torn along two creases and badly water-blotted; the second page is water-blotted at the bottom. One or more pages have gone missing, and thus the letter lacks a signature. AL (no signature). UVA.]

Littleton NH
May 20 1915

Dear John

Back here at the piled-up letters and the business of buying a farm. The letters are rather too much for me with my piled up inexperience. The transaction of buying the farm is [SEVERAL WORDS ILLEGIBLE] from the consciousness that I am an arrived poet. Buying and selling are the great levellers.

Just you hold on a bit till I know where I stand with my Boston friends and I will do so for you (and more also) as I needed someone to do for me when I was your age. At least I will try. There are a dozen sorts of thing you could do and make more money in a week than I ever could in a year. Don't count on me too much, but, as I say, I will try.

I told the family all about your family and there is nothing left but to show them to each [BALANCE OF LETTER MISSING].

[To Amy Lowell (1874–1925), poet, critic, anthologist, and collector. Lowell was named first president of the New England Poetry Club at a meeting RF attended in Boston on May 11, 1915. ALS. Harvard.]

Hail first President of the Poetry Society of New England! (bis)[107]

If I liked your poetry before, you may imagine how much more I shall like it after this.

Note rhyme and believe me

Seriously yours
Robert Frost

Littleton N.H.
May 21 1915

[To Walter Prichard Eaton (1878–1957), drama critic, author of numerous books on theater, and professor of playwriting at Yale. The poem RF mentions in closing the letter has not been identified. ALS. DCL.]

Littleton N.H.
May 26 1915

Dear Mr Eaton:

It's not your turn really. Before I have a right to answer your best letter of all there are a whole lot of perfunctory letters I ought to write to people who have been rising out of my past to express surprise that I ever should have amounted to anything. You may not believe it but I am going to have to thank one fellow for remembering the days of '81 when we went to kin[d]er-garten together and once cut up a snake into very small pieces to see if contrary to the known laws of nature we couldnt make it stop wriggling before sundown. I am going to have to thank, when I get round to it, a dear old lady for remembering me as you may say before I was born or thought of—just before—remembering that is to say my mother and father as teachers in a little Pennsylvania mountain town the year before they married.[108] You have been a literary man longer than I have: what do you make of it all? I don't say that I absolutely abhor it if it really means anything. But none of these people talk of anything but my success. They haven't read my book; possibly they

107. As a direction in a musical score, "bis" means "repeat" (it also simply means "twice").

108. The poet's father, William Prescott Frost, Jr., met his mother, Isabelle Moodie, in Lewistown, Pennsylvania, in 1872; at the time, both taught at Lewistown Academy.

have bought it out of some sort of perverted pride. Why one of them actually got hold of me when I was in Boston and tried every Yankee "line of talk" for getting it out of me whether I had grown rich, and failing with every one was finally driven to asking me point blank "Have you done well—ah—in a money way?"

It is not so much that I am busy day and night answering them; but there they are on file waiting to be answered in their turn and keeping me from answering anybody else with a clear conscience. But to Hell with a few of them tonight—with such of them as are not Unitarians and Universalists and have a Hell to go to. Suppose I pass them over on the ground that yours is an emergency case calling for instant attention and having let it go two weeks if I dont do something soon you will carry out the threat you closed your letter with and begin to write a kind of poetry calculated to bring your family to grief. Then I should be to blame partly for setting you a bad example by my book and partly for not warning you in time not to follow it.

But you say you had already followed my example a little way before I set it. W. D. Howells has been saying the same thing and sending me a book of his "The Mother and the Father" to prove it.[109] I'm glad neither of you got any farther or mine wouldn't have been the glory, such as it is. Or no, you know I don't mean that. If you had written N.O.B. first, I hope I should have just envied you as generously as you envy me and looked around for what was left to do. There is always something left to do.

I don't believe it is because you are a practiced writer that I like your letter so much and couldnt be happy till I had brushed all these other letters aside to get to yours. What I like is your unreserve, the envy you dont conceal, the temptation to sin against your family which you confess to—it's all so genuine. It stirs old memories in me and old misgivings. I have been pulled two ways and torn in two all my life. But by the Lord Harry every time I have taken the way it almost seemed as if I ought not to take I have been justified somehow by the result. It scares me to say it—I knock on wood to placate any devil who may happen to hear me. I dont say that I have done well for my family—I have done badly, but I've always made some little gain for them when I took a flyer in ideals.

109. William Dean Howells (1837–1920) favorably reviewed RF's first two volumes of poetry in the September 1915 issue of *Harper's*, writing, "Here is the old poetry as young as ever; and new only in extending the bounds of sympathy through the recorded to the unrecorded knowledge of humanity." His *The Mother and the Father: Dramatic Passages* appeared in 1909.

I liked your letter a good deal because I liked Sidney Snow.[110] You are going to be something like him when I meet you presently, meet you with him perhaps and have a chance to stand you up side by side for comparison. You needn't laugh at the notion. It wont be as formal as all that. I am really more shamefaced than I sound in a letter. And I won't say anything more about this, so that you may think that I haven't found the likeness between you that I expected to, but I am sure that I shall find that in common that I have found among all the friends I have ever cared for, though it is too subtle a thing for words and if it were not it is my secret and nobody can make me betray it.

Kinsman is the mountain that from this side looks like a wave combing? You are to be up the valley of the South Branch ten or twelve miles from Franconia?[111] How soon? There is just a fear that I may fail to get the farm my heart is set on in Franconia. It will be through no fault of mine. The bad farmer I was buying it of talked of fifty acres until it came to the showdown. The deed only calls for thirty. I myself am more amused than offended by the little discrepancy and what it says for the farmer—at least he is not indifferent. But my people are respectable and shrink physically from a lie not of their own telling. And as they hold the purse-strings—

But if I don't get down to Franconia, I shall linger on for some time at my old haunt just above Franconia at the top of Break-neck Hill—on what is known as the South Road out of Bethlehem. And you must look for me here.

The pleasure your letter gave me has lasted me clear through my answer to it. I have run on.

Sincerely yours
Robert Frost

Maybe I wouldn't have stopped here if I hadn't just thought of a poem to write on "Springs."

---

110. Sidney Bruce Snow (1878–1944), a Unitarian clergyman, assigned to King's Chapel, Boston. Snow and Eaton were classmates at Harvard (class of 1900). Eaton dedicated to Snow his 1914 volume *Boy Scouts in the White Mountains: The Story of a Long Hike* (Boston: W. A. Wilde). See also RF's November 22, 1915, letter to Charlotte Endymion Porter.

111. Where the Gale River—a thirteen-mile tributary of the Ammonoosuc River located in the northwestern New Hampshire county of Grafton—runs north through Franconia it splits into two streams, called North Branch and South Branch. The two streams reunite in Bethlehem, where the river turns westward. Kinsman Mountain, mentioned earlier, is located just south of Franconia near what is now Franconia Notch State Park.

[To Llewellyn Jones (1884–1961), literary editor of the Chicago Evening Post. *The reference in the first sentence is to Untermeyer's article "Robert Frost's 'North of Boston'" and to an editorial on RF by Jones; the two items appeared together on page 11 of the* Post *on April 23, 1915. ALS. Private collection of Pat Alger.]*

Franconia N.H.
May 26 1915

Dear Mr Jones

You'll wonder how when I say your letter gave me as much pleasure as the great spread you and Untermeyer made of me in The Post, I haven't answered it sooner. What I have been waiting for is a moment when I could call my soul my own. At about the time you wrote, a challenge I accepted to read a Phi Beta Kappa poem somewhere scared me out of a month of sincerity.[112] I quite lost the power to say real things till it was over and for sometime after it was over. The minute I begin to feel myself again I hasten (hasten is the word) to thank you for what you have seen in my books.

There can be no comparison between your reviews and what Miss Gilder wrote.[113] You were kind to me and she wasn't. And how wrong she was about Hardy. It is of course as a poet that he will be remembered: such is the best critical opinion in England. But poet or no poet I would ask no better than to be remembered as long as some of his poems will be.

I'm glad you gave the small book its share of notice. The two are the same thing at the source. Such a line as

"Till even the comforting barn grows far away" (Storm Fear)

is the spirit of both books.[114]

If you will permit me to be personal: I have a friend over yonder, a Welshman, a literary man of eminence who I believe would come to live in America if amid all the Germans in the Middle West I could point him out so

---

112. At Tufts College.

113. Newspaper correspondent, editor, and critic Jeannette Leonard Gilder (1849–1916) had cofounded with her brother Joseph the literary magazine the *Critic* in 1881, and she served as editor until 1906. She also collaborated with her brother Richard Watson Gilder in the editorship of *Scribner's Monthly*. Her December 8, 1895, review of Thomas Hardy's *Jude the Obscure* in the *New York World* had offered such judgments as "too filthy to print." Writing under the pen name "Brunswick," Gilder was also the New York correspondent of the *Boston Evening Transcript*. The article about his poems to which RF refers may have been unsigned.

114. "Storm Fear," from which RF quotes the line, appeared in *ABW*.

much as one man with a name like yours—right at both ends. His name is Edward Thomas (I wonder if you know his work) and his children are named Bronwen, Merfyn and Mifanwy. He has become a very dear friend to me and you wont mind, will you, if I use your name as a lure to draw him over with—when the war is over?

Thanks for your generous praise.

Sincerely yours
Robert Frost.

[To George Herbert Palmer. ALS. Wellesley.]

Franconia N.H.
May 26 1915

Dear Prof. Palmer:

My fault for not writing to thank you at once for the books I am so proud of. It's a bad habit I have fallen into of not acknowledging books till I have had time and more than time to decide what to make of them—bad, if for no other reason, because the longer the acknowledgment is delayed the greater becomes my obligation to say something wise and just about them.

I found a copy of "North of Boston" in the first edition nearer home than in England. I want you to have the small first book too. It will put in an appearance in time. I have had to send across for that.

Thank you for the "George Herbert."[115] The man I have this day bought a farm of facing all the Franconia range at an airline distance of three of four miles is a Herbert.[116]

Sincerely yours
Robert Frost

115. Palmer published *The English Works of George Herbert* in three volumes in 1915 (Boston: Houghton Mifflin).

116. In May 1915, RF agreed, via handshake, to purchase the Franconia farmhouse on Ridge Road, together with some 28 acres of land, from Willis E. Herbert (1868–1924) and his wife Delphine (1875–1954). The selling price was set at $1000. But when Herbert learned of RF's notoriety as a poet, he attempted to raise the price by $200, which RF refused to pay. Willis later repurchased the property when RF moved to South Shaftsbury, Vermont, in 1920. Delphine willed it to her niece, who, in turn, sold it to the town of Franconia in 1976, which, at the suggestion of David Schaffer and Evangeline Machlin (and like-minded townsfolk), established the farm as the Frost Place, a historical site and summer retreat for poets-in-residence.

[To Alfred Harcourt (1881–1954), publisher. Edward Garnett, a noted English critic, was credited with having discovered, for English audiences, both Joseph Conrad and D. H. Lawrence. His favorable review of NB*, in which he claimed that "since Whitman's death, no American poet has appeared, of so unique a quality, as Mr. Frost," was published alongside "Birches," "The Road Not Taken," and "The Sound of Trees" in the August 1915 issue of* The Atlantic Monthly. *In the upper left corner of the letter RF has drawn a hand pointing to the new address, together with the word "Notice." ALS. Princeton.]*

Franconia N.H.
May 30 1915

Dear Harcourt:

Forgive my impulsive suggestion on advertising: I was stung for a moment out of my composure by something ill-natured and not quite honest in the lady's criticism. If she has really read and found disgusting the reviews I had in England last summer I wonder what she will say to Edward Garnett's article when it appears (if it appears) in The Atlantic. Edward Garnett you know is the greatest of English critics. I am credibly informed that he has been admiring my book too much. We shall see.

Will you cause a few more copies of the lesser book to be sent to me?

I have fixed on a farm that I hope to be settled on by the end of this week.

Sincerely Yours
Robert Frost

Sedgwick[117] has just written to say that Garnett's article will appear.

[To Wilbur Rowell. Now held at the Frost Place, Franconia, New Hampshire. ALS.]

Franconia N.H.
May 31 1915

Dear Mr Rowell

You must have wondered what had become of me and my farm. I have been making slow work of the farm owing chiefly to the fact, I think, that the owner has been seeing my picture in the papers and so getting up his ideas of what he ought to get out of me. It has taken time to make him see sense.

---

117. Ellery Sedgwick, editor of *The Atlantic*.

He has himself sent to Woodsville for the records I enclose. Tell me if there is anything more you need. Mr Herbert's copy of the deed lies in a safe in a cellar in Littleton where it fell in a recent fire.[118]

You will notice the discrepancy between the owner's claim and the acreage the deed calls for. I have had a surveyor chain the farm and he makes it forty-two acres. To-day Mr Herbert is going to show me what he will throw in from his adjoining farm. Forty-two acres are enough for the money and for my purpose but we may as well have what we were promised or somewhere near it.

I should like to hurry the business up all I can so as to get to planting this week.

Thanking you again for your kindness in helping me in this matter, in going out of your way to help me, I am

Sincerely yours
Robert Frost

[To George Browne (1857–1931), cofounder of the Browne and Nichols School in Cambridge, Massachusetts. The "notes" referred to here are records Browne made of RF's talk at the Browne and Nichols School on May 10, 1915. The private school, founded in 1883, later merged with the Buckingham School and is now called Buckingham Browne and Nichols. See CPPP, *687–689. ALS. Plymouth.]*

Franconia NH
June 1 1915

My dear Browne

Will you give me a little longer with those notes? I want to do them for you: I see an object in it—look out for me.

The further I read in the pamphlets you loaded me with the surer I am that we did not meet for nothing: there was some fatality in the meeting. I see now that I could have gone a good deal deeper in my talk to the boys on images of sound and you would have had no quarrel with me. I can see a small text-book based on images of sound particularly of the kind I call vocal postures or vocal idioms that would revolutionize the teaching of English all

118. See the notes to RF's May 26, 1915 letter to Palmer.

the way up through our schools. They are the spirit of the sentence, they are the sentence.

I wish I had met you long ago when I was still a teacher and pining for someone who would see as I saw.

I am asking for more time with your notes because I am rushed to death finding buying and moving onto a farm before it is too late for this year's planting.

Sincerely yours
Robert Frost.

[To Nathan Haskell Dole. RF has drawn on the letter a hand, with the word "notice," pointing toward the address. ALS. Harvard.]

Box 82
Franconia N.H.
June 1 1915

Dear Dole:

I read your letter as far as to where you said I probably hadnt read a word of it and there I had a mind to stop but I thought I might as well go on to the end as long as the end was so near.

You are the very devil for that kind of humility.

Don't you know by this time that if you are neglected and left off a committee or anything else it is not on your merits as a poet? People can't stand the way you ring the changes on your humility. And worse than that is what I call your cultivated cheerfulness. Don't you know that you can't cultivate a thing like cheerfulness without driving everybody crazy around you and finally going crazy yourself?

You are a little older than I and I have no right to be scolding you and I'm not scolding. But you break my heart with your puns. It is not that I am offended by them in the conventional way; I am moved to tears. And other people are too: their pretense of being outraged is only a humorous cover for real pity. Your suffering is a very public secret.

I am hard on you. But harsh as I may seem, I am nothing compared with what I ought to be for the sake of your poetry. Give that a decent chance. Be sad when there is so much in your life to be sad about. Give your poetry the benefit of your sadness.

Remember that cheerfulness is only one resource in keeping up the fight in life, just as whipping is only one in bringing up a child. It may be a good one, but every method has its inherent disadvantage that forbids its being used all the time.

Now tell me to go to Hell or mind my own business. I shouldn't have said a word if you hadn't been so in the dark as to why you are not honored on committees.

Not least your friend when telling you a thing or two,

R.F.

Forgive me again.

[To John W. Haines. ALS/Photostat. DCL.]

Franconia N.H.
June 1 1915

Dear Haines

Take notice of the town name, because this is where you are coming to live some time when the Germans drive you out of your island—as they will dammit if you don't look sharp. It seems to me you haven't done as well since I came away.

I am writing in pencil because I am off here by the Gale river[119] without a pen and with nothing to dip into but water. The water is good water but I doubt if it is turbid enough to leave the least stain if I wrote with it. It runs clear and broad and shallow on cobble stones with a noise more like talking than writing. My inclination is more like talking than writing. I wish I could make you hear. I am not settled down to write. I thought I would just drop a line to tell you where I am.

Yours ever
Robert Frost

119. See notes to RF's May 26, 1915, letter to Eaton.

[To John Bartlett. The letter is undated, but the surviving envelope is postmarked June 2, 1915. ALS. UVA.]

Franconia N.H.
[circa June 2, 1915]

Dear John:

We expect to be in this place from now on for a while. It will have to do.

I think the war may end in five years in favor of the Germans. In that case Canada will join us to save herself, and all the British will steal away over here to live. North America will become the larger island of the English-speakers of the world. Maybe you don't see it as I do. But the prophecy stands. I wish I had been able to do it in ink, so that it would be more permanently of record, but I am off here by the Gale river with nothing but water to dip into if I had a pen, and all I have is a pencil.

It was good to see you all. Take care of yourself or I shall transfer to the baby all the ambitions I have had for you.[120]

Love to you all.
R.

I had best leave to Elinor to urge you to come up soon and for long. She feels sure she can prevail on Margaret.[121]

[To Wilbur Rowell. ALS. UVA.]

Franconia N.H.
June 7 1915

Dear Mr Rowell

It is just a week since I wrote you and because there are documents and money involved I begin to feel a little anxious. I am afraid my letter may not have reached you or some letter you have sent may not have reached me.

120. At the end of May, RF visited the Bartletts in Derry, New Hampshire; the couple had recently returned from Vancouver with their infant son, Forrest.

121. RF enclosed, with this letter, a second letter from Elinor to Margaret Bartlett, urging the Bartletts to visit later in the summer (an invitation the Bartletts politely declined).

This is not to press you, but simply to let you know where we stand as a precaution.

Sincerely yours
Robert Frost

[To John Bartlett. ALS. UVA.]

Franconia N.H.
June 8 1915

Dear John:

Im not going to talk of this farm yet, because it isn't paid for. There's many a slip—Still we're on it and planting it and prospecting round over it.

Come and see us if you can. I see the difficulties. But it would cost you less to make the journey than it would us. We are five full fares now.

I was far from satisfied with what Braithwaite got out of our talk together. Not but that it was good enough and very good considering.[122] But I want time with someone who will give me time. I should like a real shot at you for a week pretty soon.

A little rain today—not enough to pay for prayers at the regular pulpit price.

I should like to meet "Andy." I wonder if he ever comes this way buying. A type like that is rarer and more interesting than the college type.

Then there will be two where there was only one before and before that none. 2728 acres ought to be playground enough for them.

Our love to you all.
R.F.

---

122. W. S. Braithwaite published "Robert Frost, New American Poet" in the *Boston Evening Transcript* on May 8, 1915.

[To Alfred Harcourt. AL (with signature cut off). Princeton.]

Franconia N.H.
June 8 1915

Dear Harcourt:

I find that my sole remaining copy of N.O.B. is one that my wife doesn't want to part with—for reasons. Will it be all right if I give you a list of the corrections I should like to see made in the next edition? There are only a few, but one or two of them are important.[123]

Sedgwick is a good friend. He bought a few poems the other day. There is a story connected with Garnett's article.[124] That just naturally put in an appearance in the nick of time. Sedgwick had already handed me over to a lady professor. Give me a man any day.

Sincerely yours

[To Susan Hayes Ward. ALS. Huntington.]

Franconia N.H.
June 8 1915

Dear Miss Ward:

You must have got hold of a very old paper if it was published before I read at Tufts. I was there on May 5—there and thereabouts.[125] I thought of you, but with all I had on hand, getting to you at South Berwick was out of the question. There were forty eleven things prearranged for me and by the time I had got two-thirds through with them I was shucked out and had to come home.

Home is here in the mountains now and probably will be for some time. We have drawn off to think over what we have done. I shall probably get

---

123. RF enclosed the list of corrections, which was separated from the letter on receipt at Henry Holt and Company. As he inscribed copies of the first edition of *NB*, RF often made textual corrections to "A Hundred Collars" and "The Code." For a record of variant readings in these poems, see Edward Connery Lathem, ed., *The Poetry of Robert Frost* (New York: Holt Paperbacks, 2002), 535–537.

124. Ellery Sedgwick, editor of *The Atlantic Monthly*, had taken "Birches," "The Road Not Taken," and "The Sound of Trees"; they appeared, along with Edward Garnett's essay, "A New American Poet," in the August 1915 number of the magazine.

125. Before reading at Tufts, RF addressed the Boston Authors' Club.

south for lectures a few times in the winter and sometime soon when I am down I mean to see you. Elinor and I would both like to make a special trip to see you, but we can't afford it. I wish you would visit us here as you did years ago.

Yours always
Robert Frost

[To Louis Untermeyer. ALS. LoC.]

Franconia N.H.
June 8 1915

You Louis U!

I believe you like to see me suffer—I do it so nobly.

It reduces itself to this, that I am native, I set up to be a poet, and am generally set down for a realist. I'll tell you how you can tell whether I am the last or not: find out how I fell in love. The realist always falls in love with a girl he has grown up and gone to school with, the romanticist with a new girl from "off somewhere." Thats not to say that they dont both fall in love with the respective girls for what they dont know about them. Mystery draws both on; only in the case of the romantic it is a more obvious mystery—a less mysterious mystery.

Pretty lively news about the festering free versters and the new magazine of poetry.[126] It seems to me you could have used to advantage at the paragraph-ends some such refrain as The Bowery, the Bowery! I'll never go there any more.[127]

I see be [*sic*] the papers that you have been disporting yourself cognito at something springy and festive got up by the Classes; so you needn't try to deny it.[128] I see it stated, though, that you weren't allowed to read any of your poetry there. That was probably salutary.

---

126. Alfred Kreymborg launched *Others: A Magazine of the New Verse* in July 1915.

127. See "The Bowery," a song from the Broadway hit *A Trip to Chinatown* (1891), music by Percy Gaunt and lyrics by Charles H. Hoyt: "I was out to enjoy the sights, / There was the Bow'ry ablaze with lights; / I had one of the devil's own nights! /I'll never go there anymore," etc.

128. "Classes": a teasing reference to Untermeyer's association with *The Masses,* which sponsored in the prewar years a number of social and fund-raising events in Greenwich Village—including balls that came to be known as "pagan routs."

A thousand copies is a lot of any book of poetry to sell. Five hundred is more of an edition than many a good man sells in England. Big reputations are made on smaller sales. I venture to say that Abercrombie has never sold over three hundred of anything, yet his name is a word of awe in high places over there. I wonder how well Robinson does with his books.

Do you know, I think that a book ought to sell. Nothing is quite honest that is not commercial. Mind you I don't put it that everything commercial is honest.

The beauty of your book is that the poems in it all get together and say something with one accord. It's a long way from you down to the ladies (they are mostly ladies in this country) who find difficulty in making the lines in one poem get together like that.

The three poems you have interested yourself in are with Ellery to stay. Ellery has said it: he is going to be good to me. He is even going to print the article by my new-found friend Garnett. He says it over praises me, but never mind, it may not hurt me: he has never known a man's head turned when his hair was turned already. But—if you would try to sell me something else, when I am sure I have something.

We are not fast in our place yet. But this is where we want to live and unless something hangs up here we shall live, and here if you will stand a sort of camping out we want you to come and see us—you and your wife, on your way to or from Oguquit[129]—and this summer. Make it a week or so. I wonder if you care for the mountains. Lafe, the mountain (alt 5000f), not the man, stands right in front of us.[130] We are all pine on this farm. Apples are not a success where the winter temperature sometimes drops to 40 below.

Yours ever
R.F.

Tell me if you will come.

---

129. Ogunquit, a town on the coast of Maine.

130. Mt. Lafayette, outside Franconia, stands 5,249 feet high, at the northern end of the Franconia Range of the White Mountains.

[To Edward Garnett (1868–1937), English critic, writer, and editor. ALS. HRC.]

Franconia NH
June 12 1915

Dear Mr Garnett:

I have tried two or three times to answer your letter but everything I started to say ran off into the unpatriotic. You see I was still fighting American editors—I hadnt heard that peace had been declared, and I had quite believed Sedgwick when he told me he didnt see how he could use your article because he had already handed me over for review to some single-bed she professor with a known preference for the beautiful in poetry. I knew I should never have such another piece of good luck as your help at this moment and I was discouraged. Sedgwick was teasing me: he meant all the time to publish the article; and I should have known as much, but it has been a long fight with editors, my rage has gathered considerable headway and it's hard to leave off believing the worst of them.

Sedgwick has just written me a beautiful letter and sent me fifty-five beautiful dollars for poetry. He says he will be good to me. He says you give me "great praise, perhaps too great," but never mind, he will risk it on me as being too old to be spoiled by flattery. I have to thank you for these signs of grace in Mr Ellery Sedgwick.

What you say for me is bound to have a tremendous effect. I can see the impression you made by the way you came to judgment last winter on the novelists. We are all prepared to envy anyone you think well of.

Most of the reviewers have made hard work of me over here. That is partly because they use up their space groping for the reason of my success in England. (I was rather successful, though not with the editor of the English Review—as you observe.[131]) What you are good enough to call my method they haven't noticed. I am not supposed to have a method. I am a naive person. They get some fun out of calling me a realist, and a realist I may be if by that they mean one who before all else wants the story to sound as if it were told the way it is because it happened that way. Of course the story must release an idea, but that is a matter of touch and emphasis, the almost incredible freedom of the soul enslaved to the hard facts of experience. I hate the story that takes its rise idea-end foremost, as it were in a formula such as It's little we know what the poor think and feel—if they think and feel at all. I could name you an English poet the editor of The English Review admires,

131. Austin Harrison edited *The English Review* from 1909 to 1923.

all of whose stories are made on just that formula. The more or less fishy incidents and characters are gathered to the idea in some sort of logical arrangement, made up and patched up and clothed on.

This is not all apropos of myself. I'll tell you a poet with a method that is a method: Lawrence.[132] I came across a poem of his in a new Imagiste Anthology just published here, and it was such a poem that I wanted to go right to the man that wrote it and say something.

You must know that I am grateful to you—and to Thomas—but I was that to Thomas before.[133]

But it's hard in these times not to think nationally and owe my gratitude to England instead of to any man or men of England. We sailed from Liverpool on February 13 but we left our hearts on the other side at least for the duration of the war. We have tried to wish the States into the war. But we cant talk to our neighbors. They are too indifferent to please us. Here on the edge of it all the fight shades off into a sort of political argument no more rancorous than we are used to at election times. The Yankee will go his joking way till something hits him harder than the loss of the lives on the Lusitania. That's not to say that a very large majority of us are not on your side. I think I can explain our state of mind. We are just near enough to the Civil War to remember that we fought it and just far enough from it to have cooled off and forgotten our reasons for fighting it.[134] We have come to doubt if we ever had any reasons. We doubt if any nation ever had any reasons for any war. So passionate reasons always evaporate. But—there is this: in passion they can be renewed. Give us time to warm up. There is no hurry. The war won't be over for some years yet.

Sincerely yours
Robert Frost

You seem to have made a friend for me in W. D. Howells. There is the best American, if you want to know the truth.

R.F.

---

132. The career of D. H. Lawrence had been of considerable interest to Garnett, to whom Lawrence had dedicated *Sons and Lovers* (1913) for his role in editing it and for his efforts in nurturing Lawrence's literary reputation. In *Some Imagist Poets: An Anthology* (1915), Amy Lowell had included seven of Lawrence's brief narrative lyrics: "Ballad of Another Ophelia," "Illicit," "Fireflies in the Corn," "A Woman and Her Dead Husband," "The Mowers," "The Scent of Irises," and "Green."

133. Edward Thomas.

134. In this connection, see "The Black Cottage" in *NB*.

[To Carrie T. Hinman (1862–1949), of the St. Johnsbury, Vermont, Athenaeum. ALS. ACL.]

Franconia N.H.
June 12 1915

My dear Mrs Hinman:

I thank you for your invitation. I could give you the reading you propose and perhaps a talk on some such subject as the "Sound of Poetry."[135] I havent contemplated reading before Woman's Clubs and so you have me at a disadvantage when you ask my price. But I think it will take about twenty five dollars to entice me as far from home as St Johnsbury. The time I should leave to you.

Very truly yours
Robert Frost

[To Edwin Arlington Robinson (1869–1935), who was awarded the Pulitzer Prize for Poetry three times in the 1920s. The play in question is Van Zorn, *which Robinson had published in 1914. ALS. NYPL.]*

Franconia N.H.
June 13 1915

Dear Robinson:

Don't think I have been all this time trying to decide what your play is if it isnt a comedy. I have read it twice over but in no perplexity. It is good writing, or better than that, good speaking caught alive—every sentence of it. The speaking tones are all there on the printed page, nothing is left for the actor but to recognize and give them. And the action is in the speech where it should be, and not along beside it in antics for the body to perform. I wonder if you agree with me that the best sentences are those that convey their own tone—that haven't to be described in italics. "With feline demureness" for instance is well imagined as it is, but do you suppose it wouldnt have been possible to make the sentence to follow indicate in itself the vocal pos-

135. RF did indeed lecture on "The Sound of Poetry" in St. Johnsbury, Vermont, on September 6, 1915. See his July 12, 1915, letter to Hinman.

[To Franklin P. Rice (1852–1919), author of a number of works on genealogy. The book he sent to RF was likely Time Notes of Franklin P. Rice: My Ancestry in America, *privately printed in Worcester, Massachusetts, in 1915. It was a Ward from Abington—Susan Hayes Ward—who, in 1894, first published a poem by RF ("My Butterfly: An Elegy") in a professional journal (the* Independent*); presumably, either she or her brother William Hayes Ward told RF the story mentioned here. ALS. BU.]*

Franconia N.H.
June 17 1915

My dear Dr Rice:

A long time ago I got a small book from you that on account of its subject looked longer than I should ever read. Hitherto I have been less interested in genealogy than in those interested in genealogy (cf a poem of mine called "The Generations of Men.") I think still that I haven't the right genealogical interest in genealogy: I don't very much care who I am, though I am glad enough to be told that there is more Rice in me than ever went in at the mouth if that may be taken as assurance of long life. I have done such a thing as run over a family history or town history on the lookout for the makings of a good story like yours about the Rice who became an Indian Chief or one a friend of mine dug up in Abington Mass when in quest of Wards. It was about a man who had come to the settlement too late and found the land all taken up and all the farmers so well supplied with great sons of their own begetting that they were hiring no help. It seemed to him an evil chance and one to appeal to God and man from. So instead of treating it from a socialistic or sociological point of view and making a general inference from a particular case he wrote a simple moving poem about it which he read in town meeting. The poem is preserved in the clerks report. And it seems to have served some purpose, for presently the author or someone of his name is found taxed as a man of property. But it is for more than a stray story that I read your book. You are entertaining, and it is easy to see why: you are the first genealogist I ever came across who found his ancestors a little amusing and even his own interest in them a little amusing.

So thank you for the book and the inscription.

Sincerely yours
Robert Frost.

If you are on this way some summer (as who is not sooner or later?) will you look me up in these mountain fastnesses? R.F.

[To Sidney Cox. ALS. DCL.]

Franconia N.H.
June 24 1915

Dear Cox:

Thanks for your article.[140] It's the right stuff. I wonder how far you would dare to go in describing your directer method in teaching English. You are much safer in a paper like yours than you would be in one like the first in your magazine for instance. It takes an awful courage to come right out and tell the way you do it in so many words. Chandler's device is dead deadly wrong. And so is that of the lady who writes on An Evolution of English Teaching.

I'm blessed if I dont believe sometimes that the whole subject of English was better neglected and left outside the curriculum. School is for boning and not for luxuriating. We dont want much school even when we are young, that is to say, we want a great deal more of life than of school. And there is no use in this attempt to make school an image of life. It should be thought of as a thing that belongs to the alphabet and notation. It came into life with these. Life must be kept up at a great rate in order to absorb any considerable amount of either one or the other. Both are nonsense unless they mix well with experience. They are the past and the future and the distant, and the problem is to bring them to bear a little on the present and the near, to make them make some difference even the slightest. Too much time spent on them is either an injury to the infant or a waste of time on the infant that refuses to be injured. Literature—I dont know where literature comes in, if it comes in at all. It is ever so much more of life anyway than of school. It is almost too emotional for school handling, almost too insubordinate and unconventional. The one thing that it is bound to be is what it is not told to be. Mind I do not say what it is told not to be, though there might be reason for its being that.

I write as I feel tonight. Some of what I say is true. Run it all through a DeLaval separator.[141]

---

140. "A Plea for a More Direct Method in Teaching English," *English Journal* 4, no. 5 (May 1915): 302–305. The same number of the journal included articles by Frank W. Chandler ("A Creative Approach to the Study of Literature") and Mary Percival ("An Evolution of Oral Composition").

141. A machine that separates milk from cream.

I am up to my eyes in milk and such like farm produce. Hence this Georgic figure. And I'm too tired to be awake writing.

Hammer away at them. You are going to do a lot. You have the energy and you have the other things.

Yours ever
Robert Frost

Have you any way of finding out for me the correct spelling of the name of some professor of English in University of Penn. who seems to sign himself Cornelius Weygant.[142] Print it out for me.

[To Edward Thomas. ALS. Cardiff.]

Franconia N.H. U.S.A.
June 26 1915

Dear Edward:

Methinks thou strikest too hard in so small a matter. A tap would have settled my poem. I wonder if it was because you were trying too much out of regard for me that you failed to see that the sigh was a mock sigh, hypocritical for the fun of the thing.[143] I dont suppose I was ever sorry for anything I ever did except by assumption to see how it would feel. I may have been sorry for having given a certain kind of people a chance at me: I have passionately regretted exposing myself.

Sedgwick has come over bag and baggage. He will print the poem along with two others in his August number. I saw the proof of it a week or two ago. The line you object to has long since taken a different form. I suppose my little jest in the poem is too much between me and myself. I read it aloud before the Phi Beta Kappa of Tufts College and while I did my best to make it obvious by my manner that I was fooling, I doubt if I wasnt taken pretty seriously. Mea culpa.

I am doing this sick in bed—so to call the thing I am sleeping in till we know definitely where we are going to live. We came down here (from the

---

142. Cornelius Weygandt (1871–1957) graduated from and taught at the University of Pennsylvania.

143. "The Road Not Taken." RF meant the poem (in part) as a playful registration of Thomas's indecisiveness, a point lost on Thomas. See *EY*, 88–89.

Lynches) because our rent up there was running into such money. And yet we have no certainty that this farm is going to be ours and so we dont dare to fetch our furniture from Plymouth. There's a flaw in the owner's title as my guardian sees it. Damn the suspense.

You begin to talk as if you werent coming to America to farm. We have gone too far into the wilds for you or something. It was inconsiderate of us. But listen: this farm is intended for the lecture camp. We won't make it our winter home for more than a couple of years. It is a picturesque spot and it is in the region where I have to take refuge for two months a year from hay fever. That's all you can say for it. About all it raises is grass and trees. Some time we must have a real fruit farm again further down along. But this place will always be here for our lecture camp scheme when that shall come to anything. Meanwhile it represents a small investment: the year's interest on it is less than the rent we have been accustomed to pay for our two months stay in the mountains. I think the pine and spruce on the place will increase in value more than fifty dollars a year. I think I told you the farm is to cost $1,000.

You may be right in coming over in your literary capacity. Elinor is afraid the rawness of these back towns will be too much for you. You know I sort of like it. The postmaster asked Lesley yesterday "How's Robert?" He's a nice old nasal-organist who thinks God has given him the freedom of your heart and mind. I should say it wasn't fair to you to assume that you couldnt stand him. He might try to place you if you let him get acquainted. And then if he should decide that you were intellectual (approximately) he would start marvelling to you every time he got a chance on the latest invention he has read of in The Scientific American.

He doesn't chew tobacco—he is a good Baptist—but many do here. And shoes arent shined. It really is the Hell of a country.

The postmaster for instance traces his descent from someone named something in 500 A.D.

I dont want to scare you, but I want to be honest and fair. The worst that could happen would be no worse than Fletcher that day in St George's. I saw Fletcher by the by in Boston.[144] Such a person to exist.

September would be all right—late in September when people are getting back to town. Bring all your introductions. Some of my new friends will be

144. RF met, again, the American poet John Gould Fletcher (1886–1950) when visiting Amy Lowell's house for dinner on March 8, 1915.

good to you. Some of them arent good to me even. That is to say they persist in liking me for the wrong reasons and in otherwise disregarding my wishes.

And there's nothing licit to drink here.

Other objections as I think of them.

As for the war, damn it! You are surely getting the worst of it. You are <u>not</u> through the Dardanelles and we know that you are not. Nothing will save you but Lloyd George and a good deal of him.[145] You must quit slacking.

The Prussian hath said in his heart, Those fool Chesterton's [*sic*].[146] I say so too. All the follies that England is like to die of are gathered together in the books of those brothers. And Belloc with his estimate of two thirds of the Germans dead and the rest buried is nothing to respect.[147]

All our papers are your friends. But they all make hard work of your present predicament. I clip from The Boston Herald the most hopeful editorial I have seen lately.

The letter I enclose may amuse you.

We-all to you-all.

Yours ever
R

---

145. Then chancellor of the exchequer, David Lloyd George (1863–1945) became prime minister in 1916, organized a war cabinet, and vigorously prosecuted the war.

146. RF echoes certain phrasings in Ecclesiastes, as for example here: "Then said I in my heart, As it happeneth to the fool, so it happeneth even to me; and why was I then more wise? Then I said in my heart, that this also is vanity" (2:15).

147. British writer Gilbert Keith Chesterton (1874–1936), his journalist brother Cecil Edward Chesterton (1879–1918), and Chesterton's close friend, the poet and essayist Hillaire Belloc (1870–1953). As part of a then-secret government effort to counter German propaganda and increase support for the war effort, G. K. Chesterton had published *The Barbarism in Berlin* in 1914. In *The Two Maps of Europe and Some Other Aspects of the Great War* (1915), Belloc wrote about the proportionately far greater German casualty rate in the first years of the war and its implications for Allied victory.

[To Wilbur Rowell. ALS. UVA.]

Franconia N.H.
July 8 1915

Dear Mr Rowell

I dont feel sure that the new documents we have brought to light make the title much clearer. I send them for what they are worth. I have learned that the Esther Hunt of the will of 1863 is the Esther Marston of the quitclaim deed, as the Registrar supposes, and that she had but the two daughters who made the deed with her.[148] Will it be necessary to establish that fact by some public record?

For my part I still fail to see why the deed is quitclaim.

Of course we want to have the thing exactly right, the more so as the Herberts have been so slovenly and unbusinesslike in all their dealings with me.

It seems a shame to trouble you with so much material in so small an affair.

Sincerely yours
Robert Frost

[To Louis Untermeyer. ALS. LoC.]

Franconia N.H.
July 8 1915

Dear Untermeyer

I think Spoon River[149] is perfectly all right for them as likes it; and that is saying a good deal for a book I am not supposed to have seen. Why have you never sent along the copy you promised? And there was a book of Oppenheim's I was to have had.[150]

---

148. Esther (1822–1897; née Esther Guernsey) married Ezra G. Hunt (1821–1865), owner of the Franconia farm. Three years after Hunt died, she married Orin Marston. In 1894 she sold the property to Joseph E. Herbert and his son, Willis E. Herbert. RF bought it, in turn, from the latter. Surviving property records indicate a two-acre discrepancy in the later transactions; the unaccounted for land may have been parceled out to Esther's daughters in the 1863 will to which RF refers.

149. Edgar Lee Masters (1868–1950) published his *Spoon River Anthology* in the spring of 1915.

150. James Oppenheim (1882–1932), poet, novelist, and editor, had lately published a volume of poetry, *Songs for the New Age* (1914) and a novel, *The Beloved* (1915). He would join Untermeyer in launching the *Seven Arts* in 1916.

Forgive me my nonsense as I also forgive the nonsense of those who think they talk sense. All I insist on is that nothing is quite honest that is not commercial. You must take that as said in character. Of course I dont mean by that that it isnt true. Nothing is true except as a man or men adhere to it—to live for it, to spend themselves on it, to die for it. Not to argue for it! There's no greater mistake than to look on fighting as a form of argument. To fight is to leave words and act as if you believed—to act as if you believed. Sometimes I have my doubts of words altogether and I ask myself what is the place of them. They are worse than nothing unless they do something, unless they amount to deeds as in ultimatums and war crys. They must be flat and final like the showdown in poker from which there is no appeal. My definition of literature would be just this, words that have become deeds.[151]

Remember all I say is said in character. I urge nothing.

It is as well that you shouldn't come here now. Because we are not really here ourselves yet. I am milking a cow or two and otherwise acting as if the farm were mine, but I havent felt secure enough in it to have fetched my furniture or to have laid out any money on repairs. I have to wait on the decision of a guardian in these matters. The guardian holds a few hundred dollars in trust for me which if he thinks best he can lend me to buy the farm with. And if not, not. Don't tell my critics of this lest it should prejudice them against my unfortunate books.

You will be just beaching—quenching your "speed in the slushy sand"—your New York speed.[152] Take it easy and dont upon any consideration look for copy—as dear old Wilfrid Gibson does wherever he goes. Once we were coming home from some country races, what they call point-to-point races, when he asked me uneasily I didnt see a thing there I could use did you?[153] He counted the day lost and only asked consolation in learning that I had lost it too. Those troubles rather told on me in my last six months in England. Now I can forget them in a couple of cows that have to be anchored at both ends as a boat ought to be when you fish for perch and pout.

I'll bet there is nearly as much water here today as there is where you are. And we care personally. We have to care. We have a garden we don't want

---

151. See "Some Definitions by Robert Frost," where these sentences appear again almost verbatim (*CPRF*, 84).

152. RF borrows the quoted phrase from stanza one of Robert Browning's "Meeting at Night."

153. "Point-to-point races": amateur steeplechases involving hunting horses (usually thoroughbreds).

drowned. We easily fall into bitter apostrophe when the weather goes wrong—we dont stop to ask whom to. We talk on. I can't help thinking it is good for us after our three years detachment and disinterestedness.

Iron cross for you if you kill more than so many of my enemies at once.[154]

Yours ever
Robert Frost

[To Harold Goddard Rugg. ALS. DCL.]

Franconia N.H.
July 8 1915

Dear Mr Rugg

If you can excuse the roughness of this copy of Birches it is yours to throw where you please when you have done with it.[155]

Pleasant (for me) that you should have fallen in with Fay so soon after my visit with him at Tufts.[156] I should be almost sure from the way he treated me that he wouldn't be saying anything very bad about me behind my back.

I have your promise then that you will look for me sometime soon. You know where I am. When you get to Franconia, enquire for me at Howard's store.

Yours always
Robert Frost

[To Carrie T. Hinman. ALS. ACL.]

Franconia NH
July 12 1915

My dear Mrs Hinman:

I sha'n't mind paying my own expenses, the fare for such a short distance will be so little; and perhaps I can make the round trip in one day so as to avoid hotel expenses. Poets have to consider these things.

---

154. The Iron Cross, a Prussian military decoration awarded for valor during the Napoleonic wars, was re-commissioned for use during the Franco-Prussian War, World War I, and, later, World War II.

155. RF copied out the poem on four sheets of notepaper, enclosed with the letter (and still associated with it at DCL).

156. Charles E. Fay, professor of English at Tufts University, where RF read as Phi Beta Kappa poet on May 5 (see *CPRF*, 170).

Yes "The Sound of Poetry" will serve to describe the talk I undertake to give you before reading from my poems.[157]

September 6 then.

And thank you for your interest.

Sincerely yours
Robert Frost

[To Joseph Warren Beach (1880–1957), American poet, scholar, educator; professor of English at the University of Minnesota from 1907 until his retirement in 1948. ALS. Minnesota.]

Franconia N H
July 15 1915

My dear Mr Beach:

If I have buried myself in mountains it is not with the idea of hiding from the undesigning and inoffensive or from anyone else for that matter who seeks me as a friend. I shall be only too happy to see you for a talk on poetry and your poetical pilgrimage. I make no secret of my station on the railroad. You will have to come to Littleton N.H. where you will find a stage waiting to bring you on to Franconia. You will have to spend one night here at the very least. I wish I could say Come to us, and possibly I could a few weeks later; but we are not yet really settled on our farm: we are without a good deal of our furniture: everything is at sixes and sevens with us.

Will you remember me very specially to Braithwaite if you are seeing him?

And be sure to let me know when to look for you. I don't think you can do better than take the train arriving at Littleton at something like 4.45 P.M.

Till our meeting then!

Sincerely yours
Robert Frost

---

157. See RF's June 12, 1915, letter to Hinman.

[To Walter Prichard Eaton. ALS. UVA.]

Franconia NH
July 15 1915

My dear Mr Eaton

Will you mind if I write to thank you for a thing I have just had from Snow?[158] I mean your Barn Doors and Byways.[159] You make it perfectly clear to me why you are provoked with yourself for having let the editors put you off your poetry. I never read such books without wondering how they came to be in prose. And before this I have expostulated with their authors for doing them in prose. My British friend Edward Thomas whose work yours reminds me of in some ways has had to listen to me. Sometimes I get him to write a poem. I have had one in the post from him lately.

I think poetry itself is to blame. It seems to want to exclude too much. And if left to its own tendencies, I believe in time it would exclude everything but love and the moon. That's why it's none the worse for a little rough handling once in a while. Do it a violence, I say, if you have to to make it aware of what's going on around it.

Far be it from me though to regret that all the poetry isn't in verse. I'm sure Im glad of all the unversified poetry of Walden—and not merely nature-descriptive, but narrative as in the chapter on the play with the loon on the lake, and character-descriptive as in the beautiful passage about the French-Canadian woodchopper.[160] That last along with some things in Turgenieff must have had a good deal to do with the making of me.[161]

158. Sidney Bruce Snow (1878–1944), a Unitarian clergyman; see also the notes to RF's May 26, 1915, letter to Eaton.

159. Eaton's collection of essays, *Barn Doors and Byways,* was published in Boston by Small, Maynard and Company in 1913.

160. The loon appears in *Walden* in the chapter titled "Brute Neighbors"; the French-Canadian woodchopper turns up in "Visitors."

161. Ivan Turgenev (1818–1883), Russian novelist, short story writer, and playwright. RF has particularly in mind Turgenev's *Sketches from a Hunter's Album* (published in book form first in 1852), with is richly detailed descriptions of Russian peasant life. The title has been variously translated as *The Hunting Sketches* and *A Sportsman's Sketches*. Morris Tilley, professor of English at the University of Michigan, reported that RF cited *A Sportsman's Sketches* as one of the books that had most influenced him (*YT*, 602).

Yours is a lovely book—full of things I wish I had thought of first—so we are quits there. It is a poem just to mention driving into a strange barn to bide the passing of a thunder storm.

You were somewhere near my old haunts when you were at your grandfather's at Reading. I have been right through Reading in my walks from Lawrence to Boston and I believe I considered that at Reading I had done half my distance.[162]

And somewhere near my present haunts you say you are going to be this summer. I dont just make out where you see Moosilauke from.[163] It cant be far from here; for we see it looking southward down or rather up the valley of the Ham Branch.[164] You wont fail to make us some sign, will you? I have looked forward to meeting you.

Sincerely yours
Robert Frost

[To Llewellyn Jones, editor of the Chicago Evening Post. *In August 1915* The Atlantic Monthly *published three poems by RF ("Birches," "The Road Not Taken," and "The Sound of Trees") alongside an article about RF by the English critic Edward Garnett; the event occasioned the following letter. ALS. Private collection of Pat Alger.]*

Franconia N.H.
July 17 1915

Dear Mr Jones:

Will you, then, if you see anything in The August Atlantic you can like a little, kindly speak of it to the Western World?[165]

---

162. The passage in question appears early in the first essay in *Barn Doors and Byways*: "The earliest barn-door vista of which you have recollection was not many miles from Boston, and there looms in the foreground a great yellow stage-coach swung on straps, that used to ply between Reading and North Reading until the trolley superseded it hardly a generation ago. It was your grandfather's barn that housed this coach, after it had deposited you at grandfather's gate across the road, beneath the balm-of-Gilead tree that made cut fingers a pleasure."

163. Mt. Moosilauke is in the White Mountain Forest, just due south of Franconia.

164. The Ham Branch River originates in the town of Easton, New Hampshire, and flows north through a valley at the western base of the Kinsman Range near Franconia.

165. A Chicago newspaper, inaugurated in 1885.

I hope you are taking a vacation by water or on a mountain somewhere and that this only finds you by being forwarded.

Sincerely yours always
Robert Frost

[To John W. Haines. Text derived from SL, 183–184 (Thompson apparently omits a portion of letter); see the notes to RF's first (June 1914) letter to Haines.]

Franconia NH
July 17 1915

Dear Haines,

There's a heartache that attends remembering hopelessly distant places and it is as definite as if it were due to strains put upon actual tentacles by which the heart makes fast to all the places it ever staid overnight in. The thought of Gloucester with me not there is a melancholy. That's why it is so natural to write of haunts we aren't haunting. Next thing you know I shall be reversing my machinery and writing of England from America. What would my friends all say to that? Shall I be allowed to write of anything but New England the rest of my life? And May Hill without me for evermore[166] is as sad as the world should be without me the day after I die. You could be there, but I, though I am as free to think May Hill as you, I cannot come near it.[167]

Thomas did me a nice little picture of you out with your flower canister just as on the day when I first met you the better part of the way up from the Greenway to Little Iddens. These things are a pleasant pain.[. . .]

Some day the war will end one way or the other (decisively I trust) and then you will come to see us. I wonder what you will say to our cheerful self-sufficiency as a nation. You'd think

166. One might expect "forever more," but the phrase "for evermore" occurs scores of times in the King James Bible; RF adds, for the nonce, a slightly scriptural note of gravity. (Though the original manuscript of the letter is now missing, we have no reason to suppose Thompson mis-transcribed the phrase in *SL*.)

167. May Hill, some seventeen miles south of Ledbury, lay close to Haines's residence.

Europe might sink and the wave of her sinking sweep
And spend itself on our shores and we should not weep;
Our cities would not even turn in their sleep.[168]

We don't really care what happens over there. It doesn't touch us nearly enough. At least we can't see that it does. We stand lost in sentimental contemplation. Not one nation in the whole fight is out for anything but its own interest. We tell ourselves that the one thing we would not go to war for is self-interest. The fact of course is that that is the only thing we would go to war for. We are only able to hold the high opinions of ourselves we do because our interests are not touched. You can't make it our war any way you look at it. We can't by trying. If we look uncommonly foolish at the present moment, it is from trying overhard to enter into the spirit of a row we weren't prepared for and don't understand. I believe the Germans have written of us as having done our part to drive them to desperate measures by the step we took outward into world politics when we went to the East Indies. But we are blissfully unconscious of having done anything to make an enemy by a simple act of business expediency. We may have heard of the Germans' view, but we suspect them of being too philosophical and of looking for the bottom of things that haven't got a bottom or a bottom worth looking for.

I tell you these things for the fun of it. Be careful to distinguish between what I say as speaking for the country and as speaking for myself. You know the views I hold. I like the Germans, but they must excuse me if I want to see them exterminated. Abercrombie's poem won't do—the small one you sent me I mean. Too Bryanesque.[169]

Love to you all.

Always yours
R.F.

---

168. This never-finished or collected fragment (held now at Dartmouth) dates from 1892, and includes these additional lines: "Our faces are not that way or should not be / Our future is in the West on the other Sea."

169. That is to say, not martial enough (though it is not clear which poem RF means): William Jennings Bryan, Woodrow Wilson's secretary of state from 1913 to 1915, opposed entry into the war.

[To Louis Untermeyer. ALS. LoC.]

Franconia N.H.
July 20 1915

My dear Untermeyer:

You do just right to humor me when I am like that: one of my wife's relatives married into a family in which there was a taint of insanity.

That was a bad letter I wrote you the other day and what was worse I sent it. I dont remember what I said in it, but it was naught. Always give a fellow another chance when he behaves badly and still another chance after that. Never draw a line beyond which you wont allow a friend or anyone else to go. It is the mark of a small mind to draw the line anywhere.

I wrote of everything I believe but what was really bothering me, which was no more important a person than Richard Burton—poor dear—author of the mortal line (I don't lie): The Sough of winds in Immemorial trees, (caps not his) which brings together in some sort of relation the two worst poeticisms of our poetical bancruptcy [*sic*].[170] Why should I mind Richard, you say. I dont mind him today. But I did two or three days ago while his offense was still fresh on the floor. He had been writing to a common friend a pious wish that for my own sake I weren't quite so "daringly radical." Its the damned hypocracy [*sic*] of his daringly that seems like the whole nation against me. You see the force of it and you smell the device. It makes him seem to speak as a well-wisher. Torment his picture.

I come to you with this sorrow because you are a young feller with enough oil in your feathers to shed it for me. My own feathers are drying up with age. (Figure not necessarily drawn from the barnyard.)

Remember this if you are still in the water: There is no help in a wave when you are coming back to shore tired out. It will be going your way. For a moment you will be lifted up with hope on the crest of it. But it carries nothing with it. It will go forward itself but leave you to the mercy of any current. It is a hateful delusion when you are desperate for solid ground under your feet.

Poem—what? Willitscan?

You will be glad to hear that my cows and I have composed our differences and I now milk them anchored at one end only. They have accepted me as

170. Richard Burton (1861–1940) was an American poet and critic. RF quotes the second line of a poem entitled "An Impression," later collected in *Poems of Earth's Meaning* (1917).

their milker in place of the calves. The trouble was that I wasnt enough like the calves, which are black and ringstreaked, to impersonate them. And I lacked some of the calves' little ways. I was easily known for a changeling.

Isn't it the usual thing to wind up a bucolic like this with an Ah here we touch the realities of life? Let's make a list of the realist things we know.

We have a maple tree we call the Torch on the farm. We'll be lighting it about the time you come.

Yorn
R.F.

[To Sidney Cox. ALS. DCL.]

Franconia N.H.
July 20 1915

Dear Cox:

I want to see you intirely [*sic*] and I wonder if we can't arrange it in spite of the devil. Let me tell you first how we are fixed. We are not really in possession here yet. We are still without our furniture and sleeping cramped in borrowed beds. There has been some difficulty about the title to the place which has kept us from going ahead very far with our plans. But it might be that I could find you a room with some farmer near us and for meals you could picnic with us. That seems an inhospitable sort of invitation and if you care to wait a year you can have a better one—if we are all alive and not worse off then than we are now. What say you?

Some of the rest of them have been reprinting me without money and without price. I imagine it is good advertising. They may teach me a thing or two, as for instance how to drop -g's from words ending in -ing. The parodies in the New York papers all rebuke me for not dropping the g. I can stand being parodied in the same way I can stand being pirated. But I hate being instructed—at my age.

A place I passed at night alone something like twenty years ago made In a Vale[171] then and there in my head and I wrote it down with few changes the next morning.

171. Collected in *ABW.*

You have been a good friend to the books. You must twit your Illinois professor with the Garnett article in The Atlantic for August.[172] The Nation is nonsense. Its bragging advertisement is everywhere.[173]

I may see you, then, when you are on your walk. I am just out of Franconia—just off the Easton road at the first bridge you come to.[174]

Yours ever
R.F.

[To Edward Thomas. This letter, together with two others to Thomas, were in the hands of the collector Howard George Schmitt, an acquaintance of RF's, when Lawrance Thompson printed them in Selected Letters of Robert Frost *(1964). They have since gone missing; efforts to locate Schmitt's papers have been unsuccessful. The text given here is drawn from* SL, *184–185.]*

Franconia N.H.
July 31 1915

Dear Edward:

I am within a hair of being precisely as sorry and as glad as you are.

You are doing it for the self-same reason I shall hope to do it for if my time ever comes and I am brave enough, namely, because there seems nothing else for a man to do.[175]

You have let me follow your thought in almost every twist and turn toward this conclusion. I know pretty well how far down you have gone and how far off sideways. And I think the better of you for it all. Only the very bravest could come to the sacrifice in this way. Davies is only human but he

---

172. See the headnote to RF's May 30, 1915, letter to Harcourt.

173. The reference to "The Nation" as "nonsense" is puzzling. Lascelles Abercrombie's review of *NB* in *The Nation* (London) for June 13, 1914, was quoted widely in the United States (and RF liked it); *The Nation* (New York) had also named *NB* one of the four best books of 1915.

174. On July 25, Sidney Cox and his friend Alex Bloch began a walking trip that took them from Rutland, Vermont, to Franconia, where the two men hiked during the day and spent evenings with RF. See *RFSC*, 74–76.

175. After some hesitation, Thomas had decided to enlist in the British Army. In a letter dated July 14, 1915, he had written to RF: "It is done. The doctor passed me yesterday & I am going up again on Monday to be attested & get my uniform."

is a robber who cant forget stealing while his neighbor has anything left to steal.[176]

I have never seen anything more exquisite than the pain you have made of it. You are a terror and I admire you. For what has a man locomotion if it isnt to take him into things he is between barely and not quite standing.

I should have liked you anyway—no friend ever has to strive for my approval—but you may be sure I am not going to like you less for this.

All belief is one. And this proves you are a believer.

I cant think what you would ask my forgiveness for unless it were saying my poetry is better than it is.[177] You are forgiven as I hope to be forgiven for the same fault. I have had to [overstate] myself in the fight to get up. Some day I hope I can afford to lean back and deprecate as excessive the somewhat general praise I may have won for what I may have done.

Your last poem Aspens seems the loveliest of all. You must have a volume of poetry ready for when you come marching home.[178]

I wonder if they are going to let you write to me as often as ever.

Affectionately
R.F.

[To Wilbur Rowell. ALS. UVA.]

Franconia N.H.
Aug 6 1915

Dear Mr Rowell

I am sorry to have to seem to press you when I know how busy you are, but my position here really grows so awkward that I thought I ought to tell you. The man who sells us this place is buying another. He has actually moved to the other to make room for us on this and is counting on our

176. Welsh poet W. H. Davies (1871–1940). Thomas had been his benefactor on several occasions, raising funds to cover Davies' debts.

177. In his July 14 letter Thomas had written: "If there is anything to forgive you would forgive me, I believe. But I don't feel inclined yet for explaining myself, though if you were here I should. [W. H.] Davies by the way looked serious when I told him & said 'Well, I suppose it will be compulsion very soon.' He thinks he thinks so. Goodbye. Yours ever" (held at DCL).

178. Henry Holt and Company, RF's publisher, issued Thomas's *Poems* in the spring of 1917, at about the time Thomas was killed in action at the Battle of Arras on April 9.

money to meet his obligations with there. The whole transaction interests too many people for comfort. It has even got into The Atlantic Monthly which speaks of me as having bought a farm in Franconia. People know that I was buying a farm; they know that I have settled down on a farm; they assume the rest. It is all rather funny, but, as I have said, it is awkward too. It keeps me explaining to everybody. And the Herberts[179] seem a little tired of explanations.

Sincerely yours
Robert Frost.

[To Nathan Haskell Dole. ALS. Harvard.]

Franconia N.H.
Aug 6 1915

Dear Dole:

It isn't from a sense of having sinned that I have kept still so long. Dont think that. What I said presumptuously was wrung from me. I simply had to tell you how I suffered from your pathetic cheerfulness. I believe I never saw anything more sad and pleading than your puns. The Zend Avesta was an old story with me when I was a bad little boy in San Francisco.[180] I give you a wiser saying than that of the Zend Avesta: never be cheerful but when there is something to be cheerful about. Above all if you will wear a false cheerfulness see that it is not as easy to see through as false whiskers.

Having said so much in all sincerity and rather for my own relief than for your good (I suppose), let me turn to less controversial subjects.

We are not quite settled in our place yet, but we have been getting pleasure out of it, if few vegetables, now these two months. We name our cows fresh every day to insure the milk's being fresh. Today they were Rosalyo and Millicent: yesterday Mandragora and Moly (not Molly): the day before Hepsibah and Amariah (fem.) the day before that Lilith or Helen or Antigone. The calves we refrain from naming for fear of learning to love what

179. The family from whom RF bought the Franconia farm.

180. The Avesta is a collection of sacred Zoroastrian texts. The word *Zend* means "interpretation," and in this context refers to paraphrases of, and commentaries on, the Avesta in late Middle Persian.

must soon be slaughtered. What if we should shrink from attaching ourselves to everything on the same principle?

I am sick sick for my friends in England today. They must know that the phrase "Time fights for the Allies"[181] will not save them. They must have been in terrible straights [*sic*] these last few months that they havent struck the least stroke to help Warsaw.[182] Well, the seas are still England's.

Some time I mean to drag you up here for a visit.

You are a good man and I am

Always yours
Robert Frost.

[To Harold Monro, owner of the Poetry Bookshop in London, and editor of Poetry and Drama. *The "she" referred to in the first sentence is Mrs. Alfred Nutt, who ran the London firm of David Nutt, the publisher of RF's first two books. In the letter, RF also refers to his friend the English poet Lascelles Abercrombie. ALS. Private collection of Pat Alger.]*

Franconia N.H., U.S.A.
Aug 7 1915

Dear Monro:

The trouble has been altogether with the she who calls herself David Nutt. She has steadily refused me permission to let you have the poems for the chapbook.[183] You may know what she is to everybody. She is trying to be particularly nasty to me as being of a nation not represented on the firing line in this war. So she puts it and it sound [*sic*] patriotic. But I havent failed to discover that her real grievance against me is that I wont write war letters to the papers to get my name before the public and help her sell books.

She carries her not quite disinterested disapprobation so far that she refuses to give me an accounting. I am told that my contract with her is very bad: still it does seem to call for an annual accounting and for royalties of 12% on both my books. This is the only hope I see, namely that she may have let me out of her clutches by violating the contract. Of course I dont know but

181. A common slogan during the war.

182. German troops moved into Warsaw on August 5.

183. Monro had asked RF for a small collection of new poems, to be published as a chapbook (an "intermediate form of publication," as Monro phrased it in his August 24 reply to RF, held now at DCL).

I am going to enquire. Abercrombie very generously offers to have it out with her for me.

I had set my heart on the chapbook. And I never thought of such a thing as her standing in the way. I was within an ace of letting you go ahead with it without asking her permission, on the assumption that it was not strictly a book and so not subject to the terms of the contract. A chapbook seems more like a magazine than a book. Luckily I decided to be on the safe side—or I might have got you into trouble.

I wonder what would happen if <u>you</u> asked her for the poems. She might listen to you. I suppose she would say she was afraid of losing the American copyright. You could promise to take care of that: I will take care of it for you.

I am glad poetry goes on in spite of the war—or is it because of the war? I shouldn't like war if it were incompatible with poetry as some seem to think it is incompatible with Christianity.

Yes what you people began for me has gone merrily on over here. But I am less grateful to you than homesick for you. I often long to look in on you in your Holborn slum.[184] Will there be beds for me if I turn up there with a few more children some day?[185]

Yours ever
Robert Frost

[To John Bartlett. ALS. UVA.]

Franconia N.H.
Aug 8 1915

Dear John:

I feel as if we had gone and done it in getting settled so near and yet so far. How much better off are we than when we were 6000 miles apart? I speak on some such assumption as that we both need each other of course. I know I need you or someone like you dating back to the days when my friends were those who had brains enough to judge me for themselves. I have lately been piled on top of by a lot of people who mistake their appreciation of my re-

---

184. In the Bloomsbury district of London, where the Poetry Bookshop stood.

185. In fact Elinor Frost was, at the time, pregnant; the pregnancy ended in miscarriage in late November.

views for an understanding of me. As an honest man I am not a little disturbed by it all. I long for something old and sure to cling to.

Is this the way it stands, that I will have to go to you if I want your company? You positively wont think of trying it up here for your asthma? I see a possibility of my getting south to farm sooner or later. I am not going to be satisfied with just grass-farming. But this place will have to serve for a year or two or until I am rich enough to let it lie idle all but two or three months in the year. I should always want to keep it as a summer resort. I wish it were so we could have it together. We could be neighbors in some good fruit region down your way and up here we could all live together for the hay fever season. Wouldn't that be about right?

My scheme for a summer literary camp here is on its way toward realization. I'll tell you more of it soon if it interests you.

Elinor had the pleasantest time with you on your mountain.[186] I have been sick to see you ever since she came home with the little box of wild honey. Why would you live in such a lonely place without benefit of teachers where I couldn't have joined you even if I had tried to make my plans harmonize with yours? It's rotten—too rotten to go on about. Say something helpful in your next letter.

Affectionately
R. F.

[To Alfred Harcourt. ALS. Princeton.]

Franconia N.H.
August 12 1915

Dear Harcourt

The sight of so much of that letter apparently en bloc gave me rather a turn. But I knew I was safe in your hands. You let nothing in to give offense. The only question in my mind now is whether you let enough in to do the editors justice.[187] They probably deserve a little discredit. I love them not and

---

186. Elinor had visited the Bartletts at their summer farm in the Pawtuckaway Mountains. See the notes to RF's June 17, 1915 letter to Bartlett.

187. The "letter" in question was, as Harcourt phrased it in a July 21 letter to RF, a "literary note" on the circumstances of the publication of *NB*, to be used in advertising copy for the American edition. As for American editors, in his August 15 reply to the

I hate what they have taught people to think was American poetry. If I ran away from anything when I went to England it was the American editor. Very privately in the inmost recesses of me I suppose my Hegeira[188] was partly a protest against magazine poets and poetry. We wont insist on that now; but please remember it when I am dead and gone.

I wonder if you had the David Nutt contract that I sent you, and I wonder what you made of it.[189] It is going to take the stuff all out of me if I am going to have to write books all the rest of my life for that woman. She has gone so far as to forbid my publishing anything in a magazine.

I am asking you about this because some of my poetical friends in England are urging me to let them attack her. Would you let them or might it only make matters worse? I have been asked to contribute to an annual along with the six best poets over there and I don't even know whether I can do that without getting other people into trouble. Pity if I can't; it would do so much to spread reputation.

Was the Times editorial so bad that you thought I had best not see it?[190]

I enclose a letter for you to do what you think best about. I am all out of N.o.B.

Yours ever
Robert Frost

---

present letter Harcourt writes: "I worked your letter over very carefully for the literary note, and am glad that I did not say anything to distress you. I am rather hoping that you will have experiences with American editors that will make you glad we 'hardly did them justice' " (letter held now at DCL).

188. RF favors a spelling that, though largely out of use by 1900, had been quite common in the seventeenth and eighteenth centuries.

189. In his aforementioned August 15 reply, Harcourt says: "Yes, we have the David Nutt contract in the safe, and I am enclosing it. I have taken the liberty of keeping a copy, which we are asking our lawyer to look at closely . . . We shall need to know just where we stand before the next time of royalty payment in October. In the meantime, I cannot see what harm it would do for you to let your poetical friends in England raise all the rumpus they want to" (letter held now at DCL).

190. On August 8, 1915, the following note ran in the *New York Times* column Book World in Summer and Autumn: "Robert Frost, whose 'North of Boston' has been welcomed with acclaim in both the United States and England, explains that his book of poems was published in England merely by 'accident.' He happened to be in that country when it occurred to him that he had enough manuscripts to make a book. The collection of poems was accepted quickly and gladly by the first publisher to whom he showed it, and met when published with instant success, as it did a little later in this country."

[To George Browne. ALS. Plymouth.]

Franconia N.H.
Aug 12 1915

Dear Browne:

While I am trying to make up my mind whether I can get down to see you, why don't you take a run up through the notch to see me? From Plymouth to Franconia in a good car is nothing. Your coming here wouldnt make me any less likely to go there. On the contrary it might make me more likely by starting some subject that we couldnt finish in one visit. We could talk about tones (in tones) till the cows came home and then you could see me milk them out of doors—the cows, not the tones. You would find us in circumstances where we have to be terribly informal, so informal that you might not be able to tell off hand whether we were not so of choice. But I don't think that would bother you. Come and make a day or two of it and let me thank you in person for all the lovely things of your letter. I wish you could bring along some of the boys' papers you speak of. We must be projecting our new method in teaching English composition. I won't say that you might not carry me off if you came after me.

Yours always
Robert Frost

[To Amy Lowell. ALS. Harvard.]

Franconia N.H.
August 13 1915

My dear Miss Lowell:

There is an ominous note in your letter that seems to tell me you are getting ready to throw me over as a poet of the elect ostensibly on the ground that I am become a Best-seller when really it will be because I haven't convinced you that I like your book.[191] What's the use of my trying to say anything now when I am in a corner? You will be sure to ascribe my prettiest compliments to fear. But I leave it to Beach if I didn't tell him I liked the book

191. *Sword Blades and Poppy Seed*, Lowell's second book of poetry, appeared in 1914.

when I was a free agent.[192] You know my little weakness for dramatic tones. I go so far as to say that there is no poetry of any kind that is not made of dramatic tones. Your poetry always speaks. I wish sometimes you would leave to Browning some of the broader intonations he preempted. The accent-on-the-you sort of thing. But that's a small matter (or not so large as it might be): the great thing is that you and some of the rest of us have landed with both feet on all the little chipping poetry of a while ago. We have busted 'em up as with cavalry. We have, we have, we have. Yes I like your book and all I lay up against you is that you will not allow me a sense of humor.[193] Occurs to me a simple way to make you: I could make up my mind to stand outside your Poetry Society until you did.

Sincerely yours
Robert Frost

[To William Stanley Braithwaite. ALS. Middlebury.]

Franconia N.H.
August 14 1915

Dear Braithwaite:

Would you come up about now?—and fetch along the book you gave me? I cant say that we are quite settled yet, but we are not likely to be this year and what's that to keep us from seeing our friends if they are such as will make allowances for us without being asked to? Don't you think we could kill a week walking and talking? I am bursting with sounds I want to utter about the sound of poetry. Be careful how you refuse me. If you dont come I shall be sure it is because you are too nice to have anything to do with the author of a Best-seller (non-fiction) which is what I am told I have become. Isn't it—well hard to know how to take?

Sincerely yours
Robert Frost.

---

192. Joseph Warren Beach (1880–1957), American poet, novelist, scholar, and long-time member of the faculty at the University of Minnesota.

193. In her review of *NB*, published in *The New Republic* for February 20, 1915.

[To Rose Fay Thomas (1852–1929), widow of Theodore Thomas (1835–1905), classical violinist and first conductor of the Chicago Symphony Orchestra. ALS. Newberry.]

Franconia N.H.
Aug 15 1915

My dear Mrs Thomas:

Do you suppose I should be permitted to send the bride, your niece, for wedding present one of the books I wrote—as long as I was to have been invited to the wedding if it had not been so sudden? You would have to give me her address and write her yourself to tell her how it happened. You could say that it was with the idea of piling poetry on poetry that I send the book.

Sincerely yours
Robert Frost.

[To John Bartlett. The reference is apparently to a visit RF made to the Bartletts' farm in the Pawtuckaway Mountains (the family would soon settle in Raymond, New Hampshire). ALS. UVA.]

Franconia N.H.
Aug 24 1915

Dear John-a:

You're a good one—and a deep. I don't pretend to have fathomed you on this visit: but I got down into you far enough for my purpose: I know what I know. All I say is: You'll do. We had good talks. I like you and everything about and around you.

Affectionately
R.

[To William Stanley Braithwaite. ALS. Middlebury.]

Franconia N.H.
August 24 1915

Dear Braithwaite:

Go right ahead with your " 'anthology' " (double quotes) and come up here in October when you are free.[194] Nothing can beat October in these mountains. You wait till you see. But you must stay for more than a couple of days.

Thanks for all the good words of your letter. You contrive to be inspiring—you and Robinson.[195]

I shall be honored if you will use the poems in your book, honored enough if you will use two, honored beyond dreams if you will use three.[196]

No I haven't seen Pound's letter.[197] What new terms of abuse has he found for your review? Why would you review him? He needs letting alone. The English have ceased to give him space in their papers.

Any time, then, in September or October. Take your choice. We'll have good talks.

Sincerely yours
Robert Frost

194. Beginning in 1913, Braithwaite compiled his annual *Anthology of Magazine Verse and Yearbook of American Poetry*; the last appeared in 1939.

195. Edwin Arlington Robinson.

196. In his *Anthology of Magazine Verse* for 1915, Braithwaite included "Birches," "The Road Not Taken," and "The Death of the Hired Man."

197. In August 1915 Ezra Pound wrote from London to the editor of the *Boston Evening Transcript*: "I notice in the *Current Opinion* for June a quotation from the paper to the effect that my friend Robert Frost has done what no other American poet had done in this generation 'and that is, unheralded, unintroduced, untrumpeted he won the acceptance of an English publisher on his own terms' etc. Now seriously what about me? Your (? negro) reviewer might acquaint himself with that touching little scene in Elkin Mathews' shop some years since. Mathews: 'Ah, eh, ah, would you, now, be prepared to assist in the publication?' E.P.: 'I've a shilling in my clothes, if that's any use to you.' Mathews: 'Oh well. I want to publish 'em. Anyhow.' And he did. No sir, Frost was a bloated capitalist when he struck this island, in comparison to yours truly, and you can put that in your editorial pipe though I don't give a damn whether you print the fact." See *The Selected Letters of Ezra Pound*, D. D. Paige, ed. (New Directions): 62–63. Elkin Mathews published several of Pound's books, beginning in 1909.

[RF met Morris Palmer Tilley (1876–1947), professor of English at the University of Michigan in Ann Arbor, while the Tilleys were summering in Franconia near the farm where RF settled in June 1915. The Frosts and the Tilleys remained friends for many years. RF's sister, Jeanie, enrolled at the University of Michigan in 1916, and Morris Tilley assisted RF in looking out for her interests there; the two men saw much of each other when RF later taught at the university during the 1921–1923 and 1925–1926 academic years. ALS. UM.]

Franconia N.H.
Aug 24 1915

My dear Prof. Tilley:

Miss Newton had written of your coming and we had been wondering when we were to have the pleasure of seeing you. I should say come at once, but I am just off to read poetry to some farmers near Plymouth (N.H.) and may not be back for a few days.[198] How would Monday suit you?—or if Monday should be rainy, Tuesday?

Sincerely yours
Robert Frost

[To Sidney Cox. ALS. DCL.]

Franconia N.H.
August 30 1915

Dear Cox

I will write you a better letter than this in requital of all the lovely things you have been saying of me and Bloch[199] has been trying to say. Bloch mustn't try too hard to be adequate. We liked him and we saw that he didn't dislike us. So a good deal goes without saying.

But as I was about to say this letter is chiefly designed to deal with the business you have so gloriously stirred up for me. Money! You can thank Chase[200] for his interest and make the tentative proposal as coming from

198. RF refers to his stay with George Browne in Bridgewater, New Hampshire, some six miles outside Plymouth.

199. Alex Bloch, a German schoolteacher and friend of Cox's. See Evans, *RFSC*, 66.

200. George C. Chase, president of Bates College (Cox's alma mater). Here began a series of negotiations pertaining to a talk RF was to give in the spring of 1916 at Bates. See RF to Chase, May 5, 1916.

yourself (or from me if you think best) that I should have seventy-five dollars and pay my own expenses. You could put it as a question if you were speaking for yourself. You manage it as seems wise. If you think seventy-five too much and want me to go for less either for my sake or your own make it fifty, and expenses.

I think of you when I look into the tent.

The last state of the one who speaks in the Ode to Duty[201] is no better than the first.

I will write. Be good.

Ever yours
R.F.

[To Alfred Harcourt. ALS. Princeton.]

Franconia N.H.
Aug 30 1915

Dear Harcourt:

I received and quite understood your telegram. But I couldn't ask you to come to Boston when you were busy; and if the truth must be told, I hadn't the money in hand to pay my fare to New York. It would have been hard for me to get to New York anyway in my present hay-feverish condition. I shall be better in two or three weeks or the air down country will be better breathing and then if your invitation still stands—[202]

---

201. By William Wordsworth (1770–1850).

202. Dated August 20, the telegram reads, as quoted to RF in an August 28 letter from Harcourt: "Difficult leave town just now better come here any time next week we pay expenses if you cannot come wire and we meet Parker House Boston Monday morning" (DCL). In the same letter Harcourt informs RF that *NB* had gone into a third printing (1,500 additional copies) in its American edition. A September 2 letter to RF encloses a royalty check for $200 (worth some $4,500 in 2013 dollars), and assures the poet that he needn't concern himself with David Nutt: "Don't worry. You're going to be able to publish poetry and get your just dues" (DCL). Later in the year, on December 10, Harcourt informed RF that the firm had "cleaned out a stack of 500" copies of *NB* in one week alone ("since Monday"), and was soon to issue an additional printing of 2,000 copies (DCL). On December 14 Harcourt was able to send RF another royalty payment of $200. Holiday sales, as Holt anticipated, were brisk, a matter that may bear on the theme of "Christmas Trees," manuscripts of which RF sent to family friends in December.

You may believe I am anxious to hear of any hope of being wrested from Mrs Nutt. It seems to me that if I am to remain that lady's for life there will be no more poetry. What would be the use of writing just to be cheated out of royalties by her?

I mustn't go into harrowing details, but really I have reached a pass where I must earn a little or perish. I trust you see no reasons legal moral or ethical why I should not accept that part in the success of my book that you wanted me to have. Let me speak frankly: at this moment when I have so much to be glad of in the general approval of my book, I am actually nearer worrying about money than I have had to be for a number of years.

It will be a help to see you for a good talk.

Yours ever
Robert Frost

[To Robert Winthrop Morse (1892–1978), who attended Phillips Academy in Andover and later graduated from Bowdoin College. ALS. Bowdoin.]

Franconia N.H.
Aug 31 1915

Dear Mr Morse:

I find you a very interesting young man of twenty-three and I am going to ask you to call me friend and believe me quite literally in my explanation of why I can't take you to board this year. I am just home from England dead broke, my wife is in bad health, and we are not well started with anything like farm work.

You are not alone in having found a taste for poetry a drawback. There was a long time when I seemed to be alone in the world with poetry and in need of sympathy. I should not have known how to seek sympathy with your grace and ingenuousness. You have a happy way of throwing yourself on me that is anything but impudent. You make me like you if that is any consolation. You must write to me when you feel inclined and tell me all about yourself. I probably shan't be able to help you much. You won't be able to help yourself. You will just have to suffer through. And after all it is a noble kind of suffering. Some pains are to be preferred to all the pleasures of Pine Island.[203]

---

203. Pine Island Camp was established in 1902 near Belgrade Lakes, Maine.

You will write won't you?—and we will see what can be planned for another year.

Sincerely yours
Robert Frost.

[To Walter Prichard Eaton. ALS. UVA.]

Franconia N.H.
August 31 1915

My dear Eaton:

I hope it is to be as you lead me to expect, if for no other reason, because I had so much rather talk than write to you.[204] I will write if I have to, but oh circumstances have conspired of late to make letter writing a burden like the grasshopper.[205] I shall be on the look out for you on the road that comes up from Willow Bridge. And as Shelley says Come soon.[206]

Sincerely yours
Robert Frost

[To John Bartlett. ALS. UVA.]

Franconia N.H.
Sept 9 1915

Dear John

No it is not among the fat-headed things I have done to have fired off a revolver that wasnt loaded and almost killed my fat mother-in-law.[207]

You wont believe it, but I tell you all the same that I was certain sure you were getting too gay with that weepon [*sic*]. You see I do draw the line some-

---

204. Eaton planned a trip to Franconia, but canceled (as a September 10 letter to RF, held now at DCL, indicates).

205. See Ecclesiastes 12:5: ". . . and the grasshopper shall be a burden," etc.

206. See the last stanza of Shelley's "To Night": "belovèd Night— / Swift be thine approaching flight, / Come soon, soon!"

207. As Margaret Bartlett Anderson notes, Bartlett had accidentally discharged a shotgun while his mother-in-law Georgiana "Grammie" Abbott was visiting. No one was injured. See *RFJB*, 99–100.

where in folly. I never intend to do anything too fatally conclusive. I wouldn't for instance encourage anyone to shoot me with an empty gun just to show how careless I was of appearances. I would take some other and less final way of asserting my recklessness. After all I am but a timid calculating soul always intent on the main chance. I always mean to win. All that distinguishes me from the others that mean to win or from some others is my patience. I am perfectly willing to wait fifty seventy five or a thousand years as the fates may decree. I might be willing to be cut off at almost any time (I might) but it would have to be for something. I do nothing for nothing.

Frost has twice hit our garden hard and there is nothing more to look for from it but beets turnips and cauliflowers. So it goes. I doubt if what we have had from our summers planting has cost us any more than it would have in the market.

I wish it lay with me to straighten out the question of where you are going to live this winter. I wish it lay with me to straighten out you.

You should have seen me doing that eight miles to Raymond, mosquito-driven, scoffed at by people in wagons, but coming through with half an hour to spare.[208] I hope there was another journey or two left in the bicycle. Any way I must have improved the roads by drying them up considerably.

Enjoy yourself but try to be good.

Affectionately
R.

A large fat man that morning in a sagging light buggy stopped and stopped me dead still before he put the deliberate question[:] I wish you'd tell me what the difference is between riding a bicycle and walking.

[To Wilbur Rowell. ALS. UVA.]

Franconia NH
Sept 9 1915

Dear Mr Rowell:

My proposal was just as you state it in your letter of August 24th: I will accept the farm at its cost as the last payments of my annuity. In the meantime I am to occupy the farm and to pay the taxes, insurance premiums, and any

208. RF visited Bartlett in Raymond, New Hampshire, late in August.

other charges, and five percent on the investment. I regard the whole thing as a special favor, for which I am very grateful.

I understand that Mr Morse has sent the papers along.[209] I hope he has made everything finally satisfactory.

Sincerely yours
Robert Frost.

[To Louis Untermeyer. ALS. LoC.]

Franconia N.H.
Sept 9 1915

Dear Louis

Let me call you that in the hope of softening a little the light with which you burn too bright for these old eyes. You mustn't be so intellectual with me. I shan't be at ease till we are on emotional terms where there is no more controversy neither is there any danger of crediting one the other with more or less than we mean. Thus we shall know when we are fooling because we shall be always fooling like a pair gay with love. We shant mean anything too profoundly much except perhaps that we are friends and that nothing else matters between friends. That is the only sincerity: all else is an approximation. It sounds like the loss of something, and it is—of competition, of the sharpening of wits and of the criticism that makes us look to ourselves. But friendship is like that: it may not be as strengthening as enmity, and then again it may. At any rate it is different. The beauty of enmity is in insecurity; the beauty of friendship is in security.

Even here I am only fooling my way along as I was in the poems in The Atlantic (particularly in The Road Not Taken) as I was in what I said about

---

209. Harry Moses Morse. Born in Haverhill, Grafton County, New Hampshire, in 1857, Morse died in Littleton, New Hampshire, where he practiced law, in 1924; his wife, Helen Oakes, was a native of Franconia. The Bar Association of New Hampshire memorialized him in its *Proceedings* for 1924: "He served a number of years as Trustee of the Littleton Public Library and was for a short time a Justice of the Municipal Court. It is doubtful if there was ever a better storyteller in the State than Harry M. Morse. His supply of witty anecdotes was inexhaustible. He had pronounced literary tastes and his knowledge of general literature was extensive" (Manchester, New Hampshire, 1925): 204–205.

Spoon River.[210] I trust my meaning is not too hidden in any of these places. I can't help my way of coming at things.

It grieved me a little that you shouldnt have felt that what I wanted to say about Masters but couldnt say because it would sound strange coming from me—couldnt say in so many words at least—was that he was too romantic for my taste and by romantic I'm afraid I mean among other things false-realistic. Such are my limitations. But dont scold me. It is a small matter. It's but a qualification moreover of a real liking for the book. I like it better for what it is than for what a lot of people take it for.

But Lord why waste time in the realm of neither here nor there!

And you are naught with all that nonsense about being in W.S.B's anthology for that you can [*sic*] review it in The Post.[211] Your fault is that you are too active-minded. You may be as nimble as you please when you move; but most of the time you must plan to lie still. Otherwise you will think of something that is nothing. Only those thoughts are worth anything that we have in despite of our indolence. You mustn't larrup your faculties under penalty of being unreal. You mustnt intend to have an idea strike you any more than to have an automobile. Then if the auto strikes you—

And as for your parodies—why you are a child if you think I mind them.[212] They are not my kind of fooling; but they are a constituted kind and of course much better than mine. The best of your parody of me was that it left me in no doubt as to where I was hit. I'll bet not half a dozen people can tell who was hit and where he was hit by my Road Not Taken.[213]

What would you say if you were to see me for a moment in New York before we see you here? I may have to take a run in on business with the Holts on or about the twenty fifth. I should wish to avoid the many, but if it came right you might give me a glimpse of your Clement Wood and your James Oppenheim.[214]

---

210. For *Spoon River,* see RF's July 8, 1915, letter to Untermeyer.

211. W. S. Braithwaite placed three poems by Untermeyer in his *Anthology of Magazine Verse* for 1915: "Swimmers," "The Laughters," and "To a Gentleman Reformer."

212. Untermeyer would collect his parodies of contemporary poets (including RF) in his 1916 volume "*—and Other Poets*" (New York: Henry Holt).

213. Edward Thomas, to whom RF sent the poem. See RF's June 26, 1915, letter to him.

214. Clement Richardson Wood (1888–1950) was an American poet and novelist; James Oppenheim (1882–1932) was an American poet, novelist, and editor. Both writers shared Untermeyer's socialist politics.

With the devout Tennysonian wish that that which I have written here may He within Himself make pure[215] (I refuse to look back at it) I am, my dear Poet

Sinceriously yours
Robert Frost.

[To Carrie T. Hinman. RF had given a reading at the St. Johnsbury Athenaeum on September 6. ALS. ACL.]

Franconia N.H.
Sept 13 1915

My dear Mrs Hinman:

I was sorry I let myself be diverted from seeing more of you both before and after the reading the other day. I really wanted to show my appreciation of the pleasant arrangements you had made for me. But I walk as in a waking dream on such occasions and am in the hands of anyone who will seize hold of me. Let me thank you again for having been enough interested in my work to invite me to St Johnsbury.

Sincerely yours
Robert Frost

[To Ellery Sedgwick (1872–1960), editor of The Atlantic Monthly. *ALS. Mass. Hist.]*

Franconia N.H.
Sept 15 1915

Dear Sedgwick:

It is good for me to know that I have my enemies and I suppose it can do me no harm to know that I have my friends too who can be relied on not to go over to my enemies. You must stay on my side. It gives me real support to know that you and Mrs Sedgwick care for my books. You may have your reservations: you may draw the line of admiration well this side of where Garnett draws it. But I shouldnt want you to be entirely incredulous of me. I

215. RF quotes from Tennyson's "Morte D'Arthur": "I have lived my life, and that which I have done / May He within Himself make pure!" (244–245).

shouldnt want to be afraid you printed Garnetts paper against your better judgment out of pity for the poet's hard lot.

I should like to have heard that violent diatribe and to have encountered the diatribesman. I don't believe I mind him unless he lumped me with the wrong people. I can stand almost anything but being taxed with free verse along with Masters and my dear friend Miss Lowell. I am not of their party at all. What I write is a very simple form of blank verse, as neither Garnett nor Howells has failed to see.[216]

Never mind, I am going to get in my licks next winter when I go a-lecturing on the Sound of Poetry. Then there will be some distinctions made. Sometime when the cows aren't worrying me I mean to write an essay for <u>you</u> on the Sounds of "O" and "Oh" in Poetry.[217]

Thanks for the copies of "The Atlantic." Odd that just as you were sending them I was ordering some sent to England from No 3 Park St.[218]

Sincerely yours
Robert Frost.

[To Edwin Arlington Robinson. ALS. NYPL.]

Franconia N.H.
Sept 15 1915

Dear Robinson

Both your speculations interest me, particularly the first one as to whether or not I care what you think of me. It may not pain you to hear that as long ago as May Sinclair's paper in The Atlantic I marked you down as one of the few people I intended some day to know. Miss Sinclair didn't succeed in interesting me in Moody or Torrence.[219] What has kept me from seeking your friendship all these years is the fear that you might be troubled to find

---

216. Edgar Lee Masters (1869–1950) and Amy Lowell (1874–1925) both enjoyed success as practitioners of the new "free verse." Edward Garnett's "A New American Poet" appeared in the August 1915 *Atlantic Monthly.* William Dean Howells spoke well of RF's blank verse in his Editor's Easy Chair column in the September 1915 issue of *Harper's.*

217. See *CPRF*, 302.

218. Street address of *The Atlantic Monthly* in Boston.

219. Sinclair had published an essay entitled "Three American Poets of Today" (Robinson, William Vaughn Moody, and Ridgely Torrence) in *Atlantic Monthly* in September 1906.

anything to like in my work. I knew I liked yours: that much was right. But I should never actually seek a fellow author's friendship unless everything was right, unless he saw something in me as I saw something in him and there was little or nothing to cover up and lie about in our opinions of each other.

Your second speculation was as to whether or not I was satisfied with myself. I am in a way. I'm rather pleased to have attained to a position where I dont have to admire my work as much as I had to when no one else admired it. It's a relief not to have [to] say more for it than I mean any more.

I am afraid I can't be in Boston in time to catch you unless you are staying over into October. But I am to be in New York on the quiet soon (seeing Harcourt of Holts about my royalties), and if I could look you up there. You say you go to New York about the first of the month. Will you tell me if that is definitely decided and where I will find you by yourself in New York, if it is?

Yours ever
Robert Frost.

[To Walter Prichard Eaton. ALS. UVA.]

Franconia N.H.
Sept 18 1915

My dear Eaton:

Of course if you refuse to come within talking distance I must just do as I have to do and write you a letter (with map of the surrounding country).[220] Mind you it is not altogether from laziness that I prefer talking to letter writing. Let it not go unsaid that once I enjoyed letter writing as much as anybody. And I intend some day to have back my pleasure in it—or you may protest me the baby of a girl. All that is required of me is to deal summarily with a few people like N. H. Dole and I shall he free to. (I hope Dole isn't a particular friend of yours. Poole is I suppose?)[221]

It was nice of Howells to do what you say wasnt it? Long long ago my mother was a little schoolma'am in Columbus Ohio when he was there and I have heard her speak of meeting him once or twice in society when Columbus society was gay in the sixties. He has always stood for something to me

220. On September 10, Eaton wrote to cancel his trip to Franconia.

221. Ernest Poole (1880–1950), Chicago-born novelist and reformer, based, at the time, in New York.

away off and high up. So that I felt that I had rounded some sort of a circle when he did what you say.

You don't mention my having had a whole article to myself in The Atlantic as among my signal honors: from which I infer that you don't like the article. I wonder why. Others seem to ignore it on purpose. I wonder what's the matter.

I was grateful to both Howells and Garnett for making so little difficulty of my blank verse. I have nothing in common with the free-verse people. There is no more distressing mistake than to assume that I have. (Some of the western reviewers have been assuming it.) I am really not so very novel take it from me. I am only interesting to myself for having ventured to try to make poetry out of tones that if you can judge from the practice of other poets are not usually regarded as poetical. You can get enough of those sentence tones that suggest grandeur and sweetness everywhere in poetry. What bothers people in my blank verse is that I have tried to see what I could do with boasting tones and quizzical tones and shrugging tones (for there are such) and forty eleven other tones. All I care a cent for is to catch sentence tones that haven't been brought to book. I dont say to make them, mind you, but to catch them. No one makes them or adds to them. They are always there—living in the cave of the mouth. They are real cave things: they were before words were. And they are as definitely things as any image of sight. The most creative imagination is only their summoner. But summoning them is not all. They are only lovely when thrown and drawn and displayed across spaces of the footed line. Everyone knows that except a free-verster. It is the conventional thing. It may not be in the text-books but everyone knows it though he may have lost sight of it in an age of mere diction and word-hunting. Now Tennyson—

I bore you stiff.

You speak of going to New York. Would I find you for a talk somewhere there near the first of October. What you say about coming to Stockbridge is very tempting.[222] But I can't be away from home this fall or winter except on business. Business takes me to New York this time—pressing business with my publishers. But if we could find a corner to lunch together in—

Always yours
Robert Frost

---

222. Eaton had suggested that RF change trains at Springfield (en route to New York) and spend some time with him in Stockbridge.

near the first of October. What you say about coming to Stockbridge is very tempting. But I can't be away from home this fall or winter except on business. Business takes me to New York this time—pressing business with my publishers. But if we could find a corner to lunch together in—

Always yours
Robert Frost

The map with which Frost concludes a September 18, 1915 letter to Walter Prichard Eaton pictures the route Eaton would have traveled had he not cancelled a trip to Franconia. It completed and amplified the fond teasing with which the letter had begun: "Of course if you refuse to come within talking distance I must just do as I have to do and write you a letter (with map of the surrounding country)."

Courtesy University of Virginia Library

[To Lascelles Abercrombie. ALS. UVA.]

Franconia N.H. U.S.A.
Sept 21 1915

Dear Abercrombie

I must hurry and write you a letter before anything goes click in your mind against me and shuts me out forever.

If thoughts were letters I should have been all right: you would have had a plenty of me since we drank plum wine together out of a lime juice bottle at Leddington, and if they were visits—but they are not visits, so what's the use of iffing. All I was going to say was that if they were visits how often I should have looked in on you to see how you were bearing up under all the trouble you were having.

Catherine would take a long time recovering from such a terrible thing.[223] Wonderful to escape at all. Your news was only partly news to us. Still we did not know the worst, though we had been told there was something seriously the matter. Everyone seems to leave it to someone else to tell us what is going on over there, so that between one friend and another we learn next to nothing.

You will be sorry to hear that Elinor is altogether out of health and we are in for our share of trouble too. It is the old story—what she has been through so many times.[224] But we are not as young as we once were. I'm sure I don't know how it will be with her. The doctor frightens me about her heart. But this is something you mustnt mention in your letters.

It comes particularly hard on us just at this moment when our fortunes begin to look up a little—when people seem to want to put money in our way and make of us if we will go about and let them. Not that we haven't enjoyed life before. I dont mean anything so disloyal to the past or so unlucky to say as that. We have taken our pleasure as we went. But there have been one or two things we have had to wait for till we found help in England and one of these has been success (limited). It is something I suppose we could have done without. Nevertheless—Anyway I confess I like it so well myself that I should have been sorry if the rest of the family had had to go entirely without it.

When I say people want to give us money I dont mean Mrs Nutt and her office boy alone. Nononono! I dont mean them two at all. I have never had one penny or one word of accounting from Mrs Nutt and I should like nothing

223. Abercrombie's wife.

224. Elinor was pregnant; she would miscarry some months later, on November 29, while, as it happens, RF was in Boston to see "Home Burial" staged as a play.

better than just to cry Havoc[225] and let you loose on her. I wish you could settle her for me by yourself the way you settled the gamekeeper.[226] But I suppose there ought to be some sort of concert. I am seeing my American publisher's lawyer in New York this week to find out what can be done to save me from the fool's contract I signed. What do you say if when we are ready on this side and I say the word, you strike from that? I don't know what you think of doing. But anything you please will suit me.

I shall be only too happy to be brothers with you in your next enterprise if you will have me. I cling more than I can tell you to your friendship in poetry. Yours was the first praise over there and there will never be any other just like it. We must try to manage. But if I cant join you I can't. I have told you, I think, that Mrs Nutt forbade me to let Monro[227] have anything for a chap book. She even holds that I have no right to sell poetry to magazines. She will oppose us. You mustn't have too much trouble on my account. And then there's the question of time. How much time have we? Tell me more. I will be prompter in answering again.

Now I should like to go out into the yard and shake hands with your big cold pump till his iron tank was as full of water as my heart is of Ryton memories.

Our best to you all.

Affectionately
Robert Frost

I forgot to mention the war in this letter.

And I ought to mention it, if only to remark that I think it has made some sort of new man and a poet out of Edward Thomas.

R. F.

Sept 30 1915

I decided not to go to post with this till I knew more definitely what my predicament was with Mrs Nutt. I now know all the law in this matter. I am

---

225. In Shakespeare's *Julius Caesar* (3.i), Mark Antony says:

And Caesar's spirit, ranging for revenge,
With Ate by his side come hot from hell,
Shall in these confines with a monarch's voice
Cry 'Havoc,' and let slip the dogs of war.

226. See *EY*, 467–468. See also note 54, page 281, in the present volume.

227. Harold Monro, proprietor of the Poetry Bookshop in London, editor of *Poetry and Drama*, and a publisher.

bound by the contract unless she refuses to render an account on my two books within the sixty days I have given her. The contract calls for two more books which if I have to give them I intend to write in prose. I shall make very short work of them, padding them with quotation. I have long contemplated the possibility of having to do this dirty trick and my lawyer agrees that it may be necessary. My minister agrees that it may be justifiable. There seems to be nothing you can do at present—except countenance my practices. I should welcome any suggestion from you as to what I should write the two books on. I shall write them on the same subject from different points of view. For my own protection I intend to sink a cryptogram in the text that will say to the public when I furnish the key in the newspapers: Mrs. or Madam mistook her Man. Dont think too badly of me.

R. F.

[To Louis Untermeyer. ALS. Jones.]

Franconia N.H.
Sept 24 1915

Dear Louis:

This is to be a business trip and I shall be with Harcourt (of Holts) most of the time. We are seeing what can be done to save me from Madam Nutt. I set up to be practical, but I have got my business into the conventional entanglement of the conventionally impractical poet.

As I say, I shall be in Harcourt's hands and at his house for a day or two. Then I shall have a day with you—perhaps a night too if you have the room vacant you spoke of. I must not be gone from my cows very long.

It was Longfellow and not Whittier who wrote Felicia Hemans.[228]

Yours ever
Robert Frost

I've promised Harcourt to arrive in New York Tuesday morning. Direct anything you write me in care of Henry Holt & Co 34 West 33 St. (not to be forwarded.)

---

228. Felicia Hemans (1793–1835), a British poet, was among the most popular writers of her day. Neither Longfellow nor Whittier "wrote" a poem or anything else about, or titled after, or in homage to, Hemans. Nor does a letter from Longfellow to Hemans survive. The letters do show, however, that Longfellow admired Hemans' poetry, as did his wife Frances "Fanny" Appleton Longfellow.

[To Sidney Cox. ALS. DCL.]

Franconia N.H.
Sept 27 1915

Dear Cox:

This is just to say that I am off for New York City on pressing business with my publishers—and will there be any hope of catching a glimpse of you down there? I shall be in town from Tuesday morning (the 28th) till Thursday night—possibly Friday night. You could drop me a line in care of Henry Holt & Co (not to be forwarded)

I shall lavish thanks on you if I see you for your good offices with President Chase.[229] I suppose that is a sure go. I have heard nothing from Lewiston.[230]

Your story which is none of my business I have never the less read. I like it a lot. Elinor will tell you what she thinks of it when she is the least bit stronger. You saw the state of health she was in. I suspect you scared her a good deal by throwing yourself so completely on her judgement. The story is done without nonsense. I am afraid the ordinariness of the young man is just a little ordinary for me. Your style shoots straighter and straighter. Permit me to say so much.

Remember me to our friend Bloch.[231]

Yours ever
R.F.

[To Morris Tilley. ALS. UM.]

Franconia N.H.
October 5 1915

My dear Tilley:

I am going to confess to you first that I have been to New York and come home again without having visited your mother and sister.[232] I know that I

229. See RF's August 30, 1915, letter to Cox.

230. That is, Lewiston, Maine, where Bates College (of which Chase was then president) is located.

231. See the notes to RF's February 2, 1915, letter to Cox.

232. Tilley's mother was Lois F. Miller Tilley, and his sister, Lydia Lois Tilley.

am sorrier than they will be. You and they will understand when I tell you how it happened. I had planned on several days in the city but I was hardly there and done with the business of my contract when I got a summons home: my wife was not able to get on without me. You saw how it was with her. Unless we can find help, she is not going to be able to spare me for more than a day or two at a time this winter.

My mind was so full of pleasanter things when I was with you last that I clean forgot the matter of ten dollars you let me have the day of our expedition through bad air to 81 Johnsbury.[233] This makes amends.

I have found already a way for you here next summer. There will be no difficulty about a place to rent.

Here's hoping that classes seem a fresh interest to you after your year at large.

Always yours sincerely
Robert Frost

[To George Browne. ALS. Plymouth.]

Franconia N.H.
Oct 7 1915

My dear Browne:

I have just got your letter and am hurrying an answer to catch you in Cambridge.

I have been hoping to see you all these weeks. Come for as long a day as you think you can make of it.

What a catalogue of clubs and things your letter is. You have done wonders.

Never mind Lowell.[234]

Twelve hens were what I thought I could find room for.

I will tell you about the horse when you are here. I really have no place for a horse on the farm yet. The barn is a cow barn and not satisfactorily that as it is.

---

233. Possibly St. Johnsbury Road, Littleton, New Hampshire. The Tilley family summered in New Hampshire.

234. Amy Lowell.

I say come for a long day. I should say for more than a day but I suppose if you come with an automobile that will be out of the question.

Trusting I have forgotten nothing in my haste I'm

Yours always
Robert Frost

[To Marie A. Hodge. ALS. BU.]

Franconia N.H.
October 9 1915

My dear Mrs Hodge:

It seems too perfectly absurd for us to have kept up our friendship all this time when we were separated by the ocean and then to have lived within a few miles of each other all summer without seeing each other. We have talked of having you up here and thought of you. Elinor will tell you what has prevented our giving you a definite and pressing invitation to come.

I haven't thanked you for the Plymouth Record record of my journey to Bridgewater Hill.[235] I had a delightful time down there among the farmers and summerers (more summerers than farmers I fear.) I have had more excitement for the last year than is good for me. Time I stopped gadding and settled down to prove that my writing hand hasn't lost its cunning. Dont you say so?

Before we dig in for the winter, however, you may expect a glimpse of me when I run down for another lot of furniture.

Always sincerely yours
Robert Frost

---

235. Bridgewater Hill is a few miles south of Plymouth, New Hampshire, just below Bridgewater Mountain. RF's friend George Browne had a farm there, which the poet visited in August 1915. The *Plymouth Record* was the local newspaper.

[To Harold Monro. Text derived from SL, *194–195. At the time he prepared the latter volume in 1964, Lawrance Thompson listed the letter as in the private collection of H. Bacon Collamore. It has since gone missing and is not among the Monro letters held at the Watkinson Library.]*

Franconia NH
October 9 1915

Dear Monro:

So help me, it is exactly as I tell you and not at all as you suspect. I was pleased when you asked me for stuff for a chapbook and I went right to work on Madam Nutt to get her permission to give it.[236] I have been at her off and on ever since about this time last year. It has all been in the matter of just one thing. You must not doubt my friendship for a moment. So far as I am concerned I am not afraid to let you publish the poems. Suppose it were in violation of my contract with the Madam. It wouldn't be on me but on you she would descend for damages. I don't know very much about these things, but as I see it there is just the chance that she might have a case against you. All would depend of course on whether a chapbook could be made to appear a book in a court of law. I don't believe it is a book. You don't believe it is? The question is how much would you be willing to risk on your opinion. The risk would be all yours. You can have the poems if you want them. Only I want you to understand the situation. I don't want to get you into trouble. I ought to warn you that Madam Nutt will make trouble if she can. I haven't improved her disposition by a year's nagging and I don't suppose the success of my books in pirated editions on this side has improved it any either.

I have this suggestion to make: perhaps you will prefer to wait for the chapbook till we see what can be done to extricate me from the lady's clutches. We are considering there is a little hope for me in the fact that I am quite capable of fulfilling the rest of the contract in books of very bad prose. It wouldn't take much more to make me write her two (that's all are called for I think) books on Boston Baked Beans between now and Christmas. I am about out of love with her. Too bad to miss a chance to quote Arnold, "For I am passing weary of her love."[237] When I heard that bombs had been blowing holes in Bloomsbury it was with half a hope that perhaps a small one had

---

236. See RF to Monro, August 7, 1915.

237. The last line of Matthew Arnold's "Tristram and Iseult": "For she was passing weary of his love."

hit her in the office safe at No 6 Bloomsbury St and blown my contract into little bits of white paper the size of a moth. You see how Christian I was. I wished her no harm personally. And you see the reward of my Christianity. I wished modestly and got nothing. Instead of coming near her the Germans seem to have come within an ace of you. You must be careful to keep from under them.

I have written you this nice long letter with no other object than to keep on the good side of you so that you won't give up the idea of the chapbook but will bear it in mind till my affairs are straightened out and I am free to do what I please with what I write. Therefore don't mistake me.

Yours ever
Robert Frost

[To William Stanley Braithwaite. AL (apparently RF neglected to sign the letter). ACL.]

Franconia N.H.
October 10 1915

My Dear Braithwaite

I wrote you a letter in your official capacity the other day. But that is one thing and this is another. This is to tell you that now is the time to come if you are coming, when we are all banked high in watery gold and white winter is already looking down prepared to descend on us from the tops of the mountains. You are in print with your book and you have promised: so come you must. Let it be within a few days or it will be too late as now it is just late enough for the full effect of the region.

If you had been accesible [*sic*] by telephone I should have said this to your ear the other evening as I passed through Boston on a flying trip to New York on business.

Always yours

[To George C. Chase (1844–1919), president of Bates College. ALS. Bates.]

Franconia N.H.
October 12 1915

President George C. Chase,
Bates College,
Lewiston, Maine.

Dear Sir:

Thank you for your friendly but very perplexing letter.

Perhaps you are in a position to divide two hundred dollars by five so as to give me for my share the fifty which is the least I am getting anywhere for an evening lecture. Modesty forbids my doing it. I might lead you to expect too much of my performance as a lecturer. You understand I am not regularly in the lecture field. I shall go where I go this winter chiefly as the author of my books and the exponent of one or two ideas not entirely old on the sound of poetry. I am really a person of very small pretension such as you may not care to spend fifty dollars on. You must take my dear Sidney's word for nothing: he is my devoted friend.[238] I say all this frankly to my own hurt, and every word of it goes against me, because I shall be sorry to miss the chance of meeting you all at Bates. It is the college people, and not least the undergraduates, that I like to think I make my appeal to. Practically all my engagements for the winter are at colleges.

Very truly yours
Robert Frost

[To Harold Goddard Rugg. ALS. DCL.]

Franconia N.H.
October 15 1915

Dear Mr Rugg:

Im glad you got your train as long as you were determined to have it.

Go as far as you like in probing my life even to asking me whether at Dartmouth or elsewhere I ever did anything wrong. I never did. And feel free to use anything I have written you. Such indiscretions as I have committed to

238. That is, Sidney Cox. See RF's November 1, 1915, letter to Cox.

paper were a necessary part of my inspiration and I must be prepared to stand by them.

It is strange that there is so little to say for my literary life at Dartmouth. I was writing a good deal there. I have ways of knowing that I was as much preoccupied with poetry then as I am now. "My Butterfly" in "A Boy's Will" belongs to those days, though it was not published in The Independent till a year or two later (1894 or 1895 I think),[239] so also "Now Close the Windows" in the same book. I still like as well as anything I ever wrote the eight lines in the former beginning "The grey grass is scarce dappled with the snow."

But beyond a poem or two of my own I have no distinctly literary recollections of the period that are not chiefly interesting for their unaccountability. I remember a line of Shelley (Where music and moonlight an [*sic*] feeling are one) quoted by Prof C. F. Richardson in a swift talk on reading;[240] a poem on Lake Memphremagog by ______ Smalley in The Lit; and an elegy on the death of T. W. Parsons by Hovey in The Independent.[241] I doubt if Hovey's poem was one of his best. I have not seen it from that day to this, but I will sware [*sic*] that it talks of "horns of Elfland faintly blowing."[242] So the memory of the past resolves itself into a few bright star points set in darkness—(the sense of the present is diffuse like daylight).

Nothing of mine ever appeared in Dartmouth publications.

If you draw at all on the article in The Review of Reviews be sure not to perpetuate the error about my having taught psychology at Pinkerton Acad-

---

239. "My Butterfly" appeared in the *Independent* on November 8, 1894. "Now Close the Windows" appeared first in *ABW.*

240. Charles Francis Richardson (1851–1913), professor of English at Dartmouth, author of *A Primer of American Literature* (Boston, 1884). The line quoted is from Shelley's "To Jane: The Keen Stars Were Twinkling."

241. The underlined blank space is RF's; he'd forgotten the given name. Bertrand A. Smalley (Dartmouth class of '94) edited *Dartmouth Lyrics: A Collection of Poems from the Undergraduate Publications of Dartmouth College* in 1893 and included a poem of his own entitled "Memphremagog in Winter," which had first appeared in the Dartmouth *Literary Monthly* ("The Lit"). RF refers also to "Seaward: An Elegy on the Death of Thomas William Parsons," by Richard Hovey (1864–1900); the poem first appeared in the *Independent* on November 17, 1892, when RF was enrolled at Dartmouth.

242. See stanza XI of Hovey's "Seaward": "Grieve, marshes, though your noonday melody / Of color thrill through sorrow like a horn / Blown far in Elfland!" Hovey's lines are indebted to Canto III of Tennyson's *The Princess* (1847): "O sweet and far from cliff and scar / The horns of Elfland faintly blowing!"

emy.[243] I taught English there and psychology for a short time at Plymouth just before I went to England.

The "Listeners" is the poem![244]

I will see if I can find you Rupert Brooks [*sic*] autograph. The difficulty is that he was on first name terms with the fellows I know and signed himself simply Rupert. You can see that might not be a signature they would be willing to part with. I'll try for you though.

I shall be glad to have the Masefield.[245] Put your name in it, wont you?

Always sincerely yours
Robert Frost.

Your card has just come. Sorry I didn't get this off sooner. I don't think of anything to add. Ask and it shall be answered to you.

RF.

[To Katharine Lee Bates (1859–1929), American poet, literary scholar, editor, translator, and professor of English. ALS. Wellesley.]

Franconia N.H.
October 21 1915

My dear Miss Bates:

I base my faith on Rossetti that what two friends ask for for me I must sooner or later get.[246] If you will remember me for a lecture and reading at Wellesley when it can be thought of as being my turn. It's the colleges I look

---

243. Sylvester Baxter's "New England's New Poet" had appeared in the American *Review of Reviews* in April 1915.

244. With RF's encouragement, Henry Holt would publish an American edition of Walter de la Mare's *The Listeners and Other Poems* in 1916.

245. John Masefield (1878–1967), English poet and Poet Laureate from 1930 until his death.

246. See Dante Gabriel Rossetti's "The Blessed Damozel" (stanza 11, emphasis added), as collected in Quiller-Couch's *Oxford Book of English Verse*:

> *"I wish that he were come to me,*
> *For he will come," she said.*
> *"Have I not prayed in Heaven?—on earth,*
> *Lord, Lord, has he not pray'd?*
> Are not two prayers a perfect strength?
> *And shall I feel afraid?"*

to for the chance to say certain things on the sound of poetry that are going to trouble me as long as they remain unsaid. Not everybody would be interested in my ideas. I'm not sure that many would be outside the circles where books are made and studied. They have value I should say chiefly in education and criticism. Call them theories, if you will be careful to distinguish them from speculative theories. These are descriptive. I make them sound formidable here because I am under restraint not to go into them, but really I can be quite off-hand with them fetching them in edgewise between poems as I read. All this is for when my turn comes—if it ever does come.

Meanwhile I should be most happy to earn fifty dollars in the way you suggest. I could leave the time to you to fix. Either Thursday you name would suit me.

I am afraid I have been betrayed by the friendliness of your letter into saying a good deal for myself. Will you forgive me?

Thank you for your good words.

Sincerely yours
Robert Frost

[To John Bartlett. The "circa" in the date is RF's own. ALS. UVA.]

Franconia N.H.
circa October 21 1915

Dear John:

Be good to him![247] And that doesn't mean simply not to write poetry for a living. For his sake you are bound to shun <u>every</u> folly, ginseng, Belgian hares, squabs, wonder berries, mushrooms, Orpingtons,[248] alfalfa, Angora goats, Mexican rubber stock for the small investor and the Honduras Lottery. Those are the things as well as poetry you have to have in mind when you pray saying "Lead us not into temptation but deliver us from evil." For now you are a father twice over and must give up childish ways in favor of your children. I'd like to be your wife for about five minutes someday till I could knock the whole duty of the responsible head of a family into your head. I'd have no more of this romancing in agriculture. I speak partly from concern for your own future. Suppose your sons grow up to be sensible men.

---

247. John and Margaret Bartlett's second son, John T. Bartlett III, had just been born.

248. A breed of chicken named for Orpington, England.

How will you feel when you begin to realize that they are judging you. They will be earning fifty seventy five a hundred dollars a week. About that time you will have got round to skunks and will be starting a skunk farm—chuck full of your subject, all the lore of deodorizing skunk skins so as not to make the hair come out and of picking up a skunk by the tail without consequences—full of figures too such as these: Assuming that a skunk will produce twenty five polekittens in an off year—it ought to do say one fourth as well as a rabbit and we all know what a rabbit will do—but assuming to be on the safe side that it will produce no more than twenty-five and that except for a considerable loss in overalls which you have had to bury without benefit of clergy, the twenty five have cost you nothing to rear and the market price of a pelt—why it ought to be two dollars if it's a scent oughtn't it and so on. How will you feel, I say, if when you talk like that you catch your two solid and citizenly sons winking at each other on the sly? You will feel like as if it was a tragedy if I may speak like another Reynolds.[249] You will feel as if you had vainly wasted your life in vain.

The moral is that the least little thing starts me moralizing these days and this is not a little thing.

Bless the whole lot of you.

The score now stands 4 to 2 in favor of us.[250] But the game is young yet, or at least you are.

Affectionately
R.

---

249. Arthur W. Reynolds, Harvard class of 1898, became superintendent of schools in Derry, New Hampshire, in 1910.

250. In addition to Forrest and John (named after his father and grandfather), the Bartletts would have two children more, Margaret (named after her mother) and Richard, evening the "score" with RF and Elinor, four of whose children survived into adulthood (Lesley, Carol, Irma, and Marjorie).

[To George Browne. In the following letter, RF works out some details of a lecture trip that would take him to Cambridge, Massachusetts (where he spoke before the English Lunch Club, and also at the Browne and Nichols School), to Concord (where he spoke at the Middlesex School), and to Milton (where he spoke at Milton Academy), before returning to Franconia on November 17. ALS. Plymouth.]

Franconia N.H.
October 27 1915

My dear Browne:

It's not so much busy as sick with that cold I've been—though I've been a little busy helping Carol build the henhouse when I've felt able to be out in the wind. We got the house up and the roof on to it (and the hens into it) just before the rain came yesterday afternoon. That is something to have got off my mind. It leaves really very little to think of before winter but banking up and putting on a window or two.

I have saved one nail from the house-building to nail your schedule of dates to the wall so that I sha'n't be allowed to forget for a moment what I am in for from Friday November 12 till toward Christmas. I can't say that you haven't been busy. Time you let up and rested on your laurels. I note that it is the Friday Club, Friday, English Lunch Club, Saturday, Middlesex School, Sunday, Mrs Browne's evening, Monday. I wish it might be Milton on Tuesday. Let's not have the thing too much strung out: I mustn't be away from the family too long.

Please spare me anybody's society on Monday that I shall feel antagonistic. Bliss Perry[251] is free to think any platitudinous thing he likes about my work. I shouldn't want to meet him in such a way as to seem to have come before him for judgement. I have got on as far as I have got on in the world by brushing a good many people aside. I have no strength to spare in the frontal attack.

You understand. I never show myself but to friends. I couldn't show myself to anyone else—I couldn't, I mean, if I would. I am not the least bit of good in overcoming prejudice.

---

251. Bliss Perry (1860–1954), influential and prolific American literary critic and scholar. His edition of Emerson's journals had appeared in 1914; a book on Thomas Carlyle followed in 1915.

Perhaps Mr. and Mrs. Marks[252] would like to see me: I should like to see them.

Then there are the Hockings (Mr & Mrs Ernest Hocking) who are my great friends.[253] Could you ask them—and perhaps Mr and Mrs Sylvester Baxter of Malden.[254] For the rest I leave the inviting to Mrs Browne. It is all very good of her. She mustn't do too much or get too many together to be disappointed in me. I can't promise to be clever for her company.

You got my telegram I trust. "New Hampshire Gold" was the subject I had thought of for the New Hampshire Daughters.[255]

I doubt if I have any whole review in my trunks; but there is this folder you can have. Practically all the reviews quoted from ran into three columns.

Farewell for the moment

Always yours
Robert Frost

I am sending books

---

252. Josephine Preston Peabody Marks (1874–1922), American poet and dramatist; wife of Lionel Simeon Marks (1871–1947), professor of mechanical engineering at Harvard.

253. See RF's April 3, 1915, letter to the Hockings, William Ernest Hocking (1873–1966), professor of philosophy at Harvard, and his wife, Agnes O'Reilly Hocking; RF met them and stayed at their residence in 1915.

254. Sylvester Baxter (1850–1927) was a journalist (often writing for the *Boston Evening Transcript*), poet, and urban planner, in which latter capacity he helped design the Metropolitan Park System of Greater Boston.

255. A reference to a talk RF was scheduled to give before a meeting of the New Hampshire Daughters of the American Revolution on February 19, 1916, at the Hotel Vendome in Boston. See RF's December 2, 1915, letter to Rugg for some indication as to its theme.

[To Wilbur Lucius Cross (1862–1948), Yale professor and first dean of Yale Graduate School (1916–1930); editor of the Yale Shakespeare *and, for some three decades, of* The Yale Review. *Among his books are* The Life and Times of Laurence Sterne *(1909) and* The History of Henry Fielding *(1918). Cross served as fifty-sixth governor of Connecticut (1931–1939). ALS. Yale.]*

Franconia N.H.
October 27 1915

Prof W. L. Cross,
New Haven Conn.

Dear Sir:

Thank you for the friendly suggestion. I have been trying to think what I have to show you. There are poems—long and short; but I'm afraid not any I wouldn't rather have round the house a while yet before I part with them. I should be glad, though, if you would keep a place in your mind open for me. I ought to have something for you soon.[256]

Sincerely yours
Robert Frost

[To Frank C. Brown (1869–?), who owned a rare book shop located at 44 Bromfield Street, Boston. ALS. UVA.]

Franconia N.H.
October 27 1915

My dear Mr Brown:

The dea knows[257] I have had time enough to think of something clever to write in these books. There are any number of people, some of them friends of mine I am proud to say who would have thought of something in half the time. I envy them their wit. As you see I have thought of nothing. I have had to end ignominiously by copying you out a poem or two that I care a little

256. RF made good on the promise. In April 1916, *The Yale Review* published the poems subsequently gathered, in *MI*, under the title "The Hill Wife" (with the exception of "The Smile," which had previously appeared in *Poetry and Drama* in December 1914).

257. For this expression, an archaism RF favored, see the notes to his November 12, 1912, letter to Mosher.

for. Will you ever forgive me for being all this time to no purpose? My intentions were so good. I did so want to add something to the books to make them at least worth the publishers price.—I wonder if I shall ever dare to look in on you at your store when I am in Boston.

Sincerely yours
Robert Frost

[To George H. Browne. ALS. Plymouth.]

Franconia N.H.
Oct 29 1915

My dear Browne:

I'm really a sick person and in no mood to straighten things out for myself with all these schools. Best drop a few of them if I have gotten them into too much of a tangle for you. I haven't heard a word from St Marks or from any other school.[258] You dont mean you want me to start writing to them on my own account?

I'm just rushing a word into the mail for tomorrow morning. It is hard getting letters out of here. Only two mails a day go from the post office. Dont wait to hear from me. Anything you arrange will stand. I shall be with you for a week or so to fill all the engagements you make—unless I die or come near dying between now and November 10. You are a great friend to have and you know I know how to value what you are doing for me. I wish you would fix the dates absolutely so that I shall have nothing to worry about but my sins.

Forty thanks for all. I shall write again on Sunday. My best to Mrs Browne in her electioneering.[259]

In a devil of a haste

Yours ever
Robert Frost

---

258. St. Mark's, an Episcopalian prep school in Southborough, Massachusetts, was founded in 1865.

259. Emily Browne was a suffragette.

Fine interesting letters you enclose with yours.

RF

Make the Andover date[260] to suit you [*sic*] own notions. Let me lean on you hard.

R.F.

[To Sidney Cox. This letter is filed, at Dartmouth, with another to RF from President George Chase of Bates College (also dated November 1), on which RF has written the note reprinted here below the poet's initials. ALS. DCL.]

Franconia NH.
Nov 1 1915

Dear Cox

You wont forgive me I fear for having been a trifle humorous in my answer to your President's proposal. I wasn't really very bad but after what he promised I couldn't resist the temptation to let him know that I thought his come-down a little absurd. He even had the nerve to send me a marked catalogue to call my attention to the fact that he had had Alfie No-yes[261] in his course. Which was rather like hurting my feelings because he knows and I know he never had Alfie for lessnahunderd. All I said was "Perhaps you would be in a position to divide two hundred dollars by five so as to give me fifty for my share. Modesty forbids my doing it."[262] It finished him. But never mind. I dont care if you wont. I'm just as grateful to you for having tried to get me the chance at Bates. What counts is your friendly concern for me. That much more than the money.

I'm off to Boston for a few days soon and if nothing slips up should reap a couple of hundred on the trip. This all grows out of a little talk and reading I

---

260. See RF's November 21, 1915, letter to Browne; the Andover talk took place during the second week of November. RF would speak again in Andover at the Abbot Academy on January 13, 1916.

261. That is, Alfred Noyes (1880–1958), English poet. In 1914, Noyes accepted a post at Princeton University, which he held for nine years.

262. RF had added: "I might lead you to expect too much of my performance as a lecturer. You understand I am not regularly in the lecture field." See *RFSC*, 99; see also RF's October 12, 1915, letter to Chase.

gave free for nothing at the Browne & Nichols School in Cambridge in the spring.[263] You will be glad to hear this much good news.

I had a good letter from Dow urging me to urge myself on some New Bedford man who could give me a lecture.[264] I'd like to go to New Bedford if it were only to meet Dow whom I missed last summer. But I don't see much hope where I have to begin by telling people who I am and what in my own opinion I have done.

Schenectady sounds better. Wouldnt it be fun if I could see you for a day in your Dutch-named big American town?[265]

Remember me to Block[266] and be strong against the day of wrath.

Yours always
R.F.

Dear Cox[267]

Just like me to think I had offended by my fooling. Anybody's silence always works like madness in my brain. Damme! [*sic*]

R.F.

[To Louis Untermeyer. ALS. LoC.]

Franconia N.H.
Nov. 1 1915

Tell me, Louis,

While it is uppermost in my mind what when you are doing the high-critical, do you mean by "overtones" in poetry. Don't, whatever you do, force an explanation. If you dont mean anything frankly say so.[268] On the other

---

263. RF gave a talk at the school on May 10 (see *CPPP*, 687–689).

264. Ralph P. Dow graduated with Sidney Cox from Bates College (class of 1911) and in 1915 was teaching high school in New Bedford, Massachusetts.

265. The opportunity came soon when, on February 17, 1916, RF spoke before the Women's Evening Missionary Society of the First Presbyterian Church in Schenectady.

266. Alex Bloch, German schoolteacher and a friend of Cox's. See RF to Cox, February 2, 1915.

267. This note is inscribed on the November 1, 1915, letter from Chase to RF, which RF had sent for Cox's perusal. The letter invites RF to lecture at Bates, for a fee of fifty dollars, the following March.

268. Untermeyer replied on November 6: "Of course I mean something, darn your skeptical & untanned hide! 'Overtones'—even in poetry are perfectly tame, house-broken

hand if you mean something dont for the sake of being clever or seeming to be modest, dont I beg of you protest that you don't mean anything. It is the truth I am after in this as in all things. A wet blanket, now, on your cleverness. I must know certain things to a certainty before I go me [*sic*] into the world next week to preach the gospel of sound, which is as you remember Take care of the sound and the sense will take care of itself.

Or if you dont know what you mean yourself when you speak or anyone else speaks of overtones what do you suppose Amy Lowell for instance and to be specific but at the same time not too personal, may mean? The question comes very near the heart of life for me. Yet let me not scare you out of your casual ease by my impressiveness. The situation requires that you should speak from what comes first to your mind. Be your limpid self in speaking. (I spare you the peroration. You get my drift.)

Let's see was there anything else I felt as deeply about that wouldnt seem like an anticlimax coming after. Oh, there was Ellery. I didn't find him anywhere in Boston as I came through which served me right for not sending word ahead. I said nothing and went to bed in the north bound sleeper for home. Ellery doesnt even know I was gunning for him.[269]

Are you coming to Boston somewhere round the 27th to meet me and see The Am. Dram. Soc. (Ink.) put on The Death of the Hired and Home Burial?[270] I may not be there and then again I may.

Tell your wife that some day I am going to write you a family letter beginning Mes enfants in which I will undertake to make it clear to you why an old man would so much rather see people cunning than clever.

Ollers urn
R.F.

But I seem to see little or nothing of that book with your Swimmers in it.[271]

& useful things. It was in high-school, in my second year of physics, that Dr. Linville first introduced me to them. Sound, he told me, was made of a series of vibrations. These vibrations are the *body* of the sound—its *tone*. But every sound has its 'harmonic'—its 'overtone'—a higher & less obvious note" (letter held now at DCL).

269. Ellery Sedgwick, editor of *The Atlantic*.

270. Staged on November 27 in Huntington Chambers Hall, with RF in attendance. See RF to Charlotte Endymion Porter, November 5, 1915.

271. *The Anthology of Magazine Verse for 1915*, ed. William Stanley Braithwaite (New York: Gomme and Marshall), included Untermeyer's poem "Swimmers."

[To Henry Tunis Meigs (1855–1932), owner of The Maples, a farm in Romney, Indiana. ALS. Yale.]

Franconia N.H.
November 1 1915

Dear Mr Meigs:

You give me back my poetry in just the lines where I enjoyed it most in the writing. No one but a predestined friend could do this so unerringly. I have had to tell many people what I wanted them particularly to see in "Storm Fear." You found it without being told: "Till even the comforting barn grows far away."[272]

I wish you might be first buyer of my next book. I shall keep it on my mind to see if I can't manage it so that you shall be. The trouble is that the next one still looks a long way off in spite of such stimulation as I am constantly having from such letters as yours.

Will you write me again some time and tell me of your luck with other books you come across? I wonder how much you care for Rupert Brook's [*sic*] poetry.[273] I knew Brook rather well in England.

Sometime when I have something not too bad in MS. I will copy it out for you to put into one of my books for a keepsake. Suppose I copy a short one for you right now.[274] You needn't thank me for it. But write when you are inclined.

Sincerely your friend
Robert Frost

272. "Storm Fear" appeared first in *ABW*.

273. Rupert Brooke had died some seven months before this letter was written, aboard a hospital ship moored off Skyros, in the Aegean Sea.

274. The manuscript was separated from the letter; we do not know which poem RF enclosed.

[To George Browne. For the dramatic reading of "Home Burial," see also RF's November 5, November 22, and December 3 letters to Charlotte Endymion Porter, who directed the staging. The following letter was written on the Wednesday after election day in 1915; Browne's wife had been campaigning for women's suffrage in Massachusetts. ALS. Plymouth.]

Franconia NH.
Nov 3 1915

Dear Browne:

It hardly seems to me that you ought to unsettle anything that has been settled. You start changing dates in all this welter of them and you'll go crazy. I shall manage somehow about the Drama League recital if I decide that in courtesy and for my own instruction I ought to hear my poems when they are acted. It really ought to be worth something to me to see how much dramatic stuff they have in them just as they stand. Mrs Baxter[275] is mistaken: I never read Home Burial in public anywhere. I dread a little to see it acted. Still I authorized the giving of it. I confess to a certain curiosity as to what a dramatic society will do with what I shouldn't dare to touch.

Remember you are to please yourself in these arrangements. I only stipulate that I shan't be kept away from home too long. Better go down twice than be that.

Sorry for all honest suffragists.

Yours ever
R.F.

I have one engagement in view for one of the spare evenings. A friend in Melrose[276] has asked me what I would give a drawing room reading for charity for there. What ought I to ask? Is fifty too much?

R.F.

---

275. Lucia Millet Baxter, wife of Sylvester Baxter.

276. The Mrs. Blake mentioned in RF's November 7, 1915, letter to George Browne.

[To Charlotte Endymion Porter (née Helen Charlotte Porter) American poet, editor, and translator). With Helen Archibald Clarke, Porter edited the journal Poet Lore, *based in Boston; she also edited* Shakespeariana. *Porter (along with Clarke) arranged the event spoken of here, which was hosted by the American Drama Society in Boston on November 27, 1915. ALS. BU.]*

Franconia N.H.
November 5 [1915]

Dear Miss Porter:

My health is not what it ought to be at the present moment, but that will make no difference: unless I am made absolutely ill by the week of lecturing just ahead of me, I can promise to be with you on the 27th. For several reasons (some of them the most practical) I should be sorry to miss seeing your attempt to make drama of my poetry.[277] I am very grateful to you for that same attempt as you may expect me to assure you again when we meet.

I will read perhaps "Mending Wall" if I have the courage after hearing your reader do "A Hundred Collars."

Always sincerely yours
Robert Frost

[To Joseph Warren Beach. Above the salutation and separated from it by a diagonal line, RF has written a postscript. ALS. Minnesota.]

November 8
This is some nonsense I wrote yesterday and haven't the firmness not to send.

Franconia N.H.
November 7 1915

Dear Joe Beach:

I am worse than immoral I'm bad to have let it come to a date like that and a state of winter like this I hear blowing about the house where we two were friends last summer before getting down to do my part in the correspondence I was the one to propose. Well you mustnt complain too much of my neglect. It isn't that I havent thought of you or that anyone who has come

277. Namely, "The Death of the Hired Man" and "Home Burial," which Porter staged in Boston on November 27, with RF in attendance (and, as is indicated here, as a reader).

after you here has crowded you out of my affections. You have fared no worse than my poetry. I have put you both off till I should have got through with a kind of letter writing that I regarded as drudgery and could give myself to enjoying you even as I should like to be enjoyed. That is the simple truth. It has been less a putting off than a saving up of the best things set before me till the last.

This sounds all very well in words but to show you how sincere I am, I am not going to take advantage of it to keep your friendship: I am going to confess that in practice it has all turned out badly. I am no nearer being ready to write to you now than I was the day after you wrote from New York State (as we say) or the day after I had your card or the day after I had your poems in Poetry or the day after I came across your poem in The Atlantic.[278] And the reason is that I am just as far from the end of my drudgery as ever. I get through a lot of it every day but it seems as if more is always piled up ahead of me. It is so serious that I am not laughing a bit as I write, that I am not laughing any more at all. It has stopped my laughing: it has stopped my poetry. It has finished R.F.

Yes I could have written you a much better letter if I had let duty slide and done it when first I felt like it. As it is you get but the last of me. But you must be content with that as better than none. And you must try to realize when you hear from me or someone else that I am finally dead and out of it that if I served you ill it was through a selfishness that is absolutely essential to love: I wanted not to miss my own pleasure in writing when I wrote. Of course it was all a mistake. I have made you suffer to no purpose—I trust you have cared enough to suffer. If you are anything like me you would have been torturing yourself some of this time with trying to decide which one of your confidences had proved on consideration too much for my narrowness.

—Or what in the poems had turned me against you as a poet. It certainly wasnt anything in the "Colloquy," for I think that is the way the thing should be done and there is more there than elsewhere of what I crave of the sound of the voice. It has got to be, my dear: there will be too many sentences born unless we require this also of them that they shall say something by their tone in addition, it may even be in opposition, to the sense of the words. The joy of the artist is in finding the bounds that are to keep him in bounds—the real

278. Beach published six poems in the May 1915 number of *Poetry*, among them the two poems RF mentions later in this letter. Beach's "Urban Colloquy" appeared in *The Atlantic* in October 1915.

not artificial bounds. There is no such uneasy misgiving as when he says at a loss What is to prevent my going on at this rate forever? What is to prevent me? The everlasting limitations are these: you shall not write but of images of life in images of the speaking voice. Images.

I liked best the "Café" one in Poetry—the glass of milk, the string the bicycle—the making no more of it all than it was. I doubt if the "Cave" one is good.[279] It is tainted with easy evolution and the heap big genius fallacy. Why, do you want me to tell you in a poem someday where we see the beauty that flees before us. We see it for a flash in wave like a white arm lifted in the bay, for a moment in a solitary house-light in a hundred square miles of black mountainside but longest and strongest in a woman. We see it at first in some things like this region w[h]ere I live now: we see it at last in other things like the region where I used to live in Derry. I shall see it here for a while at first in one way and then lose it to see it again in another way later when this place is no more nor less to me than just home and succeeds with me only as Derry did by familiarity. I refrain from pursuing the homily. If this be moral, at any rate it is not literary and oh me oh my but I am sick of some words and I am sick of some ideas till you'd think I might die of them and cheat the gallows.

You get here a foretaste of what some other people will have to take in four several lectures next week. I tell you this so that you will know that I am earning money and wont have to worry about me. I won't worry about you if you will tell me you will be as good as you can. And we will talk presently about you coming here next summer and about our academy.[280]

Yours ever
Robert Frost

---

279. "Rue Bonaparte," which describes a morning in a café, and "Cave Talk," the first and last of the six poems published in *Poetry*.

280. Likely a reference to the "literary summer camp" RF wrote of establishing, in several letters in 1915; see, for example, RF to Cox, January 1, 1915, and RF to Bartlett, August 8, 1915.

[To George Browne. ALS. Plymouth.]

Franconia N.H.
November 7 1915

Dear Brown[e]

These are no kind of letters I write in such a hurry. It's nothing but business between us all the time. Your half literary queries look funny and almost out of place in your letter along with dates and lecture rates. They'll look even funnier when I write them in here in my answer.

Yeats wrote the line

"Who dreamed that beauty passes like a dream"

& T. E. Brown a schoolmaster of Gloucester England wrote the line

"O blackbird what a boy you are!"[281]

And you said you had been reading Masters and Lindsay with an exclamation point.[282]

What a week I shall be in for. From here at this moment of perfect quiet and mountain loneliness it does not look as if I should prove equal to it. But you never can tell.

I ought to say that I think from what I hear from Miss Bates that there will be nothing possible at Wellesley this year. But Miss Bates has found something else for me for Jan 10 which I will tell you more about when I see you.[283]

I have written to Mrs Blake of Melrose that I could possibly be free to read to her company Thursday evening the 18th.[284] Tell me at once if that is all right.

Yours ever
R.F.

---

281. RF quotes the first lines of Yeats's "The Rose of the World" and of Thomas Edward Brown's "Vespers."

282. American poets Edgar Lee Masters (1868–1950) and Vachel Lindsay (1879–1931).

283. Katharine Lee Bates arranged for RF to read on January 10 at the Hotel Vendome in Boston.

284. Identity uncertain. However, census records for 1920 list an Edith Blake (1878–?) in Melrose, then employed as the principal of a public school.

[To George Browne. Apparently Browne had arranged for RF to read at Winsor, a private academy for girls in Boston. ALS. Plymouth.]

Franconia NH
November 10 1915

Dear Browne:

Monday be it then unless I think better of it and decide on the night train on Saturday which would land me in Boston Sunday morning. You wouldn't mind my turning up unexpectedly if I told you I might turn up unexpectedly.

Of course I sha'n't take Winsor's good money till I earn it.

I wish I could think I ought to get down to your Friday Club. But the family have no one but me here in the mountains and it's hard for them to be without me.

Count on me to say something to your boys Tuesday morning.

Till we meet.
Yours ever
R.F.

[To Harold Goddard Rugg. Rugg arranged RF's first lecture at Dartmouth College (as this letter indicates), and he later began there what would become one of the most extensive archives of the poet's work. ALS. DCL.]

Franconia N.H.
November 10 1915

Dear Mr Rugg:

You were just off for something when you wrote and I am just off for something now. I only mention the fact because I am afraid that when I get back from what I am off for it will be some time before I shall be in the mood for any more of the same. You have guessed that I mean talking. It will be altogether at boys' schools this trip and I ought not to mind it any more than so many recitations; but I shall: it is bound to put me off my writing for a while. There is a sort of purturbation [*sic*] that I have my doubts about in this new life I have entered on for the money I can pick up. I believe it would be a mistake for me to think of setting right off for Hanover before I have had time to get well over Boston. I should like December wholly to myself to see if I can't subside and get some work done. I wonder if you sympathise enough to understand. I do want not to seem to fall out with the plans you have taken so much trouble to make for me. But here are two or three all-but-finished poems and here on file are more than as many invitations to print them. They ought to be seen to, dont you say? A matter of a month all to myself ought to settle them one way or the other. What I should like to ask you is to see if you couldnt fit me into your plans for January.[285] Of course if December were going to be my only chance ever to see Dartmouth again I should have nothing to say. I only thought I would tell you how it was with me. I have as yet no fixed dates in January except a reading for Prof Bates of Wellesley on the tenth and the Dartmouth Alumni Dinner on the twenty-seventh.

When you write again will you tell me a little more about your idea? You seem to use the plural "talks."

Glad you didn't go to Fenway Park for nothing.[286]

Have you seen a new posthumous volume of poetry by Alice Freeman Palmer?[287]

Always sincerely yours
Robert Frost

[To Joseph Warren Beach. ALS. Minnesota.]

Franconia N.H.
November 11 1915

My dear Joe Beach:

And if I didn't seem to like your poetry enough, I want to add that I liked it better than my own. I've been looking again at the Café poem[288] (it's the one one goes back to) and if it's a shade off anywhere it's in the implication

285. See RF's December 22, 1915, letter to Rugg.

286. On October 13 the Boston Red Sox defeated the Philadelphia Phillies in the 1915 World Series.

287. *A Marriage Cycle* (Boston: Houghton Mifflin, 1915), with a preface by her husband, and RF's friend, Harvard professor of English George Herbert Palmer. Alice Freeman Palmer (1855–1902) graduated from the University of Michigan in 1876, served as dean of the women's department at the University of Chicago, and taught history at Wellesley College, where she held the presidency from 1881 to 1887; she was a staunch advocate of higher education for women.

288. See RF's November 7, 1915, letter to Beach. The poem in question is "Rue Bonaparte."

that such people know at the moment that there's anything they lack. Every thing else you read out of your facts: that is the only thing you seem to me to read into them. But dear me suz[289] just see how bad I am if judged by the standards I set up for you. When I get the chance I am going to do a paper anonymously that will finally read me out of present-day literature. Whats the use of being bothered by a person like me. People have been imposed on by the way I pulled the legs of some nice Englishmen. Why I can't run a farm decently. I am at a very low ebb of courage. But believe me

Your friend and friend of all you do
Robert Frost

[To Louis Untermeyer. Included with the letter was a whimsical sketch of Hudson Bay. See RFLU, *18. ALS. LoC.]*

Franconia N.H.
November 11 1915

Dear Louis

Its all right then: there's nothing in the term that will make any difference in what I am about to say. I only wanted to be sure before I went ahead. Its just one of those bad analogies that obliterate the distinction between poetry and music. I knew you were well informed (as well as clever) and would be able to tell me everything. I never meant to imply that I had caught you talking of "overtones" (even in undertones)—never![290] I dont know what I may have said. I may have said anything and meant nothing or the very opposite—just as I may have said you were clever when you weren't even educated. You and I are not clever, Louis: we are cunning, one with the cunning of race the other with the cunning of insanity. (All women are cunning with the cunning of sex.)

Anybody can tell you are cunning by the way you phrase yourself on the subject of Braithwaite's five best poems. The selection "staggers you."[291] That

289. Variant spelling of "sirs" (*Oxford English Dictionary*).

290. See RF to Untermeyer, November 1, 1915.

291. William Stanley Braithwaite had published, in the *Boston Evening Transcript*, a summary review of the best poetry of autumn 1915. The poems to which RF specifically refers in these paragraphs are "Patterns" by Amy Lowell, "The Adventurer" by Odell Shepard, "Peter Quince at the Clavier" by Wallace Stevens ("Susanna's music touched

is to say you dont say it isn't good and you wont say you dont know what good is. You seem to allow that the poems have merit though you dont see it. They have none. Amy's is just nothing to the eye ear or peritoneum. How completely outside herself she gets and how completely outside of everybody else she keeps. She executes a frightfulness. Somewhere else she brings in the Peeping-Tom idea. The Adventurer is a Blissful Carmen[292]—a voice from the nineties. Mosher would like it.[293] But to be novel you have to revive something older than the nineties. Sussanner simply bothers me. A priori I ought to like any latter-day poem that uses the word bawdy. I don't know why I dont like this one unless it is because it purports to make me think. A bawdy poem should go as easy as a song: "In Amsterdam there lived a maid," frinstance.

But why try to discriminate in this world? It ill becomes the author of poems not to like the other fellows' poems, because the more he doesnt like other people's poems the more he seems to his suspectors to like his own. Me for Hudson Bay!

And whatever we do Louis let us never take the Poet as a subject as if so in love with the idea of being poets that we dont realize that in Whos Who poets are rated lower than aldermen. A man has a right to be a poet if he can climb into the Poetry Society but he neednt go to calling himself sticky names like Gayheart in public.

I wish you wouldn't keep reminding me of the poetry societies I belong to.

Can you drore pitchers? Let me do you one of our new home (not yet finished or begun) on the Shores of Hudson Bay.

I profess myself an idealist in pictorial art. I have four children who are enhanced as I take it by not being represented in the picture. Art has ever

---

the bawdy strings . . ."), and "Gayheart: A Story of Defeat" by Dana Burnet. In his reply, dated November 23, Untermeyer writes: "I'm willing to be stunning—even clever—even cute. But I'll be ground to bone fertilizer & spread out over the grave of Alfred Austin before I'll let you hint that I'm a compromiser. I repeat, Braithwaite's selection 'staggered' me. And I repeat that nobody but a Yankee or a poet (or both) could have misunderstood me. 'Staggered' by what—by their capital letter Beauty? Pish, tush & folderiddle!" (letter held now at DCL).

292. Whimsical reference to the style of the Canadian poet Bliss Carman (1861–1929), who made his career in the 1890s, publishing, over the course of the decade, eight volumes (some in collaboration with Richard Hovey).

293. Thomas Bird Mosher (1852–1923), American publisher, best remembered now for his *Bibelot* series of yearly anthologies (1895–1914). See RF's February 19, 1912, letter to Mosher.

been my lifelong solace when things have been going wrong at the front. The object with the long matted hair is me neglecting the fur business to go fishing on the immemorial sea in carnadine[294]—I might as well have said neglecting one thing to do another as always. How it all comes back to me from the future. (It would come forward to me from the past, you!) The boat is named the New Moon to put it in the moon series with Henrick Hudson's Half Moon.[295] The dog is behind the house barking at an Indian or something mysterious astir in the forest of Eld. My wife—I dont mean to desert my wife: she is there too—is cooking linseed doughnuts in bear-grease. Nearest neighbors—not any. Nearest library Carnegie at Newhernhut.[296] You come too.

R.F.

As you say few of these poets are much bothered by anything that is in them. I wish you would give them all Hell and relieve my feelings without involving me in the odium of seeming jealous of anybody. You have a scourging pen. Scourge away.

[To David Emerson Greenaway (1885–1950?), Amherst graduate (1905), local historian, and a history teacher at the Springfield (Massachusetts) Technical High School at the time of his correspondence with RF. ALS. Private collection.]

Franconia N.H.
November 12 1915

Dear Mr. Greenaway:

Thanks for the clipping. Frank Sanborn makes considerable difficulty of me.[297] Really, you know, I haven't the least thing in common with Whitman.

---

294. See *Macbeth* (2.i): "this my hand will rather / The multitudinous seas incarnadine, / Making the green one red."

295. In 1609, the Dutch East India Company commissioned Henry Hudson to find a Northeast Passage to China; the ship he commanded was named the *Half Moon*.

296. German name for the capital of Greenland.

297. Franklin Benjamin Sanborn (1831–1917), Concord schoolteacher, abolitionist, and adviser to John Brown. Sanborn was also a special correspondent for the *Springfield Daily Republican*. In his Boston Literary Letter in the November 10 issue, he compared RF to Walt Whitman and then said: "Now Mr. Frost has capacities for pleasing verse . . . but in his larger and later volume he neglects them for a plainer and barer style. . . . Frost's 'North of Boston' is colloquial in another sense; it uses the prose conversational form, as

He drew no character, he presented no action, he was almost never specific and particular. All I know of Sanborn is that he is the Concord movement on its dear old last legs. I think he doesn't mean ill by me. But he is quite out in most respects. It is a safe bet that he thinks he knows Milton's blank verse without ever having read Samson Agonistes.

There are few things that I am likely to remember longer than our walk up Bridgewater Hill together.[298] I shall hope to see more of you sometime not too far off—and to hear from you again now and then when your thoughts run on poetry.

Sincerely yours
Robert Frost

[To George Browne. Elinor Frost was ill and pregnant at the time; she suffered a miscarriage later in the month, on the twenty-ninth. The "production" RF alludes to was a dramatic staging of several of the poems from NB, *including "Home Burial"; for details of the event, see RF's November 5, November 22, and December 3 letters to Charlotte Endymion Porter. ALS. Plymouth.]*

Franconia Nov 21 [1915]

Dear Browne

Home again and laid out straight for the space of two days not noticed in the passing.

I suppose it was a good week but I only counted three or four things really successful—your Monday, Mrs Hocking's infant class, the Poetry Club in the graduate School, the Friday Club and possibly your school. Andover was a trifle worse than Milton. The church at Andover seemed too large for me. I may be able to get my effects in such a place, but I shall have to try again. Mine is the intimate way. I am best with a few people near me.[299]

Horace did in his Satires, which the gay Roman termed 'sermo merus' or 'common talk.' Though this may have the form of verse, and often of effective verse, it is not poesy, and does not give pleasure, in Wordsworth's meaning of the word. It is apt to depress the soul, instead of raising it."

298. Near Plymouth, New Hampshire, where Greenaway summered.

299. A reference to a series of no less than five readings RF gave in the Boston area from November 13 to November 16. Agnes O'Reilly Hocking was the wife of RF's friend Ernest Hocking; see RF's April 3, 1915, letter to both.

There is nothing new to say about Elinor—Mrs Frost. Mrs Browne may write and I shall be glad to have her say any cheering thing she can, but she will hardly be able to coax Elinor to Cambridge. We are well fixed where we are and the long journey seems to have terrors.

Thanks for this letter of Groce's. It tells its own story of what you went through on my behalf after I was out of the way. You seem to have had to be my champion.[300]

I will give you more dates as I make them—if I make them.

I shall probably be down for the production next Sat. but it will be the barest run in.

Thanks for everything and forgive me that I cant keep thanking you and Mrs Browne till I have used this paper up.

Always yours
Robert Frost

---

300. Byron Groce (1878–1915) was English Master at the Boston Latin School and president of the Friday Night Club (a literary society). At the Club's November 12 meeting, at which RF seems to have made a brief appearance, Browne "championed" the poet's theories about "sentence sounds," apparently to little effect. In the letter referred to here (dated November 13), Groce explains that, though he admires RF's work, he considers much of it (in *NB*) "shredded prose." He then writes: "I confess I don't get the idea of [RF's] sentence-sound theory. If he should report conversations just as spoken the sentences would be prose, and yet would report the sound with the sense. Is there some art he claims by which a spoken sentence of plain prose may be made over to suggest the sound and thus become poetry?" Here Browne added, in ink of another color, three exclamation points of frustration. Groce concludes, in a passage Browne lightly canceled: "But I must not impose an answer on you. Nobody in our club could do the stimulating, fine thing you did to-night, except you. Your enthusiasm and your acumen were well mixed" (letter held now at Plymouth).

[To Charlotte Endymion Porter, who would stage dramatizations of two poems by RF in Boston on the twenty-seventh. Helen Clarke, whose name RF misspells, was Porter's long-time companion and collaborator on a number of literary projects. ALS. BU.]

Franconia N.H.
November 22 1915

My dear Miss Porter:

Thank you for all your kindness. I look forward to seeing what you have done for what you call my folk-plays, though I confess not without misgiving in the case of Home Burial. If you succeed with that, you may have it.

I am sorry, but Mrs Clark's invitation comes too late. I am already promised to my King's Chapel friend Sydney [*sic*] Snow.[301] Can I show my appreciation by going to lunch with Mrs Clark on Saturday?

Till we meet then.

Sincerely yours
Robert Frost.

Am I wrong in thinking the hour on Saturday is 4 P.M.? I have been telling friends that. Unfortunately I have kept none of the printed notices for myself.

[To Ellery Sedgwick. ALS. Mass. Hist.]

Franconia N.H.
November 22 1915

Dear Sedgwick:

Will Monday evening the twenty-ninth be convenient for you? I shall plan to hold over till then from my Saturday engagement at Huntington Hall.[302]

Always yours sincerely
Robert Frost

301. See RF to Eaton, May 26, 1915. RF visited Snow in Boston in late November.

302. Again, Charlotte Endymion Porter's staging of "Home Burial" and "The Death of the Hired Man."

[To Alfred Harcourt, then of Henry Holt and Company, RF's American publisher. He and Holt's legal team had been trying to sort out problems in RF's contract with David Nutt (RF's London publisher, presided over by its namesake's widow: here, "Madam"). ALS. Princeton.]

Franconia NH.
November 22 1915

Dear Harcourt:

The enclosed tells its own story. The postmark dates are mysterious without and within. No other word or sign from Madam.

I was so-so in my work last week; and now I am home again for reflection.

Prof. George Palmer[303] came to the Monday evening at Browne's (Cambridge) to tell me I had been chosen Phi Beta Kappa Poet at Harvard for next June. So it goes.

Yours always,
R.F.

[To Edward Thomas. ALS. Cardiff.]

Franconia NH.
November 23 1915

Dear Edward

I have reached a point this evening where no letter to or from you will take the place of seeing you. I am simply down on the floor kicking and thrashing with resentment against everything as it is. I like nothing, neither being here with you there and so hard to talk to nor being so ineffectual at my years to help myself or anyone else. How am I going to tell you in cold writing that I tried to place your Four-and-twenty Blackbirds with Holt and failed. I know it was something I didn't say or do to bear down the publishers doubts of the book as too English for the American mother and child. It is not too English—someone will see it yet—and I tried to make the publisher see it by not saying too much and by not saying too little. But if I haven't succeeded in doing anything for you, I havent succeeded in doing anything for myself. If I seem to have made any headway with the American reading crowd, it is by what was done for me before I left England. You over there

303. George Herbert Palmer, of Harvard; see RF's April 2, 1915, letter to him.

brought it about that I was named the other day in the "Queries" department of a school paper as perhaps the equal of Ella Wheeler Wilcox and James Whitcomb Riley.[304] Don't think I am bitter. You know how little I ask. Only I wish I could have the credit for getting a little of it for myself and perhaps sharing a little of it with someone else. I havent even dug in on this farm yet. I am still a beggar for the roof over our heads. And you know how it is with us; Elinor is so sick day and night as to affect the judgement of both of us: we cant see anything hopefully though we know from experience that even the worst nine months must somehow come to an end. The devil says "One way or another." And thats what Elinor says too this time. There is really cause for anxiety. We are not now the strength we were.

Is this in the miserable confidential tone they are curing you of by manly discipline? You wont be able [to] hit it off with the like of me by the time the war is over. You'll be wondering how you ever found pleasure in grovelling with me in such self-abasement—walking about the fields of Leddington—in the days that were. Couldn't we run ourselves down then without fear of losing too much favor with each other?

Do you want me to tell you the best thing that has come to me for a long long time, let you take it as you will from the will to be agreeable or from perversity. It is the news that the country may not ask of you all that you have shown yourself ready to give. I dont want you to die (I confess I wanted you to face the possibility of death): I want you to live to come over here and begin all over the life we had in St Martin's Lane at Tyler's Green at White Leaved Oak and at Balham.[305] Use should decide it for you. If you can be more useful living than dying I dont see that you have to go behind that. Dont be run away with by your nonsense.

You know I haven't tried to be troubled by the war. But I believe it is half of what's ailed me ever since August 1914. Lately I have almost despaired of England at times. I've almost been afraid that she might be beaten on land and brought to terms which might prove the end of her in fifty years. We say a disturbance of the balance of power was what caused the war. It shows how little the balance was really disturbed—the fight is so equal and so desperate. I agree with what Pat said to Pat and with what Pat answered. Pat said "It's a

---

304. American poets Ella Wheeler Wilcox (1850–1919) and James Whitcomb Riley (1849–1916) were very widely read.

305. St. Martin's Lane and Balham are locations in London; Tylers Green is a village in Buckinghamshire; White Leaved Oak is in Herefordshire.

terrible war!" And Pat answered "Terrible, but after all it's better than no war at all."

I'll write you in a better vein than this within a week.

Tell Baba our silly President thinks well of widows too.[306] Damn some people that get in my light.

Goodbye Soldier
R.

Say something pleasant and characteristic for me to everybody not excluding Miss Farjeon and Maitland Radford.[307]

[To Walter Prichard Eaton. Frost refers to his appearance at King's Chapel at the behest of Sidney Snow. ALS. UVA.]

Franconia N.H.
November 25 1915

My dear Eaton:

Have this from me[308] and remember I often think of you and wonder when we will be where we can exchange thoughts for a little while in some easier way than by writing. I suppose you wouldnt be in Boston on Monday? I am to be at Snow's Sunday night.

I liked your Woodchuck. The Woodchuck is a sacred bird. He occurs in the best thing Thoreau ever wrote.[309]

Always sincerely yours
Robert Frost.

---

306. Edward Thomas' daughter, Myfanwy, was nicknamed "Baba."

307. Eleanor Farjeon (1881–1965), English poet and author of children's books; she was close to Edward Thomas and his wife, Helen. Maitland Radford (1884–1944?), English poet and physician.

308. RF enclosed a fair copy of "Putting in the Seed."

309. See the opening of "Higher Laws," in *Walden:* "As I came home through the woods with my string of fish, trailing my pole, it being now quite dark, I caught a glimpse of a woodchuck stealing across my path, and felt a strange thrill of savage delight, and was strongly tempted to seize and devour him raw; not that I was hungry then, except for that wildness which he represented." Eaton's descriptive essay "The Ways of the Woodchuck," with illustrations by Walter King Stone, had appeared in the November 1915 issue of *Harper's*.

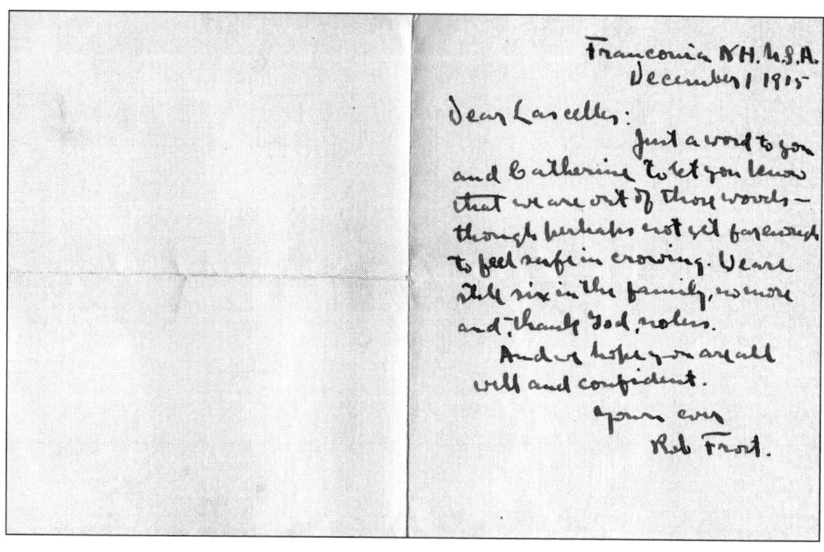

Franconia NH. U.S.A.
December 1 1915

Dear Lascelles:

Just a word to you and Catherine to let you know that we are out of those woods—though perhaps not yet far enough to feel safe in crowing. We are still six in the family, no more and, thank God, no less.

And we hope you are all well and confident.

Yours ever
Rob Frost.

Brief as it is, Frost's note to English friend Lascelles Abercrombie conveys his compounded emotions of fright and relief at Elinor's having survived three months of a difficult pregnancy and a traumatic miscarriage on November 29, 1915.

Courtesy Jones Library (Amherst, Massachusetts).

[To George Browne. This letter dates Elinor's miscarriage, following a serious illness throughout which RF feared for her life, as having taken place on Monday, November 29. Among the poems "acted" the evening of the twenty-seventh in Boston—as RF sat in the audience, anxious about his wife's condition—was "Home Burial." (He'd explained to Browne several weeks earlier, on November 11: "I never read Home Burial in public anywhere. I dread a little to see it acted.") ALS. Plymouth.]

Franconia NH.
December 1 1915

My dear Browne:

We are out of those woods—though perhaps not far enough to feel safe in crowing yet; and we are still six in the family, no more and, thank God, no less.—I was called home by telephone Monday morning and left everything and fled with explanations to nobody. I got here to find the worst over.

I was less sorry not to see you to talk over the poems as acted than not to see you to say goodbye. What was there to say about the poems that wouldn't be obvious to everyone?—or to nearly everyone? Country people are not so peculiar as through some fallacy peculiar to city-dwellers my characters were made. Ask Alice Brown if you ever meet her.[310] But that is all.

Our best to you both.

Yours ever
R.F.

[To Lascelles Abercrombie. ALS. Jones.]

Franconia NH. U.S.A.
December 1 1915

Dear Lascelles:

Just a word to you and Catherine to let you know that we are out of those woods—though perhaps not yet far enough to feel safe in crowing. We are still six in the family, no more and, thank God, no less.

And we hope you are all well and confident.

Yours ever
Rob Frost.

[To Harold Goddard Rugg. ALS. DCL.]

Franconia N.H.
December 2 1915

Dear Mr Rugg:

Mrs Frost has been very ill for some days and is still in a serious condition. You will forgive my having put off writing to you.

January 22 will suit me.

I should like not to get very far from the subject of sound in my talk. How would "Imagination and the Voice" do?—or "New Sounds in Poetry"? I could give you "New Hampshire Gold" which would be a homily on the exceptional in life and poetry. My own preference would be for "New Sounds in Poetry." Something would depend of course on the character of the audience you have in mind for me. I gave this, or virtually this, five times last week. It was most successful with the new poetry society in the Harvard Graduate School and with a group of Cambridge people, professors, and their wives.

310. New Hampshire novelist and poet Alice Brown (1856–1948).

I should like seventy-five dollars for my pains.

I wonder if you would be interested in this glimpse of English poets in war-time. I like friends here to know that my friends over there are not recreant. I spoke to Wilfrid about the autograph you wanted. He neglects to mention the matter.[311] I'll jog him again.

Sincerely yours
Robert Frost

[To John Bartlett. ALS. UVA.]

Franconia N.H.
December 2 1915

Dear Johnah:

We are suddenly out of our misery and nothing to show for it. It has been so much worse than we remembered it from times past that we had begun to suspect that something must be wrong. It turns out that nothing has been right for three months. Elinor has been unspeakably sick. But I think we are safely out of the woods now. I will write in a better frame of mind when I write again.

Affectionately
R.

[To Charlotte Endymion Porter. ALS. BU.]

Franconia N.H.
December 3 1915

My dear Miss Porter:

Thank you again for holding me up to myself so effectively. I saw how a number of things would be that I had been wondering about. Who knows but that you may have put me in the way of becoming a dramatist?

---

311. Wilfrid Gibson. It is not clear which volume RF refers to in speaking of a "glimpse of English poets in war-time." Apparently not (given the plural) Gibson's 1915 volume *Battle* (New York: Macmillan). The autograph spoken of is the one Rugg wanted from Rupert Brooke; see RF to Rugg, October 15, 1915.

I must write my thanks to Mr Watson and Miss Shull too.[312] They got my essential meaning so sympathetically.

I suppose the friendly praise of your little speech gave me the happiest moment of the evening.

Some time you and I must talk over this matter of folk drama. You seem to have thought of things that have occurred to me too.

Sincerely yours
Robert Frost.

[To Louis Untermeyer. ALS. LoC.]

Franconia N.H.
Decem 3 [1915]

Dear Louis:

I think I told you what we were in for. But we are not in for it any longer. We have just passed through one of those family crises that leave nothing to show for themselves. We are lucky in all being still alive. I am nurse cook and chambermaid to the crowd and that discouraged it would do my enemies (see roster of the Poetry Society of America) good to see me.

Sometime I will do as you tell me—write a little more poetry and a little prose too. Not now.

You needn't tell anyone I am so down or I shall have everybody on top of me. You know what a wolf pack we are.

Goodbye—goodbye
R.F.

It's a joy to me that you have come in with us. Let's start a great period in American letters. (Some people in Boston dont like my levity in such remarks as that.) Harcourt is the best ever.[313]

---

312. The actors who performed the "The Death of the Hired Man" and "Home Burial"; see *YT*, 534–535.

313. Untermeyer had become associated with Alfred Harcourt, an editor at Henry Holt and Company.

[To John W. Haines. ALS/Photostat. DCL.]

Franconia N.H.
December 3 1915

Dear Haines:

(I always put the Jack on in my mind, though I have never ventured to say or write it.)

We are suddenly out of our fear and anxiety in a way we hadnt looked for. It has been a bad bad summer for us as you may have inferred from what I have and haven't written. We had our mouths set for a worse winter. But suddenly, as I say, we are clean out of it (with nothing to show for it) and ready to begin life all over. Well I cant caper yet: I'm not sure that the caper isn't all gone out of me: I may never caper again. Still I can see that I am glad, theoretically glad at least—as glad as a dead person might be at being buried in a place of honor or at being thought enough of to be embalmed or something equally gratifying to the dead.

Don't mind anything I say, will you? There is really a good deal more to be thankful for than in this mood I am willing to admit except to a friend who wont use it against me. We are still six in the family, the same six no more no less. One of us is very ill at this moment, but visably [*sic*] improving all the time. In a week or two there should be nothing to worry about but a living. You can see from the enclosed what my publisher is doing to make my books earn that. They'll never do it of course. But a penny earned is better than two pennies saved. We begin to get real royalties out of the piratical Holt which is something we never got out of Madam Nutt.[314]

Another good thing: my publisher's lawyer has given the Madam sixty days to render me an account in. As he reads us the law if within that time she doesn't comply, my contract becomes void. The sixty days is nearly out. Two or three days more and I may be a free man. Then for business. I vow I never intended to write another poem tied to that woman.

---

314. RF's contract with David Nutt, London publisher of *ABW* and *NB*, called for him to be paid a 12 percent royalty on copies sold beyond the initial 250. Mrs. M. L. Nutt had directed the firm since her husband died. The reference to Holt, RF's American publisher, as "piratical" is done in irony; they had yet to reach terms with David Nutt.

Still another: I grow famous as fame goes in these parts where the Boston Trans[315] acclaims fifty-two poets of distinction a year, which is one a week. The proof of my fame is the latest honor that has come to me from the college I ran away from in 1899: I am to be the Phi Beta Kappa poet at Harvard next June.[316] This is as high as we go officially over here. It means nothing to you. Never mind: I wouldn't have it mean too much. Be still the friend of my obscurity and don't take too much stock in anyone who thinks he sees more in me than you have seen. I am coming back to you someday after I am forgotten over here, and you shall pour me sherry by the open fire in Hucclecote and comfort me for what I have had only to lose.[317]

Im talking myself sadder and sadder and it wont do at all in a letter due in England somewhere near Christmas.

My love to you, all three.[318]
Always yours
Robert Frost

[To Amy Lowell. ALS. Harvard.]

Franconia N.H.
December 5 1915

Dear Miss Lowell:

Thanks for this large—this spacious—book, and especially for the Paul Fort of it. Between his French and your English I'm not sure that I dont come nearer some idea of him than ever I did of foreign poet before. How he manages to keep off everyone else's preserve. Analytic clown-clown! Do you know he's the only one of your six who shows with any vividness the sounds I am after in poetry. I'll tell you what we did with the Henry III. My daughter and I read it together, I with my head tipped one way following your English aloud she with her head tipped the other way following his French in silence, the book being open at two places at once you understand. And even under

315. The *Boston Evening Transcript*, which had reviewed RF's work favorably in a number of notices.

316. On June 19, 1916, RF read "The Bonfire" as Phi Beta Kappa poet.

317. Hucclecote: a village in Gloucestershire, where Haines resided.

318. "All three" being Haines, his wife, Dorothy, and their son, Robin.

those unfavorable circumstances I brought tears of excitement to my daughters eyes. And she is a young thing.[319]

Well you didnt want all this letter about it. You wouldnt have sent the book if you thought you were going to bring down endless thanks on your head. No excuse for being long-winded when we are not paid at space rates.

I meant to ask you if I couldnt call on you when I was in town. But as you may have heard I was summoned home two days before my time by serious illness in the family.

Sincerely yours
Robert Frost

[To Ellery Sedgwick. ALS. Mass. Hist.]

Franconia N.H.
December 5 1915

Dear Sedgwick:

Forgive my running away from you on Monday. I was sincerely sorry to miss seeing you and Mrs Sedgwick. Tell Mrs Sedgwick so from me, won't you? I wasn't quite sure you got my explanation: I spoke in some confusion. I had just been called home in haste to my wife who had been taken ill in the night. I found her a very sick person. She is better now, but it will be some time before she is up and around again.

Wilfrid writes that both he and Lascelles Abercrombie have tried to enlist and been rejected.[320] I'm glad they took the step: I'm prouder to call them friends. I know one husky young poet who considers it braver to stay out

---

319. Lowell's *Six French Poets* (1915) included a chapter on Paul Fort along with others devoted to Émile Verhaeren, Albert Samain, Remy de Gourmont, Henri de Régnier, and Francis Jammes. In a lengthy appendix, Lowell provided original English translations of all poems quoted in the six chapters, including *Henri III*, by Fort. In a December 9 reply, Lowell writes: "Of course you like Paul Fort best. He is dramatic, as you are. 'Sound posturing,' well, well, call it what you like, it is dramatic, all the same. It is strange, but more and more I come to feel that the dramatic is the great interest in poetry. Not plays . . . but what Browning called 'Dramatic Lyrics' " (DCL).

320. Neither Wilfrid Gibson nor Abercrombie ever saw the front. The latter worked at a munitions factory in Liverpool. After four attempts at enlistment, Gibson was finally accepted, in October 1917, as a private in the Army Service Corps Motor Transport; he later worked in London as a medical clerk.

than to go in as things are in England at the present time. He expects to get the Victoria Cross for staying out. Another fine fellow I mustnt name rises to the spirit of the hour by calling the whole thing "too stupid to be true." Well, I wonder where we shall be found when it comes our turn.

Congratulations on your election to the Academy.[321]

Always sincerely yours
Robert Frost

[To Wilbur Rowell. ALS. UVA.]

Franconia N.H.
December 15 1915

Dear Mr Rowell:

Will you forgive me if I trouble you further about this farm? I have long felt uneasy about my obligation to the Herberts.[322] They have shown themselves decent kindly people. They have been more or less urgent for a settlement but they have never pursued us with ill nature and lately out of consideration for my wife who has been seriously ill they have let up on us entirely. All the same I can see that they are as unhappy about their obligation to the man they are buying their farm of as we are about our obligation to them. It would really be a mercy in keeping with the season to a whole lot of people at once if I could do something for them soon. At least I wish I could give them their answer one way or the other. The thing grows too complicated to go into in a letter: my wife or I could get down to lay it all before you sometime just after Christmas—if there is need.

Sincerely yours
Robert Frost

321. Sedgwick was elected to the American Academy of Arts and Letters in 1915.

322. The family from whom RF bought his Franconia farm; see the notes to RF's May 26, 1915 letter to Palmer.

[To Nathan Haskell Dole. ALS. Harvard.]

Franconia N.H.
December 19 1915

Dear Dole:

I was quite content with you and Mosher[323] the other night though you may not have found me demonstrative except toward the cake. I think a lot of you, Dole, and I hate to hear you say awful things about yourself. You must be good to yourself. I wish you could have heard the nice things an old classmate (and a distinguished one) of yours at Harvard said to me when I was last in Cambridge.

But we'll drop all that. You are going to be good to yourself when I am around.

After you have had the merry Christmas that I am wishing you (it was on other days I have asked you to be frankly a little sad) after you have had that and a week or two to get over it, we are to meet again.

I am going to speak or read in three parts at the Vendome—so be prepared—Antedeluvian Deluvian [*sic*] and Posthumous.[324] It will be for you to put me together again and send me home to my wife. Shall I look you up at your house sometime on Monday and go under your care?

Yours ever
Robert Frost

[To Harold Goddard Rugg. ALS. DCL.]

Franconia N.H.
December 19 1915

Dear Mr Rugg:

Let's stop right where we are for a moment till I explain. I simply mustn't be put before Dartmouth as standing out for any particular price. I named seventy five dollars more or less off hand with no very definite idea in mind

---

323. The publisher Thomas Bird Mosher (1852–1923). Mosher had written to Dole on November 5, 1915, asking if Dole and his wife might join him in Boston, on November 27, to meet RF (DCL holds a photostat of the letter).

324. Katharine Lee Bates arranged for RF to give a reading on January 10, 1916, at the Hotel Vendome in Boston.

of what I was going to at Hanover.[325] I thought if it was to be some thing you charged admission to, you would want me to have as much as you could. It is never for a moment a matter of what I am worth. I am probably worth nothing. Really I ought not to be asked to set a price. I am not in the business and you are—and you ought to [know] what I ought to have. I am getting all sorts of fees. I shall get no more than fifty dollars for what is my chief honor, the Phi Betta Kappa at Harvard in June.[326] So you just straighten the matter out to suit yourself and in the way to make the least noise. Whatever else I may be worth I am certainly worth no noise. Fifty dollars will be all right.

I was sorry not to be able to ask you to look in on us at Thanksgiving, but we were too badly off to be seeing anyone

I thought that what Gibson thanked God for might prove mildly interesting to you.[327] Potes [*sic*] as are Poets are what they are.

Sincerely yours
Robert Frost

[To Lois Tilley, daughter of Morris P. Tilley, professor of English at the University of Michigan in Ann Arbor. RF met the Tilleys first when they summered in Franconia near the farm RF bought in June 1915. The Frosts and the Tilleys remained friends for many years. The text of "Christmas Trees" herein differs in several details from the text as published in Mountain Interval. *ALS. UM.]*

Franconia N.H.
December 19 1915

My dear Miss Tilley

I'm afraid I took shameful advantage of you by my suddenness last week.[328] I didn't give you time to decide that you couldn't take the trouble I asked you to. But you and your mother are good and will forgive me and sometime I shall hope to pay you back with something better than this Christmas thing the children and I have been playing with. You will believe that I am infi-

---

325. RF would speak at Dartmouth on January 22, 1916.

326. On June 19, 1916, RF read "The Bonfire" as Phi Beta Kappa poet.

327. A reference, perhaps, to a line by Wilfrid Gibson in a book RF gave to Rugg: see RF's December 2, 1915, letter to him.

328. RF had taken up Lois Tilley and her mother, Mabel, on their offer to have him stay with them in their apartment in New York City (as conveyed in a November 28, 1915, letter held now at DCL).

nitely more grateful to you both than Merfyn was and I trust he was grateful enough for a boy.[329]

We are in better spirits here than we have been, for we have Mrs Frost up and around with us again. I hope you are past the worst of your cold and that both you and your mother may be well for Christmas.

Thanks again and then again for your kindness.

Sincerely yours
Robert Frost

CHRISTMAS TREES

The city had withdrawn into itself
And left at last the country to the country,
When between whirls of snow not come to lie
And whirls of faded foliage not yet laid
There drove one day a stranger to my door
Who did in country-fashion in that there
He sat and waited till he drew us out,
A-buttoning coats, to ask him who he was.
He proved to be the town come back to look
For something in the country it had left
And could not do without and keep its Christmas.
He asked if I would sell my Christmas trees.
My woods!—the young fir-balsams like a town
Where houses all are churches and have spires.
I hadn't thought of them as Christmas Trees.
I doubt if I was tempted for a moment
To sell them off their stumps to go in cars
And leave behind the house all cold the slope
Where the sun shines now no warmer than the moon.
I wouldn't have them know it if I was.
Yet who would have his trees to be but as
The trees of others, who refuse for them,
Beyond the natural time allowed for growth,
Trial by market that all things must come to?
I dallied so much with the thought of selling.
Then whether from mistaken courtesy

329. Merfyn is Mervyn Thomas, the son of Edward Thomas.

And fear to seem too short of speech, or whether
From hope of hearing good of what was mine
I owned a doubt if there would be enough
To make them worth his while.
  "You'd be surprised
To find how many they would cut you, Mister.
I could soon tell you somewhere near how many
If I could look them over."
  "You could look
But don't expect I'm going to let you have them."

Pasture they spring in, some in clumps too close
That lop each other and leave few branches green.
He shook his head at those. But not a few
Stood solitary and had equal boughs
All round and round. He nodded Yes to those
Or paused to say beneath some lovelier one
With the trader's moderation, "That would do."
We climbed the pasture on the south, crossed over
And came down on the north.
  He said, "A thousand."

"A thousand Christmas trees!—at what apiece?"

"A thousand trees would come to thirty dollars."

I knew for certain I had never meant
To let him have them. I concealed surprise.
Yet thirty dollars seemed so very small
Beside the extent of pasture I should strip
Three cents so small beside the dollar friends
I should be writing to within the hour
Would pay in cities for great trees like those,
Some of them vestry trees, whole Sunday Schools
Could hang enough on to pick off enough.

A thousand Christmas trees I didn't know I had!—
Worth more it seemed to give away than sell.
Too bad I cannot lay one in a letter.
I cant help wishing I could send you one

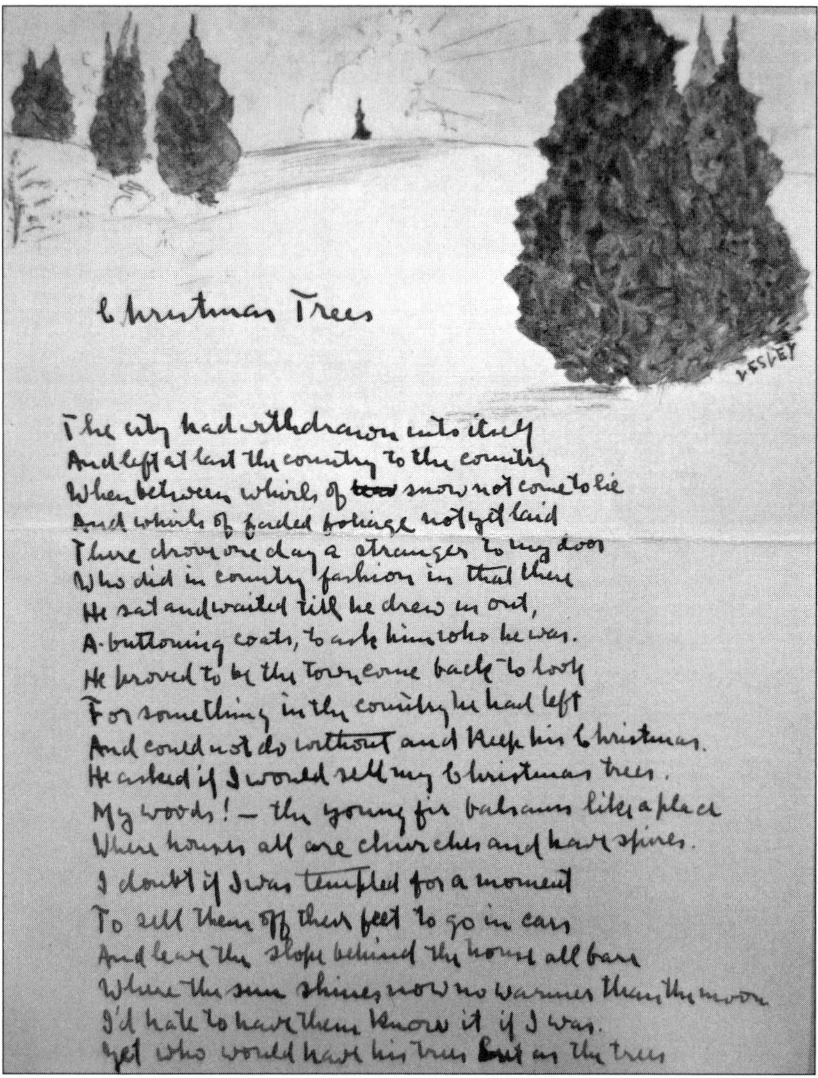

Christmas Trees

LESLEY

The city had withdrawn into itself
And left at last the country to the country
When between whirls of ~~too~~ snow not come to lie
And whirls of faded foliage not yet laid
There drove one day a stranger to my door
Who did in country fashion in that there
He sat and waited till he drew us out,
A-buttoning coats, to ask him who he was.
He proved to be the town come back to look
For something in the country he had left
And could not do without and keep his Christmas.
He asked if I would sell my Christmas trees.
My woods! — the young fir balsams like a place
Where houses all are churches and have spires.
I doubt if I was tempted for a moment
To sell them off their feet to go in cars
And leave the slope behind the house all bare
Where the sun shines now no warmer than the moon.
I'd hate to have them know it if I was.
Yet who would have his trees ~~but~~ as the trees

An early anticipation of the Christmas cards Frost would have designed and printed beginning in 1934, "Christmas Trees," illustrated in watercolor by Lesley Frost, was sent to Louis Untermeyer on December 22, 1915. An earlier version, with a simpler pencil sketch by Lesley, was sent to Lois Tilley on December 19, 1915.

Courtesy Library of Congress.

(I could spare one and never feel the difference)
In wishing you herewith
A Merry Christmas.

For
Miss Tilley and her mother
from
Robert Frost
and the children.

And Mrs Frost wishes to be remembered though she had no part in this nonsense.

[To Louis Untermeyer. RF's scurrilous (and "polluting") reference is to W. S. Braithwaite. ALS. LoC.]

Franconia NH
December 22 1915

Dear Louis:

Sometime at a worse season I will tell you what I think of niggers and having said so much to pollute this letter I will break off here and begin over on a fresh sheet which I will mail under a separate cover.[330]

Nobody's but yours
R.

---

330. Under separate cover RF sent Untermeyer a fair copy of "Christmas Trees," accompanied, again, by a watercolor sketch done by his daughter Lesley, and with the following note appended: "For a few Untermeyers (three to be exact) from a many Frosts (six to be exact)." See *RFLU*, 20–21. The poem elicited the following reply on December 27: "That was the finest Christmas letter any of our friends sent. And, what's more, it is one of the nicest Christmas poems I've read. It cheers my radical young heart to know that a Yuletide poem can be written without reference to 'babes' (with or without capitals), to mangers, wise men, peace, gold, frankincense or myrrh" (letter held now at DCL).

[To Katharine Lee Bates. ALS. Wellesley.]

Franconia N.H.
December 28 1915

My dear Miss Bates:

Thank you for your suggestions as to my program.[331] I think it might be a good idea for me to break the monotony of my reading by a little off-hand talk on a subject not unrelated to my poems.

I am sending the program to you because I seem not to have any other very definite address to send it to. May I ask you kindly to pass it along to its proper destination?

And one thing more: will you just run your pen through one or the other of the two poems I have offered as alternatives? I should like to leave the choice to you here because you have just had to listen to "A Hundred Collars"[332] and may not care to so soon again.

Well, the time draws near enough now so that I take an occasional long breath at the thought of it. I am booked for five appearances in public in a space of four days.

Sincerely yours
Robert Frost

[To Morris Tilley. ALS. UM.]

Franconia N.H.
December 29 1915

My dear Tilley:

Thank you for the pictures of us and where we live: and thank you for trying to make the professors out there like me. It was a good deal if you interested them even a little. It is an axiom that the further you get from London and Paris in the world and the further you get from Boston and New York in this country the less likely you are to find intellectual courage that is really intellectual. (The courage to take up with free silver and eugenics and uplift

331. For RF's upcoming appearance at the Hotel Vendome in Boston.

332. On November 27, RF read the poem at Huntington Chambers Hall, Boston, as a part of the program that also featured "Home Burial" and "The Death of the Hired Man" staged as plays.

movements generaly [*sic*] must not be mistaken for intellectual.) What bothers the worthy English Dept at Ann Arbor and at Minnesota[333] too I have reason to suspect, seems no such stumbling block at Harvard or Yale; or so I infer from the fact that I am to be Phi Beta Kappa poet at Harvard this year and the Yale Review keeps asking me for copy.[334] I am only considered radical on the frontier.

We have had a good deal of snow but to our surprise it hardly shows white on Lafayette at all. Except in a certain slant of the sun the mountains remain black.

We have had all sorts of sickness or I should have written you a real letter before this. I have been very much down myself lately. The truth is I dont just see how I am going to get into shape for all the lecturing I have ahead.

I enjoyed reading your notes on Shakespeare. I must pass them along to J. C. Smith who is editing the new Oxford edition of the plays.[335]

Always sincerely yours
Robert Frost.

[To Louis Untermeyer. ALS. LoC.]

[Franconia, NH]
[January 1, 1916]

Dear Louis:

And again: to be niggerly is not necessarily to be niggardly. It is niggerly for instance to single out Fannie Stearns Davis for dispraise, but it cant be called niggardly to name nobody else in the world but to praise him. In the case of Fannie you can't help suspecting something in the woodpile, a nigger scorned or slighted or not properly played up to.

---

333. Where RF's friend Joseph Warren Beach taught.

334. See RF's October 27, 1915, letter to Wilbur Cross.

335. James Cruikshank Smith, whom RF met in Scotland in 1913, was general editor of the *Selected Plays of Shakespeare* (Oxford, 1912–1916). RF may refer to any one of several essays by Tilley: "The Organic Unity of Twelfth Night" (*PMLA* 29, no. 4 [1914]: 550–566), "Two Shakespearean Notes" (*Modern Language Notes* 25, no.8 [December 1910]: 262–263), or "The 'White Hand' of Shakespeare's Heroines" (*Sewanee Review* 19, no. 2 [April 1911]: 207–212).

Mind you I haven't read Fannie and I haven't read Braithwaite's g.d. book[336]—I got one of the children to read it for me and tell me about it. All that saved the fat obstacle from the worst fate that overtakes paper was your name and mine on the flyleaf.

No I didn't read the book. I'll tell you what I did do, though. I took the Midnight Horror out of Littleton not long ago and on the train with me I had about as many good-looking boys and girls as there are great poets in the book. They were of the Lisbon High School which had just beaten at basketball for a second time the Littleton High School. And they were yelling glad. And this is what they kept saying all together and out loud: it came somewhere near expressing my feelings, though at the same time it shocked me: since as you know I am not a swearing man: I couldnt help liking the liberty taken in the rhyme: all the old rhyme pairs are so worn out that I'm ready to permit anything for the sake of a fresh combination: this was a new one to me—it may not be to you: well here goes: I mustn't put you off any longer: this is what the good looking children said:

Lisbon once—Lisbon twice!
Holy jumping Jesus Christ!

Maybe you dont like me to talk this way. I can see that I am going to make enemies if I keep on. Still that wont be anything new or strange. I had nothing but enemies three years ago this Christmas.

Why go into details? Granted that there are a few good poems in the book—I read yours and liked it because it says something, first felt and then unfolded in thought as the poem wrote itself.[337] That's what makes a poem. A poem is never a put up job so to speak. It begins as a lump in the throat a sense of wrong, a homesickness a lovesickness. It is never a thought to begin with. It is at its best when it is a tantalizing vagueness. It finds its thought and succeeds, or doesnt find it and comes to nothing. It finds its thought or makes its thought. I suppose it finds it lying around with others not so much to its

336. *Anthology of Magazine Verse for 1915: and Year Book of American Poetry,* ed. William Stanley Braithwaite (New York: Gomme and Marshall, 1915). In the "Year Book" section of the volume, Braithwaite had unkind things to say about *Crack o' Dawn* (New York: Macmillan, 1915), by the American poet Fannie Stearns Davis (1884–1966).

337. "Swimmers," later collected in Untermeyer's 1917 volume *These Times* (New York: Henry Holt).

purpose in a more or less full mind. That's why it oftener comes to nothing in youth before experience has filled the mind with thoughts. It may be a big big emotion then and yet find nothing it can embody in. It finds the thought and the thought finds the words. Let's say again: A poem positively must not begin thought first.[338]

Say! When I get started! What?

Thanks for your defense in The Call.[339] You and I have got inside of each others breast works. I shall be glad when you can like anything I do. But don't feel obliged to like it (I know you wont—you are an honest man) I mean to hang on to you as a friend whatever you have to say to my poetry.

I shall come to see you if I stop more than three hours in New York. That dinner comes just wrong. I have engagements for a little money on the day before it and the day after—and by rights just on it.

I'm glad for your wife she has found a backer in Amy Lowell.[340] I'm hoping to be more and more her backer when I see more of her work. Theres an opening there she's making for herself—I dont mean with any person or persons—I mean in a realm.

You mustn't mind me. Some days you would think I knew it all to see me on paper. In reality I am only a poor man on ration. Its a hard winter and I'm hard up and sometimes I harden my heart against nearly everything.

You came into our Christmas to make us a good deal happier. We're all your friends—friends of all of you.

---

338. See RF's 1939 essay "The Figure a Poem Makes": "It is but a trick poem and no poem at all if the best of it was thought of first and saved for the last. It finds its own name as it goes and discovers the best waiting for it in some final phrase at once wise and sad—the happy-sad blend of the drinking song" (*CPRF*, 132). See also *Some Definitions by Robert Frost*: "A poem begins with a lump in the throat; a home-sickness or a love-sickness. It is a reaching-out toward expression; an effort to find fulfilment. A complete poem is one where an emotion has found its thought and the thought has found the words" (*CPRF*, 84).

339. The allusion is to the *New York Call* (shorthand for the *New York Evening Call*), a socialist newspaper with which Untermeyer was affiliated. However, we have been unable to track down the "defense" RF refers to.

340. Lowell was an early supporter of Jean Starr Untermeyer's poetry. Poems by both appeared in the October 1917 issue of *Seven Arts*; the two women exchanged a number of letters and occasionally dined together.

If there were no God—but there is one—that's just the point—he's come back at the smell of blood on his altars—and he hasnt come back in pieces (two or more) like Biela's comet the last time it turned up—He is still One.[341]

R.F.

Looking for the Yale Review and that puts me in mind of something else to thank you for, but not this time—later.

[To William Rose Benét (1886–1950), American poet. At the time, Benét edited the Century. *Later he edited the literary supplement of the* New York Evening Post, *which, in turn, led him to found the* Saturday Review of Literature *in 1924. ALS. ACL.]*

Franconia N.H.
January 3 1916

Dear Benét:

Your letter came pleasantly to hand to help our Christmas—your good card too, as from the family. This has to be my answer, wishing you a Happy New Year both on and off the job. This is the first time I have written the sixteen, and the first poetry I have shown an editor for more than a year—except the Phi Beta Kappa things the Atlantic had.[342] But for my old fear of editors which your kindness does so much to allay but can't be expected to cure all at once, I should have included one of my sardonics, a bit of narrative on voting the right ticket.[343]

Thanks for thinking of me in connection with the two whose poetry I admire most of all that is going.

Sincerely yours
Robert Frost

---

341. Biela's Comet was first recorded in 1772; it subsequently split apart, and now only remnants of it survive, appearing, periodically, as a meteor shower.

342. Perhaps "In the Home Stretch," which appeared in the *Century* in June 1916. On May 5, 1915, RF had read "The Road Not Taken, "The Sound of Trees," and "Birches" as Phi Beta Kappa poet at Tufts University; the three were published in *The Atlantic* in August 1915.

343. Title unknown; no poem answering to the description survives.

[To Wilbur Lucius Cross, professor at Yale University, and editor of The Yale Review *for almost thirty years. ALS. Yale.]*

Franconia N.H.
January 3 1916

Dear Prof. Cross:

I am sending you a few of my more recent poems that I seem to care for. Thank you for this opportunity to show them to the editor himself.[344]

The Encounter, The Gum-gatherer, An Old Man's Winter Night are of course in no way related to one another but at the same time I should like very much to sell them to be printed in a group.[345]

I look forward to seeing the copy of The Review that Untermeyer says he has asked you to send me for a poem of his it contains.[346] The other copy of The Review you sent was gratefully received in these solitudes where there isnt much on the public library table but the big flat thin things.

Sincerely yours
Robert Frost

---

344. RF here replies to a December 20, 1915, letter from Cross: "Some time ago, I think you said that you might be able to send a poem in to the Yale Review. Are you still of the same mind? If so, when may I see it?" (letter held now at DCL). See also RF's October 27, 1915, letter to Cross.

345. None of these appeared in *The Yale Review.* Instead, Cross published, in the April 1916 number, the poems subsequently gathered, in *MI*, under the title "The Hill Wife" (with the exception of "The Smile," which had already appeared in the December 1914 number of *Poetry and Drama*).

346. See notes to RF's January 1, 1916, letter to Untermeyer.

[To Louis Untermeyer. Dating derived from postmark. ALS. LoC.]

[Franconia, NH]
[January 7, 1916]

Dear Louis:

Will you tell me who Willa Sibert Cather is? Is the name a man's? That's what I want particularly to know. Is he (or she) some poet I ought to have read?[347]

R.F.

[To Willa Cather (1873–1947), Pulitzer Prize–winning novelist and managing editor of McClure's Magazine. *The letter is written on stationery bearing the letterhead of Abbot Academy, Andover, Massachusetts, where RF had given a reading on January 13. See the notes to RF's January 7 letter to Untermeyer. ALS. BU.]*

January 15 1916

My dear Miss Cather:

I sit down beside the way (of the transgressor) to answer your good letter which was corsive to some of the wounds I have had of late.[348] I should be willing to put it this way: if Masters is a poet, then I am not; if he is not then I may be. You for one see that I am not only not a free-verse writer, but not a

---

347. On December 17, 1915, Cather had written to RF: "Will you pardon an expression of gratitude from one who is very willing but utterly unable to derive much pleasure from the crackling little fire of poetical activity which is being fanned, so to speak, by a wind off Spoon River? Your two books contain the only American verse printed since I began to read verse, in which I have been able to feel much interest—the only verse of highly individual quality. The appearance of such verse seems to be a very important event, and the warmth of appreciation which it kindles in one is a pleasure to feel. I would like to believe in the whole army of poets catalogued by Mr. [Witter] Bynner and Miss [Jessie] Rittenhouse; but if Ezra Pound and Mr. [Edgar Lee] Masters are poets, clearly you are none. One comes to feel ashamed of being unable to share any of this enthusiasm about 'new poets,' and ashamed of one's desire to ridicule. So let me thank you for the pleasure of admiring your verse, which is 'new' enough and which yet contains so many of the oldest elements of poetry. Very sincerely yours, Willa Sibert Cather" (letter held now at DCL).

348. In opening his reply, RF echoes Proverbs 13:15: "Good understanding giveth favour: but the way of transgressors is hard." "Corsive" is an alternate spelling of "corrosive," which had, in the sixteenth and seventeenth centuries, a medical meaning now lost.

free-thinker nor a free anything. It is better to be praised for what you aren't than to be blamed for what you aren't, but nothing in the world can quite compare with being praised for what in some degree you are. I thank you for everything you say and especially for bringing in my first book for a word of approval. I wish I might have the chance to add to these thanks in person next week when my wife and I are to be in New York (probably with Mr Alfred Harcourt of Henry Holt & Co.) for the annual dinner of the Poetry Society.[349]

Sincerely yours
Robert Frost

[To Helena T. Goessmann (1868–1926), instructor in English at the Massachusetts Agricultural College in Amherst (now the University of Massachusetts). The dramatization RF refers to took place on November 27, 1915, in Boston; he was present for it (see RF's several letters dating to November 1915 to Charlotte Endymion Porter, who arranged the event). ALS. BU.]

Methuen Mass
January 15 1916

Dear Miss Goessmann:

I have been away from home on my lecturing or I should have attended to your letter more promptly. Excuse me if I make but a hasty word of this.

I shall be only too happy to have you do anything you will with and for my poems. The dramatising of "The Death of the Hired Man" and "Home Burial" amounted to little more, to nothing more in fact, than leaving out the introductory descriptive passages. You can dramatise them to suit yourself. Tell me how you come out with them. I really think myself that they lose by being dramatised. All they need is a rather dramatic reading.

I am endlessly grateful to you and your boys for your interest in my books. Sometime I am going to meet you somewhere for a shake of the hand.

Sincerely yours
Robert Frost

When you write about your success with the poems use my Franconia [*sic*]. I mean to get back there in time to freeze to death this winter.

R.F.

349. On January 25 RF gave a talk at the sixth annual meeting of the Poetry Society.

[To Jessie Belle Rittenhouse (1869–1948), a popular poet and anthologist, and a founder and secretary of the Poetry Society of America. The letter is written on letterhead from Abbot Academy, a preparatory school in Andover, Massachusetts, at which RF gave a reading on January 13. The date is written in a different hand above the letterhead. ALS. Rollins.]

Abbot Academy
Andover, Massachusetts
[January 15, 1916]

My dear Miss Rittenhouse:

Your letter overtakes me "as I ride."[350] And a good generous letter it is. Of course I am pleased that you should be seeing more in my book with time. Let me thank you in haste now and leave the rest to say when I see you on the twenty-third.[351] I am going to undertake to get to New York then though to do it I shall have to take a midnight train out of Hanover N.H. after a lecture and a reading there in the evening.[352] I shall hope to have my wife with me to share in the pleasure of meeting you and your friends.

Sincerely yours
Robert Frost

[To Julia Ellsworth Ford (1859–1950), a New York collector, socialite, and philanthropist. ALS. Yale.]

Methuen Mass
January 15 [1916]

My dear Mrs. Ford:

I'm sorry your letter should have had to go unanswered so long. It has just overtaken me on my travels. I shall not be free on the sixteenth or I should be most happy to accept your invitation to meet Mr Masefield.[353] The fact is I am just getting in my last work as a lecturer before the great Englishman drives

350. See the refrain in Robert Browning's "Through the Metodja to Abd-El-Kadr" ("As I ride, as I ride / With a full heart for my guide," etc. . .").

351. Apparently RF was to be entertained in anticipation of the reading he would give two days later.

352. RF gave a talk on "New Sounds in Poetry" at Dartmouth on January 22.

353. John Masefield (1878–1967), English poet (and poet laureate of Great Britain from 1940 to 1967). He was recruited by the British Ministry of Information to go on an Ameri-

all little Americans from the field. It might tend to give him some pangs of conscience if you were [to] tell him this from me with my compliments.

Thanking you for your distinguishing letter I am

Sincerely yours
Robert Frost.

[To Alice Brown (1856–1948), American novelist, poet, and playwright, best known as a writer of New England local color stories, most notably Tiverton Tales *(1899). RF misdates the letter "1915"; almost certainly it dates from 1916, when RF was on a lecturing junket in eastern Massachusetts. ALS. UVA.]*

Methuen Mass
Jan 18 [1916]

My dear Miss Brown:

Thank you for your good letter. It is less in need of an answer now that Miss Lowell has arranged matters with you.[354] As I understand it, several of us are to read to you on Feb 2. Count on me to do my part with pleasure.

Sincerely yours
Robert Frost

[To Ashley H. Thorndike (1871–1933), an editor, along with his fellow Columbia University professor John Cunliffe, of the thirty-volume Warner Library of the World's Best Literature. *ALS. Columbia.]*

Amherst Mass
January 25 1916

Dear Mr Thorndike:

I am so very busy with my new work here and my general reading and lecturing that I'm afraid I shall have to give up the idea of doing Gibson for you for Warner's Library. I don't know why I entertained the idea for a moment unless it was out of friendship for Gibson. Writing about writers is something I have never done nor wanted to do. I doubt if I should do it as

---

can lecture tour in the winter of 1915–1916; his secondary mission was to gather opinions from Americans concerning World War I.

354. Amy Lowell.

well as a dozen others you will think of in connection with Gibson. Lascelles Abercrombie is really the man to give Gibson his due.[355]

Thanking you just the same for this chance to earn an honest penny, I am,

Sincerely yours
Robert Frost

[To Louis Untermeyer, as dictated to Lesley Frost. ALS (in Lesley's hand). LoC.]

Franconia N.H.
Feb 3, 1916.

Dear Louis;—

Just to protest that though in bed with the temperature of a setting hen I ain't a'goin' to die to please

Ella Wheeler Wilcox
Robert Underwood Johnson
Richard Le Gallienne
Abbie Farwell Browne
Benjamin R.C Low
Brian Hooker
Joyce Kilmer
Cale Young Rice
Florence Earle Coates
Richard Burton
Arther [*sic*] Guiterman
Olive Tilford Dargan[356]
or any other
Old-believer.
whatsoever

R.F.
by Lesley.

355. Instead, Thorndike recruited Harry M. Ayres to write the entry on Wilfrid Gibson, which appears in volume eleven of the series.

356. All popular poets of the day.

*[To John Bartlett. The letter is undated, but the specifics of the whirlwind touring RF describes would indicate February 1916. Thompson provides an account of these speaking engagements (*YT*, 72–75). ALS. UVA.]*

[Franconia, NH]
[February 1916]

Dear John:

I was badly disappointed when you failed me at the eleven o'clock train. I stood on the step as we pulled out hoping you were going to turn up from somewhere on the run and catch the train at the last minute. I was on the point of dropping off when you didn't, but I remembered my luggage which I had left in my seat where I couldnt get it and get off before we were moving too fast. I assumed of course that you had been delayed by some accident and might think of coming along on the next train. At Haverhill I stopped over and telephoned back to the station agent at Exeter to ask him to look and see if he saw the likes of you about the station. I boarded the next train when it came but there was no you on it. So I gave you up. I got the leaves you tore out of your note-book three or four days afterward at home in Franconia.

The Exeter evening was better than the Dartmouth Dinner. I never can tell when I am going to like my job. Lawrence was rather a success: most of the schools and colleges have been. The Dartmouth Dinner was for the politicians. I felt rather lost with my brief poem in all the smoke and noise. I would do better another time; for I would bargain for an early place on the program and should know from experience how to make more of my voice and manner. I wasnt particularly good at the New York Dinner either. There I struck too serious a note. Dinners are all new to me.

There was a reasonable chance of our dropping in on you at Raymond as we came along up. But that went glimmering when Elinor was taken sick in Cambridge and I had to leave her there in bed while I came home to see about the children. I had no sooner got here than I was taken sick myself and the children had to see about me. So our bust busted. Better luck next time!

Fifteen below here this morning. Twenty-five below the morning I left for my last tour. Hope it will moderate before my next which begins in five days. I jump clear to Schenectady this time.

Be good to your Rhode Island Reds![357]
As allers
R.

---

357. A breed of chicken raised for meat, eggs, and also for showing.

[To Wilbur L. Cross. ALS. Yale.]

Franconia N.H.
February 5 [1916]

Dear Prof. Cross

I should like you to know that sickness and nothing else had kept me from answering your letter of some two weeks ago. I had thought of asking you for a little more than the thirty dollars for the three poems. You left me the opening for that. I should have been willing however to leave a good deal to you. And I am now. Pay me what The Review can afford. Any comparison between The Review and Century was not mine. Harcourt is my good friend and knows how literally poor I am. You mustnt blame him if he wants me to get the most possible for what can't bring me very much anyway.

It occurs to me that you might prefer the Hill Wife sequence to the group of three but for the knife that put you off. I see your point there. The knife would be better out of the way and the line made to read

And once she went to break a bough
Of the black alder.[358]

Sincerely yours
Robert Frost

[The following letter is to Llewellyn Jones, literary editor of the Chicago Evening Post, *who had proposed to do an article on RF. The "Louis" referred to is Louis Untermeyer; the "jamboree" to which RF refers is a spate of readings and talks he gave early in 1916 at a number of sites in New England. ALS. Private collection of Pat Alger.]*

Franconia N.H.
February 7 1916

Dear Jones:

I have been all over the lot lately, not doing myself or anybody else much good but always haunted with a sense of something unattended to which

358. Lines from the last section ("The Impulse") of the suite of poems collected, in *MI*, under the title "The Hill Wife." Cross published them in *The Yale Review* in April 1916 (the one exception being "The Smile," which had appeared, without the subtitle it eventually bore ["Her Word"], in the December 1914 number of *Poetry and Drama*). For the "group of three [poems]" RF mentions, see his January 3, 1916, letter to Cross.

was of course your letter asking me to open my heart to you on the matter you wot of.[359] I couldn't attend to it as I rode in the trains because they joggled my pencil so always suggesting the question whether they didn't joggle more than English trains and so sending me off on a train of odious comparisons between things English and things American in which I lost myself for the duration of that particular mental spurt.

I wonder if I am disposed to write thus nonsensically by having met you at Louis' where all is always hilarious and so having come to have a feeling of intimacy with you that may not seem quite respectful to your editorial dignity. Forgive me everything at once and let me just say that I shall be only too happy to tell you the notions I entertain on the subject of the double duty a sentence must do in prose or verse. I think it must convey as it stands alone or with the help of the context an extra meaning over and above the meaning of the mere words by some tone indicated by the words. For instance is it six o'clock? is no good because it conveys no extra meaning by tone. What, is it six o'clock? is better because besides asking the question it says that the questioner is surprised. Have I told you once, it is six o'clock? is better still because the extra meaning (over and above the query) is more interesting.

The great thing to insist on is that there are so many definite significant sounds peculiar to the human throat, only so many of them, and it is the main part of the writers business to summons them with the imagination of the ear and so catch them in the meshes of the words of sentences—one to a sentence—that they will remain fast there for all time or for the life of the language.

This is nothing new: the tones are never anything new; we never add to them by invention. My complaint is that poetry of late has been getting along on too few of them from an atrophy of the particular kind of imagination—that of the ear—whose function it is to summons them. We have no tones at all or none but the time-honored sweet or magnificent. We have none anyway that havent been previously brought to book. You would suppose that no one had taken a fresh listen to the speaking voice for a hundred years. I exaggerate of course—for my purpose. We have asked that every poet should give proof of having looked for himself at life. I havent heard that anyone has asked that he should give proof of having listened for himself to life as it speaks in tones that say more than words.

---

359. Again, RF favors a phrasing with a seventeenth-century savor.

Never mind if I dont make this all clear at once. Lets talk about it before you attempt it in print. I really didn't set out to go into it tonight. I was going to say I was sorry I hadn't written before and I would be writing just as soon as I was recovered from my grip and my late jamboree. Speaking of my late jamboree, it was on that that I got up a story I told first in bad sentences and then in good to show the difference from my point of view.

> The dog is in the room. I will put him out. But he will come back.
>
> There's that dog got in. Out you get, you brute! Whats the use—he'll be right in again?

I say there are no tones in the first version and I hear three different tones all quite distinct and all in black and white on the page unmistakable for anyone who knows the language in the second.

And I say Swinburne[360] is N.G. because he hasnt enough tones to last him over night!!! Next!

Remember I dont confine myself to a theory of colloquial writing. I expect tones of everybody and many tones—one a sentence. Suppose I began a poem to the fools of the age

> Out of my light, ye darkeners!

You'd know the tone and you'd not set it down for vulgar or anything but high and angry.

Well I leave it there for this time. What say you?

Sincerely yours
Robert Frost

360. Algernon Charles Swinburne (1837–1909), English poet, playwright, novelist, and critic. For more on Swinburne, see RF's July 4, 1913, letter to John Bartlett.

[To David Emerson Greenaway. The Republican *is a daily newspaper published in Springfield, Massachusetts. ALS. Private collection.]*

Franconia N.H.
February 7 1916

My dear Greenaway:

Thanks for the much mistaken article from The Republican. The wonder about the Republican is that it can seem so intelligent without ever being right on any subject.[361] Perhaps that is a good receipt for seeming intelligent or at least intellectual—always to be wrong in an able, bookish style.

Couldnt you as a friend do combat for me in a letter to the editor. Tell 'em that no one who knows anything thinks of me as a free-verse writer. I write straight blank verse and The Republican be blanked. I suppose you saw Garnetts article in the August Atlantic. Here's some more material to think over. You don't think I'm a vers-libertine, as Louis Untermeyer puts it.

The Yale Review will have something of mine sometime within the year: so also will The Century. Some others too probably if I get to sending out things. I have only written a little in the last two years.

Sincerely yours
Robert Frost

361. See RF's November 12, 1915, letter to Greenaway, concerning an article in the Springfield *Republican*. RF may refer also to another article in the same paper, reprinted from the *Boston Evening Transcript* and dated November 20, 1915. It reads, in part: "Mr. Frost has come up like a rocket, and for the present, at least, he stays up. His work has the essence of poetry at least, for it awakens the ear and kindles the heart. In reading it, we find ourselves close to the heart of things. The reader's mood is strangely caught up and swept into the mood of the poet. We often find it impossible to call Mr. Frost's efforts verse, but somehow we cannot help finding them poetry. He is easily the best of all those who have treated the old metric laws as a mere scrap of paper."

[To Walter Prichard Eaton. The letter is undated and unaddressed; dating is derived from the preserved envelope. ALS. UVA.]

[Franconia, NH]
[February 8, 1916]

"You and I, gentle reader, saw James A. Hearne [*sic*] in Shore Acres."[362]

So we did, so we did, gentle writer.

This house has been twice warmed by word from you once in the friend's letter you sent and once in the Christmas card and still no thanks from me. I'm a bad person. But I dont want to write letters: I want to see you. I just missed doing that I believe the last time you were at Snows. Too bad.

Yours always
Robert Frost

[To George Noyes Whipple (1856–1940), who graduated from Amherst in 1878 and began a business career as a warehouse manager in Boston and then moved into advertising. Author of a number of class and fraternity (Psi Upsilon) hymns and odes and a member of the American Folk-Lore Society, Whipple had by 1915 established a Boston-based lyceum-lecture bureau he called the Players, "A National Association of Lecturers and Musicians." Willa Cather was among his clients. ALS. UNH.]

Franconia N.H.
February 12 1916

My dear Mr Whipple:

How can I tell you in a letter what is troubling me? If I thought you could get me not less than two thousand dollars clear for twenty-five or thirty lectures all crowded into not more than ten weeks, why I should be with you. But I just mustn't enter into any agreement that might take me away from home off and on all next winter. I have had enough of running this year under my own management. I have had about twenty engagements for fifty

362. RF quotes loosely from the opening paragraph of Eaton's article "Great Acting" in the February 1916 issue of *American Magazine*. "You and I, gentle reader, remember Mansfield; we remember Jefferson's Rip, and Julia Marlowe's Juliet; we saw Irving and Terry, Duse and Coquelin, John Hare as Lord Quex, James A. Herne in 'Shore Acres.' Ah, what wonderful things didn't we see!" James A. Herne, playwright and actor, performed the lead role in his *Shore Acres* for a number of years, including an extended run at the Boston Museum theater in the mid-1890s.

dollars or over and there wasn't any of the money they brought in that I didn't know how to use, and still I'm far from sure that they haven't been a folly. They have broken up my time and put me off my writing. I could only listen to your proposals if you could do much better for me than I have done for myself. Both my wife and my publisher are against my going any further with the lecturing at the expense of my writing. The writing of course must be the first consideration now that I am where I can afford to make it so (as it appears.) Nevertheless the lecturing if you could take it in hand and keep it in bounds for me has still some attraction as a second consideration. But you see how it is. I seem to ask you to make too special a case of me. How would you draw up a business agreement between us so as to cover all my requirements? Wouldn't it be too irregular to fit into your system? You see I am really rather a nuisance.

Sincerely yours
Robert Frost

[To Clarissa Hall (1891–1988), formerly a student of RF's at Pinkerton Academy and at the Plymouth State Normal School. ALS. UNH.]

Franconia N.H.
February 26 1916

My dear Miss Hall:

We were glad of a word from you. Not that we needed any to be reminded of old friends. We have often spoken of you since we saw you last. My wife has been on the point of writing to you; but you know how that would be with all she has to do.

If I get to Whitefield for you I'm afraid it would better be next fall. My calendar is so full of the engagements by which I earn a living that I hardly have a day for the next three months that I can call my own. Next fall Mrs Frost and I would think it a pleasure to make a little journey over to see you.

I would know without being told that school was going well with you. And if I had to be told it wouldn't have to be by you because I have been told by others.

With best wishes from us both and all I am

Sincerely yours
Robert Frost

[To Louis Untermeyer. ALS. LoC.]

Franconia NH
February 28 1916

Friend of the Poor and Neglected:

Your dedication if I get it will make up to me for many things I havent had in life.[363] You seem bent on being good to me whether I deserve it or not—as I think I have said before. (Never mind, so long as no one else has said it. But perhaps your wife has or some one of your friends who is acquainted with the facts of the case, viz, my unworthiness and your generosity.) I shall accept the poems and ask no questions. And all that are no worse than "The Swimmers" I promise to read and love for their own sake as well as yours. And the next time we are in New York together won't we open a bottle of the Illor Wellor Wheelcox brand of apricot cocktail on it![364]

I'm sorry for your brother.[365] I hope he comes out right soon. Is it the brother I met that night?—that night! If so and I may claim acquaintance, remember me to him.

God delivers me even from having been where I would have had to treat as my superior the likes of O. Shepard and a Stark Youth.[366] I'm glad Jean made hay.[367] I should like to hear her read some time, but where there were no particular drawbacks.

Looking over your letter again has just given me an idea for a suicide poem of my own in which a butcher by trade kills himself cuts himself up and distributes the pieces in corners and closets from garret to cellar. Very

---

363. Untermeyer had asked permission to dedicate his next volume of poetry to RF. The book, dedicated "to Robert Frost / Poet and Person," is *These Times* (1917). "Swimmers," mentioned here, is the first poem in the first section of the volume.

364. The joke concerns the poet Ella Wheeler Wilcox. Kentuckian William Larue Weller (1825–1899) was a celebrated distiller; a number of cocktails call for bourbon and apricot brandy.

365. Martin Untermeyer (Louis's only brother).

366. Odell Shepard (1884–1967), American poet, professor of English at Yale and at Trinity College, and Stark Young (1881–1963), American poet, playwright—and, subsequently, colleague of RF on the faculty at Amherst College—had delivered speeches at a recent meeting of the New England Poetry Society; see *RFLU*, 25.

367. Jean Starr Untermeyer (1886–1970), Louis's first wife; also a poet. Her first book, *Growing Pains*, appeared in 1918.

gruesome—also mysterious till you know the solution. Classification: historical-pastoral.[368]

Your guess would be that the order is wrong and he cut himself up and then killed himself. I have know[n] of such a case. The victim—but I spare you the details. The motive was to cast suspicion on an enemy. The scene was a sawmill where there were things enough to cut with. I dont like this story. No chance for psychological gags. Some day I'll do you the other. And then there's the tale of the dentist and the illegal operation. I forget what to call it. I guess I wont write it till I get a good name for it. A Dream of Julius Caesar. How would that be?[369]

I was thinking I would let Benét have the poem you spoke of. It was among those I sent to Harcourt, was it? I must ask it back. Benét had an idea it would do for his chimerical scheme. You dont dislike it, then? I mean the poem—not the chimerical scheme. Any chimerical scheme is good per se.[370]

You wait till I start roasting friends when I go on the road next fall with my stock lecture "New Sound in Poetry"! Of course something may interfere to prevent my going. Let's hope so.

We are all well of some things but we are sick of some others. Something that appeared in The Post a week or so ago nearly finished us.[371] But the necklace came and it was all lovely. And thanks for the sonnet.[372] Hit 'em again.

---

368. See *Hamlet* (2.ii), where Polonius speaks of "the best actors in the world, either for tragedy, comedy, history, pastoral, pastoral-comical, historical-pastoral, tragical-historical, tragical-comical-historical-pastoral; scene individable, or poem unlimited."

369. RF published a poem titled "A Dream of Julius Caesar" in the Lawrence (Massachusetts) High School's *Bulletin* in May 1891. See *CPPP,* 490.

370. William Rose Benét (1886–1950), American poet, writer, and editor; older brother of Stephen Vincent Benét. Alfred Harcourt was RF's editor at Henry Holt and Company.

371. Carl Wilmore's interview with RF, conducted in Franconia, had appeared in the *Boston Post* on February 14, 1916. He described RF as "the least known man in American letters, and one of the most delightful, lackadaisical, lazy, whimsical, promising makers of verse in contemporaneous literature."

372. Untermeyer, a jeweler, had sent Elinor Frost a necklace of his own design, accompanied by a sonnet.

You tell Dick[373] that I will talk moon to him next time if I have to talk in verse to do it.

Always yours,
R.F.

A sonnet comes about as near being a cube to the eye—or at least a square as any poetic form we have. But you want me to believe it isn't cubism!

[To George Browne. ALS. Plymouth.]

Franconia N.H.
March 2 1916

Dear Browne:

All right then: I see my way under that title right to the proposal I want to make to your teachers. It's something definite, as you know it would be. It seems as if this next bout ought to be an end of my failures through purturbation [*sic*]. I dont mind being scared. But to be scared out of my precious sense of humor that Amy Lowell says I haven't got!—as I was in New York.[374]

Why not write it as you see it for The Independent and then send it to me for approval before it goes into print.[375] I forbid you to compare me with Shakespeare. Otherwise feel that you have a pretty free hand. Strike one good blow for the sentence that does double duty. But don't make much [of] it. Give the lyrics their due by naming them, October, Mowing, Going for Water, A Line Storm Song, My November Guest, Reluctance, and The Thawing Wind, perhaps quoting the last in full if you thought there was space.[376] You are going to be personal rather than critical, but you can say one decisive word for the lyrics and rest my friend forever. But dont say it combatively as

373. Richard Starr Untermeyer (1907–1927), Louis and Jean's first son.

374. RF was still smarting from what he regarded as an error in judgment on Lowell's part in her February 20, 1915, review of *NB* in *The New Republic*; it would continue to rankle him, insofar as the review provided, in part, the basis for Lowell's chapter on RF in her *Tendencies in Modern American Poetry* (New York: Macmillan, 1917).

375. The article in question became Browne's "Robert Frost: A Poet of Speech," published in the *Independent* on May 22, 1916. See also RF's letters to Browne dated March 5 and May 22, 1916, and his letter to Alice Brown of May 26, 1916.

376. Poems collected in *ABW*.

if anyone disagreed with you. Wow! Listen to me telling you. What do I care what you say if you don't get journalistic!

Harcourt spoke of having enjoyed meeting you.

Glad you had things your way in N.Y.

Our best to you all.

Yours ever
Robert Frost

[To Amy Lowell. The letter is undated but "March 1916" is written in pencil in the upper right corner in another hand. ALS. Harvard.]

[Franconia, NH]
[March 1916]

Dear Miss Lowell:

You are too sudden for me. You dont give me time to begin to get ready to commence to get my typewriter into working order. You throw me into such confusion of mind that I can't tell patriotism from decadence. Here are these to choose from. Look out for them: one or two of them may be unwholesome or something. I won't tell you which I like best for fear I should be giving you too many lines for your money—either that or seeming to try to satisfy you with too few lines for your money.

This in haste. I run, I run in response to your telegram.

Always sincerely yours
Robert Frost

Two of these are in very free verse for me. I call them "experiments in vanishing metres."[377]

---

377. It is not clear which poems RF enclosed. Lowell was, at the time, preparing her 1917 volume *Tendencies in Modern American Poetry*, which would reprint, in full, several of RF's poems. However, only one of these was as yet unpublished in March 1916 (and it is indeed in blank verse uncharacteristically "free," at least by RF's standards): "An Old Man's Winter Night."

[To George H. Browne. For the photo here mentioned, see page 256. ALS. Plymouth.]

[Franconia, NH]
March 5 1916

Dear Browne:—

Foolish of me to set out to tell you what to say in your paper for The Independent.[378] Say what you golbung please. I doubt if I want to see it before it's in print either. If I can't trust you to take care of my good name—

Any thing you say is bound to be all right.

We are interested in the photographs. Don't keep us waiting very long. I should like some on some cheap mount to give to friends who ask for something now and then. I'll foot any bills.

Winter shows not the least sign of breaking yet.

Our best to you all

Ever yours
R.F.

[To Wilbur Cross. ALS. Yale.]

Franconia N.H.
March 6 1916

My dear Prof. Cross:

Thank you for the generous check.

As for the poem "Not to Keep,"[379] I should like nothing better than to have you have it if it is anything to you. But first I shall have to find out where it is. I think it is in a lot of poems I let Harcourt take to market for me.

Sincerely yours
Robert Frost

---

378. See RF to Browne, March 2, 1916.

379. Published in *The Yale Review* (which Cross edited) in January 1917.

[To Harold Goddard Rugg. ALS. DCL.]

Franconia N.H.
March 6 1916

Dear Mr Rugg:

O.K. was it? I simply spread myself all over those books to try to show you fellows what a good time I had with you in Hanover.[380]

I should like to have seen your winter sports. Maybe next year I can get over and bring a child with me. We ski a little every day by the book—yours.[381] But we still know a whole lot more than we can perform.

With best wishes.

Sincerely yours
Robert Frost

[To Harriet Monroe. ALS. Chicago.]

Franconia N.H.
March 8 1916

Dear Miss Monroe:

Here is this I particularly wanted you to see.[382] I have been on the point of sending it for some time. But it is not a year old yet and I am so accustomed to having things around for years and years that I find them hard to part with under a year old. You have had some warning of the length of this. It isn't as long as the heavy paper makes it look. Still it is long enough. I should like awfully well to get not much less than two hundred dollars for it—if that doesn't take your breath away.

With thanks for the kindness of your last letter I am

Sincerely yours
Robert Frost

---

380. A reference, again, to RF's talk on "New Sounds in Poetry," given at Dartmouth on January 22.

381. Rugg was an avid skier and hiker, and often accompanied the Dartmouth Outing Club on its expeditions. He enjoyed some renown in this regard, and was mentioned, for example, in the *Boston Evening Transcript* on February 21, 1914 ("The Mountaineer: The Dartmouth Outing Club's Trip among the Green Mountains—The Ascent of Mansfield"). RF and Rugg also had in common a keen interest in ferns.

382. The manuscript of "Snow," which Monroe published in *Poetry* in November 1916, the month before it appeared in *MI*.

[To Wilbur Cross. ALS. Yale.]

Franconia N.H.
March 21 1916

Dear Prof. Cross

I'm glad if you've found somewhere near what you want in "Not to Keep."[383] But please don't like it any better than "The Hill Wife."[384] Between you and me "The Smile" and "The Impulse" in that are about as poems should be.

Sincerely yours
Robert Frost

Have I acknowledged the check you sent? I had meant to thank you for it.
R.F.

[To William Stanley Braithwaite. Throughout his career, RF struggled—occasionally to the point of illness—to write "on demand" or for special occasions. ALS. Middlebury.]

Franconia N.H.
March 21 1916

Dear Braithwaite:

You shall have the poem on Shakespeare if I can write it—and nothing said of pay.[385] You rather scare me by asking for anything I haven't written. My faculties scattered like a brood of young partriges [*sic*] the minute you spoke. I'm ashamed of myself for being like this. Don't lay it up too much against me. I may be able to come to time. Other redoubtable fellows will anyway from Maine to Indiana; so that Shakespeare sha'n't lack for praise nor you for material to fill your space.

---

383. RF replies to a March 9, 1916, letter from Cross, which begins: "[Alfred] Harcourt has sent me your 'Not to Keep.' I like it intensely" (letter now held at DCL).

384. Published in *The Yale Review* in April 1916.

385. Perhaps for a series of poems on the occasion of the tercentenary of Shakespeare's death, to be printed in Braithwaite's new venture, the *Poetry Review of America*, inaugurated in May 1916, with a special note on Shakespeare.

I heard good word of you at Mount Holyoke.[386] These are piping times and surely you are one of the pipers.

Remember: if I possibly can!

Sincerely yours
Robert Frost

[To Louis Untermeyer. ALS. LoC.]

Franconia N.H.
March 21 1916

Dear Louis:

I wish I could remember where-all I've been in the past week or so and who-all I've baptized into my heresies. Here I am home again in disgrace with those who see through me and ready with pen and the same kind of note paper to resume inkling. You first!

Im glad you found it in you to give Robinson his due because he gave you yours you devil the night of the Poetry Meal.[387] The way he snickered over you was the next best thing to you there, confirming me in what I had about made up my mind was the best quality in his books. You are only more witty than he.

Sometimes I think you are a blinding flash—as in that preface to "—and Other Poets."[388] And dont think that because I don't think you as successful with me as with Masefield Yeats Lindsay Masters Pound and some others I don't like the whole book as well as any part of it. There ain't been no such book for brilliance.

Im too faint with the pleasure you give me with your Review of Reviews review[389] to meet it with objections. I cant help suspecting you know what

386. On March 14 RF gave a reading at Mount Holyoke College.

387. E. A. Robinson. Possibly a reference to the sixth annual meeting of the Poetry Society of America in New York City, January 25, 1916, which RF attended.

388. That is, Untermeyer's "*—and Other Poets*" (New York: Holt, 1916), a book of parodies, including send-ups of (among many others) all the poets here named (John Masefield, W. B. Yeats, Vachel Lindsay, Edgar Lee Masters, and Ezra Pound). Untermeyer based his parody of RF on "The Death of the Hired Man."

389. RF may be mistaken. The review in question is, perhaps, Untermeyer's article on W. S. Braithwaite's *Anthology of Magazine Verse* for 1915, published in the February 1916 number of *The Masses* (8.4: 6). In it, Untermeyer wrote, in terms that must have pleased

you are talking about. You speak not without having had time to think me over.

Baxter axt me the same question he asked you as to your three and whether you meant them dead or alive.[390] I shall tell him Riley Ella and me and all congenitally dead from the waist up.[391] "They told me, Heracleitus, they told me I was dead. They brought me bitter tears to hear and bitter news to shed."[392]

And Harold Goddard Rugg is a young librarian at Dartmouth who it's a safe guess has been writing to you to ask you some such question as Baxter's. I slept with him when I was at Hanover for my lecture in the winter (as distinguished from the spring if it ever comes); so naturally he has an interest in finding out what he was entertaining unawares.

Very zeroic weather here yet.

Probability of our being in New York week after next.

All yours by this time
R.

RF: "This volume shows . . . that, as poetry has come nearer to people in thought, it has come closer to them in speech. It is using the language of the majority, not of the few. It is a pliant, democratized speech the poets are using today—as rich and racy as the soils from which it flowers. One of the newest voices, Robert Frost, with a directness equaled only by Edwin Arlington Robinson, reveals a wealth of poetic quality in hitherto unpoetic names and things."

390. Untermeyer explains in a note: "[Sylvester] Baxter's question . . . concerned a remark I had been making in my lectures on 'Modern American Poetry' about Robert Frost's being one of our three most important and most recognizably native poets. Later I named the other two: Walt Whitman and Emily Dickinson" (*RFLU*, 26).

391. James Whitcomb Riley and Ella Wheeler Wilcox.

392. Heraclitus of Ephesia (ca. 535–475 BC), one of the pre-Socratics, was dubbed "the weeping philosopher" owing to his fabled melancholy. RF mischievously misquotes "Heraclitus," by the British poet William Johnson Cory (1823–1892).

[To Alfred Knopf (1892–1984), American publisher. The reference is to the British poet Ralph Hodgson (1871–1962), whom RF met in England in 1913 (it was Hodgson who introduced RF to Edward Thomas). Knopf had founded his publishing house in 1915. However, he did not secure Hodgson for his list; instead, the poet's first American volume was published in 1917 by Macmillan. ALS. BU.]

Franconia N.H.
March 22 1916

Dear Mr Knopf:

Glad to do anything I can to put you in the way of giving Hodgson an American chance. He is with some division of the army somewhere at the present time. The best way to reach him is in care of the Poetry Book-shop Devonshire St., Theobalds Road, London, W.C. He is always in and out there.

Very truly yours
Robert Frost

[To Harriet Monroe. ALS. Chicago.]

Franconia N.H.
March 22 1916

My dear Miss Monroe:

Greedy, I must seem. I don't want to be that even for the sake of variety. It would take too long to tell you in self-defense how I figured it out that I ought to have two hundred for my "Snow." It was probably partly on the basis of what you paid me for something else aforetime. But I am always open to conviction. Lave [*sic*] us talk the matter over, as the Germans would say to Wilson.

You aren't going to be in Philadelphia by any chance when you are in New York are you? Because if you are you could easily run across us there by a little contriving. I shall be with Cornelius Weygandt[393] of the University of Penn. from the first to the third and possibly fourth of April. I should like

393. Cornelius Weygandt (1871–1957), historian, biographer, nature writer, and professor of history at the University of Pennsylvania. RF stayed with Weygandt at his home in Germantown, Pennsylvania, from April 1 to 3. While there, the poet gave a reading before the Science and Art Club of Germantown, and a reading and talk (the latter, again, on "New Sounds in Poetry") at College Hall Chapel at the University of Pennsylvania, with (as Lawrance Thompson reports) some 500 students in attendance.

very much to see you if a way could be found. Let's see if we can't manage it. I write principally to say this, and not to haggle over the price of poetry.

Sincerely yours
Robert Frost

Send any letter to Franconia, N.H. that has a chance of reaching here before March 29.

[To Ellery Sedgwick. ALS. Mass. Hist.]

Franconia N.H.
March 22 1916

Dear Sedgwick:

How would a week from Friday do for our talk? We are off for Philadelphia, Mrs Frost and I, on Saturday and we could just as well start a day or so earlier and take you in on the way. I want you and Mrs Sedgwick to meet my wife this time. We had bad luck the last time we were down: Mrs Frost fell ill and was able to see no one.

I shall have talked my idea pretty well over with a good many audiences before I get it down in writing. I've had all sorts of adventures with it lately.

The saw-mill poem is gone.[394] Harcourt sold it in New York. I'm sorry. I should have liked you to have it. Something about it seems to impress people. However it's not the only poem I ever wrote. I ought to be able to show you something else you will care for.

You mustn't teas [*sic*] me about teas. For you know very well it is not teas that keep me away from my friends when I am in Boston, but bitter constraint and hard work lecturing.

Sincerely yours
Robert Frost

---

394. " 'Out, Out—,' " published in *McClure's Magazine* (Alfred Harcourt facilitated the arrangement) in July 1916. RF collected the poem in *MI*.

[To Mabel Cabot Sedgwick (wife of Ellery Sedgwick). ALS. Mass. Hist.]

Franconia N.H.
March 29 1916

My dear Mrs Sedgwick:

Once more it will have to be me without Mrs Frost. We are sorry. Children's ailments! Mrs Frost may be able to come after me, but not in time to go to dinner with me on Friday. I am on my way to Philadelphia for a number of readings and planning to enjoy an hour or two with you between trains.

Thanking you for your kindness I am

Always sincerely yours
Robert Frost

[To Ray Timothy Gile (1852–1939), surveyor for the state of New Hampshire. ALS. UFL.]

Franconia NH
March 30 1916

Dear Mr Gile:

The publisher of that queer book is Henry Holt and Co. 34 West 33 St. New York City. Perhaps I have no right to assume from your question that you are thinking of buying it. So I wont advise you not to buy it.[395]

Very truly yours
Robert Frost

[To Joseph Warren Beach. ALS. Minnesota.]

Franconia N.H.
April 25 1916

My dear Beach (wherever you are):

I have been thinking you and How d'ye-spell-im over and I find you both wrong in ascribing loyalty to weakness and I like you, at least, too well to fail to tell you so though it cost me your friendship and do you no good. But it

395. The book in question, given Gile's interests, is almost certainly *NB*.

won't cost me your friendship because you are loyal (and strong) and would cast me off for no reason but that you had been cast off by me.

Disloyalty fumbles life. It goes looking for the chance to live the past over in the hope of bettering it. This is enough to say against it, if it is said by the right person.

My dear man I wanted you to come to Franconia and I didnt want you to come. I was on the point of telegraphing "Yes and no." You wouldn't have liked it here if for no other reason because you couldnt have had much of me this winter. I have been off lecturing half the time and when I have been at home I have had endless worries about the family. Elinor was seriously ill when you wrote and Carol has been an anxiety in several ways all winter. He has been having unaccountable rises of temperature.

But the frogs are speaking up and the side hill is saturated. We now put winter thoughts behind us so completely that by the time you get here in the summer you won't be able to tell that we ever had any. I've been burning brush all afternoon. The twelve hens laid ten eggs today. There are six woodchucks dodging in and out where we can see them from our window right in the mowing field. Carol and I have been gunning for them for a week and we havent got one yet—we may as well admit it. And that isnt all: a neighbor from uphill came to offer me seeds for sale and sat with me at the round table in the dining room for a while. The first thing he says say[s] he How are your books doing? I had a mind to ask him what books but didn't. And the next thing he says says he, What do you ask for them? And then as if God was afraid I hadnt been properly shucked out he had to finish off with "Poetry exclusively?" I hadn't taken my hat off when I came in with him for fear I should live to be sorry for it if I treated him too decently. But I was almost on the point of taking it off when what he said made me decide to keep it on. He had taken his hat off. He put it back on after a while not to be outdone in incivility. What was there about this misfortune that reminded me of what the Poetry Society did to me in New York the other night in reading for abuse a poem of mine they must have stolen from somewhere since it has never been in print and I certainly never lent it them for their filthy purposes. I hate to end on this note but I had been thinking all along that I would end on this <u>note paper.</u> Where are you now and do you seem to be getting any nearer Franconia? I will send you a picture of me as I have come to be. This isnt far enough away from some people but you are not one of them. Come east.

R.F.

[To Stark Young (1881–1963), an American playwright, novelist, painter, and literary critic. A native of Mississippi, he taught English at Amherst College from 1915 until 1921. In the spring of 1916, Young invited RF to read at Amherst and helped facilitate his subsequent appointment to the faculty there in 1917. ALS. HRC.]

Franconia N.H.
April 27 1916

My dear Young:

I got home swinked.[396] For a week I lay in a blessed swound before I began to recall even the greatest of my obligations. Then the minute I recovered what Amy Lowell says I never had viz my sense of humor I smiled at that dollar you had piled on top of my honorarium. I said I will write to that Southern (ballad style) and tell him in so many words how it came there. Because I know. It is the fifty cents I may be supposed to have paid for our ride to the station—for some reason multiplied by two. You would never have thought of it if somehow word hadn't come to you of the row I made over it. I never should have thought of it if the stage driver hadnt demanded it of me in his worst New England manner. I judged from the way he came at me that he would have had me arrested before he would have let me leave town without paying it. I was surprised into a show of temper. I trust I didn't disgrace you. Edward Thomas thinks I am overfond of a fight. It is not for me to say. (Business of piously lifting the eyes as in adoration-mural.)

You will come soon and see the homely tasks we immerse ourselves in to forget failure. To-day we have been burning brush. We had the mountain on fire like a volcano. To-day five fowl came from Weygandt.[397] They are Dominique, of the oldest strain in America.[398] We shall have to take good care of a gift like that.

---

396. Exhausted, worn out. An archaic term (as per the *Oxford English Dictionary*), derived from John Milton's *Comus* (RF staged a production of the masque with his students at Pinkerton Academy, and often quoted from it in letters and talks): "That time the laboured Oxe / In his loose traces from the furrow came, / And the swink't hedger at his Supper sate."

397. Shortly before reading at Amherst, RF had read in Philadelphia at the behest of Cornelius Weygandt, professor of English at the University of Pennsylvania.

398. The Dominique (variously called the Dominicker or the Pilgrim Fowl) is a breed of chicken peculiar to America; its origins date to the colonial period.

We were happy with you. There were forty things I sha'n't forget. Our best to you and forgive me. Elinor will write a note to your Aunt.

Always yours
Robert Frost

[To Louis Untermeyer. Dating provided by Untermeyer. ALS. LoC.]

[Franconia, NH]
[May 4, 1916]

Dear Old Louis

When I have borne in memory what has tamed Great Poets, hey? Am I to be blamed etc? No you aint. Or as Browning (masc.) has it:

That was I that died last night
When there shone no moon at all
Nor to pierce the strained and tight
Tent of heaven one planet small.
Might was dead and so was Right.[399]

Not to be anymore obvious than I have to be to set at rest your brotherly fears for my future which I have no doubt you assume to be somehow or other wrapped up in me, I am going to tell you something I never but once let out of the bag before and that was just after I reached London and before I had begun to value myself for what I was worth.* It is a very damaging secret and you may not thank me for taking you into it when I tell you that I have often wished I could be sure that the other sharer of it had perished in the war. It is this. The poet in me died nearly ten years ago. Fortunately he had run through several phases, four to be exact, all well-defined, before he went. The calf I was in the nineties I merely take to market. I am become my own salesman. Two of my phases you have been so what shall I say as to like.

---

399. A riff on Robert Browning's "A Serenade at the Villa":

That was I, you heard last night,
When there rose no moon at all,
Nor, to pierce the strained and tight
Tent of heaven, a planet small:
Life was dead and so was light.

Take care that you don't get your mouth set to declare the other two (as I release them) a falling off of power, for that is what they cant be whatever else they may be, since they were almost inextricably mixed with the first two in the writing and only my sagacity has separated or sorted them in the afterthought for putting on the market. Did you ever hear of quite such a case of Scotch-Yankee calculation? You should have seen the look on the face of the Englishman I first confessed this to. I won't name him lest it should bring you two together. While he has never actually betrayed me, he has made himself an enemy of me and all my works. He regards me as a little heinous. As you look back dont you see how a lot of things I have said begin to take meaning from this? Well.

But anyway you are freed from anxiety about my running all to philosophy. It makes no difference what I run to now. I neednt be the least bit tender of myself. Of course I'm glad it's all up with Masters my hated rival. He wasn't foresighted enough I'll bet to provide against the evil day that is come to him. He failed to take warning from the example of Shelley who philosophized and died young. But me, the day I did The Trial by Existence (Boys Will) says I to myself, this is the way of all flesh. I was not much over twenty, but I was wise for my years. I knew then that it was a race between me the poet and that in me that would be flirting with the entelechies, or the coming on of that in me. I must get as much done as possible before thirty. I tell you, Louis, its all over at thirty. People expect us to keep right on and it is as well to have something to show for our time on earth. Anyway that was the way I thought I might feel. And I took measures accordingly. And now my time is my own. I have myself all in a strong box where I can unfold as a personality at discretion. Someone asks with a teasing eye "Have you done that Phi Beta Kappa poem yet?"[400] "No I don't know that I have as you may say." "You seem not to be particularly uneasy about it." "Oh that's because I know where it's coming from don't you know." Great effect of strength and mastery!

Now you know more about me than anyone else knows except that Londoner we wont count because he may be dead of a lachrymous.

And don't think mention of the war is anything to go by. I could give you proof that twenty years ago in a small book I did on Boeme and the Tech-

400. On June 19 RF read "The Bonfire" at Harvard before the Phi Beta Kappa Society.

nique of Sincerity[401] I was saying "The heroic emotions like all the rest of the emotions never know when they ought to be felt after the first time. Either they will be felt too soon or too late from fear of being felt too soon."

Ever thine
R.F.

I must give you a sample from the fourth book "Pitchblende."[402] As a matter of fact and to be perfectly honest with you there is a fifth unnamed as yet, the

---

401. That is, German theologian and mystic Jakob Böhme (1575–1624), whose name is Anglicized, variously, Jacob Boehme and Jacob Behmen. Emerson refers to him often, though RF's mother's Swedenborgianism would also have led him there. Much might be said of these remarks on "the technique of sincerity," coming, as they do, hard upon RF's "confession" of "Scotch-Yankee calculation," and upon his claim to have kept himself "all in a strong box where [he] can unfold as a personality at discretion," the better to achieve a "great *effect*" of "strength and mastery": the letter playfully blurs the distinction between sincerity and insincerity. The flippant ease with which RF here imagines a "small" book on so large a subject as "[Boehme] and the Technique of Sincerity" probably mocks the pretensions of such literary philosophizers as Ezra Pound. The reference to Boehme may be a joke at the expense of W.B. Yeats, whose mysticism derived, in part, from the German theologian (though it is also possible that RF simply has fun with the quasi-Emersonian idea that mystical experiences are uniquely authentic [see the opening paragraph of "The Over-Soul"]). RF almost certainly refers to Pound's remarks in "Credo," published in *Poetry Review* in February 1912: "I believe in technique as the test of a man's sincerity." Mischief aside, RF took the matter seriously. He lectured on "The Technique of Sincerity" at the University of Chicago on March 14, 1917, and the theme concerned him enduringly. In the "Letter to *The Amherst Student*" (1935), and in "The Constant Symbol" (1946), RF muses upon the relation between commitments to form and technique on the one hand, and commitments to "sincerity" on the other. Alluding to modernists who had broken with "form," RF says, in the "Letter": "They can write huge shapeless novels, huge gobs of raw sincerity bellowing with pain and that's all that they can write" (*CPRF*, 114–115). In "The Constant Symbol," he says: "Jeremiah, it seems, has had his sincerity questioned because the anguish of his lamentations was tamable to the form of twenty-two stanzas for the twenty-two letters of the alphabet. The Hebrew alphabet has been kept to the twenty-two letters it came out of Egypt with, so the number twenty-two means as much form as ever" (*CPRF*, 150). See also RF's hints, "In the Constant Symbol," as to how the strictures of the sonnet form led Shakespeare into certain insincerities ("Between us, what's the use in pretending he was a freer agent than he had any ambition to be . . . he doesn't even have the say of how long his piece will be," etc.) (*CPRF*, 149–150). Finally, as to "effects" of "intimacy" and "sincerity," see RF's March 22, 1915 letter to Braithwaite.

402. A mineral containing uranium oxide and radium (the latter produced as the uranium decays).

only one unnamed (the third has been long known as "Mountain Interval") and I think the most surprising of the lot (circa 1903). But none of that now.

*Toop.[403]

OLD AGE.
My old uncle is long and narrow.
And when he starts to rise
After his after dinner nap
I think to myself
He may do it this once more
But this is the last time.
He let's one leg slip off the lounge
And fall to the floor.
But still he lies
And looks to God through the ceiling.
The next thing is to get to his outside elbow
And so to a sitting posture
And so to his feet.
I avert my eyes for him till he does it.
Once I said from the heart,
"What is it, Uncle,—
Pain or just Weakness?
Can't we do anything for it?"
He said "It's Specific Gravity"
"Do you mean by that that it's grave?"
"No, not as bad as that yet, child,
But it's the Grave coming on."
Then I knew he didnt mean Seriousness
When he said Gravity,
Old age may not be kittenish
But it is not necessarily serious.

R.F.

Someone writes to tell me that the Poetry Society had one of my poems to abuse in manuscript the other night. Absolutely without my knowledge and

403. That is, a tuppence.

consent. I dont mind their abuse, but I do mind their trying to make it look as if I was fool enough to come before them for judgement except with something I had cooked up for their limitations. Protest for me will you. I wonder how in the world they got the manuscript.

[To George C. Chase. ALS. Bates.]

Franconia N.H.
May 5 1916

My dear Dr. Chase:

You mustnt think it took this stray envelope I have just come across to remind me of what I owe you for my ride from Lewiston to Portland. I am <u>almost</u> as far from forgetting that as I am from forgetting the pleasant time you gave me in Lewiston, you and Miss Chase and the College and your friends of the Lewiston Sun.

With best regards.

Sincerely yours
Robert Frost

[To Amy Lowell. ALS. Harvard.]

Franconia N.H.
May 14 1916

Dear Miss Lowell:

Your "without hesitation" is good supreme court stuff. I wish I could tell one poem from another with that assurance. The best I can do is to tell what some poems mean sometimes better than anybody seems to be able to tell what my recent poems in The Yale Review mean.[404] I consented to act as judge in two contests of poetry lately and I confess before I had done I couldnt tell an indifferent poem from a bad one, I had so worked myself into a state of overconscientiousness. Very important in our business to know an indifferent poem from a bad one.

---

404. See RF's February 5, 1916, letter to Wilbur Cross.

I am sorry sorry but I cant really afford to make the trip to Boston for your meeting this week. Ask me in June or if not then, in January or February of 1917 when I expect to be down along on purpose for just such things for awhile. I hate to seem to stand outside of anything—I am always grieved when asked if I belong to the Masons or the Rebeccas to have to say No[405]—and if I could be persuaded that I could do the Poetry Society any good or it could do me any harm I don't know but that I'd begin to save up money etc etc making the most of the want of money in my apology in forma pauperis all the way.

But seriousness aside (I guess you'd think it was serious if all you had to keep an establishment on was an occasional ten dollars for a poem you only wrote for fun anyway), I shall hope to see you sometime a good deal sooner than I can promise to be at the Poetry Society to be reduced to the ranks.

I've been trying to tell Louis of New York, but I haven't got around to write it out yet, that I was asked to read poetry at the movies the other night to give the people time to get into their seats before the main part of the show began. I was advertised on the bill like this: Prayer by the Rev So-and-so. Poems by R.F. Pictures Life of Christ, 5000 feet. I was advertised first and invited afterwards. I wasn't there.

You may not believe that and if you don't you wont believe this: a neighbor got into the house on the pretext of wanting to sell me seeds. He began on me the minute he sat down with "How are the books coming on Mr Frost?" Next he said "Poetry exclusively I believe it is with you?" Next very respectfully, "What do you ask apiece for them?" And when I answered "Seventy-five cents and one dollar and twenty-five cents," he told me "Poole gets one dollar and fifty." Poole of "The Harbor" summers further up the mountain.[406] All I ask is your sympathy.

Shall you be where I can find you in the middle of June?

Always sincerely yours
Robert Frost

---

405. RF refers to the Rebekah Assemblies, first organized, in 1851, as an all-female auxiliary to the International Order of Odd Fellows. The assemblies now admit men as members.

406. A journalist and labor reformer, Ernest Poole had published *The Harbor*, a novel about trade unions, in 1915.

[To Wilbur Cross. ALS. Yale.]

Franconia NH.
May 14 1916

My dear Prof. Cross:

Browne tells me you don't like the poem so well now that you find yourself saddled with it.[407] How too bad for you to keep it then. Why not wait till I can give you just what you want? I am the furthest possible from being in a hurry to publish anything for my mere necessary food. You can be perfectly frank with me. If by the length or lurch of the fourth line or by anything else the poem offends you please speak right out. Let this make it easy for you: that I may decide against it myself tomorrow. I have possibly kept it as long as I have chiefly as a record of the little I saw of the war.

Sincerely yours
Robert Frost.

[To Charles Louis Townsend (1887–1962), a Canadian-American scholar. A graduate of McGill University (1909), Townsend completed a PhD at Harvard (1915) and taught briefly at Trinity College and Duke University before joining the faculty of Southwestern Presbyterian University in 1917. ALS. BU.]

Franconia N.H.
May 15 1916

Dear Mr. Townsend:

I believe I have been of the impression that you were sending me copies of my books to autograph. I find on reference to my letter file that it was to be with my permission. I am sorry I have not given it sooner. By all means send them. And accept my thanks for your review.

If I have a book this year, it will not be made up altogether of material gathered since my last book. I am not of the book-a-year brotherhood.

Sincerely yours
Robert Frost

407. "Not to Keep"; see RF's March 6, 1916, letter to Cross.

[To George Browne. Hamilton Holt (1872–1951) was editor of the Independent *from 1897 to 1921; he had also been a founding member of the National Association for the Advancement of Colored People (NAACP). After an unsuccessful run for the U.S. Senate in Connecticut in 1924, he assumed the presidency of Rollins College, where he remained until shortly before his death. ALS. Plymouth.]*

Franconia N.H.
May 22 1916

Dear Browne:

We are so full of our troubles, that I haven't felt much like writing lately. But thanks for all you have done. I'm sure the paper in "The Independent" must set 'em a-going again. Hamilton Holt shows very friendly in his letters to you. Guess he's another good man—like you.

Carol has had another setback that puzzles the doctors. He has been in bed for two days with we don't pretend to know what except that it is feverish. It seems a serious matter. Of course it knocks everything if he is going to be a sick boy. We had quite cheered up over him since he came out of school. He and I had gone about the spring work and I had forgotten the scare of a while back. We were just thinking he would soon be strong enough for the operation on his tonsils.

It's the mischief. And youve got yourself so to sympathize with that I mustnt ask you to sympathize with us. Damn an east wind. We can get together in saying that. It is safe to lay it down as a general proposition however, that climates are bad for people. It isnt just east winds and the New England climate.

Oh I was going to ask you to see if you can find a little book of verse at your house Bliss Perry wanted me to read. I must have left it kicking round there. My name in it. Would you send it along?

Our love to you all.

Always yours
Robert Frost.

[To Shirley Wilcox Harvey (1892–1983), author of The Christmas Trail and Other Poems *(Concord, New Hampshire: 1916). ALS. DCL.]*

Franconia N.H.
May 22 1916

Dear Harvey:

One thing and another—especially sicknesses in the family—have kept me from answering you sooner. The poem is the important thing, so since time is short let me address myself almost wholly to that. Some other letter I can be more discursive. I shall want to write to you and keep track of you, but you must let me be desultory.

I like the poem.[408] I could have used it to confute the critic of my Tuft of Flowers who wouldnt have it that "the mower in the dew" there could have spared the butterfly weed for any reason except because it wasnt good fodder. Your poem if he could have had it would have set him right and perhaps taken some of his smartness out of him.

So you see I had touched on the theme you take for yours, but not in North of Boston. Twice in fact I have come near it in A Boys Will. See Rose Pogonias and A Tuft of Flowers. That's not to say that it's not decidedly yours not by right of the way you treat it (let's never use that as a justification) but by right of your having caught it fresh <u>out of living unhelped by reading.</u> Go after more such material. We have to begin there with things observations preferences that are our own, content with them so long as they are our own however slight and few and far between they are at first, if we are ever going to rise to the great thoughts we can call our own. I don't know that I think it much matters about the great thoughts. The thing is not to be traversing other people's ground. I believe a lot of talkers have no sense of when they are simply saying

---

408. Harvey enclosed a poem, in his hand, which begins:

"MOWING"
Why is it that one hates to mow a flower?
The swale-glass bunches on your swinging scythe
And you don't think of it. But only let
A blazing cardinal or white arrow-leaf
Tumble among the heap; and then you feel
As though you must stoop down and pick it up,
As least I do. I somehow wish that I
Could make it live and grow again. I feel
As though perhaps I oughtn't to have cut it . . .

what others have said. I suspect the beauty of a comparison I noticed in the June Century (Burges Johnson) would be lost on them.[409] Something was as harmless as a piece of glass worn smooth by the action of the waves. Just to have brought in that wave-worn piece of glass is worth all the rest of the poetry in that number of the Century put together. But enough for now.

I am a bad reviser. At least I regard myself as such, though I sometimes surprise myself by improving a poem a good deal when I take it up long after writing it. But my best work always goes right first off—my worst work too. I have to throw a good deal away. They are not lost if they have given you practice in the best way you can get it, viz, when you don't know you are writing for practice. It comes hard to throw away what you thought you were writing for keeps—not so hard though if you wait a year or so before judging. A poem you throw away or the idea of it may turn up as a figure or illustration to enrich some other poem. I could show you in my books where poems I threw aside and thought I had forgotten have shrunk to one good line in a better poem. Well!

Always sincerely yours
Robert Frost

I'll send along the book soon

---

409. All the more notable in that RF refers not to a poem but to Burges Johnson's essay "The Everyday Profanity of Our Best People," published first in the *Century* and then collected in Johnson's 1917 volume, *The Well of English and the Bucket*: "The interjectional oaths," Johnson writes, provide "profanity for our best people. This division covers a field of expression so broad and so vaguely defined that a hasty definition might be viewed as offensive personal criticism by the gentlest reader. 'Jove!' 'Gee whiz!' 'Jiminy crickets!' 'Oh my!' 'Oh dear!' 'Gosh!' 'I'll be dinged!' 'Shiver my timbers!' 'Gracious!' 'Goodness!' 'Peste!' 'Carramba!' 'Donner und Blitzen!'—all were once asseverative or denunciatory, but time has rubbed away their keen points and biting edges, just as waves and sand in time render harmless a bit of glass on the sea-shore" (118–119).

[To Louis Untermeyer. Accompanying the letter is an enclosure headed, "Anybody Want to Hear R. Frost on Anything?" ALS. LoC.]

Franconia N.H.
May 24 1916

Dear Old Louis:

Seriously I am fooling. And so are you with your crocadile [*sic*] you'llyou'llations. Come off. I thought you and me was going to be rebels together. And being rebels doesnt mean being radical, it means being reckless like Eva Tanguay.[410] It means busting something just when everybody begins to think it so sacred it's safe. (See Rheims Cathedral—next time you're in France.[411])

These folks that get on by logical steps like a fly that's climbed out of the molasses a little way up the side of the cup—them I have no use for. I'm all for abruption. There is no gift like that of suddenly turning up somewhere else. I like a young fellow as says, "My father's generation thought that, did they? Well that was the Hell of a way to think wasn't it? Lets think something else for a change." A disconnective young fellow with a plenty of extrication in his make up. You bet you're [*sic*] sweet life. What would the editors of the Masses say to such onprincipled—what shall I call it?

The only sorrow is that I ain't as reckless as I used to be. That is to say not in as many departments.

The sacred theory that you may not have theories is one I might not hesitate to lay hands on. But dear me it will have to wait till I have a day off. There's the planting to think of and the Phibetakappa poem and I can't tell you what all.[412]

Meanwhile and till I can go to join him here's a sigh and tear for poor old Masters. That stuff on the outside of Sandburg's book is enough to prove my original suspicion, not that Masters is just dead but that he was never very much alive.[413] A fellow that's that way can't ever have been any other way. But we wont labor that. We wont labor or belabor anything and so we shall

---

410. Eva Tanguay (1879–1947) billed herself as "the girl who made vaudeville famous"; her signature songs included "I Want Someone to Go Wild with Me" and "I Don't Care."

411. On September 20, 1914, German artillery severely damaged parts of the cathedral.

412. On Monday, June 19, RF read "The Bonfire" at Harvard University as the Phi Beta Kappa poet. Later the same day he read "The Ax-Helve" for the first time.

413. Edgar Lee Masters supplied extensive jacket copy for Carl Sandburg's celebrated first book, *Chicago Poems* (New York: Henry Holt, 1916), beginning with this: "It is with high explosives that Carl Sandburg blasts from the mass of Chicago life these autochtho-

save ourselves from all things dire. Nothing but what I am "forced to think" forced to feel forced to say so help me my contempt for everything and everybody but a few real friends.

You are one of the realest of them. Who else has struck for me so often in swift succession. I had seen what you wrote in Masses. The devil of it is I am getting so I rather expect it of you. Don't fail me!

Markhams circular made me wonder if I hadn't a series of lectures in me that I could give.[414] So I blocked out a few. They are not much like what I have been giving for my salt. And yet perhaps they are or nearer it than the set talks I would give for instance in school. I sort of fool along.

And by the way I'm going to teach for a week or so at a summer school in July.[415]

And by the way I'm going to do something in Philadelphia on June 1st—I cant tell what till I get there.[416] I cant stop in New York because there is sickness and trouble here at home that I must hurry back to. You will come over to Boston when I go down for June 19th (I think it is). I take you at your word.

Dont mind me, but let me carry on for a rest. We havent got to be a blasted thing, now, have we? Lets make it easy for each other.

Always yours
R.

I liked James' book. It has more things of heaven and earth in it than Sandburg's.[417]

Anybody Want to Hear R. Frost on Anything?
Partial list of subjects in stock:

---

nous masks and figures of modern circumstance." RF recurs to the blurb in his mock list of lecture topics.

414. Charles Edwin Anson Markham (1852–1940), American author of the ubiquitous poem "The Man with the Hoe" (1898), was a popular lecturer.

415. See RF to Bartlett, May 30, 1916.

416. On this date RF read before the Browning Society of Philadelphia.

417. RF refers to James Oppenheim's *Songs of the New Age* (New York: Century, 1914), and, again, to Sandburg's *Chicago Poems*.

* * *

Booty. Derivation of the word from beauty. Two words interchangeable in age of bride snatching. Poetry the bride of the elemental nature. Richard Le Gallienne. Kale Young Rice. Edith Thomas.[418]

The Unattainable. How much ought a poet to get for showing (Hamlet Act III scene II[419]) in public? How much is fifty dollars? Are the English overpaid? Masefield. Yeats. Noyes.[420] Base suggestion that poetry is as often gloating over what you have as hankering after what you haven't. Strabismus and idealismus.

Poetry and Science. Is the conflick irreconcilable? How long will the war last? Piece of Utrecht and other memorable pieces. Aphasia. Pompadour. Nell Gwyn.[421] Resolved that evolution is like walking on a rolling barrel. The walker isnt so much interested in where the barrel is going as he is in keeping on top of it. The Labarynthodont, the Sozodont,[422] the Cotoledon, the Dodecahedron, the Plesiosaurus, the Thesaurus (and Rhyming Dictionary) the Megatheorem, the Pterodactyl, the Spondee, the Concordance, and Sappho.*

The Inevitable; and how to postpone or avoid it. How to keep from attaining what you dont want. Query, if what Shelley meant by Prometheus wasn't the philosophizing poet. Shelley himself. The world's gain could he have stood fate off for one year. Two years. Five years. Ten years. Futility of speculation. Distance between speculation and insight. Shelley's mistake in developing a system. (See Masters on the cover of Sandburg's Chicago.) How he

418. For Gallienne and Rice, see RF's February 3, 1916, letter to Untermeyer. American poet Edith Matilda Thomas (1854–1925), to whose career Helen Hunt Jackson notably gave a boost, was widely read in the late 19th century.

419. In which Claudius deputes Rosencrantz and Guildenstern to dispatch with Hamlet, and Polonius announces his intention to hide behind the arras in the Queen's chamber, where he meets his death.

420. British poet Alfred Noyes lectured in America in 1913 and 1914, after which he took a position at Yale. His countryman John Masefield, later poet laureate of England, lectured in America in 1915, in part on assignment from the British Foreign Office to sound out American attitudes toward the war.

421. "Pompadour": Jeanne Antoinette Poisson, Marquise de Pompadour (1721–1764), a courtesan and mistress of King Louis XV. Eleanor "Nell" Gwyn (1650–1687) was a mistress of Charles II; she appears in the diary of Samuel Pepys as "pretty witty Nell, at the King's house."

422. Sozodont was a popular toothpaste (of sorts) in late nineteenth- and early twentieth-century America. RF whimsically mingles zoological names (e.g., Labyrinthodont) with commercial names, and ultimately with terms borrowed from geometry and prosody.

could have saved himself. (See Drummond: You can't get drowned on Lake Champlain so long as you stay on shore.[423]) Osler stuff.[424] First symptom: Thinking. E. A Robinson, Doughty, Masters, Author of Eve.[425]

The Harrison Law.[426] Some dull opiate to the drains. Swinburne's famous adjuration to his sister: Swallow, my sister, oh sister, swallow![427] Picture: We were the first that ever burst,[428] or the danger of mixing no-license drinks. Jamaica Ginger.[429] A plain talk to druggists. Given in England under the title, A plain talk to chemists. The Manchester Guardian said, If everybody had went to this that greatly longed to there wouldn't have been anybody left for them to take with him. Jane Austen, Emily Brontë Aphra Benn, Sidney's Sister, Pembroke's Mother.[430]

---

423. A reference to "The Wreck of the Julie Plante" by William Henry Drummond (1854–1907), French-Canadian dialect poet:

"Den the wind may blow like hurricane
And spose she's blow some more,
You can't get drowned on Lac St. Clair
So long you stop on shore."

424. Sir William Osler (1849–1919), Canadian-born physician and one of the founders of the Johns Hopkins Hospital in Baltimore; his surname figures in the names of a number of diseases that he was noted for having classified.

425. In addition to the poets Robinson and Edgar Lee Masters, RF refers to Charles Montagu Doughty (1843–1926), British poet and the author of celebrated travel books, most notably *Travels in Arabia Deserta* (1888), and perhaps also to the Reverend Sabine Baring Gould (1834–1924), British novelist, antiquarian, hagiographer, and author of "Onward, Christian Soldiers"; Gould published *Eve: A Novel* in 1891.

426. The Harrison Narcotics Tax Act regulated and taxed the production, importation, and distribution of opiates; Congress passed it on December 14, 1914.

427. See Charles Algernon Swinburne's "Itylus," where the "swallow" has nothing to do with opiates ingested: "Swallow, my sister, O sister swallow, / How can thine heart be full of the spring? / A thousand summers are over and dead."

428. See Part two of Samuel Taylor Coleridge's "Rime of the Ancient Mariner":

"The fair breeze blew, the white foam flew,
The furrow followed free;
We were the first that ever burst
Into that silent sea."

429. Jamaica Ginger extract was sold in the late nineteenth century as a patent medicine; later, it offered a convenient way around Prohibition laws (the concoction was 70–80 percent alcohol by weight).

430. RF traces a line of celebrated women writers from Brontë, through Austen, and back to the dramatist, poet, and novelist Aphra Behn (1640–1689), who was among the

Moanism and Swounding. On larruping an emotion. Men's tears tragic, women's a nuisance (so let 'em vote!) Heightening. Niehardt [*sic*]. In this I make it clear by repeated assertion that I can use any adjective that anyone else can.

True Story of My Life. Stealing pigs from the stockyards in San Francisco. Learn to whistle at five. Abandon senatorial ambitions to come to New York but settle in New Hampshire by mistake on account of the high rents in both places. Invention of cotton gin. Supercedes potato whiskey on the market. A bobbin boy in the mills of Lawrence. Nailing shanks. Preadamite honors. Rose Marie. La Gioconda. Astrolabe. Novum Organum. David Harum.[431] Cosmogony versus Cosmography. Visit General Electric Company, Synechdoche, N.Y. Advance theory of matter (whats the matter) that becomes obsession. Try to stop thinking by immersing myself in White Wyandottes. Monograph on the "Multiplication in Biela's Comet by Scission"[432] "North of Boston." Address Great Poetry Meal. Decline. Later works. Don't seem to die. Attempt to write Crossing the Bar.[433] International copyright. Chief occupation (according to Who's Who) pursuit of glory; most noticeable trait, patience in the pursuit of glory. Time three hours. Very intimate and baffling.

Adventures We Can't Use; and whether the new liberty permits us <u>not</u> to use them.

New Hampshire Gold.[434] Adventure with an examining doctor for an insurance company who after looking me over and taking samples of me decided I was just the romantic kind he could unload a small wild farm on be-

---

first commercially successful women writers in England. Mary Sidney (1561–1621), herself a poet and the sister of Sir Philip Sidney (1554–1586), married Henry Herbert, 2nd Earl of Pembroke; some speculate that their son William Herbert, 3rd Earl of Pembroke (1580–1630), was the addressee of Shakespeare's sonnets.

431. John G. Neihardt (1881–1973): American poet. Pre-Adamite arguments, which hold that a separate creation of men predates that of Adam, have been deployed to various ends (in the nineteenth century and early twentieth century, to racist ends) for centuries. RF may refer to "My Rose Marie," a 1910 song by James MacElwee (though other songs by that name, or simply by the name "Rose Marie," were current in the mid-1910s). Francis Bacon (1561–1626) is the author of the philosophical treatise *Novum Organum,* published first in Latin in 1620. La Gioconda is another name for da Vinci's "Mona Lisa." Edward Noyes Westcott's novel *David Harum: A Story of American Life* was a bestseller in 1899.

432. Biela's Comet, first recorded in 1772, split apart; now only remnants of it survive, appearing, periodically, as a meteor shower.

433. The author of "Crossing the Bar," is Alfred Lord Tennyson (1809–1892).

434. RF indeed lectured on the topic "New Hampshire Gold"; see his December 2, 1915, letter to Rugg.

Anybody Want to Hear
R. Frost on Anything?

Partial list of subjects in stock:

Booty. Derivation of the word from beauty. Two words interchangeable in age of bride snatching. Poetry the bride of the elemental nature. Richard Le Gallienne. Cale Young Rice. Edith Thomas.

The Unattainable. How much ought a poet to get for showing (Hamlet Act III scene II) in public? How much is fifty dollars? Are the English overpaid? Masefield, Yeats, Noyes. Base suggestion that poetry is as often gloating over what you have as hankering after what you haven't. Strabismus and idealismus.

Poetry and Science. Is the conflict irreconcilable? How long will the war last? Piece of [illegible] and other memorable pieces. Aphasia. Pomphalous. Nell Gwynn. Resolved that evolution is like walking on a rolling barrel. The walker isn't so much interested in where the barrel is going as he is in keeping on top of it. The Labyrinthodont, the Gogodont, the Cotoledon, the Dodeca-

Appended to a letter to Louis Untermeyer of May 24, 1916, this mock circular playfully describes a series of lectures through which Frost could, as he declares, "sort of fool along."

Courtesy Library of Congress.

cause it was blessed with a gold mine that had been worked to the extent of producing two or three wedding and engagement rings. The moral being that I am not romantic.

NOTE

Some of these lectures are more intelligible if taken in combination with all the rest together the same afternoon or evening.

Dollar a minute or sixty minutes for fifty dollars. I have to ask a little more where I introduce my adjectives immediately after instead of before my nouns—as in The House Disorderly.[435] Lists of nouns and adjectives I am accustomed to use with them furnished in advance to guard against surprise.

*Displacement

[To Alice Brown. The letter is undated but a date is provided in a penciled annotation in an unknown hand. ALS. UVA.]

[Franconia, NH]
[May 26, 1916]

Dear Miss Brown:

Most of the books that come to our house are for one or two of us, but this is for all six.[436] So much of it is just the kind of fun I like to have with children. It is all lovely. You may think of us as picking it up a good many times together.

And thanks for the dedication. It goes to my heart to have you see, as you show you do there, that I have not suffered from New England, not meant to make anyone else suffer. To like folks at all, our folks or any others, I find I have to like them for their bitter as well as their sweet. It is a provision of my nature against melodramatic despair.

It was a brown day when your book came, for in addition to your book in the mail there was an ear of corn to plant from Alice Brown and a letter from

---

435. In English jurisprudence, a "disorderly house" is one in which the conduct of its inhabitants becomes a manifest public nuisance, or outrages public decency.

436. The title of the book to which RF refers is unclear. Perhaps he refers to Brown's *Children of Earth; a Play of New England* (Macmillan, 1915); Macmillan would also publish Brown's novel *The Prisoner* in June 1916. Neither is dedicated to RF in print, nor is any other of Brown's books dating from the midteens; RF probably refers to an inscription.

George Browne to tell me that he was out in The Independent with something about me.[437] A pleasant brown day.

Sincerely yours
Robert Frost

[To Marie A. Hodge. ALS. BU.]

Franconia N.H.
May 28 1916

My dear Mrs Hodge:

Just a word in haste in answer to your letter. You know how grateful I am for your interest in me.

I know you will want to give me for my reading as much as you would give anyone. We'll go by that, rather than by what I am getting now as a rule. Reading in your entertainment course would be one thing, an afternoon affair another. You don't say which it would be.

I am going to Plymouth on your terms. I shall let you name them.

You will see something of us this summer—that is if you dont run away when we make our descent on you by the Pemigewasset Valley.[438]

I am running away from here again. I am off for Philadelphia and Providence tomorrow.[439]

I'm glad the poem was a fit.

Always sincerely yours
Robert Frost

---

437. See George H. Browne's "Robert Frost: A Poet of Speech," published in the *Independent* on May 22, 1916. See RF's letters to Browne dated March 2, March 5, and May 22, 1916.

438. The Pemigewasset River runs south from Bristol, New Hampshire, toward Franklin, in the area below Plymouth.

439. On May 30 RF embarked on a junket of readings that took him to the Browning Society of Philadelphia (where he was the guest of poet Charles Wharton Stork) and to Providence.

[To John Bartlett. Thompson dates the letter May 30; we follow him here. ALS. UVA.]

Franconia
May [30] '16

Dear John

A letter once in a while can do no harm to him that sends or him that receives, though damn letters as a rule. There are a few people I might enjoy writing to if there weren't so many I had to write to. I remember the time when I looked forward to an evening of writing to you. I'd rather see you now than write to you. Strange, aint it?

Of course theres a whole lot about the art of writing that none of us ever masters. We all remain duffers and properly dissatisfied with ourselves. I'm not speaking of the art of letter writing but of the larger art of writing for the Country Gentleman. It is touch and go with any of us. Now we get it for a little run of sentences and now we don't.

There are tones of voice that mean more than words. Sentences may be so shaped as definitely to indicate these tones. Only when we are making sentences so shaped are we really writing. And that is flat. A sentence must convey a meaning by tone of voice and it must be the particular meaning the writer intended. The reader must have no choice in the matter. The tone of voice and its meaning must be in black and white on the page.

I will take a look around for you up here.[440] I had counted on the Lynches.[441] But from what I hear they may be too crowded to take any one in this summer. A son has come home with his family to stay with them for a while. I'll see them however as soon as I get back from this trip. I'll find somebody to take you in.

I wish I could see you this time. But I can't honestly. I'm longer away than I ought to be every time as it is. I'll leave here on the 2 P.M. tomorrow—leave the house at 1 P.M.—get to Boston at 9 P.M., take the midnight for New York, reach New York at 7 AM Thursday, take the 8 A.M. for Philadelphia, reach Philadelphia at 10 AM, read, get away on the midnight for New York, take 7 AM train Friday for Providence read, sleep, take early morning train for Boston for a little business and then scoot for home. You see the kind of jaunts I take.

---

440. RF hoped to assist Bartlett (both men suffered from allergies) in finding a place of refuge above the hay-fever line.

441. The John Lynch family in Bethlehem, New Hampshire, had been friends of the Frosts for more than a decade.

The Harvard one on the 19th will be the last.[442] (You must get down to Boston for that to please me.) Sometime in July the family will move down to Plymouth for a week while I talk to the summer school seven or eight times.[443] But that is another thing. None of us will suffer by that particularly.

Well old man <u>stay</u> on the map. Elinor will write and tell Margaret what to do. But you stay on the map.

As always
R

[To Louis Untermeyer. RF refers, in the letter's opening, to Untermeyer's invitation to join the editorial board of the Seven Arts, *founded in 1916 under the general editorship of James Oppenheim. ALS. LoC.]*

Franconia N.H.
June 6 1916

Dear Louis:

Count me in of course. It sounds to me. What couldn't you hope to do to R. Burton, T. Garrison and the like with an engine of that range?[444] Death to the dead ones!

Never give up trying to make me "a prominent New Englander" till you make me one. Think of me on an Advisory Board! <u>Cave Poetam</u> when he gets a little power in his hands.[445]

No but seriousness aside, I should like nothing better than having some little part in your enterprise.

You dont mean that I should work—very hard anyway, except hemming and hawing and rubbing up my spectacles in my best Supreme Court manner.

I seen your Post impression of me and have forgiven you, since you speak of it, your mixing me up with Masters. Next time you mention me in the

---

442. On June 19 RF read "The Bonfire" as Phi Beta Kappa poet at Harvard.

443. From July 24 to July 29 RF gave talks and readings at a summer seminar held at Plymouth Normal School, where he had taught in 1911–1912.

444. Theodosia Pickering Garrison (1874–1944) was an American poet; Richard Burton (1861–1940) was the author of *Masters of the English Novel* (New York: Henry Holt, 1915), among other volumes of literary criticism.

445. The Latin phrase means "Beware a poet."

Catalogue of the Ships put me in a different boat from the mighty Chicagoan.[446] We are two separate aJackses.

This is more haste than is good for me at my age—but the habits of a lifetime, my child, the habits of a lifetime.

I'll tell you more when I know more myself.

Always yours
R.

[To Alfred Harcourt. Dating from internal evidence. ALS. Princeton.]

[Franconia, NH]
[circa June 14, 1916]

Dear Harcourt:

We don't know definitely about Carol yet. We hope to hear from the doctor's examination that there is nothing worse the matter with him than bad tonsils—as I think I told you. One thing is sure: I sha'n't try to winter with him at this altitude another year.

We are just off for the Phi Beta Kappa festival at Harvard. Some of our great neighbors of the summer colony are taking care of the girls. We are taking Carol with us. So-called festival.

Introducing Madame Nutt the Avenger. I almost welcome her as a diversion in the present circumstances. Wonder what she will do to me. She being the only out-and-out Frencher I happen to know, naturally I am not wasting any particular sympathy on the French in this war.[447] The English have been my friends and I refuse to believe they were licked off Jutland.[448]

Always yours
R.F.

---

446. "The mighty Chicagoan" is Carl Sandburg; RF felt no more affinity with him than he did with Edgar Lee Masters. "Catalogue of the Ships": see *The Iliad*, Book II.

447. RF's London publisher, Mrs. M. L. Nutt, widow of Alfred T. Nutt (son of the firm's founder, David Nutt), was French by birth. RF had forwarded to Harcourt a recent letter from her regarding his contracts for *ABW* and *NB*. Harcourt replied on June 28, after consulting Holt's lawyer, who made the following report: "I advise you [Harcourt] that in my opinion it is not necessary for Mr. Frost to reply to the letter to him from David Nutt, dated May 15, 1916, and that it does not seem advisable at the present time for him to make any reply thereto" (letter held at DCL).

448. The Battle of Jutland, a naval battle fought in the North Sea near Jutland, Denmark, on May 31 and June 1, 1916, was inconclusive. Both the British and the Germans claimed victory.

[To Emily Isabel Meador [Mrs. Frank T.] Easton (1870–1942), an American educator. Enclosed with the letter was a reserved-seat ticket for RF's appearance, as Harvard's Phi Beta Kappa poet for 1916, at the Sanders Theatre in Cambridge, Massachusetts, on the afternoon of Monday, June 19; RF read "The Bonfire" (and then, later in the day, at a dinner, "The Ax-Helve"). ALS. BU.]

Franconia N.H.
June 15 1916

Dear Mrs. Easton:

The book for Carol was particularly good of you. Two or three of us have read it clear through already.

I found that there were tickets and I found this ticket for you. Don't feel obliged to use it.

We are farming away in the wet. Carol is enjoying himself and I hope to hear from the doctor when he sees him that there is nothing much the matter. Tell Robert that Carol will have some stamps for him.

Mrs Frost joins me in the hope that we may all see more of each other before long.

Sincerely yours
Robert Frost

[To Louis Untermeyer. ALS. LoC.]

Franconia NH.
June 15 1916

Dear Louis:

This is it.[449] I don't advise you're [*sic*] coming over to hear me. There is an orator you might care to hear, though I have made a point of not learning who he is, in order to be beforehand with him in case he should be up to ignoring poetry in the person of me. He is doubtless a statesman—and I know these statesmen.

I've been keeping under cover a couple of things called An Axe-helve and The Bonfire for this occasion neither of them except by a stretch of the words can be called either timely or appropriate. That much may be said in their

449. Untermeyer's note identifies "it" as a ticket to RF's Phi Beta Kappa reading at Harvard. Harvard professor Theodore William Richards delivered the oration.

favor. One is old old and the other is new and so older than the first because it is written by an older man.

Thanks for a glimpse of Harriette in mid career. Of course I can do nothing with King Solomon because it is not self-expressing. Simon Lagree will do for fun with the children but you will admit that it is a very cheap gallop of verses. The way John Brown gets into the Negro folk thought affects me. Vachel is at least more interesting than a lot of us.[450]

Of yours I like better the second, though you may not expect it of me from what you know of my own work. I am emboldened by that. It tells me why we are friends.

It was no very lyric time at Baxter's.[451] I was there to see about taking Carol to Mrs Baxter's brother who is a specialist of the lungs. They have been extraordinarily good about Carol. All distinctions are off.

If you do come over—but I don't advise you to this time. I sha'n't be myself and I shall be pull-hauling in every direction. I can let you see the poems in MS one at a time and you can stand them that way.

Always yours
Robert F

James Oppenheim says he doesnt know what I am talking about in my letter to him, but he can get an explanation out of you. Don't you give it to him. I am trying to cultivate a little obscurity to save myself from the crowd.

---

450. Untermeyer notes that "Harriette" is Harriet Monroe, mentioned here because she championed Vachel Lindsay. RF refers to the following parts of Lindsay's "Booker Washington Trilogy": "Simon Legree: A Negro Sermon," "John Brown," and "King Solomon and the Queen of Sheba."

451. Frost family friend Sylvester Baxter, journalist, poet, and urban planner. His wife's brother, Charles Sumner Millet (1858–1929), developed a treatment for tuberculosis.

[To Marie A. Hodge. RF spent the week of July 24–29 with his family in Plymouth, New Hampshire, where he gave a series of five talks at the summer session of the Plymouth Normal School. The family was the guest of Ernest Silver, head of the school. ALS. BU.]

Franconia NH
June 26 1916

My dear Mrs Hodge:

You may count on me. And when we meet we can decide on a date for my reading.

I am asking Mr Silver if he can have us for the last week of July. We all look forward to seeing something of Plymouth again. You must be sure to be there when we are.

Sincerely yours
Robert Frost

[To Ellery Sedgwick. The letter concerns RF's poem "The Encounter," which Sedgwick placed in The Atlantic *for November 1916, paying the poet a fee of $40. ALS. Mass. Hist.]*

Franconia N.H.
June 28 1916

Dear Sedgwick:

This runs into a few more lines than I thought. But you <u>will</u> try to find a place for it as soon as possible, won't you? Once an editor kept a poem of mine in a pigeon-hole for five years after accepting it, and I have never been the same man since.

The war may hold off, but the rain doesn't.

Always yours sincerely,
Robert Frost

[To Alfred Harcourt, of Henry Holt and Company. The book discussed in the letter is MI, *which Holt released on November 27, 1916. ALS. Princeton.]*

Franconia NH
June 29 1916

Dear Harcourt:

You can't come a minute too soon for us. I've seen and heard so much of you on your home grounds that I can't help wondering how you will look and sound on mine. You are coming to camp down and stay with us some days, n'est-ce pas? Let it be "Yes," and be damned to those who will protest that in indulging us you will be denying them. There are things that may not be transacted in less than days. I should like it if our differences touching the next book would resolve into a sort of pow wow or battle of wits like a horse trade in which time is no object and in which the decision goes to the best talker. The decision once reached, we would climb Lafayette on it.[452]

You see the two big arguments against my giving you a book to publish this year? I may as well let them out of the bag now so that you may be ready to meet them when we meet. The first is that perhaps I sha'n't have the book and the second that perhaps I sha'n't dare to give it to you with Mrs Nutt hanging over me in the way she undeniably is. I can see that she is going to cost me a penny before all is said and done and I begin to think it might be more restful to have her over with before I go much further with You and Co. I confess I rather hate the prospect of having to divide all I am ever likely to earn by writing between her and the lawyers. It would put me all out of sorts—quite fundamentally out of sorts.

---

452. The differences had to do with whether a new book should be released in 1916 (as *MI* ultimately was). Harcourt had written to RF on June 22: "I have [made] bold to ask what has been on my mind for some weeks. It's time to decide if we may make a book for you this fall. You have, I'm quite sure, enough in bulk and good enough, surely. Again, you and [Edgar Lee] Masters have been coupled, as you know, all along. I don't know why. Well, his new book [*Songs and Satires*] is having nothing like the success of Spoon River [1915]. I think this is a good year to get the differentiation across that your respective courses are"—whereupon follows a pen and ink chart sketched out by Harcourt, and showing RF on an ever-rising trajectory and Masters peaking and falling precipitously (letter held now at DCL).

Carol is going to be an anxiety—that much is settled by our conference with the doctors. Richard Cabot took the more cheerful view.[453] The way he put it was When in doubt, avoid the sanatarium [*sic*]. The other doctor (who runs a sanatarium) would have you turn to the sanatarium when in doubt. Well! The one certainty is that I shall have to be making money somehow to provide for the family in new quarters next winter.

Come for the earlier part of your vacation. I shall be teaching in Plymouth for the week July 24–30.

And may the best man have his way.

Always yours
Robert Frost

Will you cause someone to send me a copy of DeLaMare?[454]

[To John W. Haines. Transcribed from a typescript copy of the original letter, presumably made by Haines. RF refers to the Battle of the Somme. TL (copy). Gloucester.]

Franconia, N.H., U.S.A.
July 4. 1916.

Dear Jack,

I have said that I would start praying for you just the minute there was a good forward movement for my prayers to join forces with. And I believe the forward movement has come. They are off, and my heart's with them with all the love I bear England for the time I met you or we met you first between the Greenway and Leddington with your canister for tall flowers, for May Hill, for the fern we groped on the little cliff for by the light of a match in your English winter twilight and for the evenings by your books of all the poets (those I can stand and those I can't stand). Just you and I and your wife together. Old man, I shouldn't have seen you at all if I wasn't going to see more of you. I shouldn't have seen England if I wasn't going to see more of her. You both become an increasing pain as you are. I can't say much of my

453. Richard Clarke Cabot (1868–1939) taught at Harvard Medical School. RF had taken Carol to see him on June 20. Cabot and RF remained in touch through July 24 about Carol's condition (as indicated in a letter of that date from Cabot to RF, now held at DCL). The other doctor mentioned is Charles Sumner Millet, who ran a sanitarium.

454. Walter de la Mare's *The Listeners and Other Poems*, the American edition of which Henry Holt and Company had recently published.

affection for you because I seem not in a position to do anything to prove it. Probably I am saying more now than the Censor will pass if he opens this. He will say talk is cheap: why don't I come over and fight for England if I love her so? But its not like that. A Censor couldn't be expected to understand. My politics are wholly American. I follow my country in regions where the best of us walk blind. I suppose I care for my country in all the elemental ways in which I care for myself. My love of country is my self-love. My love of England is my love of friends. That may be the higher kind of love, but it is not the kind to make me quite dangerous. Which is the point. But I want you to win now!—on this drive—come on!—and be done with your troubles, so that you and I can sit down and talk again in peace of mind either here on a White Mountain or there on a Malvern among old fortifications where your race long ago perhaps extended itself in every faculty as desperately as they are straining today. Carol says "In Berlin tomorrow!" All backward to the German Rhine! How is it the German song goes?

Affectionately,
Robert Frost.

[To Ellery Sedgwick. The poem under discussion is, apparently, "The Encounter"; see RF to Sedgwick, June 28, 1916. RF's eldest daughter, Lesley, often typed manuscripts for him in the late teens. ALS. Mass. Hist.]

Franconia NH.
July 8 1916

Dear Sedgwick:

And here is this also sans phrase. You rouse my curiosity.

Yours in haste
R. F.

I think my daughter does the typewriting rather well—say what you will to the poem itself.

[To Harriet Monroe. ALS. Chicago.]

Franconia N.H.
July 13 1916

Dear Miss Monroe:

I was on the point of suggesting that it might be well to hold "Snow" over till as late as early next year.[455] Timeliness is no particular object with you I suppose; just the same when a thing is so obviously of January February or March I dont see how it can lose anything in coming out in one of those months. What do you say if I have the manuscript for a while again to look over and touch up when I happen to light on it lying around? Have no anxiety about the money. Where we are now we can live on our debts. I wouldn't play into your hands by admitting so much if I were writing to you merely as an editor. It is between poets I say it and I make no bones of it.

Sincerely yours
Robert Frost

[To Louis Untermeyer. ALS. LoC.]

Franconia N.H.
July 17 1916

Dear Louis:

There are as many as four hypothetical questions I should like to put to you if I didnt have to do it in writing. One is asto [*sic*] inversions, whether they are all of one kind; another is asto a poem[456] I have here in pickle which the same I hadnt any doubts of till I used it as a Phi Beta Kapper and almost scared myself out of conceit with it; another is asto a play[457] I wrote once and might, under certain circumstances and if I was sure you weren't overstocked with plays already, offer for an early number of the Seven Arts, and another still is asto the advisability of memorializing Harriet Monroe on the subject of the poem she seems to assume I entered in the late poetry Event of the Poetry Society. It dirks me to have anyone suspect me for a moment of

---

455. See RF to Monroe, March 8, 1916. The poem appeared in *Poetry* in November 1916 and was collected later the same month in *MI;* at this point, in July, RF did not anticipate so early a publication date for the new volume.

456. That is, "The Bonfire," which RF read as Phi Beta Kappa poet at Harvard on June 19.

457. *A Way Out*, published first in the *Seven Arts* in February 1917.

having appealed to Wheeler for judgement:[458] and of course I should like nothing better than to have it generally known that I was the only living poet that Wheeler cared enough for to want to have him appear as if appealing to Wheeler for judgement.

Shall I begin or have I said enough? as Milton's Elder Brother hath it.[459] Don't you think I'd better wait a day or two to see if I wont feel fluenter before attempting to formulate such important questions?

Harcourt has been and gone. He says I am out this fall with a book to be known as Mountain Interval.

Last year I advised you on waves. A word on sharks. I always find it efficacious in dealing with the Suns-of-Gons [*sic*] to keep the body exactly at right angles with the line of their smile. When they turn on their side and smile perpendicularly in the act of biting, the body must be thrown instantly to a horizontal position as in floating so that they shall be warded off by bumping their own noses. There must be no hesitation. And remember the body must never be presented either end on. That is said to be fatal: as are also a few other things I'm too plug inert to go into here, among them speculation, theory and all uncertainty.

Luck to The Seven! Couldnt a poem be done on them to demonstrate as in Wordsworth that they <u>are</u> Seven, though several of them have gone to heaven. Anyway it could do no harm to use for a legend on the title page "kind Master, we are Seven."[460] Are they seven honestly? I never counted them. Well there may be seven arts; but there are only two voices.

To voyses ah there, won is of the see,
Won of the mountings, Louis, you and me.[461]

Love to you all.

Never doubt me yours
R.F.

---

458. Edward Jewitt Wheeler (1859–1922) was the first to petition the president of Columbia University to offer a Pulitzer Prize in poetry (RF would eventually win four).

459. A reference to *Comus*, lines 779–780: "Shall I go on? / Or have I said enough?" The line (in fact) is spoken by the Lady.

460. The allusion is to William Wordsworth's poem "We Are Seven": "O Master! We are seven."

461. RF parodies the opening of Wordsworth's "Thought of a Briton on the Subjugation of Switzerland": "Two voices are there; one is of the sea, / One of the mountains."

[To Wilbur Rowell. ALS. UVA.]

Franconia N.H.
July 18 1916

Dear Mr Rowell:

We are just as grateful as if you had done everything for us we know you have wanted to do. We have come to understand your position and we trust you understand ours in not having released you from your promise sooner. We can release you now. You will be pleased for more reasons than one to hear that we are going to be able to buy the farm with our own money.

If you consider that I have any claim on your generosity still unsatisfied, will you let me take it out in asking you to do something for my sister? She thinks a word from me might warrant you in advancing her a hundred dollars now from the far end of her final annuity. I am ashamed not to be able to help her myself. But I have let her have all I could for the present.

It gives me pleasure to know that you and Mrs Rowell cared for my poem in The Century.[462] Thank you both.

Is there any caution you wish to give me with regard to buying the farm? If I remember rightly, there is record of a considerable undischarged mortgage among the papers you have. Whose assurance is sufficient that the mortgage is being paid off with the money I am handing over?

With real regard I am

Sincerely yours
Robert Frost

[To Ellery Sedgwick. RF had offered "The Bonfire" to Sedgwick for The Atlantic; *the editor declined the offer and the poem appeared instead in the inaugural issue of the* Seven Arts *in November 1916. ALS. Mass. Hist.]*

Franconia N.H.
July 18 1916

Dear Sedgwick:

So be it, then. You have to "say it as you see it." The Bonfire is a bad example of something you particularly object to in poetry—I don't just make out what. I should mind your decision less if it hadn't from the nature of the

462. "In the Home Stretch" appeared in the *Century* in July 1916.

case to be so public—so very public. Many people will ask me why I saved the poem from other editors for you. And I shall have to admit that it was at my own risk as I now realize, though I didn't realize it at the time.

Sincerely yours
Robert Frost

[To Louis Untermeyer. RF read "The Bonfire" as Phi Beta Kappa poet at Harvard on June 19; many took the poem topically, as if it were merely a response to the war. Date and place derived from internal evidence. ALS. LoC.]

[Franconia, NH]
[July 21, 1916]

Dear Louis:

What disheartened me about this Bonfire was that it made everybody think or so many think that it was saying something on one side of [*sic*] the other of a "question of the day." Dammit.

What should you say?

More anon. I'm just off to Plymouth for a weeks work.[463]

Love your country,

As allers
R.F.

[To Louis Untermeyer. ALS. LoC.]

Wonalancet N.H.
Aug 1 1916

Dear Louis:

That ere poem has been forwarded from Franconia to Plymouth to here and I'm just confronted with it.[464] Give me a moment longer. I'm afraid the

463. As noted earlier, RF spent July 24–29 in Plymouth, New Hampshire, where he gave a series of talks and readings at the Plymouth Normal School (he had taught there during the 1911–1912 academic year).

464. Untermeyer explains in *RFLU*: "The poem referred to . . . was a confused semi-autobiographical narrative by a professor whom I had met on one of my lecture tours. I had incautiously referred to my friendship with Robert, and the professor, who later

theme doesnt come clear enough to make me sure it is anything. Tell me in two words what you think it says as a whole and let me see if it agrees with what I think I get out of it. I have my doubts.

In hot haste
R.F.

[To James Oppenheim (1882–1932), American poet, novelist, and editor. The magazine referred to is the Seven Arts, *on whose editorial board (along with Louis Untermeyer and others) RF had agreed to serve. Oppenheim founded the magazine in 1916; it ceased publication in 1917, and merged with* The Dial. *As has been noted (see RF to Sedgwick, July 18, 1916), "The Bonfire" (for which RF was paid $50) appeared in the November 1916 inaugural number of the* Seven Arts, *just before it was collected in* MI, *RF's third volume of poetry, released on November 27; his one-act play* A Way Out *appeared in the February 1917 number. ALS. BU.]*

[Franconia, NH]
[early August 1916]

Dear James Oppenheim:

(And next time I may venture to do without all that Oppenheim as long as we are to see more of each other, as I hope, in the enterprise you have in hand.)

I wish I might have seen something of you for a little talk before you took the final decision in the matter of Robinsons poem.[465] I'm still afraid you may lose Robinson by letting the poem go. But I'm confessedly more timid in my dealing with folks than in my judgement of their deeds and works. I'm sure that sisterly talk was only good in spots. For all its seeming palpitation it didn't come to anything palpable.

I begin to catch fire at the thought of the new magazine. You are probably full of things that we shall see unfold. I'm glad you counted me in for the

---

turned on both of us for failing to acclaim him, prevailed upon me to act as intermediary for his work" (39).

465. For more on the poem by E. A. Robinson, see *RFLU*, 40–41. See also RF to Untermeyer, August 8, 1916; given what he says there, the poem in question may be "Rahel to Varnhagen"—about a couple who figured in intellectual circles in nineteenth-century Berlin—to which Robinson affixed the following note when he collected it in his 1920 volume *The Three Taverns:* "Rahel Robert and Varnhagen von Ense were married, after many protestations on her part, in 1814. The marriage—so far as he was concerned at any rate—appears to have been satisfactory." The poem did not appear in *Seven Arts* or in any other magazine prior to its publication in *The Three Taverns.*

adventure for whatever I may be worth to it. I hope and really expect to be where we can all have talks before long.

I'm glad you could find it in your heart to like The Bonfire. I like the money you sent me for it. Try not to hold it back too late for the book, wont you?[466]

I'll settle down to make the list of names you ask for right away.

Always sincerely yours
Robert Frost

[To Louis Untermeyer. The reference at the beginning of the letter is to a brochure prepared by the publicity department at Holt. ALS. LoC.]

Franconia N.H.
Aug 7 1916

Dear Louis:

Help me, will you? Harcourt sent me this to develop into something about myself and I find that I can do nothing with it. It ain't that I'm overnice. I simply dont seem to know how to advertise my own work. It may be because I can't find anything good enough to say. Man that is borne of woman is apt to be as vain as his mother. I turn to you. Just a few touches to this are wanted. The sentences dont run clear enough. Some of the items of comment are all right, but I'm not sure that the aspersion toward the end on North of B. ought to stand as it is. "As hard and lonely as in some of the poems in" it might better read. I have been counting and I find that seven out of fifteen of the poems in N. of Boston are almost humorous—four are almost jokes: The Mountain, A Hundred Collars, The Code, The Generations of Men. It won't do to go into all that. But something saving could be said.

But I want to leave the whole thing to you. Won't you sketch it freshly and then let me make the compromise with what A.H.[467] has done? Of course if you think this is good enough, why we'll let it stand.

You had my letter as to Robinson's poem. I must confess the thing bothers me. It seems to me to state nothing that I can state after him in words of my own. There are good owlish things in it as always with Robinson. But its only a fairly good poem as a whole. I shouldn't say <u>not</u> to publish it. You want to hold Robinson. He will be giving you something better than this if you get

466. *MI.*

467. Alfred Harcourt.

him coming. And I dare say its better than much you will have to accept. But probably you ask no more of me than my opinion of the poem as a poem. It's dubious.[468]

I really think you may like my one-act play. It can wait till a little later. I'd like to have a poem in the first number of The Seven so that it would be out ahead of the book.[469]

In hot haste but yours as ever
R.F.

[To Louis Untermeyer. ALS. LoC.]

Franconia N.H.
Aug 8 1916

Dear Louis:

I had written you my last letter before either of your last two came.

Fifty is all right for The Bonfire. I'm glad you and James liked it.[470]

As to Robinson's poem, it still seems to me splay or something. Regarded as an attack of early-marriage nerves, it seems even a little funny. But what I say stands: it's probably better than a good many poems you will have to print if you are going to print poetry at all. And I suppose you want to hang on to Robinson. Dont mind my not being enthusiastic over him in this particular poem. I'm willing to be counted with those on the fence.

The pennant for Boston in both leagues![471]

Love to yous [*sic*]
R.F.

Thanks for writing your address on your envelope. It's so long since I have seen it that I was needing confirmation of my recollection of it.

---

468. See *RFLU*, 41, for an account of this episode.

469. The *Seven Arts*, a magazine launched in November 1916 under the general editorship of James Oppenheim; RF was on its advisory board. His play *A Way Out* appeared in the fourth number of the magazine (February 1917).

470. RF's "The Bonfire" appeared in the inaugural issue of the *Seven Arts* in November 1916.

471. The Boston Red Sox (American League) went on to win the 1916 World Series, defeating the Brooklyn Robins 4–1. The Boston Braves, however, placed third in the National League.

[To Edward Thomas. ALS. Cardiff.]

Franconia N.H.
August 15 1916

Dear Edward:

First I want to give you an accounting. I got here a year ago last March, didn't I? I have earned by poetry alone in the year and a half about a thousand dollars—it never can happen again—and by lecturing nearly another thousand. It has cost us more than it used to to live—partly on account of the war and partly on account of the ill health of the youngsters. Still one feels that we ought to have something to show for all that swag; and we have: we have this farm bought and nearly paid for. Such is poetry when the right people boom it. I dont say how much longer the boom can last. You can fool some of the people some of the time, but you can't fool all of them all the time, as Lincoln more or less put it.[472] It may be that the gulfs will wash us down. Nevertheless what we have done, we have done (and may He within Himself make it pure, as the poem has it).[473]

I was going to add that nobody can take it away from us. But that's not so absolutely certain. Mrs Nutt threatens from the right flank. The what-shall-I-call-her has never given me one cent or one word of accounting since she took my first book. The lawyers say she has forfeited all claim on me. She can get nothing out of me. But she can make me trouble and expense if she wants to go to the expense herself. I tell you that so that you will know the whole story. I may have to put the farm into my wife's name for protection. Some day soon I'll have Lesley make you a copy of the lawyer's advice in the matter.

---

472. Reported to have been said by Lincoln in a speech at Clinton, Illinois, on September 2, 1858; no contemporary evidence confirms the accuracy of the attribution.

473. RF quotes from Tennyson's "Morte D'Arthur" (1842):

And slowly answer'd Arthur from the barge:
"The old order changeth, yielding place to new,
And God fulfills Himself in many ways,
Lest one good custom should corrupt the world.
Comfort thyself: what comfort is in me?
I have lived my life, and that which I have done
May He within Himself make pure! but thou,
If thou shouldst never see my face again,
Pray for my soul.

Whats mine is yours. I say that from the heart, dear man. I may be a bad letter writer. I have been spoiled for letter writing by a mob of new friends who don't care what becomes of me so long as they get my autograph once in so often. My whole nature simply leaps at times to cross the ocean to see you for one good talk. It seems as if I couldn't bear it not to follow my inclination. I had a thought of you trying to induct me into clay pipes and all the old days swept back over me. I can never live here any more without longing for there, nor there without longing for here. What kind of a predicament do you call that?

But as I said, what's mine is yours. Here are a house and forty odd acres of land you can think of as a home and a refuge when your war is over. We shall be waiting for you.

My interest in the war news has picked up of late. Lloyd George is a great man. I have wanted to do something for your cause if it came in my way to. I thought of writing to the papers, but everybody was taking all the space and drowning everybody else out. I did my first material bit the other day when I read to a small audience for "the wounded in France"—not for the Red Cross.[474] A collection of a hundred dollars was taken up. I'm to read twice more within a week for the same cause. I only mention this in self defense. I believe the money reaches its destination through Edith Wharton our novelist who is living in France.[475]

Dorothy Canfield Fisher one of our good writers whom you should know has gone to France with her husband and two babies to help what she can.[476] Her husband has organized a repair shop for automobile ambulances. She will be into something herself before long. Not all of us are indifferent. You should hear the standard Bostonian on the subject of the Fryatt case.[477]

---

474. On August 9 RF read at a benefit at the Forest Hill House in Franconia. He would read again in Franconia, this time to benefit the Red Cross, on August 15 (raising some $200).

475. American novelist Edith Wharton (1862–1937) maintained a residence in Paris throughout the war; she worked tirelessly on behalf of refugees.

476. When Fisher's husband went to France as an ambulance driver, she followed and worked with blinded soldiers. She also established a convalescent home for refugee French children from the invaded areas.

477. Captain Charles Algernon Fryatt of the British steamship *Brussels* was court-martialed and executed in Germany in July 1916 for having attempted to ram a German U-boat in March 1915. Since the U-boat had surfaced and Fryatt's crew and passengers were in no immediate danger, the case caused considerable international controversy.

Send me more poetry when you have any. I have a long thing about Snow you might care for a little. I wonder if it would be likely to get to you.

It seems to me Merfyn is going the best way. I'm just Yankee enough to be sure of that. I saw yesterday the two friends, Mrs and Miss Tilley, who had him with them in New York before he sailed.[478] They said the loveliest things of him. They are Southerners of the old school and see nothing in anyone who is not first of all "gentle." They were evidently pleased with Merfyn for the pleasure he made them believe they gave him.

Do you think you could help me get up an anthology of the homely in poetry to be called The Old Cloak after the poem of that name?[479] Or are you too busy? I should want to claim a place on the title page along with you for my part in having got up the idea (great idea). But you would have to think of most of the material.

About time I heard from you again.

My love to you as you look in that last tall picture Helen sent.

Always and forever yours
Robert Frost.

[To Harriet Monroe. ALS. Chicago.]

Franconia N.H.
August 17 1916

Dear Miss Monroe:

I was born to be an awful bother. It now looks as if I were not going to get out of giving Harcourt another book this fall.[480] And I shall need every poem I have written in the last three years to swell it to book like proportions. That as good as takes "Snow" away from you, doesn't it?[481] It makes me sorry. I had set my heart on having another poem in "Poetry" before I turned to play-and-novel-writing. What can you say to relieve me? I suppose you couldnt think of lugging me in prematurely in October?

---

478. Family friends Mabel L. Tilley (wife of Morris Palmer Tilley) and her daughter, Lois Frances Tilley.

479. RF refers to the anonymous fifteenth-century ballad of that title.

480. That book would become *MI*.

481. In fact, "Snow" appeared in *Poetry* in November 1916.

I should be glad to go to Chicago for $150 and take my chances on picking up a little more. The money would be much—we won't say it wouldn't—but the great thing would be to see you and Vachel Lindsay.[482]

I have been meeting friends of yours, Mrs George Glessner and Miss Wilson (?) on my little front porch lately.[483]

Sincerely yours
Robert Frost

[To George Browne. The occasion for the following August 18 letter to RF's friend George Browne requires considerable explanation. The man mentioned in it, Charles Payson Gurley Scott (1853–1936), was an eminent philologist, and the author of, among other works, The Devil and His Imps: An Etymological Inquisition *(American Philological Association, 1895). RF inscribed the letter to Browne on a sheet bearing a typed paragraph in which Scott gives a detailed account of the word "interval," the use of which in the title of RF's third book,* Mountain Interval *(1916), Browne had disputed. "Intervale, with its present pronunciation and meaning"—according to Scott, in the paragraph RF passed along to his friend—"arose from a mistake."*

> *It was not formed from inter +vale; nor would that mode of formation have been used, I think, at the time and place at which the word arose. Though some formations of this apparent kind, with inter-, as it were, an adjective, equivalent to intervening, are of older date (for example, INTERSPACE) they were not really of this kind. The explanation, which is a little subtle, involves the inherent ambiguity or two-sidedness of inter, between, and similar terms. The original word was INTERVAL. This word was spelled, in the 17th century, interval, intervall, and rarely intervale; also enterval, entervall, and rarely entervale, the spelling enter—probably representing a Scottish pronunciation between short i and short e. Apart from this point, all these spellings represented the same pronunciation, namely in-ter-val, the last syllable being pronounced like Val for Valentine. Certain it is, that the word*

482. Nicholas Vachel Lindsay (1879–1931) was an American poet best known for singing his verses, many on a midwestern theme.

483. Alice Hamlin Glessner, wife of George Glessner (1871–1929), son of John Glessner (1843–1936), founder of the International Harvester Company. The Glessner family was based in Chicago but owned an estate (named The Rocks) near Bethlehem, New Hampshire, not far from Franconia. The "Miss Wilson" is unidentified.

1

My old friend George Brown of Brown and Nichols School started all this by disputing my right to use the word Interval in the title of my book. He said the word was a vulgarism of the "natives". I wanted it for its double meaning. I believe Emerson and Thoreau wrote no other. My neighbors spoke no other.

R. F.

The dedication of Mountain Interval is but part of the controversy.

49 Arthur street, Yonkers, N.Y.,

August 7, 1916

ROBERT FROST, Esq., Franconia, N. H.

Dear Sir:

My friend Dr. Child* has askt me to send you a statement of my opinion concerning the phrase A MOUNTAIN INTERVAL as a title for a new book of poems. I understand that your publisher prefers A MOUNTAIN INTERVALE. I take pleasure in sending you this reply, thru Dr. Child, who, being at intervals an inhabitant of the intervales, and a leaper of fences, and a reader of the signs of the times, black and blue, is of course interested in all sides of the subject.

I went into the subject soon after I went into the intervales, and from the accessible quotations stated the case to my own satisfaction. The facts are briefly these: INTERVALE, pronounced as <u>inter-</u> + <u>vale</u>, and assumed to mean 'an intervening vale', is comparatively modern. It began to be accepted, in that pronunciation and meaning, some time before 1780, and is now establisht as a good word, indeed an apt and poetical word, belonging to 'the New England dialect' (to use a large term), but used also, in a literary way, outside of that favored tract. In this and in some other respects it is analogous with the word FELL, as used in the Lake district and elsewhere for another special geografical feature..

* Child was called in by Cornelius Weygandt of the University of Pennsylvania, author of White Hills

Intervale, with its present pronunciation and meaning, arose from a mistake. It was not formed from inter- + vale: nor would that mode of formation have been used, I think, at the time and place at which the word arose. Though some formations of this apparent kind, with inter-, as it were, an adjective, equivalent to intervening, are of older date (for example, INTERSPACE) they were not really of this kind. The explanation, which is a little subtle, involves the inherent ambiguity or twosidedness of inter, between, and similar terms. The original word was INTERVAL. This word was spelled, in the 17th century, interval, intervall, and rarely intervale: also enterval, entervall, and rarely entervale, the spelling enter- probably representing a Scottish pronunciation between short i and short e. Apart from this point, all these spellings represented the same pronunciation, namely in·ter-val, the last syllable being pronounced like Val for Valentine. Certain it is, that the word spelled in the 17th century interval, intervall, or intervale, would have become, and did become, interval in the 19th century. Its distinctive application to a low level tract of land (originally, to one of a series of such tracts, found at intervals by travelers or surveyors) arose in a natural way, and there was no need to vary its pronunciation. It is my guess, indeed, that the pronunciation now given to intervale arose as a literary pronunciation, among persons who saw the word spelled intervale, meaning interval, in maps and deeds. So far as the word is in the inherited speech of the oldest inhabitants, it must be pronounced in·ter-val, and not in·ter-vale.

Dear Browne:

You might suppose this to be my own statement of my own position. It is the way Charles P. G. Scott puts the case for interval. My purpose in sending it is not to disqualify you as an authority, or to persuade you of anything, but to teach you not to assume too lightly that nobody but yourself has a reason for what he does. While you are about it, you might profit by looking to see if you can't find interval (so-spelled) in Emerson's Monadnoc.

Over

All this is not to say that intervale is not a good word, though an accident, a sophistication, and a mistake; only that interval is another good word.

Nearly everyone would know who Charles P. G. Scott is.

So cheer up, and don't make a long-face to everyone about how hard you have tried to educate me in the New English language and nothing to show for your pains.

I heartily wish you were a well man.

As ever
Robert Frost.

This cluster of documents—letters, notes, and notes on notes—records the imbroglio that resulted from George H. Browne's having disputed Frost's use of *interval*, rather than *intervale*, in titling his third book, *Mountain Interval*, in 1916.

Courtesy Plymouth State University Library [for RF to Browne] and the Jones Library [for Scott to RF].

spelled in the 17th century interval, intervall, or intervale, would have become, and did become, interval in the 19th century. Its distinctive application to a low level tract of land (originally, to one of a series of such tracts, found at intervals by travelers or surveyors) arose in a natural way, and there was no need to vary its pronunciation. It is my guess, indeed, that the pronunciation now given to intervale arose as a literary pronunciation, among persons who saw the word spelled intervale, meaning interval, in maps and deeds. So far as the word is in the inherited speech of the oldest inhabitants, it must be pronounced in-ter-val, and not in-ter-vale.

This paragraph was copied out in type—perhaps by RF's daughter Lesley—from a four-page typed treatise that Scott had composed at the request of Professor Francis James Child of Harvard, Child's advice having been sought in the first place by RF's friend Cornelius Weygandt (on the faculty at the University of Pennsylvania). In short, in answer to Browne's challenge, RF marshaled the combined authority of Penn, Harvard, and the inimitable Charles P. G. Scott, who wrote to RF as follows in the August 7, 1916, letter the poet quotes in his August 18 riposte to Browne.

> *My friend Dr. Child has askt me to send you a statement of my opinion concerning the phrase A MOUNTAIN INTERVAL as a title for a new book of poems. I understand that your publisher prefers A MOUNTAIN INTERVALE.*[484] *I take pleasure in sending you this reply, thru Dr. Child, who, being at intervals an inhabitant of the intervales, and a leaper of fences, and a reader of the signs of the times, black and blue, is of course interested in all sides of the subject.*

After some three pages of discussion, including the paragraph forwarded to Browne with Frost's own letter, Scott concludes:

> *If you adopt the title A MOUNTAIN INTERVAL, what will the reader understand by the title, before he sees the book or reads an explanation? The phrase could bear four meanings:*
>
> *1. An interval of land that is, or consists of, mountain.*
>
> *2. An interval of land that is on or by a mountain.*
>
> *3. An interval of low and level land on a mountain or among mountains (=A Mountain Intervale).*
>
> *4. An interval of time spent in traveling or living on a mountain or among mountains.*
>
> *I think that only a few readers would at first think of the third meaning.*
>
> *But what of that? It is the mark of a poet to choose titles and words that are distinctive, or that make his own special thought distinct and rememberable tomorrow. The moment he chooses, or avoids, the unusual because*

484. On July 30 Alfred Harcourt had queried RF: "Do we call the book Mountain *Interval* or Mountain *Intervale*? Interval say I" (letter held now at DCL). See also RF's August 29 letter to Charles Payson Gurley Scott.

it is unusual, or chooses the trite because that *happens to be in fashion, he chooses the road of Safety first—and Oblivion soon after. Even Wordsworth, who was a great Pedestrian, used some words that were not of the common or garden kind; and I, for one, never thought the less of a poet who adds Notes.*

My *notes, as above written, at Intervals, are calculated for the region 'North of Boston,' and likewise West and Northwest and in the face of the East wind. If they help to confirm you or Dr. Child, in any opinion already fixt, so; if not, why, then, kill the next Percy yourself.*

Don't mind what the publisher says. A publisher is a man who succeeds in literature by keeping steadily in the narrow path that separates Knowledge from ignorance, Thought from vacuity and Taste from popularity; on good terms with both sides, but not a slave to either.

Yours truly,
Charles P. G. Scott

On the first page of this letter, where Scott first mentions Child, RF has added an asterisk referring to a note he added below: "Child was called in by Cornelius Weygandt of the University of Pennsylvania, author of White Hills." The reference to The White Hills: Mountain New Hampshire, Winnepesaukee to Washington *dates the annotation to no earlier than 1934, the year the book was brought out by Holt (RF's publisher). And to this annotation RF has added still another, though it is not clear for whose eyes it was intended: "My old friend George Brown [sic] of the Brown [sic] and Nichols School started all this by disputing my right to use the word Interval in the title of my book. He said the word was a vulgarism of the 'natives.' I wanted it for its double meaning. I believe Emerson and Thoreau wrote no other. My neighbors spoke no other. R.F. The dedication of Mountain Interval is but part of the controversy." The dedication to* Mountain Interval *(addressed to the poet's wife, Elinor) reads: "TO YOU who least need reminding that before this interval of the South Branch under black mountains, there was another interval, the Upper at Plymouth, where we walked in spring beyond the covered bridge; but that the first interval was the old farm, our brook interval, so called by the man we had it from in sale." George Browne himself lived in a New Hampshire "interval"—on the Webster Farm, below Bridgewater Mountain, to which address the letter transcribed below was directed. The letter to Browne is held now at Plymouth State University in New Hampshire; the letter from Scott to RF, bearing the poet's annotations, is held now at the Jones Li-*

brary, Amherst, Massachusetts. Dating derived from postmark. ALS (on the typed document described above). Plymouth.]

[August 18, 1916]

Dear Browne:

You might suppose this to be my own statement of my own position. It is the way Charles P. G. Scott puts the case for interval. My purpose in sending it is not to disqualify you as an authority, or to persuade you of anything, but to teach you not to assume too lightly that nobody but yourself has a reason for what he does. While you are about it, you might profit by looking to see if you can't find interval (so-spelled) in Emerson's Monadnoc.[485]

All this is not to say that intervale is not a good word, though an accident, a sophistication, and a mistake; only that interval is another good word.

Nearly everyone would know who Charles P. G. Scott is.

So cheer up, and don't make a long-face to everyone about how hard you have tried to educate me in the New English language and nothing to show for your pains.

I heartily wish you were a well man.

As ever
Robert Frost

---

485. RF refers to these lines from "Monadnoc":

Thousand minstrels woke within me,
"Our music's in the hills;"—
Gayest pictures rose to win me,
Leopard-colored rills.
Up!—If thou knew'st who calls
To twilight parks of beech and pine,
High over the river intervals,
Above the ploughman's highest line,
Over the owner's farthest walls!

[To F. S. Flint. ALS. HRC.]

Franconia N.H.
August 24 1916

Dear Flint:

You and a bare one or two others are England to me. It will be you I shall be going back to when I go back to England. It won't be Gibson and Monro. You didn't think it would, now did you?

I've had your two anthologies out a good many times lately with visitors, particularly for your poems in them and more particularly for your Trees, Gloom and Easter.[486] I wrung Gloom from you by betraying Pound. I'm a very little ashamed of myself now. But make allowances for me.

Some of your allies I have always seen: Aldington and H.D. and Lawrence.[487] Amy Lowell will do. At any rate, she's useful to you part as trans-Atlantic Barker and politician in the ring. She sometimes gets something. I suppose some of you like her Whoop-la! But on what principles, I wonder, did you let in Fletcher. It must have been a principle of rhetoric or oratory. There are some people you have to lay it down to that poetry is in things—things that happen to you and things that occur to you without your seeking. I should never want to say anything else to the like of Fletcher. I know there are others you have to turn right around the other way with and tell them that poetry lies in words or the way things affect you. You sit on a bent pin, for example, and what is of importance to literature is not the pin itself but the words struck out of you by the pin. But oh dear. I only mean that Fletcher is a rotter willing to profess what he cant understand and to cant in terms of Imagism for the sake of being allowed.

I suppose I oughtn't to have exhorted you to send your little book of translations till I told you where I was.[488] Come on with it. Lesley and I are fairly deep in our Latin. You know my weakness for Virgil's Eclogues. I believe I

486. "Trees" appears in the annual anthology *Some Imagist Poets* (Boston: Houghton Mifflin, 1915), "Easter" and "Gloom" in the volume for 1916.

487. Richard Aldington, Hilda Doolittle (H. D.), Amy Lowell, and D. H. Lawrence all contributed to *Some Imagist Poets,* as did John Gould Fletcher.

488. Flint translated *The Love Poems of Emile Verhaeren* (London: Constable, 1916); he also translated *Philip II* for *The Plays of Emile Verhaeren* (Boston: Houghton Mifflin, 1916); three other plays, translated by Arthur Symons, Osman Edwards, and Jethro Bithell, rounded out the volume.

like the Georgics a good deal too. But you are all for intenser poets than Virgil.

Poor dear Gibson! Whatever else has been corrupting me since last I saw you bare headed in Oxford St. it hasn't been Gibson. No sooner had I got down into the country near him than I began defining my positions with regard to him—and you know what that means. It means sheering off from him. Abercrombie was another sort. I really liked him, though I saw less of him than I saw of his house. He lent us his house to live in that last winter when he went off to live with the Hewletts.[489]

After all it's all in guts—or nearly all. Of course I would have the guts kept in. You won't misunderstand me.

Not Masters. He went about it wrong. How would he hope to succeed in a string of things done all in one mood and on one formula. Childish formula too: All apparently good people are bad, and all apparently bad are good. That and Watch your wife.[490] Perhaps some novelty lies in asserting that she will bear watching as much as in the days of the horns joke. But pay no attention to me. You know how hard to please I must be at forty odd.

You wont mind if I give Edward Thomas your address? I want him to look you up and describe you to me sometime. He's more or less a wanderer since he enlisted or I could give you his address. I believe he's just gone into the artillery. I wish you two fellows could like each other a little on account of me, who am your common loss.

I keep somewhere about me a very melancholy letter I wrote you the night we lay in the Mersy River at Liverpool to send ashore before we sailed.[491] No mail was permitted to go ashore, so you never got the letter. Sometime when we meet again, here or there, we will open it together to see just how melancholy I was that night when I thought of myself of [*sic*] leaving you behind me. It is sealed in an envelope of the American Liner St Paul.

Here or there, I say. I wish I could get you where I could show you our farm in the mountains. Our forty five acres of land runs up the mountain behind the house about half a mile. In front of us the ground falls away two

---

489. Maurice Henry Hewlett (1861–1923), English novelist, poet, and essayist; his wife was Hilda Beatrice Hewlett (1864–1943), the first female aviator in England, and founder of Hewlett and Blondeau, an airplane manufacturer in Leagrave, Luton, England.

490. The allusion is to Edgar Lee Masters's *Spoon River Anthology* (New York: Macmillan, 1915).

491. See RF to Flint, February 2, 1915.

or three hundred feet to the very flat flood plain of the Ammonoosuc River. Beyond that, right over against us not three miles away are Lafayette and the Franconia Range of Mountains rising to five thousand feet. Not Switzerland, but rugged enough. We are too cold to do much farming. Grass and forest trees are our products. In the hunting season we can shoot bear and deer, or buy meat of both out of the butcher's cart. One of the forest trees, the rock maple, yields the maple sugar you may have read of—worth about twice as much as white cane sugar—no longer used on the farms for general purposes, but sold mainly as a sweet in the candy stores.

You must come over and see it all. Others come lecturing. Why can't you?

Love to you all. I should like to see Ianthe.[492] Is she too big a girl to ride where she did the day we were on Hamstead [*sic*] Heath together?

Have I let myself be too nasty to some of my contemporaries. War is war and sometimes I think peace is too. Damn, there goes an epigram.

You may and you may not find a piece of MS in this—all will depend on how I happen to feel when I am sealing up. If you do, it will be something about conscientious voting done for the divil of it in an insuffragable mood. Got to vote pretty soon for Wilson or the same man with a different name.

Yours more than ever
Robert Frost

Franconia N.H. U.S.A. finds me.

[To Philip Darrell Sherman (1881–1957), professor of English at Oberlin College and a noted book collector. ALS. Brown.]

Franconia N.H.
August 26 1916

Dear Prof. Sherman:

Have I or have I not answered the question of your letter of a month ago? I should have said that I had; but here is your letter in my file of letters still undealt with. At the risk of repeating myself, let me say that "North of Boston" was first published by David Nutt in London in 1914, my other book "A Boy's Will" by David Nutt in London in 1913. Henry Holt published both in

---

492. Flint's daughter. Hampstead Heath is a 790-acre park in London.

this country in 1915. Henry Holt will be publishing my third book, Mountain Interval, this fall.

Thanking you for the interest that prompted your enquiry I am

Sincerely yours
Robert Frost

[To Cornelius Weygandt (1871–1957), professor of English at the University of Pennsylvania. ALS. DCL.]

Franconia, N.H.
August 26 1916

Dear Weygandt:

You will be getting away home without our seeing you again if you don't come right away and take your chances on the weather. Of course we want to climb Lafayette and we want to catch it clear. But the main thing is to get you here. I was wondering if it wouldnt be fun to have someone put us down at the foot of the Garfield trail, climb that, sleep in the hut up there and then go along the range past Lafayette to Liberty for another sleep in the hut above the Flume.[493] It would mean a good deal to tote (if that's the way to spell that word: I have seen it spelled toat on a guideboard near Willoughby).

Browne sayeth. He began by telling me that interval was a shriveled form of intervale. Now that he has heard what Scott has to say: he turns round and calls interval obsolete and a piece of pedantry as I contemplate using it. He goes into my reasons for using it and finds them unworthy and contemptible. Emerson he ignores. All this in spite of the fact that he has lived for years where he must have heard the Higher Interval and the Lower Interval at Plymouth named almost every day. I spell them only as he himself must pronounce them to be understood in the neighborhood. But I guess it's foolish to be bothered with him any further.

Scott's letter was a joy.[494]

---

493. The Garfield Trail ascends Mt. Garfield (elev. 3,000 ft.), in the White Mountains of New Hampshire, near Mt. Lafayette, Mt. Liberty, and Mt. Flume, the latter rising above the Flume Bridge. Lake Willoughby is in Vermont.

494. For this letter, and for explanation of RF's remarks about Browne, see RF to Browne, August 18, 1916 (pages 477–483).

The book has filled my time in the intervale since I saw you. I always have a few lines I find it hard to leave as they are at the last minute. But the thing is done now and gone to the printers. And the MS I promised you is yours—mainly for An Old Man's Winter Night: you may not want to keep much else in it. I'm ashamed of the jumble some of the copy is in.

Our love to you all. Carol wants particularly to be remembered to Louie.[495] I have never seen him have so much pleasure with any other boy.

Every yours
Robert Frost

MS separately

[To Washington Irving Lincoln Adams, Jr. (1865–1946), an American businessman, photographer, and author. The party may have been for his wife, Grace Wilson Adams, whose birthday was September 22. Though the couple resided in Montclair, New Jersey, they had a summer retreat in Littleton, New Hampshire, not far from Franconia. ALS. Jones.]

Franconia
August 29 1916

Dear Mr. Adams:

My wife and I were very sorry we missed seeing you last summer and shall be glad of the chance to make it up to ourselves by being of the birthday party at your house on September 4th. It is so very good of you to think of us and to offer to send for us in this way.

Sincerely yours
Robert Frost

495. Likely the nickname of Cornelius Nolen Weygandt, son of Weygandt and his wife, Sara Matlack Roberts Weygandt, and two years Carol's junior.

[To Charles Payson Gurley Scott (1853–1936), American philologist, editor, and Orientalist. Draft of a letter on six leaves, a finished copy of which was, presumably, sent. We have combined text from the several sheets to arrive at a proximate reading of the whole letter, insofar as it survives. AL (unsigned). DCL.]

Franconia N.H.
August 29 1916

Dear Mr Scott:

Then my experience picks up where yours leaves off. When I came to this part of the country and bought in, so to speak, among the farmers I had never heard the word interval for a plane [*sic*] interval among mountains. Squire Bartlett of Derry who made out the papers when I took over my farm remarked that he believed the farm included a piece of interval. That was longer ago than 1901 and Squire Bartlett was at the time an old-timer of say forty-five years of age and had law offices in Derry and Boston. Later when I went to live at Plymouth, this state, I heard the word in almost daily use with old and young as applied to two parts of the town where the valley flattens out along the Pemigiwasset River, the Upper Interval and the Lower Interval.[496] The deuce of it is that the worst enemy of my word is a teacher-man who summers just there where no one would know what he meant by any names but Upper and Lower Interval.[497] His contention is that interval is a corruption from intervale by shriveling—that the original idea was intervalley. He knows and I know local people who write the word with, though they say it as without, a final e. The most he could do, though, was scare me for my spelling. I was sure enough of the pronunciation among my own folks. And I thought I was sure the word was quite detached in meaning from vale and valley. It is same here in Franconia: we live where we look at Lafayette and Moosilauke across and up the Ham Branch Interval. My doubt was whether the word might not have come all the way down to us in writing with a final forceless e: In that case I should have to spell it on the cover of my book with an apostrophe in the place of the e to guard against a pronunciation some people seem to want to fall into. This is where you come in so interestingly with your history of the word as almost to make me wish I had

496. RF refers to Nathaniel Cilley Bartlett (1858–1921). The Pemigewasset originates near Franconia, flows south through the White Mountains, merging with the Winnipesaukee to form the Merrimack River at Franklin.

497. George Browne. See RF to Browne, August 18, 1916, and also RF to Weygandt, August 26, 1916.

gone in for philology as a career instead of poetry. Your letter is bully fun as well as a gratification.[498] You must let me show you how Interval looks on my book when it appears.

[To Josephine Preston Peabody Marks (1874–1922), American poet and dramatist, and husband of Lionel Simeon Marks, British-born professor of mechanical engineering at Harvard. ALS. Harvard.]

Franconia N.H.
September 2 1916

Dear Mrs. Marks:

Only because I was going to have to ask you so soon to read a whole book.[499] I wanted to save you for that. But since you will have these particular poems now—since you won't be denied—why, here they are and more also.

I will make you this offer in the way of a bargain: if you will like what I send you herewith, The Gum-gatherer included, you will be excused from liking the book.

One wonders about the Blue Hill—what it is blue with—blueberries, distance or the blues. Not the last, God send.[500]

Our best to you all.

Sincerely yours
Robert Frost

---

498. See the headnote to RF's August 18, 1916, letter to George Browne.

499. *MI*, RF's third book (then in press) was issued by Henry Holt and Company on November 27, 1916; "The Gum-Gatherer" appears there. It is not clear which other poems RF sent: the enclosures have been separated from the letter.

500. The reference is obscure, though RF may have in mind "The Enchanted Sheepfold," a poem collected first in Marks's 1903 volume *The Singing Leaves: A Book of Songs and Spells* (Macmillan) and later several times anthologized. It begins:

"The hills far-off were blue, blue,
The hills at hand were brown;
And all the herd-bells called to me
As I came by the down."

[To Harriet Monroe. ALS. Chicago.]

Franconia N.H.
Sept 4 1916

Dear Miss Monroe:

Harcourt writes me that you've got snow in Chicago already. Sounds wintry.

After you've got me off your mind, I wish you could find time to look at a few little poems an English friend of mine has been writing since he turned soldier.[501] He is known for prose rather than for verse. If you care at all for what I enclose I shall be tempted to tell you who he is. He has a quality.

I have had a frivolous summer. Too many pleasant people in the neighborhood. It will be different when—to quote from a poem you may never have seen—

The city has withdrawn into itself
And left at last the country to the country.[502]

Sincerely yours
Robert Frost

[To Louis Untermeyer. ALS. LoC.]

Franconia N.H.
Sept 9 1916

Dear Louis:

Here are a few bona fide addresses. There are more to follow.

Beautiful day or two.

Winter in the morning air though, and migratory impulses.

I promise you the play before long.[503] You have no idea how I am kept from work by pleasant people. They don't seem to care a damn what they leave of me.

You and Jean are still without the youngster I suppose and will have to continue to be awhile longer. Hard on you and on him. Bad time.

Bless you in haste.

R.

---

501. The reference is to Edward Thomas.

502. Opening lines of "Christmas Trees," soon to be collected in *MI*.

503. *A Way Out* would appear in the *Seven Arts* in February 1917.

[To Ellery Sedgwick. ALS. Mass. Hist.]

Franconia N.H.
September 20 1916

Dear Sedgwick:

We aren't going to have you "bitterly disappointed" about "The Axe-helve." You like it, you have made your plans for it, and you ought to have it. Harcourt thinks and I think that we must try to get along without it in the book.[504]

It is no wonder you were not looking for a book from me this fall. I wasn't myself. Still when you stop to think of it, it is three years since I published "North of Boston," and it would be strange if in that time I hadn't gathered material enough for the next book. Harcourt persuaded me that I had anyway.

I dont want any of my poetry left out of The Atlantic that can be possibly got in.

Yours sincerely
Robert Frost

Not but that I am going to miss The Axe-helve in the book.

504. Alfred Harcourt (1881–1954), RF's editor at Henry Holt. "The Axe-Helve" was published in the September 1917 *Atlantic* and later collected in *New Hampshire* in 1923. A September 11, 1916, letter from Alfred Harcourt to RF explains why. Harcourt forwarded, with the letter, the following note from Sedgwick: "Nobody told me that I must hurry with the publication of Frost's poems, and I deliberately kept them for announcement in our Almanac. I have two—'An Encounter' and 'The Axe Helve' both of which are rendered worthless by the publication of your book on November 2. Would it not be possible to omit 'The Ax-Helve' from the book? The other I might, at a pinch, print in November. Of course, I should not have accepted the longer poem ['The Axe-Helve'] had there been a time limit on it" (Harcourt's letter, quoting Sedgwick's note, is held now at DCL). An additional September 19 letter from Harcourt to RF (also at DCL) advises him that they ought to omit the poem from *MI*.

[To John Bartlett. The letter, as we now have it, is missing one or more pages. We supply the lost text, enclosed in brackets, from Margaret Bartlett Anderson's Robert Frost and John Bartlett: The Record of a Friendship *(New York: Holt, Rinehart, Winston, 1963), 108. ALS, supplemented by the text as printed in* RFJB. *UVA.]*

Franconia N.H.
September 28, 1916

Dear John:

Twice. The first time before you cleared out for good, I judge. I don't know where you all were. It was late in the afternoon and showery. Not finding anyone around I didn't dare to wait for you when it meant missing a chance to ride home.

I supposed something abysmal was up. I didn't blame you, and you don't care if I did: [which is where you are right. You seem to feel as if you had everything to gain and nothing to lose by anything that can happen.

I'm feeling advisory. You sign all the notes they will let you so long as you are paid to. I shouldn't suppose it was recovering on them they were thinking of. They simply want it to be as if you were getting now what would be coming to you if your parents ever died. Let's hope they'll] never die. You don't care when they die if you can only begin to inherit their property now when you want it.

Beastly way to talk. Sounds as if I was on your side instead of your parents': I'm not. I hold with them that it's time you did something to get well. I share their anxiety for you. Get well. Nothing else matters. You are playing nearer the edge than ever I dared play.

I wish you could have come here to live. But I can see the advantage of Claremont, pop 8000, alt 500, and not too far from what's going on.[505] I shouldn't root too deeply there for fear the climate would wear out [*sic*] and you might want to come to the mountains.

I've bet good money on you: so take care of yourself on my account—not to please me but to save me loss. Have you done anything to stop the mouth breathing?

Yours always
Robert Frost

505. Claremont is in central western New Hampshire.

[To Edward Thomas. RF's postscript is written in the left margin of the letter's first leaf. ALS. Cardiff.]

Franconia N.H.
September 28 1916

Dear Edward:

I began to think our positions were reversed—you had got well-minded from having plunged into things and I had got soul-sick from having plunged out of them. Your letter shows you can still undertalk me when you like. A little vaccination and a little cold and you are down where it makes me dizzy to look in after you. You are so good at black talk that I believe your record will stand unbroken for years to come. It's as if somebody should do the hundred yards in five seconds flat.

But look at Lloyd George. You may be down-hearted, and I may be with you. But we have to admit that it is just as well to be able to say things and see things as courageously as he is. I say that quite for its face value. Lloyd George is one of the very great men. I wish I could expect my sins to be forgiven me as a Yankee, when I return to England, in the measure of my admiration for him. I'm afraid Englishmen aren't liking Americans very much just now. Should I dare to go back to England at this moment? I often long to. The hardest part of it would be to be treated badly for what is none of my fault personally.

Let's let the Old Cloak hang on the hat-tree till you put off soldier's uniform.[506] Meanwhile I wish you could let me have copies of just the poems you are putting into book form. I am not a person of half the influence I should have thought I would be by this time. Nevertheless I must see what I can do to find you a publisher here and save you your copyright. I failed in a way that was no discredit to you with the Four and Twenty Blackbirds. "Too insular" was the praise our publishers damned it with for American purposes. I can see the way Henry Holt looked at it.[507] And then it might have fared better if I could have thrust it upon him in book form—as I did The

506. See RF to Thomas, August 15, 1916, and notes.

507. In an October 4, 1915, letter to RF, Alfred Harcourt (his editor at Holt) had written: "I have read Thomas's 'Four and Twenty Blackbirds,' and I am awfully sorry that I cannot convince myself that it is worth trying here. It is slight, and it is so British that it would be under a handicap with many American parents who might otherwise enjoy reading it to their children" (letter held now at DCL).

Listeners.[508] That might have helped the matter. I am making a clean breast of all this to give you a chance to refuse to let me see what I can do with the poems. You needn't feel obliged to humour me (as I do you in that spelling.) I sha'n't go to Holt this time; but to someone else who dropped in on me lately for a talk on what was doing in English writing. Never mind who it was for the present. Get up no hopes—as I know you are incapable of getting up any. Only let me try. It's a shame you shouldn't have something on someone's list over here where I find so many who know and like you. One of my professors at the University of Pennsylvania was liking the "perfect texture" of your prose just the other day—thought he had read all you had written.[509] Mosher of Portland seemed to have a large knowledge of you.[510] I'm not saying this to cheer you up, damn you. You know the worth of your bays. And I'm nobody to cheer anyone else when I can't cheer myself of late. And winter coming on.

I'm going to write you some all fired stuff every week of my life.

Tell me, if you think of it, what your final opinion of Rupert's work is.[511]

Our love.

Always yours
Robert Frost

I wonder if there's the least chance of your being allowed to come over here on leave and say goodbye to us before you go out.

[To Louis Untermeyer. The letter is undated, but the envelope survives and is postmarked Franconia, October 2, 1916. ALS. LoC.]

[Franconia, NH]
[October 2, 1916]

Dear Louis

You couldnt come out here for that talk?

Yours bluly
R.

---

508. With RF's encouragement, Henry Holt had published Walter de la Mare's *The Listeners and Other Poems* in 1916.

509. Cornelius Weygandt.

510. Thomas Bird Mosher (1852–1923), publisher.

511. RF refers to Rupert Brooke, whose *Collected Poems* had been published posthumously in 1915.

[To Wilbur Rowell. Beneath RF's signature is a notation in another hand, probably Rowell's: "Oct. 11/16 N. Y. draft for Jeanie Frost for 62.—" ALS. UVA.]

Franconia N.H.
October 10 1916

Dear Mr. Rowell:

I am glad you have found a way to do for Jean what I wish I could do myself. I am sure we are both grateful.

Winter here this morning—snow on the roof and a wind that says, Time to bank up the house.

Sincerely yours
Robert Frost

[To Louis Untermeyer. RF dates the letter-poem "Octodecem," which Untermeyer, in preparing his edition, takes as December 8. However, given his habit of putting month before date, RF meant "October 10." The envelope survives, postmarked October 13, 1916. The poem herein was eventually collected as "A Cloud Shadow" in RF's 1942 volume A Witness Tree. *ALS. LoC.]*

Franconia Octodecem [1916]

Dear Louis

A breeze discovered my open book
And began to flutter the leaves to look
For a poem about the season, Spring.
I tried to tell her "There's no such thing."

For whom would a poem on Spring be by?
The breeze disdained to make reply.
And a cloud-shadow crossed her face
For fear I should make her pass the place.

I just thought you ought to know it whether it was so or not.

R.

[To Joseph Warren Beach. The letter-poem is dated "Franconia October," but "Oct 11 1916" is written in another hand beneath RF's postscript. RF never published the poem. ALS. Minnesota.]

Franconia
October [11, 1916]

My dear Joseph Warren:

Winter has beaten Summer in fight
And shaken the Summer state.
He has come to her capital city of Trees
To find but an open gate,

None to resist him; Summer herself
Gone from her windy towers,
First having hurried away her birds
And hidden away her flowers.

He has set her desert citadel
In one autumnal blaze,
Whereover the crows like something charred
Rise and fall in the haze.

So has he served her Summer pride
And punished a royal fault.
And he has appointed a day to sow
Her ruined city with salt.

But perhaps you don't allow me in this kind of verse being what I am

Your poor old
R.F.

I couldn't accept less than three of yours in exchange.

[To Louis Untermeyer. ALS. LoC.]

Franconia N.H.
October 13 1916

Dear Louis:

I can't make any of these seem very important. "Prelude" may be one or two things. I'm sure the rest are nothing distinct. The adjectives taken anywhere give the case away. It cost no effort of any kind to bring "vagrant" to "hair" nor "garish" to "day" nor "sultry" to "summer." They were all there already. Somebody fetched them sometime from a good way, no doubt, at considerable expense of spirit; but it wasn't Clement Wood.[512] It's the same all the way through: Clement gets out of it too easily. He simply ought to be made to learn (without being told) that he must narrow down to what he actually catches himself at, to what he finds himself forced to think feel say and do in mid career. It will reduce his output for a while. It will make him feel pretty fragmentary—as if he hadnt enough to round out a whole of anything. Then let him be as fragmentary as he feels.

The last two lines of "Prelude" are bad. I should wish to get rid of "As I lie aching for the touch of you," as well.

Sorry to have to say it of Clement,

R F.

[To Morris Tilley, who was on the faculty at the University of Michigan, where RF's sister, Jeanie Florence Frost, had recently enrolled. ALS. UM.]

Franconia N.H.
October 15 1916

Dear Tilley:

You will do it just right with Jean, I am sure. She is particularly bad at taking advice. She will probably take a little more of it from you than she would

512. Clement Wood (1888–1950) was an American poet, novelist, journalist, lawyer, and prolific author of fifty-seven titles in the Haldeman-Julius *Little Blue Book* series on subjects as various as love, sex, life in Greenwich Village, botany, Emerson, nursery rhymes, and the history of religion. As published in the December 1916 issue of the *Seven Arts*, "Prelude" does not contain the line to which RF objected; however, Wood restored it when he collected the poem in his 1917 volume *Glad of Earth* (New York: Laurence J. Gomme, 1917), where it concludes as follows:

You slowly put out the light
And the love-knitting night floods all of the room
As I lie aching for the touch of you.
The one red spark of the joss-taper glows tenderly from the mantel,
One star, alone in a heaven so near that I can touch it.
And now, out of the dear darkness,
Your fingers find mine.

from me. What will do most to keep her where she is is an occasional sign of special consideration. It's a sad case, still not so sad as it might be. There are worse places you can come to in your old age than college and some of them are jail, the poorhouse, and the madhouse. Some of her eccentricity you can put down to imperfect submission. In a recent letter she speaks of Winkler as friendly.[513] Let me know sometime how he speaks of her prospects.

You are all kindness, Tilley, in this matter and I shall always remember it. I trust you feel braced for your year's work. Elinor joins me in best wishes.

Always sincerely yours
Robert Frost

[To Edward Thomas. ALS. NYPL.]

Franconia N.H.
October 15 1916

Dear Edward:

You <u>will</u> send along the selection of poems you have made for the book, won't you? I must try to see what I can do with it before you lose the copyright by publishing it first in England.

You may have noticed that the editor of Poetry (Chicago) has been liking Edward Eastaway's Lob.[514]

I am up to my eyes in work around the place. Winter is white on the mountain tops and blowing cold at us down here in the river "interval."

This is chiefly to press you for the poems. You will understand, though, how little I am sure of doing. But let me try.

Our love to you all.

Affectionately,
Robert Frost

---

513. Possibly Max Winkler (1866–1930), professor of German at the University of Michigan; he offered courses in the literature of the Reformation and in lyric poetry.

514. "Edward Eastaway" was Thomas's pseudonym. Harriet Monroe, editor of *Poetry* magazine, praised a poem by Eastaway, "Lob," in a review of the then-new quarterly *Form* that appeared in the September 1916 issue of *Poetry* under the title "A New Quarterly." Later, in February 1917, Monroe published three poems under the name Edward Eastaway in *Poetry*: "Old Man," "The Word," and "The Unknown."

[To Edith Hill Blaney (1868–1930), an American socialite and patron of the arts; she was married to the landscape artist Dwight Blaney. ALS. UVA.]

Franconia N.H.
October 15, 1916

My dear Mrs Blaney:

Will you have the books sent right along? I shall be only too glad of the chance to autograph them.

And if autographs are anything, you must let me send you an autographed copy of North of Boston for yourself. I have been intending to carry you one this long time, but I have become so mercenary that I believe I have lost the art of going anywhere except on business. It may not be quite as bad as that; still it is bad enough and time I took myself in hand and went to a few places for pleasure as a discipline. One of the first of them will be your door in Mt Vernon St[515] to tell you how far I am from forgetting the pleasant evening you gave me there last year. It was several kinds of a lovely evening.

I have wanted you to meet my wife. She has been in Boston with me twice, but both times there were worries about sickness and we got nowhere.

Sincerely yours
Robert Frost

[To Susan Hayes Ward. ALS. Huntington.]

Franconia N.H.
October 15 1916

Dear Miss Ward:

We have been thinking of you a great deal of late. I have been so sorry that neither of [us] got to see you in your new old home before your circle was broken.[516] I was near sending Elinor off once, but she was obdurate and wouldnt leave the children when it came to the point. And once I was as near seeing you myself as this: I was at Rockingham Junction with half a day or so on my hands and I thought if I could be sure of finding you at home I might manage to run up to South Berwick for a call. So I tried to get you on the telephone. But I failed and had to go on my way to the next lecture, thinking

515. In Boston.

516. Susan's brother, William Hayes Ward, had died on August 29, 1916.

that it was perhaps just as well anyway since a mere glimpse would be so little better than nothing. You may have heard how busy I was all the year earning a living—rather more of a living than I ever made before—you will be glad to hear that.

I am surely going to see you this winter when I am south along. I shall hope to find you well and ready for a poem or two of not too new a kind.

Our united best love.

Always your friend
Robert Frost

[To Philip Darrell Sherman (1881–1957), professor of English at Oberlin College, and a collector to whose attention RF hoped to bring the new journal. ALS. Brown.]

Franconia N.H.
October 22 1916

Dear Mr Sherman:

Perhaps I took a liberty in mentioning you to my fellow editors of The Seven Arts as one who might be interested in our venture—at least in my part of it. For I am expected to do something for it once in so often in prose or verse. I don't know that I am qualified to speak of its aims. I suppose it wants to be the freshest the most signal thing in American magazines. I shall have next to nothing to do with shaping its destinies. I am no more than a contributing editor. James Oppenheim and Louis Untermeyer are going to make it what it is going to be; and they are both fine fellows and writers of distinction.

I'm afraid you weren't asked to notice the new magazine in just the terms I myself would have chosen. The letters that have gone out from the business department have given offense to one or two of my friends. The letter that has come round to me is in very bad taste and calculated to put me in a very false light. I am sure that none of my editorial friends had anything to do with formulating it.

The magazine may be badly advertised. I think it will be a good magazine. Let's hope that it will even be stirring.

Always sincerely yours
Robert Frost

[To Helen I. Fraser (1893–1992), an American educator. Born in Georgia of Canadian parents who subsequently settled near Manchester, New Hampshire, Fraser graduated from Plymouth Normal School the year RF taught there (1912), and enjoyed a long career as an elementary school teacher. ALS. Plymouth.]

Franconia N.H.
November 5 1916

Dear Miss Fraser:

Remember as if it were yesterday—both you and your tall father. I like to think I connect people with their towns. Unless I am much mistaken you were from Reed's Ferry.[517] Anyway you were one of my friends and one of the children's friends in our year at Plymouth.

I'm glad that things come round this way and that you can say you dont dislike as a poet one whom I trust you didnt dislike too much as a teacher.

Tell the two farmer ladies I knew I was right about storm-fear because I have suffered from it more or less myself.[518] But I am none the less grateful for their testimony in corroboration.

If the literary society in your high school persists in doing anything so foolish as to name itself after me, what less can I do to show my appreciation than to send it a complete set of my works to date. This might well be offered as a prize for literary work in the society as the best way to get rid of it—the set of my works, not the society.

Always sincerely yours
Robert Frost

[To Edward Thomas. ALS. Cardiff.]

Franconia N.H.
November 6 1916

Dear Edward:

Tomorrow we vote—I vote for once; and you mustn't be disappointed if we don't turn Wilson out of office. We probably shall turn him out from a mistaken idea of what we are about. But don't be disappointed if we don't. By comparison with a number of Americans I could name he has been a real

---

517. Reed's Ferry is about six miles south of Manchester, New Hampshire.

518. See RF's poem "Storm Fear," collected first in *ABW*.

friend of the Allies' cause. Roosevelt is the only man we have who could have lead [*sic*] us into war with the Germans. And he would have had to betray us into it. It would have had to be almost betrayal; because though we are very much on your side, we seem to have no general wish to be in the fighting. You will see how it will be with Hughes if he is elected.[519] He will set himself simply to beat Wilson at his own game. Granting that Wilson has given us a good deal of peace with some honour, Hughes' aim will be to give us more peace with more honour—especially the more honour. He's a confident fool who thinks he sees how it will be easy to do this. He is one of these Sunday school products who is going to be every bit as good as he has brains to be. None of him for me.

And yet you know how I feel about the war. I have stopped asseverating from a sense of fitness. You rather shut me up by enlisting. Talk is almost too cheap when all your friends are facing bullets. I don't believe I ought to enlist (since I am of course an American), but if I can't enlist, at least I refuse to talk sympathy beyond a certain point. I did set myself to wish this country into the war. I made a little noise on the subject, but soon found I wasn't half as good at the noise as some who cared less. (Has Harold Begbie enlisted?)[520] When all the world is facing danger, it's a shame not to be facing danger for any reason, old age, sickness, or any other. Words wont make the shame less. There's no use trying to make out that the shame we suffer makes up for the more heroic things we don't suffer. No more of this for a long time. Are not the magazines chuckfull of it?

I hear from a friend of mine who if he doesnt love the Germans as against the British at least loves the Irish against them, that De la Mare is to dine or lunch or something with him when he gets to New York. The time named is so near that I guess De la Mare isn't going to make me a port of call or he would have got some word to me before this. Is it that he doesn't know that you and Garnett[521] and he and Abercrombie and one or two others have made

---

519. The Republican presidential candidate was Charles Evans Hughes of New York.

520. Edward Harold Begbie (1871–1929) was an English author and journalist. In 1915 he published *Kitchener: Organizer of Victory,* a study of Field Marshal Horatio Herbert Kitchener as man and legend and the symbolic significance of his appointment to the War Office. Begbie may have come to RF's attention as the author of *Twice-Born Men: A Clinic in Regeneration; A Footnote in Narrative to Professor William James's "The Varieties of Religious Experience"* (1909).

521. British critic Edward Garnett. Walter de la Mare was coming to accept the Henry E. Howland Memorial prize (Yale) on behalf of his friend Rupert Brooke.

me even more distinguished than he is in this country. I'm a little hurt. Of course we are a little out of the way. Masefield wrote that he meant to get out here (uninvited), but his agent rushed him off his feet up to the last moment of his stay and he couldnt make it. Very likely Masefield wanted to see my Dominique (pronounced Dominik) hens.[522]

Is there the least use in beseeching you to come over for a week or two out of my pocket? Could you get leave? I wish it beyond anything. I should think it ought to be possible. We could find you a few lectures. Taking the fast boats you ought not to have to be gone more than three weeks. Does this sound so very unmilitary? They ought to consider that you were literary before you were military. I have a play I shall be half afraid of till you tell me how it strikes you. Its the same old one I tried to make you read once before when I first knew you—if you remember—and you sidestepped it. It is called An Assumed Part.[523]

I (personally) am in what is known as an "interesting state." I may have news for you in my next letter. Oh, by the way, I came across my Gibsonian lines On Being about to Become a Parent just lately. Now don't misunderstand me. There are other offspring than of our bodies.

Farewell and adieu to you with a fa la la la la la la, and don't forget your old shipmate

Robert Frost, the Frisco-Digger,
Boston
Beauty, etc.

[To Louis Untermeyer. The letter is undated, but the envelope survives and is postmarked Franconia, November 14, 1916. Perhaps because he had crowded the closing sentences along the left margin of the last page, Frost neglected to sign the letter. AL (unsigned). LoC.]

[Franconia, NH]
[November 14, 1916]

Dear Louis

If I agree to look in on you for one day, the twenty-third or twenty-fourth of the month, that is next week, will you promise not to let a soul know of

522. John Masefield (1878–1967), English poet and Poet Laureate from 1930 until his death.

523. *A Way Out*, first printed in *Seven Arts* in February 1917.

my being in town? I want to see you, but there are a lot of people I like but dont want to see because I simply cant afford the distraction in my now state of mind. What they don't hear of my being in town wont hurt their feelings.

I have been in no mood to meet De la Mare. He is one of the open questions with me like what to do with Mexico. He has only treated Edward Thomas, to whom he owes more than half, measurably well. Personally I am indifferent about him and have been these three years. Don't think I asked Harcourt to do the Listeners on De la Mare's account.[524] The sum of it is that without much to go on I suspect that the man who rhymes with Delaware is a bit of a British snob and will bear fighting shy of. I shall probably have to invite him here, because my mother was so sure she had taught me manners and I shouldn't want her to be mistaken. But I'm almost sure he scorns America and has only come over for what he can get out of us and against us. And I have his poems to save. If he is half as bad as I am afraid he is, he might spoil the poems. You know how many poems you have lost by meeting the man who wrote them. My not meeting De la Mare in England was rather accidentally on purpose.

The magazine was right. I'll leave it to talk over with you. I'll just say now that your part in it was as brilliant as any. The preface to your Heine wont be the worst of it: you needn't prepare me for it with anything deprecatory.[525]

I have been in the depths without a diving-suit. Surely you wont mind my taking a little common ordinary satisfaction in the election of Wilson. You don't think such things matter for yourself. I am even helped by the way New Hampshire went.[526] Make allowances for me. As a child I did what I could by marching and shouting and burning oil to throw the country to Cleveland in '84. And yet I lived to vote for Debs.

---

524. In 1916 Henry Holt and Company issued an American edition of Walter de la Mare's *The Listeners and Other Poems* (London: Constable, 1912). See also RF's September 28, 1916, letter to Edward Thomas.

525. Untermeyer translated, and wrote the preface to, *Poems of Heinrich Heine* (New York: Henry Holt, 1917).

526. New Hampshire was the only state in New England that went for Wilson.

[To Mary Goodwillie. Mary C. Goodwillie (1870–1949) was associated with many charitable and literary organizations in Baltimore, including the Baltimore Poetry Society and the Friends of the Johns Hopkins University Library. ALS. Hopkins.]

Franconia N.H.
November 15 1916

Dear Miss Goodwillie:

It seems but yesterday that we made friends with you under this roof and now you are away down south where all we can see of you is your handwriting. And if it seems no time at all since you were with us, what may it be supposed to seem since your first letter came to ask me to read for you? Yet here comes your second letter to tell me that there has been time enough for me to have answered you and more too. Will you forgive me for not being more prompt?

Of course I shall be happy to read for you.[527] What should you say to February first for the day? I am promised to Philadelphians for January twenty-ninth and perhaps I ought to allow the thirtieth for parting from them. I shall be at Princeton on the thirty-first. I should come back to you from there—my wife with me, if we can manage it as you so kindly propose.

The snow that you saw still aloof on the mountain tops has come down into our yards and made it winter.

Sincerely yours
Robert Frost

[To Harriet Monroe. ALS. Chicago.]

Franconia N.H.
November 20 1916

Dear Miss Monroe:

I believe I left dates out altogether. I read in Baltimore on February 1st.[528] It would be as lovely as a "track event" if I could make one jump from that to

527. RF gave a talk and reading at Goodwillie's home on the afternoon of January 28, 1917; he gave a talk that evening before the Contemporary Club in Baltimore.

528. Actually (again) the date was on January 28. Then, after reading in Amherst, at Brown University, and in Springfield, Massachusetts, in late February, RF traveled to Chicago to give talks on March 14 at the University of Chicago and on March 15 before the Chicago Women's Club.

something in Chicago on February 3rd. I could allow three or four days for Chicago and anything that may turn up there and then get away in time to speak at Bloomington Ind. on the morning of February 7th—if they will have me—as I am hoping they will.

I realize that this is making you my agent in a troublesome business. But back out without notice whenever you please. Your kindness has got you into this. I have conveniently forgotten any part I may have had in getting you in. Did I fish very brazenly I wonder.

I have been liking your poem to your brother.[529]

Sincerely yours
Robert Frost

[To Louis Untermeyer. The letter is undated but the envelope survives and is postmarked November 20, 1916, Franconia, N.H. ALS. LoC.]

[Franconia, NH]
[November 20, 1916]

Dear Louis

Unless something breaks it will be Friday night with you. Alfred[530] wants you and me to ride with him Friday day. But probably he told you when you were in there coruscating.

And won't we give things a going over!

Play under one arm.

Yours stealthily
R.

529. "To W. J. C.," published in the November 1916 issue of *Poetry*. Monroe's brother-in-law, William J. Calhoun (1847–1916), was an associate of William McKinley, an attorney, and special envoy to China under William Howard Taft; he died of a stroke on September 19, 1916, in Chicago.

530. Alfred Harcourt, of Henry Holt and Company.

[To Joseph Warren Beach. The letter is undated, but at the top left "Dec 1916" is written in another hand. ALS. Minnesota.]

Franconia [NH]
[December 1916]

Dear Joe Beach:

Sick in bed with a feverish cold but a great deal cheered by your letter. If you get anything like as much emotion out of my book[531] as I get out of your letter all I can say is you must get out nearly as much as I put in say ninety percent of it, which represents a very small loss in transmission. I should think you could do anything you pleased with anybody with a gift of letter writing like yours. I remember the sting of all your letters from that very first one that you arrived here right on top of.

But I mustn't make you self-conscious you unconscious devil.

If you and I and one person more are agreed that The Old Man's Winter Night is the one, that settles it. Three are a perfect strength. We don't care a hang who prefers Dryden's From Eavenly Armony, do we?[532]

Would you were here.

Suppose I got west as far as Chicago for a lecture or two, what would my chance be of seeing you?

What have you else of your own you want me to see. I liked what you sent. My name is connected with The Seven Arts magazine of New York and the Universe. It is not to be understood that I have anything to do with passing on MS. I am a sort of contributing editor. I'm on the magazine for what I can sell to it. That seems to be the understanding. But I ought to have a little influence with some of the editors to save them from narrowing down to a clique. There are two or three people I want them to take into consideration

---

531. *MI*, published on November 27, 1916; "An Old Man's Winter Night" is collected there. Advance orders for *MI* had exceeded 2,000 as of November 14.

532. See John Dryden's "A Song for St. Cecilia's Day" (1687):

From harmony, from heavenly harmony,
This universal frame began:
From harmony to harmony
Through all the compass of the notes it ran,
The diapason closing full in Man.

and you are one of them. Have you anything in the kind of that one with the bicycle and the glass of milk and the piece of string?[533]

Forever yours
R.F.

[To Wilbur Rowell. ALS. UVA.]

Franconia N.H.
December 1 1916

Dear Mr Rowell:

If you could let me have two hundred dollars now I could go on with certain improvements here that will otherwise have to stand still till I begin to realize on my lecturing later in the winter. We have been making more room, but we are not going to get the good of it unless we put a furnace into the cellar. Shall you feel like helping me do this? You must say if you don't see your way.

Sincerely yours
Robert Frost

I shall want you to have a copy of my new book from my hand to put with the other two.

533. RF refers to Beach's poem "Rue Bonaparte," first published in *Poetry* in May 1915.

[To H. L. Mencken (1880–1956), American journalist, editor, essayist, and scholar. The letter is a typed transcription. In an unknown hand at the top left is written "The 'Genius,'" and typed beneath is the following statement: "CONFIDENTIAL—Not to be used in evidence without the author's permission. H. L. Mencken." Mencken had solicited testimonials of noted American authors in defense of Theodore Dreiser's novel The Genius *(1915) against censure by the New York Society for the Suppression of Vice. The Comstock Act (1873)—named for Anthony Comstock, the crusading head of the New York society—made it a federal crime to send obscene materials through the mail. Typed transcription. Penn.]*

Franconia, N.H.
Dec. 6, 1916.

Dear Mr. Mencken:

With all my heart—on general principles—though I don't know much about Dreiser's books beyond that they are honest and though I don't care a hang for the "ridicule and contempt of other nations." I'm only afraid I'm too late in with my signature.[534] Your letter has been lying here beside me and I too sick to attend to it.

I hadn't heard that the Comstockians were after Dreiser. These fools should consider where H. G. Wells has come safely out in his latest by being left entirely alone to think things out for himself.[535] The way our wildest attempts to think free always end in the same conclusions is the saddest proof that no other conclusions are possible.

Sincerely yours,
(Signed) Robert Frost.

---

534. RF had, it appears, not replied to Mencken's initial query. On November 22, 1916, Mencken had written: "I surely hope your failure to sign the Dreiser Protest is not deliberate. His fight, in the last analysis, is the fight of all of us. The list of signers is already very formidable and such men as Arnold Bennett and H. G. Wells have cabled offers of support from England. Certainly the writers of America must stand by him as firmly as the writers of France stood by Zola in a similar situation. The prosecution is arbitrary and disingenuous: Dreiser is too big and too honest a man to be sacrificed to comstockery" (letter held now at DCL). Mencken thanked RF for the above letter on December 12: "Dreiser, I am sure, will be delighted to hear that you have added your name. You state the case against the Comstocks succinctly and effectively. As for me, I find it difficult to see any merit whatever in such things" (letter held now at DCL).

535. RF's reference to Wells may be in regard to the publication in 1914 of a pamphlet addressing the antiwar and pacifist elements in Britain, entitled "The War That Will End War." The heretofore pacifist Wells had changed his mind in speaking out against German imperial aggression.

[To Alfred Harcourt. The letter is dated merely "December," but it must have been written early in the month: Amherst College publicly announced the appointment herein referred to on December 17. ALS. Princeton.]

[Franconia]
December [circa 7,] 1916

Dear Alfred:

Better. Bad cold—that was all, but too close on the heels of the other one. I was in bed a week.

I may not feel equal to New York for a while yet. I wish I could see you though.

Here's this damned Hell-I-Can turned up again with the base insinuation that people like what I write because of the reputation you have made for me.[536] I don't like the business but I dont want to antagonize anyone whose friendship wont hurt us. Am I too hard on O'Brien. Do you approve of that pair (him and Braithwaite)? I get to railing and I can rail myself into damning my best friends to Hell. Sometimes I think I need holding in.

A case in point. You remember how I flew off the handle because I suspected a certain poet got me to read my poetry at his college in order to get me to find him a publisher for his poetry.[537] Well I didnt find him a publisher did I? And here he comes with an invitation to me to give two half courses at his college from January on for two thousand dollars. I'm humiliated. And it aint the first time in forty years. I seem to go plum crazy.

This about the college must be a secret. I havent decided yet.

---

536. Edward J. O'Brien, along with W. S. Braithwaite, one of the organizers of the New England Poetry Club.

537. Stark Young. An April 13, 1916, letter to RF from Alfred Harcourt, his editor at Holt, reads in part: "Stark Young of Amherst writes that he has had two fine days with you and that you went over his verses and liked them, and wanted him to bring them down to me. He wants to come down for the weekend. I am sorry to have to write to him that both this weekend and the next weekend are full, but I am asking him to send the verses down so that I can have a good look at them before we talk, since we cannot talk right off. What do you think of them, in confidence, as always" (letter held now at DCL). Holt did not, in the event, publish Young.

Tell me about de la Mare. It comes to me round the ring that you are to have another book of his.[538] Is that right? I mustn't be too hard on de la Mare either. I have little enough to go on with regard to him. Tell me.

More when I am more scrumptious.

Love to all.
Always yours
Robert

[To Mark Antony DeWolfe Howe. ALS. DCL.]

Franconia N.H.
December 7 1916

Dear Mr Howe:

I impulsively copied some impulsive lines into some of the books I sent along to-day.[539] I trust if they come to your eye you won't view them too critically. They should have aged a little in my notebook before I ventured into public with them. They are past recall now!

I usually keep my poems about me for some time before printing them. I found that easier to do in the old days when you were nearly the only editor who would pay money for them.[540]

And speaking of keeping poems a long time, there's a sonnet-shaped thing in my new book called Range Finding that you (I think it was you) once wrote me a nice letter about as long ago as 1906.

With gratitude for the way you helped me over those leanest years I am

Sincerely yours
Robert Frost

---

538. Henry Holt and Company published Walter de la Mare's *Motley and Other Poems* in 1918.

539. "On Talk of Peace at This Time," which RF never collected. It is printed in *CPPP,* 531. A facsimile of the poem as inscribed by RF was published first in *Robert Frost 100: A Centennial Publication* (Boston: David Godine, 1974), 33.

540. Howe edited *The Youth's Companion* from 1899 to 1913, during which period several of RF's poems appeared in the magazine.

[To Edward Thomas. ALS. Cardiff.]

Franconia N.H.
December 7 1916

Dear Edward:

I have been down sick in bed for a week and a half; thats where I have been and thats why you haven't heard from me. Port wine is what I need now if I am going to shine. But I'm not. I find that the chief thing on my mind is not a personal one, whats going to become of you and me—nothing like that—but a political one[:] the change in the government in England and the possibilities of great changes in France. What becomes of my hopes of three months ago when the drive on the Somme began? Something has gone wrong. How can we be happy any more—for a while. Lloyd George is the great man and he belongs where he now takes his place. But would he ever have arrived there with Bonar Law and Carson [*sic*] on his right and left, but for some desperate need.[541] Silly fools are full of peace talk over here. It is out of friendliness of a kind to the Allies: they act as if they thought you were waiting for them to say the word to quit. It's none of my business what you do: but neither is it any of theirs. I wrote some lines I've copied on the other side of this about the way I am struck. When I get to writing in this vein you may know I am sick or sad or something.[542]

Robert

541. Lloyd George's coalition government, which assumed power in December 1916, having displaced the government headed by H. H. Asquith, depended on the support of Lord Curzon (George Nathaniel Curzon, 1859–1925), Conservative leader of the House of Lords, and Andrew Bonar Law (1858–1923), Conservative leader of the House of Commons.

542. "Suggested by Talk of Peace at This Time," which argues in a high rhetorical style highly unusual for RF (hence "in this vein") against a compromise peace. RF had also inscribed the poem (with variant title and wording) on the flyleaf of a copy of *MI* sent to Mark Anthony DeWolfe Howe (see RF to Howe, December 7, 1916).

[To Sidney Cox. RF's reply is dated simply "December 1916," but the envelope survives; its postmark supplies the more precise dating given here. ALS. DCL.]

[Franconia, NH]
December [10,] 1916

Dear Cox

It gives me real pleasure to hear of your pleasure and your friend's pleasure in the book. Why mar it by raising the specter of your poor past professor to argue with? It can do me no good to be reminded of him. It's uncomfortable to be at a feast with a fellow who suddenly pushes back his chair and gets up to gesticulate with his napkin at somebody nobody else can see.

I know you do it from conscientiousness—not to hide from me anything that may be bothering you. You needn't be so scrupulous with me. I shall forgive you if you keep some unimportant doubts from me.

You do awfully well with the book. I could ask no more generous reviewer than you would be. But you mustn't be mislead [*sic*] by anything that may have been laid down to you in school into exaggerating the importance of a little sententious tag to a not over important poem. The large things in the book—well I won't name them—you know better than to think the Oven Bird is of them. Probably the best thing in the book is The Old Man's Winter Night. That seems to be the consensus of opinion among the professors I get letters from—if we are going to leave it to professors.

I like different people to like different things. I shouldn't mind your exalting the Oven Bird so much if your reasons were better. Let's not strain, let's not worry. Have a good time most of the time.[543]

I shall be off professoring a little on my own pretty soon and if I have a chance I shall try to find you in New York.[544] The trouble with New York is it thinks people ought to be glad to read to it for nothing. Thats why I keep away from it.

Always yours
Robert Frost

---

543. RF is responding to a November 16 letter from Cox that opened with the salutation "Dear Oven Bird"; Cox had reported that, of all the poems collected in *MI,* issued on November 27, "The Oven Bird" stirred him most. In a postscript he writes: "I doubt if you intended any reference to your poetic aims when you described the oven bird. Perhaps no such significance suggested itself to you even after it was written. Your voice as a poet is not loud, certainly."

544. RF had accepted a position in the Department of English at Amherst College; see the next letter, to Stark Young.

[To Stark Young. The letter is undated, but Frost met with Amherst president Alexander Meiklejohn on December 15 (a Friday). On Sunday, December 17, Meiklejohn made a formal announcement of RF's appointment, to begin in January 1917, at $2,000 a semester. ALS. HRC.]

[Franconia, NH]
[circa December 12, 1916]

Dear Stark:

I am going to take a train from here Saturday morning that should get me to Northampton at something after three in the afternoon. I thought of taking it Friday morning. But one more day at home will be better for me. Dr Meiklejohn proposed meeting me in Boston. But if I go there I sha'n't see you and I shall get into things that I am not quite up to yet. I have just got his letter—late for doing anything about it. He gives no Boston address either. I dont see anything to be saved or gained by Boston. I shall just wire him that I shall get to Amherst Saturday afternoon there to wait till he finds it convenient to see me—unless he wires me instructions to the contrary.[545]

I shall have a book in my pocket for you when I come; so be a good boy.

Always yours
R.

[To Louis Untermeyer. ALS. LoC.]

Franconia N.H.
Dec 14 1916

Dear Louis:

Try you again. I undertake to be in New York not later than Wednesday next to stay till I see you for a talk. I have had a lot of love letters in print from you but they are not the same thing as seeing you. I go to work for a living in

545. The meeting almost certainly took place on the fifteenth. On December 16 Meiklejohn wrote to RF: "This morning at the chapel service I read 'The Road Not Taken' and then told the boys you were coming. They applauded vigorously and were evidently much delighted at the prospect. I can assure you of an eager and hearty welcome in the community" (letter held now at DCL). Meiklejohn then explained the pay schedule: RF would receive a check for $350 on January 1, and then, on the first of each of the next six months, a check for $275 (about $5,000 in 2013 dollars).

two or three weeks and then goodbye to friends and poetry for awhile. I must tell you about it. Damn writing.

Love me forever.
R.

Extracts from the diary of a backwoods poet kept at intervals during the period of The High Cost of Living (Rotogravure.)[546]

October 15
This day hunted bear without success.
October 16
This day hunted bear without success.
October 17
This day hunted bear without success.
October 27
This day hunted bear without success.
November 1
This day hunted bear without
November 8
HE WAS ELECTED SAVED!!!!!!![547]

In the entry of November 1 there is a pathetic reference (almost illegible) to having spent the day in bed reading the Sears Roebuck catalogue.

[To Francis Charles MacDonald (1874–1952), professor of English at Princeton. MacDonald had joined the faculty in 1905 as one of then-President Woodrow Wilson's original group of 'preceptors'—young scholars hired to strengthen the newly established English Department. ALS. Princeton.]

Franconia N.H.
December 15 1916

Dear Mr MacDonald:

This is very kind of you to want me to see something of the undergraduates at Princeton when I am there. I shall be most happy to read for you. I have usually had about fifty dollars of the colleges, but if that sounds out of proportion to the size or wealth of your society, will you be kind enough to

546. RF's ersatz diary is composed in increasingly shaky and illegible handwriting.

547. On November 7, President Woodrow Wilson had been elected to a second term.

tell me?—and we will make it what you think right.[548] I do not like to keep these matters entirely on a business footing.

Sincerely yours
Robert Frost

[To Stark Young. ALS. HRC.]

Franconia N.H.
December 28 1916

Dear Stark Young:

Nothing better to say of a book inscribed to you with love and admiration than that you could praise it as tactful and labored and that you easily awarded it the palm in a kind of verse you soon tired of. If it is your real self speaks there and not just some momentary unhappiness how shall I be ashamed enough of having assumed that you wanted me at Amherst for something you saw in my poetry.

I wish I were altogether sure of the innocence of your "labor" and "tact." They sound dangerously like the kind of dispraise some of us think we are clever enough to palm off on fools as praise. Yet I am loth to think you would practise on me with delusive criticism.

Will you try to persuade George Browne sometime that narratives I do in verse in three or four or at most five hours and then practically never touch again may still be labored in some sense of the word? Yeats told me he was nine hours doing the three verses of the Song of the Wandering Aengus; I did The Home Stretch in less than half that time. But if mine seems labored (to some one who confessedly doesnt like the kind of poem) and Yeats' doesnt seem labored, that's all there is to it: mine is labored and Yeats' isn't.

I say these things now in writing so that we may have our time when we are together to talk of more important things.

The inscription in the book stands; the first part of it stands at any rate. I still love you though you slay me.

Robert Frost

---

548. The front page of the *Daily Princetonian* for January 29, 1917, announced the circumstances of RF's visit: "The Freneau Club, the literary society recently organized in the University, will hold its next meeting on January 31st. Robert Frost, the young American poet, has been engaged to give a reading from his own works."

[To Philip Darrell Sherman. The letter is tipped-in to a copy of MI, *which is inscribed: "Your friend / Robert Frost / Franconia / Jan. 1 1917." ALS. Brown.]*

Franconia NH
December 28 1916

Dear Mr Sherman:

Thanks for the warmth of your letter, and thanks for knowing so well how to take me. It's by what you put your finger on that you show your understanding. Some people think we mention stoves and telephone poles and kitchen sinks and wallpaper just to see what we can lug into poetry, but we mention them because they haunt us with old memories and for no other reason. Isn't that so?[549]

I shall be glad to write in the lines you like.

I am to profess English at Amherst for six months. If you are on this way, don't fail to look me up.

Sincerely yours
Robert Frost

[To Harold Goddard Rugg. ALS. DCL.]

Franconia N.H.
December 29 1916

My dear Rugg:

Just as sure as it is possible I shall get to see you this winter or spring. I shall be more disappointed than you if it can't be with Carol to see the Carnival.[550]

I am full of my plans for teaching again. Good of Dr Meiklejohn to ask me to Amherst for a school interval, wasn't it?

I am not much of a person to get autographs but what I can do for you with de la Mare and Gibson, that I will.

Always sincerely yours
Robert Frost

549. "In the Home Stretch" devotes some sixteen lines to the installation of a stove and begins "She stood against the kitchen sink." For the telephone pole, see "The Encounter." The wallpaper turns up in "The Bonfire." All are in *MI*.

550. Since 1911, the Dartmouth Outing Club had held a winter carnival.

PS. And this leaves my thanks for the book you sent for my postscript. It was to thank you for the book that I began my letter. So it goes in the rush of these days. I hardly know what I am about. I look forward to reading the book when I am at rest in Amherst.

R.F.

[To Louis Untermeyer, whose family jewelry business (mentioned here) had offices in Manhattan. RF refers to French entomologist Jean-Henri Fabre, whose The Hunting Wasps *appeared in English in 1915, and to Henri Bergson, whose* Creative Evolution *RF read in 1911; both books trouble the "modern [Darwinian] theory of instinct," as Fabre puts it. "A Side Street" was collected in Untermeyer's* These Times *(1917). Dating derived from postmark. ALS. LoC.]*

[Franconia, NH]
[January 1, 1917]
Address me at Amherst next.

Dear Louis:

You gave us a good part of our good Christmas. We are a bejeweled family.

And speaking of families how like the family affairs we flatter ourselves we only find in country villages was that shop of yours I had a glimpse of in the middle of the greatest city in the world where everybody seemed to know everybody else if everybody wasnt quite related to everybody else. I should be jealous of you for having such an institution in a modern city where it doesnt belong according to all our theories, if I wasnt so fond of seeing our theories knocked into cocked hats. What I like about Bergson and Fabre is that they have bothered our evolutionism so much with the cases of instinct they have brought up. You get more credit for thinking if you restate formulae or cite cases that fall in easily under formulae, but all the fun is outside saying things that suggest formulae that won't formulate—that almost but don't quite formulate. I should like to be so subtle at this game as to seem to the casual person altogether obvious. The casual person would assume that I meant nothing or else I came near enough meaning something he was familiar with to mean it for all practical purposes. Well well well.

R.

I have never known you better than you are In a Side Street. It is the solid stuff, especially from "I see them there" on to the end. You are so clever you have to be careful about not cheating yourself about your rhyme words. You can make yourself think they are not there just for the rhyme when they really are. Lowell perishes of just that self-deception.[551] Your rhymes justify this time very well. Excuse this troubling thought. In a Side Street is a lovely thing.

[To Harriet Monroe. The letter is undated but stamped "JAN 9 1917" in the upper left. Edward Eastaway is the poetic nom de plume of Edward Thomas. ALS. Chicago.]

[Franconia, NH]
[January 9, 1917]

Dear Miss Monroe:

Here I sit admiring these beautiful poems but not daring to urge them on anyone else for fear I shall be suspected of admiring them for love of their author. If Edward Eastaway gets killed before the war is over (he is with the artillery) there will be plenty found to like them and then where will my credit be for having liked them first. After all is it any worse for me to like them because I know their author (but I don't like them for that reason) than for others to like them because they know he is dead.

I'm afraid all these I send are coming out in an Annual the Georgian group will publish in February.[552] I wish you could think you could crowd just one of them into your February Poetry so as to be ahead of the Annual—the Annual wouldn't get over here perhaps before March and it might not then. "Old Man" is the flower of the lot, isn't it?[553]

You may not have heard that I am just off to profess poetry at Amherst for six months. So when you write again think of me as in Amherst Mass.

Sincerely yours
Robert Frost

---

551. Amy Lowell. RF may have particularly in mind her *Men, Women, and Ghosts*, published in October 1916. Though heralded (by Lowell) in the preface as a singular experiment in *vers libre*, a substantial number of the poems gathered in the book are in rhyme (if not in meter).

552. The annual apparently referred to here *(Georgian Poetry 1916–1917)* did not, in fact, print the poems in question.

553. Three poems by Edward Eastaway, "The Unknown," "The Word," and "Old Man," were published in *Poetry* in February 1917.

Robert Frost circa 1916 in Bridgewater, New Hampshire while visiting George H. Browne.

Courtesy Plymouth State University Library.

Amherst

January 1917–February 1920

If Miss Waite or any other school-fool gives you that chance again by asking what your father will say or said you answer My father knows teachers and my father knows me: and then go on to inform them that your father has dealt in marks and dealt with people who dealt in marks in every kind of school there is in America.

—Robert Frost to Lesley Frost, November 13, 1917

[To David Emerson Greenaway, a teacher in Springfield, Massachusetts. ALS. Private collection.]

Amherst Mass
January 23 1917

Dear Mr Greenaway

Ascribe my dilitoriness [*sic*] partly to my having been off on my travels partly to my having been rushed off my feet by school and social affairs since we moved to Amherst. The letters are just piled up here against me that I have been leaving unanswered.

It is good of you to want me to read to you at Springfield and I wish I could brush aside money considerations as between friends.[1] But I have had to try to think of myself as worthy of my hire in these reading engagements. I get pretty much the same price from everyone—fifty dollars—never less than that.

Could you use me on March 2, 7, or 9?

Sincerely yours
Robert Frost

I am really doing this in haste now that I am started.

---

1. RF read before the Teachers Association in Springfield, Massachusetts, on March 7, and before students at the Technical High School in Springfield on March 8.

[To Burges Johnson (1877–1963), journalist and author of a number of volumes of light verse. He wrote for the New York Evening Post. *After leaving Port Washington, New York (on Long Island), in 1915, Johnson took a teaching position at Vassar College; he contributed articles to the* Amherst Graduates' Quarterly *in 1916 and 1917. Dating derived from internal evidence: RF assumed his first appointment at Amherst College in January 1917. ALS. ACL.]*

[Amherst, MA]
[late January 1917]

My dear Johnson:

For goodness sake send along your books. I had not noticed that you were waiting for my permission. I like your article about me in The Post. It smacked of New Hampshire and my up-country audiences. I saw what you were doing; you were speaking for the little churches and schools in the mountain towns.

I don't suppose there are many ways in which I am fearfully like Will Carlton.[2] But you are perfectly free to say I am like him in some ways. At least I trust I am no rotter, as he was no rotter.

With best wishes to you and Mrs Johnson[3] I am

Always your friend
Robert Frost

Send the books to Amherst Mass where I am now teaching for my meals.

[To Francis C. MacDonald. ALS. Princeton.]

Amherst Mass
January 24 1917

Dear Mr MacDonald:

I shall be leaving these parts for your general direction tomorrow. Just a word before cutting loose from my communications to assure you that I

2. William McKendree Carleton (1845–1912), popularly known as "Will"; Michigan-born author of many volumes of poetry and fiction, and a celebrated lecturer.

3. Constance Fuller Wheeler Johnson (1879–1955), author of several children's books.

have our arrangements well in mind and may be counted on to turn up in Princeton on the thirty-first—my complete works under my arm.[4]

I am looking forward to the pleasure of being with you.

Sincerely yours
Robert Frost

[To Charles Franc Goddard. A New York City lawyer, Goddard was a graduate of Columbia University and an occasional reviewer with a particular interest in Emerson and Thoreau. RF's birth records had been lost in the San Francisco earthquake of 1906, and for many years he believed he had been born in 1875 and not 1874. The letter is undated, but a postmarked envelope survives. ALS. UVA.]

Amherst Mass
[February 1, 1917]

Dear Mr Goddard:

Since I have no way of knowing that you are not in a hurry for the information you seek, I am going to give it to you now, though I shall have to be briefer with you than I should at another time when I wasnt on the point of departure on my travels as a lecturer. The fact is I am just this hour off for Princeton Philadelphia and Baltimore.

I agree with you that my theories are of much less importance than what I have written and when I wrote it. The "time when" is of first importance both in judging and in predicting.

---

4. RF read before the Freneau Club at Princeton on February 1. F. Scott Fitzgerald, then a student, was in attendance and penned the following double-limerick in response:

A rugged young rhymer named Frost
Once tried to be strong at all cost
The mote in his eye
May be barley or rye
But his right in that beauty is lost.
Though the meek shall inherit the land,
He prefers a tough bird in the hand,
He puts him in inns,
And feeds him on gins,
And the high brows say, "Isn't he grand?"

I was born in San Francisco in 1875. I wrote My Butterfly (A Boys Will) in 1893. You will find it in The Independent of 1894 or 1895 just about as I have reprinted it in my book. Now Close the Windows belongs to the same year. The others in the book string along over the years 1895 to 1910. My November Guest belongs to about 1900. So does October. To the Thawing Wind is later. Trial by Existance [*sic*] is an early one.

The Death of the Hired Man, The Black Cottage and The Housekeeper belong to 1905. Nearly all the others in North of Boston were written in England between 1911 and 1913.

What you ask for is soon told. Will you be good enough to ask again, if there is more? I shall be back here in Amherst next week.

Thanking you for your friendly interest and proud to have drawn it to the people of my books (May I ask you to like my Mountain Interval people too?) I am

Sincerely yours
Robert Frost

[To Helen Thomas. Three months later Edward Thomas was killed by an artillery shell at the Battle of Arras, on April 9. ALS/Photostat. DCL.]

Amherst Mass
February 6 1917

My dear Helen:

I am writing this to you because I think it may be the quickest way to reach Edward with questions I must have an answer to as soon as possible.

I have found a publisher for his poems in America.[5] But there are several things to be cleared up before we can go ahead.

Has Edward sold the 'world' rights to his English publisher or only the English rights? That is to say is he free to deal directly with an American publisher?

Dont you think he ought to throw off the pen-name and use his real name under the circumstances? Shall we make him? Tell him I insist.

---

5. Henry Holt and Company, RF's publisher, issued Thomas's *Poems* in 1917.

Would he object very much if I took it into my head at the publishers [*sic*] suggestion to write a little preface to the book to take the place of the dedication?[6]

I am not going to ask permission to take up with the offer of ten percent royalty. Any royalty is all right. The thing is to get the poems out where they may be read.

My hope is that Edward hasn't lost the right to let us set the book up over here.

I have just sold two or three of the poems to Harriet Monroe of Poetry, Chicago.[7] The money will have to come to me and so to you unless we decide at once to use real names.

Isn't this rather pleasant news for the soldier?—damn his eyes.

I am a teacher again for the moment and we are all here at Amherst, Mass, the town of my college.

I wonder if it would be too much trouble for Merfyn to write a pretty little note to Frederick Howe[8] Commissioner of Immigration Ellis Island New York to thank him for the glimpse he gave him of these United States and to tell him that he is safely back in his own country and promised as a soldier when his country shall want him? I have meant to ask Merfyn myself. I had a nice letter from him awhile ago.

I doubt if his country is going to need him. I suspect that all that is happening is some ingenuity of the Germans to bring the war to an early close without having to seem beaten. I don't know just what they are up to. I think, though, they are looking for a way to let go of the lions [*sic*] tail. I begin to think we shall be seeing you all again before long.

Always yours
Robert

---

6. Thomas dedicated the book to RF who, in fact, did not write a preface.

7. See RF to Monroe, January 9, 1917.

8. Frederic C. Howe (1867–1940), Ohio-born politician and, at the time this letter was written, commissioner of immigration for the Port of New York.

[To Louis Untermeyer, who identifies the "Girl with All Those Names" as Blanche Shoemaker Wagstaff (1888–1959), the American poet. At the time, Untermeyer was putting together the first of his many anthologies of modern American and British poetry. ALS. LoC.]

Amherst Mass
February 8 1917

Dear Louis:

The Girl with All Those Names got hers—and poetic justice is done—the eternal verities are verified. Now she can kiss anything she pleases.

You dont tell me, though!—I won't believe she writes poetry about kissing dead Adonis anywhere. Anywhere in America.

> Me art hakes Anna numness panes me cents.[9]

Go in and kill them all off with my love.

The latest thing in the schools is to know that you have nothing to say in the days of thy youth, but that those days may well be put in in learning how to say something 'gainst when the evil days draw near when thou shalt have something to say. Damn these separations of the form from the substance. I don't know how long I could stand them.

No Chicago this trip. The dates were too sprawling. At most three or four days were all I had a right to steal from the college.

Thumbs down to Mr Brown.[10] I dont seem to know who he would be unless he is the fellow who tried to pull my leg once by mentioning you. His poetry may be good, but I dont like his business methods.

Roedker (spell him!) is another story.[11] He was all round London knocking at preferment's door, but he kept within the decencies and I'm glad if you find one of his poems to like.

I'm going to have you out here before long to give us what for and see how we live.

---

9. Frostian Cockney for the opening lines of Keats's "Ode to a Nightingale": "My heart aches, and a drowsy numbness pains / My sense . . ." "Anna" may have been, given that RF capitalizes it, the first name of a poet he particularly disliked, perhaps Anna Hempstead Branch (1875–1937), whom Untermeyer anthologized.

10. Unidentified.

11. John Rodker (1894–1955), British writer and poet.

I aint so s'anguine[12] about the war as you are. I am getting ready to use it to advertise my last book. Goodbye—

R.F.

[To Albert Stanburough Cook (1853–1927), a scholar of Old and Middle English and a friend of William Ernest Hocking. ALS. Yale.]

Amherst Mass
February 13 1917

Dear Mr Cook:

I shall be glad to judge your boys' poetry according to the light that is given me.[13] You will notice that I write from Amherst where I am a professor for the time being with boys of my own to make poets of.

The Hockings are my very dear friends.[14] You remind me that it is overlong since I saw them last.

Sincerely yours
Robert Frost

[To John Bartlett. His wife had been diagnosed with tuberculosis. ALS. UVA.]

Amherst Mass
February 13 1917

Dear John:

You will have heard I am teaching again. I have to do something for the country once in so often even when it isn't at war.

---

12. The joke is a bit obscure, but the whimsical spelling "s'anguine" is genuine; "anguine" means (via its Latin root *anguis*) "of or resembling a snake or serpent" *(Oxford English Dictionary)*.

13. For a number of years Cook had awarded a prize for the best unpublished poem (or group of poems) written by a Yale student; the competition was open to all students enrolled at the university. In 1925, Cook made a bequest to Yale to ensure that the award (known as the Cook Prize) would survive him. Winner of the award in 1917, when RF served as judge, was "The Drug-Shop, or, Endymion in Edmonstoun," by Stephen Vincent Benét.

14. William Ernest Hocking and his wife, Agnes; see RF's April 3, 1915, letter to the Hockings.

And speaking of war, what kind of a trouble have you children got yourselves into? Didn't I tell you you would have to stick at nothing to get over these hard times? You have still your reserves—things you wont give up. But you'll have to give up everything for a little while. Those boys ought to go on a visit to one of their grandmothers. You can do a lot for them. But if you're the least like me, not enough to take them entirely off Margaret's mind. She's got to be relieved of them to get well. That's sure. She can't afford to be foolish for a moment, and neither can you. I have seen right in my own family one person lost by not taking instant and out-and-out measures[15] and another person saved by taking them. The business can go either way you want it to, but I'm afraid generally as most of us are entangled in life and obligations, it inclines to go the wrong way. Cut and run away from every care: that is the rule. Nothing else will do. No paltering. I saw the way my father fed his hopes on one concession after another. It was my first tragedy.

Sometime when you are near a bank will you cash this check and use it for any little thing for Margaret? You can pay it back to me when I am old and neglected, with interest at one tenth of one percent—or as much more as you like if I am very much neglected.

I mean to get up to see you, but I can hardly make it now. I am expected to stay on the job most of the time.

Tell me a lot about things.

Affectionately
Rob

[To Louis Untermeyer. Otto Tod Mallery (1881–1956) of Philadelphia had a distinguished career as a public works administrator, author, and philanthropist. A graduate of Princeton, he was active in his support of a broad range of cultural enterprises, among them, The Forge, *a short-lived literary journal that published Frost's "Locked Out" in February 1917. ALS. LoC.]*

Amherst Mass
February 13 1917

Dear Louis:

Would you want to let me have one of the best of your good poems to see how much I could get you for it from some friends of mine who are publishing

15. A reference to RF and Elinor's first child, Elliott, who died of cholera on July 8, 1900.

a magazine in Philadelphia. The magazine is mostly given up to themselves, all amateurs, but they think they want one poem a month by a professional poet so to speak to be to them for an example. The money they will give is not the whole point if it is any of it. They are good folks having a good time and I'm not sure that nothing will come of their venture. Masefield gave them their head poem for the first number.[16] I gave them one for the second. Will you come in for my sake their sake your own sake or Gods sake?

Yours for business
R.

[To Amy Lowell. ALS. Harvard.]

Amherst Mass
February 13 1917

Dear Miss Lowell

Would you want to let me have a good poem (not too long) to see how much I could get you for it from some friends of mine who are publishing a magazine in Philadelphia.[17] They do the magazine mostly themselves but they want to sort of set themselves a good example in the shape of one poem a number by the likes of you and me and Louis and not many more to lead off with. They are good folks—worth influenzing—they all seem to want the influenza. Will you give it to them?

I heard nothing but the best of you where I came after you at Princeton.[18]

Sincerely yours
Robert Frost

---

16. British poet John Masefield (1878–1967).
17. Again, *The Forge.*
18. See the note to RF's January 24, 1917 letter to MacDonald.

[To Amy Lowell. The letter is undated, but at top right "Feb. 1917 (after Feb. 14)" is written in pencil in another hand. ALS. Harvard.]

Amherst Mass
[mid-February 1917]

Dear Miss Lowell:

I liked both the poems—the Customer particularly well. She was a Customer to evoke all that color. You might have called her The Gray Customer for the sake of the contrast. But the contrast is all there between what she is and what she summons.

I should have written you sooner; but there has been some hitch in Philadelphia. My editorial friend of The Forge (his name is Otto Mallery) has dropped his job almost before taking it up, and I dont know what is happening to The Forge. The new editors ought to go ahead with Mallerys plan which was to have one poem a month by a writer of fame; but they may decide not to—I don't know them and so don't know what they are likely to do. I only asked for the poems as a friend of Mallery. I shall hear one way or another about these matters within a day or two.

I want you to know that I was elected a horficer of the Poetry Society without my knowledge or consent.[19] I think it best not to do anything to undo what has been done. Best let things slide. My being elected in such an irregular way does not make me of the party of those who elected me that I can see.

I am sorry Mrs Marks has gone to war with you.[20] What is the matter with her? She ought not to let herself be made unhappy by another person's success. Let's not be too hard on her. I understand she is seriously an invalid.

The sender of the valentine is another person. I suppose there is no hope of finding him. Someone who has seen your name in the papers, probably, and mixed you up in his mind with enemy politicians and ball-players. Your position is an exposed one at the head of a fighting movement in art. Forget

---

19. On February 8 RF was named vice-president of the New England Poetry Club in absentia, with Josephine Preston Peabody named president. Amy Lowell served as the first president of the Club, when it was founded in 1915.

20. Josephine Preston Peabody (Mrs. Lionel Marks) attacked free verse in an interview with Joyce Kilmer published in the *New York Times* on January 23, 1916. The headline: "Free Verse Hampers Poets and is Undemocratic," the sub-headline: "Nevertheless, the War is Making Poetry Less Exclusive and the Imagiste Cult Will Be Swept Away."

it all and write poetry. I shall have to send north for my picture.[21] How soon will be in time?

Your distinguished brother sent some hot shot into our quasi pacifism here yesterday when he spoke of some differences between countries that can only be cut through with the sword and when he told us that the League to Enforce Peace printed the word Enforce in red letters.[22] I have had a course of upwards of five lectures under him this year (that is to say since last June). I should think that many ought to count as a course shouldn't you?—especially since I liked them a whole lot.

Well I am

Sincerely yours
Robert Frost

[To Thomas Curtis Clark (1877–1953), an editor, anthologist, and poet. ALS. Indiana.]

Amherst Mass
February 16 1917

Dear Mr Clark:

Thank you for caring enough for my poems to want to show me some of yours.

Tonight I am more than commonly sympathetic with all the good fellows who are looking for some one to read what they write. It is a hard road to travel for them as I have reason to know. I wish I knew how to help them, but I have to confess I dont know how. They must just see it through themselves. The editors are not always good judges but they are the only judges we have—properly constituted judges. The only thing I could do for your poems would be to carry them to some editor and use my authority to urge them upon him. I can't do that because I have rather over drawn on my authority

---

21. To be used in Lowell's *Tendencies in Modern American Poetry* (1917). The now-famous photograph shows RF at work in his Morris chair, writing on a lap desk.

22. Abbott Lawrence Lowell (1856—1943), Amy Lowell's brother, was an educator and legal scholar who served as president of Harvard University from 1909 to 1933. In June 1915 a group of one hundred prominent Americans had founded the League to Enforce Peace and proposed an international accord in which participating nations would agree to use economic and military force against any member nation that went to war against another. Abbott Lowell was a member of the league's executive committee.

of late. I have been urging other people's poetry on the friendly publisher—poetry I happen to think very very highly of.

Sail in to the editors yourself. It won't hurt you if it takes you a few years to conquer them.

Sincerely yours
Robert Frost

[To Clement Wood (1888–1950), newspaper columnist, novelist, and poet. Born and raised in Alabama, Wood relocated to Greenwich Village in New York to pursue his literary career. He published numerous works of fiction and poetry, and was the anonymous author of fifty-seven books on various subjects in the Little Blue Book series. Wood's first book of poetry, Glad of Earth, *was published in 1917. ALS. Brown.]*

Amherst Mass
February 16 1917

Dear Clement Wood

Now what have I gone and forgotten and left undone that I ought to have done a year ago. I just have a vision of that Spoon River[23] as it stands on the book shelf of my closed house two hundred miles from here by rail and then seven by mountain highway. You wont ask me to go clear up there for it at a cost of ten dollars and two days time at the inside. I could offer to buy you another copy and I hereby do, but I know that what you want is your own copy with your own interesting notes in it. What shall I do but take my punishment in your diminished favor. I have sinned so far already as to have failed in your judgement with my play.[24] Let me sin much more and I shall expect never to succeed again in your judgement either in prose or verse.

I honestly am sorry. How shall I make it right with you. Propose anything and I will tell you frankly whether it lies in me to do it.

Sincerely yours
Robert Frost

I'm so utterly prostrated about having to be asked for the Masters book, that I forgot to say I should like to have your book.

R.F.

---

23. Edgar Lee Masters's *Spoon River Anthology*, which was often, to RF's chagrin, spoken of in connection with his own *NB*: both had been published in America in 1915 (though *NB* was previously issued in London in 1914).

24. *A Way Out*, published in the February 1917 number of the *Seven Arts*.

[To Louis Untermeyer. AL (RF neglected to sign the letter). LoC.]

Amherst Mass
Feb 20 [1917]

Dear Louis:

Vision of you whirling me terribly by the ankle round and round your head (never stopping to recover your derby which you have knocked off) as you advance to the demolition of our masters.[25] Hit' im with me! I suppose it mayn't do me as much good as it does him harm; but it has to be.

I forgot you. There is you to consider too. Will it do you any good? Or dont you care? I ought to be able to stand it if you are.

Clement Wood took an inclement little slap at me in a letter yestre'en. Nothing serious, only just as much as to say (unasked) you write poetry, Robbie Frost, and so do I, and just as you dont like all I write, so I don't like all you write—me publisher is Gomme.[26] He wood, Would he, claim equality with me? More claimant than clement. What are you going to do with him when his book is sent you for review? It is bound to be bad in any binding.

The magazine I begged a poem for is The Forge. Masefield set it going. Otto Mallory [*sic*], 1427 Spruce St, Philadelphia, edits it and I think it asks nothing of poets in general: it aims at a good time for a dozen or twenty people who intend to fill its pages themselves. They are none of them writers by profession and I believe they are none of them as yet jealous rivals of the likes of you and me. They are comfortable people to get along with. Where we come in is at my suggestion with one poem a number for them to emulate. They had already had a poem by Masefield and one by me when I made the suggestion. They have paid me too well for mine.[27] I can see something here that I dont see in some other ventures.

As I said on the envelope of my last, When is your book?[28]

Hoping to receive a copy I am,

I may say I am.

---

25. "Our masters": yet another play on Edgar Lee.

26. Laurence J. Gomme (New York) published Clement Wood's first book, *Glad of Earth*, in 1917.

27. RF's poem "Locked Out" (a poem he later added to the contents of *MI* in his 1930 *Collected Poems*) appeared first in *The Forge* in February 1917. For details, see RF's mid-February 1917 letter to Lowell.

28. *These Times* (New York: Henry Holt, 1917).

I mean—well never mind what I mean. Only I dont mean any play on the name of the Deity.[29]

[To Sidney Cox. ALS. DCL.]

Amherst Mass
March 3 1917

Dear Sidney Cox:

Dont you want to come out here and talk over some weekend. I've meant to look you up in New York but I been [*sic*] on nothing but the fly and the jump every time I've been through New York this winter. I'd write you a letter but that I've soured on letter writing for good and all.

Keep a stiff upper lip and maybe the Germans won't hurt you.

Where shall we loch Block?—I mean if we start interning. Things begin to look pretty internal for the stray Hun.[30]

Laugh and the world laughs with you.

---

29. Exodus 3:14: "And God said unto Moses, I AM THAT I AM: and he said, Thus shalt thou say unto the children of Israel, I AM hath sent me unto you."

30. Cox's friend Alex Bloch, a German teacher then in America. RF likely has in mind recent revelations concerning the so-called Zimmermann Telegram, sent in code by German Foreign Secretary Arthur Zimmermann to the German ambassador in Mexico on January 19, 1917; it inflamed anti-German (and anti-German-American) sentiment. British intelligence intercepted the telegram, decoded it, and made it available, in February, to the United States embassy in Berlin, whence it made its way to Washington. The telegram proposed that, in the event that the United States entered the war on the side of the Entente Powers, Mexico ally itself with Germany and make war on the United States to re-conquer territories lost in the Mexican-American War. On March 1, 1917, two days before RF wrote to Cox, the *New York Times* ran a sensational article on the matter, headlined: "WASHINGTON EXPOSES PLOT; Our Government Has Zimmermann's Note of Jan. 19. BIG PROMISES TO MEXICO Conquest of Texas, New Mexico, and Arizona Held Out as a Lure to Her." On March 3, 1917, Zimmerman publicly announced that the telegram was genuine (many had believed it a British forgery). A month later Wilson asked Congress for a declaration of war and got it. Many German-Americans (and German nationals in America) would soon be charged under the Espionage Act of June 1917 and, later, under the Sedition Act of 1918.

I'm now a third-rate authority on The Four PP, Gammer Gurton and such.[31]

Allers yourn,
Robert Frost

[To Harriet Moody (1857–1932), widow of the midwestern poet William Vaughn Moody (1869–1910). Telegram on Western Union stationery; handwritten beneath the message are dates and locations for the lectures RF was confirming: "Univ [of Chicago] Wed Mar. 14 / [Chicago] Woman's Club Thursday' 15." TG. Chicago.]

[Amherst, MA]
[March 7, 1917]

MRS WM VAUGHN MOODY
2970 ELLIS AVE CHGO

DATES ALL RIGHT SUBJECTS TECHNIQUE OF SINCERITY AND COMPOSING IN THINGS

ROBERT FROST

[To Louis Untermeyer. Dating supplied by Untermeyer, though it almost certainly reflects the date he received the letter. The book mentioned in closing is, again, Untermeyer's third volume of poetry, These Times *(1917). ALS. LoC.]*

[Amherst, MA]
[March 13, 1917]

Dear Louis:

Your Post review encourages me to think I ought to keep writing. You believe in me and I do too. I wonder if we are both wrong.

---

31. *The Four PP* by John Heywood (ca. 1497–ca. 1580) and *Gammer Gurton's Needle,* whose author is believed to have been William Stevenson (1530–1575). One of the three courses RF taught at Amherst in the spring 1917 semester dealt with pre-Shakespearean drama.

I may still go to Chicago. I am in fact promising to go this week—14th and 15th.[32] I last saw the city in 1885. Where were you in 1885?[33]

I dont know what I think of teaching again after once having put all that behind me.

War will settle many things in many a man's private affairs. That much may be safely said of it.

Waiting for your book, I am,

Yours while I wait
Robert

[To Amy Lowell. ALS. Harvard.]

Amherst Mass
March 18 1917

Dear Miss Lowell:

I will get after those Philadelphian friends at once.[34] They quite understand that the poems were not submitted to them for judgement but were conferred on them as a favor. The trouble with them is they are an amateur lot and are all mixed up in their editorship. They want the help we can give them, (they look on it I know as help) and they will be sorry to have you withdraw from them the light of your countenance. Really they are worth being good to, not for the publicity they can pretend to give us but just because they are good people and disposed to be seriously interested in new poetry. But I'll get after them.

My, but I have just been to Chicago! I got home this morning after five days of it. I'm working too hard for my limitations.

I didnt just mean that I had had a valentine this year, merely that I have had valentines in my time and lived to tell the tale. Damn the senders.

---

32. As his March 7, 1917, telegram to Moody indicates, RF did indeed lecture in Chicago—at the University of Chicago on March 14 (taking as his topic "The Technique of Sincerity"), and at the Chicago Women's Club on March 15 (on the topic "Composing in Things").

33. In 1885, RF passed through Chicago with his mother and sister Jeanie Florence; his father had died in San Francisco on May 5, and the family was en route to Lawrence, Massachusetts, to resettle, temporarily, with RF's paternal grandfather. As for Untermeyer in the spring of 1885: he was in utero (born on October 1 that year).

34. Otto Tod Mallery and the editors of *The Forge*.

A few days more at most and then bluebirds. I suppose winter doesnt matter to your poetry. I find it does to mine. I want spring and I wish I was far far from here a-farming.

Always yours sincerely
Robert Frost

[To Helen Hannah Herrick (Mrs. Harry S. Churchill) (1898–1977), the daughter of a Chicago schoolteacher. When this letter was written, Herrick was a member of the Eulexia Literary Society at Northwestern University. ALS. Private collection of Pat Alger.]

Amherst Mass
March 21 1917

My dear Miss Herrick:

I am glad to tell you what I know about myself. I was born in San Francisco forty-three years ago.[35] I came to New England after the death of my father in 1885. I went to school in Salem N.H. and in Lawrence Mass. I was at Dartmouth for a while and at Harvard for a longer while. I have no degrees but I am a member of Phi Beta Kappa, if you can read that riddle. I published poems in the New York Independent as early as 1894. Some of these have survived to reappear in book form lately. My first book A Boy's Will was published in England in 1913 and again here by Holt in 1915. My second book, North of Boston, was published in England in 1914 and again here by Holt in 1915. My third and latest book, Mountain Interval, was published here by Holt in 1916. I have never lived by writing (that is to say I am not a literary man), but rather by farming and when the farming went too hard, by teaching. I have taught in every kind of school from the primary up through grammar, high school normal school and college. I am teaching for six months now at Amherst College. I have read in public a good deal lately. I read and talked on such matters as "Technique and Sincerity" and "Composing in Things" in Chicago this month. And I think that is all, except to say that I was a farmer ten years, which is longer than I have been anything else without interruption.

---

35. In 1874, not, as he believed at this date, in 1875; his biographer (Lawrance Thompson) discovered the error in the late 1930s (records had been destroyed in the 1906 San Francisco earthquake and fire).

The Review of Reviews for May 1915 and The Atlantic for August 1915 had important articles about my work.[36]

My best book, if I may be allowed to express a preference, is Mountain Interval.

Sincerely yours
Robert Frost

[To Harriet Monroe. ALS. Chicago.]

Amherst Mass
March 24 1917

Dear Miss Monroe:

I'm not so much ashamed of having kept this too long as of having kept it too long to no purpose. I don't really feel as if I had got anywhere with it even helped as I have been by wifely counsel. There's stir in the poem of the Poundian kind and I can't say that I don't like it. But it leaves me partly baffled. I suppose that is the Sordello of it: I grant him the Sordello form. I suppose the meaning is meant just to elude you going out as you come in. That kind of meaning that won't pin down is one of the resources of poetry, or so I have always held. I could name poems I love for it. And yet, and yet—

You're not asking me whether you ought to publish it, are you?[37] All you want is my impression of the poem as a poem and not as a magazine availability. I'm weak on the availabilities. I more than half like the poem: I trust I make that clear. I'd be half inclined to publish it and let the public be

---

36. Sylvester Baxter's "New England's New Poet" had appeared in the *Review of Reviews* in April (not May) 1915. Edward Garnett's "A New American Poet" appeared in *The Atlantic Monthly* in August of the same year.

37. Monroe published Ezra Pound's "Three Cantos" in the June and July 1917 issues of *Poetry*. RF has the phrasing of the first of these in mind (Robert Browning's "Sordello" appeared in 1840):

> *Hang it all, there can be but one* Sordello!
> *But say I want to, say I take your whole bag of tricks,*
> *Let in your quirks and tweeks, and say the thing's an art-form,*
> *Your* Sordello, *and that the modern world*
> *Needs such a rag-bag to stuff all its thought in . . .*

damned. Them's my sentiments. But you know better than I just how well your magazine can stand the strain.

Asking your forgiveness for the time I have taken for this little result I'm

Always sincerely yours
Robert Frost

Get better but don't get out. March air is good to keep in out of.

[To Ellen Knowles Eayres, a secretary at Henry Holt and Company, and an acquaintance of RF's daughter Lesley. She later married Alfred Harcourt. ALS. Princeton.]

Amherst Mass
March 24 1917

Dear Miss Eayre [*sic*]:

Thank you for taking all the trouble all those separate books must have been. A certain proportion of them will be sure to get through the barred zone sent that way. I hope it won't be the worst of them.[38] I may ask you to send one or two more (including my own autographed) as I think of them.

Sincerely yours
Robert Frost

[To Louis Untermeyer. RF refers to Untermeyer's third volume of poetry, These Times *(1917). ALS. LoC.]*

Amherst March 28
[1917]

Dear Louis:

Everywhere I dip into the book, pleasure—and no uncertain pleasure such as tortures me in the reading of most books lately. The book came on

38. RF refers (ironically) to the so-called "Barred Zone" act of February 5, 1917 (H.R. 10384), passed over President Wilson's veto. Formally known as the Immigration Act of 1917, the measure banned immigration into the United States of what it termed "all idiots, imbeciles, feeble-minded persons, epileptics, insane persons; persons who have had one or more attacks of insanity at any time previously; persons of constitutional psychopathic inferiority; persons with chronic alcoholism; paupers; professional beggars; vagrants," etc.

my birthday which was not observed as a holiday in this state: I had to work just as on any other day and so I have had no time for more than dipping. But I can see it's a full-flavored book as delightful as self-indulgence. It's still all before me. I have something special to live for for a week or two.

The preface is another thing.[39] That is brilliant. You ought not to do any more journalism and I only let you go on doing it because you represent the cause so well at the front: we need you to fight for us: I dont know what we should do if you dropped out of the fighting line. But you really ought to be let off for more important prose, not to mention your poetry at all.

I'm not very angry with you for what you did to Breathweight.[40] Only I wonder if he's worth your pains. Perhaps he is. We are taught that we must try not to look down on anyone.

I'm going home for a few days to see how the house is coming on for next year. I'll take your book in my bag. The next one will be waiting for me here when I get back I suppose.

Both of them are going to have a go, I predict. You're going to stand out more and more. I see you loom!

But whether you loomed more or less, came or went, I believe I should continue

Yours always
Robert

I must see about those poems. They'll want one of them down there in Philadelphia. But there's some hitch about the magazine; The Forge it's called. I'll get after Mallory [*sic*].[41]

R

39. *These Times* contains no preface. RF may allude to "The New Spirit in American Poetry," issued first as a pamphlet by Henry Holt and Company (1916) and later incorporated into Untermeyer's 1919 volume *The New Era in American Poetry* (New York: Henry Holt).

40. Poet, critic, and anthologist William Stanley Braithwaite.

41. See RF's February 13, 1917, letter to Untermeyer.

[To Louis Untermeyer, who supplied the dating. Untermeyer dedicated his 1917 volume These Times *to "Robert Frost / Poet and Person." ALS. LoC.]*

[Amherst, MA]
[April 1, 1917]

Dear Louis

I'm sick as hell of this Stark Young imbroglio[42] and I'm thinking of going out and getting shot where it will do some good. Before I do anything so desperate, however, I'd like to take a run down to you for a little talk with you on what kind of a book it is you have been dedicating to me. It's all full of lovely things in a strong clear sound. Erskine was welcome to praise you with all the praises.[43] But you know in your heart that I like you better than he does and with better understanding. Therefore you didnt let him get you away from me. You dedicated your book to me instead of to him. And I take it that by dedicating it to me as a poet (who know another poet when I see one) and in addition to that as a person, you meant that long after I cease to be a poet you will be sticking to me as a person and a personal friend. This poetry ain't all there is between us, is it now? Because if it is I shall surely not be dissuaded from going out as aforesaid and getting shot where it will do some good.

I am going to take Elinor and get down to see you next week probably, but if not next week then the week after.[44] Till then suffer with me in what I have got into. It is the incredibility of it!

But never mind me.

R.

---

42. See *YT,* 105–106. See also Jay Parini, *Robert Frost: A Life* (New York: Henry Holt, 1999): 185–186. When a student of RF's reported that Young (RF's colleague) had made unwelcome sexual advances toward him, RF brought the matter to President Meiklejohn's attention. RF was infuriated when the administration took no action, and his anger abided.

43. John Erskine (1879–1951), professor of English at Columbia University. His laudatory review of Untermeyer's 1914 volume, *Challenge,* was used in advertising *These Times.*

44. The visit came after RF read, on May 18, before the Elizabethan Club at Yale University.

[To Henry Seidel Canby (1878–1961), editor, critic, and professor of English at Yale; he helped found, along with William Rose Benét, the Saturday Review of Literature. *ALS. Yale.]*

Amherst Mass
April 5 1917

Dear Mr. Canby:

I ought to be glad of the chance of getting in a word for Davies in The Yale Review where it will do some good.[45] But I have about determined not to be drawn into the field of special criticism for a good many years yet if ever. So it is just a question of refusing your offer politely enough. I hope you will understand. And I hope you will find someone to write Davies' praises in the same measure I would use. The English may overrate him somewhat, but I think Americans underrate him more. Why not hand him over to Louis Untermeyer to see how he will deal with him?

Sincerely yours
Robert Frost

[To Alfred Harcourt. ALS. Princeton.]

Amherst Mass
April 20 1917

Dear Alfred:

Thank you for letting me know where you have gone to with all my money. I am counting on that money to keep me while I write another poem. I dont know why I should want to write another poem except that I have always planned to and there seems to be a demand for such a thing especially if it could turn out a war poem.

So don't let me lose track of you till I have got the poem written anyway.

Sounds sad—sounds like the last of me, doesn't it? Well it's about the last of all of us—the way things are going. This college is melting away under us (let 'er melt); you say your business is pickéd;[46] and there's certainly something nightmarish in the elasticity of a modern battle line by which you can

45. Welsh poet W. H. Davies (1871–1940).

46. Scottish dialect: meager. On April 6, President Wilson had asked for, and received, a declaration of war.

push into it as far as you like almost anywhere but you cant push through it or pinch ahold of it.

The great question is what shall the poem be about, since there is only to be one more. But we can talk that over the last time I come to see you in a few weeks. We may as well have it about something elementary or do I mean elemental or what do I mean? Suppose we call it Vale and then enlist either in the Potato Army or in the Ship Building Army like these blooded young heroes of the College and leave it to vain-glorious hot-heads to throw themselves away in battle. It seems so immodest to set up to be a hero.

Franconia beckons to us. We have had enough of Stark Young's stark disingenuousness. Welcome the wilderness where no one comes or has come except in an expensive touring car. Sun-treader (as Browning says) there are a lot of good things I believe in, but for the life of me I can't always enumerate them at a moments notice.[47]

The best of misunderstanding anyone is that it sort of disposes of him and clears your mind of him and so leaves you with one less detail in life to be bothered with. Of course it is the same with understanding. Of what use is either misunderstanding or understanding unless it simplifies by taking away from the sum and burden of what you have to consider? There are a hundred odd poets in a new anthology for example; I get rid of one half of them by understanding of the other half by misunderstanding—and the danger of my mind's being overcrowded with poets of my poor brain's being congested with 'em is passed. What a thing misunderstanding is. I sing misunderstanding.

Always yours
Robert Frost

47. See Browning's "Pauline: A Fragment of a Confession," in which the poet Shelley figures under the epithet "Sun-treader": "Sun-treader, I believe in God, and truth, / And love," etc.

[To Louis Untermeyer. "Amerced" is RF's whimsical way of spelling the name as pronounced by locals in Amherst. Otto Tod Mallery founded the very short-lived magazine The Forge, *for which RF had solicited poems from Untermeyer and Amy Lowell. See RF's February 13, 1917, letter to Untermeyer. ALS. LoC.]*

Amerced 4/22 17

Dear Louis:

This is the upshot of my little action between friends. I thought I was going to give you more money for your poems than most editors give and I thought I was going to give The Forge some real poetry. I guess I was intended by nature to mind my own business. Mallory's [*sic*] letter explains itself with the help of the one touch I've given it with the pen. Will you read it in my exhonoration[48] and then return it so that I can send it to Amy. I don't know when I have done as much mischief where my intentions were so good. You may forgive me, but Amy never!

Why, I'm utterly glad of Erskine's admiration for your work and I was only being jealous not of you but of him for what he said of you. I was pretending to think that I was in danger of losing you because somebody had got ahead of me in praising you. I was melancholy when I wrote and disposed to play with sad things. I'm still melancholy. He may be stark young but I'll say this if he was much stark younger I should go stark crazy before I got back to my sidehill. He has spoiled everything here that the coming of the war hasn't spoiled. And he's so foxy about it. He walks up close to me on the street and passes candy from his pockets to mine like a collier passing coal to a warship at sea. It makes everybody think that he must say with sorrow everything he says against me when he loves me so much in spite of all. But it will make a melodrama.[49]

When I have time I mean to make you my particular list of your poems.

Dont mind your Clement Wood[50] and I won't mind Stark Young. You did him more than justice.

Never again will I write you so troublous a letter as this—not though I live ten lives of mortal men.

Always yours
Robert Frost

---

48. The whimsical spelling is deliberate.

49. For Stark Young, see RF to Untermeyer, April 1, 1917.

50. See RF to Untermeyer, February 20, 1917.

[To John Bartlett. ALS. UVA.]

Amherst
April 25 [1917]

Dear John:

It seems to me the best thing might be for you to go west and see what you could find to do out there. Part-time work if you could find it would be the idea. You must save as much as you can of yourself for the writing; because the writing is going to be the whole thing with you sooner or later—I have no doubt sooner. For the present though and to shake off these family troubles, which may have a good deal to do with keeping you down in health, I should see what I could do with a limited regular job under favorable climatic conditions. I should want it to be for short hours so that you could give one hour a day to writing. And I should make the one hour a hard and fast rule. You can do a lot in an hour if you come to it with your thoughts already somewhat shaped—and you can even if your thoughts aren't shaped. I should hold myself in a while for health's sake. You've got to tighten up on your follies no matter how amiable or admirable they may be.

This is the advice you ask for. I should know better what to tell you to do with yourself if I were surer what I ought to do with myself in the present crisis.

To put it in few words, my program for you would be five hours work a day for small pay and one hour's writing in some part of the country where you will breathe easier.[51]

Your mother's letter does not please me, though no doubt she means well. She appears willing that you should die for your father and mother and sister and brother, but glad that your asthma keeps you from dying for your country. Your situation becomes ignominious. You must win your independence, I feel sure, before you can hope to get well for good.

This is a funny world.

Affectionately
Rob

---

51. The Bartletts soon moved to Colorado over the opposition of John's mother.

[To Helen Thomas. Her husband, Edward Thomas, had been killed in action during the Battle of Arras on April 9. ALS/Photostat. DCL.]

Amherst Mass
April 27 1917

Dear Helen:

People have been praised for self-possession in danger. I have heard Edward doubt if he was as brave as the bravest. But who was ever so completely himself right up to the verge of destruction, so sure of his thought, so sure of his word? He was the bravest and best and dearest man you and I have ever known. I knew from the moment when I first met him at his unhappiest that he would some day clear his mind and save his life. I have had four wonderful years with him. I know he has done this all for you: he is all yours. But you must let me cry my cry for him as if he were <u>almost</u> all mine too.

Of the three ways out of here, by death where there is no choice, by death where there is a noble choice, and by death where there is a choice not so noble, he found the greatest way. There is no regret—nothing that I will call a regret. Only I can't help wishing he could have saved his life without so wholly losing it and come back from France not too much hurt to enjoy our pride in him. I want to see him to tell him something. I want to tell him, what I think he liked to hear from me, that he was a poet. I want to tell him that I love those he loved and hate those he hated. (But the hating will wait: there will be a time for hate.[52]) I had meant to talk endlessly with him still, either here in our mountains as we had said or, as I found my longing was more and more, there at Leddington where we first talked of war.

It was beautiful as he did it. And I don't suppose there is anything for us to do to show our admiration but to love him forever.

Robert

Other things for other letters.

---

52. Ecclesiastes 3:8: "A time to love, and a time to hate; a time of war, and a time of peace."

[To John W. Haines. Text derived from SL, 216; see the notes to RF's first (June 1914) letter to Haines (page 200).]

Amherst Mass
April 27 1917

Dear Jack

I haven't written for a long time because there was nothing to write except that I was sick at heart.[53] There is nothing to write now except that Edward Thomas was killed at Arras on Easter Monday which is no more than you already knew. But what are we going to do about it? I wish I could see you.

Robert

[To Cornelius Weygandt. ALS. DCL.]

Amherst Mass
April 29 1917

Dear Weygandt:

Edward Thomas was killed by a shell at Arras on Easter Monday—if I can make you know how much that means to me. I'm glad you liked so much of his poetry. I had just been telling him about your letter in a letter he will never see.

This is the story of that man: he twice refused to be diverted from destruction, once when he was offered the chance to stay at home and teach map drawing, and once not many days before he died when he was offered a place on some officers staff, was in fact summoned to it and went and then begged off to go back to his gun. The last I heard of him he was firing his gun (a big one) four hundred times a day. He must have been going in to the thick of it then. He was as brave as the best of them. And he wasn't in love with death. He went to death because he didn't like going. I meant to have you know him.

Always yours
Robert Frost

---

53. Haines replied on May 15: "I also am sick at heart. Directly I heard the news I wrote to you at once to Franconia telling you of my last meeting with him [Thomas] a few nights before he sailed for France. I fear you may not have had the letter; let me know. He had largely taken your place with Dollie [Haines's wife, Dorothy] and me & we had come to base all our arrangements on the thought of his comings and goings" (letter held at DCL).

[To Edward Garnett. AL (unsigned). HRC.]

Amherst Mass
April 29 1917

Dear Mr Garnett:

Edward Thomas was the only brother I ever had. I fail to see how we can have been so much to each other, he an Englishman and I an American and our first meeting put off till we were both in middle life. I hadn't a plan for the future that didn't include him.

You must like his poetry as well as I do and do everything you can for it. His last word to me, his "pen ultimate word," as he called it, was that what he cared most for was the name of poet. His poetry is so very brave—so unconsciously brave. He didn't think of it for a moment as war poetry, though that is what it is. It ought to be called Roads to France. "Now all roads lead to France, and heavy is the tread of the living, but the dead, returning, lightly dance," he says.[54] He was so impurturbably [*sic*] the poet through everything to the end. If there is any merit in self possession, I can say I never saw anyone less put off himself by unaccustomed danger, less put off his game. His concern to the last was what it had always been, to touch earthly things and come as near them in words as words could come.

Do what you can for him and never mind me for the present. I sent you a copy of Mountain Interval, but perhaps it is as well you didnt get it for your review if you were not going to be pleased with it. I can hear Edward Thomas saying in defense of In the Home Stretch that it would cut just as it is into a dozen or more of your Chinese impressionistic poems and perhaps gain something by the cutting for the reader whose taste has been formed on the kiln-dried tabule[55] poetry of your Pounds and Masterses. I look on theirs as synthetical chemical products put together after a formula. It's too long a story to go into with any one I'm not sure it wouldn't bore. There's something in the living sentence (in the shape of it) that is more important than any phrasing or chosen word. And it's something you can only achieve when going free. The Hill Wife ought to be some sort of answer to you. It is just as much one poem as the other but more articulated so to speak. It shows its

54. RF quotes Thomas's poem "Roads."

55. Flat and compressed, as is a tablet. "In the Home Stretch" is a narrative poem in blank verse, rather like those collected in *NB*.

parts and it shows that they may be taken by themselves as poems of fashionable length.[56]

[To Louis Untermeyer. ALS. LoC.]

Amherst
May 7 [1917]

Dear Louis

Just two words to ask you if you can't stay a day or two with us. Everything has gone to pieces with the coming of the war or I should arrange about the lecture. The boys are pretty well gone glimmering a gun.

Say you'll stay.

R.

Trust you dont see too much in Davies.[57] He's overrated.

[To Myrtle Blanch Raitt (Mrs. Harold W. Hollis) (1898–1935), who lived in Derry, New Hampshire, during the years RF taught at Pinkerton. Although too young to have had RF as a teacher, she would have been acquainted with him through her brother Vernon (1887–1972), eleven years her senior, who played on the Pinkerton football team. RF enclosed with this letter a fair copy manuscript of the poem "Forest Flowers," which was published in the Pinkerton Annual *for 1917; very likely Raitt had requested the poem for the* Annual*; she would have been a senior at Pinkerton at the time. The poem is reprinted in* CPPP *(533). ALS. UNH.]*

Amherst Mass
May 15 1917

Dear Miss Raitt:

It is kind of you to be thinking of me when I am so long gone from good old Pinkerton. I hope I am in time with what you want and I hope it <u>is</u> what you want.

Remember me to your folks at home and if Vernon is where you see him tell him I haven't forgotten the days when we played ball together and hope he hasn't.

Sincerely yours
Robert Frost

---

56. "The Hill Wife" (collected in *MI*) is a suite of five lyric poems.

57. W. H. Davies. See RF's April 5, 1917, letter to Canby.

[To Hermann Hagedorn (1882–1964), American poet and popular biographer of Theodore Roosevelt. Hagedorn was a firm and early supporter of the American war effort, even to the point of arguing, in 1917, for the wartime suppression of the German-language press in the United States. ALS. BU.]

Amherst Mass
May 24 1917

My dear Hermann Hagedorn:

This third call to war-song is the most irresistible of all, being a war-song itself, and a better one than I thought could be written for an occasion. I suspect that not all your Vigilantes collaborated in the work however: it would have had to come to splitting words and doing a syllable apiece for all of you to have had a hand in it. You wrote the whole thing alone and it is an inspired bit. Almost thou persuadest me to be a Tyrtaean. (Why didn't you call yourselves The Tyrtaeans?[58]) But I know too well how calling myself anything is likely to scare everything out of me. I'm of no earthly use except to write about a stray cow or collar now and then when I'm least expecting to. If you let me alone and don't look at me and even neglect me a little shamefully theres a bare possibility that I might happen to write a poem about the war or not unconnected with the war before the war is all over. If I do write one, you shall have it in friendship. But I sha'n't write it if I'm billed to write it. So don't bill me, will you?

This is deplorable I know, but have mercy upon me: don't blame me too much.

Sincerely a friend of your cause
Robert Frost

58. Tyrtaeus was a Greek poet of the seventh century BCE; he often wrote on martial themes. Hagedorn had organized "The Vigilantes," a group of writers agitating for the United States' entry into the war. They published a patriotic anthology of war poetry titled *Fifes and Drums: A Collection of Poems of Americans at War* (New York: George H. Doran, 1917). The volume bore a prefatory poem by Hagedorn, with the refrain, "Surely the time for making songs has come" (to which RF refers in opening the letter).

[To Amy Lowell. Lowell's home was in Brookline, Massachusetts. ALS. Harvard.]

Amerced Mass
May 24 1917

Dear Miss Lowell:

All thanks for letting me off so easily on the poems. I deserved no mercy for having got you in for The Forge. I don't like those Philadelphians any more. I wonder who they think they are.

I don't think Mallery brought out a number of The Forge after he got the poems.[59] If he did he lied to me.

"A far hour shall wreak
And pile on human heads the mountain of my curse!
That curse shall be Forgiveness."[60]

I sent you my picture twice over and leave you to take your choice or order me to the barber's and then the photographer's for another still. We Frosts like the haggard-just-out-of-bed-at-ten-o clock in-the-morning-looking face-simile best.[61]

Oh I don't know about teaching after all. When I am fifty, say—ten years from now—when the war is over. I want to write a few things first if I can only happen to.

As for you I suppose you go write on righting all the time. I envy but don't blame you.

Some day before another winter I ought to look in on you at Brookline.

Always your friend
R.F.

---

59. Otto Tod Mallery. See RF's February 13, 1917, letters to Untermeyer and to Lowell, together with the mid-February letter to Lowell that succeeds them.

60. RF quotes with some accuracy from Canto IV, stanzas CXXXIV and CXXXV, of Byron's *Childe Harold's Pilgrimage.*

Not in the air shall these my words disperse,
Though I be ashes; a far hour shall wreak
The deep prophetic fulness of this verse,
And pile on human heads the mountain of my curse!

CXXXV
That curse shall be Forgiveness.

61. Another reference to Lowell's request for a photograph to be used in her *Tendencies in Modern American Poetry.*

[To Henry Meigs. ALS. Yale.]

Amherst Mass
May 24 1917

Dear Mr Meigs:

It is good to see your handwriting again (though I find it a hard one to decipher.)

You hadn't heard that I had been professing English at Amherst College for a while or you wouldn't have wondered why I hadn't been writing much lately. I've been up to my ears in the work of other writers, young hopefuls that don't really give me much hope. Its only for the rest of this term now, and then I shall be getting back to my New Hampshire farm.

You always put your finger on the poems I like to have you like—and on the phrases too. You know whats very especially mine in a thing like "Not to Keep."[62] Miss Monroe dealt fairly intelligently with me, but there is something in Putting in the Seed you wouldnt expect her to see. Not many people get the drift of Christmas Trees.[63] They take it as sentimental when it is altogether practical in spirit.

You dont know how much I thank you for your understanding. I should be better in telling you by word of mouth than I am in letters. I hope some time to meet you. You will come east some day or I shall get west. You must do your part to keep up the friendship by letter till we do meet. You must do your part and some of my part too. I'm a bad letter-writer: I've been spoiled by having so many business letters to write in the last two years.

You have missed none of my poems. "Not to Keep" is the only one of recent composition that didn't get into Mountain Interval. There'll be more soon I hope and you hope—we both hope.

Always your friend
Robert Frost.

---

62. Published in *The Yale Review* for January 1917.

63. RF collected "Putting in the Seed" and "Christmas Trees" in *MI*; "Not to Keep" he held over for *NH*. In an article published in *Poetry* in January 1917 under the title "Frost and Masters," Harriet Monroe had written (quoting a phrase from "Putting in the Seed"): "And 'a springtime passion for the earth,' with human life—yes, and brute life—as a part of it, burns in such poems as *In the Home Stretch, Putting in the Seed, Birches,* and *The Cow in Apple Time.*"

[To Edward Bliss Reed (1872–1940), professor of English at Yale; poet (author of Sea Moods and Other Poems *[Yale, 1917]); editor and scholar of Shakespeare; and member of the Elizabethan Club at Yale, before which RF gave a reading on Friday May 18, 1917, an event alluded to at the end of the following letter. ALS. Yale.]*

Amherst Mass
May 24 1917

Dear Mr Reed:

I'll tell you what I always do when the gunners are out for minor poets: I always try to act as if I myself wasn't a minor poet. I try to look like a stump or like a fence post buttoned to three strands of barbed wire.

But truthfully, I wasn't aware of having aimed anything at the minor poets. It is not like me to want to make anyone sorrowful. I think you would say so on better acquaintance. I have been too often sorrowful myself.

The Boston Transcript for May 12th had an interesting note on Edward Thomas.

I shall send the poems along just as soon as I can have copies of them made. They are beautiful poems I know you will say. Edward Thomas was more beautiful than the poems.

It was good-natured of you fellows to let me have it all my own way the other night and I sha'n't forget it.

Sincerely yours
Robert Frost

[To Katharine Lee Bates. Earlier in 1917, on April 13, RF had spoken at Wellesley at the invitation of Bates. In opening, RF speaks of the New England Poetry Club, founded in 1915. ALS. Wellesley.]

Amherst Mass
June 13 1917

Dear Miss Bates

I have just learned by accident that the meeting of the Poetry Society was last Saturday! And I had thought all the time it was to be next Saturday. How did I make such a mistake and how will you ever forgive me unless I make you realize how sick we have all been and how confused in mind we have had good reason for being. Five out of six of us have been sick in bed. Can I make amends by offering to come and talk to one of your classes next year or will that only be making a bad matter worse?

Yours abjectly
Robert Frost

[To Harriet Monroe. ALS. Chicago.]

Franconia N.H.
June 15 1917

Dear Miss Monroe:

I always think of you as a champion of the cause of poetry with a little no less than with a big P. Do you think it doesn't need anyone to champion it against the sort of "literature" I enclose?[64] Am I over-solicitous for it in thinking it does? Duty, philanthropy, propaganda! If it doesnt make you boil, send it back please with a few soothing words and I will see what I can do to stop boiling myself. I wish I knew what we were coming to, so as to know what to wear for the occasion. I don't care as long as I'm dressed for it.

Always faithfully yours
Robert Frost

[To Louis Untermeyer. The editors of the Masses, *of which Untermeyer was one, had been indicted on two counts, owing to their opposition to U.S. involvement in the war (conspiracy to effect insubordination in the armed forces, and conspiracy to obstruct enlistment). The affair ended in a mistrial; a second effort to prosecute the staff also failed. The Pennsylvania judge is likely RF's friend Robert von Moschzisker. ALS. LoC.]*

Franconia Once More
July 15 1917

Dear Louis

I do hope they will take a good look and see how practically out of that crowd you are before they decide to do anything harsh that will simply drop

64. The enclosure has not survived.

you back into it for good and all. This without prejudice to the crowd.[65] But you know how it is when anything is climbing up a wall out of anywhere: the best thing to do is to let him alone: you touch him with a finger to help him or boost him and all he does is let go and flop back down into whatever it was he was climbing out of and drying off from to have it all to do over again if he doesnt land feet up and die of discouragement.

I feel that this is a critical moment with you. You need expert watching. If the Postmaster General[66] jugs you and starts despitefully using you I am coming down to N.Y. as a sort of lay lawyer to defend you as Thoreau offered to defend John Brown.[67] I can say things for you that you will be too cusséd to say for yourself. And they will be truer things than you would say yourself. That is the mischief. Say go ahead and let them lock you up. I'd like to see if I wouldnt be rather eloquent in such a situation. Your youth, your genius, your only child, your only wife, your sincerity that would rather be right and appear wrong than appear right and be wrong or even than appear right and be right, what you said you would do if Teddy went over with an army[68]—why with such a chance I'll bet you another five cents I could wring tears from yourself to hear yourself described, make you fall forward in the prisoners box and weep on the ballustrade. (You see I am familiar with court proceedings, having recently sat with the judge of the Criminal Court of Pennsylvania at the trial of a—well, Braithwaite, if you will pardon the euphemism for stealing twelve dominicks.[69])

Not to make too light of what may be proving a serious matter, let me beg of you to be good at your age before the evil days draw nigh, and let who will be clever. You can discuss with the children the difference between formal liberty, which is a state structure like the Parthenon in all parts consistent with itself, and scott-free impulse which is nothing but what everything

---

65. Max Eastman, Floyd Dell, and Art Young, also on the editorial staff.

66. Albert Sidney Burleson (1863–1937), infamous for having segregated the U.S. postal service, for having fired African American postal workers in the South, and for his vigorous enforcement of the 1917 Espionage Act under the auspices of which the editorial staff of *The Masses* was prosecuted.

67. Thoreau delivered "A Plea for Captain John Brown" to audiences in Concord, Boston, and Worcester, Massachusetts, between October 3 and November 3, 1859.

68. Theodore Roosevelt attempted to raise a volunteer infantry division when the United States entered the war in April; Woodrow Wilson blocked the effort.

69. The Dominick (variant spelling of Dominique) is a breed of chickens.

comes from and everything is built out of when it cools off a little and hardens enough for the builders to cut and handle it. Eloquent! My stars!

We'll do as Elinor says in her letter unless you insist on something else.

Always yours
R.F.

[To Nelson Carry Haskell, a physician practicing, at the time, at 50 Main Street in Amherst, Massachusetts. ALS. BU.]

Franconia N.H.
July 19 1917

Dear Dr Haskell:

By an unfortunate mistake in arithmetic I have been led to overdraw my account in the Amherst bank and the bank has most courteously notified me of the fact and at one and the same time refused payment on my checks. The check I sent you is just outside the limit of my deposit with them and so may not have been honored. If so this is to make [it] easy for you to tell me. I shall be glad to write you another on a bank that would trust me for the amount I owe you even if I had no money on deposit in it.

Sincerely yours
Robert Frost

[To Wilbur Rowell. ALS. UVA.]

Franconia N.H.
July 31 1917

Dear Mr Rowell:

The check found the mark all right on the second trial. Thank you. No one was inconvenienced.

You may be interested to know that at this point the annuity begins to pay for my eldest daughter's education at college.[70] So far you have seen us.

Sincerely yours
Robert Frost

70. RF's eldest child, Lesley, entered Wellesley College in the fall of 1917.

[To Otto Manthey-Zorn (1879–1964), American scholar and educator; professor of German at Amherst. ALS. ACL.]

Franconia NH.
August 4 1917

Dear Zorn:

Time flies and the pollen flies and at this rate it will be hay fever time before I find you a possible refuge I can recommend. My old friends the Lynches[71] won't do because it turns out that they are all overrun with barkers or strippers or peelers or whatever it is they call the fellows that skin the spruce for pulping. I find that you can get board the three of you for from thirty to thirty eight dollars a week at some of the smaller hotels which are pleasanter this year than usual because they are less than usually crowded. But I dont want you to go to any of those till I learn whether you couldn't have a little furnished house I know of in the village in a side street under the mountain not far from the Gale river and not too far from us. It's the place for you and you can have it if it isn't sold. I shall know definitely if it isn't within a day or two. So will you hold on till I write again?

We came in for our share of the continental roast—touched ninety-one in the shade.[72] But from now on nothing but cool or cold at these altitudes. You have to come with a fair amount of clothes for comfort.

The kids will take a proprietary pleasure in showing Billy up our five thousand foot mountain.[73]

We have just been to the hospital with a case of tonsils and adenoids. Did Billy pull through without surgery?

I assume unless you state the contrary (whatever the contrary is) that your hay fever doesn't set in till 2 P.M. August 15th. It's heresy or bad form or lese majesty or treason or abnormal or something other than hay fever if it doesnt have a regular day and hour for starting off with a sneeze.

Best wishes from us six to you three.

Always yours friendly
R Frost.

---

71. John and Margaret Lynch owned a farm in Bethlehem, New Hampshire.

72. In July and August of 1917 a severe heat wave swept east out of the Midwest, where record high temperatures had been recorded; scores of people died.

73. Billy was Manthey-Zorn's son. Mt. Lafayette, in the White Mountains, and not far from Franconia, rises to 5,249 feet.

[To James Ormsbee Chapin (1887–1975), American painter and illustrator. The letter is dated to 1917 by the contextual evidence of subsequent letters to Chapin. ALS. DCL.]

Franconia
August 6 [1917]

Dear Mr Chapin:

We have been on the look-out for you for some time. Come when you can. You'll see plenty of outdoors. I want you to see some of the indoors too. I suppose you know how you are going to manage it.

With best wishes
Robert Frost

[To Harriet Moody, widow of the poet William Vaughan Moody (mentioned toward the end of the letter). Although she resided in Chicago, Moody maintained an apartment in New York and a farm in West Cummington, Massachusetts, some thirty miles from Amherst. ALS. Chicago.]

Franconia N.H.
August 12 1917

Dear Mrs Moody:

Unless I put off writing awhile longer I can no longer conceal from you that when you are in West Cummington and we are in Franconia the distance that separates us is almost hopeless. It is not for a practical-poetical like me to teach geography to a poetical-practical like you but by the map I should say that one of us would have to set at naught some two hundred miles to reach the other. (Let it be said in contraction that they are beautiful miles.) It seems to me you ought to be the one to do the setting at naught—you with your automobiles and your superannuated horses. Come to Franconia and adopt the rest of the family as you adopted me in Chicago.[74] We can't feed you because we haven't earned enough to feed ourselves yet in the right caterer's sense of the word, but we can surround you, the six of us as I calculate, with one continuous smile of welcome. I require of you that you shall come as an act penitential for not having come to West Cummington before we left Amherst and for probably not intending to stay in West Cum-

74. RF had given two lectures in Chicago at Moody's invitation. See his March 7, 1917, telegram to her.

mington till we can get back to Amherst. I am past the help I particularly wanted of you in June, namely, advice against a step I was about to take, because I have taken the step.[75] There is nothing left but to help me not to think too hardly of myself. Come and give me that.

No, but you will come, won't you?

And I will tell you when I see you how much I care for Will Moody's poetry. Just rough enough with beauty to show a man's assurance that beauty can't get along without him.

Always sincerely yours
Robert Frost.

[To Sidney Cox. Cox interrupted his graduate studies at Columbia University to enlist in the army, in which he was commissioned a second lieutenant in the summer of 1917. Before going overseas he married his fiancée, Alice Macy Ray, on August 15 in Waverley, Massachusetts. The couple did, in fact, take a brief wedding trip up to Franconia to see the Frost family. ALS. DCL.]

Franconia
August 12 1917

Dear Sidney:

I am going to be very sorry not to be at your war-wedding and you are going to be sorry not to have me there. But I can only be with you in thought. I promise to be wholly that on the forenoon of August 16th. I can't be more. My own marriage keeps me from your marriage so to speak. That is to say things that follow in the train of marriage keep me—babies and the fear of babies. Since some time before you were with us we havent known just what we were in for. We don't know now. It seemed like a last putting forth. At times we have been afraid it was something more serious if no more solemn. At any rate I dont think I ought to be away from Elinor as she is.[76]

But you must come to us and receive our blessing as soon as you can. It wont be safe to go without it too long. You are [to] stay a day or two with us—not to be entertained—you will take us as you find us and take potluck

75. RF had accepted an offer to continue his appointment at Amherst College as professor of English.

76. In November 1915, Elinor Frost had suffered a miscarriage that put her life at risk; the family feared another.

with us—but to say our hearts out to each other on the eve of what is to come.

Always yours
Robert Frost

[To John Bartlett. The letter is undated, but "August 13, 1917 / Franconia N.H." is written at the top in another hand. ALS. UVA.]

[Franconia, NH]
[August 13, 1917]

Dear John:

I dont see how I am to get down to see you—I really don't. Elinor has been sick for a long time. We dont know what is the matter with her unless it is something that may come to an end abruptly at any moment. I ought not to be far from her—at any rate till we know more certainly how it is with her. We are all going back to Amherst next month. But you have determined to get away before then. I very much want a talk with you. Would you come here for a day and night if I would foot the bill? This in haste on impulse.

Rob

[To George Browne. ALS. Plymouth.]

Franconia N.H.
August 14 1917

Dear Browne:

As to your coming to see us: Come hurrying! It seems too long since I saw you last. It is only new friends that bore me—in the first stages of friendship when I don't know whether I am ever going to meet them again and can't say their names offhand. You begin to be in the class of old friends. You could even take liberties with me, so long as you continued to live up to the best that was in you. But coming to see me for two hours is no liberty that you should ask my permission to come. Come at any time for longer without asking.

As to their drafting Jack: I'm damned if I can believe it of them.[77] A man who has been through what he has been through has seen and done enough.

---

77. John "Jack" Gallishaw, husband of Browne's daughter Eleanor.

They'll say so when they look into his case. I'm a hard man and I won't say anything against war on general principles or against a young man's going to war any more than I will talk against life at its worst as something we have a right to get out of by suicide. I am for sparing no one the risks he ought to take. But once he has taken them and come through them I think we ought to be thankful for him and make the most of him and hang on to him for a storied relic if for nothing else. The rewarding part of our nature demands satisfaction. We have got to have some one to expend it on. But who will there be to expend it on if we persist in throwing every body back into the fire just the moment he has come manfully through it.

As to Thomas' Four and Twenty Blackbirds: I fear we are too late to take the responsibility of offering it directly to a publisher in this country.[78] As I understand it, it has already been published in England; in which case we could only offer it to Houghton Mifflin as a book they might like to obtain sheets of from the English publisher. Perhaps you may as well let them pass on the MS as long as you have gone as far as you have with them in innocence of heart and leave it to me to set things right when they come to me. I want the book published on this side. It wont be cheating to let them go as far as seeing whether they like it before we refer them to the English publisher. What Harcourt has of the poems is sheets from the English publisher. But more of this when I see you.

As to Lewis Chase: I went to see him to see what he was like.[79] I don't know what I think of him and I dont know what I think of the situation I find myself in with him. If you dont approve of him, find a substitute for him or assassinate him.

All those who change old friends for new
Pray God they change for worse.[80]

R.F.

---

78. Edward Thomas's *Four and Twenty Blackbirds* was published in London by Duckworth in 1915; it wasn't released in America until long after Thomas died.

79. Lewis Nathaniel Chase (1873–1937) was a literary critic.

80. RF adapts two lines from George Peele's "Fair and Fair" (also known as "Cupid's Curse"), as collected in Quiller-Couch's *Oxford Book of English Verse*: "They that do change old love for new, / Pray gods they change for worse!"

[To Nathan Haskell Dole. ALS. Harvard.]

Franconia N.H.
August 15 1917

Dear Dole:

Just saying I must look you up for a few lessons in socialistic Russian before I go to Russia to ask the porters waiters chambermaids bootblacks and barbers What, if anything, 's the matter, when providentially comes me in your letter to let me know "you love me still the same that you loved me"[81] at the old address and probably couldn't refuse me instruction in anything short of the thirty-second degree Masonic secrets. So I can go ahead and engage passage for Russia. (I advise myself to go the long way round by the Pacific Ocean and Siberia. Don't you?)

But seriousness aside, would you say Russia [*sic*] would be too hard for me (to have my children learn) at my age?[82] In general which part of the mouth is it spoken from? I have heard that it scrapes the throat and cleans the teeth. Is this very true? Is the part of the mouth it is spoken from likely to have atrophied or have been pulled out in an adult American? What difference would that make in theory? In practice?

You are probably at that famous beach with J. K. Bangs combing the concealed puns out of our language.[83] There's but one I hope may escape you. That lies hardly concealed at all almost too obviously awful in something I

---

81. The line "you love me still the same that you loved me" is likely an echo of "The Gypsy Girl's Dream; or, I Dreamt I Dwelt in Marble Halls" (1843), which is sung in *The Bohemian Girl* (words by Alfred Bunn, music by Michael William Balfe). See stanza one:

> *I had riches too great to count, could boast*
> *Of a high ancestral name.*
> *But I also dreamt, which pleas'd me most*
> *That you loved me still the same, that you loved me, you loved me still the same,*
> *That you loved me, you loved me still the same.*

82. Dole published a number of books about Russia, and translated, in four volumes, Tolstoy's *War and Peace* (New York: Thomas Y. Crowell, 1889). RF may have in mind Dole's remarks, in the preface to the translation, about the "bluntness and vigor" of the original Russian.

83. John Kendrick Bangs (1862–1922), American editor (working at *Life*, *Harper's*, and other periodicals), poet, novelist, author of children's books. Banks lived in Ogunquit, Maine, at the time, a popular seaside resort; Dole and his family summered there.

once wrote.[84] Your Madam Bovary one gave one person great joy—E. A. Robinson.

I dont know what you think about the war. I trust it isn't what everybody else thinks. I mean I hope for variety's sake it looks and sounds different but comes to the same thing in action. I make it a rule to be as individual as I can in speech without committing myself to any particularly jailable individuality of action.

We mustn't let anybody know how sad we are.

Always yours friendly
Robert Frost

[To Alexander Meiklejohn (1872–1964), philosopher, university administrator, president of Amherst College. RF had recently accepted a continuation of his appointment as professor of English. ALS. Wisc. Hist.]

Franconia N.H.
August 17, 1917

Dear Mr Meiklejohn:

Though happy in the thought that it is for and with you I am going to work, I am probably not half as happy as I should have been if I hadnt had to ask so much for my services. It can't be helped however. It is the hard fate of the unworldly to have to be more worldly than the worldly sometimes to make up for the other times when they are less worldly. I suppose you understand this in your involved philosophical way or you wouldn't take me in my mercenary demands so beautifully. I know what I ought to do in requital. But I'm blessed if I offer to do it—though it tear me not to.

But we thought you were coming this way this summer.

Mrs Frost joins me in sending our best to you and Mrs Meiklejohn.

And we are all yours and Amherst's.

Robert Frost.

---

84. Reference unclear. However, in letters RF often puns on his own surname; more than one critic has suggested that he does the same in the poetry (at times, as in the opening of "Mending Wall," obliquely: "the frozen ground swell"—i.e., frost).

[To Wilbur Lucius Cross. ALS. Yale.]

Franconia N.H.
August 17 1917

Dear Mr Cross:

Of course I should like nothing better than to see "The Hill Wife" prolonged in a Yale Review Anthology.[85]

I promised Mr. Reed some poems of Edward Thomas' to look over.[86] Should I be too late if I sent them now? I've been holding them to see if I wouldn't feel like writing something to go with them. But it's too soon yet: I care too much.

Always sincerely yours
Robert Frost

[To Louis Untermeyer. The opening reference is to Elihu Root (1845–1937), whom Woodrow Wilson dispatched as emissary to the Russian government, then headed by Alexander Fyodorovich Kerensky, whom he hoped might prosecute the war against Germany more vigorously. ALS. LoC.]

Franconia N.H.
August 18 1917

Dear Louis:

Let me not argue with you as to what Root saw in Russia to inspire confidence, but let me instead tell you what I think he thinks will happen in Russia and not only in Russia but in every other country in the world. I have very little in common with Root, but though I come at things from almost an opposite direction from him, still my guess is his guess on this war. Middle class government, which is to say liberal democratic government, has won a seat in Russia and it is going to keep its seat for the duration of the war and share with us in the end in a solid out-and-out middle class triumph such as the Germans enjoyed when they marched into Paris. The lower class seeing

---

85. Cross and his co-editors reprinted "The Hill Wife" in *A Book of Yale Review Verse* (New Haven: Yale University Press, 1917). In a short foreword, the editors struck a wistful wartime note: "For our generation, at least, there is between these covers a brief but moving picture of American and English minds and hearts in the years that began the war and felt its progress, justifying such an anthology, and adding another interest certainly to those merits of good verse that are not dependent upon time or place" (vi).

86. See RF's May 24, 1917, letter to Reed.

nothing in all this for itself may do its worst to create diversions, but it will fail. This may be the last war between bounded nations in the old fashioned patriotism. The next war may be between class and class. But this one will be to the end what it was in the beginning, a struggle for commercial supremacy between nations. I will not guess further ahead than that. The lower class will kick a little on street corners and where it can find a chance in journalistic corners. But it will be suppressed—more and more brutally suppressed as the middle class gains in confidence and sees its title clearer. We are still surer of nationality than we are of anything else in the world—ninety-nine million of us are in this country. I don't say this to discourage you—merely to define my position to myself. Live in hope or fear of your revolution. You will see no revolution this time even in Germany until Germany goes down with a perceptible crash and I'm not so sure you'll see one there even then. Everybody is entitled to three guesses and this is one of mine. You can have my other two to add to your own three. You'll need that many as you keep shifting your position to adjust yourself to events that will be going continually against you.

Sometime the world will try cutting the middle class out of our middle. But my mind misgives me that the experiment will fail just as the eighteenth century experiment of getting rid of the lowest class by cutting it out and dumping it on distant islands failed. You know how the lowest class renewed itself from somewhere as fast as it was cut out.

What I love best in man is definiteness of position. I dont care what the position is so long as it is definite enough. I mean I don't half care. Take a position and try it out no matter who sets up to call you an unhanged traitor. My God how I adore some people who stand right out in history with distinct meaning.

We wept for you a little (which is a lot for us) as you went out of sight down the road—we actually wept.

Yours for all the higher
forms of excitement
Robert Frost

Those Nevinson pictures were beautiful in the way they found material for futurist treatment.[87]

---

87. C. R. W. Nevinson (1889–1946), British painter; he befriended, for a time, Filippo Tommaso Emilio Marinetti (1876–1944), Italian poet and leader of the futurist movement, but soon cut his ties to the group.

And much that Max says is true.[88] But we are concerned, for the moment, with predicting what will come true.

[To Alexander Meiklejohn. ALS. Wisc. Hist.]

Franconia N.H.
August 21 1917

Dear Mr Meiklejohn:

I wonder if you do get me. You speak of acting on an intuition. It cant be the right intuition then, for if it were it would be nothing to act on. Everything looks to me done and concluded. You have bid 1800 for me and I am yours.

I'm afraid you take me as sorry to have to ask for more than 1800, whereas I only wrote myself as sorry I had had to ask for more than 1500. Let us be almost contractual in our clearness. I knew I ought not to have asked for more than 1500 but I had asked for it and I was going to take the 1800 you offered. And I didnt want you to think too hardly of me for my selfishness. That's all I meant to say. I trust I have said it now.

Fortunately it was as a philosopher I wrote that letter—didnt you notice my attempts to be sententious?—it is always as a philosopher I address myself to you. So if it was a bad letter all the worse for philosophy and all the better for me: it only proves me a bad philosopher and bad philosopher good poet, I am told. You never knew why I didn't mind seeming to you such a bad philosopher. All the time I was saying to myself, At least this goes to confute the critics who think me too much of a philosopher to be a poet. Of course I may be too good a philosopher to be a poet and yet not be a good philosopher. I have thought of that.

Let this be a lesson to you not to act on an intuition. (Chance waived to get in something about tuition being your proper sphere.)

Always yours
Robert Frost

88. Max Forrester Eastman (1883–1969), American poet, social activist, and journalist (including an editorial stint at *The Masses*); he was an associate of Untermeyer's, through whom RF knew him.

[To William Stanley Braithwaite. ALS. Middlebury.]

Franconia N.H.
September 2 1917

My dear Braithwaite:

I'm not dead but sleeping. This is the first letter I have written in I don't know how long.

Of course any thing you please of mine for this year's anthology and the obligation all mine. Also for five years' anthology.[89]

I'll tell you presently where I'll have you send a copy or two of those older anthologies you have on hand.

I've heard of you indirectly at the Peterboro Camp where I suppose you all write a whole lot of poetry and have a high old time reading it to each other.[90] Some time you will be doing a book on the camp.

Sincerely yours
Robert Frost

[To Harriet Moody, who had a house in West Cummington, Massachusetts. ALS. Chicago.]

Franconia N.H.
September 2 1917

Dear Mrs Moody:

All hearts are set on Thanksgiving with you at West Cummington. Here's looking forward!

And if you think you could stand seeing me twice in the same winter, get me the readings in Chicago. They would have to be crowded into short space: I mustn't be away from my college long. I should be grateful for the break in the college winter however and I can't say I should object to the extra money to pay my war-time expenses.

---

89. In the *Anthology of Magazine Verse* for 1917, Braithwaite included "The Bonfire" and "Not to Keep." What RF called the "five years anthology" would be published in 1918 as *The Golden Treasury of Magazine Verse.* It included "Birches," "The Road Not Taken," "The Hill Wife," "The Bonfire," and "The Death of the Hired Man."

90. RF refers to the MacDowell Colony in Peterborough, New Hampshire, founded in 1907. Edwin Arlington Robinson was among its most notable early residents.

A few more favors like these and you will have earned the right to come right out and scold me for having tied up with Amherst. I wonder if I have made a very great mistake. It can't be a great mistake when I can so easily undo it. Dont think too discouragingly of me or I shall feel the depression even at this distance and even though you don't speak.

Do you make out just what the name of the place in West Malvern is where Wilfrid abides?[91] Print it on a post card for me if you do and end my perplexity. I didn't pay attention when Wilfrid said it and he writes it as badly as some people write poetry.

Always sincerely yours
Robert Frost

[To George Browne. ALS. Plymouth.]

Franconia N.H.
September 2 1917

Dear Browne:

I take it from the nature of your printed response to my letter that you wanted to come up and you wood of come up if you hadnt been too busy living up to what you preached about swimming in a home-made barrel-pipe aqueduct. Or is this cruelly to misunderstand you?

Here's a letter I opened by not looking at the superscripture.

Aint it funny about the English language?

But it aint no funnier than it is about the German. I heard a schollard expostulating with another for electing German. "What's the use of studding (did you ever see the themist spell it thataway?) the German language," he said. "When the war's over, there wont be any German language." And yet old Emeritus can talk of stalemate.

Allers thine
R.F.

---

91. Wilfrid Gibson, one of the "Georgian" poets with whom RF associated while in England. The Malvern Hills (in and around the towns of West Malvern, Little Malvern, and Great Malvern) are in Worcestershire, England; Gibson hiked them, and one in particular (Ragged Stone Hill) lent its name to his "The Ragged Stone," collected in *A Treasury of War Poetry, British and American Poems of the World War* (1917), ed. George Herbert Clarke.

[To Sidney Cox. Date derived from postmark (RF supplied only the month and year in his heading). ALS. DCL.]

Franconia N.H.
September [17] 1917

Dear Sidney:

Here it is, then, in all its sympathy understanding and devotion. Do you remember the misunderstanding we began in that night when we watched the normal school dance from among the empty chairs along the wall?[92] I didnt suspect then that we were to live to owe each other so much. You do owe me something, too, I think. Not much, but a little. Not enough to make your wife jealous of me, because it is nothing in comparison with what you owe her for being what she is. It made us happy to see you so happy on your way with her. Keep her my friend as I shall remain

Always friend of both of you
Robert Frost.

[To Lesley Frost. ALS. UVA.]

Franconia N.H.
September 26 1917

Dear Lesley:

You've given us Miss Pendleton[93] and some of the girls. (It was terrible about the poor thing with the Hope Chest—terrible that she should have been allowed to make her life out of one expectation. Probably she had been indifferent about her studies and her family had been driven to use every appeal of imagination and sentiment to wake her up.) Next you must give us what seems to be the idea of your course in English. I wonder if your teacher will let you into his mind in the matter or will simply start off with an assignment of work. I began last Thursday with an effort more or less vain I suppose to tell my one class how I wished to be taken. My course

92. RF and Cox met in Plymouth, New Hampshire, in 1911; at the time, RF taught at the Plymouth Normal School, Cox at Plymouth High School.

93. Ellen Fitz Pendleton (1864–1936), president of Wellesley College from 1911 until her retirement in 1936, shortly before her death.

is intended for students who like myself write. I shall not judge them by the amount they write during the year but by their one best piece of writing. The theme in which they transcend their ordinary school level—that is for me. But more important than that they achieve anything is that they lead a literary life. The only out and out failure will be failing to convince me that they have failed to lead a literary life. They will naturally ask what they must do to convince me. Why the first thing to do will be to lead the life honestly and not in pretense. I dont see much hope of their convincing me unless they begin by doing that. They may have to talk to me a little so as to show that they have the art of writing at heart and they may have to show me a little of their writing. But a little of both writing and talk will go a long way. I can promise to do them more justice than the world commonly does us if they will do their part and lead the life I ask. And it's for them to find out what I mean by a literary life. One thing I suppose it means is outbursts of writing without self-criticism. You must not always be self-watchful. You must let go. The self-criticism belongs to lulls in inspiration. And it's only when you get far enough away from your work to begin to be critical of it yourself that anyone's else criticism can be tolerable and helpful to you. A teacher's talk is an outrage on fresh work that your mind still glows with. Always be far ahead with your writing. Bring only to class old and cold things that you begin to know what you think of yourself.

This is some of what I said and some of what I shall say tomorrow night when I meet the class again. Writing out this way will make it easier to say it.

Affectionately
Rob

[To Lesley Frost. The letter is not dated, but contextual evidence suggests early autumn 1917, when Lesley was in her first term at Wellesley College. ALS. UVA.]

Pelham Mass
but address us at
Amherst Mass
R.F.D. No 2
[Autumn 1917]

Dear Lesley:

We don't want to make ourselves obnoxious or even nuisances, but I think we owe it both to ourselves and those girls to find out why you failed to make the team when other girls you defeated have made it and why you were dismissed by that senior from a game you were winning. Either one of three things: you did something you ought not to do or the senior did something she ought not to do or the terms of the contest were not what you thought they were.

It may very well be that the selection wasn't made for skill in tennis but rather for skill in tennis combined with social qualifications we dont know anything about and that that is generally understood in the college. You could ask your sophomore without any show of feeling in a spirit of honest inquiry. Or it may be that the team is made up of as good players as possible who shall all be entirely congenial to each other. We really ought to know if you went out under a misapprehension.

Then again in your inexperience you may have overstepped some rule of the game. That hardly seems possible. There must have been some referee to call your attention to any fault you were committing whether accidentally or on purpose. Still I should want to ask.

What I like least is your dismissal from the court in the middle of a game you were winning. How do you know that it doesnt reflect on your honor in some way? The least you could have asked would have been in Cordelias [*sic*] words, "Let me the knowledge of my fault bear with me."[94] Demanding an explanation may get you a chance to give an explanation. There is something to clear up on one side or the other or both sides.

If no one did you an injustice you dont want to do yourself the injustice of looking on yourself as much injured when you are not.

---

94. RF misidentifies the speaker. In *As You Like It* Rosalind says, "I do beseech your Grace, / Let me the knowledge of my fault bear with me" (3.iii).

The thing to do is to make a record at once of the names of the girls you beat and the scores you beat them by, and the name of the girl who sent you from the court in the middle of a game you were winning. (Make sure of this girl for my benefit.) Then feel your way toward action. Talk with your sophomore and possibly with the senior at your house. Perhaps one of them will go with you and merely listen while you ask the senior who dismissed you a few plain questions. After that I should carry the matter up to the member of the faculty who has supervision of athletics or to your faculty advisor if you have one.

I shouldn't drag Mr Young[95] into it at all. But I sha'n't refuse to be dragged into it and even to come down to Wellesley unless it is made more intelligible at once. Keep this letter as your warrant to show if there is any question of your judgement in finding out your rights. I may want you to show it to Mr Young before all's said and done.

Very disagreeable—the whole business. My way at your age would have been to shut up in my shell. I was always too inclined to give up wanting anything that was denied me unjustly and take it out in a feeling of injured superiority. I think that was because I took it too seriously. There would be such a thing as not taking it seriously enough to want to understand and be understood. It will be taking it just about right if you follow the course I advise you here. So it seems to me as I write any way. Say what you think. At least you must get me the names and scores I ask for.

Here's ten dollars to use as you think best. I know you wont be ambitious to match pennies with really rich girls. Dont apologize for needing what you need.

Love from us all
Papa

95. Charles Lowell Young (1865–1937), professor of English at Wellesley, and a Frost family friend.

[To Lesley Frost. Dating derived from internal evidence. Text derived from FL, *9–10; the manuscript of the letter has gone missing since Arnold Grade prepared the latter volume. In addition, as printed in* FL, *the first portion of the letter is missing.]*

[Amherst, MA]
[Autumn 1917]

[. . .] bit. Keep your eye on it and get what you can out of it for the money it costs and try not to let it cost any more than the money. What a show that was at Miss Bates.[96] I should be sorry now if an "opportunity" like that had fooled you. It would be damnable, if it had pleased you. You could have followed me round on my lecturing these last two winters and seen forty such rediculous rites [*sic*]—flatter rapture and all. I doubt if Miss Bates is a very wise person. I doubt if many people we meet are thoroughly sound and wise. We cant afford to be guided by anyone but ourselves and thats not because we are perfect but because we are no more imperfect than others and if we are going to be lead [*sic*] by blindness, the blindness may as well be our own. It has the chance of being better suited to our particular cases anyway.

Keep your balance—that's all. Your marks don't matter. I like to have the Latin and French present a good hard resistance. You'll get a lot out of them, marks or no marks. The converting of stories into Latin is just what I should think you would rise to sooner or later. Your memorizing of so much Latin should have stocked your mind with idiom. You'll find it will come out as you work it. Memorize some of the Livy—find time. Read in the grammar a little, I should too, and take special notice of the cases given in illustration. Some of those are worth remembering for their ideas as well as for their interesting forms.

Technical faults! I suppose that would be the reason they would give for putting you off the court.[97] Well what you say sounds sensible. You seem to be taking the right way with such people. We mustn't mind them. Whatever else we do we mustnt be driven into a hole or corner by them. Put not your faith in them but laugh with and at them and beat them at their own game if it's a game you like to play.

We ought not to mind when things don't go too well with you because hard times will tend to throw you back on us.

Affectionately
Papa

---

96. Katharine Lee Bates, professor of English at Wellesley College.

97. Lesley had failed to make the college tennis team.

[To James Chapin. The letter is dated to 1917 by the contextual evidence of other letters to Chapin. ALS. DCL.]

Franconia N H
October 4 [1917]

Dear Chapin

Unless you want to come as far as Franconia for another look in before it fades you'd better hold off for a week or two. We haven't found a roof to our backs down in Amherst yet.

I'll be considering what pose to assume.[98]

Here's your chance to see winter come down the mountains we climbed I was going to say at the rate of a mile a week, but that sounds as if it were our rate.

R F.

[To James Chapin. ALS. DCL.]

Amherst Mass
R.F.D No 2
October 19 1917

Dear Chapin:

I understand that Hamilton's been saying that if he ever gets out of those bogs on the Garfield trail he's going to ask you a question; he's going to ask you why you ran away and left him in there.[99] I only tell you so you may know what to expect. On the whole I think it might be as well for you to keep away from Franconia for a while. But there's no reason why you shouldn't come to Amherst right now. The lot of us will be glad to see you again. We have only one chair to sit in as yet; so that if you have the bad taste to accept that when we offer it to you, you will force me to sit for my picture on the bare floor. I have heard a good deal of late of the sufferings of the

98. Chapin would do several portraits of RF. But this is likely a reference to the portrait that would appear as frontispiece to the 1919 edition of *NB* (which Chapin also illustrated).

99. The Garfield Trail is a five-mile, 3,000-foot climb in the White Mountains to the summit of 4,500-foot Mt. Garfield. There is an area with several stream crossings early in the hike that were, especially in wet weather, boggy. We have been unable to identify "Hamilton"; he is almost certainly not Hamilton Holt (1872–1951), referred to elsewhere in the letters.

poor, but who ever heard of anything worse than having to sit for one's picture on the bare floor.

Always yours friendly
Robert Frost

[To Martha E. D. White (b. 1863), a political progressive active in the Women's Clubs of New England, about which she had written for New England Magazine *in 1903 and for* Harper's *in 1904. She resided in Arlington, Massachusetts, outside of Boston. Later she served as a publicist for the League of Women Voters. Her husband, mentioned at the head of the letter, was True W. White, manager of the Teacher's Exchange in Boston. ALS. ACL.]*

Amherst Mass
October 21 1917

Dear Mrs White:

You see from the above where I am and can infer what I am probably doing to bad boys. Mr White can testify as to how well I am probably doing it because he has seen me in action. You know I am a disciplinarian or rather say my wife and I together amount to one. We recently drew back from taking a house when we discovered that it contained not a single closet. We asked how we could bring up a family of children with no closets to put them in on occasion.

I am rather tied down to this job for the winter; at least I think it the decent thing for me to regard myself as tied down and not to allow myself more than a few lectures away from home. We have put it at six in important places like Boston New York and Chicago (I dont mean to flatter Boston). New York and Chicago are arranged for and I should be glad if you could get me something in Boston. Suppose I let you fix the date and price. Get me what you think becomes me. The Womans City Club ought to be able to find seventy-five or a hundred dollars for the sixth greatest living American poet (see Amy Lowell's Tendencies in Modern American Poetry).[100] But I will take fifty and my expenses if you tell me I must.

I shall bring Mrs Frost with me when I come and you and she can talk about Canton while Mr White and I get to the bottom of axe-helves.[101] I've

100. Lowell's *Tendencies* (1917) treats, at length, only six poets: E. A. Robinson, RF, Edgar Lee Masters, Carl Sandburg, H. D., and John Gould Fletcher.

101. White was born in Hopkinton, New York, about twenty-five miles from Canton, where Elinor Frost attended college (at St. Lawrence University).

looked for Mr White two summers now up there in the mountains. If it is Lafayette he is afraid of, he needn't feel that he's got to climb it simply because he tried to make me believe he could: he can lounge and talk at the foot of it as I do and I shall think none the worse of him.

Always your friendly
Robert Frost

[To Amy Lowell. The letter is undated but at the upper right "Oct. 22nd 1917" is written in pencil in another hand. The subject of the letter is Lowell's recently published Tendencies in Modern American Poetry *(New York: Macmillan, 1917), which contains a lengthy—and generally laudatory—chapter on RF. ALS. Harvard.]*

[Amherst, MA]
[October 22, 1917]

Dear Miss Lowell

I could have fared even badly at your hands and still have had to confess that I liked your book. But I didnt fare badly. What are your few doubts (groundless doubts) of my humor, my ability to go farther or my wisdom in not using dialect as weighed against all you say in my favor. Your generosity from the first has had so much to do with making me that if from now on you reversed yourself and tried to unmake me, I should never be brought to believe you were anything but my friend.

Considering all you found to say of me, it seems to me you have fallen into very few errors of fact, and I may be to blame for those. Please spell it Elinor Frost in the two places where you name my wife. The word should be "shock" instead of "shook" in the quotation from A Hundred Collars. Little Iddens was a house in Leddington near Ledbury, Herefordshire, where I lived neighborly with Gibson and Abercrombie from April 1914 to September 1914, about five months.[102] Even if you don't care to bother with the correction in your next edition, I wish you would make a marginal note of the fact that I didn't meet Gibson till I was putting the last touches on North of Boston and I didn't meet Abercrombie till after the MS was in David Nutts hands. It was the book that got me invited down to live with those fellows in the country. I had begun writing it in 1905. I wrote the bulk of it in 1913.

One month after the war broke out we left Little Iddens to live with the Abercrombies at their house called The Gallows at Ryton near Dymock,

102. English poets of the "Georgian" school: Lascelles Abercrombie and Wilfrid Gibson.

Gloucestershire, three miles away. You see if any of my work was in danger of Gibsonian or Abercrombian influence it was what I wrote of Mountain Interval in 1914, Birches and The Hill Wife and Putting in the Seed and The Sound of Trees. None of this greatly matters, but since you seem bent on accuracy, you might make a marginal note of it, as I say, in script in your copy of your own book.

And for the fun of it you might record in the margin of your book that RF makes no merit of not having used dialect in North of Boston. He says he doesn't put dialect into the mouths of his people because not one of them, not one, spoke dialect.

I don't know that I ever told you, but the closest I ever came in friendship to anyone in England or anywhere else in the world I think was with Edward Thomas who was killed at Vimy last Spring. He more than anyone else was accessory to what I had done and was doing. We were together to the exclusion of every other person and interest all through 1914—1914 was our year. I never had, I never shall have another such year of friendship.

Would it amuse you to learn that Range Finding belongs to a set of war poems I wrote in time of profound peace (circa 1902)? Most of them have gone the way of waste paper. Range Finding was only saved from going the same way by Edward Thomas who liked it and asked about it now and then and very particularly in a letter last Spring—he thought it so good a description of No Man's Land. So you see my poems about this war narrow down to The Bonfire and that is more of New England than of what is going on over yonder.

My address is Amherst Mass, though really we are living in the abandoned town of Pelham so close to the woods that if the woods burn our house must go too.

Thanks for everything. But thanks specially for giving An Old Man's Winter Night its due.[103]

Always yours sincerely
Robert Frost

---

103. After quoting the poem (one of RF's own favorites), Lowell wrote: "Nowhere in Mr. Frost's work is there a finer thing than that, in spite of the false accent in the eighteenth line. There is sound, and sight, and suggestion, and all painting surely and reticently the tragedy of lonely old age. The poem is superb; with what it says and what it does not say" (134–135).

[To Clarissa Hall (1891–1988), formerly a student of RF's at Pinkerton Academy and at the Plymouth State Normal School. Whitefield, New Hampshire, where Hall taught, lies just above the White Mountains, near Littleton and Bethlehem, in Coös County. ALS. UNH.]

Amherst Mass
October 26 1917

Dear Miss Hall:

You see from the above where I am and how difficult it would be for me to get to Whitefield this year. I'm sorry. I should like to see you and hear you on the subject of special teaching. Or perhaps it is not special teaching in English you are doing. You only mean you are teaching your English in a special way that you are good enough to say I gave you or partly gave you the idea of. I can't imagine you doing anything other than well. My method, so to call it, is sure not to suffer at your hands. You are the kind of person who would be a credit to anyone who taught you just as you would have been a credit to yourself if you had happened to stay at home and teach yourself. That is to say I dont think my teaching or anyone's teaching has anything to do with what you are. You'd prove capable of anything you set yourself to anyway.

I'm sending you a copy of my last book for old time's sake.[104]

Sincerely yours
Robert Frost

[To Louis Untermeyer. ALS. LoC.]

Amherst Mass
October 27 1917

Dear Louis:

Under separate cover I have told you why I ain't got no sympathy for your total loss of all the arts.[105] You tried to have too many at the present price of certified milk. Why would you be a pig instead of something like a horse or a cow that only has one in a litter, albeit with six legs sometimes, for I have

104. *MI.*

105. The *Seven Arts,* on whose editorial board RF sat, had recently folded for lack of funding.

seen such in my old mad glad circus-going days. But that's all put behind me since I discovered that do or say my dambdest I cant be other than orthodox in politics love and religion: I can't escape salvation: I can't burn if I was born into this world to shine without heat. And I try not to think of it as often as I can lest in the general deliquescence I should find myself a party to the literature of irresponsible, boy-again, freedom. No, I can promise you that whatever else I write or may have been writing for the last twenty-five years to disprove Amy's theory that I never got anything except out of the soil of New England, there's one thing I shan't write in the past, present, or future, and that is glad mad stuff or mad glad stuff. The conviction closes in on me that I was cast for gloom as the sparks fly upward, I was about to say: I am of deep shadow all compact like onion within onion and the savor of me is oil of tears. I have heard laughter by daylight when I thought it was my own because at that moment when it broke I had parted my lips to take food. Just so I have been afraid of myself and caught at my throat when I thought I was making some terrible din of a mill whistle that happened to come on the same instant with the opening of my mouth to yawn. But I have not laughed. No man can tell you the sound or the way of my laughter. I have neighed at night in the woods behind a house like vampires. But there are no vampires there are no ghouls there are no demons, there is no nothing but me. And I have all the dead New England things held back by one hand as by a dam in the long deep wooded valley of Whippoorwill, where many as they are, though, they do not flow together by their own weight more than so many piled-up chairs (and by the way your two chairs have come[106]). I hold them easily,—too easily for assurance that they will go with a rush when I let them go. I may have to extricate them one by one and throw them. If so I shall throw them with what imaginative excess I am capable of, already past the height of my powers (see Amy the next time you are in Boston).

I suppose it's a safe bet that the form your pacifism, your Protean pacifism, takes at this moment is "Down with Mitchel."[107] Next it will be—you say! Do

---

106. A gift from Untermeyer to the Frosts.

107. John Purror Mitchel (1879–1918), mayor of New York from 1914–1917. In the fall of 1917 widespread protests against a school reform program he advocated—the so-called "Gary System," based on reforms first introduced in Gary, Indiana—broke out across the city. Newspaper reports of the unrest spoke of banners reading "Down with Mitchel."

you see these transmogrifications more than one or two ahead? Aw say be a nationalist. By the love you bear Teddy!

Yours while you're still
bad enough to need me,
Robert Frost

[To Martha E. D. White. Her husband, True W. White, mentioned toward the end of the letter, managed the Teacher's Exchange in Boston. ALS. ACL.]

Amherst Mass
November 2, 1917

Dear Mrs White:

March 11 be it, and thank you for the favor. Mrs Frost and I will plan to get to you at Arlington Heights sometime on March 9. Like your New England Woman's Club we are limiting ourselves to a few chosen pleasures this winter, this visit with you, one with Mrs William Vaughn Moody, and perhaps we will get away to New York together and go to the Brooklyn Institute. I am dug in here for good and all as a teacher it appears but not to teach very hard: I only meet one class a week I only meet it once and for not more than an hour at a time. When I remember my years of five classes a day five days in the week! I can speak of these things to you and Mr White with some hope of your appreciating the contrast in my fortunes because you both know teaching.

Mrs Frost joins me in regards to you both.

Sincerely yours
Robert Frost

[To Harriet Monroe. The letter is a typescript copy. In the upper left corner it is stamped "DEC 11 / ANSD H.M." and beneath that in an unknown hand "1917." At the top center is a handwritten notation: "Original sent to [illegible] (Mr Loeb)." TL (unsigned). Chicago.]

Amherst, Mass
Nov. 2, 1917

Dear Miss Monroe:

My congratulations to you and your fellow editors of POETRY on what is bound to prove a very popular award in this family.[108] I was feeling blue when like a bolt from the blue came so much wealth and glory. I am the more sensible of it all that it is my first real prize in a long life. Hitherto my utmost had been a few dollars for running at a Caldonia [*sic*] Club Picnic, a part interest in a pair of ear-rings, and a part interest in a gold-headed cane for impersonations at a masquerade, a gold medal for sheer goodness in a high school, and a Detur for scholarship at Harvard.[109]

Always sincerely yours,
Robert Frost.

[To Louis Untermeyer. Date derived from postmark. Randolph Bourne published several articles in the Seven Arts *critical of U.S. policy during the war; RF suspected that these were responsible, in large part, for the magazine's demise after its twelfth issue. ALS. LoC.]*

[Amherst, MA]
[November 3, 1917]

Dear Louis:

This under separate cover, under cover of darkness in fact, not because I am ashamed of the sentiment, but because I havent time in the press of reading Religio Medici[110] to polish it off as I like to polish things off:

---

108. The November 1917 issue of *Poetry* announced prizes awarded for poems published in the magazine during 1916. RF was awarded $100 for "Snow," published in November 1916.

109. The Detur Prize is awarded to Harvard students who earn high marks in their first year at the college.

110. Sir Thomas Browne (1605–1682) published his *Religio Medici* (The Religion of a Doctor) in 1643.

THE SEVEN ARTS
In the Dawn of Creation that Morning
I remember I gave you fair warning
The Arts are but Six
You add on Politics
And the Seven will all die a-Bourneing.

R.F.

I am sitting in both the chairs at once and thinking of no one but Jean and you. And Dick! I'm thinking of Dick of course too.[111] Tell Dick Gee I wish I had someone to bet with on the election. Well he and I can bet on it after it's over sometime when I'm down there.

R.F.

[To Louis Untermeyer. ALS. LoC.]

Amherst Mass
November 7 1917

Dear Louis:

Do you want to be the repository of one or two facts that Amy leaves out of account?[112]

For twenty-five out of the first forty years of my life I lived in San Francisco, Lawrence Mass, Boston, Cambridge Mass, New York and Beaconsfield, a suburb of London.

For seven I lived in the villages of Salem Derry and Plymouth New Hampshire.

For eight I lived on a farm at Derry though part of that time I was teaching in the Academy there.

I began to read to myself at thirteen. Before that time I had been a poor scholar and had staid out of school all I could. At about that time I began to take first place in my classes.

I read my first poem at 15, wrote my first poem at 16, wrote My Butterfly at eighteen. That was my first poem published.[113]

---

111. Richard Untermeyer, Louis and Jean Starr Untermeyer's son.

112. In her chapter on RF in *Tendencies in Modern American Poetry* (1917).

113. See RF's April 22, 1894, to Susan Hayes Ward.

With Elinor I shared the valedictory honor when I graduated from the High School at Lawrence Mass.

I was among the first men at Amy's brother's old college, during my two years there, winning a Detur and a considerable scholarship.[114] In those days I used to suspect I was looked on as more or less of a grind—

—Though as a matter of fact I was always rather athletic. I ran well. I played on town school ball teams and on the High School football team. I had my share of fights, the last a rather public one in Lawrence in 1896 that cost me the humiliation of going in to court and a ten dollar fine.[115]

It is not fair to farmers to make me out a very good or laborious farmer. I have known hard times, but no special shovel-slavery. I dreamed my way through all sorts of fortunes without any realizing sense of what I was enduring. You should have seen me, I wish I could have seen myself, when I was working in the Arlington Mills at Lawrence, working in the shoe shop in Salem N.H. tramping and beating my way on trains down South, reporting on a Lawrence paper, promoting for a Shakespearean reader (whom I abandoned because after trying him on a distinguished audience I got him in Boston, I decided he wasn't truly great).[116] Nothing seemed to come within a row of apple trees of where I really lived. I was so far from being discouraged by my failure to get any where that I only dimly realized that anyone else was discouraged by it. This is where the countryman came in: I would work at almost anything rather well for a while, but every once in so often I had to run off for a walk in the woods or for a term's teaching in a lonely district school or a summer's work haying or picking fruit on a farm or cutting heels in a shed by the woods in Salem. Gee Whiz, I should say I was just the most everyday sort of person except for the way I didn't mind looking unambitious as much as you would mind for example. Of course it's no credit to me.

---

114. RF refers to the Sewall Scholarship, awarded to students for academic excellence. Abbott Lawrence Lowell, Amy Lowell's brother, was president of Harvard from 1909 to 1933.

115. See *EY*, 225–227.

116. RF's go at managing a Shakespearean reader probably dates to 1895; readers were in fashion at the time, and he had lately read Sidney Lanier's celebration of one (Charlotte Cushman) in *The Science of English Verse* (1880), given him by Susan Hayes Ward in the spring of 1894. RF worked for a short stint at the Arlington Mills in 1893–1894; he "tramped down south" in the autumn of 1894 (*EY*, 173ff.), and worked briefly as a reporter for the Lawrence, Massachusetts, *Daily American*, and also for the *Sentinel*, in the spring of 1895 (see *CPRF*, 256–259).

I knew what I was about well enough and was pretty sure where I would come out.

Amy is welcome to make me out anything she pleases. I have decided I like her and, since she likes me, anything she says will do so long as it is entertaining. She has been trying to lay at my door all the little slips she has made in the paper on me. She gets it all wrong about me and Gibson and Abercrombie for example. I knew neither of those fellows till North of Boston was all written. All I wrote in the neighborhood of those two was part of Mountain Interval. I doubt if she is right in making me so grim, not to say morbid. I may not be funny enough for Life or Punch, but I have sense of humor enough, I must believe, to laugh when the joke is on me as it is in some of this book of Amy's.

I really like the least her mistakes about Elinor. That's an unpardonable attempt to do her as the conventional helpmeet of genius. Elinor has never been of any earthly use to me.[117] She hasn't cared whether I went to school or worked or earned anything. She has resisted every inch of the way my efforts to get money. She is not too sure that she cares about my reputation. She wouldn't lift a hand or have me lift a hand to increase my reputation or even save it. And this isn't all from devotion to my art at its highest. She seems to have the same weakness I have for a life that goes rather poetically; only I should say she is worse than I. It isn't what might be expected to come from such a life—poetry that she is after. And it isn't that she doesnt think I am a good poet either. She always knew I was a good poet, but that was between her and me and there I think she would have liked it if it had remained at least until we were dead. I don't know that I can make you understand the kind of person. Catch her getting any satisfaction out of what her housekeeping may have done to feed a poet! Rats! She hates housekeeping. She has worked because the work has piled on top of her. But she hasn't pre-

---

117. Among the offending remarks: "One of [RF's] fellow pupils at the High School was Miss Eleanor Miriam White, the lady he afterwards married. Miss White was a good scholar and a serious young woman, and Mr. Frost owes an immeasurable debt to the steadfast purpose of his wife . . . In 1893, Mr. Frost graduated from the High School, and the following autumn he entered Dartmouth College . . . He could not learn from his teachers; he could get no mental pabulum from the prescribed courses. Miss White was no longer at his side to spur him on . . . Possibly it was her influence which led him to return again to the idea of an ordered course of study. At any rate, in 1897, he moved his little family to Cambridge and entered Harvard, especially to study Latin" (88–91).

tended to like housework even for my sake. If she has liked anything it has been what I may call living it on the high. She's especially wary of honors that derogate from the poetic life she fancies us living. What a cheap common unindividualized picture Amy makes of her. But as I say never mind. Amy means well and perhaps you will come to our rescue without coming in conflict with Amy or contradicting her to her face.

I wish for a joke I could do myself, shifting the stress entirely from the Yankee realist to the Scotch symbolist.

Burn this if you think you ought for my protection.

Always yourn
R.

[To Lesley Frost. ALS. UVA.]

Amherst November 13 '17

Dear Lesley:

If Miss Waite[118] or any other school-fool gives you that chance again by asking what your father will say or said you answer My father knows teachers and my father knows me: and then go on to inform them that your father has dealt in marks and dealt with people who dealt in marks in every kind of school there is in America.

And you tell the Latin bitch that it is none of her business how you started in Latin: all she has to do is to mark you as low as she can to satisfy her nature. I mean tell her that if she tries any more of her obiter dicta on you. Or perhaps you might tell her if it was ridiculous to start Latin with reading then it was ridiculous to start it at all and anyway it was ridiculous to teach it the way she teaches it with no sense of literary values.[119]

Dont let them scare you out of what you know must be right. Remember Mr Gardner was on my side and he knew more Latin than all Wellesley put together.[120] Only the other day Prof Litchfield here said he didn't see how any love of Latin was going to be saved or inspired unless by some such way as

118. Alice Vinton Waite, dean of the college and professor of language and literature.

119. Caroline Rebecca Fletcher was associate professor of Latin at Wellesley College in 1917.

120. Ernest Arthur Gardner, whom the Frosts met while in England (see *EY*, 424–425).

ours.[121] But it doesnt matter. Your she professor has a right to kill you as an example of what befalls anyone who reflects by word or deed on her own little commonness.

The worst is Miss Waites remark that seems to imply belief in the verdict of marks. I was telling Whicher[122] that I supposed we couldnt run a class so as to give all kinds of minds the same chance in it. Every attitude a teacher takes toward a subject is bound to work some injustice and occasionally even great injustice to some pupils. The greatest safeguard then of good teaching is to keep it always before the class that the teachers judgment is ridiculously far from final. I make a business of laughing at my marks all I can. I make light of it all for my own protection and the protection of those who might suffer innocently under me. The understanding is that there is always appeal from my judgment to the judgment of other teachers the judgment of the world (which rather scorns teachers) and the judgment of God. I wish I thought Miss Waite was joking the joke I joke when she said "you have some hope of yourself then?" The chances are that being a woman she wasnt joking.

Now lets look at this as a game to lose a little sleep over but not much sleep. You can win it even with the umpire against you. I mean Latin as one horse teachers would like to make out. But you must just put in a few months now and settle those verbs and declensions and rules. I believe you will have a freer use of them for having come to them the way you have. But you must get them and have the job over with. You must learn the principal parts of every verb in your lesson and you must write out the conjugation from the models in your grammar or beginners book of two a day. Write out the declension of a couple of nouns or adjectives too. Make these extra exercises for yourself. Tend to that list of a hundred rules near the end of the grammar. Keep a little note book of interesting expressions and idioms. Of course measure this to your strength, remembering always that the main thing is the English and you are free to let everything except that and even including that go to devil when you please.

---

121. Henry W. Litchfield, author of (among other things) "Latin and the Liberal College," an essay published in the *Classical Journal* in October 1918 (vol. 1, no. 1): 6–25. It begins: "The following outline is motived by the writer's belief that the methods and content of Latin instruction in most American liberal colleges are destined soon to undergo certain radical changes if that instruction is to make in future valid claim to the attention of any considerable number of undergraduates."

122. George Whicher, RF's friend and colleague in the English department at Amherst.

I was sick all night last night with anger and so was mamma. You ought to have heard what mamma called them all every time she woke up. It's not so much anything as it is our own stupidity in letting such people get one on us. Damn their loathsomeness.

But do it on the high minded. Never be brought to take a low school view of literature, English French Spanish or Latin. English has come up out of that Egypt that Latin is still in within the years since I studied it (a very little) in college. A great many teachers would be ashamed to teach English now as you say Sheffield was mauling that poem. (Sheffield is a clever cut-and-dried mind, but he is a survival. Remember he drove me out of Harvard.[123]) English has come to realize that it has a soul to take into consideration. It has in a good many quarters. It can still be pretty awful in the hands of some teachers. And there is this consolation that it is better to have a bad Latin teacher than a bad English teacher. I think I should want to take you away from a bad English teacher whether you wanted to stay in college or not. What you suffer in Latin after all is not right at the center of your being.

Oh and in conclusion be reminded that your safety in a subject you succeed in has to be provided for. You mustn't let praise keep you from stretching away ahead where praise at a given time can't follow you. Good writing is away beyond teachers to do justice to. Write it rich, fill it with everything.

Remember to tell em, if they ask, that I know teachers and I know you.

Affectionately
Papa

I made it end exactly with the paper!

---

123. Alfred Dwight Sheffield (1871–1961) was a teaching assistant in English at Harvard during RF's time there (1897–1999), and, later, professor of English. Sheffield awarded RF a grade of "B" in a composition course for which he had submitted "A Tuft of Flowers," an important early poem later collected in *ABW*.

[To Wilbur L. Cross, editor of The Yale Review. *ALS. Yale.]*

Amherst Mass
November 22 1917

Dear Mr Cross:

Have I done wrong in letting the Houghton Mifflin Company take "Not to Keep" without referring them to you for permission?[124] Come to think of it, I can't remember their saying anything about you or about crediting you. I shall be disgusted if I have helped them circumvent you, because I owe the firm nothing and something less than nothing. I didn't actually know that they had taken the poem. They have never made me any acknowlegement [*sic*] in the shape either of thanks or of a complimentary copy of their blessed book and the only advertisement of the book I have seen named every poet in the world as contributing except me.

I'm so bad at letters that I have been hoping against hope that I should be down along some day and could look in on you for a talk that would save me from having to write this.

I have wanted to say a word to you to explain my failure to do anything about Edward Thomas. I find he was too near me. Sometime I shall write about him. Perhaps it will come to me to write in verse. As yet I feel too much the loss of the best friend I ever had. And by that I dont mean I am overwhelmed with grief. Something in me refuses to take the risk—angrily refuses to take the risk—of seeming to use a grief for literary purposes. When I care less, I can do more.

Always sincerely yours
Robert Frost

---

124. "Not to Keep," originally appeared in *The Yale Review* in January 1917 (see RF's March 6, 1916, letter to Cross). George Herbert Clarke reprinted it in his *Treasury of War Poetry: British and American Poems of the First World War* (Boston: Houghton Mifflin, 1917).

[To Louis Untermeyer. The whimsical spellings are, of course, in the original. ALS, on the letterhead of the Department of English, Amherst College. LoC.]

[Amherst]
December 1 1917

Dear Louis:

I seize this department stationery to give you a new sense of what a merely important person I am become in my decline from greatness. Will you please by return boastage make us knowing to any honors or emolients you have been unable to understand from under?

I notice that there are a number of poems by various people in the magazines for last month and this month—or rather I assume there are: I haven't looked to see.

Answers in full to all your recent questions by telegram are going forward to you by slow fright.

Always and forever yours
Robert

[To Alfred Harcourt. ALS, on Amherst College letterhead. DCL.]

December 1 1917

Dear Alfred:

Undoubtedly those are the pictures and there is nothing the matter with James Chapin.[125]

Sanguinely
Robertus

125. James Chapin, illustrator of a special edition of *NB* (issued in 1919), had studied at the Antwerp Royal Academy and the Society of Independent Painters of America.

[To Amy Lowell. The letter continues Frost's response to Lowell's portrayal of him in Tendencies in Modern American Poetry *(1917). See also RF to Untermeyer, November 7, 1917, and RF to Lowell, October 22. ALS, on the letterhead of the Department of English, Amherst College. Harvard.]*

[Amherst, MA]
December 2 1917

Dear Miss Lowell:

A good way to show forgiveness if you are capable of such an emotion would be to have my young daughter over from Wellesley someday to see you where you sit enthroned. It would mean a lot to her for a long long time afterward not only to have seen you but to have heard you and yes to have been heard a little by you.

I must see you myself before long if only to put it to you while the business is still before the house why I am not by your own showing the least provincial, the most national of American poets—why I ought not to be anyway. Doesnt the wonder grow that I have never written anything or as you say never published anything except about New England farms when you consider the jumble I am? Mother Scotch immigrant. Father oldest New England stock unmixed. Ten years in West. Thirty years in East. Three years in England. Not less than six months in any of these: San Francisco, New York, Boston, Cambridge Lawrence, London. Lived in Maine, N.H., Vt., Mass. Twenty five years in cities, nine in villages, nine on farms. Saw the South on foot. Dartmouth. Harvard two years. Shoe-worker, mill-hand farm-hand, editor, reporter, insurance agent, agent for Shakespearean reader, reader myself, teacher in every kind of school public and private including psychological normal school and college.[126] Prize for running at Caledonia Club picnic; 2 prizes for assumed parts at masquerade balls; medal for goodness in high school; detur for scholarship at Harvard; money for verse. Knew Henry George well and saw much at one time (by way of contrast) of a noted boss.[127] Presbeterian [*sic*], Unitarian, Swedenborgian, Nothing. All the vices but disloyalty and chewing gum or tobacco.

---

126. From 1911–1912, RF taught at Plymouth Normal School (now Plymouth State University), assigning, among other things, William James's *Psychology: The Briefer Course.*

127. RF's father and mother met Henry George (1839–1897), author of *Progress and Poverty* (1879), in San Francisco when he edited the *San Francisco Evening Post,* for which RF's father, William Prescott Frost, worked in 1875. RF also met, as a consequence of his fa-

I liked what you wrote about Robinson as well as he liked what you wrote about me. So he and I are quits there. I liked some of the things you put your finger on in the Masters paper. Not the least of your merits in handling us is your eye for the quotable in our work. You put the best front on all of us by your quotations. I know you must have surprised some prejudiced people with what you were able to find in good old Sandburg.[128]

Always yours sincerely
Robert Frost

[To Lesley Frost. ALS, on the letterhead of the Department of English, Amherst College. UVA.]

[Amherst, MA]
December 3 1917

Dear Lesley:

Be sure to keep a copy of the poem in French.[129] You may be able to use it when you write sometime on A Year in College. And keep everything you do

ther's politicking, the infamous saloonkeeper and Democratic Party boss in San Francisco, Christopher Augustine "Blind Boss" Buckley (1845–1922).

128. In addition to the chapter on RF, *Tendencies in Modern American Poetry* devotes separate chapters to Edwin Arlington Robinson, Edgar Lee Masters and Carl Sandburg, and still another to the imagist poets H. D. (Hilda Doolittle) and John Gould Fletcher.

129. In *FL*, editor Arnold Grade adds this note: "Lesley's poem—'La Vie et la Mort'—survives. For a Frost poem, it begins intriguingly 'At the edge of the deep woods . . .' and reflects the influence of symbolist poetry. Along with a full page of conservative corrections, the unnamed teacher has appended a comment—in French—which suggests that the original assignment called for prose: 'You obviously have some talent but, for the moment, you should rather concentrate on the very real and very great difficulties of good prose. It is the best way to acquire the feeling and taste for, and the mastery of, a language; [qualities] without which one cannot write as correctly and elegantly as poetry demands' " (20–21). The "unmanned teacher" is, in fact, Osmond Thomas Robert (1878–1945), associate professor of French at Wellesley College. He was born in Guernsey, a British Crown dependency in the English Channel off the coast of Normandy (in which both French and English are official languages). Hence RF's application to him, later in the letter, of the epithet "Whitechapel," the implication being that Robert, a British national, is an ersatz, cheap substitute for a genuine "Frenchman." Subsequent to his time at Wellesley, and RF's doubts notwithstanding, Robert enjoyed a long career teaching French at Smith College. RF has at him again in the next letter, to Young.

and have done in everything else. You'll live to get some fun out of it yet. I'd like to know if the Whitechapel Frenchman brought up the subject of your presumption in having attempted a poem in French himself. You could make an audience laugh with the story of that adventure. Prosody (spelled with an o) is the science of versification or meters. It is something most modern poets take pride in professing to know nothing about. There is really very little to it in either English or French anyway. You could learn all that is practicable in it in ten minutes. But the fact is you know it already or your ear knows it and what you would be learning if you turned your attention to it would be merely the technical names for things that are second nature to you. We've talked about it a little already, more as a help to scanning Latin poetry (which we never read without scanning). Hendecasyllables is one of the technical words I mean in prosody. Hexameter is another. But what's the use! You should have heard Wilfrid confessing complete ignorance of the business to the assembled professors of Chicago University last winter.[130] They thought none the less of him but rather the more. Possibly that was because he was an Englishman and a reputation. They might have skun him alive if he had been a mere pupil in their classes. And then again they might not. They were obviously larger men than your Whitechapel Frenchman.

I wonder if Young got no more satisfaction out of the swab than that.[131] Dont let him make you give two thoughts extra to his course. Tend to the Latin, the algebra, and, then if you have any extra energy left, to the Spanish. And dont let Miss Drew suspect for a moment that you may be neglecting her subject.[132] Enjoy that and give her all the pleasure you can. She at least has something of our view of things and you can be yourself with her. I'm looking forward to the essay on Hiawatha. Remember you are to lay most stress on the source books you go to. Longfellows poem mustn't take too much space in proportion. The reason for that being the nature of the essay called for by the authorities at Wellesley.

I've been looking up aedes. And I find it has that form in the nominative singular (as well as in the plural.) It is one of those words with the stem ending in i. Most of them have is in the nominative singular but some have es and they dont lengthen in the genitive. Amnis amnis amni amnem etc. They

130. Wilfrid Gibson.

131. Charles Lowell Young; see the next letter.

132. Helen Louisa Drew, instructor in rhetoric and composition at Wellesley (derided in the next letter, to Young, as "that precisian in syntax").

all have ium in the genitive plural; whereas the common third declension genitive plural ending is a simple um. (I'd like to bet that once on a time all genitive plurals were orum or arum and they got cramped into um.) See what you can find out in the grammar about these ium genitives. I wish there was some rule about their ablative singular. It isnt always i.

You've got enough material already to write your A Year in College. You dont have to worry.

Rah rah rah for some other college than Wellesley.

Papa.

[To Charles Lowell Young (1865–1937), professor of English at Wellesley College. When Lesley Frost's midterm grades were unsatisfactory for what the family thought were unsatisfactory reasons, RF intervened, as did Young, a family friend. ALS. Wellesley.]

Amherst Mass
December 7 1917

My dear Young:

You are a great friend and we are fortunate in our misfortunes to have one so great. You may not know all you have done to be called great. Among a lot of other things you have given us support, and what is better and harder to give, self-support.

As for that precisian in syntax I can't quite get over her. She is nothing new mind you. If I showed surprise in running into her it is not because I had never seen her before, it is because I hadn't seen her for so long I had begun to fool myself into the notion that I had talked her off the face of the earth—laughed her off the face of the earth. I had fallen into a mellow reminiscent way about her in my public utterances that was almost good-natured and forgiving. Now I get my punishment (and not alone) for letting myself believe even for the least division of an hour that there is any such thing as progress. Mea culpa. The fault is mine and the punishment is half Lesley's. I gave a lecture somewhere once upon a time on "The Waiting Spirit: How Long Will It Wait," in which I showed how I thought we had revised our teaching in English and ought to revise it in other subjects to give the spirit its chance from the very first day in school and every step along the way, not counting on it to wait at all. I asserted that there wasnt an English teach [*sic*] left who would be for putting off the day of the spirit in reading and writing till the hard mechanics of the subject could be learned. It has been found that the spirit won't be put off. Either it will be engaged at once and kept engaged or it will take sanctuary in the sun returning unto the God who gave it. So I said in folly and so I made Lesley believe we all believed. And then on top of all the pains your Latin department takes to make Latin painful, comes your French department to exclaim against a child for so far forgetting herself as to write a poem in French before she had studied French prosody. "Let the spirit wait," says your Whitechapel Frenchman: and the spirit can wait or go—it is all one to him. I remember four lines to the tune of Tararaboom-deay I once addressed to Sheffy when I was a patient at Harvard:[133]

Perhaps you think I am going to wait
Till I can write like a graduate
Before I write to my friends any more
You prig stick, what do you take me for.

How it all comes back to me! You see I was angry at the general disposition to take everything written by an undergraduate as an exercise. I never wrote exercises in my life. I was the same sixpence then as now and so is Lesley's Latin teacher the same old scourge blight and destitution that held marks over me for seven years of Latin and then left me nowhere in the end. It's sure she's an argument against taking Latin as literature but isnt she just as much an argument against taking it as a discipline in the hope that the close thinking it calls for in accurate translation will serve in any other walk of life than Latin. Precise in syntax, you would say, precise in business, precise in justice. But not so. I say I have seen Miss Fletcher before.[134] And never in all the years have I found her able to think closely of anything but Latin. I have always found her miserably minded. Was Miss Fletchers handling of the crime she thought she had caught Lesley at precise? It was slovenly. I hope I made her look ridiculous to herself. And it didnt take me five questions. Yet I hardly feel as if I had had satisfaction. She may have to hear further from me. She is a bad woman. To Hell with her piddling accuracy in Latin. I should know it could come to nothing lovely and to nothing lovely it came.

But you have thought of all this in a lifetime of teaching and dismissed it for something the matter with it that I dont see. You don't listen with much patience, I notice.

---

133. Alfred D. Sheffield, from whom RF took English at Harvard.

134. Caroline Rebecca Fletcher, associate professor of Latin at Wellesley College.

Lesley says you had a talk with the Whitechapel Frenchman. I wonder if you found him implacable in his magisterial self-importance. Has Lesley the least hope of success with him? Prosody! I was hoping the mere word might be kept from Lesley as long as possible. I've been telling Lesley how little embarrassed Wilfred Gibson was when he had to confess before all the assembled professors at Chicago last winter that he didn't know one form of verse from another. I believe I don't know a single poet who knows any prosody, except always Robert Bridges. I once asked De la Mare if he had noticed anything queer about the verse in his own The Listeners and he answered that he hadnt noticed anything at all about the verse in it queer or unqueer.[135]

But blast all this. What a father I am! I promise never to talk to you about my children again—any of them. That is if you will forgive my having talked this time and the last time and the time before that and so on back to the day on top of Lafayette. They are really not worth talking about. Lesley in particular is not. She is no good. You can tell her I said so.

I shall intend to see you before the Christmas vacation. Anything to get back to the original footing with you of untroubled literary fellowship. Kindest regards to Mrs Young.

Always yours sincerely
Robert Frost

Did Lesley try to tell you about the pictures (not illustrations) Chapin has been doing for NoB?[136]

[To Lesley Frost. Amy Lowell published Men, Women and Ghosts, *a collection of "story" poems in 1916. ALS. UVA.]*

Amherst Mass
December 9 1917

Dear Lesley:

Read Amy's "Men Women and Ghosts" if you can possibly find time right away so that if Amy invites you over to see her you'll be ready for her. You

135. For Robert Bridges on prosody, see RF's January 19, 1914, letter to Cox. At RF's encouragement, Henry Holt and Company issued Walter de la Mare's *The Listeners and Other Poems* in 1916 (the London edition had appeared in 1912).

136. James Chapin.

won't perhaps care for the longer poems and of course you won't go far in any poem that doesn't get hold of you. Find something to like though. I know you can. Be fairer to her than some people have been to you. She's not going to examine you and see how well you know and like her. You simply wont want to feel lost in the dark should she happen to illustrate what she means by cadence rhythm and such things from her own work. She won't talk about meter. She scorns the very word. Prosody, too, she hates the name of. She may try to tell you what determines the ending place of a line in free verse. She'll be interesting. You'll find that there'll be a lot in what she says.

But perhaps if she writes to you and invites you just now, you had better say you will feel safer to wait till I can come in and show you the way across the city. Tell her I shall be in town toward the end of the week.

I mean to get to Wellesley on the coming Thursday or Friday.

I don't think you had much of any chance to look at any of my boys' work when you were here. You can let that wait till you are home again. But enclosed is one blessed little poem by someone I never heard of and another of not much worth by Raymond Holden.[137] Keep the good one.

I'm not going to talk Latin every time I write. But I've just been having a good look at conjunctions in coordinate sentences. Coordinate are sentences on equal terms neither one subordinate to the other. Both use the indicative. They are joined together by copulative conjunctions, disjunctive conjunctions and adversative conjunctions. Copulative conjunctions are et que at que: they simply hold together the two members—that is to say the two equal sentences. Disjunctive conjunctions sort of put apart at the same time they hold together the two equal sentences. Aut and sed are examples. Adversative conjunctions connect the sentences but in some way contrast the meaning. They give something of the idea of "on the other hand." I speak of these things mostly to increase your "grammatical vocabulary." We have the same lingo in English, copulative disjunctive and adversative. They cover the whole subject of coordinate conjunction. Subordinate conjunctions such as ut are a little harder because they involve the subjunctive mood and "sequence of tenses." Alii . . . alii . . . and some words used like that amount to

---

137. RF met Raymond Holden in Franconia, when the young man (who had recently dropped out of Princeton University in his fourth year) moved to a farm (Sugar Hill) near the Frost family house in Franconia, New Hampshire. Holden purchased part of RF's farm in 1919 and, in the 1920s and 1930s, launched a career as a novelist, poet, and editor.

adversative conjunctions in idea. You translate them Some did so and so and others (on the other hand) did something else.

I wrote a rather red letter to Young. But I mean not to keep myself excited any longer. The worst is Miss Fletcher. But the Frenchman annoys me too.

Affectionately
Papa

[To Louis Untermeyer. This one-line holiday sigh reached Untermeyer, as he notes on the manuscript, on Christmas Day 1917. ALS. LoC.]

[Amherst, MA]
[circa December 23, 1917]

Ah, my dear Louis———

[To Harriet Moody. ALS. Chicago.]

Amherst Mass
December 25 1917

Dear Mrs Moody:

We get a sense from your pranks of your being all around us but at the same time invisable [*sic*] like a deus ex machina. (Do you know that I never noticed before that "the duce" by which we swear is no more than the deus with the "eu" pronounced as in Zeus?) We meet someone who has met someone who has but just now seen you and heard you speak right here in Amherst, we hear you speak ourselves out of the empty air, we are fed by you with candy in a tin box like a bolt from the blue, we get your promise in writing that if we are good and have faith our eyes shall some day (some day this winter) see a better land than this, namely Chicago—"Where never wind blows loudly, but it lies etc." You know the rest—all that boastful Sandburgian, or should I say burgundian "with beaded bubbles winking at the brim."[138]

---

138. In teasing Moody about Carl Sandburg, RF quotes Tennyson's description of Avilion in "Morte D'Arthur" (1842):

> *Where falls not hail, or rain, or any snow,*
> *Nor ever wind blows loudly; but it lies*
> *Deep-meadow'd, happy, fair with orchard-lawns*

I suspect he was paid to do it by the Consolidated Real Estate Agencies to boom Chicago farms. And that was why he was winking. And you can tell him I said so.

But it is hard to have faith in these days when you can actually hear it preached from the pulpit that if those who have only one talent dont know enough to bury it themselves a committee of eugenists should bury it for them and I own to a growing doubt whether you exist as a person at all, whether you may not never have been anything more than a principle of good or evil whose promises aren't worth the paper they are written on. Nevertheless I am, I Profess,

Yours as faith-fully as
circumstances permit
Professor F.

[To Wilbur Rowell. ALS. UVA.]

Amherst College
Amherst Mass
December 31 1917

Dear Mr Rowell:

Would it be too much to ask you for two hundred and fifty dollars of this year's money now? If it isn't one extra expense, it seems to be another in these kaleidoscopic times. Last year I was getting established in Franconia; this year I am straining my resources to set up housekeeping here. I think I told you that I had come to a professorship at Amherst. I came last year to fill the place temporarily of another man who was on leave of absence and seem to have made a place of my own.[139] I get talked about as a farmer but I am not

---

And bowery hollows crown'd with summer sea,
Where I will heal me of my grievous wound.

And Keats' "Ode to a Nightingale" (1819):

O for a beaker full of the warm South!
Full of the true, the blushful Hippocrene,
With beaded bubbles winking at the brim,
And purple-stainèd mouth . . .

139. Professor George B. Churchill had left the Department of English temporarily to serve in the Massachusetts state senate (1917–1919).

versatile enough to make a good farmer. I am a much better teacher than farmer, and that not just in my own estimation. This seems to be a pleasant solution of the living problem for the kind of writer I am.

With the season's greetings.

Sincerely yours
Robert Frost

[To Morris Palmer Tilley, a professor of English at the University of Michigan whose family often summered near Franconia, New Hampshire. ALS. UM.]

Amherst Mass
January 20 1918

Dear Tilley:

We missed you last summer. I suppose you took the air somewhere nearer home. Perhaps if it wasn't easy on your apparatus, we may hope to see you back in Franconia for another breath of our air.

Don't let your difficulty with my sister trouble you in the least. She's a good girl, but hard to do anything for. The only way is to leave her to herself. She has been learning a lot of German. I wonder if it will be any good to her in the present state of prejudice against it.[140] I hope she may fall on better times soon.

I've just toned down a few places in your notes where I [*sic*] afraid you make me sound too heroic.[141] I thought too, I wouldn't be made to say any-

---

140. Jeanie Frost was then a student at the University of Michigan. As to her course of study, RF had ample cause for concern. Anti-German feeling ran high in Ann Arbor. In October 1917, the university's Board of Regents dismissed Carl E. Eggert from the German Department on charges of "seditious conduct" in the classroom. In 1918, when Jeanie was studying the language, a group of alumni petitioned the university to drop German from its curriculum. The request was ignored, but enrollment in the German department fell from 1,300 to 500. (See "The University in Time of War," a website maintained by the University of Michigan.) Jeanie's troubles only grew worse, and her oncoming insanity, at times, took the war as an idiom of distress; see RF's June 6, 1919, letter to Rowell. See also his March 21, 1920, letter to Rowell (*SL*, 245–246), and his April 12, 1920, letter to Untermeyer (*SL*, 247); these will appear in volume two of the present edition.

141. Tilley's "Notes from Conversations with Robert Frost" are held now at the Bentley Historical Library at the University of Michigan.

thing against Pound in which he would be recognized. Your interest that prompted these notes is of course flattering. You are a good friend.

Come to Franconia next summer.

Yours ever
Robert Frost

[To Wilbur L. Cross. ALS. Yale.]

Amherst Mass
February 18 1918

Dear Mr. Cross:

I wonder if you would let my friend George Whicher of our faculty write a paper for you on Edward Thomas. Whicher is a writer of experience and a poet of quality himself who knows and cares for Thomas's work.[142] I should do what I could to help him make the paper somewhat personal. Sometime I shall have something of my own to show you about Thomas (it will probably be in verse), but not right away.

These are overwhelming times. I feel as if my poetry and pretty much all the rest of me underneath a heap of jarring atoms lay.[143]

Always sincerely yours
Robert Frost

---

142. Whicher's essay on Thomas appeared in *The Yale Review* 9 (1919): 556–567.

143. From John Dryden's "Song for St. Cecelia's Day, 1687" (the quasi-Lucretian atomism of which would have appealed to RF):

From Harmony, from heav'nly Harmony
This universal Frame began.
When Nature underneath a heap
Of jarring Atoms lay,
And could not heave her Head,
The tuneful Voice was heard from high,
Arise ye more than dead.

[To Louis Untermeyer. In RFLU *Untermeyer mistakes RF's abbreviation of the year for the day of the month. The bracketed date given here derives from a chronology Lawrance Thompson maintained (held now at UVA). ALS. LoC.]*

Am Feb [28] '18

Dear Louis:

Elinor is just a little afraid from my report of your paper on Thomas that you haven't said all you can in his praise.[144] Like him all you can. It was little but condescension he got from that gang over there. Have your reservations in the first part, but if you could make the last part bulk a little larger by naming or even quoting a few more of the good things—

Always yours
R.F.

enclosed see if you can find my poem—for the Sullivan Garland.[145]

[To Martha E. D. White. Year derived from internal evidence: RF was scheduled to give a talk in Arlington, Massachusetts, where White lived, on March 11, 1918; see RF to Martha E. D. White, November 2, 1917. ALS. ACL.]

Amherst March 6 [1918]

Dear Mrs White

I have waited till the last moment for better news of Mrs Frost than I was afraid I was going to be able to give you. She has been thinking she ought not to leave the children as they are. It stands this way at the present writing. She will go with me if I will wait till Sunday for her and not keep her away more than two nights.

So unless something turns up to change her mind I shall have her with me when I arrive at Arlington on Sunday. I know she will be glad if I keep her to her present resolution. We'll all have a pleasant old talk.

---

144. Untermeyer's essay was later published in the *North American Review* for February 1919: 263–266.

145. See *RFLU,* 64–65. Vachel Lindsay had invited RF and a number of other poets to compose tributes to the boxer John L. Sullivan; RF took the occasion to parody Lindsay's "General William Booth Enters into Heaven," enclosing, with this letter, a poem titled: "John L. Sullivan Enters into Heaven (To be sung to the tune of 'Heaven Overarches You and Me')" (ibid., 65–66).

Am I too late to be naming people for you to invite to my eloquence? There would be Miss Alice Brown, 11 Pinkney [*sic*] St Boston, Mrs & Mr George H. Browne, Chauncy St. Cambridge,[146] and gracious I dont know who for the fourth without giving offence to someone we didnt invite.

Here's looking forward.

Sincerely yours
Robert Frost

[To George Browne. Year derived from postmark. ALS. Plymouth.]

Amherst March 6 [1918]

Dear Browne:

I'm coming in to thank you Monday or Tuesday for the good time you gave Lesley at the Carnival.[147] Her last letter was full of it.

You could put me up Tuesday night maybe.[148]

Ever yours
R.F.

[To Josephine Preston Peabody Marks. Year derived from internal evidence, and from the record of her correspondence (held at Harvard). ALS. Harvard.]

Amherst March 6 [1918]

Dear Mrs Marks

Much as I appreciate your invitation and much as I should like to be with you and Colum[149] (and all Boston I suppose I should add) I don't for the life of me see how I can get away from my afternoon lecture on Monday in time to

---

146. Here RF has crossed out the name of Charles Lowell Young, a family friend and professor of English at Wellesley. The American novelist, poet, and playwright Alice Brown (1856–1948) was an early admirer of *NB*.

147. Possibly the Winter Carnival held annually (at the time) at Wellesley; it took place in February.

148. On March 13, RF spoke on the subject "The Unmade Word, or, Fetching and Far-Fetching" at the Browne and Nichols School in Cambridge, Massachusetts. For the text of the talk, see *CPPP*, 694–697.

149. The Irish poet, novelist, and playwright Padraic Colum (1881–1972), who had come to the United States in 1914 for a visit that ultimately lasted some eight years. See

get ready for a dinner as early as six-thirty—the two engagements call for such different and in fact almost opposite ways of doing the hair. Seriously and honestly! I have given the matter long thought. So will you accept my regrets and make it right with Colum, the Bard?

Mrs Frost's excuses are her own and begin nearer home in the children who are not well and whom she has decided at the last moment as usual not to leave.

She joins me in thanks for thinking of us and in best wishes.

Always sincerely yours
Robert Frost

[To Lesley Frost. ALS. UVA.]

March 18 1918
Amherst

Dear Lesley:

We'll all be together again soon telling funny stories.

This is the day in the week when I get a chance to do to others as still others do to you. I wonder if truth were told how many of my underlings suffer from my exactions as you suffer from poor Miss Drew's.

Do you know I half suspect Miss Drew meant to take your sarcasm to herself by her correction of "teacher" to "instructor."[150] It was as much as to say "teacher" is too general. "You aimed at me; so say instructor and be done with it." Were you shooting at her?

First blue bird for us this morning.

Tell us your train on Friday and perhaps we can be at Northampton to meet you.

Affectionately
Papa

Enclosed is five

---

also RF to Josephine Preston Peabody Marks, April 15, 1918; as it turned out, he was apparently able to attend the dinner spoken of here.

150. Helen Louisa Drew, instructor in rhetoric and composition at Wellesley College.

[To Josephine Preston Peabody Marks. ALS. Harvard.]

Amherst Mass
April 15 1918

Dear Mrs Marks:

May I accept your invitation now and wait till I get back from the West late next week to talk definitely about a day for the meeting of the Poetry Society?[151] I do want to see the Poetry Society before I get much older and both of us, Elinor and I, want to see more of you soon than we were able to see when we were with you in the crowd at Padraic Colum's to-do. I can't say that I think a great many new poets have occurred since last we met, but enough has happened in poetry for some talk before we catch up with it.

I am dedicating the swag of my journey this time to Liberty Bonds.[152] Please remember that when you are tempted to think ill of me and my works. Remember too that I never think ill of you and your works, wont you?

Sincerely yours
Robert Frost

[To Harold Goddard Rugg. ALS. DCL.]

Amherst Mass
May 5 1918

My dear Rugg

Of course come to see us. Most happy to have you.

Im just in from the west and write this in haste.

Always yours
Robert Frost

151. From April 18 to April 24 RF traveled to Chicago and Minneapolis to give a series of readings.

152. On April 5, 1918, the third "Liberty Loan" program was launched to support the war effort.

[To James Chapin. ALS. DCL.]

Amherst Mass.
May 10 1918

Dear Chapin:

It's the best news that you have decided to go in for happiness. You know how much my heart's with you in your enterprise because I told you beforehand. It's a gay world, I sometimes think, and I cant help swaying a little when I walk in it. I must say I contemplated you with romantic pleasure. What more can I say unless it be that someone is getting an artist.[153]

The more we see of you in the summer the better, if you are going to be such a good boy as all this.

Would our home in Pelham be of any use to you for a stop over for any length of time on your way northward?[154] It will be locked up for several months. I could send you a key.

Elinor joins me in beseeching you to get us in just right, both of us, with the lady. That means you must neither overpraise nor underpraise us; but you must use a lot of tact.

Always your friend
Robert Frost

[To Lesley Frost. ALS. UVA.]

Amherst May 13 1918

Dear Lesley:

Just as much as this gives room for to tell you a disappointment, namely, that we can't get away before Wednesday and possibly Thursday afternoon on account of ill health in the head of the family who am in bed at this moment with something the doctor doesn't no [*sic*] what to call because he hasnt been called in to look at me. As near as he can make out by telephone

---

153. Chapin married Abigail Beal Forbes in 1918. Their only son, James Forbes Chapin, who became a notable jazz musician, was born in 1919, and they divorced shortly thereafter.

154. The house in which the Frosts had resided since October 1917 was just across the Amherst town line in West Pelham, Massachusetts. It would be empty once they relocated to Franconia for the summer.

it seems to be this here throatal (throttle) epidemic that seems to be epidemic in Amherst.[155] And if that weren't enough there is additional reason in the professional reasoner Ernest Hocking who is to do the Phi Beta Kappa here this week and in whose audience I really ought to show myself.[156] So we may as well say it won't be till Thursday afternoon on the four o'clock from here arriving in Boston at eight in the evening, too late for anything that day. We'll be beginning Boston then only on Friday and as you will get free the next day you wont have long to be disturbed by our being so near you and you unable to see us. Lot of things to tell and listen to, though except in an academic way I have had an adventureless year. Same with you—a[d]ventureless except in an academic way. But in that way Oh my! I beat you in one respect. I get an honorary M.A. from Amherst.[157] Then it is fixed that I am to do 1/3 time for 1/2 pay (that is 1/2 of 5000). I haven't made myself particularly detested yet—that's all that means. Give me another year to get into trouble. I don't suppose I have done anything to distinguish myself except to do one chapel talk that made talk and got me chosen to give the talk at what is called Senior Chapel at the end of the year. Without having distinguished yourself as a mere student you have apparently made people like you, or they wouldnt be trying as hard to entangle you in next year's courses. After all it's been an exciting and varigated [*sic*] year for you—really just the kind of experience mere tuition can't buy. Only fortune can bestow it, and she cant do it entirely from without: she has to do much of it from within. I dont quite get over my resentment against some of Wellesley but <u>nearly</u> the last vestige goes with the joke of your agreeing to take Latin Composition with Miss Fletcher.[158] That puts us on top of it all with a laugh. <u>Aint</u> it the funny world? Well that is about all I can write in this position. I can tell you of the ups and downs of my Western trip later. I personally conducted the elopement of Joseph Warren Beach that awful sinner with an assistant of his in the graduate school.[159] I never saw craziness as near the surface as it is in Beach. He's a darn fool but

155. RF fell ill during the influenza pandemic of 1918–1919; it took him some months to recover.

156. William Ernest Hocking (1873–1966), professor of philosophy at Harvard, was a close family friend.

157. Awarded in May 1918.

158. Caroline Rebecca Fletcher, associate professor of Latin at Wellesley College.

159. RF was present at the wedding of Joseph Warren Beach and Dagmar Doneghy on April 24, 1918 (a wedding RF had, indeed, instigated); it was Beach's second marriage, his first having dissolved in 1917.

he makes me laugh when I'm near him—laugh and cut up. It was cruel of me to marry him off, but I had to do it—I was cutting up. It was like some Shakespearean confusion.

Wish we could see you play ball.

Anxious to see the story.

Affectionately
Papa

Boston address by Thursday night 97 Pinkney St.[160]

[In this letter to Louis Untermeyer, RF whimsically assumes the persona of Untermeyer, and under that auspice addresses himself. Dating assigned by Untermeyer. ALS. LoC.]

[Franconia, NH]
[June 6, 1918]
Date to suit

Dear Robt

Sorry you found nothing in the Liberator you inordinately liked but my attack on Masters.[161] I can see how you might like that for personal reasons; and as a matter of fact it was a pretty piece of writing, especially the first part of it, which I rather liked myself. But on the whole the merits of the magazine as an aphrodisiac were thrown away on you. To the pure all things are poor.

I can just know how the very naughty love story of Philip Dru[162] will put you off the main interest of this book which is political and right in your line. Yes my dear Robt you were disposed from that early San Francisco training to a life of intrigue and machination.[163] Love is a kickshaw and dalliance

---

160. The home of Alice Brown.

161. *The Liberator* succeeded *The Masses,* which the Wilson administration had forced out of print. In the new periodical, Untermeyer had published (in June 1918) a review of Edgar Lee Master's book *Toward the Gulf* (New York: Macmillan, 1918).

162. Edward Mandell House (aka "Colonel House") (1858–1938), a close advisor to Woodrow Wilson, published, anonymously, a futurist novel titled *Philip Dru: Administrator: A Story of Tomorrow, 1920–1935* (New York: B. W. Huebsch, 1912); his authorship of the book was an open secret.

163. RF's father, William Prescott Frost, Jr., was involved in San Francisco politics when Christopher Augustine "Blind Boss" Buckley (1845–1922) ran the Democratic Party machine there in the 1870s and 1880s. See also RF's July 18, 1918, letter to Untermeyer.

naught, but give you a field like poetry that calls to the pulling of wires and the manipulation of ropes, to the climbing of every black reviewer's back stairs for preferment and you are there with a suit case in both hands "like an old stone savage armed." (I know you dont mind my quoting from your published works.[164]) I wish I could say something to prepare you for what is before you in Philip Dru. There is no more to it than this: Philip meets Gloria (so named from the umbrella goods of commerce) quite properly through her brother a classmate at West Point. Nothing to take exception to thus far. They walk out into a Mexican desert together. She faints from the heat. He has to carry her and in carrying her loses his sight from the alkali dust he kicks up as he stumbles along with his precious burden. Nothing is insinuated of his having overstepped the proprieties at this time. Neither has anything to reproach the other with. I cant believe that Col House means Philip to have carried her other than as a perfect gentleman else how would she have consented to come to dinner with Philip (and Col House too; for I make no doubt Col House was at the dinner if anyone was) that memorable day after Philips great victory over the armies of plutocracy? Unless he did nothing he ought not to do how was Gloria left wondering all those years while he was busy reforming the U.S.A. and tout le monde and hadnt time to see much of her whether he loved her or not. You must remember that this isnt a novel by Hardy where every little accident has a significance in sex. In the end when he honorably can marry her when all his obligations to the state are discharged, that is to say when he has a minute to spare he looks around for Gloria and marries her. That's another thing that makes me almost sure that the desert episode was quite all right—at least that it is possible to put a good construction on it in the work of a man like Col House: Philip's love sounds so like true love—the love that would not be so much loved it not honor more.[165]

---

164. Here, RF has "Untermeyer" quote "Mending Wall" in a disparaging reference to William Stanley Braithwaite.

165. An allusion to the last stanza of Richard Lovelace's "To Lucasta, Going to the Wars":

> *Yet this inconstancy is such*
> *As you too shall adore;*
> *I could not love thee, dear, so much,*
> *Loved I not honor more.*

But whatever you make of Philips relations with women (and I have pretty well covered them in the foregoing) for your own sake don't let them blind you to the beauty of such poetry as that of Col House's chapter on reforming our burial practices.[166] You can plainly hear the voice of Col House saying to his good friend the President after the war is over and the captains and the kings are licked: "And now, Woodrow, what do you say to our doing away with this awful habit of letting dead people down into a hole in the ground and throwing earth onto their coffin lid when it would seem so much pleasanter to gather as friends and relatives and see them shoved into a fiery oven and cooked to ashes. Next after the social revolution (I am sorry it had to be so bloody—over a million killed wounded and missing—I can't help wondering where the missing went) next after the social revolution nothing is so dear to me as cremation. And I think chewing is a good thing too. Don't you think something could be done about that. Couldn't the noon hour of the laboring classes be lengthened say ten minutes with the express understanding that unless the actual time consumed in consumption—but I leave to you the formulation of the statute. I never thought when I was half the age I am now that I would ever have a chance to put a notion into practice just because I found I couldnt put it into words. And say Woodrow what's the matter with making a law that if anyone dreams a dream often enough to indicate that theres something he wants that he can't have and dont dare to ask for but if he submits his dream in writing to the department of Labor and Parturition and it be found that what he says is true and he really has the dream and often enough to be called habitual and nothing else will take the place of what is lacking in his life, such as more furniture or a different wife or a reputation as a novelist or a kind of food that will agree with him, well then what do you say Woodrow if some other department that shall herein after be provided for and gotten up and authorized by Congress shall do everything in its power to make that man happy. Do you feel with me in these aspirations?"

Please legitimatize by signing on this line

---

166. Chapter fifty-five of *Philip Dru*.

[To George Whicher (1889–1954), American scholar and educator; professor of English at Amherst from 1915 to 1954. ALS. ACL.]

Franconia N.H.
June 21 1918

Dear Whicher:

Two weeks' farming has made me think better of teaching than I did when I left it at Commencement in the first stages of asthma but the last of agoraphobia. When you come right down to it such ills of teaching as man's ingratitude and benefits forgot are as nothing compared with the freezing of one bitter sky in mid-June.[167] Our thermometer dropped to 25 night before last and thirty last night losing us all our seed and a month's growth where months are more precious than they are in your region. That worst night the large farmers fought the cold with fire and water; the small farmers wrapped their gardens up in their own clothes and bed clothes and went without themselves. A lot of good it did. My favorite tomato froze right in my heavy winter overcoat. Our local Buddist [*sic*] blames it all on the eclipse in conjunction with the new star in Aquila.[168] She was educated at the New Hampshire State Normal School (where I taught) and belongs to the Baptist Church, but she professes Buddism [*sic*] at the evening meetings, practices transmigration and derives the present more from the future than from the past. For this latitude she insists that cucumbers and watermelons shall be planted before sunrise on the Sunday before the first rain in June—if at all.

Oh, yes, my novel. I want that to take rank with the epic I accounted for my time with to my friends in England. Just keep that in mind—that I am

---

167. RF borrows his phrasing from *As You Like It* (2.vii):

Blow, blow, thou winter wind,
Thou art not so unkind
As man's ingratitude;
Thy tooth is not so keen,
Because thou art not seen,
Although thy breath be rude. . . .
Freeze, freeze, thou bitter sky,
That dost not bite so nigh
As benefits forgot . . .

168. On June 8, 1918, a supernova (scientific name *Nova Aquilae 1918*) appeared in the constellation Aquila.

known to be at work on a novel and you will be a valuable witness to call when I am taken under the law to 'press loafers.

Write a lot. Enjoy the war. I've made up my mind to do the second anyway. I dont see why the fact that I can't be in a fight should keep me from liking the fight.

Our best to you all.
Always yours
Robert Frost

[To James Chapin. ALS. DCL]

Franconia N.H.
June 24 1918

Dear Chapin:

Come along with your tent and your painter's tackle—your paint-pots ropes pulleys hooks and ladders. We'll paint Mrs Elinor F. all the colors of the rainbow. I know just where to find her when we want her. But you know all about that now that you are happily married. All our felicitations.

I cant promise you any Hamilton this summer to show your wife, but there will be Bissell enough to go round.[169]

Here's looking forward. Expect you'll look twice as numerous as you did.

Always yours
Robert Frost

[To Ernest Silver. Sent via registered mail. ALS. DCL.]

Franconia N.H.
June 27 1918

Dear Mr Silver:

Politics any day in preference to business. A lot has happened in the State since last I saw you. But that will have to wait I suppose till I drop off the train sometime at Plymouth.

---

169. The Samuel Bissell family lived in Sugar Hill (near Franconia), and occasionally took in Frost family guests. "Hamilton" we have been unable to identify.

Meanwhile about that check for $15. Your version of it is perhaps near enough the truth, but the exact facts of the matter are these: I got the check all right and put it with a letter into an envelope addressed to Mr Hardy. I am sure of that much. I could even do fairly well at reproducing the letter—mostly a pleasantry about an adventure of his and mine going with umbrellas to rescue a lot of kids caught out on a picnic in the rain. The rest's a blank. I assume that I mailed the letter. But it seems it never turned up. I may have lost it, some one I entrusted it to may have lost it, or Uncle Sam may have. Let's blame Uncle Sam: everybody's shying something at Burleson: he's used to it.[170] I'm sorry to have caused all this trouble. Will you have another check made out and we'll see if we can't do better with it this time.[171]

The only Plymouthian I've seen is Miss Hilliard (teaching here at Franconia) and I had only a few minutes' gossip with her. I didn't hear that there was much new with you down there except teachers: those of course are always coming and going. The interesting thing is not those that come and go but those that stay like Dr Lamson.[172] He's the useful citizen. Remember me to him, will you?

Im back at my old tricks again I suppose you've heard—teaching. Funny game.

Sincerely yours
Robert Frost

---

170. Albert S. Burleson (1863–1937), postmaster general under Wilson, infamous for enforcing antiobscenity and antisedition statutes.

171. In his reply to RF, written on June 27, 1918, Silver wrote: "I have taken up the matter of that last check with Mr. Plummer, the state treasurer, and find that it never has been presented for payment. Mr. Plummer has drawn a new check which I will ask you to be kind enough to endorse" (the letter is held now at DCL).

172. Herbert H. Lamson, a teacher of science whom RF met while at Plymouth Normal School (1911–1912), and in honor of whom the Lamson Library at Plymouth State University (as the institution is now known) is named.

[To Louis Untermeyer. ALS. LoC.]

Franconia N.H.
June 27 1918

Dear Louis:

Why when you can write poetry like Jerusalem Delivered[173] will you continue to mess with the Masses (or is it mass with the messes?). Is it because I am an aristocrat as someone in a review accused me of being that I so object to your social revolutionary antics? No it is because I am as ambitious for you as a mother. Havent I told you once that your social revolution, yes and my world war, are nothing but politics which is a game you and I know what we think of when we see partizans of the old line at it. Politics is a joke because it is as speculative as philosophy. I lump them together, politics and philosophy, as things a young fellow might toy with in his salad days. Once on a time I fooled with philosophy myself—wrote a little book in fact (which may you never see) on Staving Off Results, the theme being the result of staving off results. But, dear me, you, and everybody, I thought you were putting away childish things. You are President of a manufacturing concern now. What do you want to be—President of the U.S.? That's where your political agitation will land you if you dont watch out. And then what will Dick think of his father? Will he think he's farther? I axe you. We all want you to be a poet. Poetry is the only wildness excusable in a person who has attained to your dignities, and that for the simple reason that it's the only wildness that can be hoped to carry you beyond those dignities. It may not carry you beyond them, but ah it may. (Privately I think it has carried you already, but it's not to my purpose to say so here.) We want you to immortalize. Don't for God's sake spoil everything for us by turning out a Philip Dru. (By the way I didn't tell you Huebsh[174] writes he suspects you of having written Philip.) Be great.

---

173. "Jerusalem Delivered" appeared in *The Yale Review* 7 (1918): 742–747. It was subsequently reprinted, as was RF's "Not to Keep," in *War Poems from the Yale Review* (New Haven: Yale University Press, 1918). The occasion for Untermeyer's poem was the Battle of Jerusalem (November–December 1917), as a result of which the British acquired control of the ancient city from the Ottoman Empire.

174. B. W. Huebsch was the publisher—later, he served on the board of Viking Press—who released (anonymously) *Philip Dru: Administrator: A Story of Tomorrow, 1920–1935*. See the notes to RF's June 6, 1918, letter to Untermeyer.

To be frank I'm not much in favor of your going on with your book of criticism just now when the whole world is doing books of criticism. Thats another thing I oppose you in. You just deliberately lose yourself in the ruck of Phelpses and all.[175] Of course you can do it to tease me, making a virtue of humility all the way. But it's foolish and it's dangerous. You should know better what you are after. For my part I live in fear lest I shall get so I can't tell politics and criticism from the warmth that called and clasped me to my kind. It wouldnt hurt you to cultivate the same fear in yourself.

If you really value that letter of Vachel's you put yourself in my power by letting me have it.[176] You'll have to be mighty good to get it back. Would you be willing to abandon politics to get it back? And criticism? I've about made up my mind you'll have to.

Now don't run tattling to Jean about my cruelty. She'll just take my side if you do. What does she want of anything but the poet in you?

Tell Dick hurrah for the Fourth.[177] Tell him I'm what I call a Fourth-of-July American and what does he call himself?

Forever yours
Robt Frost

Robt—perfect passive participle, preferred by some to form ending in ed.

[To Louis Untermeyer. ALS. LoC.]

Franconia N.H.
July 13 1918

Dear Louis:

You may say of me if you like that when Allen B. [*sic*] Thurman Samuel J. Tilden and David Bennett Hill had read to them what I proposed (in a prospectus) to write about the campaigns of '76, '80 and 84 disrespectively if they didn't come across, all three sat down with one bump on the same park

175. William Lyon Phelps (1865–1943) was a professor of English at Yale; he authored a number of popular books of literary criticism.

176. See the notes to RF's to February 17, 1919, letter to Untermeyer.

177. Jean Starr Untermeyer was, at the time, Untermeyer's wife; their son was named Richard (Dick).

bench and cried.[178] But wait till I tell you what they cried. They cried: "Blackmail! We will have to come across, or I believe the little cuss will be as good as his word. He has all the qualifications: he can write: he was born in time to speak from personal knowledge: he is unscrupulous in his origin; his grandfather was out in Shays Rebellion: and his father was a delegate to the convention at Cincinatti [*sic*] that nominated General Hancock and a close friend of that Buckley the blind boss of San Francisco who died a fugitive from justice in Hawaii before the Yankee Imperialists stole the islands from Queen Liliahhowdoyouspellher.[179] This menacing boy was one of the plain people whom Garfield was survived by in 1881 when he was shot by Gitteau where stands the brass star in the floor of the R.R. station in Baltimore (which see), whom McKinley was survived by when he was shot by Emma's admirer, the youthful Czolgosz, at the Pan American Exposition at Bluffalo, got up to disarm the suspicions of the small American Reps that what we were after was them. We have of course to steer a course about midway between the treasonable and the libelous in these days when all courts tend to degenerate into courts martial;[180] but we say it without fear of consequences, we had far rather pension this boy here and now right out of the public

178. Allen G. Thurman (1813–1895), eminent politician in the Democratic Party and its nominee for vice president in 1888, helped broker the compromise that resolved the disputed election of 1876, whereby the Republican Rutherford B. Hayes (1822–1893) prevailed over Democratic Party presidential nominee Samuel J. Tilden (1814–1886). David Bennett Hill (1843–1910), a Democrat, served as governor of New York (1885–1891) and then as senator from New York (1892–1897).

179. RF's paternal grandfather, William Prescott Frost (1823–1901) could not, needless to say, have taken part in Shays's Rebellion (1786–1787). But his father, William Prescott Frost Jr. (1850–1885), was indeed a delegate to the convention that nominated General Winfield Scott Hancock (1824–1886) as the Democrats' unsuccessful standard-bearer in the 1880 campaign against James Garfield (1831–1881). Christopher Augustine "Blind Boss" Buckley (mentioned already in these pages) was the Democratic Party boss in San Francisco; RF's father knew him. He traveled to Hawaii in the mid-1880s, on hiatus from politics, but did not, as RF whimsically suggests, die there a fugitive from justice; he died in San Francisco at his Clay Street home. In January 1893, in a coup ultimately supported by the United States, Queen Liliuokalani was overthrown and replaced by a government composed of members of the so-called Committee of Safety (comprised of Americans, Europeans, and Hawaiian collaborators).

180. A reference to the severity with which the Espionage Act of 1917 and the Sedition Act of 1918 were then enforced.

pocket, than see him launched with all his inside knowledge, his gift of frankness and his love of the picturesque on an Epic of Politics that unless something intervened to stop it might go on forever. Absolutely fatal as was the loss of the electoral votes of Florida and Louisiana, there are worse things in the world (and out of it too for the matter of that) than being robbed by an empire especially since in the election of 1876 we had our own weakness chiefly to blame in not having made a more thorough job of disfranchising the nigger. No this boy knows too much. He has lived through more times already than the Wandering Jew. Better infanticide than homocide [*sic*]: shall we kill him now? All these in favor of this result make it none by the usual motion."[181]

So they cried like push-cart pedlars in a side street. Then having cried they wept. Like the true Democrats it is hoped to make the world safe for,[182] they managed this without handkerchiefs, dashing the tears from their eyes and noses with the back of fists, all except Allen Thurman who used his symbolic red bandanna,[183] the democratic theory of which in the campaign of 1892 was that one copy of it will last a life time: it will take care of a nose running with grief or a cold, a nose bleeding with love or a fight; a snap in the wind as it is pulled endwise from the pocket and it is as presentable as if it had been to the laundry: no one could tell whether the last thing had in it was a cold or a nosebleed. We hardly made the most of Thurman's red bandanna though reference to the public prints of that day will convince you that we did not

181. Charles J. Guiteau shot President Garfield in Washington, D.C., on July 2, 1881; Garfield died eleven weeks later. Leon Czolgosz, an admirer of the radical Emma Goldman, assassinated President William McKinley on September 6 at the Pan-American Exposition in Buffalo, New York. Disputed electoral votes from Florida and Louisiana (among other states) led to the crisis alluded to above in the campaign of 1876; Hayes ultimately assumed the presidency in a deal that ended Reconstruction, effectively opening the way for Southern states, under a resurgent Democratic Party, to disenfranchise African American voters.

182. A reference to Wilson's April 2, 1917, speech, asking Congress for a declaration of war: "The world must be made safe for democracy. Its peace must be planted upon the tested foundations of political liberty. We have no selfish ends to serve. We desire no conquest, no dominion. We seek no indemnities for ourselves, no material compensation for the sacrifices we shall freely make. We are but one of the champions of the rights of mankind."

183. The Democratic ticket of Grover Cleveland and Allen Thurman sported a red bandanna as its campaign flag.

fail to correlate it with the way Thomas Jefferson rode to his inaugural alone and tied his horse to a post outside the White House with his own hand.

You are free to use any or all of the foregoing you can make head or tail of except what Thurman Tilden and Hill as with one voice cried, which I consider so tributary that I am reserving it to have it cut on my tombstone as a surprise to my enemies and critics, and I'd a little rather not have it released till then. A public character has got to keep something up his sleeve for when he is dead.

Anybody must be a baby not to see from my origin in such corruption that I am really strong meat for men, though I advertently admit that Masters may be a great man too.[184] Moreover though I mewed my infancy among political bosses and in party bigotry, it must never fail to be mentioned once an hour or so while the world lasts that I have always liked reformers who went in for radishes. You knew I gave Henry George his start. I remember once, when I was a very small boy, going to his house in San Francisco and before dinner or supper going with him to a very sandy garden to get radishes. (I state but the truth.[185])

Thats the kind of a hairpin I am, if posterity asks you anything about me. I have been associated to my lasting good with all the reformers from him to you—all the reformers at any rate who go in for radishes. But all the time it has been my purpose to keep away from as many poets as I could and not hurt their feelings.

And by the way I should hardly want to prescribe for your radishes without seeing them. I have always found it dangerous and unsatisfactory to prescribe for or treat radishes in absentia. Only as an emergency measure, you might try thinning them to four feet apart in the row if your row is not less than four feet in length and then consult Davies the tree specialist.[186] They may be suffering from crevices (so-called) in which case the crevices should be scraped out, treated with some reliable antisceptic and filled with cement. You must act at once, as the life of a radish is very short at best and they will have gone by or been eaten before you can make them comfortable. Whatever you do, dont be persuaded to spray them with Paris green

184. The poet Edgar Lee Masters.

185. RF's parents did indeed meet Henry George (1839–1897), the author of *Progress and Poverty,* in San Francisco.

186. Possibly a joke at the expense of Welsh poet W. H. Davies (1871–1940). In a May 18, 1914, letter to Cox, RF derides Davies' pretensions as a naturalist.

too immediately before you eat them. Better salt than Paris green if you think you must eat them.[187]

I concede that your criticism will differ from theirs in being criticism, but how will people know this if you publish yours in the same year with theirs?

Robt Frost

Next letter will deal with the Maria Halpin scandal, campaign of '84.[188]

[To Wilbur Rowell. ALS. UVA.]

Franconia N.H.
July 23 1918

Dear Mr Rowell:

The check for this year hasn't come. I thought perhaps I ought to tell you so that if it has been sent and gone astray we can be getting on the track of it. We have been so busy farming that we didnt think of it till a day or two ago.

With best wishes.

Always sincerely yours
Robert Frost

[To Charles Lowell Young. ALS. Wellesley.]

Franconia N.H.
August 8 1918

My dear Young:

Isn't it just our luck! Mrs Lator is baby-farming this year and couldn't take you if you'd come—and you wouldn't come under the circumstances if she'd take you. I've tried to find somewhere else to lay your head not too far off, but there seems nowhere except the Spooner Farm[189] which I'm afraid is too

187. Paris green (copper acetoarsenite) is a potent pesticide.

188. In the campaign of 1884, Grover Cleveland's Republican opponents charged that he'd fathered an illegitimate child by Maria Crofts Halpin; he admitted having paid Halpin child support since 1874 (though it was not clear whether he or one of his associates was actually the father of her child).

189. Now known as the Franconia Inn, the Spooner Farm (purchased by Henry Spooner in 1865), regularly took in summer boarders (a practice common among farmers in the area, including, apparently, the Lator family, referred to near the start of the letter).

public a place to please Mrs Young. You know about what it is. I haven't liked to ask how full it is (that being a point hotels are sensitive on) but I should judge by the looks that it wasnt full enough to be called drunk, I was going to say. I mean it isnt so full that you couldnt find room there to be by yourselves. Then there are places in the village; but I don't want you to be away off down town. I'll tell you what: I dont think the Spooner Farm would be so bad this quiet year. And anyway what if there are some of commoner sort on the Spooner piazza? After all they are only less human than we are. Everything is relative. To the German all Americans seem niggers and Indians.

I've wasted some time in accomplishing nothing, so perhaps you had best wire me if you want me to see what I can do for you at the Spooner Farm.

Beautiful rain on the gardens and there's a crane wading in a big rain-pool below us on the meadow.

We're looking forward to seeing you both. So don't fail us.

Always yours
Robert Frost

Glorious war, isn't it?

[To Charles Lowell Young. The letter is undated and without heading but accompanied by an envelope postmarked August 9, 1918. Wellesley.]

[Franconia, NH]
[August 9, 1918]

Dear Young

At your service. Command me. But be sure to arrange it with Miss Bates so I'll run into no conflicts.[190] As a poet I have to be particularly careful about being taken care of.

Of course you understand I am coming to Wellesley only because I swore I would never come there again after what you told me. We must have discipline.

We'll go right on from where we left off in Peru.[191]

Ever yours
Robert Frost

190. Katharine Lee Bates, professor of English at Wellesley College.

191. Peru is a small village in Vermont's Green Mountain forest, some twenty miles north of Bennington; RF and Young had hiked there previously.

[To Charles Lowell Young. ALS. Wellesley.]

Franconia N.H.
August 14 1918

My dear Young:

You must come, both of you, or we shall be disappointed. I'm just right for your purposes: I'm good enough for company: any better and I should be good enough for writing and too good for company. The war's what's the matter with me. It keeps me down to a low conversational level of spirit. But dont pretend to be sorry for a loss of mine that is obviously your gain. Now is the time to make the most of me before I withdraw in cloud.

Beautiful upon the mountains.

With forward looking thoughts

Always yours
Robert Frost

[To Louis Untermeyer. Untermeyer dates the letter to 1918. Evidence suggests that it was written in mid-August, quite likely after the nineteenth (RF and his family summered in Franconia in 1918). The Christmas greeting at the end is a joke. ALS. LoC.]

Franconia N.H.
August something [1918]

Dear Untermeyer

Was it you were asking about my liver? Thanks but I ain't got no liver—and only one lung. There cant be anything the matter with what I aint got. What ails me is what in high poetic parlance is known as an imposthume of the spirit; for which you will probably have to see Beaumont and Fletcher though you may find it in Stephen and Percy.[192] The Poetic Drama! Oh my God!

---

192. The word "imposthume" appears in Beaumont and Fletcher's *The Humorous Lieutenant,* though it was not at all uncommon in Elizabethan and Jacobean literature. It refers to (as the *Oxford English Dictionary* has it) "a purulent swelling or cyst in any part of the body; an abscess," or, when used figuratively, "moral corruption in the individual." RF may have in mind also *Hamlet* (4.iv): "This is the imposthume of much wealth and peace, / That inward breaks, and shows no cause without / Why the man dies." The allusion to "Stephen and Percy" is obscure, but RF likely refers to his contemporaries Ste-

That sounds like a person who knows what he doesn't like and I always hold that we get forward as much by hating as by loving—just as in swimming we advance as much by kicking with our feet as by reaching with our hands. But I can't say for certain that I don't like Spoon River. I believe I do like it in a way. I should be able to tell you better if you hadn't asked me. I could wish it weren't so nearly the ordinary thing in its attitude toward respectability. How shall we treat respectability? That is not for me to say: I am not treating it. All I know with any conviction is that an idea has to be a little new to be at all true and if you say a thing three times it ceases to be so. Mind you I am not finding fault—I never am—only—to be frank, the book chews tobacco I'm afraid. Perhaps thats <u>why</u> I like it.

So if you're looking for anything out of me on the subject that you can use against me, you will have to wait till next time. So much depends on the clothes a man has on when he speaks that I would rather, if you don't mind, defer handing down an opinion on my fellow in art till I have you here with me and can deliver myself by word of mouth.

You are coming before many months now. I hope the ground will be wet, so that we can have a bonfire of spruce boughs to talk around. This is a lovely region. It is away off.

If you knew the true inwardness of what The Atlantic has just been through for my sake![193] When everything else gives out there will still be the story of Me and The Atlantic to write a book on. One good thing: it will be well documented.

I am going to thank Wood for all that lively stuff the next thing I do.[194]

Wishing you a merry Christmas I am,

"Not worth a breakfast in the cheapest country under the cope."[195]

Robert Frost.

---

phen Phillips and Percy MacKaye, both of whom where dramatists; we thank Mark Scott for the suggestion.

193. In *RFLU* Untermeyer explains: "It was rumored that Robert was seriously ill, that he had come out publicly against [Edgar Lee Masters's] *Spoon River Anthology,* that several old subscribers to *The Atlantic Monthly* had objected to the way in which the magazine was favoring 'the new poetry,' particularly Frost's" (75).

194. The poet and writer Clement Richardson Wood (1888–1950).

195. RF quotes Boult's lines in Shakespeare's *Pericles* (4.vi): "If your peevish chastity, which is not worth a breakfast in the cheapest country under the cope, shall undo a whole household, let me be gelded like a spaniel."

[To Louis Untermeyer. Though RF speaks whimsically of Calcutta, Indiana, and so on—which explains his signing off as Tagore—he was writing from Franconia, where he and his family were summering. ALS. LoC.]

Calcutta Bombay Indiana
~~Amherst Mass~~
August 19 (Approximately) [1918]

Dear Louis:

While I am I and you are you, you are never to doubt me; and I promise never to doubt you except as to your sanity. You are wise and clever and deep and wide and noble and impulsive (look at the way you made friends with the lower classes of Franconia in the person of Pearley last summer.[196] He borrowed your "These Times" from me the minute your back was turned and has decided to keep it, he likes it so well with your inscription in it) and having conceded so much I should think I might have earned the right to go further in attribution and say that you are mad too—divinely mad in the common every day sense of the word, though if you were to ask me whom at I should just have to create a diversion by asking in turn if the locution "whom at" doesnt fall on your ears a little—what shall I say? You're not mad at me and I'm not mad at you. We are agreed in too many things for that especially in wanting all the freedom we can get before prohibition becomes national. I for my part still get all that's good for me though I have to confess by resort to constantly lower and more humiliating subterfuge. I haven't fallen so low as going to Poetical Dinners or Jay Writtenhome's at house however and I dont think you have.[197] At any rate I think I can stay away from them if it will help you to stay away and lead a cleaner life. Stick to your writing my child. You write so well. Etc. Etc.

No, but seriousness aside I sha'n't have time for any thing in Poetry Carnival Week. I have you and Alfred to see and a lot of other hard work to cram into a few days.[198] And it does seem to me you do the reviewing better and better. It has no business to be thrown off as mere reviewing. It is criticism and you know it and it ought to be done in a form that declares itself.

Believe me or not, I am
Rabindranath Tagore

PS. I forgot to say damn your politics. Was there something else?

---

196. Unidentified. Untermeyer's volume of poetry, *These Times,* had appeared in 1917.
197. "Jay Writtenhome" is a play on poet and critic Jessie Rittenhouse's name.
198. Alfred Harcourt, of Henry Holt and Company.

[To Alexander Meiklejohn. ALS. Wisc. Hist.]

Franconia N.H.
August 28 1918

Dear Mr Meiklejohn:

I am certain it was terrible for Harris to go out of sight and hearing like that.[199] Other boys have had to give up everything just when they were finding what to set their hearts on, but it was not for nothing in their case. Poor Harris had to leave everything for nothing. He let me see how he hated the war as an interruption. Well, he had to be shown a worse one. It was the most cruel kind of war-time death. And the swiftness of it. With all the start of him the other boys had in having enlisted, Harris beats them to the tape. I wonder what he thought. He was so good at thinking.

He was good at many things that now nothing will ever come of. There you have about the long and short of my loss in him—that I sha'n't see the fulfillment of his promise. I admired him more than I had learned to love him as yet and I had hardly got the hang of him personally. But I know he was a good boy and a fine boy and a gifted boy.

It was interruption with a vengeance.

It's an age of interruption. Who of us hasnt been more or less or completely interrupted in the last four years? Theres a fern called Interrupted that I'd put on and wear all round my hat for a twelve month and a day in place of any badge of war I am likely to win, but it's too large: it would cover me up.[200]

Unless I assure you that I am better than most of this sounds you wont want to see me as soon again as I want to see you. Potatoes beets and carrots have done wonders for me—the sight of them growing I mean. Even peas and beans have helped me, though not so radically of course, not being root

---

199. The *Amherst College Biographical Record, Centennial Edition* (1821–1921), contains the following entry: "Harris, Alvin Emerson. S. of George H. and Lulu I. (Goodnow), b. Shelburne Falls, F. 26, 1897. Phi Beta Kappa; Delta Tau Delta. Prepared Arms Acad., Shelburne Falls. Asst. in English A. C., 1918; inspected shells in munitions factory, Erie, Penn., 1918. D. Erie, Penn., Aug. 3, 1918."

200. The "interrupted fern" (*Osmunda claytoniana*) has fronds extending from two to four feet.

crops. I shall hold on I guess till we get some real satisfaction out of the Germans other than verbal and oral.

Best wishes to you and Mrs Meiklejohn.

Always faithfully yours
Robert Frost

[To Louis Untermeyer. ALS. LoC.]

Franc: Sept. 16 '18

O Dear Louis

Comfort me with a Hartmann picture[201] console me with anything you can say, for I am desolate and sick of the whole business. How shall I sing the John L. song that Vachel requires of me?[202] Open thine eyes eterne and sphere them round and see if there is anything left to do thats worth a breakfast in the cheapest country under the cope.[203] Till when I stand pat while this machine is to me

Yourn
Robert Frost

[To Wilbur Rowell. ALS. UVA.]

Franconia N.H.
September 23 1918

Dear Mr Rowell:

If there were a hundred or two dollars where you could easily put your hand on them I should be glad of them to tide us over the opening of school and college. We find ourselves short for the autumn mobilization after a year of more or less voluntary giving and lending to our Uncle Sam and my sister Jean and I'm a little afraid that in its present transitional disorganization college may not be ready with our salaries exactly on time next month.

201. C. Bertram Hartmann, a friend of Untermeyer's and a painter; RF kept one of his watercolors in the Franconia house.

202. See RF's February 28, 1918, letter to Untermeyer for the reference to Vachel Lindsay and John L. Sullivan.

203. RF echoes (again) Boult's lines in *Pericles* (4.vi) after quoting line 117 of John Keats's "Hyperion" ("Open thine eyes eterne," etc.).

College is opening again but it is a changed college. Poor President Meiklejohn hardly knows what to make of it all. But it's good for us and he can be counted on to turn present disadvantages to our advantage in the long run.

With best wishes.

Sincerely yours
Robert Frost

[To Lesley Frost. ALS. UVA.]

Franconia N.H.
September 28 1918

Dear Lesley:

Not much to say this time but this much money (check for $25 enclosed.) Irma has Boston Grippe as her nurses prefer to call it there, and we are wondering if you havent it too. We are anxious to hear from you. The taking care really just begins when you think you are getting well enough to go out. That's the time to stay in longer.

But possibly your cold hasn't proved to be the Distemper. That would be great.

I'll tell you next letter about Hendricks and how too much flying has sickened him of the air.[204] It's a wild game up there—and yet not various enough to fill the mind with the days work and keep it off the subject of death.

Affectionately
Papa

But I think we hear a noise like the Central Powers squealing.

[To Lesley Frost. ALS. UVA.]

Amherst Mass
October 18 1918

Dear Lesley:

Your adventures are partly ours and we enjoy them with you but it seems to us that just your being free from college and exactly where you choose to

204. Walter Hendricks (Amherst College, 1917), an officer in the U.S. Army Air Corps, was a flight instructor and a Frost family friend.

be in an aeroplane factory ought to be nearly adventure enough for one year for all of us, you and mamma and me and the children, without your casting about for further excitement that we know not of.[205] In other words please try to restrict your adventures to your work, keep them within the walls of the Curtis [*sic*] factory if you care anything for our peace of mind. I liked the propeller episode.[206] But that ought to mark a limit. You surely took risk enough there for all practical purposes. You took a chance and luck smiled broadly on you. That's all clean business and the worst that could have come of it would have made no difference to you or us in the long run. We simply howled with pleasure at the way Mr Lunt came into the story in the nick of time. You were bold and you were rewarded with heaven-sent help. But the yachting with Mr Weeler [*sic*] doesn't yield us the same kind of thrills—if it yields us anything but chills. I wasn't there and don't know all that was in the air, but I doubt very much if Mr Wheeler should have taken you into his boat. In these things there is no sure ground under our feet. We dont want to think too much about them lest we grow too suspicious and even evil-minded, but also we don't want to have too much to do with them. The best way I find is to observe a few simple rules laid down by sensible people for keeping out of danger where men and women meet. Be conventional pretty nearly always with men and always with these fellows "old enough to be your father." It's a funny world. You don't want to boast that you have scared as reckless a father as I am into chronic sleeplessness.

College still hangs off. We are grip-bound. The boys march march and that's all.

Amherst gathered on the common yesterday and subscribed its quota of $450000 viva voce. The air was full of money in handfuls and bagfuls. Showers of money all over hats and shoulders like confetti at a wedding. A rivalry got going between the Amerst [*sic*] College army and the M. A. C.[207] army who were drawn up in battle array behind the civilian crowd. I think our

205. Susan Wanvig, a family friend, had suggested the possibility of Lesley's working at the aircraft factory in Marblehead and arranged for her board; the Burgess Company of Marblehead, Massachusetts, became a subsidiary of the Curtiss Aeroplane Company in February 1916. Monroe Wheeler (mentioned subsequently) was a director at Curtiss.

206. In *FL*, Arnold Grade explains: "Under consideration for promotion from factory work to the final shaping of mahogany propellers, Lesley was asked if she had had woodworking experience" (35). "Mr. Lunt" (mentioned subsequently): Winfield W. Lunt.

207. The Massachusetts Agricultural College (now the University of Massachusetts, Amherst); or the "Aggies," as RF later calls the students.

boys started it by offering to give a thousand if the Aggies would give a thousand. It looked as if it was going to be rough on someone or someone's father before it was over. Probably we could have stood it a good deal better than they could. But someone was sensible to stop it with a joke in time. And anyway just then the hand went to 450,000 on the clock. Money! You'd have thought the town was lousy with it. I went in under the excitement rather too much myself. I dont know what I shall do if there's another loan floated.

There's a good autobiography of Conrad's you ought to read. And I myself like Franklins awfully well. While you're reading either or both of those I'll be thinking up some more. Both James and Howells have written good autobiography. I have forgotten what they call the books. You would probably recognize them somehow by their names.[208]

Remember me cordially to Mrs Wanvig. Tell her I hope your youthful vicissitudes may divert her a little from too much thinking of her part in the war, and so compensate her somewhat for what trouble we have cost her.

Come on with the letters.

Affectionately
Papa

[To Lesley Frost. ALS. UVA.]

Amherst Mass
October 24 1918

Dear Lesley:

Didn't we tell you about Hendricks? He had been sick, you know, and as I saw at once when he got here, had lost his nerve for flying. He seems to have been a good flyer. He won his commission early and has taught some three hundred men to fly. But the flying field is nearer the front than anything else on this side of the Atlantic. The ships are always getting "cracked up" and hardly a week passes without somebody's getting killed or injured. The service has a reckless fatalistic way of taking itself that would be funny if it wasn't so tragic. It jokes with Death as the presiding presence. Two ambulances stand conspicuously waiting for you always on the field. You may fly a

---

208. RF refers to William Dean Howells's *Years of My Youth* (1916), to Henry James's *A Small Boy and Others* (1913) and *Notes of a Son and Brother* (1914), and either to Joseph Conrad's *The Mirror of the Sea* (1906) or to his *A Personal Record* (1912).

month you may fly at best a year. But It will get you soon or late. You will make some day very likely through no fault of your own, what is known as a Mat landing which calls for the motorcycle the ambulance and the truck. The ambulance or meat wagon is for you personally and maybe for your cadet but not so certainly for him because he rides in the back seat where in the crash he has a good chance, whereas you are pretty sure to die by "getting the engine in your lap." It is thrown right back into you, you see, when the nose of the fusilage [*sic*] dives into the ground. The teacher takes the big risk that the pupil is apt to be the one to incur. Hendricks had made a number of "forced landings," that is without power, but had had but one serious smash up. In that he had made one big hole in the ground, bounced and made another. The truck took home what was left of the engine and he walked home on his own legs after having made a bonfire of the wings and fusilage. But I doubt if it was that sort of thing that had shaken him or if he ever dreaded a particular flight. It was just that the shadow of Death over the whole place had spoiled him for sleep. He got a terrible shock I suspect from seeing a fellow flyer die in the next bed to him when he was in hospital. The doctor holding the poor boys teeth apart to let the blood gush and the last two or three breaths draw free—that will be a picture on his mind (and on mine) for life, though in the stamping of the impression it was no more than a matter of moments. I wonder if he is going to get back into condition. He can gamble with the rest of the boys and he can joke and talk the language of the Morituri, but unless I'm mistaken he's nearly insane for want of sleep.[209] You'd think the excitement would bear him up. They all complain that there is no excitement in flying after you have learned what little there is to it say half a dozen to a dozen maneuvers. You have to learn straight flying without fussing your controls, you have to learn to go into a tail spin in order to learn how to come out of one (because when you stall or go wrong in almost any way you almost certainly fall into a tail-spin and it's death if you haven't the art of undoing it) and you have to learn to make a "three-point landing" that is on your two wheels and skid simultaneously (because if you bounce ever so little with the skid you'll tip up onto your crank shaft and spoil a two hundred dollar propeller.—That's called a "crank-shaft landing") and you have to

---

209. Referring to the pilots as "Morituri" likens their jaunty fatalism to that of the Roman gladiators in Suetonius, *De Vita Caesarum:* "Ave, Imperator, morituri te salutant" ("Hail, Emperor, those who are about to die salute you").

learn to make a "verticle [*sic*] bank" to turn on and an Immelmann turn[210] and a good loop—this last to go over your pursuer and get behind where you can pursue him. Thats about the extent of it. Theres a "spinning nose-dive" which I believe they don't know how to handle when they get into it. It is death just as the "tail-spin" was for a long time. In the tail spin the whole ship slowly revolves wing over wing and the tail describes great circles. In the "spinning nose-dive" it is the same except that the nose describes great circles. After you get so much learned apparently you perish slowly of the monotony and for want of exercise. The French have a name for the nervous malady flyers suffer from. I didnt get it. But I have been careful with all the technical language I have used and am sure of it all except the "Immelmann turn." It's Immelmann something—I think "turn." Hendricks has made a reputation for "vertical banks" and landing in a small space. He made a forced landing once in a road between two fences facing one of them where there wouldnt have been room to land facing up the road. One pretty thing I forgot to mention: they make a descent with the power off just fluttering the aillerons [*sic*] a little called "falling leaf." But this is so little in the monotony of endless flying. The romance had all gone out of it for him and he doesn't know for sure why. Told about a boy who, after his first "solo," flight alone, "tail-spinning" "looping" "banking" and all, got out of his ship swearing and swearing off on that kind of excitement. He never flew again. Hendricks thinks some of the young wives get their husbands out of it and off into other work, lecturing at colleges and such like safe jobs.

Ive told you all this for a glimpse of the unheroic heroic. We are nobody to judge anybody. There are all sorts of ways to go through with danger. We haven't all got to like it, though I have no doubt a great many like it alot [*sic*].

Affectionately
Papa

---

210. "Immelmann turn": an aerobatic move named for its inventor, World War I German ace Max Immelmann. It involves going into a steep climb and beginning a loop, but executing a roll at the top.

[To Louis Untermeyer. Dating derived from postmark. Untermeyer was ill at the time, as had been RF, and he had jokingly asked RF to write an obituary, even supplying him with the expected date of his death. ALS. LoC.]

[Amherst, MA]
[October 28, 1918]

Dear Louis

I have made a bad start in medias res on that obituary con amore, but before I can go any further I shall have to know at whose hands or of what you are concluding on Dec 17 if I remember rightly. I find it will make a difference in my wording which it is to be a case of, influenza, war, or the critics. It is just possible that you do not know yourself definitely, but then how can you be so definite about the date? Is there something here that I should be able to figure out for myself if I were as wise as a New Yorker and as harmless as I am? Ought I to be able to diagnose the disease, that is to say, from the length of the run from the beginning of the end to the end. Too long for influenza it seems too short for most of the critics I have heard of or for due process of law. The government hasn't sent you as a gentle hint a snakeskin sausage with gunpowder stuffing and the motto We leave it to you? Such times we live in in the twilight of the subter-gods. Not that I want you on my account to feel that you must go ahead and die because you have sent out for your announcements and invited people to the funeral. I hate to have my friends feel committed to anything. I should hate to have the Kaiser feel committed to this war. He must quit just the moment he has had enough and I shan't think much of any the less of him (that would be impossible), though I must confess it is in his honor, you may tell my friend Dick if you see him, we have gone into half-yellow. So please excuse this stationary.

Tubby serious. This is a war college and I am teaching war issues; so it's a lucky thing I have always taken a sensible view of the universe and everything in it. Otherwise I might have to knuckle to the war department were it ever so little or else go to jail like good old Gene Debs.[211] I am out to see a world full of small-fry democracies even if we have to pile them two deep or even three deep in some places.

211. On June 16, 1918, Eugene Debs spoke in Canton, Ohio, urging resistance to the draft. He was arrested on June 30, charged with ten counts of sedition, and convicted on September 12.

Lesley is worse than I am. She is manufacturing hydroplanes with the Curtiss company and I'm afraid if she wasnt so fond of seeing people licked, anybody licked, she might want to see the war go on forever.[212] In other words she is one of the interests.

Too much war! I swear if there's another war on top of this one I shall refuse to know anything about it. I have ordered all my papers and magazines discontinued after July 4 1919. No more politics for me in this world, once I am sure all throwns are throne down.

Commend me to everybody. What fun we'll have when we can get back to poetry and the form of things is once more all or nearly all. Me heart celebrates. Let's go to Palestine for a visit at least. Shall we fix it up?[213]

blessed if we don't.

R.F.

[To Amy Lowell. ALS. Harvard.]

Amherst
November 1918

Dear Miss Lowell:

(So to call you formally to your face, whatever liberties your greatness as a poet and as a friend may tempt us to take with you behind your back):

I didn't think that was the bad book you may have been lead [*sic*] to suppose from the length of time it has taken me to acknowledge it.[214] I thought it was a very splendid book both when I read it aloud and when I didn't read

212. The Curtiss Aeroplane Company was the single largest producer of aircraft during World War I.

213. British foreign minister Arthur Balfour had issued the so-called Balfour Declaration in 1917, which promised to establish a Jewish national home in Palestine once the Ottomans had been expelled. The British Egyptian Expeditionary Force, commanded by Edmund Allen, captured Jerusalem on December 9, 1917.

214. Lowell's 1918 volume *Can Grande's Castle*. Her preface begins: "The four poems in this book are more closely related to one another than may at first appear. They all owe their existence to the war, for I suppose that, had there been no war, I should never have thought of them. They are scarcely war poems, in the strict sense of the word, nor are they allegories in which the present is made to masquerade as the past. Rather, they are the result of a vision thrown suddenly back upon remote events to explain a strange and terrible reality."

it aloud. I delight to see you plank it down to them so-fashion. It's the very next thing this precocious young republic is going to be able to live on. We come on. The war has helped, I'm sure, and besides one thing leads to another. Americans are something at last to go up against. We no longer have to think so much of coaxing 'em along into objective existence. We've got 'em where we can jab it to 'em stiff without fear of having them all to create over again. They can stand art. And by the ton you've given it to 'em!

After all which 'ems I might be excused for signing off Sincerely yours, Emmer, but I prefer to sign myself as of old and always

Your admiring friend
Robert Frost

And by the way when you feel that you can afford it wont you send me an autographed Dome of Many Colored Glass for completeness?[215] Then if none of my boys here steals any of the books you have given me I shall be all right.

I don't suppose you can tell me the addresses of F. S. Flint and Solomon de la Selva?[216]

Judgematical of Fletcher to say what he did in Youth about Thomas.[217]

R.F.

Louis is coming this week.

R.F.

---

215. *A Dome of Many-Colored Glass* (1912) was Lowell's first book.

216. A friend of Lowell's, Salomón de la Selva (1893–1959), born in Nicaragua, had come to the United States at age thirteen, and later graduated from Williams College. In 1918 he published his first volume of poetry, *Tropical Town and Other Poems,* which was written in English. Determined to fight for the Allied cause in World War I but denied enlistment in the American army, de la Selva—whose maternal grandmother was a British citizen—had joined the British army in July 1918. His regiment was deployed in Belgium in October, a month before the war ended.

217. RF may refer to John Gould Fletcher's dismissive remarks about Edward Thomas in a review—published in *Poetry* in August 1918—otherwise devoted to D. H. Lawrence: "The press can make a great to-do about the innocuous, blameless and essentially minor poetry of Edward Thomas (to take but one example); they politely refuse to discuss the questionable, but essentially major effort of a D. H. Lawrence. Is it any wonder that such an attitude drives a man to sheer fanaticism?"

[To Alice Brown. ALS. UVA.]

Amherst Mass
November 2 1918

Dear Miss Brown:

I must accept your congratulations though you are tardier with them than I am with the books I was going to inscribe. But we are both poets and I don't know what easement belongs to us as such if it isn't from being punctual.

Yes I have been a full professor at Amherst from the moment I came here year before last. So you see how very behind hand you are. Mr Meiklejohn has been faultless in the honor he has done poetry in the person of me. Let it be said wherever my sad story is told.

You shall have the books almost by return mail with the poor best I can write in them. I'm afraid it will have to be some irrelevant poem out of my note books and not the smart inscription I had hoped to make it. I've been awfully unclever all summer. I don't know what's come over me. I used to be so—how shall I say it?—brilliant when I was in a corner and had to be. Do you suppose teaching has been bad for me? But then I've always taught more or less. Luckily Im humble and where I can't shine am willing to be merely serviceable and friendly. You will understand the spirit in which I carry out my promise as to the books.

The mind still tingles with the pleasure of our visit in Boston. We'll always remember that it was you who gave us the keys of the city.

Our united best wishes to you and your mother and sister.[218]

Always sincerely yours
Robert Frost

Oh! I forgot to tell you. The War is Won.

---

218. Alice Brown's mother was Elizabeth Lucas Brown.

[To Louis Untermeyer. The armistice ending hostilities in World War I was signed one week after this letter was written, on November 11, but the "Central Powers" and the Ottoman Empire had already disintegrated during October. ALS. LoC.]

Amherst Mass
November 4 1918

Dear Louis:

More to us than many letters, however wild, will be the sight of you twain drawing rein, stalling your engine breaking your car or what you like to call it, before our door in Main St. Our number is 19 of that ilk; our telephone number 468W; our names respectively as professor and author Robert Lee Frost and Robert Frost.

"Come as the waves come when
Navies are stranded!"
"Come for the soul is free!"[219]

It is just the same about you as it is about Peace: the minute we let ourselves think we can have it we cease to be able to wait for it: we give way to our longing entirely and are of no more use to anybody for anything.

For God's sake don't disappoint us. And please plan to stay more than a day or two. Please—if I say please wont you?

There's twa fat hens upo the coop
Been fed this month or mair.
Well, death to them, thraw their necks about, feed for the welcome guessed!

Waithfully watching
Robert Frost

---

219. RF quotes first from Sir Walter Scott's "Highland War-Song" ("Come as the waves come when navies are stranded!"), then, later in the letter, from a poem by Bliss Carman collected in Quiller-Couch's *Oxford Book of English Verse 1250–1918* ("Come, for the soul is free!"), and, still later, from a poem by the Scottish poet William Mickle (1735–1788), "There's Nae Luck about the House": "There's twa fat hens upo' the bauk, / Been fed this month and mair, / Mak haste and thraw their necks about, / That Colin weel may fare."

[To Lesley Frost. Accompanying the letter were manuscript versions of "The Cow's in the Corn" (CPPP, *537) and "The Aim Was Song"* (CPPP, *207). The letter is undated, but the postmarked envelope survives. ALS. UVA.]*

[Amherst, MA]
[November 5, 1918]

Dear Lesley:

You seem to have more to tell in the way of sheer news than we stay-at-homes or go-from-home-to-homes. My news is nearly all new poems—some of them not so very important and some I hope more so. What do you say to these? The Lynch one is only funny I suppose.[220] You needn't copy them. I seem to arrive at the copying point slowly. You never know what will come to save a poem at the last moment.

I'm supposed to be coming back to N'York on March 15th or so. I may not feel up to it. So if any body sets up to know more about my affairs than you—

Take care of your feet and your head will take care of itself.

Affectionately
Papa

[To Sidney Cox. ALS. DCL.]

Amherst Mass
December 27 1918

Sidney Cox:

Proud memory be canned!

The way to do is to make a point of seeing me good and plain once in so often as not to depend for friendship on the letters I dont write any more. What's the matter with your bringing Alice up for a day and a night with us toward the end of next week? I'd say sooner, but I've been very sick with influenza and must give myself time to get back to my talk before I begin to meet people again.

---

220. "The Cow's in the Corn," a whimsical playlet in verse (*CPPP*, 537–538). RF based it loosely (and affectionately) on his friends John and Margaret Lynch. They had a farm in Bethlehem, New Hampshire, which the Frost family visited a number of times.

We're only three or four hours from Boston and there are no changes if you come on a morning train that starts from the North (not South) Station. You would have to look up the exact time.

Great to have a look at you and hear you on your plans and prospects. I can hardly keep from advising you what I think you ought to do next. I'll hold myself in though till I see you. (I want you to be a critic—first-class American.)

Well say you'll come and meanwhile our love to you both. Thanks be that the war has spared you to me.

Always yours
Robert Frost

[To Louis Untermeyer, who provides the precise dating. Here again RF spells "Amherst" as the locals pronounce it, as without the "h." RF had fallen ill to influenza, during the pandemic of 1918–1919. ALS. LoC.]

Amerced [January 4] 1919

Dear Louis:

Here it is as late as this (1919 A.D.), and I don't know whether or not I'm strong enough to write a letter yet. The only way I can tell that I haven't died and gone to heaven is by the fact that everything is just the same as it was on earth (all my family round me and all that) only worse, whereas, as I had been brought up in Swedenborgianism to believe, everything should be the same only better. Two possibilities remain: either I have died and gone to Hell or I haven't died. Therefore I havent died. And that's the only reason I haven't. I was sick enough to die and no doubt I deserved to die. The only question in my mind is could the world have got along without me. I leave it to you to whom I think I may safely leave it.

We'll assume then in what follows that I am alive—however unlively it may sound. I can't tell whether it is my voice speaking or my bones creaking. What bones are they that rub together so unpleasantly in the middle of you in extreme emaciation? You ought to hear them in me when I make a sweeping gesture as in tennis or oratory or attempt to dance a lá Russe some such classic as Integer Vitae. But why try to dance such a poem, you may say, till I feel more integral. Why not confine myself to the Rubaiyat? Why not simply confine myself?

Let's see what was I going to say.

Oh I guess first I shall have to ask you to call your red friends off von Moschzisker.[221] I don't want his house in Philadelphia bombed again. Do you hear? Bomb somebody that's shown some want of sympathy with the down-most man as it used to be called. He's the most sensible decent sort—the Judge is. Isnt there some mistake don't you suppose?

Yes you can have the bad shoes parable. It's Ojibway I think—think.[222]

I have read the way you say I would write Integer Vitae and I promise you I will do my best to write it that way when I write it so as not to make you a liar.[223] Everybody says it's the living breathing image of my idiom. It ought not to be hard to live up to. I will bear it in mind. Mine was good but probably not quite so good as Robinson's and Davies', n'est pas?

And by the way I saw a dazzler of yours quoted from Braithwaites Anth in the Boston Herald.

George Whicher liked Jean's book best of all he's seen lately. I'm to tell her personally how much I liked it when I get strong enough to lay it on with a baseball bat. I liked it all right.

---

221. Robert von Moschzisker was an eminent Pennsylvania lawyer and judge. He served on that state's Supreme Court from 1921 to 1930. His house had not been bombed; RF is joking. Early in his career von Moschzisker had been active in the Republican Party in Pennsylvania. The Frost family had known him and his wife since 1915.

222. Untermeyer reports that the "bad shoes" parable "emanated from a talk that Robert gave on what might be considered 'native' in poetry. Mary Austin, Natalie Curtis, and others were causing a stir with books purporting to prove that the basic American rhythm was that of the Indian and that our most indigenous poetry was in what they called the Amer-indian song. Robert was one of those who maintained that, stirring as the Indian songs may be to the Indians, they were not, and could not be, part of our cultural heritage. He proved this by reading three different versions of one Indian chant which, according to the three translators, incorporated three differing symbols and meant three different things" (*RFLU*, 81). The chant in question is almost certainly the one Frederick R. Burton translates from the Ojibway in his *American Primitive Music, With Especial Attention to the Songs of the Ojibways* (New York: Moffat, Yard and Company, 1909). There, Burton indeed discusses the difficulty of translating the song he titles, in his version, "Old Shoes," which, he further tells us, was popular among (white) children in kindergarten and grammar school.

223. Untermeyer explains: "An occasional translator, I was also a part-time parodist. A volume entitled *Including Horace* [New York: Harcourt, Brace ad Howe, 1919] began with a set of paraphrases of the Horatian 'Integer Vitae' ode rendered in the manner of twenty-five poets" (*RFLU*, 81). Among the poets were RF, W. H. Davies, and E. A. Robinson.

Lola was so-so.[224] She tries a little harder than Emerson would have us try. Easy does it.

Pellé was good reading.[225] But none of it was any news. Not a phase but was old story. It was the insight that was remarkable and the nearness to the life. Form is with the rich, material with the poor, though to the poor it sometimes may seem that material is just what they lack to eat and cover their backs with. The rich are too vague from their remoteness from things ever to make realizing artists. Things belong to the poor by their having to come to grips with things daily. And thats a good one on the poor. They are the only realists. Things are theirs and noone's else though of course it is forbidden the poor to eat or wear the things. Well there I go and I mustn't. Some time I must copy you out a poem I did on Bolshevism in 1911 as I saw it spectral over Lawrence at the time of the strike.[226] It will show you where I was.

What times they are. Jack Reed will tell you this month who licked the Germans but will he tell you next month who didn't lick Lloyd George in the English elections? If the poor promised themselves no more than vengeance in the oncoming revolution I'd be with them. It's all their nonsense about making a better or even a different world that I can't stand. The damned fools!—only less damned than the Goddamned fools over them who have made and made such a mess of industrialism. Requiescas! I started mildly enough: where have I got to!

Lets resolve to be good anyway.

Your petitioner
Rob't Frost

---

224. B. W. Huebsch issued Lola Ridge's *The Ghetto and Other Poems* and Jean Starr Untermeyer's *Growing Pains* in 1918.

225. *Pellé the Conqueror* by the Danish novelist Martin Andersen Nexø.

226. The Lawrence Massachusetts Textile Strike of 1912, often called the Bread and Roses Strike. RF alludes to his poem, "The Parlor Joke" (*CPPP*, 516–518). See also RF's June 25, 1912, letter to Rowell. John "Jack" Reed (1887–1920) chronicled the Bolshevik Revolution.

[The following letter to Zenobia Camprubí Aymar, wife of the poet Juan Ramon Jiménez (winner of the Nobel Prize in literature for 1939), concerns what appears to be the first Spanish translation of any of RF's poems. Camprubí Aymar had already translated "The Hill Wife" in collaboration with her husband. Here, RF replies to her request for permission to translate North of Boston, *permission that was in fact granted by his publisher, Henry Holt and Company. The letter was published in transcription, together with a facsimile of the manuscript, in the Spanish journal* La Torre *6, no. 23 (July–September 1958). The transcription here is from the manuscript facsimile as published in* La Torre.*]*

Amherst Mass
January 20 1919

My dear Mrs Jiminez:

I should have answered your letter from Spain long ago but for something else from Spain, far less pleasant, that, coming just after the letter, almost took my life and has left me rather badly off, I'm afraid, for the rest of the winter.[227]

What I have carried in mind all this time to say to you is that so far as I am concerned you have all the permission in the world for the pleasant thing you propose, and I can't think my publishers will make the least difficulty. I have seen your translation of The Hill Wife but have too little Spanish to judge from it for myself how fortunate I am in my translator. I am told however by a good friend whom I trust that you have caught the spirit of the poem and done me something more than justice. Of course I am very grateful.

I hardly see why I should have the five dollars for what is your work as it stands. To plant a tree with for you to find growing when you come to America? Why shouldn't you have kept the money to plant a tree with yourself for us to find growing when we come to Spain as we have been long planning to do for our children and mean to do the minute the world subsides to peaceful prices. Well the great thing is that you are planting North of Boston for me over there. I suppose I must plant you the tree in requital, though I think it ought to wait till we settle down where we know we are going to live the rest of our lives.

227. The influenza pandemic of 1918–1919 was often called the "Spanish Flu."

Sometime will you give me the pleasure of seeing An Old Man's Winter Night and perhaps The Gum Gatherer in your language? An Old Man's Winter Night is my favorite among them all in all three of the books.

And will you understand and forgive my long delay and believe me

Gratefully yours
Robert Frost[228]

[To Lesley Frost. The letter is addressed as from "Ammass," a pun on Amherst, Mass. ALS. UVA.]

Ammass
1/25/19

Dear Lesley:

We've been tempted by various considerations to go away off to Porto Rico and leave you alone to your cheerful Barnard curriculum.[229] But we probably won't go. It seems too cruel all round. Marj is the most bent on going. I wish the kids could do something for excitement. But perhaps they can hold out till next year and we can all get away to Spain together. We've got Baxter enlisted in the Porto Rico scheme.[230] We are committed to it to that extent. He'll probably let us off though if he has to.

You left a fragment of poetry around that you must go on with someday. The one about the cut-over hillside. You were just going to name some of the slain trees when you stopped. It's a good kind of poem.

New York! New York! Not all of it together and all the entertainment of it and the pleasant friends you can have in it are worth one real deed of your own in poetry. It is full of other people's deeds and accomplishments. But those can only give you something and someone to talk about. What we want is to do something for all that silly mob to talk about. Let them talk about the latest. We want to do the latest.

Great—all that about the subterranean rumblings in England. Write more when you have time. And don't fail to write a good off-hand letter to Mrs

---

228. For information about RF's acquaintance with Zenobia Camprubí Aymar and her husband, see Lesley Lee Francis, "Robert Frost in Spanish Translation," *Robert Frost Review* (Fall 1999): 1–14.

229. Lesley entered Barnard in February 1919.

230. Sylvester Baxter (1850–1927), critic, poet, and Frost family friend.

Whicher saying anything pleasant you can about any of her friends at the college you have met.[231] Or if you prefer tell me about her friends and I will pass the word along. I want to have her feel that you were pleased to have her introduce you down there.

I think it's better for us that Harcourt is staying with the Holts. Where would we be with our books spread over three publishing houses. Of course I'd go out with Harcourt in a minute. And I wouldnt stand too much from Roland if I were in his place.[232]

Carol is taking punching lessons from Tug Kennedy and seems not displeased with himself.[233] He seems to be coming to his assurance. You mustnt mention in any letter this that I'm going to tell you: it might make him too self-conscious; but he had a fight on the rink with a college freshman and knocked him down and cut his lip and got altogether the better of him. It was over a hockey stick the fellow had taken from one of the little boys. Carol had asked him several times to give it up and he had said at last "If you don't shut up I'll take yours." Carol said, "I'd like to see you try it." The fellow tried it and got hurt and badly left before all the crowd.

Let's see what else there is for family brag. Miss Bates sent a Madrid paper with the translation of The Hill Wife.[234] She wrote nice things about you. She was one good friend we had there at Wellesley.

We had a talking evening with the Oldses Esteses and Whichers (at the Oldses) the other night and a very pleasant one at the Lancasters to meet the French teacher and his wife from Smith College tonight. The French teacher is a great Emersonian, as am I also. His wife is a Lake Willoughbian as are all of us. She comes from Lyndon. He saw three years service in the French army.[235]

---

231. Harriet Whicher, wife of RF's Amherst colleague George Whicher.

232. Roland Holt, son of the founder and vice president of the publishing firm Henry Holt and Company; Harcourt did in fact leave Holt in 1919 to found Harcourt, Brace and Howe. RF remained with Holt through the end of his career.

233. Tug Kennedy was a heavyweight boxer based in Northampton, Massachusetts, and active in the sport ca. 1910–1912.

234. Katharine Lee Bates, on the faculty at Wellesley, which Lesley had left in favor of Barnard College; for the Spanish translation, see RF to Jiménez, January 20, 1919.

235. RF refers to Regis Michaud (1880–1939), the author, eventually, of several books on Emerson; his wife was Jane C. Michaud (who was born in Lyndon, Vermont, near Lake Willoughby). George Daniel Olds (1853–1931) was, at the time, professor of mathematics at Amherst (he later served as president). The "Estes" were Thomas Cushing Esty (1870–1958), professor of mathematics at Amherst College, and his wife, Annette Emer-

Tell Harcourt about the Madrid paper. I shouldn't mention it to anyone else.

Tell us about the work in the office.

The Chapins are really nice people. I like Chapin.[236] Remember me to him particularly—and to her too of course though less particularly.

The one thing I want to ask of you is that you will get your full sleep as a protection against throats. Sure!

There was a nice letter from Nichols but he hasn't blown in yet and Hendricks hasn't.[237]

Carter Goodrich lunched with us and talked politics two or three hours last week.[238] He's bound away. He expects to mix up in English labor politics all next year. He says he has looked and looked, but he sees not one sign of a revolution in America. He hopes for better reward in England.

The Frenchman from Smith College put the way I begin to suspect it will come out. Bolshevism is nothing to speak of in England France and even Germany and will come to nothing. It may serve to take some of the high

---

son Esty. RF's hosts on this "talking evening" were Henry Carrington Lancaster (1882–1954), professor of French literature at Amherst College, and his wife, Helen Clark Lancaster. (Lancaster later joined the faculty at Johns Hopkins University.) It was on this evening that RF inscribed a copy of *NB* to Michaud: "Some twenty-two lines in 'Monadnoc' beginning 'Now in sordid weeds they sleep' (I dont need to copy them out for such an Emersonian as you, Michaud) meant almost more to me than anything else on the art of writing when I was a youngster; and that not just on the art of writing colloquial verse but on the art of writing any kind of verse or prose. I suffer from the way people abuse the word colloquial. All writing, I dont care how exalted, how lyrical, or how seemingly far removed from the dramatic, must be as colloquial as this passage from 'Monadnoc' comes to. I am as sure that the colloquial is the root of every good poem as I am that the national is the root of all thought and art. It may shoot up as high as you please and flourish as widely abroad in the air, if only the roots are what and where they should be. One half of individuality is locality: and I was about venturing to say the other half was colloquiality. The beauty of the high thinking in Emerson's Uriel and Give All to Love is that it is well within the colloquial as I use the word. And so also is all the lyric in Palgrave's Treasury for that matter, no matter at what level of sentiment it is pitched. Consider Herrick's To Daffodils. But sometime more of this when we can sit down together" (the copy of *NB* bearing this inscription is held now at DCL).

236. James Chapin, illustrator of a special limited edition of *NB* (issued in 1919); his wife was Abigail Beal.

237. For Hendricks, see RF to Lesley, October 24, 1918. George H. Nichols served in the army.

238. Carter Goodrich (1897–1971) graduated from Amherst in 1918; he later distinguished himself as an economist.

mightiness out of the too rich and it may help in some rather radical changes that are coming. That will be its life. The credit for the changes will go mostly to other political parties who will be too cautious and too interested to forget the rights of property too far. I don't know, but this sounds somewhere near my sense of the situation. Wilson seems to be representative of the sentiment of the world.

Affectionately
Papa.

[To Lesley Frost. Above the salutation, RF has written "Received cheque." Along the left edge of the page he has written "Im glad you like the Chapins so much." ALS. UVA.]

Amherst
Feb 17 1919

Dear Lesley:

You can write to them in Franconia and they'll send to me or you can write to me here and I'll send to them—either way or both ways—better both ways.

I shall have to go to the theatre, I also, before it is all over for this year I expect. And the reason is that my play is to be given in Northampton and I suppose it would look funny if I didnt see it. I rather dread the ordeal, though I must say the boys who are to act the two parts do first rate in them. It will be my fault or the audience's if the thing fails. I'm prepared to call it the audience's. I doubt if the play is very bad.[239]

I pity you, having to write essays where the imagination has no chance, or next to no chance. Just one word of advice: Try to avoid strain or at any rate the appearance of strain. One way to go to work is to read your author once or twice over having an eye out for anything that occurs to you as you read whether appreciative contradictory corroborative or parallel (can't spell). There should be more or less of a jumble in your head or on your note paper after the first time and even after the second. Much that you will think of in connection will come to nothing and be wasted. But some of it ought to go together under one idea. That idea is the thing to write on and write into the title at the head of your paper. As you write you will probably want to turn

239. *A Way Out* was performed at the Northampton Academy of Music on February 24, 1919, with RF's former student, Roland Wood, in the role of Asie.

again to your author for citation and quotation to make the body of your work. One of the boys here had Longfellow to do. He read him till he saw his idea to go by. He expressed that in his title Longfellow and the Middling Virtues. Another thought that the interesting thing that rose naturally in his mind as he read Hawthorne was that some of his mysticism was just mechanical for story purposes mere ghost and mystery, but some of it was profoundly religious and real. So he will probably call his paper something like Real and Affected Mysticism of Hawthorne. Then he will go back to the passages in Hawthorne to bear him out in his idea. He wont be very long or at all pretentious if he knows his business. One idea and a few subordinate ideas—its to have those happen to you as you read and catch them—not let them escape you in your direct interest in your author. The sidelong glance is what you depend on. You look at your author but you keep the tail of your eye on what is happening over and above your author in your own mind and nature. I've never written essay, but I have the material often when I read—I'm aware of it making—not in every book by any means but in a few. Nothing happened either corroborative appreciative illustrative or very contradictory when I read Jean's book for instance and that's why I dont write her the little essay she asks for on it.[240] Out of a class of sixty boys only seven have seen what I mean by all this. The rest will put a name at the heads of their papers Hawthorne, Poe Emerson or Longfellow; and they will simply tell again what these men said and did and wrote. None of their own increment here. Receptivity is all their faculty. They seem incapable of the over-and-above stuff. I think maybe it goes on in their heads as they read but they are incapable of catching it. They are too directly intent on the reading. They cant get started looking two ways at once. I think too they are afraid of the simplicity of many things they think on the side as they read. They wouldnt have the face to connect it in writing with the great author they have been reading. It may be a childhood memory; it may be some homely simile; it may be a line or verse of mother goose. They want it to be big and bookish. But they haven't books enough in their heads to match book stuff with book stuff. Of course some of that would be all right. The game is matching your author thought for thought in any of the many possible ways. Reading then becomes converse—give and take. It is only conversation in which the reader takes part addressing himself to anything at all in the author in his subject

---

240. Jean Starr Untermeyer. B. W. Huebsch published her first book, *Growing Pains*, in 1918.

matter or form. Just as when we talk together! Being careful to hold up our end and to do our part agreeably without too much contradiction and mere opinionation. The best thing of all is going each other one better piling up the ideas anecdotes and incidents like alternating hands piled up on the knee. Well its out of conversation like this with a book that you find perhaps one idea perhaps yours perhaps the book's that will serve for other lesser ideas to center around. And there's your essay. Be brief at first. You have to be honest. You dont want to make your material seem more than it is. You wont have so much to say at first as you will have later. My defect is in not having learned to hammer my material into one lump. I haven't had experience enough. The details of essay won't come in right for me as they will in narrative. Sometimes I have gotten round the difficulty by some narrative dodge.

Of course this letter is essay. It is material that has come to the surface of my mind in reading just as frost brings stones to the surface of the ground.

I dont know you know whether its worth very much—I mean the essay—when you have it written. I'm rather afraid of it as an enemy to the really creative writing that holds scenes and things in the eye voices in the ear and whole situations as a sort of plexus in the body (I dont know just where). Take it easy with the essay whatever you do. Write it as well as you can if you have to write it. Be as concrete as the law allows in it—concrete and experiential. Don't let it scare you. Don't strain. Remember that any old thing that happens in your head as you read may be the thing you want. If nothing much seems to happen, perhaps another reading will help. Perhaps the book is bad or is not your kind—is nothing to you and can start nothing in your nature one way or another.

Affectionately
Papa

[To Louis Untermeyer. ALS. LoC]

[Amherst, MA]
[February 17, 1919]

Dear Louis:

I'm sorry to have to put off New York again, but what's the use of saying so till I am prepared to "do different."

Part of the enclosed is intended for a little surprise. I ask you can any original first gift however unexpected give you half the pleasure that you must get from the return of anything as long given up for lost as Vachel's Edgar Lee Letter (so called from henceforth).[241]

I can't say that I am not satisfied with the Thomas article.[242] In our hearts we both wanted you to write it as you saw it. I'm credibly told that theres something about me the British prefer not to have mentioned in connection with Thomas. If so you will have bothered them by what you have written. They seem to think it must diminish their poet to have him under obligations to an American. And yet he knew and freely and generously said that it was not only in verse theory but in inspiration that he was my debtor. Of course it is all nothing. But no harm in bothering them in their conceit.

Lesley cites you and Jean for distinguished attentions. The family when next it convenes will doubtless make an appropriation—to buy you medals.

The family is terribly scattered for the moment. It gives me a foretaste of what it will be like when they are grown up and gone and I don't like it any better than I should. I suppose they will have to go their ways sometime. Well then I'm not going to stop them of course if its fate. But I dont believe there's any law to keep me from turning from my own way to go after them along theirs. A father ought to have a right to follow imitate and lose himself in the careers of his children. What would Bernard Shaw say?—I mean about the aged being dragged along by the young instead of the young being held back by the old?[243]

---

241. Untermeyer explains: "This refers to a long letter, dated May 13, 1918, which Vachel Lindsay had written me in praise of Edgar Lee Masters" (*RFLU,* 81). See RF to Untermeyer, June 27, 1918.

242. Untermeyer's article on Edward Thomas appeared in the *North American Review* for January 1919. RF's diffidence arises from the fact that the article mentions him as often as it does Thomas, and avers, with regard to Thomas's first volume: "The genius, the influence, the inflection, even the idiom, of Robert Frost, can be found in almost all of these English pages. The book itself, with its logical dedication, is a tribute to Frost the person as much as Frost the poet."

243. RF refers to George Bernard Shaw's *Treatise on Parents and Children* (1910): "A child should begin to assert itself early, and shift for itself more and more not only in washing and dressing itself, but in opinions and conduct; yet as nothing is so exasperating and so unlovable as an uppish child, it is useless to expect parents and schoolmasters to inculcate this uppishness. Such unamiable precepts as Always contradict an authoritative statement, Always return a blow, Never lose a chance of a good fight, When you are scolded for a mistake ask the person who scolds you whether he or she supposes you did it on purpose, and follow the question with a blow or an insult or some other unmistakable expression of resentment, Remember that the progress of the world depends on

I've got a word to you for one of these days my friend about these people who think you spend too much time thinking of me. You know you have exalted me. The question will soon be have you done it for nothing. Seeing you such a rich man they will suspect you have fattened your purse out of me. That will be the next thing. Lets destroy our check books so that they can't prove any money connection. I'd hate to have it go down to posterity that one poet had corrupted another with money. It would be unprecedented in the annals unless you count Amy's corruption of Braithwaite and that's not a case of poet and poet so much as of poet and duodecaroon—something very special and never likely to happen again.[244] I'll tell you something else we can do to throw the poetry society (lc) off the track. Lets meet and ignore each other in a public place on the very day Holts releases your book of criticism.[245] Let's both act equally offended. Lets loudly refuse to be introduced to each other. Start cultivating the perpendicular wrinkles in front.

Meanwhile my love to you all from Dick up.

Robertus.

[To Marguerite Ogden Bigelow Wilkinson (1883–1928), poet, anthologist, and critic. See also RF to Wilkinson, April 21, 1919. ALS. Middlebury.]

Amherst Mass
February 19 1919

My dear Mrs Wilkinson:

My serious fault not to have written you sooner. I meant the best. Lesley was to have found you with a message from me long ago and we ourselves were to have been in New York where we expected to see you before this.

I am glad you decided for An Old Man's Winter Night and The Gum Gatherer. I didnt want to be the one to direct you to The Gum Gatherer; but it is a favorite of mine if for no other reason than because it is the only poem I

---

your knowing better than your elders, are just as important as those of The Sermon on the Mount; but no one has yet seen them written up in letters of gold in a schoolroom or nursery." We thank Mark Scott for the suggestion.

244. Braithwaite regularly praised Lowell in print and featured her in his yearly *Anthology of Magazine Verse.*

245. *The New Era in American Poetry* (New York: Henry Holt and Company, 1919). An essay on RF led off the volume.

know of that has found a way to speak poetically of chewing gum. The Code can very well be passed by for once. It has been reprinted rather more than its share.

Will you see to it for me that the word "fill" is changed to "keep" in the line "One aged man—one man—can't etc."[246] I dont know how it ever got printed "fill." I only noticed it lately. I think I must always have read it aloud "keep." That's the way I first wrote it.

I gather from what you let fall in your letters that you have found a fresh way to make a book about poetry.[247] It sounds to me as if it is bound to go well. I shall look forward to seeing it.

I wanted Lesley to meet you. If you have time for youngsters, won't you ask her round some afternoon? She is at Fernald Hall, Barnard College. She will tell you of my adventures with my wicked English publisher who has never paid me a cent for my books or even rendered an account. Us sufferin' authors!

With greetings to Mr Wilkinson.

Always your friendly
Robert Frost

[To Katharine Lee Bates. ALS. Wellesley.]

Amherst Mass
February 20 1919

Dear Miss Bates:

If you are still of the same mind as when you wrote some time ago I should like to propose coming to you early in March. We have had sickness on sickness in the family all winter till I haven't known what I was free to undertake. Otherwise I should have written to you sooner. We have had five

---

246. RF refers to "An Old Man's Winter Night," collected in *MI*; he replaced "fill" with "keep" when he brought the book's contents into his *Collected Poems* (1939).

247. In her critical anthology *New Voices: An Introduction to Contemporary Poetry* (New York: Macmillan, 1919), Wilkinson included an unusual assortment of Frost poems: "An Old Man's Winter Night," "Brown's Descent," "The Sound of the Trees," "The Gum Gatherer," and "The Cow in Apple Time." The book was structured as a series of essays on significant authors and defining traits in contemporary poetry, with each essay followed by an illustrative anthology of poems.

cases of influenza out of a possible six. I myself went near dying, which I take as a particular compliment from the disease since it is advertised to make itself dangerous only to the young in years, looks, dress, or feeling. I can't complain as long as I got a compliment out of it.[248] And there were other compensations, as that I had a fine time thinking my own thoughts in convalescence. I just settled back and got well slowly on purpose. I was never better in the mind than I have been since the war ended. I wonder if it is the same with you. We ought to write some poetry now. Which isnt to say that you haven't written any during the war—only that I haven't and that you haven't written as much probably as you would if you had been untroubled by it all. Of course Miss Scudder's Social Revolution is on the way—no use blinking that; but I refuse to let it worry me this spring anyway.[249] Please tell her so with my regards and also remember me appropriately to our amiable if somewhat unmanageable friend Charles Lowell Young.

We had a pleasant little visit from Miss Drew of your department the other day when Lesley happened to be at home. Wellesley is not all ill memories to Lesley. She knows what she owes you and Miss Drew and Miss Young (Math.) for a number of happy moments. But she's too young and honestly implacable to pretend that she doesnt lay it up more or less against the whole college for what Miss Fletcher and Miss Coe did to her. Those two gave her a taste of life she had never had before—particularly Miss Coe, to the bitter end. Even so it might have come out all right if Brother Young hadn't allowed that he thought Lesley's final rather triumphant marks the unjust ones if any: they had come to her on my account at his solicitation.[250] Fatal tactics.

---

248. See G. D. Shanks and J. F. Brundage, "Pathogenic Responses among Young Adults during the 1918 Influenza Pandemic," *Emerging Infectious Diseases* [serial on the Internet], February 2012: "Of the unexplained characteristics of the 1918–19 influenza pandemic, the extreme mortality rate among young adults (W-shaped mortality curve) is the foremost." American reporting contemporary with the pandemic emphasized this.

249. Vida Dutton Scudder (1861–1954), professor of English literature at Wellesley, cofounded the Episcopal Church Socialist League and was an activist on behalf of labor during, among other things, the Lawrence Textile Strike in 1912 (a strike RF knew well: see his June 25, 1912, letter to Rowell). Named also in the letter (and familiar from still others): Helen Louisa Drew, instructor in rhetoric and composition; Caroline Rebecca Fletcher, associate professor of Latin; Ada May Coe, instructor in Spanish; and Mabel Minerva Young, instructor in mathematics.

250. The aforementioned Charles Lowell Young, Bates's colleague in the Department of English, and a Frost family friend.

She's a proud youngster in a hard position, I'm afraid, as her father's daughter. But the energy is there. She'll come out all right. We all thank you for the help you gave us in getting through what remains to me even a puzzlingly bad year.

Always your friend
Robert Frost

[To Lesley Frost. The first page (or pages) of the letter is missing. Internal evidence and a note by Lesley Frost date the letter to February–March 1919. ALS. UVA.]

[Amherst, MA]
[mid-March 1919]

[. . .] allowed to try their puzzles on the whole American army. Puzzles is the word—puzzles and traps. American psychology is famed for the trick boxes it has invented to try the intelligence of monkeys guinea pigs and mice. Something is wrong with it all. As the writer of a book I have been reading says probably it is its artificiality. Glazer [*sic*], one of our best teachers here (that is he is reputed in his department one of the brilliant men of the country) passed one of the lab-test-exams recently with the rating of a child of fourteen years.[251] One of the things he failed in was imagining the pattern in a square piece of paper when it should be unfolded after having been folded four times and cut into in one or two places. He never had seen any game like that before. I played it when I was young and so would probably have done better than he with it. His failure, they told him, proved that he was weak in visual imagination. He knows himself too well to be deceived there. Visual imagination happens to be his chief strength in his particular science. If he were younger and less self experienced he might be scared by such findings.

But we have to take education as it comes in our day—awful as it may be. You can always transcend it to a certain extent even if you get somewhat worse marks for being independent in your thoughts and actions. To hell with the marks so long as you know you are better than the best marks. Think! Have thoughts! Make the most of your thoughts. That is all that matters. After that you can read if you have time so long as you make sure to keep on top of your reading by thinking. Have at least one idea of your own for every one in the books. Simile analogy example from life and experience.

251. Otto C. Glaser was professor of biology at Amherst College.

The preparation for the examination was good for you in one way though it didn't help you in the examination and the examination was probably good for you in another way though it may not have been the way intended by your teachers.

Don't mind Knapp and dont mind Boas.[252] Be pleasant to them but be natural and untruckling. There's no harm in your asking if the class couldn't translate a little. He may think the class is too large. All he has to do is say so then. I can't think he can mean to punish you for so simple a proposal. The class ought to translate. It is damnable to have to sit in every class and hear nothing but the voice of teachers. At least there's little of that dullness at Amherst.

Prime yourself for old Boas. Go and get some ideas out of Osborn's Men of the Old Stone Age and books mentioned in it.[253] One book will lead to others. You'll only have time to read patches in each of them. You'll stumble on to curious things that may come in handy in class talks. I've just been reading about the most ancient human remains in their order of antiquity Pithecanthropus Erectus (found in Java) the Piltdown Man the Neanderthal Man and the Cro-Magnon Man ranging from 200,000 to 10,000 years B.C. Good pictures of them in Osborn's book—funny too when you stop to consider what the artist had to go on.

Then one thing more: one of Whichers friends an old pupil of his at Illinois, a sort of poet-reformer-farmer, a really interesting fellow as far as I could see into him has been visiting here and now he writes from Long Island that his sister has met you at Barnard (where she is enrolled too) and wants you to go home with her some time for better acquaintance. The name is Walser.[254] They're English. It would be nice if you happened to like her and thought she wasn't trying to get into poetical society. You wouldn't

252. Charles Knapp (1868–1936) was a professor of Classical Philology at Barnard during Lesley Frost's time there. Franz Boas (1858–1942), German-American pioneer of modern anthropology, taught at Columbia University from 1896 until 1936.

253. Henry Fairfield Osborn Sr. (1857–1935) was an American geologist, paleontologist, and eugenicist, and the president of the American Museum of Natural History for twenty-five years. In 1916, he published *The Origin and Evolution of Life* and *Men of the Old Stone Age*.

254. Frank E. Walser, born in 1891 in London; in 1919 he was living in Nassau County, Long Island, New York. World War I draft records identify him as a farmer. The Charity Organization Society of New York lists him as active in 1920. He died in 1977. His sister Violet Walser (later Violet Walser Goodrich) was, in 1919, like Lesley, a student at Bar-

see Walser, her brother; he's out managing a farm somewhere in the country. The rest of the family may not be as real and out-of-the-usual as he is—or seemed. Gee! I'm on my guard against every body.[255]

I'm sorry for Cox. I wish I could do something for him here. But we are full to the back balcony. It looks as if Percy Mackay might teach with us. I like him and I'm glad in a way but it just cuts out William Benet whose name I have been proposing to Mr Meikle.[256] No word of this to Louis or anyone else.

Don't you think it would be nice for Irma to go down to see you for a while. Could she have a room with you or very near you. Poor kid she has

---

nard. Before joining the faculty at Amherst in 1915, George Whicher had taught at the University of Illinois.

255. At this point some five lines of text have been heavily scored out in ink of a color slightly different from that used to pen the letter. The canceled passage begins, "Hendricks played us false . . ."; the rest has been rendered illegible. The matter involves Irma Frost's report (she was sixteen at the time) that Walter Hendricks had made improper advances toward her. In March 1919, with RF still in Amherst, Elinor asked Hendricks to look after Carol, Marjorie, and Irma in her absence: "He is going to stay with the children while I am away," she wrote Lesley, "and he may stay here all through March, until Papa comes up for good, but he will probably go up to Bissells [local family friends] when I get home from New York" (*FL*, 60). RF returned to Franconia from Amherst on March 19. Hendricks apparently remained in or around Franconia through mid-May, after which point RF discretely broke with him. On May 18, he sent Hendricks down to Hanover bearing a cordial letter of introduction (and a book) to Dartmouth librarian Harold Rugg (letter reprinted herein). Four days later, on May 22, he wrote Lesley: "Well anyway we are rid of Walter, and keeping that pretense up for appearance' [sic] sake is over. We had to be careful that the neighborhood didnt notice anything" (again, letter reprinted herein). In short, between mid-March and mid-May, with Hendricks in or near Franconia (population 500), RF and Elinor maintained friendly relations for the sake of privacy, until RF sent him away, on May 18, bearing the aforementioned letter to Rugg. Later, RF concluded that Irma's accusations had been groundless (she began to manifest symptoms of mental illness as she matured). By October 1922, RF had made amends and thereafter he spoke of Walter Hendricks with kindness (see, e.g., *CPRF*, 152). In the third volume of his biography (completed by R. H. Winnick), Thompson incorrectly dates the trouble with Irma and Hendricks to 1917 (*LY*, 413–414).

256. Alexander Meiklejohn, president of Amherst College. William Rose Benét (1886–1950) was an American poet, writer, and editor. Cox, mentioned earlier, is Sidney Hayes Cox. The dramatist and poet Percy MacKaye would, in 1920, take up a post as Poet in Residence at Miami University (Oxford, Ohio). Neither Benét nor MacKaye joined the faculty at Amherst.

had a hard year. Say what you think of this to me, not to them up there. The children may get hold of what you write to Mama.

Long letter—what?

Affectionately
Papa.

I wonder if you want any of us down to see the Grecian Games.[257] Let me know soon either way.

[To Harriet Moody. RF apparently wrote this letter before leaving, the same day, for Franconia. ALS. Chicago.]

Amherst Mass
March 19 1919

Dear Mrs Moody

(Still to keep to a mode of address that no one else of equal pretension to your friendship seems to use):

Though I'm not as well as I ought to be and there are other obstacles in the way of our getting to Chicago to see you this spring, I am resolved to try to make it if only for a very short visit. You'll have to squeeze both the lectures into the one week, April 14–19 and leave me Tuesday the 15th free for a little talk I may do for some of the free verse gentry.

We'll talk over the summer school plans when I get there. It may be I had rather put off the summer school till a year from now. I could keep it (if it would keep) for something ahead to prolong life a moment if I should burst my bonds here as teacher and run wild again.[258] I strain at those bonds all the time and of course they only cut deeper the more I strain. It might be a good thing if you mustered against our coming your religion such as it is to help me endure what I ought to endure for my sins and my family. You can tell me your idea of duty and I'll counter you with why I think nobody that talks round poetry all the time or likes to hear talk round poetry can ever write poetry or even properly read it for that matter. I suppose simply that it is the nature of God to have it so. It is not that generalizations from poetry are so

257. The annual Greek Games held at Barnard. See RF's April 14, 1919, letter to Lesley.

258. The University of Chicago had offered summer sessions since the late nineteenth century; Moody hoped RF might teach there.

wholly bad if they make themselves as it were spontaneously and after the fact. God has only made them fatal when they are used school fashion as the approach to poetry. The general notion having been laid down by the professor it then becomes possible to enjoy the particular poem as an illustration of it or as a case under it and as nothing else.

But don't mistake my getting mad about it in your presence for getting mad at you. You may be as much to blame as you please for this or anything else it will make no difference to me: I shall remain

Always your devoted friend
Robert Frost

[To Mitchell Dawson (1890–1956), a Chicago attorney and a poet. ALS. Newberry.]

Franconia N.H.
March 19 1919

Dear Mr Dawson:

I told Kreymborg when I was in New York that I probably couldnt make Chicago this spring. He may have passed the word to you and taking it as final you may have cast me out of your plans. Would you take me back into them if I should decide to come now? And would the date you named be still open to me?—ie. April 15.[259]

I appreciate being in the list of poets you name. The only trouble with it is that though on paper it seems to bring us together, in reality it strings us out and keeps us apart as if making special provision against our all being in Chicago with you at one time. I suppose you know what's good for Chicago. It doesnt matter about Conrad Aiken Lola Ridge Carlos Williams Alfred and me.[260]

Sincerely yours
Robert Frost

---

259. Family illnesses prevented the trip.

260. A friend of Alfred Kreymborg, editor of the literary magazine *Others,* Dawson in 1919 instituted the Others Lecture Bureau and invited writers to present lectures and readings in Chicago. The series lasted only one year and RF apparently did not participate, but each of the other poets RF mentions did make an appearance.

[To Lesley Frost. ALS. UVA.]

Franconia
March 24 '19

Dear Lesley

The first thing is to ask you to look up Mrs Zorn at the Grenoble Hotel if she hasn't already looked you up. She is there for a week or so with Mrs Stewart.[261] You could locate her by telephone and then take her somewhere for entertainment. Do the honors. Suggest going with her to see Chapin's studio, or to some good play.[262] (How about the French players?) I should have written about this sooner.

The second thing is to ask you what you-all are thinking of to want me to judge in a lyric contest in which you may be entered however unbeknownst to me. Consider the risk of your winning any prize I had the disposal of. No one would believe I hadnt known what poem was yours. It would never do.

We decided it would never do before Momma told me you were in fact going in for the lyric prize. Lucky I foresaw the possibility. People would say it takes two Frosts, father and daughter, to win one prize—that is if we won it. And we ought to win it on such a good poem as this you have sent home. Gee it is a good one. Prizes are more or less accidents and of course we can't and dont count on them, having more important things to look to beyond them. Just about perfect all down through beginning with the fifth line,

I heard the morning church bells ring.

You know how I would be likely to like all that about the dead fern and leaves in his hair and hoofs. It is the kind of poetry I can hardly keep my finger out of. I should like to ask you to get in a stanza saying that where he got up from the ground was a bare spot as where you turn over a field-stone. You see how it excites my imagination. The best place of all perhaps is about the

---

261. Ethel Manthey-Zorn was the wife of RF's Amherst colleague Otto Manthey-Zorn and one of Elinor Frost's close friends. Helen Lucille Wynkoop Stewart was the wife of Walter W. Stewart (1885–1958). He had joined the Amherst faculty in 1915 as professor of economics and would resign in 1923 after Meicklejohn left (he had also been offered the presidency of the college). Later he taught at Princeton, served on the Federal Reserve and the Council of Economic Advisors, and was head of Rockefeller Foundation.

262. Painter and illustrator James Chapin.

bells not ringing true. That is returning on an old phrase with real effect. I want you to make it the bells outright like this:

because he knew
By something in the sound of them
They were not ringing true.

Everything could stand very well just as it is however for all I see. I see no real defect in the ringing true lines as they stand. But I think you could do something to fill out the meaning of the poem a little by making more of the line "A god they had with ease denied." You could stuff more into that line. The idea is Should he give back to men an older god than the one that had their bells. Why not say just about that? Gee it's a real poem—Pipes against Bells! It doesnt say how he succeeded. He simply saw a chance. But he had great confidence.

Im enclosing part of an examination I gave my boys.[263] The answers are on the back of the sheet. The boys were supposed to have read all the poems in the Oxford Book of Victorian Verse. But they also had the book open before them. They did rather badly. Their answers were strained and far-fetched. They tried too hard to preserve common sense.

I'm glad you did well with James' Varieties.[264]

If you were plumb sick and nauseated in Knapps quiz and the quiz is crucial I should think he might give you another chance.[265] If not I shouldn't mind.

Here's a check for 25 for luck.

Affectionately
Papa

263. Arnold Grade reprints the quiz and answer key in *FL* (58–59), retaining RF's misspellings (and noting that, in the enclosure as originally sent to Lesley, the answer key was written upside down). RF drew up six groups of poems from Quiller-Couch's *Oxford Book of Victorian Verse* (1912), and then asked students the following question: "On what similarity have the following groups been made?" See Grade's edition for the particulars.

264. William James's *Varieties of Religious Experience.*

265. Charles Knapp, professor of Classical Philology at Barnard.

[To Lesley Frost. ALS. UVA.]

Franconia N.H.
March 29 1919

Dear Lesley:

I want you to spend some money on entertaining people you like and I dont want you to be niggardly about it till I call a halt. I hope you had my check in time to seem free handed enough with Margaret White (Wha's [*sic*] the matter with me—blunder struck.)[266]

If that girl is mad about anything I should say it must be either because your poem is too good or because it is irreligious or rather unchristian.[267] I dont see how she can know enough to know it is too good; so I conclude she frowns on you as impious or something, though I confess that seems improbable in these days and at a metropolitan college. At Wellesley for certain you would be barred from any prize for unorthodoxy. The reason might, surely would, be suppressed, but you would find your poem unconsidered. They would say why in Hell cant she praise the Greek god without reflecting on the Christian God. They wouldnt see that it was the church, the form of worship that you found false. You say nothing against the One God. He is Pan in a manner of thinking. He includes Pan anyway, whatever else he is more than Pan.

We are in the hen business to the depth of fifteen hens and a rooster, five of the hens and the rooster being aristocracy. We are better off than last year by one small hen house Carol built. We are going to hatch a slew of chickens.

Irma and I and Carol captured about forty young wild apple trees just over the wall on that slope going down to the Pooles spring house and are setting out an orchard on the steepest slope behind the house in our mowing field.[268]

---

266. RF's parenthetical exasperation appears to refer to the number of false starts, blots, and crossings-out in his manuscript. Margaret White was, at the time, enrolled at Teachers College, Columbia University; students there could also take courses at Barnard, where Lesley was enrolled.

267. The poem in question concerned the god Pan (see *FL*, 59).

268. Perhaps William H. Poole and his wife, Anna, also residing, at the time, in Grafton County, New Hampshire.

We ordered $10.40 worth of seed of James J. H. Gregory & Son of Marblehead Mass to-day, wondering all the time if we would get it back out of the enormous crops we expect to raise this summer.[269]

Carol is into the sugaring with the Herberts.[270] Most of us are surfeited with the taste of maple in one form or another, sap, syrup, snow-candy, or sugar. Great sugar weather. Wild cold and snowy yesterday and still going it. Furnace feels good.

Wont it be rather difficult about all those boys you are going to the Plaza with?

Yes you'll have to allow yourself something to entertain good people with.

I think Irma ought to look into New York this year. She seems to want to sit around in the art gallery. You could take her there get some beneficial glimpses yourself and leave her to meditate the masters.

Affectionately
Papa

John Bartlett writes that Margaret has taken the poetry editorship of Farm Journal.[271] Funny how things come round.

[To Elizabeth Douglas Van Buren (1881–1961), archaeologist, wife of Albert William Van Buren, and author, among other books, of Symbols of God in Mesopotamian Art *(1945). ALS. BU.]*

Franconia N.H.
March 31 1919

My dear Mrs Van Buren:

What things to make my left ear burn you must be saying down there in Paradise. I do and don't deserve them. I ought of course to have dropped everything and gone south at your invitation: I was to blame and expect to be

---

269. The firm RF mentions operated a mail-order seed business; its location would have been familiar to Lesley from the work she did in Marblehead for the Curtiss Aeroplane Company during the war.

270. Possibly the Willis E. Herbert family, from whom RF had purchased the Franconia farm; however, a number of families by that name resided in Franconia

271. Established in 1877, the magazine had a circulation of about a million nationwide in 1915. See *RFJB*, 119.

punished for not accepting your invitation. But you wouldn't blame me so much for not having written to tell you why I didn't accept it if you knew how miserably off we have all been here. I myself have just been through what appeared to be a milder second attack of influenza. I have been a drag on myself and everyone else all winter.

The impulse to get up and get out of the cold was a natural one you will admit under the circumstances. I thought we were in earnest about it when we started stirring Baxter up about Porto Rico.[272] But there were things against our going away this year much as we probably needed a change of climate. We are ordinarily good at getting over obstacles in the way of our doing what we like or need. This time however energy seemed to fail us. We were so inadequate that I'm afraid we would have had to be personally conducted to get anywhere. The amount of it is we were too weak to be unscrupulous enough for action.

Sometime I wish we might see you in your warm Floridan [*sic*] winter. We are too much of a troop to impose on friends. What would draw us south would be the assurance of a small inexpensive cottage in your neighborhood where we could take care of ourselves—see a good deal of you without being a burden to you. This for some other winter.

Meanwhile we are disappointed to have had to disappoint you. You are so very kind. I wish there was something more than sending my mere photograph to show how much I appreciate what you have wanted to do for us either because you like us or like our poetry or like my having a southern name or for some reason that's beyond me.[273]

With friendliest greetings from both Mrs Frost and myself.

Sincerely yours
Robert Frost

P.S. So far from being any further south for all our pother we are actually, as you see by the address, further north—back in our own Franconia, the coldest of the cold. You have every sort of fruit all round you on trees; we have scarcely so much as an apple in a barrel in the cellar. Isnt it mournful?

R.F.

---

272. Sylvester Baxter (1850–1927), family friend, critic, and poet; for more on Puerto Rico, see RF's January 25, 1919, letter to Lesley.

273. The poet's Copperhead father, William Prescott Frost, named him after Robert E. Lee.

*[To Louis Untermeyer. The ostensible addressee is the corresponding secretary of what RF terms a "Poetry Society," one Margaret Perry. There has been some confusion as to the matter. Untermeyer believed the letter had been sent only to him, that the pretense that he was being "copied" on it was a spoof, and that Perry worked for the Poetry Society of America (*RFLU, *83). In his* Selected Letters of Robert Frost, *Thompson reprints the letter, in error, as having been sent to "Lila Cabot Perry," who was never secretary of a poetry society but was a distinguished painter and the mother of Margaret, who was born in 1876. In* YT, *Thompson refers, in his notes (see page 587), to the letter as addressed to Margaret Perry, and also refers his readers back to* SL, *where the text of the letter, as reprinted there, differs somewhat from that printed by Untermeyer, though Thompson worked from the same document (held at the Library of Congress). The society is variously referred to—by Untermeyer and Thompson—as the Poetry Society of America and as the Poetry Society of New England. However, an unpublished chronology maintained by Thompson, and held at UVA, indicates that on February 24, 1919, RF was elected, in absentia, president of the New England Poetry Club (a fact supported by RF's complaint in the April 3 letter below to Lesley Frost: "Having trouble with New England Poetry Society because I dont accept presidency"). And indeed Margaret Perry served as the Club's "corresponding secretary," as a notice in William Stanley Braithwaite's* Anthology of Magazine Verse for 1923 and Yearbook of American Poetry *indicates. The notice in Braithwaite's* Anthology *also indicates that, by 1923, RF had managed to get himself demoted to "honorary president" of the New England Poetry Club, along with Amy Lowell and Katharine Lee Bates. ALS. LoC.]*

Franconia N.H.
April 3 1919

Copy of letter to
Dear Mrs Perry
(Corresponding Sec.)

So I'm to be President of the Poetry Society because I wasn't at your last meeting to say I wouldnt be President, just as I seem to be expected at Wellesley on the eleventh for the simple reason that I havent said I wouldnt be there on the eleventh. Neither have I said that I wouldn't be there on the twelfth or the thirteenth or the fourteenth or any other day you have a mind to name. On the same principle I suppose I am writing an epic because I haven't said I wasn't and it has already made me a rich man because I haven't said it hasn't and if I am a rich man I can go any distance in the trains at three cents a mile because I haven't said that as a sick man I'm not able to. I must protest at this reverse way of being taken. Must I be assumed guilty till I am proved innocent but more than that must I be assumed guilty of every particular deed and thought that I havent specifically declared myself innocent of? (As for instance Maria Halpins baby.[274])

But seriously now do you think it was friendly of you all to make me an official when you must have seen how superstitious I am about holding office. I thought I saw a way out of it for us both in not accepting the Presidency you had imposed on me. I thought by silence I could sort of keep from myself what I was in for and in fact privately take the view that I was not a President while at the same time leaving you free to think that I was a President. Ingenious, you see—and significant: it shows how anxious I am to please you as friends and fellow poets if not as members of any society. But it wouldn't do: you had to spoil it all and make the issue acute between us by proposing to lunch me formally on my job just as you would launch a ship. I may be nervous but I cant help seeing in it a conspiracy to shear me of any wild strength I may have left after two years of teaching in college. As Vachel would say "Let Samson be comin into your mind."[275]

With protestation of the
warmest regard etc
Robert Frost

Louis, I wanted you to have a picture of me struggling to climb out of what I had got into out onto the thin ice around me. The letter is a copy of one I am sending to Mrs. Perry on the occasion of her expecting me to lunch on the eleventh of the month because I havent said I wouldnt come. Please put it up to posterity if I haven't done the best I could. Be my witness.

R.F.

Bids fair to rival the famous case of Viereck versus the Poetry Society of America only mine illustrates the difficulty of staying out while his illustrates the difficulty of staying in.[276]

R.F.

274. During the presidential campaign of 1884, Maria Halpin was rumored to be Grover Cleveland's mistress, and to have borne a child by him.

275. RF alludes to "How Samson Bore Away the Gates of Gaza" by Vachel Lindsay.

276. The German American poet George Sylvester Viereck (1884–1962) was accused of spying for the Germans during World War I and was expelled, on those grounds, from the Poetry Society of America and from the American Authors League.

[To Marguerite Ogden Bigelow Wilkinson. RF refers to the poetry of Edward Thomas. ALS. Middlebury.]

Franconia N.H.
April 3 1919

Dear Mrs Wilkinson

Just a word to say that I dont know what to say. My adventures with publishers over there have made me timid. I should think it most likely that the English publishers would want some of Thomas' poetry in your book. I know Mrs Thomas would. But I should be afraid to advise you to use the poems. How too bad we havent got about the business earlier. You havent time to wait till I can write to them for you I suppose? Say the word and I'll do anything I can.

I didnt know how to phrase this discreetly for the wire.

In hurried haste but

Faithfully yours
Robert Frost

[To Lesley Frost. Above the salutation, along the margins of each page, and beneath the signature, RF has written a number of additional remarks. They are reproduced in order as postscripts below. ALS. UVA.]

Franconia NH
April 3 1919

Dear Lesley:

This is returning you the scholarship application blank no longer blank except in the spot which should name what you are asking for. I hadnt the least idea what figure could be put in there. You put in a reasonable one. You know better than I do what you can expect.[277]

As to the contest in poetry—tralala! I could have told you—maybe I did tell you—how it would be. You can plunge into a thing of the kind if you like the excitement and the object is to get so you don't care, but you mustn't expect prizes. Probably I would have immunized myself to criticism a little if I had exposed myself earlier to some of that kind of it. One ought to get so he can pursue the evenness of his writing through everything favorable or un-

277. Lesley was, in fact, awarded a scholarship by the National Association of New England Women.

favorable. It may do you good if you can take the smash from those girls for the practice it gives you in not caring as I say. It is not so important what they decide about you. Don't let them see how you feel about it. I wish you hadnt asked them for a look at the successful poems. All is probably quite honest. Only you have to remember it is not quite impersonal. You labor under the personal disadvantage of being who you are and of not being in any class where writing is done and so not being acquainted with any of the teachers of writing. They probably knew the writing of the two girls who won and had made up their minds that it was likely to be the best before they saw it. And no doubt they liked it better than they did yours. They really may have—we have to remember that even at our maddest. I'd rather you wouldn't say much to Louis about it. To hill [*sic*] with it.

The thing is to write better and better poems. Setting our heart when we're too young on getting our poems appreciated lands us in the politics of poetry which is death. Consider the ways of the members of the poetry societies and be wise. Write, write, for this is all there is.

We'll be pleased to see the winning poems, sceptical [*sic*] as we are about their worth.

Lucky I staid out of the jury.

Bully for Miss Drew.[278]

I wish Irma could see the hoop and torch races. We wont send her down before a week from the Saturday. If she gets there on the 12th, does that make it—does she see the games? I wish I could see the games myself. But I feel ill-natured about the poem. So perhaps I had as well not be there.

Ten feet from the plate is like playing up for a bunt.

Hens are laying 10 eggs a day.

Affectionately
RF

Having trouble with New England Poetry Society because I dont accept presidency.[279]

Carol has the Blick typewriter all in pieces cleaning it.

Must send you a poem of mine some day.

---

278. Likely, again, Helen Louisa Drew, who had taught Lesley rhetoric and composition at Wellesley College.

279. See the headnote to RF's February 3, 1919, letter to Untermeyer ("Margaret Perry") for details.

Been reading some of Henry James short stories. Simply too good
Deep snow good sleighing very cold here.
Ask for what money you need always.
Grand row about Stark at Amherst.[280]
Poor Hollister, he should give up red.[281]
Jean began a letter to me, Mr Robert Frost.[282]
Did I tell you we had planted twelve apple trees.
I dont see much to Walters poetry.[283]

[To John Bartlett. ALS. UVA.]

Franconia N H.
April 7 1919

Dear John

You have yourself partly to blame for writing me such a messy little post card. But I suppose it was the best you could do you poor boy if you were sick in bed. Gee I didn't get what you were trying to tell me did I? Lets see what I did think you were saying: that Margaret had got an editorial job sifting poetry for Farm Journal and that you had all been sick but had come through all right and things were going well. To me the post card balanced up to the good. So far from intending to make light of your bad luck I was really making gay over your good luck. My mistake began and ended with my misreading of the post card. Don't be so cramped and cryptic another time. You have to be pretty broad and outright with an old fellow like me.

---

280. Stark Young, RF's colleague in the English department. As noted above, a student reported to RF that Young had made unwelcome sexual overtures. RF brought the matter to President Meiklejohn's attention and was infuriated when the administration took no action. See *YT*, 105ff.

281. Caroll Hollister, then a student at Amherst College.

282. In *FL*, Arnold Grade identifies "Jean" as Jean Starr Untermeyer. But more likely RF refers to his sister Jeanie (whom he often called "Jean"); she suffered from dementia praecox (schizophrenia) and would, in 1920, be committed to the State Asylum in Augusta, Maine. When RF went up to Maine to tend to the matter, Jeanie did not recognize him as her brother.

283. Again, Walter Hendricks. As for his poetry, see also RF to Rugg, May 18, 1919, and RF to Monroe, July 21, 1920.

How the devil would I be thinking of Marguerite Wilkinson by her first name and in connection with any story about carrots?[284] She may have heard my carrot lecture on Shakespeare or some conversational rehash of it sometime. It dealt with the problem of invention in art. Probably that's what has come to you circuitously. But it never would have entered my head.

Isnt it rotten that you should have had such a time? What right had all those associated charities in on top of you? Or did you have to have them in? Upwards of one hundred dollars a month sounds not so bad when you have your own garden and hens. Tell me more about it. You can't be so wretched. Did the doctor call in the charities? Are the neighbors gossiping about you because you are sick and literary? It all makes me sick. Say right up and down, do you want some money now. Say how much and let me see how much of it I can rake together.

Do you mean by "cards on the table" any kind of personal news good or bad? Well we haven't had Scarlet Fever but we have had five cases of influenza out of a possible six all of them bad enough but only one and that mine anywhere near fatal. Irma was sick in October and is not fully recovered yet. The year for us at Amherst was unsatisfactory what with all this sickness and the unsettlement in the college due to the war. We came away with a bad enough conscience about the money we had taken for no work to speak of and yet after all not so bad either: we managed to blame others as much as ourselves for the way things had gone. We would almost as soon have gone without the money if we could have been out of the confusion of a war-wrecked college—a rather unpatriotic one at that. Maybe we could have been writing something if we hadnt been killing time down there on salary.

I have gone rather easy on the writing for the two years last past. Breathweight had no choice in the matter of taking or leaving any poetry of mine for his anthology.[285] There was none. Nary a drop. I have shown not a poem to an editor since I gave The Ax Helve to The Atlantic summer before last.[286] So that let's the nigger out. (The first part of The Ax-Helve was a good poem the last part not. You probably didn't see it.)

---

284. Marguerite Wilkinson (1883–1928) was a Canadian American poet, critic, and anthologist. For the remarks about "carrots," see the notes to RF's April 21, 1919, letter to Wilkinson.

285. William Stanley Braithwaite (1878–1962).

286. "The Axe-Helve" appeared in *The Atlantic* in September 1917.

Not that I've absolutely stopped which puts an idea into my head. How would a book be on the Barred Plymouth Rock by the Plymouth Rock Bard?[287] Thus is literature made. Watch me.

Wet cold and wild on this mountain still. I hate to have you so far off out there and sometimes wish I could say Come on East and try this Franconia or Sugar Hill climate for the various ills your flesh is heir to.[288] But I don't know. You know best anyway. Are you on the whole better in the throat and lungs both of you? Shall you ever venture East again? I wish I could see you. I get as far as Chicago about once a year but though that seems a long way it isnt more than half way to you.

You mustnt write long letters. As you say letters are no good. You need your strength for other writing—just as I need mine. I have to nurse it out of myself always you know. Nerves nerves! Its the same with both of us only I wont claim it isnt worse with you. No you mustn't spend yourself in letters to me. What you must do though is tell me what you are writing and let me see some of it—yours and Margarets both. This is peremptory.

Peremptorily
R Frost

[To Lesley Frost. ALS. UVA.]

Franconia N.H.
April 16 1919

Dear Lesley:

Just one detail of the games did we find in The Sunday Times and that was that the Torch Race was the excitement of the day, and that your class won it.[289] I said I'd bet that was where you came in. And it seems I wasn't far wrong. I don't know whether it wouldn't have been too much for us if we had been there. It's a wild kind of a race the Torch Race when you come third and have to stand waiting for a torch that is dropping gradually behind. I'll

287. The Plymouth Rock, often called Rocks or Barred Rocks, is a cold-hardy chicken breed that originated in the United States.

288. RF echoes Hamlet's famous soliloquy (3.i): "to die, to sleep / No more; and by a sleep, to say we end / The Heart-ache, and the thousand Natural shocks / That Flesh is heir to?").

289. A reference to the annual Greek Games at Barnard.

bet you almost wanted to run without waiting for the torch. And I'll bet you went when you went as if you'd been shot out of a cannon, far as cannon are from anything Greek. There's nothing I'm more susceptible to than victory in athletics. I should have gone crazy when your will to win carried you to the front and over the line. I can just see you put in and scoot. I wonder how Irma felt till you had got ahead.

I was thinking Saturday afternoon about your taking the turns with your hoop. All I hoped was you wouldn't fumble and drop the hoop. Well you got a first with that too. And your class came out on top. Enough glory for once in a way.

That was a memorable encounter you had with Miss Dotage.[290] We'll keep the record of that for our educational novel when we write it. Why it sounds like the middle ages. Her use of will power for self-control sounds so old-fashioned. Will power is drive as we use it now-a-days. It is that in some people that simply won't be checked. Education can't install it like an engine in a Ford car. You have it or you dont have it. Education can at most steer it. At worst it can damage it so that it won't go. It is a kind of hunger, a hunger for victory, for art, for philosophy. It may be a hunger for money. We have to be thankful when it isnt for still worse things. And we have to know that when it is denied in good objects there is danger of its being diverted to bad objects. It takes an awful fool to risk trying to kill the will to poetry in a young person. Ever if your aim should be scholarship anyone but a fool would know that the more creative speed you get up the more mere knowledge you will pick up and carry along with you. The beauty of Miss Dotage is her incredibility. I should have thought there was no such animal. Will wonders never cease in the education of you?

But there is something to be said for what is known as self-control. You for instance will have to exercise a good deal of it as editor of a magazine. You mustn't print just anything of your own you happen to write. You'll have to be a good deal more on your guard than you realize at this moment. It was an unguarded thing to think of asking Irma to make the cover for a Columbia magazine. It would be as mistaken and would do you as much harm as Louis' folly (which was awful.)[291] It would hurt Irma too. Head that scheme

290. A snide reference to Eleanor Doty, instructor in physical education at Barnard College, who is mentioned again at the close of the letter.

291. Louis Untermeyer, a close family friend, had served on the judges' panel for the Greek Games; RF thought he ought to have recused himself.

off at once. What you want is a Barnardian or Columbian artist in it. Nobody else would be appropriate. You ought to be able to find someone who goes in for art or architecture. Some of the faculty that does the good detail in architecture would come in here.

Easy does it. You decide on what of your own you will print. But perhaps you had better let me have a glimpse of it for confirmation.

Mama is up around but not as she should be. I guess we have got to think of her a good deal this year.

I just learn [*sic*] that the end of school is not much more than six weeks away. We'll all be together again soon.

By the way I wish you would ask Harcourt[292] if he could help you get rid of 200 dollars worth of bonds. I shall have to have some more money for you and for the rest of us. Perhaps he can tell you where to take the bonds to sell. Miss Eayres might tell you or help you. Let me know what they suggest.

Yes we must manage to be good to Louis somehow. He means well by us.

Set up late if you have to but try to get your eight hours sleep. Sock it to the studies. Remember in your writing for yourself and for your teachers and magazine: Ideas and Imagination. Dont take any stock in Miss Doty except as a specimen.

Affectionately
Papa

Include Miss Eayres in some of your pleasures

[To Louis Untermeyer. ALS. LoC.]

Franconia N.H.
April 18 1919

Dear Louis

The point is that there isn't anybody in Gods present world that's got such a mechanical mixture of poets real and unreal going round and round and over and over each other in his head and even shassaycrossways but always

292. Alfred Harcourt, head of the trade department at Henry Holt and Company, would soon leave to establish his own firm, Harcourt, Brace and Howe. Ellen Knowles Eayres was his secretary; she would subsequently follow him into the new firm. After his first wife died (in 1923), they married.

kept off the bottom as the author of The New Era in Poetry.[293] I was afraid that book would be too good to be good for you. And it is. It is dangerous in two ways. It calls for another book like it to pile on top of it about all the poets here and in England taken together and it calls for it from you because you are plainly the only one who knows enough to do it. And then on top of that and before you are free to get back to writing your own poetry again it calls for a third book, an anthology of this century that I wish we could call The Laurels Wither on Your Brow as a taunt to the British. Of course we wont be indiscreet enough to name it that. Just the same our purpose in it would be to show the British who's writing the poetry now, i.e., who's luny now. The preface will say that it takes us over here to make a just anthology because while the English like doting islanders have been reading themselves and not us we have been reading both ourselves and them. We put you forward as probably the only man of judgement in the arts who knows all the poetry of all the poets there and here. Anybody can see you are that and the fact imposes on you a duty you are not going to shirk. When do we begin to round-up?

And the second danger of the book is that it will make you your own worst rival.

All this apart from my personal satisfaction in the book, O thou most generous one. You made the book and I may say that I also made it if only in the sense in which I made the football team in school and the last train at night. You achieved the book and I achieved a place in it. It suffices for me. I wish you could say the book came out in March. Otherwise March is a blank this year and my superstition breaks down that I always get in some signal stroke of ambition in March. Say it was in March and you make this March my best ever.[294]

I follow you in nearly all your judgements and for so stupid a person (without humor) in a surprisingly large number of your brilliancies.

I have given you a name for your next book. My next is to be The Bard Plymouth Rock by

The Plymouth Rock Barred[295]

---

293. "Shassaycrossways": a portmanteau cross-linguistic pun, derived from the French *chassé-croisé,* which describes an intermingling of people whose paths cross, but who nonetheless never stumble into one another. Untermeyer's *The New Era in American Poetry* was issued in 1919 by Henry Holt and Company, RF's publisher.

294. RF's birthday was in March, on the twenty-sixth.

295. See also RF to Bartlett, April 7, 1919.

[To Marguerite Ogden Bigelow Wilkinson. ALS. Middlebury.]

Franconia N.H.
April 21 1919

My dear Mrs Wilkinson:

I didn't telegraph because I saw nothing to object to in what you said about my processes. As nearly as I can tell that's the way I work.[296] I meant to make no particular merit of it however. I worked for twenty years as I had to by force of circumstances and I work now as I have to from force of the habit formed then. I have never been good at revising. I always thought I made things worse by recasting and retouching. I never knew what was meant by choice of words. It was one word or none. When I saw more than one possible way of saying a thing I knew I was fumbling and turned from writing. If I ever fussed a poem into shape I hated and distrusted it afterward. The great and pleasant memories are of poems that were single strokes (one stroke to the poem) carried through. I wont say I haven't learned with the years something of the tinker's art. I'm surprised to find sometimes how I have just missed the word. It wasn't that I was groping for my meaning. I had that clear enough and I had and thought I had said the word for it. But I hadn't

296. See Wilkinson's *New Voices: An Introduction to Contemporary Poetry* (New York: Macmillan, 1919): "Robert Frost, to be sure, writes rapidly and seldom revises his successful poems. But for years he wrote poems that served only as practice work and were never offered to the world. . . . More than any poet who uses regularly stressed rhythms, Robert Frost is influenced by the tunes of human conversation, and he is the greatest living master of the poetry that talks. . . . [In] all of his poems we find something of the warmth and depth and richness, the sudden humor, the droll whimsy, the characteristic innuendo and flexible intimacy of conversation. To read them is to share profound mirth, amazing tragedy, delicious irony made out of talk and of one substance with it. . . ." Wilkinson then speaks of the "warning against insincerity" that is "tacitly suggested in what Robert Frost has said about realism and idealism in literature": " 'A man who makes really good literature,' says Mr. Frost, 'is like a fellow who goes into the fields to pull carrots. He keeps on pulling them patiently enough until he finds a carrot that suggests something else to him. It is not shaped like other carrots. He takes out his knife and notches it here and there, until the two pronged roots become legs and the carrot takes on something of the semblance of a man. The real genius takes hold of that bit of life which is suggestive to him and gives it form. But the man who is merely a realist, and not a genius, will leave the carrot just as he finds it. The man who is merely an idealist and not a genius, will try to carve a donkey where no donkey is suggested by the carrot he pulls (6; 63; 207–208).' " See also RF to Bartlett, April 7, 1919.

said within a row of apple trees of it. That's the way it was I suppose with that word "fill" in the Winter Night poem.[297] I had the perfectest conviction of having said "keep" then and I believe I had read it aloud as "keep" for some time before I saw that I had written "fill." "Fill" is awful!

I sometimes I often live to dislike a poem I have dashed off like lightning out of a clear sky, but first or last I never like a poem I have written any other way. I make them in haste and repent of them at leisure. I dont know that I would have taken the leisure I took if the editors and such hadnt forced it on me. They took care that I should take time to judge my own work. Not that I like to judge it or that I have attained to security in my judgements. I'm still fearfully afraid of committing anything to print—just as you seem to be. A book on publication day is what Sherman said war was.[298] But don't you worry. Your book will be all right. It sounds to me like a good sort of thing to do and I'm absolutely sure we shall enjoy reading it.

Lesley has enjoyed knowing you. We appreciate your kindness to her.

Faithfully yours
Robert Frost

[To Harriet Moody. ALS. Chicago.]

Franconia N.H.
April 21 1919

Dear Harriet Moody:

You know I wear your collar (or rather collars: there are two or three of them and they are not worn out yet) and you can do what you please with me. But of course you wouldn't do such a thing as this comes to. Enter distinguished Englishman, exit extinguished American. Padraic may think my sympathy with his Ireland is just Blarney I give him.[299] Its not that I love Ireland more for loving England less and less. But I do love a country that loves itself. I love a country that insists on its own nationality which is the same

297. "An Old Man's Winter Night," collected in *MI*. RF replaced "fill" with "keep" when he brought the book into his *Collected Poems* (1939).

298. In his address to the graduating class of the Michigan Military Academy (June 19, 1879), General William Tecumseh Sherman famously declared that "war is Hell."

299. Irish poet Padraic Colum (1881–1972) had come to the United States in 1914 for a visit that ultimately lasted some eight years.

thing as a persons insisting on his own personality. Isn't an idea any better for its being my own out of my own life and experience? Isnt it? Isn't a literature any more to us for being our own? It is, whether you think so or not. No danger about our not insisting on our own nationality in business and diplomacy. But that is only on the material plane. My concern is that someday we shall go in to back ourselves on the intellectual and spiritual plane. Don't we seem poor stuff the way we whoop it up for anything imported in the arts? Other things being unequal, the visitor having all the advantage in other things, I should still make him feel if I were an American that, just because he was imported, he couldnt expect any more adulation than our own homegrown poet. But of course I'm not an American. Let's go back on America together.

Wretched that we should be away off up here when you are to be in Cummington. When do we meet again?

I had the good evening at your house in New York with the great-faced noble Ridgely.[300]

Always faithfully yours
Robert Frost

[To Rose Emily "Lola" Ridge (1873–1941), an anarchist poet, and an influential editor of the avant-garde magazines Others *and* Broom. *ALS. UVA.]*

Franconia N.H.
April 24 1919

My dear Lola Ridge:

Kreymborg had shown me an editorial of Jones' on your Chicago address that made me realize how much you had done for me there and I have wanted to requite it in some way.[301] But the way you ask is the hardest way. I have a few poems on hand and perhaps one or two of them are good or good

300. Moody had a house in Cummington, Massachusetts. She also had an apartment in New York City on Waverly Place, which she made available to the Frosts and to other poets, including Ridgely Torrence (1874–1950).

301. Alfred Francis Kreymborg (1883–1966) was an American poet, novelist, playwright, literary editor, and anthologist. Closely associated with William Carlos Williams and other American modernists, he founded the literary magazine *Others* in 1915. RF also refers to Lewellyn Jones, literary editor of the *Chicago Evening Post*.

enough but I shall have to think at least ten of them are good before I start publishing again. It is ten or none with me for the simple reason that I have promised at least ten people a poem if I give any one a poem. Taking a poem out of me now would be like taking out a swallowed fish hook. Not only my heart (which might not be so bad) but my lungs might have to come with it. I have wrestled with this business since your letter came. But it makes it easier between us that I am an individualist in the premises. You of all people wont want me to behave as anything else after what you said in Chicago. You, for instance, wouldn't make me president of a society I had never paid dues in and insist on keeping me president in spite of my well-known superstitions about belonging to anything or holding office in anything.[302] But there are people who would and well meaning people at that, whose only fault is that they think they know better than I myself what is good for me. What is good for me is to leave me severely even contemptuously alone for a useless [*sic*] till I shall get some more poems piled up ahead. I shall have a poem for you some day before long. But I am afraid you will be cross with me for not coming to time and won't want my poem when I want to give it. All I can say to that is that it would serve me just right.

With the best wishes and the enclosed check for Others, you must know I am

Always your friendly
Robert Frost

[To Louis Untermeyer. The book mentioned at the head of the letter is Untermeyer's The New Era in American Poetry, *issued in 1919 by Henry Holt and Company. See RF to Louis Untermeyer, April 4, 1919. ALS. LoC.]*

Franc May 6 [1919]

Dear Louis:

I ask you to say the book came out in March, my birth month, and you confound me by making it on March 26 my exact birthday. You make me drunk with superstition. I am in love with chance and though as mischance it someday slay me yet will I and so forth.

You liked my Runaway. But we wont publish it yet a while. You can show it to anybody but editors. I should think Dick might like it. I suspect <u>my</u> kids

302. Again, see RF to Untermeyer ("Margaret Perry"), April 3, 1919.

really liked it, though Carol says it is not as good as my Well[303] (a copy of which I may decide to enclose for comparison since you have probably forgotten you once saw it on my porch in Franconia.)

Do you want to send George Whicher a copy of your book with your name written in it?

What's this madness of the mad Lesley over a college magazine? I hear the wild animal won a hoop race or a torch race or something round a flower pot.[304] The audience must have had time to get almost excited. So must the performers. Once all the way around a flower pot. I never was good at long distances myself.

Irma rounded off her education nicely with her two weeks in New York.

You predict things for May. There is something uncertain about the word May per se. I dont care to predict for it. Still I doubt it will be marked by any particular occurances [*sic*] anywhere of any particular nature. The time is not yet. I'm composing a poem with the refrain "Blow their bloody hats off." "Hats" you will observe. It is addressed to the wind not to the Bolsheviks which are one and the same thing (nit).[305] Pity me for not knowing what would set everything right. When I think of all the human pains that went to uplifting Pithecanthropus Erectus into the Piltdown man and the Piltdown man into the Neanderthal and the Neanderthal into the Heidleberg and him into the likes of me and Woodrow Wilson it makes me as tired as sitting up all night on the job or doing it in my sleep.[306] It seems looking backward as if it had been largely a matter of changing bones directly or indirectly. I'm afraid it was mostly indirectly. But why couldnt we try if it could be done this

---

303. "Well": "For Once, Then, Something." RF's poem, "The Runaway," had already appeared in the *Amherst Monthly* for June 1918. But RF first collected it in a volume, with a number of significant emendations, in *NH*. "Dick" is Untermeyer's son Richard.

304. Lesley Frost won a prize as a chariot racer in the annual Greek Games at Barnard College, where she was a student. Untermeyer, as has been noted, was among the judges.

305. The Bolsheviks—whom both Max Eastman and John Reed (mentioned later in the letter) supported—did not consolidate their power over the whole of Russia until late in 1919.

306. *Homo heidelbergensis* (Heidelberg Man), an extinct species of our genus, lived some 400,000 to 600,000 years ago, and, though RF reverses the order here, antedated *Homo sapiens neanderthalensis*. The bones of the so-called Piltdown Man were not exposed as a hoax until 1953.

next time by attacking the bones directly after the Flathead Indians?[307] Why by osteopathetic manipulation for example couldnt you for instance effect the next great change of me into Max Eastman or Jack Reed. (Let it be Max if I am going to be free to choose the particular freeman free thinker or free for all I have got to be.) Oh dear! I havent got room to say what I want to about Prometheus and Polyphemus.[308] But you can guess the rest from your knowledge of

RF

[To Lesley Frost. ALS. UVA.]

Franconia
May 10 '19

Dear Lesley

The weather here makes it hard to believe you can be within three weeks of your summer vacation. I can hardly get it through my head that you are on the verge of examinations. The weather is only partly to blame for that however. You have said so little about anything but athletics and magazines lately that I had forgotten you were still studying and going to classes. Boas and Pillsbury's Psychology seem things of the distant past.[309]

We have planted nothing except a few trees, some lettuce and radishes in a cold frame and a pound or two of onion sets. Carol fishes a good deal and the rest of the time works round with the hens. He and Wilfred caught two hundred perch, big ones, over in Streeter pond today. I think that is more fish

---

307. The Flathead Indians, or, as they knew themselves, the confederation of the Bitterroot Salish, Kootenai, and Pend d'Oreilles tribes, were native to the land between the Rocky Mountains and the Cascade Range. The name "flathead" was bestowed upon them by whites under the mistaken belief that they practiced (as did some other tribes) infant head-binding.

308. The epithets apply to Max Eastman and Jack Reed—to Eastman (Prometheus) because he raised funds to send Reed to Russia, and because his articles in *The Masses* twice brought him up on trial for sedition; to Reed (Polyphemus, which means "much spoken of") not simply because of his immense fame, but also because he took an active role in the Russian Revolution.

309. RF refers to Walter Bowers Pillsbury, professor of psychology at Columbia and author of *The Fundamentals of Psychology* (1916). Anthropologist Franz Boas (1858–1942) was on the Columbia University faculty.

than I have caught in my whole life. They gave them away right and left in the village and kept enough for themselves. Perch not trout. He has caught some trout, one really good string that made a meal for all of us. But the perch aren't to be despised just because they dont compare with trout. Down country where we saw no trout we thought pretty well of perch.

There are two hens setting and we ought to have some white chickens when you get home if we hatch any and dont lose them all.

I sent you a couple of poems a week ago. Suppose I send you one or two more with this.

I ought to send you George Whicher's dispose of the May Amherst Monthly: it tells you so well if you know how to read it, of the conflict now on between the aesthetic anti-Puritan anti-American Meiklejohn-Youngs and the anti-aesthetic Puritan-American Frost-Whichers. It's a wallop in the mouth.[310]

You may remember an old bellows that lies rotting just inside the old road where it leaves the new road at the top of the hill above Lynches?[311] It has lain there for years. I thought when I was up there yesterday what a use it would be to put it if I should crate it and send it C.O.D. to Mr Meiklejohn to run the college with.

I'll have some more money somehow for you in a few days.

Affectionately
Papa

Two poems enclosed.[312]

---

310. See *YT*, 102–103, 105, 120–121, and 553, for one account of the disputes at Amherst College regarding the presidency of Alexander Meiklejohn. Stark Young and George Whicher were, with RF, on the faculty of the Department of English. The "dispose" to which RF refers is presumably a letter to him *about* the May number of the *Amherst Monthly* (Whicher published no article in it).

311. John and Margaret Lynch, friends of the Frost family since the Derry years, owned a farm near Bethlehem, New Hampshire.

312. Titles unknown; the enclosures were separated from the letter.

[To Harold Goddard Rugg. Apparently hand-carried by Walter Hendricks, not mailed. ALS. DCL.]

Franconia NH
May 18 1919

My dear Rugg

I am sending you with this a young poet friend of mine Walter Hendricks (Amherst, 1917) who wants a glimpse of Dartmouth. If you will begin by being kind to him on my account I think you will find yourself being kind to him before very long on his own account. He carries a book from me to you with best wishes.[313]

Always yours friendly
Robert Frost.

[To James Burton Pond (1889–1961), head of the Pond Lyceum Bureau, an agency that managed lecturers. ALS. BU.]

Franconia N.H.
May 19 1919

My dear Mr Pond:

I should like nothing better than to visit the West and Middle West under your management. It would have to be in one or two tours in February March and April when I shall be entirely free from college work next year. I suppose a good deal could be accomplished in two months as you are able to draw things together. I have rather tired myself out running here and there for single engagements. It would be a great relief to be taken in hand by someone who could give me real tours.

The idea of the Coast particularly attracts me. I was born in California and have always wanted to get back to the state if no more than to look round and claim native sonship.

Mrs Moody is a good friend to intercede with you for me.[314]

Will you let me know what arrangements you would propose?

Sincerely yours
Robert Frost

---

313. See the notes to RF's mid-March 1919 letter to Lesley Frost for details regarding his relationship to Hendricks.

314. Harriet Moody, widow of the poet William Vaughan Moody and a family friend.

[To Lesley Frost. ALS. UVA.]

Franconia N.H.
May 20 1919

Dear Lesley:

You've done enough to satisfy us in having fought your way to first place in your class and second place in your college in tennis. We don't ask you to win the college cup—you've had so little real experience in the game. You've had a good time and you've proved to yourself that you don't need Charles Lowell Youngs help in sports however much you may need it in Latin French and English.[315] What more should you want. It's so much as it is that you will have to be careful not to brag too much when you go visiting at Wellesley.

And while I think of it be sure you tell the same story I do when anyone asks you how you came to elect Miss Fletcher's Latin for sophomore year. Say you elected it to make it absolutely impossible for you to go back to Wellesley. Say you were afraid you might weaken in the summer (melt in the summer heat) and decide to go back if you didnt put an impassable barrier in your way. Say you have a forgiving nature and you were afraid with time you might come to forgive all your other Wellesleyan injuries, but you were sure of yourself on that injury. Sometime I shall tell Miss Bates the so-called psychology of your apparent inconsistency in electing Miss Fletcher.

I'm glad you liked the Percy MacKayes. It would be fun for you to go West with Arvia if we could spare you and if we could spare the money. I think you'd like Mrs Moody. Martha Crowfoot is what she is.[316] I wonder if she is really as simple silly as she seems. It would be almost an achievement in unsourness to keep so to her age. I wonder if her silliness may not be mechanical and kept up to cover something sour or bitter underneath. I don't believe it is though. She's an unspoiled old sentimentalist.

---

315. Charles Lowell Young and Katharine Lee Bates (mentioned later in the letter) were professors of English at Wellesley College; Caroline Rebecca Fletcher (also mentioned here) was professor of Latin. For more on Young and matter in question, see RF's December 7, 1917, letter to him.

316. Percy MacKaye (1875–1956), American dramatist and poet; Arvia was his daughter. A friend and companion of Harriet Moody's, Martha Foote Crow (1854–1924) was dean of women at Northeastern University in Chicago, and the author/editor, in 1896, of *Elizabethan Sonnet-Cycles.*

What do you say to getting in one evening with the Cambridge Brownes—the final e Brownes so to speak?[317] You will be in such a hurry to get home though. Perhaps you had better come right along as soon as you leave Wellesley. Be sure you write at the last moment to let us know definitely when to look for you—on what day and train exactly. Coming up from Boston gets you to Littleton earlier than coming up from New York. I can look up your train from Boston right now. It leaves Boston at nine in the morning and gets you to Littleton at about four in the afternoon.

And be sure you have money enough with you for emergencies.

I have a letter from Harcourt in script to tell me in confidence that he is leaving the Holts to set up for himself. I suppose the script means that not even Miss Eayres is in the secret.[318] He wants to know if we will go with him and I suppose there is only one answer possible after what has passed between us. But by jingo it throws my already confused relations with publishers into still greater confusion. This is a year of unsettlement. I am on the point of making changes here at Franconia too and at Amherst I feel all at sixes and sevens. Out of the general breaking up may come some new beginning that will be exciting and perhaps good and even great for us.

Lets feel darned friendly toward your psychology teacher for liking you to think.[319] People deserve almost more credit for appreciating what we do than we deserve for doing it.

The great things are direct thought and emotion and never to be put off our unforced natural thought and emotion in any circumstances however disturbing—not even in examinations. I never got so I was serenely myself in examination. I have rather to pick and choose my circumstances. The Carter Goodrich kind of boy is the ideal kind of examinee.[320] No Faculty can muddle his faculties.

---

317. The family of George Herbert Browne, head of the Browne and Nichols School in Cambridge.

318. Alfred Harcourt left Henry Holt and Company to establish the new firm of Harcourt, Brace and Howe in 1919. Ellen Knowles Eayres, on the staff at Holt, soon joined him there (she often typed outgoing correspondence at Holt: hence RF's reference to Harcourt's letter being "in script"). After Alfred's first wife, Susan Harreus Harcourt, died in 1923, the two married.

319. Professor Walter Bowers Pillsbury; see RF to Lesley Frost, May 10, 1919.

320. Carter Lyman Goodrich (1897–1971), economist and historian, graduated from Amherst in 1918.

Powerful flight the CN4 made to the Azores. It makes me feel strong myself. I almost wish Hawker hadn't tried it. It was too wild an adventure. But he was a brave man.[321]

Affectionately
Papa

Twelve small white chickens hatched yesterday.

[To Alfred Harcourt. ALS. DCL.]

Franconia N.H.
May 21 1919

Dear Alfred:

There is only one answer possible to your question. I am under obligations to Henry Holt & Co for endless favors. But so far as I am concerned, you are Henry Holt & Co. You are all the Henry Holt & Co I have known and dealt with. Where you go I naturally go. I am with you with all my heart. I promise to do all I can to make you a great publisher even as I expect you to do all you can to make me a great author.[322]

Always yours
Robert Frost

---

321. Harry George Hawker (1889–1921) was an Australian aviation pioneer and cofounder of Hawker Aircraft. In May 1919 he attempted to win the *London Daily Mail's* £10,000 prize for the first flight across the Atlantic in less than seventy-two consecutive hours; he was rescued after his Sopwith aircraft went down at sea. On May 14, 1919, a U.S. Navy team, in an NC4 seaplane, completed the longest leg of the transatlantic route thus far, flying from Newfoundland to the Azores. John Alcock and Arthur Whitten Brown, who flew successfully from Newfoundland to Ireland, won the *Daily Mail* prize in June 1919.

322. RF did not, as it happened, follow Harcourt into his new firm (Harcourt, Brace and Howe); he remained with Holt.

[To Lesley Frost. ALS. UVA.]

Franconia N.H.
May 22 1919

Dear Lesley:

You won't be much longer where you have to look for letters from us and some of the time in vain. It's been a vicissitudinous year. This half of it ought not to have seemed long, and it hasn't—and then again it has. It has gone fast and it was only half a year; but it had some of the attributes of a whole year. It has had as much crowded into it for you as most whole years for one attribute. What a lot we owe Mrs. Wanvig for the pretty interval between one college and another.[323] What's the prospect of your seeing her in New York before you start for home.

There must be Hell to pay in the Holts office. Poor Miss Eayres writes an excited letter.[324] She knows we know and assumes we know more than we do. I take it she doesnt know where she is going next. She's out in the world. Probably in the long run it will be better for her on the Ailleys (sp.) account.[325] Harcourt will set out to be the big publisher. He wont need much office help though for some time I imagine. He'll succeed just the same. Someone will back him where he wants for capital. And I should say he had been the whole literary side of Henry Holt and Co and would take the whole literary side off with him. He's not a person to my taste. But he has something to him. He means to do it on the great. No petty publishing for him. No mere professional standards. National standards! A great publisher with a flock of great authors—all American. Thats his ambition.

Speaking of petty standards, the pettiest and most danderously [*sic*] so are intramural college standards. I had an adventure with Walter the other day that I have had many a time with other well educated little college Walters. I had just uttered something of my own that he more than half saw the goodness of but what was his response to it? "Do they say that?" I told him "No, I say it but they would say it too if I pointed it out to them." They know of nothing not gotten from somebody else. Quotation is the height of scholar-

323. Susan Wanvig, a family friend, had suggested that Lesley work at the Curtiss Aeroplane Company in Marblehead, Massachusetts.

324. See RF's May 20, 1919, to Lesley, and notes.

325. Maxwell Aley (1889–1953) was then employed at Holt. Later, he became managing editor of *Century Magazine*.

ship and scores ten. It is best if you have an idea to attribute it to someone else so that they will feel that it has the weight of authority. They are always asking Who is your authority? I suppose their attitude of mind can hardly be helped in college where acquirement is the main object. But it is deadly and deathly. How to escape it! Well anyway we are rid of Walter, and keeping that pretense up for appearance' [*sic*] sake is over. We had to be careful that the neighborhood didnt notice anything.[326]

About now we must be as far along in Spring as you were a month ago.

Affectionately
Papa

Ive been trying Hen Dekker syllables but without much luck lately.[327]

[To George Whicher. ALS. ACL.]

Franconia N.H.
May 23 1919

Dear George:

I could lean back and listen to your review of The Monthly as the devil sucks eggs.[328] Don't tell me I mean your grandmother, after she has been taught, or a weasel. I mean exactly what I say, the devil. You'll see why sometime.

More, I prithee, more. I shall soon feel as one who has had a fight taken off his hands. I'll bet you made the injudicious grieve that time.

But that's it—that's the whole duty of man, to make his own furniture. It is to see something that isn't to be had and make it. But I mustnt get excited on the subject.

A well-educated college boy said to something I said the other day "Do they say that?" And I answered "I may say unto you for the twentieth well educated college boy I have said it unto, No! they don't say that. I say it. But they will after me presently." What's the matter with these fellows? Do they

326. For details about Walter Hendricks, see the notes to RF's mid-March 1919 letter to Lesley Frost.

327. "For Once, Then, Something," a poem in hendecasyllabics.

328. See RF to Lesley Frost, May 10, 1919.

want ideas merely authorized or do they want them authorized from abroad? Have they had to stay in the receptive attitude so long they have stiffened in it and what's worse never expect to meet in the flesh anyone who hasn't stiffened in it?

I thought of you the minute I heard of The Review. I have been wondering where we were going to turn for a real opening for what we think—the likes of you and me. You remember our joking about George Harvey's War Weekly.[329] But that wouldn't have done.

Between you and me I am having a lot of fun with Hen Dekker syllables. You'd think I might be about something more profitable.

And we aren't farming much either.

And Elinor wouldnt let us hatch too many chickens.

Does Wilson at last stand revealed to you in his last message to Congress?[330] The message should be entitled Gas the Probable Weapon of the Next War and What Measures Should Be Taken to Insure Our Having Enough of It. It seems he came not to bring peace but a League of Nations. Anyone who could use the word afraid as he does there! He is afraid we won't have to be afraid of European nations for some time yet. Does he mean he's afraid we can't look for them to give us a fight worthy of our steel industry or rather chemical industry? Is it like Richard the Lion-hearted he talks. No I'm afraid he talks like a fraud. Afraid am I?

I like not what you say about Stark if I quite understand it. Were you caught somewhat at a disadvantage because you weren't prepared to find him well-grounded in the Dionysiac?[331]

---

329. George Brinton McClellan Harvey (1864–1928) was a diplomat, journalist, and a newspaper editor. In 1918 he established the *North American Review's War Weekly* (later called *Harvey's Weekly*), which opposed the policies of the Wilson administration.

330. Woodrow Wilson delivered this message on May 20, 1919, via telegraph from Paris where he was negotiating the Treaty of Versailles. He said, in part: "The close relation between the manufacture of dyestuffs, on the one hand, and of explosive and poisonous gases, on the other, moreover, has given the industry an exceptional significance and value. Although the United States will gladly and unhesitatingly join in the programme of international disarmament, it will, nevertheless, be a policy of obvious prudence to make certain of the successful maintenance of many strong and well-equipped chemical plants."

331. RF pokes fun at the sensual bohemianism (as he saw it) of his Amherst colleague Stark Young.

Lancaster goes and Amherst loses what she hadn't enough of.[332]

Let me know when the family anxieties are past.

Don't farm hard enough yourself to lose the ability to see it partly from the weeds' point of view. If some of these weeds hold on long enough they may be received into respectability and the seed catalogues. Mark my words.

Always yours
Robert Frost

I think I won't bother you with the Mt Holyoke poems. Why should I shirk them?[333]

[To George Browne. ALS. Plymouth.]

Franc May 27 19

Dear Browne:

Instead of Elinor or me Lesley may turn up at your house toward the end of this week or first of next to ask you about your family and tell you about ours. She blows in from a different job or college every time you see her. Now she's from Barnard where she struck in in the middle of the year after she lost her aeroplane factory by fire on Armistice Day at Marblehead.[334] I think she thinks Barnard has been the place for her. What really finished Wellesley for her was the way she failed to make the Freshman tennis team there when she had beaten such girls as she had played with in the try-outs and two of the girls she had beaten made the team. The Senior who had the games in charge gave as an explanation that she hadn't had time to watch Lesley play and had taken the word of some unofficial girls for it when she happened past the court that Lesley was losing. Feminine justice, so-called. You can tell Mrs Browne for me that probably women behave better toward each other and everybody else when they work and play in the shadow of men as at Radcliff and at Barnard. Mrs Browne may laugh; but laughing is no argument. Neither is voting, though she vote next year. The joke of voting is

332. Henry Carrington Lancaster (1882–1954), professor of French, left Amherst for Johns Hopkins (where he had taken his doctorate) in 1919.

333. In 1916, RF had judged a poetry contest at the request of Jeanette Marks, professor of English at Mount Holyoke College; apparently he had been asked to do it again.

334. The Curtiss Aeroplane factory in Marblehead, Massachusetts, where Lesley Frost worked for a time during the war.

that it comes to women just at the last minute before those clear-headed realists the Bolsheviki take it away from all of us forever. What's left of democracy is hardly worth keeping women out of. No one has much interest any longer in compromise and well-enough—in the half thing called liberalism. The best in man is about to set itself free once more to seek the best by direct action and at any cost. We shall live to see leaders who will not dare to be led by a confused throng shouting yea and nay. They will refuse to be led by anything less certain than the light in themselves. Who would go by information from below when he has known what it is to catch inspiration from above? After all the votes are in, I still have to act as I see the way with my own eyes. It's a great moment in the world that rediscovers in the name of the proletariat the divine right, the divine responsibility to rule, from ideals instead of from statistics, that had been lost on battlefields in the name of kings.[335] Man stands too rapt at the prospect to care who picks his pockets of such an unconsidered trifle as the franchise.

Aw, go shake your ears![336]

I enclose a bit of metrical perfection for you to scan. I supposed you would know blank-verse when you saw it.[337]

I supposed also that you would know good Emersonian doctrine when you saw it however disguised it was in the terms of Bolshevism.

Anyway the peace terms read as if we had licked the Germans. You and your League of Nations!—and your friend

R.F.

---

335. RF would recur often to this theme; see *CPRF,* 142.

336. See *Twelfth Night* (2.iii), where Maria says the same to Sir Andrew Aguecheek

337. The "bit of metrical perfection" is a draft of "For Once, Then, Something" (RF had recently written it, under the working title "Wrong to the Light," and had also enclosed it in letters to several people). Browne, unlike some readers, had understood RF's handling of blank verse in *NB,* and he would also, RF implies, understand the meter of the new poem (which is not in blank verse but in unrhymed hendecasyllabics).

[To Helena T. Goessman, instructor of English at Massachusetts Agricultural College (now University of Massachusetts Amherst). Helen Sibley was, as it would appear, her student at the time; information about both appears in the college's yearbooks. ALS. Jones.]

Franconia N.H.
May 27 1919

Dear Miss Goessman:

I have taken the momentous decision after hovering duly in the air. Several of the papers are good, but I like Miss Sibley's best because I am surest of the personality in it. I have gone into this a little in a letter I enclose to her.[338]

Mrs Frost joins me in wishing you and your sister a pleasant summer.

Sincerely yours
Robert Frost.

[To Alexander Meiklejohn. ALS. Wisc. Hist.]

Franconia N.H.
May 30 1919

Dear Mr Meiklejohn:

In accepting with gratitude this money with blood on it, I must reserve the right to return it wholly or in part if it brings me bad luck in too tragic a form. Much would depend on whether the blood was of war or of peace. I wish you had told me. If it were no more serious than peace blood, I should anticipate no special trouble from it. I have had some experience in the blood money of peace and I find that at the rate at which it normally passes through my hands I am not much hurt by it.

You see I speak as one of the old-fashioned economists who hold that peace money is not bloodless for the obvious reason that every man's gain is some other man's loss in business. Recent events have confirmed me in that belief. The only advantage of peace blood over war blood is that it does not appear repulsively on the surface: it is congealed without being shed. And, as I gather from several readings of the President's latest message to Congress, peace blood is to lose even this advantage: the next war blood is to be congealed without being shed. The wars of the future are to be fought with gas-

338. The letter has apparently not survived.

ses and the battlefields will represent a great step forward at least from the aesthetic point of view, where everyone will have an equal chance of lying beautiful in death, ungashed, unmangled, and everything will be as dry as prohibition.[339]

Everywhere the poppies are in bloom along the edges of the receding icecap. Yesterday it snowed for the last time (we assume). The mosquitoes are back.

Mrs Frost is better than she was. The rest of us are perfect. We hope you all are too.

Faithfully yours
Robert Frost

[To Wilbur Rowell. The letter concerns RF's sister, Jeanie Florence Frost. ALS. UVA.]

Franconia N.H.
June 6 1919

Dear Mr Rowell:

I turn to you for help about the enclosed letter. You will know where Jean is to send it to her if you should decide she ought to act on it. She has instructed me to pay no attention to the writer. But I'm not so sure she can afford to ignore him. I should think he might have means of getting even with her that she hasnt taken into account such as writing further innocent letters of inquiry to other people. He could easily make her pretty public with the teachers' agencies and school journals.

It is only right to tell you that Jean may not thank you for your good offices in this matter—and then again she may. I know she never thanks me for mine in any matter. I give her outright about a hundred dollars a year which she doesn't show any gratitude for because she loftily chooses to regard it as a loan. She is too difficult a person for me. You will know better than I what you can do with or for her.

I don't know just why she is keeping out of this man's way unless it is because she is afraid if he finds her he will put the Mill River people on her track. She thinks the Mill Riverites chased her out of town for talking pro-Germanism Bolshevism and internationalism and are still after her to make

339. See notes to RF's May 23, 1919, letter to Whicher.

her salute the American flag. She had a wild time in Mill River and apparently narrowly escaped violence.[340] No need to go into this with her. I simply tell you so that you may know what there is to go on. You may decide from the premises not to stir her up at all, but to deal with the agency man yourself so as to shield her. The right word from you to him might make it all right till she should have time to earn in peace what she owes him.

Sincerely yours
Robert Frost

[To the Boy Scouts of America. ALS. Jones.]

Franconia N.H.
June 15 1919

Dear Sirs:

Please don't count on me for the kind of poem you would like for your Boy Scouts' Song Book. If I happen to write one, I shall be happy to let you have it. I am pleased to be asked to write for the boys. Who wouldnt be when he considers the immortality they can confer?

Faithfully yours
Robert Frost

[To Alexander Meiklejohn. ALS. Wisc. Hist.]

Franconia N.H.
June 16 1919

Dear Mr. Meiklejohn:

If I had realized that the blood was your blood, please believe that I wouldnt have tried to be so funny about it.

The other day I happened to read a poem of my own that made me resolve never so far to forget myself the author of it as to do another mean or hateful thing. Of course that was easier to say in the summer than in the winter, in Franconia than in Amherst, and easier to say at any time anywhere than to

340. For an account of Jeanie Florence Frost's troubles in Mill River (a town some fifteen miles north of Amherst), where she briefly taught high school, see *YT*, 128. The author of the letter RF herewith forwarded to Rowell is unknown.

live up to. Still I was still clinging to my resolution when I wrote to you: if there was anything unkind in my letter it was unintentional: I wouldn't mean to seem unappreciative of one drop of blood you may have shed for me.

Thus my poetry makes me a better man, or at least a man more like a mosquito, who bites and knows it not. But so it is with all ecstacy: it keeps us happy in ill-doing: it enables us to do evil without feeling wicked.

Don't think I don't wish you didn't have those committee meetings to attend down there in the heat.

Always yours
Robert Frost

[To Jessie B. Rittenhouse. ALS. Rollins.]

Franconia NH
June 16 1919

Dear Miss Rittenhouse:

That's a side of my work my charming daughter my wife and I are all grateful to you for seeing and wanting to make others see. You have our unanimous approval of the selection you make, our all but unanimous approval of the one pointed omission it involves. The Smile has something sinister that I personally cling to but I am willing to defer to your adverse opinion in the matter especially since it is backed by Mrs Frost's. She has always thought I dragged The Smile in from an entirely different kind of poem I must have been writing at the same time I wrote The Hill Wife.

But if I sacrifice The Smile mayn't I ask you to make it up to me by adding to your selection just one least lyric from A Boy's Will, such as Flower Gathering, Reluctance, To the Thawing Wind or, if lyricality isnt essential, Storm Fear or if leastness isnt essential The Tuft of Flowers?[341] I know I ought to be above trying to influence your judgement even this much (next I shall be telling the critics what to say about me in their reviews), but Mrs Wilkinson[342] spoiled me by letting me choose a poem for her book and moreover I

341. Rittenhouse included "The Road Not Taken," "Birches," "After Apple-Picking," and "The Hill Wife" (with "The Smile" omitted) in her *Second Book of Modern Verse* (Boston: Houghton Mifflin, 1919).

342. Marguerite Wilkinson edited a number of poetry anthologies for Macmillan's Modern Readers series, among them *New Voices: An Introduction to Contemporary Poetry*

grow more unscrupulous in everything but the art of writing itself as I grow older. I suppose you don't[,] living in the city. The half of the temptation of life in the country has never been told.

With best wishes for you and the book I am

Sincerely yours
Robert Frost

[To Louis Untermeyer. ALS. LoC.]

Franc June 30 [1919]

Dear Looiss

Your Child's Garden of Erse hadn't escaped me. I've been having The Post regularly for some time so as to keep an eye on you in the Saturday number.[343] I dont want to seem to avert my gaze from anything you do as if I were ashamed of you. Pun your damnedest: I am not afraid of your compromising <u>me.</u> A mother can follow an erring son even to the gallows and beyond in tears to his grave in quicklime without in any way sharing in his guilt. So I should hope could a friend of my known devotion to you.

You are down there among the Daylight Savers letting off puns you don't intend and I am up here among the Anti Daylight Savers not writing the epics I do intend. It shows the difference between town and country.[344]

One of the epics I intend is dental. I talked it up the other night to indicate what could be done that hadn't to my knowledge been done yet. If Amy has done it please apprize me and I wont go ahead with it which will be easy enough as I wouldnt go ahead with it anyway.[345] The Care of the Teeth is the name of the whole work and An Aseptic or Well-cleaned Cavity the name of the first chapter. I should want it to be expressive of the major and minor Satisfactions of a Dentists Life. Shouldnt you? And I should want it to run

---

(New York: Macmillan, 1919), which reprinted "The Sound of Trees," "The Gum Gatherer," "An Old Man's Winter Night," "The Cow in Apple Time," and "Brown's Descent" (all from RF's third volume, *MI*).

343. Untermeyer explains: " 'A Child's Garden of Erse' is a caption I used for a review of a banal collection of Irish poetry" (*RFLU*, 89).

344. Summer Time (as Daylight Savings Time was then known) was put into effect in the United States on March 9, 1918; after farmers vehemently objected, the Federal Daylight Saving Time law was repealed, over the veto of President Wilson, in August 1919.

345. Amy Lowell.

serially in some good dentifrice's advertising. I feel that we are right at the turning point in these things: we are right at the shift of interest on the part of both the writer and reader from the literary section of the magazines to the advertising section. The serial epic of advertising will settle it in favor of the advertising section for good and all. I am ambitious to be the one to mark the final disappearance of the literary section; that is to say I could be ambitious to be that one if I had the least encouragement. Why dont you encourage me? Probably you want to know more about this epic of dentistry before you commit yourself to the project. Well it will be narrative of course as an epic should be. The plot is something I came across in the old days before success isolated me and cut me off from meeting ordinary people on equal terms. It is really no more than the life of a dentist I used to know who had gone out from a New England hill farm to learn dentistry and become dentist to a crowned head of South America, the Emperor Dom Pedro of Brazil.[346] In the end he had retired to the New England hill farm with a pocket full of Brazilian diamonds. Once Dom Pedro leant him to the king of Portugal for a while and he always averred that gold was so scarce in Portugal that he had to scrape a bit of it here and a bit there from out of the way corners of the kings crown to fill The Kings front teeth with: his back teeth he stopped up with Spanish cork. Consider the Americanness of it all. American dentistry was our first and perhaps till Menken [*sic*] wrote The American Language our only signal contribution to civilization.[347] Our pride as a people rested on where our dentists had penetrated to.

Speaking of Menken I can tell you what he would like to say if he had time to think it out. He would like to say that America isnt American enough for her authors to be very American yet. There may be a few fools trying to anticipate their future selves and write poetry as of 4000 AD so as to be more American than the facts warrant. But most of us are willing to take our lifes as given us. About all we can do is write about things that have happened to us in America in the language we have grown up to in America. It's not so long ago that most of America except Jim Thorpe[348] came from Europe—its

346. Emperor Dom Pedro II of Brazil died in 1891.

347. Alfred Knopf published the first edition of H. L. Mencken's *The American Language* in 1919.

348. Jacobus Franciscus "Jim" Thorpe (1888–1953), gold medalist in the pentathlon and the decathlon in the 1912 Olympics, and pro-football star, was of Native American ancestry; he traced his line back through both the Sac and Maskwaki (Fox) nations.

so short a time ago that it may be said to be coming yet. Look at me. Half of me has been here nine generations the other half one generation: which makes me more representative I think than if I was altogether of old stock. I'm an ideal combination of been-here-since-the-beginning and just-come-over. My ideas may be such, most of them, as I could have got in Europe. They are over there as well as here. But what are the chances I didnt come by them honestly here where I lived totally immersed in them for thirty seven years before I saw Europe or much of anybody from Europe? If I got them in America I have faith that they are touched with Americanism. They may be European, but they have been here long enough to be tanned and freckled with the American sun.

Time we defined, I suppose, what it is to be American. Lets say it is never to have gone out of the country except to lick another country. That saves the soldiers and when you come to consider it doesnt leave me out. No one except Menken has ever accused me of having gone to England for anything but to get the better of the English.

And so I might go on writing nonsense indefinitely if I didnt see the end of this piece of paper just ahead.

Great scheme your text book.[349] It ought to have an <u>un</u>academic chapter on versification. You are on the high school end. Lesley and I are writing An Expressive First Reader for kids. Straight goods. Please include Death of Hired Man.

till further notice yours
R F.

---

349. Untermeyer's *Modern American Poetry: An Introduction* (New York: Harcourt, Brace and Howe, 1919), which reprinted "Mending Wall," "The Road Not Taken," "Birches," and "The Tuft of Flowers." "The Death of the Hired Man" didn't make the cut.

[To Charles Lowell Young. Inscribed on a signed typescript of "Wrong to the Light" (working title of "For Once, Then, Something"). Dating uncertain. However, RF sent a typescript of the poem under the same title to Untermeyer during the summer of 1919, and reference is made here to the "end of [the] term,"—at Wellesley, that is, where Young taught; both details suggest that the letter dates from about June of that year. ALS. Wellesley.]

[Franconia, N.H.]
[circa June 1919]

My dear Young

Lesley says you seemed in fine fettle for the end of a term.[350] I wish I could have seen you for myself. If you are so vigorous why don't you do something to stop some of the nonsense they are all saying about Whitman. Just how much of Whitman do you think wasn't Emerson?

I wonder which of these poems you'll care for.

Ever yours
Robert Frost

[To George Whicher. At RF's suggestion, Whicher wrote an essay on Edward Thomas that was published in The Yale Review *9, no. 3 (April 1920): 556–567. RF's poem "To E.T.," mentioned herein, accompanied it. ALS. ACL.]*

Franc July 1919

Dear George

I am going to send you the ET poem to show you that it is something more than a mere project. The truth is it is probably as complete as it will ever be. I'm not keeping it back to go on with it. Perhaps I can tell you why I have hesitated over it. Edward Thomas was the closest friend I ever had and I was the closest friend he ever had; and this was something I didn't wait to realize after he had died. It makes his death almost too much to talk about in The Yale Review in the hearing of Wm. Lyon Phelps even at two years distance.[351] Just one little poem however ought not to do any harm if I'm sure of my motives in printing it—and I think I am. They are practical, non-

350. Lesley Frost had just visited Wellesley and Cambridge. See RF's May 20, 1919, letter to her.

351. William Lyon Phelps (1865–1943), professor of English at Yale, often published in *The Yale Review.*

sentimental and sufficiently removed from my impulses (not motives) in writing it. I'm one person in writing and I'm another or if cornered can become another for purposes of publication. I've about reached the point where I am willing to wrong whatever may be wronged by publishing this poem. Some part of an ideal is sacrificed to some god in every deed done and the old formal sacrifice of one child out of so many to Moloch was no more than symbolic recognition of the fact.

Which brings me round to children.

Happy to make the acquaintance of a boy that though new has already so many marks besides his three names to distinguish him from other boys.[352] I don't mind his having fewer legs than hairs, so long as he has legs. Not in commission till by and by I suppose? Meanwhile he insists on using other peoples' legs to walk the floor at night. Large head, indicative good judgement. Can't make his hands much more than meet above it. I'm glad you didn't name him Lorenzo de Medici just at this time. It would have looked like defection or a disposition to curry favor with Mrs Meiklejohn. As it is he comes in safely between Calvinism and Quakerism where he can fall either way and not fall into aestheticism.

Why couldn't I have seen that Williams game for one last loyal thrill before I declare myself the enemy of that Amherst that aspires

In unconsidered elegance to feel?

Please publish it as widely as possible that I will make common cause with simply anybody who is out to fight such sentiments on earth.

What do you think the chances are of our getting the Parker house for five months?[353] I wonder where they are to ask about it. They may want a foolish price. I should like to be down there by you.

R.F.

---

352. RF refers to the Whichers' second son, Stephen Emerson Whicher, then aged about four (he was born on June 16, 1915). He would later distinguish himself as a scholar of Emerson and as a professor at Harvard, Swarthmore, and Cornell. His *Freedom and Fate: An Inner Life of Ralph Waldo Emerson* appeared in 1953, soon to be followed by his innovative edition of Emerson's writings, *Selections from Ralph Waldo Emerson: An Organic Anthology* (1957). He took his own life on November 13, 1961.

353. The Frosts were looking for a place to rent in Amherst for the upcoming term.

[To Alfred Harcourt. ALS. DCL.]

Franconia N.H.
July 4 1919

Dear Alfred:

It reads like a fairy story, you've got so nearly what you always wanted—so exactly I should say. I never look on at anything like that but I wish I was in it. Why wasn't I brought up to publishing instead of to writing so that I could have added a fourth to your firm name.[354] Perhaps it is long enough to say familiarly now. It must be the longest going as it is. I don't think of any other trinity publishing.

I suppose I should be more excited if I hadn't been looking for it to happen ever since something you said to me somewhere in a narrow side street as we walked across town to lunch two or three years ago.

I shall hope to have a book in on one of the earliest lists of the new firm. But we will try to have my affairs straightened out so that I won't have Mrs Nutt hanging over me, however, shadowily when next I publish, won't we?

Of course I know and like both Brace and Gehrs. Howe I have heard a lot about. I have never met him, though I have read for him at one of his assemblies, so called. As I knock about lecturing I hear a good deal about practically everybody in my department. I could almost write you a biography out of what I have picked up about Will Howe without half listening. He seems to be a stirring sort.

We have quite a writing young fellow on our faculty whom you ought to get something out of some day. I'll watch him for you. Some day presently when he's just ripe I'll send him to you.

Our best [to] you and herself and Hastings[355]

Always yours
Robertus

---

354. Alfred Harcourt (as has been noted) left Henry Holt and Company to found Harcourt, Brace and Howe. Donald Brace (1881–1955) had been a classmate of Harcourt's at Columbia University; Will David Howe (1873–1946) left his position in the Department of English at Indiana University to join Harcourt and Brace. Later in the letter RF misspells Henry Ghers's name. Ghers (1886–1960) was head of sales at Holt when he followed Harcourt into the new firm. We thank John Lancaster for assistance in identifying Ghers.

355. Hastings Harcourt (1907–1981), son of Alfred and his first wife, Susan Harreus Harcourt.

[To Jesse B. Rittenhouse. ALS. Rollins.]

Franconia N.H.
July 5 1919

Dear Miss Rittenhouse:

Having selections made from me is a form of criticism I rather like: it feelingly persuades me what I am; whereas the other forms are apt at times to try to persuade me unfeelingly. But for it to mean anything, I ought not to interfere in it. I am going to let you decide entirely for yourself about omitting or including The Smile or about having or not having something from my first book in your anthology.[356] I mustn't influence you one way or the other. I didn't influence you in my last letter. I'm not influencing you now. No, I'm sure I'm not.

Do you know I half suspect you of not owning a copy of my first book—let alone not having one with you in Shaftsbury? I believe I will have to send you one. It is something you ought never to be without.

So if you find a suspicious looking parcel in your mail some morning, dont drop it in a pail of water and send for the police as you do in the case of a bomb, but open it fearlessly as probably no more dangerous than a book of verse from

Your friend
Robert Frost

[To K. F. Truman, eastern manager at the Pond Lyceum Bureau; see RF's May 19, 1919, letter to Pond. ALS. LoC.]

Franconia N.H.
July 6 1919

Dear Mr Truman:

I begin to think I am not going to be equal to making a lecture tour next winter. I havent recovered from the influenza as well as I expected to this summer and I think to be on the safe side I ought to plan to take life easy for a while and be free to get away south for the worst of the cold weather.

I am sorry to miss this chance to see the west under Mr Pond, but perhaps he will have me in mind for another year. Then I should be more ready for

356. See RF's June 16, 1919, letter to Rittenhouse.

his catalogue than I am now. I am off here in the country where it is hard for me to raise a picture of myself that hasnt been used too much already or to rake together any press notices I may have kept. I'm afraid I have kept very few about my lectures; there is a good deal in books and magazines about my writing I could furnish you with if I were where I could lay my hands on it. Another year I could start early enough with you and do the thing right—that is if I keep till then. I shall look forward to our better acquaintance.

Always faithfully yours
Robert Frost

[To Louis Untermeyer. The text of this brief letter parodies "Papyrus," a poem by Ezra Pound, and also queries Untermeyer as to how long RF would have to wait for a much-anticipated visit. ALS. LoC.]

[Franconia, NH]
[August 4, 1919]

August!
How long
Gongula?

[To John Bartlett. The first page of the letter is missing. As he occasionally did when writing at length, RF numbered the pages. At the top of page 2, "late summer 1919?" is written in another hand. ALS. UVA.]

[circa August 1919]

[. . .] It will take the homesickness out of living away off so far from New Hampshire to have had your father and mother with you for a long stay.[357] Your mother especially carries so much New Hampshire with her wherever she goes that I'm sure she is bound to leave a tone and atmosphere of it wherever she has come and gone. Both your father and mother are the best kind of folks. Its great they took the notion they could desert their clients and star-boarders to go visiting their Western son. (Chance there to do something with westering and sun but I've gone by it and it won't do to go back.)

---

357. The Bartletts had moved to Colorado in 1917 for health reasons; in 1919 they lived near the town of Pleasant View.

Awful stuff some of the poor ladies write about us but I suppose it must be to earn a living. Possibly its to see themselves in print. It can't advance them in fame or me either I should think. My publisher would say it might sell books. It sort of disseminates me. You could say that such a mouthful as you quote was me getting down to the women's clubs. Thats only a guess. It's got so I don't see much thats said about me. It's understood with my publishers that I dont want to be bothered with either the pros or cons and I have never subscribed to a clippings agency. What reaches me leaks in by accident. Once in a while some editor sends some marked passage in his magazine about me. I take most of it rather badly—that is to say I am apt to wonder too long what it means and if there is anything to it whether friendly or unfriendly. There's better business I can be about. The main thing is to pursue the even tenor. I never wrote to write right: I wrote for the fun of it. Thats all I can hope to write for. For the fun of it in the larger sense—for the devil of it—to myself where I could bother the critics, not where the critics could bother me. Of course they count in the long run. Sooner or later its theirs to dispose of me. I'm only concerned with the distant result however. I should waste myself in paying any attention to their daily whiffle. And some of them are too entirely minor to have much of anything to do with even the distant result, the ultimate verdict.

I do have a look to them [*sic*] when they do it in book form though. There was Amy Lowells book of Tendencies.[358] Did you see [PAGE OR PAGES MISSING] [. . .] grew with you. I suppose you were too late to get in a garden this year. But its a pleasure to have other people's gardens flourishing around you. Hold forth on the subject. Its the ruling passion with me.

Being writers does give us certain freedoms and if it doesn't take us at least lets us go to interesting places to live. No place is out of the way to writers. And our kids get something out of this. It makes up to them for some losses. I can just see it making it up to the two boys as photographed.

Oh I was just going to forget to mention that the same old gentle unassuming Seavey walked in on us the other day from Littleton where he is preaching the Gospel.[359] What impression he made was not by word of mouth.

---

358. Amy Lowell, *Tendencies in Modern American Poetry* (1917).

359. George Seavey was a student of RF's and a classmate of Bartlett's at Pinkerton Academy. He is listed in the program RF prepared for a series of dramatic performances in 1910 (see *CPRF*, 75–77). After graduating from Middlebury College in 1914, he attended Berkeley Divinity School in Middletown, Connecticut.

His education (and he has had twenty years of it) absolutely doesn't show anywhere unless it is in his smile to make it respond to things, subjects, it wouldn't perhaps brighten to in an untaught man. That is to say I could tell by his smile that he was not unfamiliar with certain ideas I broached though he was too modest to say so. But I was pretty sure that he had grown into a good man not given to seeking his own advantage, not anxious to score, perhaps better than a lot of us who know how to put ourselves forward more[.]

Affectionately
Rob

[To Jessie B. Rittenhouse. ALS. Rollins.]

Franconia N H.
August 16 1919

Dear Miss Rittenhouse:

Well then we'll have a chance to see how The Hill Wife looks in print without The Smile, since fate so wills it in the person of the artistically disinterested publisher.[360] You see him as fate. I should be willing to bow the knee to him as justice blindfolded and weighing in his scales size of book against amount of money. Not that I am a particularly resigned sufferer when I have to suffer, but I rather enjoy the sensation, one of relief to the reasoning part of the mind, as often as I come on new proof that some higher justice, fate or luck shapes our ends and not just we ourselves.

I am surprised that anyone can see Home Burial other than as you see it. But nearly everyone makes the mistake of taking sides as between the man and woman. The good young artist who is illustrating the book misses here.[361] He understands the woman in the poem as the man in the poem understands her not as the man or woman outside of the poem ought to understand her. I had to tell Amy Lowell once that one difference between her New England work and mine was that in hers everybody was to blame and

---

360. Again, see RF's June 16, 1919, letter to Rittenhouse.

361. James Chapin did the illustrations for a 1919 limited edition of *NB,* issued by Holt in a run of 500 copies.

in mine nobody was to blame. "In tragic life God wot no villain need be."[362] It might amuse you to hear that the first of all my funny adventures with Home Burial befell in Edinburgh where a literary club asked me to settle a controversy that has arisen among the members as to which I had meant to put in the wrong the man or the woman of the poem.

Thanks for the call to greater things. I mustn't say I shall write a play some day for fear that will keep me from writing it. All the same I regard plays as great things to write.

Best wishes for your book.

Sincerely yours
Robert Frost

[To Edward Bristol of Henry Holt and Company. Zenobia Camprubí Aymar, wife of the poet Juan Ramon Jiménez, translated NB *into Spanish. See RF's January 20, 1919, letter to her. ALS. Princeton.]*

Franconia N.H.
Aug 16 1919

Dear Mr Bristol:

I should think it a good idea to let Mrs Jiménez have my works on the terms she proposes without reservation. There wont be a great amount of money made in them to scramble for anyway—unless of course I should decide to put in my vacations in a succession of South American countries stirring up an interest in my poetry.

Our weather hasn't much on yours this year I'm afraid. You get too much rain; we don't get enough to put out the forest fires and clear the air of smoke.

Sincerely yours
Robert Frost

---

362. Cf. stanza XLIII of George Meredith's "Modern Love" (1862):

'Tis morning; but no morning can restore
What we have forfeited. I see no sin;
The wrong is mixed. In tragic life, God wot,
No villain need be! Passions spin the plot;
We are betrayed by what is false within.

[To Jessie B. Rittenhouse. The letter is dated in an unknown hand above the salutation and lacks a heading. ALS. Rollins.]

[Franconia, NH]
[August 27, 1919]

Dear Miss Rittenhouse:

I wired this morning to accept your invitation if you could make the day Wednesday or Thursday of next week.[363] After that would be too late for Mrs Frost who leaves here on Saturday for Amherst with a child to put into school.

There's this to say about me at this time of year: I almost never leave the mountains even for a plunge into the hay fever. I'm afraid if I should sleep below the Franconia range the night before I read I should be too stuffed up to read at all tolerably. So I thought I would plan to make the journey on the day of the reading. We ought to get there somehow in time for an afternoon reading in case you should have announced one—though an evening one would have one advantage—it will give me a chance to rest a little before I was called on to give tongue.

It turns out to be rather further than you or I perhaps realized from Franconia to Arlington. It comes to nearly one hundred and fifty miles. The question is wouldn't it be the cheapest way out of it for me to hire a car here for the round trip if I could get one for not over thirty-five or forty dollars. The expenses by rail would mount up at this rate: two dollars to the train, train fare for two from Littleton to Burlington to Arlington about twelve dollars, hotel bills overnight at Burlington about five dollars, or about twenty dollars going and then if it wasnt convenient for you to bring us back as much more coming.

But I leave a good deal of this for you to decide. In any case we should want to stay with you and your friends over the night after the reading. I should just stand the hay fever once the reading was over.

This is all in haste to catch the R.F.D. man. You'll pardon any confusion. I'm anxious to meet friendly engagements like this. I've sworn off on all others. I have just had to give up Pond on account of my health.[364] But half a

363. RF read before the Poetry Society of Southern Vermont in Arlington, Vermont, on September 3, 1919.

364. See RF's July 6, 1919, letter to K. F. Truman.

dozen public appearances a year can do no harm we think—that is if they are with and for personal friends.

Sincerely yours
Robert Frost

[To Mrs. Halley Phillips Gilchrist (1876–1944), secretary of the Poetry Society of Southern Vermont. RF omits the year; 1919 is interpolated in pencil in another hand. ALS. Middlebury.]

Franconia N.H.
August 29 [1919]

Dear Mrs Gilchrist:

I had some idea I would be in friendly country in Arlington. I knew Mrs. Fisher and Miss Cleghorn were there and I hoped I might find the Harcourts still there if I came soon enough.[365] But for reasons of health late enough is more important to me than soon enough. I am much more certain to be in reading condition in Arlington on September 13th than on September 6th. By the middle of the month the hay-fever season will be waning and I can begin to think of going almost anywhere with comparative safety. You mustn't take it as any reflection on your Green Mts if as the greatest living authority on where hay-fever is or isn't to be had, I have to tell you there is no refuge in Vermont from it till you come to Stowe and Danville any more than there is in New Hampshire till you come through the Crawford and Franconia Notches.

But as I say the poison flood will be ebbing from the air by the 12th or 13th of the month; it will be fun to let you carry us off on trial; and then if we find breathing good, like Noah's dove we can simply not come back to Franconia but go on to Amherst.

We shall look forward to the ride across states and to seeing you all at Arlington—even a little to reading to you, though I'm not the minstrel I sometimes wish I were and don't pretend to give or experience the pleasure Vachel Lindsay does in public performance.

365. RF refers to Vermont writers and Arlington residents Dorothy Canfield Fisher and Sarah Cleghorn and to editor/publisher Alfred Harcourt, a summer visitor.

Glad to hear that the New England hired man persists with you. It was my purpose to immortalize him in death.[366]

Sincerely yours
Robert Frost

[To Louis Untermeyer. ALS. LoC.]

[Franconia, NH]
[August 29, 1919]

Dear Louis

What we want to know before we go any further in any direction is are you home alive and getting well. Because if you're not what's the use of anything?

But if you are I may or I may not want to address myself in a few words to the subject of your two school books.[367] Not that they need any ideas from me. Thats my consolation: if I find I cant say anything to help you about them, they will probably be the better for it. As they stand I see their sufficient value. They easily beat what any one else can do. Only I just dont want you to be too intemperate about the past. My efforts, should I rise and put forth any, would be toward begging you on bended knee to give the past half a show. (You'd think I was pleading for a lady with a past, but no, it is the past alone I am concerned for.)

Look what Amy's pig-eyed young bear cat done all over the Dial for want of a little historical sense. Amy ought to be ashamed of him.[368] Right through his diapers! Let's withdraw from such society and go into the maple sugar business. I swear!

Be good to Jean on our account.

More yours every time I see you
Robert Frost.

---

366. In "The Death of the Hired Man," collected first in *NB*.

367. *Modern American Poetry: An Introduction* (New York: Harcourt, Brace and Howe, 1919), and *Modern British Poetry* (which Harcourt, Brace and Howe would issue in 1920).

368. Amy Lowell's "bear cat" is John Gould Fletcher (1886–1950), who reviewed Untermeyer's *New Era in American Poetry* in an article titled "A Jazz Critic" in *The Dial* 67 (August 23, 1919): 155–156.

[To Frederic Melcher (1879–1963), publisher, editor, and bookseller. During the foregoing week, RF had been driving (with his family) from Franconia down to Amherst, stopping off along the way (on September 3) for a reading for the Poetry Society of Southern Vermont in Arlington, Vermont. ALS. UVA.]

Amherst Mass
September 22 1919

Dear Mr Melcher:

The extenuating circumstances are that I have been all round everywhere lately not getting my mail most of the time and not attending to it when I got it. And then I'm just a plain bad lot lazy and unbusinesslike. I dont defend myself. I ought not to have made it necessary for you to write me three letters.

To come immediately to what time presses me to tell you—we can leave swapping New Hampshire memories till we sit down together in your New Jersey home: what should you say to some night <u>early</u> in December? Will you name one?[369]

I shall intend to read to your audience and perhaps talk to them a little on Vocal Reality

You will forgive me I hope for such of my sins as are against you.

Sincerely yours
Robert Frost

[To Katharine Lee Bates. RF gave a talk and reading at Wellesley College on October 31. ALS. Wellesley.]

Amherst Mass
September 29 1919

Dear Miss Bates:

I have put off answering you till I should know how my classes were to be distributed through the week and whether I was to be left any more free for out-of-town visits at one end of the week than the other. I should say that I was going to be able to get away best after Wednesdays. And I should like it

369. The reading and lecture took place at the Unity Institute (of the Unitarian Church) in Montclair, New Jersey, on December 4, 1919. While in Montclair, RF stayed with Melcher.

pretty well if you would have me early in the season while I am still fresh from the mountains and fresh on a subject I have been having ideas on lately, namely Vocal Reality. There lies the root of the whole matter I feel for the moment. Just wait till you hear.

With the same sincere regard as always I'm

Yours truly
Robert Frost

[To Frederic Melcher. ALS. UVA.]

Amherst Mass
September 29 1919

Dear Mr Melcher:

The one noticeable thing about professors now-a-days is the way they do their best to forget what they are. Their ambition is to be unacademic and not to be called Professor. So you see how safe you are in calling me Mister even at Amherst.

It looks now from my schedule of classes as if December 1st would do though December 3rd would be a little easier. Let's consider chiefly your end of the business. You choose the day most favorable for an audience. My only objection to December 1st is, it would make me hurry home rather precipitately for class the next day at two o'clock. But thats not too serious a matter.

Sincerely yours
Robert Frost

[To Katharine Lee Bates. Bates had arranged for RF to appear at Wellesley on the thirty-first. ALS. Wellesley.]

Amherst Mass
October 8 1919

Dear Miss Bates:

October 31 couldn't be bettered for me.

It seems a long time since last we encountered—was it in the Mt Holyoke poetry contest (as judges)?[370] Do you get excited about all the nonsense that is

370. See RF's May 23, 1919, letter to Whicher.

being said about free rhythms? Free rhythms are as disorderly as nature; meters are as orderly as human nature and take their rise in rhythms just as human nature rises out of nature. I wonder if you dont get impatient with some people who give their sentiment divine against the being of a line between prose and verse.[371] I shall want to hear what you have to say.

Sincerely yours
Robert Frost

[To Frederic Melcher. ALS. UVA.]

Amherst Mass
October 9 [1919]

Dear Melcher:

I have just discovered in entering my date for lecturing you that it is Wednesday December 3rd. Now when I named December 3rd I thought it came on Thursday for some reason. Wednesday is my very busiest day in Amherst. Is it too late to amend this? If so, let it go. But I wish it could be made December 4th—Thursday. I must have read the calendar wrong.

Sincerely yours
Robert Frost

371. See Emerson's "Uriel":

One, with low tones that decide,
And doubt and reverend use defied,
With a look that solved the sphere,
And stirr'd the devils everywhere,
Gave his sentiment divine
Against the being of a line.
"Line in nature is not found;
Unit and universe are round;
In vain produced, all rays return;
Evil will bless, and ice will burn."

[To Louis Untermeyer. ALS. LoC.]

Amherst Mass
October 15 1919

Dear Louis:

No need to tell you how sure I am that no one succeeds in any of the arts without observing at least some one of the various realities. That's the way he gets his originality whatever it comes to. He may be as romantic as a girl of eighteen in subject matter and in vocabulary: you'll find him trying to make it up to you in vocal reality or some other reality. He must get back to the source of sanity and energy somewhere. Every form of romance is but an exhalation from some form of reality. The common speech is always giving off, you and I know how, the special vocabulary of poetry. The same thing happens with the tones of every day talk. They have emanations of grandeur and dignity and reverence and heroism and terror. No matter how realistic we are we go up with these and float on them like charred paper balancing on the updraft above a fire. That is to say the realist is that much a romantic. The romanticist differs from the realist only in being more romantic than he. He starts where the realist leaves off. He refines on refinement and thats all he cares about refining on. He still persists long after his refining touch becomes imperceptible. Never mind if he is happy. Etc etc. Here comes a boy I shall have to go on with this to if I am to go on with it at all. Maybe it will prove to be Everett Glass.[372] Not for myself any more do I think but for boys we can only hope can make better use of it than I can. We are asked to believe that if I teach them enough they will go beyond me in accomplishment so that I can well afford to go no further myself.

Yours sadly
R.F.

---

372. Everett Glass (1891–1966), Amherst College class of 1914; subsequently an actor and playwright. He appeared in (among other films) *Invasion of the Body Snatchers* (1956).

[To Frederic Melcher. The letter is undated and was typed—in RF's behalf—by Ellen Knowles Eayres ("E.K.E."), a secretary at Henry Holt, on company letterhead ("19 West 44th Street, New York, NY"). In the upper right, "1919?" is written in an unknown hand, likely Melcher's. RF is discussing the illustrations James Chapin had done for a new, limited edition of NB. *Reference to his pressing Chapin's illustrations "in several quarters during the summer" places this letter in the fall. TLS. UVA.]*

I pressed Chapin's pictures in several quarters during the summer, but nowhere to any definite conclusion. I thought von Morch . . . (I can't read the name. E.K.E.)[373] might write about them, but in a letter just at hand he fails to mention them. To be perfectly frank with you in confidence, most of my friends make uphill work of them. They complain that the Grandsire is a Dutchman with a long Dutch pipe, that the figures in the Housekeeper picture are French or at any rate, old World or Art World, that the Sinister Staircase is Poesque and Art World anything but New England. His part of the book in a word, is cosmopolite. And they don't just see instantly how it goes with the work of a person who is known to hold that nine-tenths of personality is locality. The pictures seem to them from everywhere and so from nowhere. That's where they stick. We left it that they should take time to think it over. They recognized the distinction of the work as work. And they didn't ask that Chapin should use the same symbolism with me. They expected him, though, to smack of the same place.

R F

[To Charles Lowell Young. ALS. Wellesley.]

Amherst Mass
October 25 1919

Dear Young:

As it looks now I ought not to be away over Sunday, and I must show some consideration for that poor Poetry Society that keeps electing me to I know not what offices. Suppose I get to Wellesley early enough on Friday for a talk with Miss Bates, give Friday night to barding, give you all day Saturday and then go to Norreys O'Conor's to meet the Poetry Crowd Saturday eve-

---

373. The "von Morch" with whom the typist struggles—the parenthesis is her addition—is Robert von Moschzisker, a Pennsylvania Supreme Court justice whom RF befriended in 1915.

ning.[374] You would get more of me than anyone else would by that arrangement. And would it suffice to prove faithful friendship, I want to hear what these women are trying to do to you, and I want to help you stand them off. I could perhaps stretch a point and get in some of Sunday at Wellesley if I should have to for the cause of right teaching.

I'd sleep at Tower Court[375] Friday night and so not come on Mrs Young for more than a meal or two. Probability is Elinor will be with me.

Ever yours
Robert Frost

[To Lesley Frost. ALS. UVA.]

Amherst Mass
November 4 1919

Dear Lesley:

Been to Wellesley where I saw Margaret White[376] and to Boston where I saw Amy Lowell and presided over the Poetry Society so it couldnt be said I never do what I dont want to do. Told the assembled girls about my new classroom game "salon" destined to displace the older games of "quiz" "lecture with notes" "lecture without notes" "pupil—teacher," "examination" and "debating society." In "salon" the players come to class determined to show as wise, witty, and well-read (anything else, too, that counts in good company.) The scoring, which is my concern, is rather indirect than direct. I incline to give some credit for initial remarks for their face value, but estimate them chiefly by their prevocative and suggestive effect on conversation. Remarks that provoke comment of any kind sympathetic or unsympathetic from four I give A: from three I give B: from two I give C: from one I give D: from none I give E. I told the girls how one of my boys said this would be all right from the point of view of the class but he didnt see where I came in, because the class would simply stand together and see to it that I had to give everyone A. It was the greatest surprise to him when I asked what more could I want than to see them help each other get a high mark.

374. Norreys Jephson O'Conor was president of the New England Poetry Club, where, as it turned out, RF spoke on Thursday, October 30.

375. A residence hall at Wellesley.

376. Margaret White had been Lesley's housemate at Wellesley.

Did he suppose my object in teaching would be to make pupils fail? Evidently from the laugh I got out of both boys and girls that was about what he supposed.

I'm speaking for the group of languages (all the languages) here on Friday before the visiting alumni—that is if I'm up and around by that time—I'm in bed now from overexertion in Wellesley and Boston.[377] Shall have to tell them that the mainstays in a language department should always be men who refuse to put a book to any use it wasn't designed for by the author. The best books are to read: the best of the best to read and reread—not to philosophize over, not even to study—not to translate any more than need be—the sooner we reach an understanding of them without translation the happier for us and the books. Shall have to tell them a pedagogue is a person who has been willing to do violence to anything in himself or in the great books or even in the student for the sake of making the books pedagogically useful, laborious and disciplinary in class. Shall have to tell them that language courses ought to be most fruitional of all so to call them. They ought to be where most we come into the enjoyment of what we are and of what by pains and more or less ugly effort expended elsewhere we have come to be. In writing and reading we come home with the reminiscent spoils of all our adventure and experience in life and books.

Speaking of books: ask Chapin will you to give you one of the new N.O.B.s with his autograph. Tell him I wont beg a book of Rolan Dolt and I'm damned if I'll buy one.[378] Arent they behaving small?

Ask Miss Eayres where Harcourt is—what address I'm to use in writing him.

I told Young (Chas Lowell) and Margaret White how you covered yourself with blue ribbons. I saw Sheffy and he looked unutterable things about my publicity.[379] Miss Bates was friendly. How she hates Amy the poetic politician.

Affectionately

Papa

---

377. On November 7, RF addressed the Amherst Alumni Council. The text of his talk was subsequently published in *Proceedings of the Alumni Council of Amherst College At The Meeting Held In Amherst November 7–9, 1919* (Amherst: The Alumni Council, 1920). See *CPRF*, 80–81 and 260–262.

378. "Rolan Dolt" is Roland Holt, then vice president of Henry Holt and Company.

379. "Sheffy" is Alfred Dwight Sheffield, who had been RF's English instructor at Harvard.

[To Frederic Melcher. On the evening of December 4 RF spoke on "Vocal Reality" at the Unity Institute in Montclair, New Jersey, and was the guest, there, at the home of the Melchers. ALS. UVA.]

Amherst Mass
November 18 1919

Dear Melcher:

Don't have the Montclair Blues about it whatever you do. I shall manage to make the college accommodate itself to us. Let's call it December 4th—and bid our will avouch it.[380]

I think I will look you up at your office in New York in the middle of the afternoon. You say just when.

I suppose Sandburg sang you the Livery Stable Blues too.[381] There's a whole Blues Cycle I wish I had. I heard one yesterday that went off

If I die in Arkansaw
Send my body to my mother in law
If she refuse me send me to my pa
If my pa refuse me send me to my girl
If my girl refuse me throw me in the sea
Where the whales and fishes make a fuss over me.[382]

Yours faithfully
Robert Frost

380. RF (again) borrows a favorite phrase from *Macbeth* (3.i): "and though I could / With barefaced power sweep him from my sight / And bid my will avouch it, yet I must not."

381. See Carl Sandburg's "Vaudeville Dancer," soon to be collected in Sandburg's 1920 volume *Smoke and Steel*. The lines in question read: "Elsie Flimmerwon, you got a job now with a jazz outfit in vaudeville. / The houses go wild when you finish the act shimmying a fast shimmy to The Livery Stable Blues."

382. The folk song exists in a number of forms.

[To Charles Wharton Stork (1881–1971), poet, playwright, novelist; editor of the magazine Contemporary Verse *(from 1917 to 1925); professor of English at the University of Pennsylvania; and member of the Philadelphia Athenaeum. ALS. Yale.]*

Amherst Mass
Nov 19 1919

Dear Stork:

Perhaps as your plan is already so much made, you would do better not to try to accommodate it to us. We would keep till another year, and you could call on us or not then as you liked. I'm sure I speak somewhere near the common sentiment when I say that we dont want to seem to make any one poem out so much better than the others of the year as giving it a first prize would imply.

I could tell you more if we met sometime this winter.

Can't you Philadelphians keep from quarreling with a quiet inoffensive girl like Amy?[383]

I liked the sonnet you sent. But you shouldnt let yourself be seen in the act of changing a line in it that way. Privacy for some acts.

Always your friend
Robert Frost

[To Louis Untermeyer. ALS. LoC.]

Amassed Mass
Dec 8 1919

Dear Louis

That's a sturdy friend! I knew I could count on you not to doubt me even when appearances were most against me.

Brooks Moore means nothing to me. Who is he? But Stork!—both denotatively and connotatively![384] Not the father of twenty children, many of them twins, can show more purturbation [*sic*] than I at sound of that dread name. Stork! Almost more unwelcome to the married ear than cucoo even.

---

383. Amy Lowell.

384. John Brooks More (1884–1960), literary critic and brother of Paul Elmer More; for Charles Wharton Stork, see the November 19, 1919, letter to him, above.

Had a good journey home with the illustrator of any books of mine hereafter to be illustrated.[385]

Yours everly
Robertus.

[To Charles Wharton Stork. ALS. Yale.]

December 10 1919
Amherst Mass

Dear Stork:

I'm not quite pleased that you should have gone ahead and made me one of your judges when we were still in the middle of negotiations. I don't like being a judge any too well anyhow and was only bringing myself to act for you this time for what concessions I could get from you in a matter or two of taste. I don't get the concessions, so of course you can't expect to get me. Be careful—won't you?—in the name of friendship, not to say in dropping me that I have withdrawn. I cant withdraw from what I have never gone into. Please put it this way if you mention me at all: that my name was used by mistake or through a misunderstanding. I'd like it if you would say just that. Perhaps some time you will let me cooperate with you when it shall be more convenient for you to give me some say in the conditions.

Sincerely yours
Robert Frost

---

385. James Chapin. Remarks here notwithstanding, the illustrator with whom RF would be most closely associated (from 1923 on) was the woodcut artist J. J. Lankes (1884–1960).

[To E. Merrill Root (1895–1973), American poet, educator, and (in his later years) an anticommunist activist. He taught at Earlham College in Indiana from 1920 to 1960, having graduated in 1917 from Amherst College, where he was RF's student. Dating derived from postmark and internal evidence. ALS. ACL.]

Tuesday
[December 16, 1919]
[Amherst, MA]

Dear Root:

I shall be only too glad to see you again and hear about your plans. Dont expect too much of me though in the way of wisdom.

I shall be free either Friday afternoon or Friday evening.

Faithfully yours
Robert Frost

[To Lincoln MacVeagh (1890–1972), soldier, diplomat, businessman, founder of Dial Press in 1923; after the war he worked for Henry Holt and Company. At a later date, MacVeagh penciled in a note on the letter: "Written when I was going to England for Henry Holt & Co. for the 1st time, after I came home from France." ALS. Jones.]

Amherst Mass
Dec 27 1919

Dear Mr MacVeagh:

I thought I might be able to get down to see you to-day. Too many things on top of each other here. I shall have to be content with a word this way.

Harold Monro (Poetry Book Shop, Devonshire St, Theobald's Road, London W.C.) will have had a letter warning him against you and your coming by the time you get round to him.

I leave Mrs Nutt entirely to your judgement. I know you won't compromise our position with her. I rather hate to have her offered terms. But you are in the business and know what is ideal and practical.

I enclose Heinemanns list with suggestions of addition and substitution.[386] I'm sure you're right about The Gum-gatherer, The Old Man's Winter Night,

386. William Heinemann published the English edition of RF's *Selected Poems* in 1923; apparently Holt was already, at this early date, in negotiation with him about that volume. Heinemann had written to Holt in April 1919 intimating that, in his first book, RF borrowed several lines from an old English ballad and another line from Shakespeare

Amherst Mass
Dec 27 1919

Dear Mr MacVeagh:

I thought I might be able to get down to see you to-day. Too many things on top of each other here. I shall have to be content with a word this way.

Harold Monro (Poetry Book Shop, Devonshire St, Theobald's Road, London W.C.) will have had a letter warning him against you and your coming by the time you get round to him.

I leave Mrs Nutt entirely to your judgement. I know you wont

written when I was going to England for H. Holt & Co. for the 1st time after I came home from France.

compromise our position with her.
I rather hate to have her offered terms.
But you are in the business and
know what is ideal and practical.

I enclose Heinemanns list with
suggestions of addition and substitution.
I'm sure you're right about The
Gum-gatherer, The Old Man's Winter
Night, and The Death of the Hired Man.
I think my other suggestions are
important too.

This is in some haste to catch
you before you sail.

Happy New Year and good
voyage to you.

Faithfully yours
Robert Frost

Robert Frost to Lincoln MacVeagh, December 27, 1919.

Courtesy Jones Library (Amherst, Massachusetts).

and The Death of the Hired Man. I think my other suggestions are important too.

This is in some haste to catch you before you sail.

Happy New Year and good voyage to you.

Faithfully yours
Robert Frost

[To Harold Monro. ALS. Trinity.]

Amherst Mass U.S.A.
January 1 1920

Dear Monro:

This is wishing you a good year for poetry—and may I ask will you receive almost if not quite as kindly as someday I hope you will me the friend I am sending you for the present instead of coming to England to face my creditors myself. He will be, when he turns up, Mr Lincoln MacVeagh, my publisher (head of the literary as distinguished from the school-text department of Henry Holt & Co), and officer of the American Expeditionary Army and a scion, so to speak, of one of our first families in the government—no less.[387] You are both publishers: you ought to prove mutually advantageous. At least you ought not to want for something to say to each other. I think it is MacVeagh's first journey to England in quest of books. You must know of something important enough to import. Any help you give him you will be giving me. I shall requite it if I have to exceed my natural span to keep my word.

We weep inwardly with something like homesickness when we remember the days we had with you in our rooms over the Bookshop. The question is not could we live them over again, but can we, for before long we mean to try.

What is new in your own work? I start hard after being so long laid off by the war.

Always yours
Robert Frost

(see *YT*, 649–650); however, the allusion here is to a proposed table of contents for what would become the 1923 volume.

387. Lincoln MacVeagh's grandfather, Wayne MacVeagh, served as Attorney General under President Garfield; his great uncle Franklin MacVeagh was Secretary of the Treasury under William Howard Taft; and his father Charles would later serve as Calvin Coolidge's ambassador to Japan.

[To Wilbur L. Cross. ALS. Yale.]

Amherst Mass
January 1 1920

Dear Mr Cross:

Here then, out of the freshness of my resolutions to be good this year is what I have been promising you and Mr Canby.[388] Best wishes to you both.

Always yours faithfully
Robert Frost

I mean to look in on you some day.

[To Sidney Hayes Cox. ALS. DCL.]

Amherst Mass
Jan 5 1920

Dear Sidney:

The further from New York the better for a whole lot of reasons. Out there there ought to be something new for you to get the hang of for yourself.[389] In New York there is next to nothing that somebody else hasnt already got the hang of for you. New York's as completely formulated as Abraham Lincoln. The last Englishman to arrive knows as much about it as the most pains-taking Greenwich Villager is ever likely to know. Our minds are so crowded with what we have been told to look for there that they have no room for accidental discoveries. And that's the way with whole tracts of knowledge. We can only turn away from them to Montana.

And even at three cents a mile I dont suppose Montana is as far off as California we'll say. And where are you in California when you get there? Almost brought through on the other side again—nearer East culturally than you would be in Montana at any rate.

The worst of it is that the difference between East and West or between this country and Europe seems to want to be blotted out in colleges. Col-

---

388. Henry Seidel Canby (1878–1964) was at the time Cross's editorial assistant at *The Yale Review*; RF likely enclosed, with this letter, a copy of "To E.T.," a poem written in memory of Edward Thomas and published in *The Yale Review* in April 1920.

389. In the fall of 1920, Cox had taken a position as assistant professor of English at the State University of Montana at Missoula.

leges will be colleges wherever found—colorless and cosmopolitan. But I shall trust you to take measures to keep from missing Montana people in your preoccupation with a college faculty probably largely transplanted from Eastern colleges and mostly wishing they were in London or Paris at this moment.

Why do we oppose the introduction into English of idioms not English such as "gives upon"? Does it seem so small minded of us? And yet we are asked to let in all their continental sex notions. I say lets try to get hold of what we have here however accidental and then hold on to it to the exclusion of everything foreign the importer has a pocket-interest in importing. There ought to be something springing from Montana soil that needs a friend to keep the trampling foreign off it.

We have a little mountain pony that came to us with the name Beauty which we couldnt stand: so without her finding out we changed her name by imperceptible stages to Beaut to Butte and Montana Butte, or Butte, Montana. That will give us a fellow feeling with you as long as we keep the pony and you stay in Montana.

What New Year's resolution did you discover worth taking? I resolved not to let anybody put a book to any use it wasnt intended for by its author—if I could help it. Some will ask how they are going to kill three hours a week in an English course and not put an occasional book to an occasional use it wasnt intended for by its author. Embarrassedly twiddling thumbs if necessary. Or if that suggests too much a country courting, let them read aloud a good deal and teach others to read aloud. Shakespeare says good orators, when they are out, spit.[390] There is something will suggest itself when other things fail.

You may have heard that at the time you wrote me about your proposed book I was hung as it were between two publishers and not in a position to do anything for you with either. Harcourt my friend had quarreled with my friend Henry Holt and started a new firm of publishers, Harcourt Brace and Howe. It looks now as if I would belong to Henry Holt because he refuses to surrender me to Alfred Harcourt on demand and representation. I'm like the lady who didn't care much either way as long as it was settled one way or the other. I'm not sure about the value of your anthology for schools. Everybody is doing it. I told a friend in Houghton and Mifflin without getting any partic-

390. *As You Like It* (4.i.7): "Very good orators, when they are out, they will spit."

ular encouragement. You'll have other ideas for books I can help you with. Let me know when you do. Only keep a-thinking. You've got things where they can't happen too fast for you now.

The unhappiness that attached to me in your dream wasnt so far wrong. I don't believe I am very happy about this college. And yet it is a better college than plenty of colleges. It tries hard to deny its nature. I musnt ask it to dissolve into a mere school of experience to please me.

I promised to send you a poem or two. These can wait and take the place of a letter some day when I am less in the mood for a letter than I am today.[391]

Go at it now for genuineness. A minimum of class work and all kinds of work for mere exercise. Remember that some of us have got by without ever having written a thing for exercise. Dorothy Canfield was telling me the other day that she had. She's a Doc of Phil of Columbia too.[392] Make it real and you'll beat the Dutch.

Best wishes to you and Alice from us all.[393]

Affectionately
Robert Frost

---

391. Enclosed with the letter were "Fire and Ice," "The Onset," "Plowmen," "Silver Lizards" (i.e., "A Hillside Thaw"), "A Star in a Stone Boat," and "Two Look at Two." As Evans notes in *RFSC,* line five of "Fire and Ice," in the typescript RF enclosed, reads "But if I had to perish twice," and that line one of "Plowmen" reads "I hear men say they plow the snow."

392. Dorothy Canfield Fisher (1879–1958) received her doctorate in romance languages from Columbia in 1904.

393. Cox and his wife, Alice, would soon have a son (Arthur), born in May.

[To Louis Untermeyer. The following jeu d'esprit is written in ink on the typed letter it answers, in which Untermeyer, addressing RF as "Dear Rob," says: "I expect to send my introduction to 'Modern English Poetry' to the printer in two or three weeks. Before this happens I must arrange the volume chronologically. Would you be so helpful as to fill in what blanks you can, fold on the dotted line, detach and return to me." RF did not do as instructed. He did indeed inscribe the ages for Abercrombie, Gibson, and Flint (where Untermeyer had typed them out). But he did not fold and detach the bottom of the sheet to return to Untermeyer. Instead, RF added, above the dotted line, the legend "Sign here," beneath which he supplied his signature; he then gratuitously pasted in, under the heading "photograph," a five pfennig Bavarian stamp issued in 1911 and bearing the image of Prinzregent Luitpold Karl Joseph Wilhelm Ludwig von Bayern (1821–1912); and, finally, inside a box drawn for the purpose, underneath the heading "Thumb," RF adorned the letter with his own thumbprint. The body of the letter itself is given as a footnote to the (typed) name "Wilfred W. Gibson." The envelope survives and supplies the dating. ALS. LoC.]

[Amherst, MA]
[January 5, 1920]

Lascelles Abercrombie is approximately 38 years old
*Wilfred W. Gibson " " 42 " "
D. H. Lawrence " " ? " "
F. S. Flint " " 32 " "

*Isnt it Sturge Moore who says Wilfrid Gibson is older than most sheep, but not so old as the rose bush is; he is about as pretty as the former. Isn't it Tennyson who says D. H. Lawrence is old damsell, old and hard. Jean Ingelow says Lascelles Abercrombie is old, so old he can't write a letter. Flint, though young, is old enough to be the putative father of free verse in England.

Visaed for State Dept
W J Bryan[394]

---

394. RF cracks a number of whimsical jokes. William Jennings Bryan (1860–1925) served as secretary of state under Woodrow Wilson from 1913 to 1915 (the poet, perhaps acknowledging Bryan's advanced age, signs the name in an ostentatiously shaky hand). RF also alludes to "Chorus of Grecian Girls" by English poet Thomas Sturge Moore (1870–1944): "We maidens are older than most sheep, / Though not so old as the rose-bush is; / We are only as pretty as that." Also in play is the following passage from the "Gareth and Lynette" section of Tennyson's *Idylls of the King:*

Then the third brother shouted o'er the bridge,
'O brother-star, why shine ye here so low?
Thy ward is higher up: but have ye slain
The damsel's champion?' and the damsel cried,

[To Margery Swett Mansfield (1895–1984), an American poet, journalist, and editor. A graduate of Smith College (1917), Mansfield published a number of poems and reviews in Poetry *and other magazines during the 1920s, including a review of Gorham Munson's* Robert Frost: A Study in Sensibility and Good Sense *(1928). In 1928, she was named secretary to the Poetry Society of America. With her husband, Jay Van Everen, an early modernist painter and illustrator, she published* Workers in Fire: A Book about Poetry *in 1937. In the same year, she published a critical anthology entitled* American Women Poets. *After Van Everen's death in 1947, she married poet and editor Edmund Kelly Janes. ALS. UVA.]*

Amherst Mass
January 20 1920

My dear Mrs Mansfield:

Of course if you are going to say pleasant things about my talk at Garden City I shall have no choice in the matter: I shall have to accept your invitation to talk in New York too. March 17th will be right for me. Will that be in the afternoon?[395]

Thanking you for your kindness I am

Sincerely yours
Robert Frost

'No star of thine, but shot from Arthur's heaven
With all disaster unto thine and thee!
For both thy younger brethren have gone down
Before this youth; and so wilt thou, Sir Star;
Art thou not old?'
'Old, damsel, old and hard,
Old, with the might and breath of twenty boys.'

Jean Ingelow, English poet and novelist, died in 1897 at the age of seventy-seven when Lascelles Abercrombie was only sixteen. F. S. Flint was associated with the free-verse "imagist" movement of the mid-teens.

395. RF did speak in Garden City, Long Island, on "Vocal Reality"; but (according to notes compiled by Lawrance Thompson) on January 30, not on March 17.

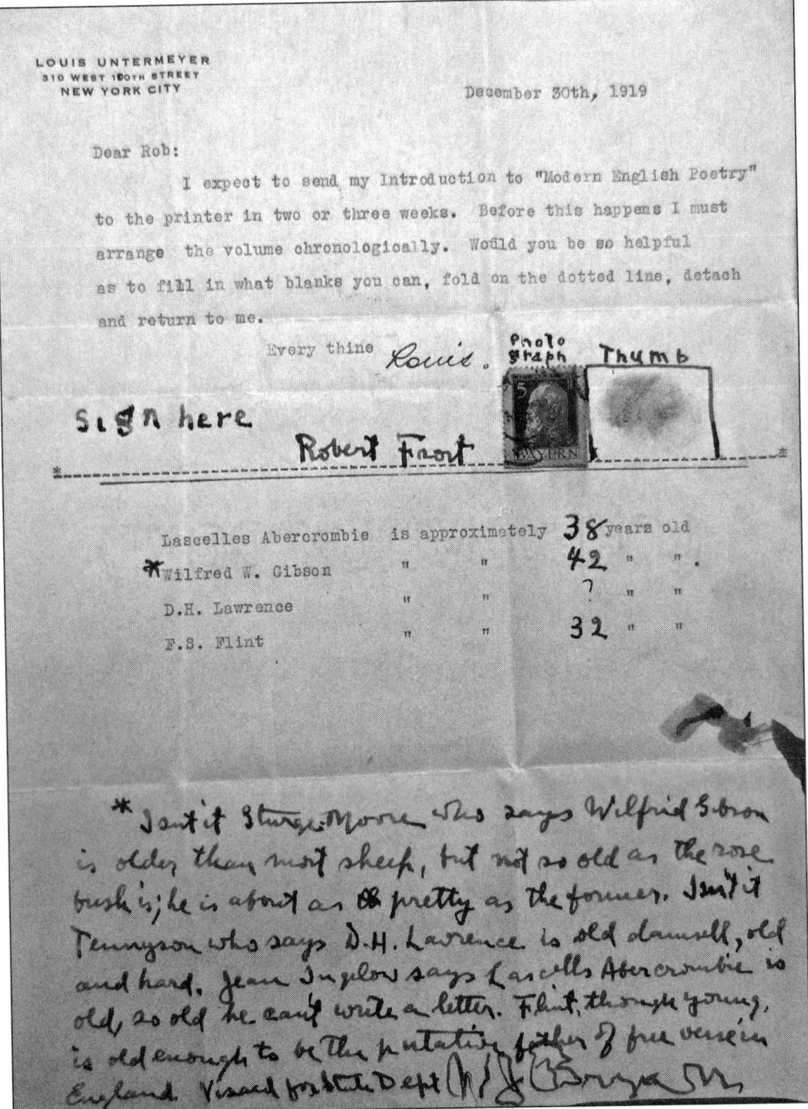

LOUIS UNTERMEYER
310 WEST 100TH STREET
NEW YORK CITY

December 30th, 1919

Dear Rob:

I expect to send my Introduction to "Modern English Poetry" to the printer in two or three weeks. Before this happens I must arrange the volume chronologically. Would you be so helpful as to fill in what blanks you can, fold on the dotted line, detach and return to me.

Every thine Louis.

Photo graph Thumb

Sign here Robert Frost

Lascelles Abercrombie	is approximately	38	years	old
*Wilfred W. Gibson	" "	42	"	".
D.H. Lawrence	" "	?	"	"
F.S. Flint	" "	32	"	"

*Isn't it Sturge Moore who says Wilfrid Gibson is older than most sheep, but not so old as the rose bush is; he is about as pretty as the former. Isn't it Tennyson who says D.H. Lawrence is old damsell, old and hard. Jean Ingelow says Lascells Abercrombie is old, so old he can't write a letter. Flint, though young, is old enough to be the putative father of free verse in England. Visaed for State Dept

The tongue-in-cheek mischievousness of this January 5, 1920 response to a straightforward inquiry was a frequent feature of Frost's correspondence with the witty and articulate Untermeyer.

Courtesy Library of Congress.

[To Lesley Frost. ALS. UVA.]

Amherst Mass
January 28 1920

Dear Lesley

You get neglected with things going the way they are. I've been trying to give the boys good measure at the last moment and mama's been taking care of sick children till she's had to give up sick herself. We don't get our minds made up about your going to Paris and if we got them made up in our present state I doubt if we could keep them so. I rather hate to have you go so far off right now. Still I don't want to hang on to you. Can you wait to decide till I am down on the fourteenth of February? Decisions come hard now-a-days. We don't have to decide much on farms, though, because there aren't any. Amherst is as full as the bases in Pussy-wants-a-corner and we are as left out as Pussy. To-day we were on the point of telephoning to Mr Glover to make ready the Franconia house to receive us and to the Fishers to ask if they knew of any furnished house in Arlington we could have for the spring.[396] It sounds as undignified as a retreat from Moscow.

And speaking of Moscow, I should think it was about to become one of the great capitals of the world with a government we are going to treat with respect whether we like it or fear it. It only goes to show how easy it is to lie to us till we are thoroughly unprepared for anything that happens.

Marge is being examined here you there. I heard Marge wishing all her history examination would be by maps. She says she can make and fill out all sorts of maps but she can't spell well enough to answer questions in writing. Take it easy and have good luck.

The same notion haunts me that I had last year at this time. If I knew of a furnished flat in New York I should be tempted to try it down there for a month or two. It wouldnt do though. What we need is a home and settled life right off soon. My observations of mama's health convince me of that.

I've been wanting to say the word, Come home for your free week; but I don't know that you wouldn't be better off where you are. You've got an infirmary to go to if you are sick (you neednt think I'm asking you to be sick) and you haven't any responsibility for other sick people. By staying, too, you avoid two train journeys more or less risky the way things are. What do you say?

---

396. The Dorothy Canfield Fisher family owned a house in Arlington, Vermont.

Joseph Anthony seemed an able-minded boy when I talked with him here. He ought to go a long way.

He said there was no immediate rush for the poems for Harpers. Wells is out of the office for the moment and no one else ought to have the handling of them.[397] I shall send them to you to copy when I have regarded them a little longer. Overhauling them has stopped me writing new ones for the moment. How are the dailies coming—any as good as the rain-wet window?

Here's one Whicher thought too hard. Joseph Anthony got it quickly enough.

PLOWMEN

I hear men say to plow the snow.
They cannot mean to plant it, though—
Unless in bitterness, to mock
At having cultivated rock.

R.

I keep trying for the word I want in your line about the withering silver on the back of a looking glass.

Affectionately
Papa

[To William Constable Breed (1871–1951), a partner in the New York City law firm of Breed, Abbot, and Morgan. At the time this letter was written, Breed (Amherst class of 1893) was chairman of the New York Amherst Alumni Association, before which RF had been asked to speak. The letter was later published in the New York World *as a part of an article by Walter Lippmann ("The Fall of President Meiklejohn [of Amherst College]," June 24, 1923, page 13E). RF did indeed resign his position at Amherst in February 1920. TL (copy). Jones.]*

Amherst, Mass.
Feb. 2, 1920

Dear Mr. Breed:

I am forced after all to give up the idea of speaking at the Amherst dinner, and I owe you something more than a telegram in explanation. I have de-

397. Joseph Anthony managed publicity for Harper and Brothers. Thomas B. Wells was the editor of *Harper's Monthly* magazine, which published four poems by RF in the July 1920 issue: "Fragmentary Blue," "Good-by and Keep Cold," "Place for a Third," and "For Once, Then, Something."

cided to leave teaching and go back to farming and writing. Strangely enough, I was helped to this decision by your invitation. It was in turning over in my mind my subject chosen for the dinner that I came to the conclusion that I was too much out of sympathy with what the present administration seems bent on doing with this old New England college. I suppose I might say that I am too much outraged in the historical sense for loyalty. I can't complain that I haven't enjoyed the "academic freedom" to be entirely myself under Mr. Meiklejohn. While he detests my dangerously rationalistic and anti-intellectualistic philosophy, he thinks he is willing to have it represented here. But probably it will be better represented by some one who can take it less seriously than I.

There are regrets that I mustn't go into here. The main thing is that I am out of Amherst and it won't be fitting that I should speak for Amherst at the dinner.

Believe me deeply sensible of the friendly treatment I have had from Amherst men, and

Most sincerely yours,
Robert Frost.

Biographical Glossary of Correspondents

Chronology

Acknowledgments

Index

Biographical Glossary of Correspondents

Abercrombie, Lascelles (1881–1938), British poet and literary critic. A major figure among the "Georgians," he was also one of the "Dymock poets" among whom Frost lived and worked in 1914–1915. After the First World War, he embarked on a successful professorial career that culminated in a readership at the University of Oxford (1935–1938).

Adams, W. I. Lincoln (1865–1946), American businessman, photographer, and author. A descendant of the Adams presidential family, and son of the president of the Scovill & Adams Mfg. Co., he took particular interest in the manufacture of photographic equipment and assumed editorship of *Photographic Times* and *American Annual of Photography*. In 1901, he published *Woodland and Meadow: Out of Door Papers Written on a New Hampshire Farm*, a book of observations drawn from life at Hilltop Farm, a family retreat in Littleton New Hampshire.

Bartlett, John T. (1892–1941), journalist. He was a student of Frost's at Pinkerton Academy, from which he graduated in 1909. Bartlett married another Pinkerton student, Margaret Abbott, and pursued a journalism career in Vancouver, British Columbia, and then in Colorado. Frost maintained an active and lifelong interest in his life and career.

Bates, Katharine Lee (1859–1929), American poet, literary scholar, editor, translator, and professor of English. A member of the second graduating class at Wellesley College, in (1880), Bates studied at Oxford, earned a graduate degree at Wellesley, and joined the faculty there in 1883. She retired from her position as professor and chair of the English department in 1925. Her thirty-two books include works of poetry, children's literature, literary criticism, and travel writing. She is perhaps best known as the author of the lyrics to the song "America the Beautiful."

Beach, Joseph Warren (1880–1957), American poet, novelist, critic, and scholar. Beach taught English at the University of Minnesota from 1907 until 1948. Among his most notable publications are *The Method of Henry James* (1918), *The Twentieth-Century Novel* (1932), *The Concept of Nature in Nineteenth-Century English Poetry* (1936), and *American Fiction, 1920–1940* (1941).

Benét, William Rose (1886–1950), American poet, editor, critic, and columnist. After graduating from Yale in 1907 he worked at the *Literary Review, New York Evening Post,* and *Century Magazine.* In 1924, Benét cofounded (with Henry Seidel Canby and others) the *Saturday Review of Literature,* where he worked as an editor and wrote a column, "The Phoenix Nest," for the remainder of his life. A prolific writer, he published his first volume of poetry, *Merchants of Cathay,* in 1913; he won the Pulitzer Prize for Poetry in 1942 for a verse autobiography entitled *The Dust Which Is God* (1941).

Binyon, R. Laurence (1869–1943), British poet, dramatist, and art scholar. Too old to enlist during World War I, Robert Laurence Binyon volunteered in war hospitals in France, and from that experience he wrote one of the most widely read poems of the Great War: "For the Fallen." He worked for many years at the British Museum, and wrote influential studies of Japanese and Chinese art and a well received translation of Dante's *Divine Comedy.* In 1933–1934, he was Norton Professor of Poetry at Harvard.

Blaney, Edith H. (1868–1930), American socialite and art patron. Daughter of the owner of the Eastern Steamship Co., she married artist Dwight Blaney in 1893. She is portrayed in Childe Hassam's *Portrait of Edith Blaney* (1894) and John Singer Sargent's *On the Verandah* (1920).

Braithwaite, W. S. (1878–1962), African American poet, literary critic, editor, and anthologist. In addition to authoring numerous books of poetry and criticism, William Stanley Braithwaite served as literary editor of the *Boston Evening Transcript,* editor of the *Poetry Journal* (Boston), and editor of the annual *Anthology of Magazine Verse and Year Book of American Poetry,* published from 1913 to 1939.

Breed, William C. (1871–1951), American attorney. Educated at Amherst (BA 1893) and the University of the State of New York (LLB 1895), William Constable Breed was a partner in the New York City law firm of Breed, Abbot, and Morgan. He served as president of the NY State Bar Association in 1928 and was a longstanding member of the board of directors of the New York Chapter of the American Red Cross. In 1918, he became a trustee of Amherst College and was also president of the Amherst College Alumni Association in 1920.

Briggs, LeBaron Russell (1855–1934), American educator. Educated at Harvard (AB 1875, AM 1882), Briggs joined the Harvard English faculty in 1883 and retired as Boylston Professor of Rhetoric in 1925. He also served as dean of

Harvard College (1891–1902), dean of the Faculty of Arts and Sciences (1902–1925), and president of Radcliffe College (1903–1925).

Bristol, Edward N. (1860–1946), American businessman and publisher. Educated at Williston Seminary, Edward Newell Bristol began a teaching career in Litchfield, Connecticut before taking a position at Henry Holt & Co. in 1882. He was made a director and secretary in 1903, vice president and general manager in 1918, president in 1926, and chairman of the board in 1932. He retired in 1940. His first responsibility at Holt was to develop the educational textbook department.

Brown, Frank C. (1869–?), American bookseller. He operated a rare books shop on Bromfield Street in Boston.

Brown, Harry Alvin (1879–1949), director of the New Hampshire Bureau of Educational Research. He later served as president of Oshkosh State Teachers College (1917–1930) and Illinois State Normal University (1930–1933).

Browne, George (1857–1931), American educator. George Henry Browne graduated from Harvard with honors in classics in 1878. He and former classmate Edgar H. Nichols founded the Browne and Nichols School in Cambridge, Massachusetts in 1882. Browne and Frost met in 1915 at Frost's Phi Beta Kappa reading at Tufts College. Between 1915 and 1920, the Frosts were frequent guests at Browne's farm in Bridgewater, New Hampshire. In addition to a profile of Frost, Browne published a treatise on Shakespeare's versification and a number of works on figure skating.

Canby, Henry Seidel (1878–1961), American critic, editor, and educator. After graduating from Yale in 1899 and completing his PhD in 1905, Canby joined the Yale English faculty. He edited *The Yale Review* (1911–1922) and championed American literature as a field of study. In 1920, he founded the *Literary Review* as a supplement of the *New York Evening Post*. In 1924, Canby and co-editors Christopher Morley and William Rose Benét launched the *Saturday Review of Literature*, which Canby edited until 1936. Beginning in 1926, Canby chaired the editorial board of the newly established Book of the Month Club. Notable among his many books are *Classic Americans* (1931), *Thoreau* (1939), *Whitman* (1943), and *Turn West, Turn East: Mark Twain and Henry James* (1951).

Cather, Willa (1873–1947), American novelist. Born in Virginia, Wilella "Willa" Cather moved to Nebraska at age nine; she graduated from the University of Nebraska in 1895. She began her career as a journalist, first in Pittsburgh and then in New York, where she was managing editor of *McClure's Magazine*. She published a volume of verse, *April Twilights* (1903), and then two collections of short stories. The first of her major novels, *O Pioneers!*, appeared in 1913. *The Song of the Lark* (1915) and *My Antonia* (1918) followed, both epic treatments of her heroic immigrant theme. Cather received the Pulitzer Prize in 1923 for *One of Ours* and is remembered as well for *A Lost Lady* (1923) and *Death Comes for the Archbishop* (1927).

Chapin, James (1887–1975), American painter and illustrator. After taking evening classes at Cooper Union and the Art Students League, James Ormsbee Chapin studied at the Royal Academy in Antwerp and in Paris. For financial reasons, he returned to the United States in 1912 and took work as an illustrator. He met Frost at the offices of Holt and Company, for whom he designed books. In 1924, he left New York and commercial art to live on a farm in New Jersey. His paintings of the Marvin family engaged in their daily farm work established his reputation and were influential in the development of American regional painting. Throughout his career, he was in demand as a portraitist. In the 1930s he taught briefly at the Pennsylvania Academy of the Fine Arts and in California. He returned to New York and then bought a farm in New Jersey. Opposed to American foreign policy during the Vietnam War, he moved to Canada in 1969. He died in Toronto in 1975.

Chase, George C. (1844–1919), professor and president of Bates College. George Colby Chase graduated from Bates College in Lewiston, Maine, in 1868. In 1872, having decided against a career in the ministry and after spending a year in English graduate studies at Harvard, he returned to Bates, where he taught for twenty-two years. In 1894 he became the college's second president, a position he held until days before his death in 1919.

Clark, Thomas Curtis (1877–1953), American poet, editor, and hymnist. Clark studied at University of Chicago (1901–1902) and served as office manager and poetry editor of the *Christian Century* from 1912 until 1948. Among his notable volumes of poetry are *Love Off to the War* (1918), *Home Roads and Far Horizons: Songs and Sonnets* (1935), and *God's Dreams* (1943); among his many anthologies are *Poems of Justice* (1927), *The Golden Book of Religious Verse* (1931), and *Poems for Life* (1941).

Cook, Albert S. (1853–1927), American scholar. With degrees in both science and literature from Rutgers College (BSc 1872, MSc 1875, AM 1882) and a PhD from Jena University (1882), Albert Stanburrough Cook joined the English faculty of the University of California in 1882 before moving to Yale in 1889.

He is best known for his work in Old English and in poetics, publishing annotated editions of Sidney's *Defense of Poesie* (1890), Shelley's *Defense of Poetry* (1891), Newman's *Poetry* (1891), and Leigh Hunt's *What Is Poetry* (1893), among others. He was president of the Modern Language Association (1897). In 1898, he established the Albert Stanburrough Cook Prize for the best group of unpublished poems by a Yale student; he established the Emily Chamberlain Cook Prize in Poetry at Berkeley in 1909.

Cournos, John (1881–1966), poet and novelist. Cournos was born in the Ukraine and emigrated to Britain in 1912, where he began his career as a poet and novelist and, after 1917, as an anti-Bolshevik and anti-Soviet propagandist. He later relocated to the United States. In 1914 he was associated with the Imagist poets.

Cox, Sidney (1889–1952), American scholar, critic, and educator. Sidney Hayes Cox met Frost in 1911 when he was teaching high school English in Plymouth, New Hampshire. Cox went on to teach English and creative writing at the University of Montana before joining the Dartmouth faculty in 1926. He had a distinguished forty-year teaching career at Dartmouth, during which he wrote two books about Frost—*Robert Frost: Original "Ordinary Man"* (1929) and *A Swinger of Birches* (1957). His other works include *The Teaching of English: Avowals and Ventures* (1928), *Indirections for Those Who Want to Write* (1947), and a popular anthology-textbook *Prose Preferences* (1926).

Cross, Wilbur (1862–1948), American scholar, editor, educator, and political figure. After earning a BA (1885) and PhD (1889) from Yale, Wilbur Lucius Cross taught in the university's English department from 1894 until 1916, when he became dean of the Yale Graduate School. After retiring from Yale in 1930, Cross was elected governor of Connecticut, an office he held from 1931 until 1939. In 1911 Cross had become the editor of *The Yale Review*, and he continued in that role, despite changes in position and responsibility, until 1941. Noteworthy among his scholarly books are *The Life and Times of Laurence Sterne* (1909) and *The History of Henry Fielding* (1918).

Dawson, Mitchell (1890–1956), American attorney and poet. Educated at the University of Chicago (PhB 1911; JD 1914), Dawson practiced law in Chicago until his retirement in 1954. In the years before World War I, his poems appeared in *Poetry*, *The Little Review*, and *Others*. He supported as a patron and contributed as a writer to Chicago's literary renaissance. In the 1920s and after, he wrote a legal advice column called "Advice of Counsel" that appeared in *The Saturday Evening Post*, *The New Yorker*, and *Esquire*.

Dole, Nathan Haskell (1852–1935), American poet, music historian, editor, and translator. A regular contributor to the *Boston Evening Transcript* and the *Independent*, Dole was a prominent and popular figure in Boston art and literary circles for many years.

Easton, Emily (1870–1942), American educator. Emily Isabel Meador [Mrs. Frank T.] Easton graduated from Wellesley (1891) and taught English at the Providence (Rhode Island) Classical High School. Married to a prominent attorney and the mother of two children, she contributed regularly to educational journals and authored *Roger Williams: Prophet and Pioneer* (1930).

Eaton, Walter Prichard (1878–1957), American drama critic and author. After graduating from Harvard, Eaton worked as a drama critic at the *New York Tribune* (1902–1907), the *New York Sun* (1907–1908), and *American Magazine* (1909–1918). He was professor of playwriting at Yale from 1933 to 1947. In addition to theater history and literary criticism, Eaton wrote extensively about nature and outdoor life.

Eayres, Ellen Knowles (1889–1984), American publisher and philanthropist. After graduating from Vassar (1911), Eayres worked for Henry Holt and Co. as Alfred Harcourt's secretary. When Harcourt and Donald Brace left Holt to establish their own publishing house, she joined, and invested in, the new firm. She was made a director of Harcourt, Brace and Company in 1921, worked until 1930, and remained a director until 1939. She and Harcourt married in 1924 after the death of his first wife. In 1962, she formed the Alfred Harcourt Foundation and served as its president until her death.

Filsinger, Ernst B. (1880–1937), American businessman. Born in Saint Louis, Ernst Balthasar Filsinger married American poet Sara Teasdale, also from Saint Louis, in December 1914. In 1916, the couple moved to New York; Teasdale divorced Filsinger in 1929. An expert on foreign trade, Filsinger was president of the New York Export Managers Club (1927–1929). As president of Filsinger, Hines and Campbell, he represented the company's interests in Asia from offices in Shanghai. His *New York Times* obituary noted that he had "delivered several lectures at the Harvard Graduate School of Business Administration and was the author of 'Exporting to Latin America' and 'The Commercial Travelers Guide to Latin America.'"

Flint, F. S. (1885–1960), British poet and translator. Forced to leave school at age thirteen, Frank Stuart Flint continued his education in a workingman's night school while employed as a civil servant. Combining his poetry reading with study of Latin and French, he made himself a leading authority on modern French poetry. Flint's literary reputation rests upon his early work as an imagist poet and theorist. His notable works include *In the Net of the Stars* (1909), *Cadences* (1915), and *Otherworld: Cadences* (1920).

Ford, Julia (1859–1950), American collector, philanthropist, and author of children's books. The wife of financier Simeon Ford, she was a fixture in New York literary, artistic, and social circles, hosting a salon that featured such luminaries as W. B. Yeats, Kahlil Gibran, and Isadora Duncan. Her best known work, *Snickerty Nick and the Giant* (1919), featured illustrations by Arthur Rackham and rhymes by Witter Bynner. In 1934, she established the Julia Ellsworth Ford Foundation for the encouragement of young people's literature.

Fraser, Helen (1893–1992), American educator. Born of Canadian parents who settled near Manchester, New Hampshire, Fraser graduated from Plymouth Normal School (1912) and had a long career as an elementary school teacher, briefly in New Hampshire and then in Salem and New London, Connecticut. After retirement, she worked at the New London County Historical Society.

Gardner, Mary (?–1936), wife of Ernest Gardner. Mary Wilson Gardner met Frost at the Poetry Bookshop in London in January of 1913. The Frost family visited the Gardner home in Scotland in August 1913. Ernest Arthur Gardner (1862–1939) served as director of the British School of Archaeology at Athens (1887–1895) and as professor of archaeology (1896–1929) and vice chancellor at the University College London.

Garnett, Edward (1868–1937), British writer, critic, and editor. As mentor and friend, he encouraged the careers of Joseph Conrad and D. H. Lawrence. In publishing his own banned play, *The Breaking Point*, in 1907, he took an active role in the censorship battles over the English stage.

Gilchrist, Halley Phillips (1876–1944), vice president and secretary of the Southern Vermont Poetry Society. Born and raised in Vermont, Gilchrist trained in elocution and public speaking and completed a two-year program at the School of Expression in Boston in 1897. During the 1920s, she toured eastern cities with a program of readings in modern poetry. She later served as house mother for Smith College's Hubbard House.

Gile, Ray T. (1852–1939), American surveyor and engineer. Graduate of Dartmouth (1877) and the Thayer School of Civil Engineering (1879), Ray Timothy Gile was a highly regarded railroad surveyor. He worked primarily in

Coös and Grafton Counties and was appointed as surveyor for the state of New Hampshire when the boundary with Massachusetts was redrawn in the 1890s. He was a lifelong resident of Littleton, New Hampshire.

Goddard, Charles F. (1862–1954), American attorney. Educated at Columbia (AB 1887, AM 1888, LLB 1889), Charles Franc Goddard practiced law in New York City.

Goessmann, Helena T. (1868–1926), American educator and writer. Educated at Ohio State University (PhM 1895), Helena Theresa Goessman in 1910 joined the faculty in English at the Massachusetts Agricultural College in Amherst, where her father, Charles Goessmann, was a distinguished professor of Chemistry. First as assistant and then as instructor, she taught until her death in 1926. A regular participant in the Catholic Summer School of America, she published *The Christian Woman in Philanthropy* (1895) and a book of poems, *A Score of Songs* (1887).

Goodwillie, Mary C. (1870–1949), American philanthropist. Active in a variety of social and charitable organizations in Baltimore, she was chair of the Southern District of Federated Charities, president of the Baltimore Social Service Exchange from 1924–1945, president of the Friends of the Johns Hopkins University Library, and instrumental in establishing the Baltimore Poetry Society. In 1940, she was awarded an honorary MA degree by Johns Hopkins.

Greenaway, David (1885–1950?), American educator. David Emerson Greenaway graduated from Amherst College in 1905. A history teacher at the Springfield (Massachusetts) Technical High School for many years, he published a volume titled *History: Connecticut Valley Scotch-Irish Society* in 1922.

Hagedorn, Hermann (1882–1964), American novelist, poet, and biographer. Educated at Harvard (1907), he studied at the University of Berlin before returning to Harvard as an English instructor (1909–1911). He published *A Troop of the Guard: And Other Poems* (1909) and *Poems and Ballads* (1913) before involving himself with issues of war preparedness and German-American patriotism. In 1916, he led the formation of a group of writers called the Vigilantes and in 1918 published *Where Do You Stand?: An Appeal to Americans of German Origin*. In 1919, he published the first of his eight books on Roosevelt and became director of the Theodore Roosevelt Association. He wrote biographies of Leonard Wood, E. A. Robinson, and Albert Schweitzer, among others.

Haines, John W. (1875–1966), British lawyer, botanist, and poet. A prominent citizen of Gloucester, John Wilton Haines was friend, legal adviser, and patron to many of the Georgian poets.

Hall, Clarissa (1891–1988), American educator and bookkeeper. A student of Frost's at both Pinkerton Academy and Plymouth Normal School, Clarissa Gertrude Hall taught for a number of years in Whitefield, New Hampshire, before leaving the classroom to work as a bookkeeper in Manchester.

Harcourt, Alfred (1881–1954), American publisher. After graduating from Columbia University in 1904, Harcourt worked for Henry Holt and Company until 1919, when he founded—along with classmate and colleague Donald Brace—the publishing firm of Harcourt, Brace and Howe.

Harvey, Shirley (1892–1983), American poet and educator. After graduating from Dartmouth (1916), Shirley Wilcox Harvey taught English at Tufts College and completed an AM at Harvard (1918). He worked as a banker before joining the faculty of the Massachusetts College of Pharmacy. He then earned a PhD from Boston University (1936). He published a number of poems in journals, including *Poetry*, and one volume: *The Christmas Trail and Other Poems* (1916).

Haskell, Nelson (1866–1952), American physician. Educated at Amherst (1887), Nelson Carry Haskell completed a medical degree at Bowdoin College (1890) and practiced medicine in Amherst for fifty-five years. He was president of the New England Pediatrics Society from 1932 to 1933.

Herrick, Helen H. (1898–1977), American educator. Helen Hannah Herrick graduated from Northwestern University (1920), married Harry S. Churchill in 1921, and had three children. In the early 1930s, the family relocated to Florida, where she worked as a schoolteacher through the 1940s. When she wrote to Frost in 1917, she was a member of the Eulexia Literary Society at Northwestern.

Hinman, Carrie (1862–1949), assistant at the Athanaeum in Saint Johnsbury, Vermont. Carrie T. Hinman's husband, Jason (1885), and son George (1917), were both graduates of Amherst College.

Hocking, Ernest (1873–1966), American philosopher and professor at Harvard. Having studied with Josiah Royce, William Ernest Hocking elucidated his own version of idealist philosophy and developed what he called "negative pragmatism" in two major works: *The Meaning of God in Human Experience*

(1912) and *Morale and Its Enemies* (1918). Although his primary interest was in the philosophy of religion, Hocking also wrote extensively on issues of political philosophy. Hocking married Agnes O'Reilly, daughter of the journalist and poet John Boyle O'Reilly.

Hodge, Marie (1856–1944), American educator. Hodge graduated from Plymouth Normal School and worked as a schoolteacher until her marriage in 1883. Widowed in 1893, she returned to Plymouth Normal and served as a residence hall preceptress from 1910 to 1916. Subsequently she was a librarian in Plymouth for many years and published studies of local history.

Howe, M. A. DeWolfe (1864–1960), American editor and author. After graduating from Lehigh University (1886) and completing a master's degree at Harvard (1888), Mark Antony DeWolfe Howe served as associate editor of *The Youth's Companion* (1888–1893 and 1899–1913), assistant editor of *The Atlantic Monthly* (1893–1895), and vice president of the Atlantic Monthly Company (1911–1929). Prolific as both editor and author, he edited *The Beacon Biographies* (thirty-one volumes, 1899–1910), *The Memory of Lincoln* (1889), and *Home Letters of General Sherman* (1909), among other works; he authored volumes of Boston and regional history and biographies of Phillips Brooks, George Bancroft, Bishop Hare, and others, and won the Pulitzer Prize for Biography in 1925 for *Wendell Barrett and His Letters*. He also published one volume of poetry, *Harmonics*, in 1909.

Jacobs, H. G. (1880–1936), reporter, foreign correspondent, and editor. Harry Gordon Jacobs had a long career at the *Brooklyn Eagle* and wrote regularly on the literary and theatrical scene. His article on Frost was titled "A New Poet of the Hills. *North of Boston* by Robert Frost, Sounds a New Note in Our Literature."

Jewell, Ernest C. (1872–1938), American educator. Ernest Clarence Jewell attended Lawrence High School with Robert Frost and edited the *High School Bulletin* in which Frost's first poem, "La Noche Triste," was published. After graduating from Harvard (1896), he taught mathematics at Lawrence High School for many years.

Jiménez, Zenobia (1887–1956), Spanish translator and author. Translator of Bengali poet Rabindranath Tagore, Zenobia Camprubí Aymar Jiménez married poet Juan Ramón Jiménez in 1916. They fled Spain during the Civil War in 1936 and lived in Cuba, Puerto Rico, Florida, and Washington, DC, before settling in Puerto Rico in 1951. In addition to her many translations, she published poetry and four volumes of memoirs, the three volumes of *Diarios* (1937–1956) and *Juan Ramón y Yo* (1954). She died two days after Jiménez was awarded the Nobel Prize in Literature.

Johnson, Burges (1877–1963), American journalist, poet, and educator. A graduate of Amherst College (1899; LittD 1924), he was a reporter for the *New York Evening Post*. In 1915, he joined the English faculty at Vassar, teaching journalism and directing the college's public relations. He left Vassar in 1926 to teach at Syracuse University and then taught at Union College from 1935 until 1944. He served on the staffs of both Bread Loaf and the Rocky Mountains Writers' Conference. In addition to multiple volumes of light verse and frequent contributions to *Harpers*, *The Century*, and other magazines, he published *Essaying the Essay* (1927) and *Campus Versus Classroom: A Candid Appraisal of the American College* (1946).

Jones, Llewellyn (1884–1961), British-born editor and literary critic. From 1914 to 1932 he was the literary editor of the *Chicago Evening Post*. During the 1920s, he also taught writing at the University of Chicago and at Northwestern University.

Knopf, Alfred (1892–1984), American publisher. Born in New York and educated at Columbia (BA 1912), Alfred Abraham Knopf, Sr. clerked briefly at Doubleday before founding his own publishing house in 1915. Specializing initially in European literature, he developed an American list that included Theodore Dreiser, Langston Hughes, Vachel Lindsay, H. L. Mencken, and Knopf's personal favorite, Willa Cather. From 1924 to 1934, he published the literary magazine founded by Mencken and George Jean Nathan, *The American Mercury*.

Lloyd, Claude T. (1894–1968), American educator. Claude Thaddeus Lloyd graduated from Simmons College (1917) in Abilene TX and completed a PhD at Yale (1925). After teaching at the University of New Hampshire (1924–1931), he joined the English faculty at Phillips Exeter Academy (1931–1962) and became chair of the department in 1936. He was made Odlin Professor of English there in 1939.

Lowell, Amy (1874–1925), American poet, critic, anthologist, and collector. Born into the prominent Lowell family of Brookline, Massachusetts, Amy Lawrence Lowell did much to advance the cause of poetry in modern America. She published the first of her six books of poetry in 1912, the title of which—*A Dome of Many-Coloured Glass*—suggests her abiding interest in Keats, of whom she published a biography in 1925. Her second volume, *Sword*

Blades and Poppy Seed (1914), was written in free verse and "polyphonic prose" and revealed her immersion in the aesthetics of Imagism, the American emergence of which she facilitated through *Some Imagist Poets*, an annual anthology published in 1915, 1916, and 1917. Although a champion of free verse, she wrote a laudatory review of *North of Boston* and devoted a chapter to Frost in her *Tendencies in Modern American Poetry* (1917).

MacDonald, Francis C. (1874–1952), American educator, novelist, and poet. MacDonald graduated from Princeton (1896) and joined the English faculty there in 1905 as one of then-president Woodrow Wilson's original group of "preceptors"—young scholars hired to strengthen the newly established department. Between 1905 and his retirement in 1936, the only interruption of his service on the Princeton faculty came between 1917 and 1920 when he was in Tokyo as secretary to the American ambassador. His noteworthy publications include a novel, *Sorcery* (1919), and a volume of poetry, *Devices and Desires* (1922).

MacVeagh, Lincoln (1890–1972), American diplomat, archaeologist, and publisher. After graduating from Harvard in 1913 and studying languages at the Sorbonne, MacVeagh served with distinction as a U.S. Army officer in World War I. He joined Henry Holt and Company after the war and left in 1923 to establish the Dial Press. Between 1933 and 1953, MacVeagh served the Roosevelt and Truman administrations as ambassador to Greece, Iceland, South Africa, and Spain. During his years in Greece, he conducted excavations beneath the Acropolis and made contributions to the National Archaeological Museum of Athens.

Mansfield, Margery (1895–1984), American poet, journalist, and editor. A graduate of Smith College (1917), Margery Swett Mansfield published a number of poems and reviews in *Poetry* and other magazines during the 1920s, including a review of Gorham Munson's *Robert Frost: A Study in Sensibility and Good Sense* (1928). In 1928, she was named secretary to the Poetry Society of America. With her husband, Jay Van Everen, an early modernist painter and illustrator, she published *Workers in Fire: A Book about Poetry* in 1937. In the same year, she published a critical anthology entitled *American Women Poets*. After Van Everen's death in 1947, she married poet and editor Edmund Kelly Janes.

Manthey-Zorn, Otto (1879–1964), American scholar and educator. After graduating from Western Reserve University (1901), Manthey-Zorn completed a PhD at the University of Leipzig (1904). He joined the Amherst faculty in

1906 and was a professor of German there until he retired in 1955. In 1907 he married Canadian-born Ethel K. Bray. Among his notable works are *Germany in Travail* (1922) and *Dionysus: The Tragedy of Nietzsche* (1956).

Marks, Josephine Preston Peabody (1874–1922), American poet and dramatist. She taught at Wellesley College from 1901 to 1903 and authored numerous books, including *The Wayfarers: A Book of Verse* (1898), *Fortune and Men's Eyes: New Poems, with a Play* (1900), *The Singing Leaves: A Book of Songs and Spells* (1903), *The Wolf of Gubbio: A Comedy in Three Acts* (1913). In 1906 she married Lionel Simeon Marks, British-born professor of mechanical engineering at Harvard. She won the Stratford-on-Avon Prize for *The Piper: A Play in Four Acts* (1909), produced first in England (in 1910) and then in New York (in 1911).

McQuesten, Gertrude I. (1864–1931), American educator. A teacher at the Emerson College of Oratory and the New England Conservatory of Music in Boston, she met Frost in 1911 when she gave a reading at Pinkerton Academy. Her family lived in Plymouth, New Hampshire, and the Frosts became friends with her mother when Frost taught at Plymouth Normal School.

Meigs, Henry Tunis (1855–1932), owner of The Maples farm in Romney, Indiana.

Meiklejohn, Alexander (1872–1964), American philosopher and educator. Born in England, he was educated at Brown University (BA 1893; MA 1895) and Cornell University (PhD 1897). He joined the Brown Philosophy department in 1897 and in 1901 was made dean of the college, a position he held until he accepted the presidency at Amherst in 1913. He resigned from Amherst in 1923 and taught philosophy at the University of Wisconsin, where he started the University's Experimental College (1928–1932). He remained at Wisconsin until 1938 and spent the closing years of his career involved with adult education in San Francisco. He was the author of *The Liberal College* (1920), *Freedom and the College* (1923), *Free Speech and Its Relation to Self-Government* (1948), and *Political Freedom; the Constitutional Powers of the People* in (1960). A free-speech advocate, he was a member of the National Committee of the American Civil Liberties Union and was awarded the Presidential Medal of Freedom in 1963.

Melcher, Frederic G. (1879–1963), American publisher, editor, and bookseller. Although he had planned to attend Massachusetts Institute of Technology, financial circumstances led Frederic Gershom Melcher to accept a job in the mailroom of Estes and Lauriat Bookstore in Boston. Moving into sales, he developed what would be a lifetime commitment to children's books. After managing a bookstore in Indianapolis, he assumed the editorship of *Publishers' Weekly* in 1918. At the death of R. R. Bowker in 1933, he became president of the firm and then chairman of the board of directors in 1959. Throughout his career, he not only served the bookselling profession as head of many trade associations and programs but also advanced the field of library science and nurtured the development of children's literature. He established the Newbery Medal in 1922 and the Caldecott Medal in 1937.

Mencken, H. L. (1880–1956), American journalist, editor, essayist, and scholar. With a high school diploma from the Baltimore Polytechnic Institute and a correspondence course in writing, Henry Louis Mencken became the most influential journalist of his age. At the *Baltimore Morning Herald* (1899–1906) and the *Baltimore Sun* (1906–1941), he was a reporter, editor, columnist, and theater critic. In 1908, he joined the staff of *The Smart Set* and in 1914 became co-editor with George Jean Nathan. In his fifteen years at *The Smart Set*, he reviewed about 2,000 books, wrote nearly 200 articles, and established himself as one of the most significant critics of the day. From 1924 until 1933, he edited the *American Mercury*. He was the author of some thirty books and collections of essays and criticism, including the acclaimed philological study, *The American Language* (1919, 1945, 1948); and volumes on politics, religion, and ethics including *Notes on Democracy* (1926), *Treatise on the Gods* (1930), and *Treatise on Right and Wrong* (1934).

Monro, Harold (1879–1932), British poet and proprietor of the Poetry Bookshop in London, which served as a gathering place, reading venue, and temporary housing for many contemporary poets. Educated at Cambridge, Monro edited and published a series of influential magazines, the *Poetry Review, Poetry and Drama*, and *The Chapbook*, and was the publisher of the *Georgian Poetry* anthologies.

Monroe, Harriet (1860–1936), American poet, editor, publisher, and critic. While working as a freelance correspondent and art critic for the *Chicago Tribune*, Monroe convinced one hundred prominent Chicago business leaders to sponsor a magazine devoted to the new poetry. After founding *Poetry: A Magazine of Verse* in 1912, she served as its editor until 1936.

Moody, Harriet (1857–1932), American educator, entrepreneur, and patron of the arts. Born Harriet Tilden, the daughter of a wealthy Chicago businessman, she graduated from Cornell (1876) and completed a year of study at the Women's Medical College in Philadelphia before leaving to enter Chicago society. Her first marriage, to Edwin Brainard, a Chicago lawyer, ended in divorce. The death of her father led her in 1889 to seek employment as a high school English teacher. To support her invalid mother, she supplemented her income by launching a gourmet-delicacies business, which flourished until 1929. In 1909, after a ten-year friendship turned courtship, she married poet William Vaughn Moody, who died suddenly in 1910. In her later years, she maintained a residence in Chicago and an apartment in Greenwich Village, and she opened both to a host of younger writers and poets to whom she offered encouragement, friendship, and support.

Morse, Robert (1892–1978), American educator and civil servant. Robert Winthrop Morse graduated from Andover Phillips Academy in 1913, where he won a number of prizes in composition and oratory. He entered Bowdoin College, enlisted in the navy in 1918, and eventually graduated from Bowdoin in 1921. He began graduate study in literature at Yale but left in 1923, accepting a government appointment to teach in the Philippines. In subsequent documents, he identified his occupation as "clerical."

Mosher, Thomas Bird (1852–1923), American publisher and bibliophile. In addition to fine-press editions, Mosher published a magazine entitled the *Bibelot.* His list was focused primarily on the works of the Irish revival, the English aesthetes and Pre-Raphaelites, and the French symbolists, but he also published the first facsimile reprint of Whitman's 1855 *Leaves of Grass.*

Oppenheim, James (1882–1932), American poet, novelist, and editor. After attending Columbia (1901–1903), Oppenheim began a career as a teacher and social worker. His *Songs for the New Age* (1914) was a collection of Whitmanian free verse poems on themes of social justice. With Waldo Frank, Louis Untermeyer, and others, he founded *The Seven Arts* in 1916 to which he contributed editorials in free verse. Progressive in politics and a Jungian lay-analyst, he published thirteen books of poetry, fiction, and popular psychology.

Palmer, George Herbert (1842–1933), American scholar, translator, and philosopher. A professor of natural religion and moral philosophy at Harvard, Palmer translated Homer and authored studies of the works of George Herbert and Shakespeare. His important philosophical works include *The Field of Ethics* (1901), *The Nature of Goodness* (1904), and *Altruism: Its Nature and Varieties* (1919).

Peabody, Sabra (1876–1939?), Frost's childhood sweetheart. Sabra Jane Peabody was the daughter of Ephraim Peabody; her brother, Charles, was also a playmate of the young Frost. Thompson reports that Charlie taught the San

Francisco–born Frost to "swing" birches. The Peabody family lived along the rail line connecting Lawrence, Massachusetts, to Salem Depot, where the poet's mother taught school. Charles remained near Lawrence and joined the family construction business. Sabra Peabody did not marry until 1922, when, at age forty-five, she wed Levi Woodbury, age eighty-eight, who had amassed a considerable fortune in hotel and transportation businesses in Washington D.C. She was widowed in 1925 and last listed in the DC directory and as a shareholder in the Washington Railway & Electric Company in 1938.

Perry, Margaret (1876–1970), American poet. Daughter of Harvard professor and historian Thomas Sergeant Perry and painter Lily Cabot Perry, Margaret LaFarge Perry grew up in the center of Boston's intellectual and literary circles, counting Howells and James as family friends. She also enjoyed a friendship and correspondence with E. A. Robinson. She published a book of poems titled *Something Singing* in 1916. In the late teens and early 1920s, she was Corresponding Secretary to the New England Poetry Club. (It is not clear whether she actually received the letter addressed to her here, which RF sent to Louis Untermeyer.)

Phillips, Le Roy (1870–?), American editor and playwright. After graduating from Amherst College (1892), Phillips worked for *The Youth's Companion, Illustrated American,* and Ginn and Company. Bibliographer and editor of Henry James, he also published works about R. L. Stevenson and G. B. Shaw. He was also the author of a number of plays, largely one-act comedies.

Pond, James B. (1889–1961), American businessman. Son of Civil War hero and famed impresario, Major James Burton Pond (1838–1903), James Burton Pond, Jr. owned and managed the Pond Lyceum Bureau that his father had established in 1874. The bureau filed for bankruptcy in 1920, but Pond kept it afloat until 1933 and the depths of the Depression, when a second bankruptcy brought the enterprise to an end.

Porter, Charlotte (1857–1942), American poet, editor, and translator. Charlotte Endymion Porter, born Helen Charlotte Porter, was cofounder and editor of *Poet Lore* and editor of *Shakespeariana*. She also published editions of the works of Shakespeare, Robert Browning, and Elizabeth Barrett Browning.

Raitt, Myrtle (1898–1935). Myrtle Blanch Raitt [Mrs. Harold W. Hollis] lived in Derry, New Hampshire, during the years that Frost taught at Pinkerton. Although too young to have had Frost as a teacher, they would have been acquainted through her brother Vernon, eleven years her senior, who played on the Pinkerton football team. She married in 1927, moved first to Ohio and then Massachusetts, and had two children. She and a young son both died of pneumonia in 1935. Vernon Raitt (1887–1972) moved to Lawrence, Massachusetts and worked for the Boston-Maine railroad.

Reed, Edward Bliss (1872–1940), American scholar and poet. Educated at Yale (BA 1894; PhD 1896), he joined the English faculty in 1900 and was later a professor of both English and music. In addition to a collection of poems, *Sea Moods and Other Poems* (1917), and books on English lyric poetry, eighteenth-century English literature, and Shakespeare, he was an authority on medieval Christmas carols. He was assistant editor of *The Yale Review* from 1911 to 1928.

Reynardson, Margaret (1861–1930), British socialite. Wife of Aubrey H. Birch Reynardson, gentleman and solicitor at Gray's Inn, London, she was born Margaret Spring-Rice and was the sister of Sir Cecil Arthur Spring-Rice, British ambassador to the United States from 1912 to 1918.

Rice, Franklin P. (1852–1919), American printer and publisher. In the early 1870s Franklin Pierce Rice bought a printing press and undertook to preserve and publish the vital records of the towns of Worcester County, Massachusetts, dating back to colonial times. A lifelong project, his work did much to foster interest in historical preservation and genealogy in New England.

Ridge, Lola (1873–1941), Irish-born poet and editor. After a childhood in Dublin, Rose Emily "Lola" Ridge moved to New Zealand in 1887 and lived there and in Australia for twenty years. Briefly married in New Zealand, she moved to Sydney, Australia to study painting at Trinity College. She emigrated to the United States in 1907. In April 1918, *The New Republic* devoted three pages to "The Ghetto," a sequence of poems which would form the core of her collection *The Ghetto, and Other Poems* (1918). Additional volumes of poetry followed: *Sun-Up, and Other Poems* (1920), *Red Flag* (1927), *Firehead* (1929), and *Dance of Fire* (1935). She was a contributor, publicist, and editor at *Others* (1918–1919) and *Broom* (1922–1923).

Rittenhouse, Jessie (1869–1948), American poet and anthologist. After teaching school and working as a reporter in Rochester, New York, Jessie Belle Rittenhouse Scollard moved to Boston in 1899 and then to New York, where from 1905–1915 she was poetry reviewer for the *New York Times Book Review.* In 1914 Rittenhouse helped to found the Poetry Society of America, of which she was secretary until 1924. Active on the lecture and reading circuit, she published four books of poems, including *The Door of Dreams* (1918) and *Moving Tide: New and Selected Lyrics* (1939), and edited a series of influential anthologies including *Little Book of Modern Verse* (1913) and *Little Book of American Poets* (1915). In 1924, she married American poet Clinton Scollard (1860–1932). In 1930, she was the first recipient of the Poetry Society of America's Robert Frost Medal.

Robinson, E. A. (1869–1935), American poet. Born in Gardiner, Maine, Edwin Arlington Robinson established himself as a major poet and literary voice of New England with the publications of *Children of the Night* (1897) and *The Town Down the River* (1910). He won the Pulitzer Prize for Poetry three times during the 1920s for *Collected Poems* (1921), *The Man Who Died Twice* (1924), and *Tristram* (1927). Throughout his career, Robinson alternated between lyric poetry and book-length dramatic narratives, publishing twenty-eight volumes in total.

Root, E. Merrill (1895–1973), American poet, essayist, and educator. After graduating from Amherst (1917), Edward Merrill Root went to France as a member of the American Friends Service Committee and returned to study at Andover Theological Seminary. In 1920, he joined the English faculty at Earlham College in Indiana and taught there until his retirement in 1960. In the late 1930s his personal political position shifted from Quaker pacifism to extreme conservatism. His books *Collectivism on the Campus* (1954) and *Brainwashing in the High Schools* (1958) were vitriolic condemnations of American liberalism and the communism he saw as rampant in American education. In retirement, Root became an editor of *American Opinion*, the bimonthly magazine of the John Birch Society. Among his volumes of poetry are *Dawn Is Forever* (1938), *Before the Swallow Dares* (1947), and *Ulysses to Penelope* (1952), a sonnet sequence.

Rowell, Wilbur E. (1862–1946), prominent attorney, banker, and district court judge in Lawrence, Massachusetts. A graduate of Harvard Law School, in 1912 Rowell published an article in the *Survey* condemning the Lawrence textile workers' strike. He served as executor of the estate of William P. Frost, the poet's grandfather.

Rugg, Harold G. (1883–1957), librarian, historian, naturalist, and collector. A graduate of Dartmouth College (1906), Harold Goddard Rugg began his career as a library secretary in 1906, became executive assistant to the librarian in 1912, and was promoted to assistant librarian in 1919. He also held a faculty position in the Art Department, offering courses on the history of book design and printing. For thirty-nine years he served as the literary editor of the *Dartmouth Alumni Magazine*. He retired in 1953.

Scott, Charles P. G. (1853–1936), American philologist, editor, and Orientalist. Educated at Lafayette College (AB 1878) and Columbia (PhD 1881), Charles Payson Gurley Scott briefly taught Greek and Anglo-Saxon at Columbia. In 1883 he was appointed assistant editor and etymologist of the new *Century Dictionary* (1889) and he remained etymological editor through subsequent editions. In 1892 he was appointed editor in chief of the Lippincott Company's revision of Worcester's dictionary, a project that was not completed. He was a member of the Spelling Reform Association, and in 1905 he was appointed secretary of the Simplified Spelling Board. His notes on "A Dictionary of Etymological Terms," consisting of some 120,000 note cards, are in the Manuscript Collection at Columbia.

Sedgwick, Ellery (1872–1960), American journalist and editor. After graduating from Harvard in 1894, Sedgwick was assistant editor of *The Youth's Companion* in Boston (1896–1900) and editor of *Leslie's Monthly Magazine* (1900–1905) and the *American Magazine* (1906–1907) in New York. He purchased the Boston-based *The Atlantic Monthly* in 1908 and served as editor from 1909 until 1938. Under Sedgwick's direction, *The Atlantic Monthly* became a magazine of national social and literary influence.

Shaw, Albert (1857–1947), American journalist, author, and editor. Shaw published a number of works about international law and political institutions, and was editor in chief of the American edition of *Review of Reviews* from 1891 until 1937.

Sherman, Philip (1881–1957), American scholar and book collector. Educated at Brown University (AB 1902, AM 1903), Philip Darrell Sherman briefly taught German at Brown and English at Ohio Wesleyan, and matriculated in the PhD program in English at Johns Hopkins. He joined the English faculty at Oberlin in 1907 and remained there until retirement in 1942. His extensive library was bequeathed to Brown University.

Silver, Ernest L. (1878–1949), American educator. Ernest Leroy Silver was educated at Pinkerton Academy and Dartmouth College (BL 1899). He served as superintendent of schools in Rochester and Portsmouth, New Hampshire, and as principal of Pinkerton Academy before becoming principal of Plymouth Normal School, where Frost taught psychology (among other things) from 1911 to 1912. For thirty-five years, Silver served as principal, director, and president of the school that became Plymouth Teachers College in 1939 (now Plymouth State University).

Stork, Charles Wharton (1881–1971), American poet, playwright, editor, critic, and translator. Educated at Haverford College (AB 1902), Harvard (AM 1903), and the University of Pennsylvania (PhD 1905), Stork taught at Penn from 1908 to 1916 before resigning to devote himself to literary work. He was the editor of *Contemporary Verse* from 1917 to 1925. In addition to volumes of his own verse, drama, and criticism, he published translations of Norwegian, Danish, and Swedish writers and compiled anthologies of poetry translated from those languages.

Thomas, Edward (1878–1917), British poet, essayist, biographer, and reviewer. After taking a history degree at Oxford, Philip Edward Thomas earned a living as a reviewer for the *Daily Chronicle* and other publications while building a reputation as an essayist—largely on themes of nature and travel in England—and a biographical critic: *Richard Jefferies* (1909), *Maurice Maeterlinck* (1911), *Algernon Charles Swinburne* (1912), and *Walter Pater* (1913). After moving his family to the country in 1913, Thomas began to write fiction. Shortly thereafter, he met Frost, who persuaded him to follow what had long been his desire and write poetry. He enlisted in the British army in July 1915 and was killed at Arras, in France, in April 1917. Between 1914 and 1916 Thomas wrote 140 poems, none of which he would see published.

Thomas, Helen (1877–1967), British educator and author. Daughter of journalist James Ashcroft Noble, Helen Noble Thomas was educated at the Wintersdorf School. She worked as a governess before her marriage to Edward Thomas in 1899 and then as a schoolteacher. After Thomas's death, she wrote two autobiographical works about their life together: *As It Was* (1926) and *World without End* (1931).

Thomas, Rose Fay (1853–1929), American decorative artist and music critic. Daughter of a prominent Vermont Episcopal bishop, Rose Emily Fay Thomas was married to Theodore Thomas (1835–1905), concert violinist, and founder and first music director of the Chicago Symphony Orchestra.

Thorndike, Ashley H. (1871–1933), American editor and scholar. Educated at Wesleyan University (1893) and Harvard (PhD 1898), Ashley Horace Thorndike taught at Western Reserve and Northwestern before joining the English department at Columbia (1900–1933). A Shakespeare scholar, his publications include *Shakespeare's Theater* (1916) and *Shakespeare in America* (1927). With fellow Columbia professor John Cunliffe, he edited the thirty volume *Warner Library of the World's Best Literature* (1917). He was the first president of the

Shakespeare Association of America and secretary of the National Institute of Arts and Letters.

Tilley, Lois (1907–1976), American social worker. The daughter of Morris Tilley, Lois Frances Tilley Schneider Lewis graduated from the University of Michigan in 1930. She was married to Samuel Schneider, a photographer, and lived briefly in New York before returning to Ann Arbor. In 1969, she married the Reverend Henry C. Lewis, retired rector of Saint Andrew's Episcopal Church.

Tilley, Morris (1876–1947), American scholar and educator. A professor of English at the University of Michigan from 1906 until 1946. Morris Palmer Tilley earned a BA (1897) and MA (1899) in English from the University of Virginia; Tilley was also a student of German and completed a PhD in language and literature at the University of Leipzig in 1902. Tilley's most notable scholarly work was *A Dictionary of the Proverbs in England in the Sixteenth and Seventeenth Centuries* (1950).

Townsend, Charles (1887–1962), Canadian-American scholar. A graduate of McGill University (1909), Charles Louis Townsend completed a PhD at Harvard (1915) and taught briefly at Trinity College and Duke University before joining the faculty of Southwestern Presbyterian University in 1917 where he taught until retirement in 1954. Among his publications are *The Foes of Shakespeare* (1924) and *Problems on Nine Plays of Shakespeare* (1929). Southwestern Presbyterian became Southwestern University in 1925 and was renamed Rhodes College in 1984.

Untermeyer, Louis (1885–1977), American poet, anthologist, critic, and editor. Having left high school to work in his father's jewelry firm, Untermeyer published his first book of poems in 1911. Sympathetic to socialist causes, he wrote for many of the radical magazines of the time, including *The Masses* and *The Liberator.* In 1923 he left business to devote himself to writing. Over the next fifty years he wrote, edited, or translated more than one hundred books, including several volumes of his own poetry. His anthologies, notably *Modern American Poetry* (1919) and *Modern British Poetry* (1920) were regularly reissued and became classroom standards. As an anthologist and critic, he was an influential figure in the creation of a modern poetic canon. One of the original panelists on the TV game show *What's My Line,* he was blacklisted from television in 1951 as a communist sympathizer. In 1956 Untermeyer was awarded a Gold Medal by the Poetry Society of America. He was consultant in English poetry for the Library of Congress from 1961 until 1963.

Van Buren, E. Douglas (1881–1961), British archaeologist and wife of Albert William Van Buren, professor of archeology and head librarian at the American Academy in Rome. Educated at Cambridge University and a prolific author of scholarly books and articles, Elizabeth Douglas Van Buren was particularly renowned as an expert on Mesopotamian art and culture.

Ward, Susan Hayes (1828–1924), American art critic and editor. The sister of William Hayes Ward, she was educated at Wheaton Seminary, studied art in New York and Paris, and later attended the New England Female Medical College in Boston. She taught at the Berwick Academy in Maine, the Guilford Institute in Connecticut, and Knox Seminary in Galesburg, Illinois. Art critic of the New York *Independent* from 1883 to 1893 and its office editor from 1892 until 1898, she also wrote numerous articles on the household arts and mission work. Her publications include church histories, biographies, *The Green Guess Book* (1897)—a collection of riddle poems—and a meditation on Holman Hunt's painting *Christ at the Door* (1872).

Ward, William Hayes (1835–1916), American clergyman, editor, and Orientalist. After graduating from Amherst College (1856) and the Andover Theological Seminary (1859), Ward served briefly as pastor of a church in Kansas and as professor of Latin at Ripon College in Wisconsin. He joined the editorial staff of the New York *Independent* in 1868 and was editor in chief from 1896 until 1913. He wrote the biographical "memorial" that prefaces Mary Lanier's edition, *Poems of Sidney Lanier* (1884; subsequently reprinted numerous times).

Weygandt, Cornelius (1871–1957), American scholar and author. Educated at the University of Pennsylvania (1891), he worked five years as a newspaper reporter before joining the English faculty at Penn as an instructor in 1897. After completing a PhD in 1901, he rose to the rank of professor, and taught until retirement in 1952. He was responsible for bringing contemporary literature into the curriculum. His interest in the Celtic Renaissance led to *Irish Plays and Playwrights* (1914); *A Century of the English Novel* followed in 1925. In fifteen books between 1929 and 1946, he wrote about the heritage of his own Pennsylvania Dutch and about nature and folkways in Pennsylvania and New Hampshire.

Whicher, George (1889–1954), American scholar and educator. After graduating from Amherst (1910), George Frisbee Whicher completed his MA (1911) and PhD at Columbia (1915). He was professor of English at Amherst from 1915 to 1954. Notable among his many published works are *This Was a Poet: A*

Critical Biography of Emily Dickinson (1938), *The Goliard Poets: Medieval Latin Songs and Satires* (1949), and *Poetry and Civilization* (1955).

Whipple, George N. (1856–1940), American entrepeneur. George Noyes Whipple graduated from Amherst in 1878, began a business career as a warehouse manager in Boston, and then moved into advertising. Author of a number of class and fraternity (Psi Upsilon) hymns and odes, and a member of the American Folklore Society, Whipple had by 1915 established a Boston-based lyceum-lecture bureau he called the Players, "A National Association of Lecturers and Musicians." Willa Cather was among his clients.

White, Martha (1863–1944), American journalist and educator. A suffragette and a progressive, Martha E. D. White published a number of articles and reviews in *New England Magazine* under such titles as "The Work of Women's Clubs" and "New England in Contemporary Verse." In the 1920s she worked as a publicist for the League of Women Voters and published a primer on citizenship. She was married in 1890 to True Worthy White.

Wilkinson, Marguerite (1883–1928), American poet, anthologist, and critic. Canadian-born, Marguerite Ogden Bigelow Wilkinson grew up in Evanston IL and attended Northwestern University as a special student (1906–1908). Between 1910 and 1925, she published three volumes of poetry—*In Vivid Gardens* (1911), *Bluestone* (1920), and *The Great Dream* (1923)—a book of essays on contemporary poetry—*New Voices* (1919)—and an anthology—*Contemporary Poetry Prior to 1915* (1923). She was a regular contributor of poems, reviews, and essays to *Touchstone* and other journals and lectured widely on modern poetry.

Wood, Clement (1888–1950), American attorney, journalist, teacher, novelist, and poet. Educated at the University of Alabama (1909), Clement Richardson Wood received a law degree from Yale in 1911. He practiced law in Birmingham, Alabama, was assistant city attorney in 1912, and served as chief presiding magistrate of the Central Recorder's Court in 1913. Choosing a writing career over the law, he moved to Greenwich Village. Beginning with *Glad of Earth* (1917), he published fifteen volumes of poetry. He also published novels, mysteries, spy stories, literary criticism, biography, history, and writing guides. Anonymously, he contributed fifty-nine volumes to the *Little Blue Book* series. He was an active member of the Poetry Society of America.

Young, Charles Lowell (1865–1937), American scholar and teacher. After graduating from Harvard (AB 1893), Young joined the faculty at Wellesley in 1898;

he retired as a professor of American Literature in 1933. Young's most notable scholarly work, *Emerson's Montaigne*, was published posthumously in 1941.

Young, Stark (1881–1963), American playwright, novelist, painter, and literary critic. Young graduated from the University of Mississippi (1901), completed an MA at Columbia (1902), and joined the English faculty at Mississippi in 1905. He moved to the University of Texas in 1907 and then to Amherst College in 1915. He resigned in 1921 to become drama critic at *The New Republic*, from which he retired in 1947. In 1930, he contributed to the Agrarian manifesto *I'll Take My Stand*. In addition to five plays, a volume of poetry, and seven books on drama and the theater, he published four novels on Southern themes, the most successful of which was *So Red the Rose* (1934).

Chronology: 1874–February 1920

1874 Born on March 26 in San Francisco, California, first child of Isabelle Moodie and William Prescott Frost Jr., and named Robert Lee Frost after Confederate general Robert E. Lee. Mother, born 1844 in Alloa, Scotland, was the daughter of a sea captain who died soon after her birth; she was brought up by her father's parents, and after her grandfather's death she came to America in 1856 to live with her uncle in Columbus, Ohio, where she taught school (and once met William Dean Howells; RF would later write Walter Prichard Eaton: "Long long ago my mother was a little schoolma'am in Columbus Ohio when [Howells] was there and I have heard her speak of meeting him once or twice in society when Columbus society was gay in the sixties"). Father, born 1850 in Kingston, New Hampshire, was the only child of an old New England farming family. As a teenager during the Civil War he had run away from home to join the Army of Northern Virginia under Lee, getting as far as Philadelphia before he was caught and sent home. A Phi Beta Kappa graduate of Harvard, he met his wife in Lewistown, Pennsylvania, where they were both teaching; they were married in March 1873 (RF would later write, again to Eaton: "I am going to have to thank, when I get round to it, a dear old lady for remembering me as you may say before I was born or thought of—just before—remembering that is to say my mother and father as teachers in a little Pennsylvania mountain town the year before they married"). They moved to San Francisco soon after, and his father obtained a job as a journalist. (RF would later write Amy Lowell: "Doesnt the wonder grow that I have never written anything or as you say never published anything except about New England farms when you consider the jumble I am? Mother Scotch immigrant. Father oldest New England stock unmixed. Ten years in West.")

1875 Father becomes city editor of the *San Francisco Daily Evening Post*, edited by social reformer Henry George, a family friend (mother will later write book reviews and poems for the paper, and RF would several times speak of having met George in childhood).

1876 Travels east in spring with mother, who is expecting another child and is upset about father's drinking and gambling. Sister, Jeanie Florence, is born in grandparents' home in Lawrence, Massachusetts, on June 25. Spends autumn with maternal relatives in Columbus, Ohio. Returns to San Francisco in late November with mother, sister, and mother's old friend Blanche Rankin ("Aunt Blanche"), who will live with family for four years. Father is diagnosed as consumptive after defeating celebrated walker Dan O'Leary in six-day walking race.

1877–1878 Lives in Abbotsford House hotel (family moves often during years in San Francisco, living in both apartments and hotels). Receives religious instruction from mother, who reads stories from the Bible, and attends Sunday school at the Swedenborgian church. Father is stern and short-tempered.

1879 Goes to kindergarten for one day but suffers severe nervous pain in stomach and does not return.

1880 Father is elected as delegate to the Democratic National Convention in Cincinnati, which nominates General Winfield S. Hancock for president, and writes short campaign biography of General William S. Rosecrans, who is running for Congress. (RF would later write Ernest Silver: "Your politics fresh from Concord [NH] stir something in me that I must inherit from a politician father.") Grandparents visit in summer. RF enters first grade in public school, but soon drops out when nervous stomach pain returns and is educated by mother for the remainder of the school year; takes walks with her around San Francisco to learn the city's geography and history. Accompanies father to campaign events in San Francisco. (RF would later write, in "A Poet's Boyhood": "My father was chairman of the Democratic City Committee and my health not being very good I was kept out of school and taken down town with him to his office many, many days. I rode around with him in a buggy electioneering and tacking his card to the ceilings of saloons with a silver dollar for tack hammer. I often acted as his errand boy to the City Hall and to the office of the Democratic boss, Buckley, who was my kind friend. I had my lunches free off the saloon counters.") Though Rosecrans wins congressional race, father is deeply depressed by defeat of Hancock by Republican congressman James A. Garfield in presidential election.

1881 RF enters second grade. Baptized in mother's Swedenborgian church. He would later quip, in a letter to Amy Lowell, that he'd been "Presbeterian [*sic*], Unitarian, Swedenborgian, Nothing."

1882 Drops out of school in February when nervous pain in stomach returns and continues education at home. Goes with mother and sister to visit Aunt Blanche, now married and living in the Napa Valley, north of San Francisco.

1883 Enjoys hearing mother tell stories about Joan of Arc and characters in the Bible, myths, and fairy tales; she also reads aloud from works of Shakespeare, Poe, and George MacDonald (mother will later read aloud from *Tom Brown's School Days,* Emerson, Burns, Wordsworth, Bryant, Tennyson, and Longfellow). Sometimes hears voices when left alone and is told by mother that he shares her gift for "second hearing" and "second sight." Family vacations in summer at Bohemian Club camp in Sausalito (father is member). RF watches with terror while father takes long swims in San Francisco Bay. Father continues to drink as his health deteriorates.

1884 Accepted in a neighborhood gang after proving his courage by fighting two boys at once. Works briefly as paperboy. With sister, Jeanie, spends six weeks visiting Aunt Blanche in Napa Valley. Works enthusiastically in campaign of father, who has resigned his newspaper job to run for city tax collector on the Democratic ticket. Father loses election and is deeply depressed; with his health declining, he has difficulty finding and keeping work. Mother publishes children's story "The Land of Crystal."

1885 Father dies of tuberculosis on May 5, leaving family with only eight dollars after expenses are paid. Grandfather sends money, and family takes father's body to Lawrence, Massachusetts, for burial. Family lives with grandfather, now retired from job as mill supervisor, and grandmother, a former leader of the local suffragist movement. RF and Jeanie dislike grandparents' sternness and rigorous discipline and feel homesick for California. Family goes to Amherst, New Hampshire, in summer to stay at the farm of great-aunt Sarah Frost and her husband, Benjamin S. Messer. RF enjoys living with Messers and helping with berry picking, but dislikes the local teacher when school begins in the fall. Returns to Lawrence with mother and sister, where they move into their own apartment. Takes school placement tests and is placed in the third grade, while Jeanie qualifies for the fourth grade. Henry George visits the family while on a lecture tour in the Northeast.

1886 Moves with family to nearby Salem Depot, New Hampshire, where mother begins teaching the fifth to eighth grades in the district school. Enters the fifth-grade class with Jeanie. Learns to whittle and play baseball, and becomes close friends with Charles "Charlie" Peabody (son of Ephraim

Peabody), who teaches him how to climb and "swing" birches, trap animals, and collect birds' nests. Briefly works in shoe factory, then begins making shoe heels in leather shop of their landlord, Loren Bailey. Learns to box from older men in the shop. Becomes infatuated with Sabra Jane Peabody, Charlie's sister, and writes letters to her in September, the first letters that would survive ("There are not many girls I like," the young RF wrote, "but when I like them I fall dead in love with them"). Returns to school in fall.

1887 While mother continues to read aloud from works such as Scott's *Tale's of a Grandfather*, Percy's *Reliques*, and *The Poems of Ossian*, RF begins to enjoy reading on his own, starting with Jane Porter's *The Scottish Chiefs*. Studies geography, arithmetic, history, grammar, and reading in his mother's class. Memorizes Fitz-Greene Halleck's poem "Marco Bozzaris."

1888 Passes entrance examinations for Lawrence High School in June. Commutes with Jeanie by train from Salem Depot. Enrolls in the "classical" (college preparatory) program, taking courses in Latin, Greek history, Roman history, and algebra. Angered when complaints by some parents about mother's lax discipline and favoritism toward high school–bound students forces her resignation from the Salem Depot district school.

1889 Finishes school year at the head of the class, for the first time getting better grades than Jeanie. Pursues interest in Indian lore and history by reading Cooper's *Leatherstocking Tales*, Mary Hartwell Catherwood's *Romance of Dollard*, and William Hickling Prescott's *History of the Conquest of Mexico*. Works on Bailey's farm, and learns to sharpen a scythe and mow hay. Returns to Lawrence High School, taking courses in Greek, Latin, European history, and geometry; befriends older student, Carl Burell, who introduces him to works by American humorists Artemus Ward, Josh Billings, Petroleum V. Nasby, and Mark Twain, and to books on botany, astronomy, and evolutionary theory ("botanizing," as RF phrased it, would remain a lifelong avocation).

1890 After mother obtains teaching job in nearby Methuen, Massachusetts, family returns to Lawrence in February. With help from his mother, RF earns telescope by selling subscriptions to *The Youth's Companion*. Observes planets and stars, using astronomical maps from the Lawrence Public Library. First published poem, "La Noche Triste," based on an episode in Prescott's *Conquest of Mexico*, appears in the *Lawrence High School Bulletin* in April; a second poem, "The Song of the Wave," appears in the *Bulletin* in May. Joins the high school debating society. Finishes school year at the head of his class.

During the summer, family works at hotel in Ocean Park, Maine, where RF learns to play tennis. Takes Greek and Latin composition in the fall.

1891 Passes preliminary entrance examinations for Harvard College in Greek, Latin, Greek history, Roman history, algebra, geometry, and English literature. Elected chief editor of the *Bulletin* for the 1891–1892 school year. Publishes poem "A Dream of Julius Caesar" in May *Bulletin*. Maintains position as head of his class. Spends three weeks in the summer doing odd jobs on farm near Canobie Lake, New Hampshire. Works in the Braithwaite Woolen Mill in Lawrence for eleven hours a day, six days a week, until midsummer, when the workers force the mills to give them Saturday afternoons off. Meets and falls in love with fellow student Elinor Miriam White (born 1872) during the fall. Writes several editorials and articles for the *Bulletin* and plays on high school football team as right end. Jeanie is hospitalized in December with typhoid fever and is forced to drop out of school.

1892 Resigns as editor of the *Bulletin* when other students fail to do their share of the work. Begins to read widely in poetry and gives books by Emily Dickinson (*Poems*, first published in 1890) and Edward Rowland Sill to Elinor White. Shares valedictory honors with Elinor at graduation, and delivers address titled "A Monument to After-Thought Unveiled." Writes lyric for commencement hymn as class poet and is awarded prize for scholastic excellence. Works during summer as clerical assistant at mill in Lawrence. Becomes engaged to Elinor; they exchange rings in private ceremony as a pledge of love. Dependent on grandparents for financial support, enters Dartmouth College instead of Harvard because it is cheaper, and because grandparents blame Harvard for his father's bad habits. Takes courses in Greek, Latin, and mathematics. Buys copy of Francis Turner Palgrave's *The Golden Treasury of Songs and Lyrics* and reads intensively on his own in English lyric poetry. Restless, and bored by college life, leaves Dartmouth at the end of December. (He would later write Harold Goddard Rugg, a librarian at Dartmouth: "I'm afraid I wasn't much of a college man in your sense of the word. I was getting past the point when I could show any great interest in any task not self-imposed. . . . For the rest I wrote a good deal and was off in such places as the Vale of Tempe and on the walk east of the town that I called the Five Mile Round. I wrote one of the poems I still care for at about that time. It is preserved in my first book, 'A Boys Will.' I wrote while the ashes accumulated on the floor in front of my stove door and would have gone on accumulating to the room door if my mother hadn't sent a friend a hundred miles to shovel up and clean house for me.")

1893 Takes over mother's unruly eighth-grade class in Methuen for several weeks and canes several students. Quits teaching job to help Elinor's mother and ailing sister Ada; finds house for them in Salem and lives with them through the summer. When Elinor returns from St. Lawrence University in Canton, New York, in April, RF tries to persuade her to leave college and marry him, but she returns to college in September. Works at the Arlington Woolen Mill in Lawrence, changing carbon filaments in ceiling arc lamps. Studies Shakespeare during spare hours while living with mother and sister in an apartment in Lawrence. Beaten up by former students he had caned earlier in the year.

1894 Quits job at the mill in February. Begins teaching grades one through six in Salem. Learns in March that the *Independent* will publish his poem "My Butterfly: An Elegy" and pay him fifteen dollars for it. With an April 22 letter, begins long correspondence with Susan Hayes Ward, literary editor of the *Independent,* and writes her that his four favorite poems are Keats's "Hyperion," Shelley's "Prometheus," Tennyson's "Morte D'Arthur," and Browning's "Saul" (and also adds: "to betray myself utterly, such an one am I that even in my failures I find all the promise I require to justify the astonishing magnitude of my ambition"). Writes to Ward on June 10, acknowledging receipt of *Poems of Sidney Lanier* (Scribner's, 1891) edited by the poet's wife, Mary D. Lanier, with a "memorial" written by Hayes's brother, William Hayes Ward ("As you expected I have been very much interested in the memorial; and I have been enthused over what I conceive to be Lanier's theories of art. I wish I had the Elizabethan knack of expressing gratitude"). Tries unsuccessfully to convince Elinor to marry him at once. Works unhappily at odd jobs in the summer, convinced that Elinor is engaged to another man. Has local printer prepare two copies of *Twilight*, containing his poems "Twilight," "My Butterfly: An Elegy," "Summering," "The Falls," and "An Unhistoric Spot." Goes in the fall to St. Lawrence University to present Elinor with a copy but is thrown into despair by her cool reception; destroys his own copy and returns home. Still distraught, decides to go to the Dismal Swamp on the Virginia–North Carolina border. Leaves Lawrence on November 6 and travels by train and boat to Norfolk, Virginia, then follows wagon road and walks for miles into the swamp at night. Meets a party of boatmen at canal lock who agree to take him through swamp to Elizabeth City, North

Carolina. Stays with boat as it crosses Albemarle Sound to Nags Head on the Atlantic coast. Begins return journey by hopping freight cars from Elizabeth City to Baltimore. Exhausted and frightened, writes mother for return fare and arrives in Lawrence on November 30. Learns that "My Butterfly: An Elegy" had appeared in the *Independent* on November 8. (Will continue to publish poems in that journal.)

1895 Briefly works as journalist for the *Lawrence Daily American* and for the *Sentinel*, also published in Lawrence (in a January 30 letter to Susan Hayes Ward he writes: "You are not to pardon my remissness: but it is the truth that you have wished me well to such a good purpose that I have been busy night and day for two weeks. I am a reporter on a local newspaper!"). Tutors students in school started by his mother and sister. Rents cabin at Ossipee Mountain, New Hampshire, to be near Elinor, who has graduated from St. Lawrence and is spending the summer with her sister Leona White Harvey, a portrait painter. Tutors two students who stay with him for several weeks. Returns to help mother find better accommodations for her private school, where Elinor begins teaching in the fall. RF teaches at Salem district school. Marries Elinor White in Lawrence on December 19 in ceremony conducted by Swedenborgian pastor.

1896 Lives with Elinor and his mother and sister. Writes poems but feels they are not good enough (writes to Ward: "I fear I am not a poet, or but a very incomprehensible one"). Suffers from nervous ailments and stomach pains. Goes with Elinor on delayed honeymoon to rural Allenstown, New Hampshire, where they rent a cottage near the home of their high school friend Carl Burrell. Under Burrell's influence, RF renews his interest in botany; makes frequent collecting forays into the countryside and reads with pleasure Mrs. William Starr Dana's *How to Know the Wild Flowers*. Dismayed when Burrell is severely injured while working in a box factory. Returns to Lawrence and helps move mother's school into house on Haverhill Street; RF and Elinor take apartment on second floor. Teaches older students in mother's school. Son Elliott is born on September 25. Fined ten dollars in December for hitting lodger during quarrel.

1897 Publishes poem "Greece," inspired by the Greco-Turkish War, in the *Boston Evening Transcript* on April 30. Spends summer with wife and son in Amesbury, Massachusetts. Passes Harvard College entrance examinations in Greek, Latin, ancient history, English, French, and physical science (writes to Dean LeBaron Russell Brigs on September 11: "I desire to enter Harvard this fall, if possible a candidate for a degree from the outset. It came to me as a surprise only the other day that I might reasonably hope to do so consequently I find myself somewhat unprepared for examination. This is the great difficulty. . . . In particular I have neglected my Greek. If proficiency in English were any consideration, I make no doubt I could pass an examination in that. You will find verses of my inditing in the current number of the Independent and others better in back numbers. I might possibly pass in French also and in Physics and Astronomy for that matter but in Greek I fear not. You'll say it doesn't sound very encouraging.") With money borrowed from grandfather, enters Harvard as a freshman. Moves into a single room in Cambridge and takes part-time job at a North Cambridge night school. Studies German, English composition, and Latin. Joined by Elinor, Elliott, and his mother-in-law in late fall; moves with them into larger apartment in Cambridge.

1898 Awarded Sewall Scholarship for academic excellence. Spends summer in Amesbury, Massachusetts. Suffers from chills and chest pains, which doctor thinks may be consumption. Returns to Harvard in the fall; Elinor, who is again pregnant, remains in Lawrence. Takes Greek, Latin, and philosophy, studying with George Santayana, and Hugo Munsterberg, who assigns William James's *Psychology: The Briefer Course* as course text, and with George Herbert Palmer (he would write Palmer seventeen years later: "Any time these twenty years if I had been asked to name my own judges to judge me when I was ready I should have chosen you for one. You may wonder where I have come near you to have learned such respect for your judgement. It is not altogether in your writing; for I have sat with you in the room walled all on one side with poetry and heard you talk of Old Walt and of the farmers' wives in Boxford [Massachusetts] (I think) who liked to hear you read 'The Ring and the Book' "). About James RF would later say: "My greatest inspiration, when I was a student, was a man whose classes I never attended." Returns to Lawrence once a week to see Elinor and teach evening classes in mother's school.

1899 Continues regular studies and audits Nathaniel Shaler's course in historical geology. Suffers recurrence of chest pains and chills and worries about Elinor's pregnancy and his mother's health. Withdraws from Harvard on March 31. Daughter Lesley is born on April 28. After doctor warns that sedentary work would harm his health, takes up poultry farming with financial help from grandfather. Rents a house and barn in Methuen, Massachusetts, and buys 200 eggs for incubation. Insists that his mother see a doctor and learns that she has advanced cancer; she comes to live with family in Methuen.

1900 Enjoys tending chickens. Elliott dies of cholera on July 8 and is buried in Lawrence. Elinor suffers severe depression. RF's health declines, as recurring chest pains, fevers, and frequent nightmares cause him to fear consumption. Mother enters sanatorium in Penacook, New Hampshire. RF moves family to thirty-acre farm in Derry, New Hampshire, purchased by grandfather, who arranges to have Carl Burrell and his grandfather, Jonathan Eastman, move in to help with farming chores. Mother dies of cancer on November 2 and is buried in Lawrence.

1901 Writes poems at night despite depression, then begins to feel better when spring arrives. Botanizes with Burrell, often taking Lesley along. Reads Thoreau's *Walden* for the first time. Grandfather William Prescott Frost dies on July 10; his will gives RF a $500 annuity and use of the Derry farm for ten years, after which the annuity is to be increased to $800 and RF is to be given ownership of the farm.

1902 Takes over most of the farming duties in spring when Burrell leaves after Jonathan Eastman dies. Borrows money from high-school friend Ernest Jewell to expand poultry business; years later, dispute arises as to whether RF duly repaid the debt. Son Carol is born on May 27.

1903 Publishes short story "Trap Nests" in *The Eastern Poultryman* in February (will publish total of eleven stories and articles in *The Poultryman* and in *Farm-Poultry*, 1903 to 1905). Vacations in March with family in New York City; makes several calls on editors but is unable to interest them in his poetry. Daughter Irma is born on June 27.

1904 Continues to write poetry at night at the kitchen table. Enjoys company of neighbor Napoleon Guay and deepens friendship with poultryman John Hall.

1905 Daughter Marjorie is born on March 28.

1906 Secures part-time position teaching English literature at Pinkerton Academy in Derry. Publishes poem "The Tuft of Flowers" in the *Derry Enterprise* in March. Goes alone to Bethlehem, New Hampshire, in the White Mountains in August to relieve the severe hay fever that increasingly troubles him. Stays with John and Mary Lynch, who become family friends. Assumes full-time teaching post at Pinkerton Academy (writes to Susan Hayes

Ward on December 26: "I had just begun teaching at Pinkerton Academy when my poem about the heretofore ['The Trial By Existence'] turned up in the school library. Its effect was startling. From the moment of its appearance, all the teachers abruptly broke off all but the most diplomatic relations with me. Put to it for a reason, I thought at first my poem had led them to question my orthodoxy [if not my sanity.] Then I thought that a flock of teachers would be more apt to loathe me for misspelling Derry than for grafting Schopenhauer upon Christianity. Mr Merriam [a clergyman in Derry] says that I was twice wrong. I had made myself unpopular by the simple act of neglecting to give Pinkerton the credit for harboring the poet that wrote the poem. It was too funny"). Works on poems in sonnet form in an effort to master it.

1907–1908 Writes poem "The Later Minstrel" for the Pinkerton celebration of the one-hundredth anniversary of Longfellow's birth. Contracts pneumonia in March and is sick throughout the spring term. Daughter Elinor Bettina is born on June 18 and dies on June 21, 1907. Takes family to Bethlehem, New Hampshire, in August 1907, where they stay with the Lynches for six weeks (will also visit in the summer of 1908 and, later still, in the spring of 1915); Susan Hayes Ward visits the family while there. Resumes teaching at Pinkerton ("my little capacities have been taxed to the utmost in getting our English department to rights at school," he writes to Ward on November 4. "On top of everything else I have been asked to prepare a historical article on the Academy—in prose"); one of his students, John Bartlett, star pupil and captain of the football team, will become a lifelong friend and correspondent. Continues to write poems at night.

1909 Impresses Henry C. Morrison, New Hampshire superintendent of public instruction, when he visits Pinkerton; Morrison arranges for RF to lecture about his teaching methods before several conventions of New Hampshire teachers. Poem "Into Mine Own" appears in *New England Magazine* in May. Sells remaining poultry and moves family from the farm to apartment in nearby Derry Village. Takes family on camping and botanizing trip to Lake Willoughby in Vermont. Supervises *The Pinkerton Critic*, student literary magazine.

1910 Directs students in series of five plays (Marlowe's *Doctor Faustus*, Milton's *Comus*, Sheridan's *The Rivals*, and Yeats's *The Land of Heart's Desire* and *Cathleen ni Houlihan*). (Pens a notice for the local paper: "Beginning Thursday, May 26, and continuing at intervals of a week, the editorial board of the

Pinkerton Critic will give in Academy Hall a series of noted plays illustrating four periods of English dramatic literature. . . . The set, five in all [two of which will be given the same evening as being by the same author], will constitute a good short course in literature, intended to cultivate in school a taste for the better written sort of plays. But while all are literary and the object in staging them is largely educational, it must not be inferred that they have not been selected without regard to the entertainment they are likely to afford"). Revises English curriculum for the Pinkerton Academy and develops program emphasizing an informal, conversational teaching style. (Writes in school catalog: "The general aim of the course in English is twofold: to bring our students under the influence of the great books, and to teach them the satisfactions of superior speech.") Father-in-law Edwin White dies of heart disease while visiting the Frost family on May 26. Family vacations with the Lynches in Bethlehem in August.

1911 Accepts offer from former Pinkerton headmaster Ernest LeRoy Silver to teach at the State Normal School and moves family to Plymouth. Teaches courses in education and psychology; assigns works by Pestalozzi, Rousseau, Plato, and William James's *Psychology: The Briefer Course* and *Talks to Teachers on Psychology and to Students on Some of Life's Ideals*. Befriends Sidney Cox, a young teacher at Plymouth High School (will often write to him in later years). Sells the Derry farm in November. Sews together a booklet of seventeen poems and sends it to Susan Hayes Ward, literary editor of the *Independent*, as a Christmas gift. (Writes to her: "It represents . . . not the long deferred forward movement you are living in wait for, but only the grim stand it was necessary for me to make until I gather myself together. The forward movement is to begin next year.") Visits the Wards in New York City during Christmas vacation. Reads Henri Bergson's *Creative Evolution* en route.

1912 On February 19 begins a correspondence with Thomas Bird Mosher, publisher, and editor of *The Bibelot*, enclosing with the letter a fair copy of "Reluctance," which had lately been rejected by *The Atlantic Monthly*. On learning that "Reluctance" and "My November Guest" are to be published in the fall (in, respectively, *The Youth's Companion* and *The Forum*), writes to Mosher on March 4: "I do not say that either of them heralds a new force in literature. Indeed I think I have others still under cover that more nearly represent what I am going to be." Spends time with family in Franconia, New Hampshire, after school ends in summer and considers buying a farm there (he would do so three years later, in the spring of 1915). Decides to live in England for a few years and devote himself to writing full time. Resigns teaching position and sails from Boston with family on August 23, arriving in London on September 2. Stays in London for a week, attending the theater, before renting a cottage in Beaconsfield, Buckinghamshire, twenty miles north of the city (writes to Susan Hayes Ward on September 15: "Here we are between high hedges of laurel and red-osier dogwood, within a mile or two of where Milton finished Paradise Lost on the one hand and a mile or two of where Grey [Thomas Gray] lies buried on the other and within as many rods or furlongs of the house where Chesterton tries truth to see if it wont prove as true upside down as it does right side up. To London town what is it but a run?"). Prepares manuscript of *A Boy's Will* in October and submits it to London firm of David Nutt and Company, which accepts it for publication. In November, learns that Mosher wants to publish the book, and replies by letter: "The Dea knows I should like nothing better than to see my first book, 'A Boy's Will,' in your Lyric Garland Series. . . . If I ever published anything, I fully expected it would be through some American publisher. But see how little I knew myself. Wholly on impulse one day I took my MS. of A Boy's Will to London and left it with the publisher whose imprint was the first I had noticed in a volume of minor verse on arriving in England, viz., David Nutt. I suppose I did it to see what would happen, as once on a time I short-circuited a dynamo with a two-foot length of wire held between the brushes. What happened pleased me at first—in the case of the MS., I mean. I am not so sure how I feel about it now. David Nutt made me a proposal on a royalty basis. I have signed no contract as yet, but after what has passed, I suppose I am bound to sign, if pressed, almost anything that doesn't seem too one-sided." Signs contract with David Nutt in December. On Christmas Day, writes to Ernest Silver: "Very little of what I have done lately goes to swell the first book, just one or two things to round out the idea. You may look for a slender thing with a slender psychological interest to eke out the lyrical. Call it a study in a certain kind of waywardness. My publisher is David Nutt of London and Paris, a friend as it turns out of [Henri] Bergson's."

1913 On January 8, attends opening of Harold Monro's Poetry Bookshop in Kensington, where he meets poet Frank S. Flint, who later introduces him to Ezra Pound. Begins correspondence with Harriet Monroe (editor of *Poetry* magazine) in late January. Through Pound, meets, as the winter and spring unfold, Richard Aldington, Hilda Doolittle, Maurice Hewlett, Ford Hermann Hueffer (Ford Madox Ford), May Sinclair, Ernest Rhys, and William Butler Yeats (who tells Pound that *A Boy's Will* is "the best poetry written in America for a long time"). *A Boy's Will* is published on April 1 and is favorably reviewed by Pound in *Poetry*, by Flint in *Poetry and Drama*, and by Norman Douglas in *The English Review*. In June and July, RF meets with T. E. Hulme and Flint to discuss poetics; begins (in July) to set down ideas about "the sounds of sense with all their irregularity of accent across the regular beat of the metre" in series of letters to American friends John Bartlett and Sidney Cox. Friendship with Pound is strained (writes to Mosher in July: "He says I must write something much more like *vers libre* or he will let me perish by neglect. He really threatens"). Vacations with family in Scotland in late summer. Resumes literary contacts in London, meeting Walter de la Mare, Rupert Brooke, Laurence Binyon, W. H. Davies, Wilfrid Gibson, Lascelles Abercrombie, and Robert Bridges, and attending weekly gatherings at homes of Hulme and Yeats. Forms close friendship with essayist and critic Edward Thomas, whom he meets in October. Writes to Bartlett in November: "There is a kind of success called 'of esteem' and it butters no parsnips. It means a success with the critical few who are supposed to know. But really to arrive where I can stand on my legs as a poet and nothing else I must get outside that circle to the general reader who buys books in their thousands. I may not be able to do that. I believe in doing it—dont you doubt me there. I want to be a poet for all sorts and kinds. I could never make a merit of being caviare [*sic*] to the crowd the way my quasi-friend Pound does. I want to reach out, and would if it were a thing I could do by taking thought." Prepares manuscript of *North of Boston* during the fall. Introduces Edward Thomas ("that gentle person," as he put it in a letter) to Flint in December.

1914 In January, offers *North of Boston* to Sherman-French and Company (in Boston), until David Nutt informs him that his contract forbids it. Meets W. H. Davies (author of *Autobiography of a Supertramp*) in February. In May, resettles the family in old house near Dymock, Gloucestershire, to be near friends Gibson and Abercrombie. *North of Boston* is published on May 15 by David Nutt and Company and is favorably reviewed in *The Nation* (London), the *Outlook*, the *Times Literary Supplement*, *Pall Mall Gazette*, *The English Review*, the *Bookman*, the *Daily News*, and other periodicals. Spends much time with Thomas and encourages him to write poetry. In June, becomes friends with Gloucestershire barrister and botanist John W. Haines. Writes to John Cournos in July: "My versification [in *North of Boston*] seems to bother people more than I should have expected—I suppose because I have been so long accustomed to thinking of it in my own private way. It is as simple as this: there are the very regular pre-established accent and measure of blank verse; and there are the very irregular accent and measure of speaking intonation. I am never more pleased than when I can get these into strained relation. I like to drag and break the intonation across the metre as waves first comb and then break stumbling on the shingle." Is amused when local people think he may be a spy after the outbreak of World War I in August. Writes to Sidney Cox on the twentieth: "The war is an ill wind to me. It ends for the time being the thought of publishing any more books. Our game is up. There will really be genuine suffering among the younger writers. My friends have all been notified by the editors they live on that there will be no more space for special articles and reviews till the war is over. . . . So we may be coming home if we can find the fare or a job to pay the fare after we get there." In September, moves in with Abercrombie family (at "The Gallows") to save expenses. Travels with daughter Lesley to Scotland to see his friend, the gentleman-scholar James Cruickshank Smith, returning to The Gallows in early October. Learns (also in October) that New York publishing firm of Henry Holt and Company will publish his books in the United States. Decides, late in the year, to return to America, borrowing money from friends to help finance passage. Worries (in December) that review of *North of Boston* by Pound in *Poetry* may cause Americans to consider him to be one of Pound's "party of American literary refugees."

1915 In January, makes a quick trip to Scotland to see (again) James Cruickshank Smith. Briefly visits Edward Thomas (in Petersfield) in early February. Sails from Liverpool on February 13 with family and Thomas's fifteen-year-old son, Mervyn (who is to visit friends in New Hampshire); entertains the idea of bringing Thomas to New England, where the two might form a kind of "literary summer camp" or writers' colony. Arrives in New York February 23 and learns that *North of Boston* was published by Henry Holt and Company on February 20. Remains in New York City while family goes to the John Lynch farm in Bethlehem, New Hampshire (where RF will be based until he buys, in May, a farm in nearby Franconia). Meets with Holt editor Alfred Harcourt and editors of *The New Republic*, which had recently published "The Death of the Hired Man" and a favorable review of *North of Boston* by Amy Lowell. Visits sister, Jeanie, now teaching in Pennsylvania and increasingly troubled, and convinces her to attend college (she will receive bachelor of arts degree from the University of Michigan in 1918). On March 22, writes the first of what will be scores of letters to poet, critic, and anthologist Louis Untermeyer, initiating an important and lifelong friendship. Travels to Boston in April and meets poet and literary editor of the *Boston Evening Transcript*, William Stanley Braithwaite, *The Atlantic Monthly* editor Ellery Sedgwick, Alice Brown (the novelist), Albert Shaw (an editor), Sylvester Baxter (a critic), Amy Lowell, John Gould Fletcher, and Nathan Haskell Dole (among others). Rejoins family in Bethlehem. *A Boy's Will* is published by Henry Holt and Company in April; RF is surprised by number of good reviews. In May, buys farm in Franconia, New Hampshire (population 504, in the 1910 census). Suffers great nervousness while addressing Boston Authors Club the same month, but feels more at ease when reading poems "Birches," "The Road Not Taken," and "The Sound of Trees" at Tufts College on the fifth; gives informal talks at the Browne and Nichols School in Cambridge on the twentieth, and befriends its cofounder George Browne (who has a place not far from Franconia). Meets poet Edwin Arlington Robinson, whom he admires. Favorable article on RF and *North of Boston* appears in the *Chicago Evening Post*. Moves to farm in Franconia in June and, making frequent forays to Boston and elsewhere as the year unfolds, embarks on a busy schedule of lectures and readings on "The Sound of Poetry" and other themes (is paid $50 to $75 per appearance, and will, within a year or two, command as much as $100 to $150). When at home in Franconia, writes poems on a homemade writing board that attaches to a Morris chair. Writes to Edward Thomas on June 26: "You begin to talk as if you werent coming to America to farm. We have gone too far into the wilds for you or something. It was inconsiderate of us. But listen: this farm is intended for the lecture camp. We won't make it our winter home for more than a couple of years. It is a picturesque spot and it is in the region where I have to take refuge for two months a year from hay fever. That's all you can say for it. . . . But this place will always be here for our lecture camp scheme when that shall come to anything." Learns that *North of Boston* is selling very well. In August, *The Atlantic Monthly* publishes "Birches," "The Road Not Taken," and "The Sound of Trees," along with an important essay on RF by the English critic Edward Garnett. Sends children to public school (they had been educated at home since the family left Plymouth in 1912). Visits John Bartlett in Raymond, New Hampshire, in late August. Visits William Dean Howells at the New York offices of *Harper's Magazine* in early September. Befriends Katharine Lee Bates and opens a correspondence with her, writing, on October 21: "If you *will* remember me for a lecture and reading at Wellesley when it can be thought of as being my turn. It's the colleges I look to for the chance to say certain things on the sound of poetry that are going to trouble me as long as they remain unsaid. Not everybody would be interested in my ideas. I'm not sure that many would be outside the circles where books are made and studied. They have value I should say chiefly in education and criticism." Lectures in Cambridge, and in Concord, Andover, and Milton (Massachusetts) in November. On November 27, attends a staging of "Home Burial" in Boston (arranged by the critic and poet Charlotte Endymion Porter). Frightened when Elinor, who is pregnant and has a weak heart, becomes very ill; she recovers after suffering a miscarriage on November 29. (Writes to Lascelles Abercrombie on December 1: "Just a word to you and Catherine to let you know that we are out of those woods—though perhaps not yet far enough to feel safe in crowing. We are still six in the family, no more and, thank God, no less.")

1916 In January, gives talks and readings in Massachusetts and New Hampshire. On January 25 addresses the Poetry Society of America in New York. In April, lectures and reads in and around Philadelphia, and at Amherst College. Reads before the Browning Society in Philadelphia on June 1, and then in Providence, Rhode Island. At Untermeyer's request, joins the editorial board of a new literary magazine, the *Seven Arts*. Reads "The Bonfire" before the Phi Beta Kappa Society at Harvard on June 19. From July 24 to July 29 gives talks and readings at a summer seminar held at Plymouth Normal School (New Hampshire), where he taught in 1911–1912. Stays above the hay-fever line on the farm in Franconia during most of late summer. In consultation with his publisher, decides to issue a third volume of poetry late in the year. On August 15 writes to Edward Thomas: "First I want to give you an accounting. I got here a year ago last March, didn't I? I have earned by poetry alone in the year and a half about a thousand dollars—it never can happen again—and by lecturing nearly another thousand. It has cost us more than it used to to live—partly on account of the war and partly on account of the ill health of the youngsters. Still one feels that we ought to have something to show for all that swag; and we have: we have this farm bought and nearly paid for. Such is poetry when the right people boom it." In September, urges Harriet Monroe (editor of *Poetry*) to read some of Thomas's poetry; tries without success to interest Henry Holt and Company in Thomas's book *Four and Twenty Blackbirds* (though he will succeed in placing with Holt Thomas's first volume of poetry, which he asked Thomas to send him on October 15).

In October writes his friend Morris Tilley (professor of English at the University of Michigan), seeking assistance for his sister, Jeanie, who is a student in Ann Arbor. Elected to the National Institute of Arts and Letters. Visits New York to inscribe copies of *Mountain Interval*, published by Holt on November 27; advance orders exceed 2,000 copies. On December 15 meets with Alexander Meiklejohn, president of Amherst College, and accepts an appointment to teach (at the rank of full professor) for one semester at a salary of $2,000.

1917 On January 9, again speaks of Edward Thomas's poems in a letter to Harriet Monroe ("Here I sit admiring these beautiful poems but not daring to urge them on anyone else for fear I shall be suspected of admiring them for love of their author. If Edward Eastaway [Thomas's nom de plume] gets killed before the war is over [he is with the artillery] there will be plenty found to like them and then where will my credit be for having liked them first.") Moves family to Amherst, Massachusetts, settling, by January 23, in a house on Dana Street. Begins teaching courses in poetry appreciation and in pre-Shakespearean drama. One-act play *A Way Out* is published in the *Seven Arts* in February. Continues to give talks and readings, appearing before the Freneau Club at Princeton University on February 1 (the young F. Scott Fitzgerald is in the audience, and pens a double limerick sending up the evening [see notes to RF's January 24 letter to MacDonald]). In early February learns that Henry Holt will issue Thomas's *Poems* in 1917 (writes to Thomas's wife, Helen: "Isn't this rather pleasant news for the soldier?—damn his eyes. . . . I doubt if his country is going to need him. I suspect that all that is happening is some ingenuity of the Germans to bring the war to an early close without having to seem beaten. I don't know just what they are up to. I think, though, they are looking for a way to let go of the lion's tail. I begin to think we shall be seeing you all again before long"). Speaks twice in Springfield on March 7 and 8, addressing teachers' associations and high school students; appears also before an audience at the University of Chicago on March 14, and before the Chicago Women's Club the following day (while in town, visits Harriet Moody, widow of poet William Vaughn Moody, who becomes a close friend of the family). Deeply grieved by death of Edward Thomas, killed by an artillery shell in France on April 9 at the battle of Arras (writes a few weeks later to English critic Edward Garnett: "Edward Thomas was the only brother I ever had. I fail to see how we can have been so much to each other, he an Englishman and I an American and our first meeting put off till we were both in middle life. I hadn't a plan for the future that didn't include him"). On April 13 is back speaking at Wellesley College; on the eighteenth speaks at the Massachusetts Agricultural College (now the University of Massachusetts, Amherst). Generally supports the United States' entry into the war. In June, accepts offer to extend teaching appointment at Amherst; returns with family to Franconia for the summer. Meets and befriends painter James Chapin, who will do a portrait of RF for the frontispiece to a special reissue of *North of Boston* (published in 1919), and illustrate some of his poems. Lesley enters Wellesley College in the fall term, drawing for tuition on what remains of the annuity RF's paternal grandfather had bequeathed the family (throughout the academic year RF will advise and encourage her, in what are the first important family letters to survive). Returns with family to Amherst in early October to resume his professorship. On November 1 wins $100 prize given by *Poetry: A Magazine of Verse* for "Snow" (writes in gratitude to Harriet Monroe: "I was feeling blue when like a bolt from the blue came so much wealth and glory. I am the more sensible of it all that it is my first real prize in a long life"). Is chagrinned at Amy Lowell's remarks about his wife, Elinor, in the 1917 volume *Tendencies in Modern American Poetry* ("That's an unpardonable attempt to do her as the conventional helpmeet of genius," he writes to Untermeyer on 7 November. "What a cheap common unindividualized picture Amy makes of her"). Spends the Christmas holidays in Amherst.

1918 Meets Vachel Lindsay, Sara Teasdale, and James Oppenheim at party given by Untermeyer in New York on 21 February. Arranges (in February) for Wilbur Cross to publish, in *The Yale Review,* an essay on Edward Thomas by Amherst colleague and family friend George Whicher (it would appear in 1919). In March and April speaks again at the Browne and Nichols School in Cambridge, before heading west to speak in Chicago and Minneapolis. Awarded honorary master of arts degree by Amherst College in May; reappointed professor of English with teaching responsibilities limited to the first semester of each year (writes to Lesley on May 13: "Lot of things to tell and listen to, though except in an academic way I have had an adventureless year. Same with you—adventureless except in an academic way. But in that way Oh my! I beat you in one respect. I get an honorary M.A. from Amherst. Then it is fixed that I am to do 1/3 time for 1/2 pay (that is 1/2 of $5000). I haven't made myself particularly detested yet—that's all that means. Give me another year to get into trouble"). In June takes family with him to summer in Franconia (writes to George Whicher on the twenty-first: "Two weeks' farming has made me think better of teaching than I did when I left it at Commencement in the first stages of asthma but the last of agoraphobia. When you come right down to it such ills of teaching as man's ingratitude and benefits forgot are as nothing compared with the freezing of one bitter sky in mid-June"). In late June, sits for a portrait by James Chapin (in Franconia). Pleased when Lesley leaves college after her freshman year to do war work for the Curtiss Aeroplane and Motor Corporation in Marblehead, Massachusetts ("Your adventures are partly ours," RF would write her in October, "and we enjoy them with you but it seems to us that just your being free from college and exactly where you choose to be in an aeroplane factory ought to be nearly adventure enough for one year for all of us"). Enjoys discussing aviation with family friend Walter Hendricks, a flight instructor for the Army Air Corps. In September, daughter Irma falls ill with influenza, which will affect nearly every member of the household. During the great pandemic (which began in 1918) RF suffers severe case that lasts for months.

1919 Sick with influenza, RF writes Untermeyer on January 4: "Here it is as late as this (1919 A.D.), and I don't know whether or not I'm strong enough to write a letter yet. The only way I can tell that I haven't died and gone to heaven is by the fact that everything is just the same as it was on earth (all my family round me and all that) only worse, whereas, as I had been brought up in Swedenborgianism to believe, everything should be the same only better. Two possibilities remain: either I have died and gone to Hell or I haven't died. Therefore I havent died." Is pleased when Zenobia Camprudi Jiménez, wife of the poet Juan Ramon Jiménez, undertakes a translation into Spanish of *North of Boston*. Son Carol takes boxing lessons from retired heavyweight Tug Kennedy. Enjoys friendships of Amherst colleagues George Daniel Olds and Thomas Cushing Esty (both professors of mathematics), and Otto Manthey-Zorn. Attends the premiere performance of his play *A Way Out* given by Amherst students in Northampton, Massachusetts, on February 24. That same month Lesley, having left Wellesley the previous year, enrolls at Barnard College (where she studies with Franz Boas, among others). Elected president of the New England Poetry Club in February (though he is not present for the event, and resents being named in absentia). In March, with Carol's help, lays out a small apple orchard at his place in Franconia. During March visit to New York City, meets and becomes friends with poets Ridgely Torrence and Padraic Colum. Falls seriously ill again with influenza (writes to John Bartlett on April 7: "We have had five cases of influenza out of a possible six all of them bad enough but only one and that mine anywhere near fatal. Irma was sick in October and is not fully recovered yet"). Returns from Franconia to Amherst in September to take up his teaching duties. Continues to give talks and readings during fall semester at Amherst (appearing before the Poetry Society of Southern Vermont, the New England Poetry Club in Boston, at Wellesley College, and in Montclair, New Jersey, where he stays with family friend Frederic G. Melcher, coeditor of *Publishers' Weekly*). In December meets woodcut artist J. J. Lankes, beginning a decades-long friendship with the man who would illustrate his books (beginning in 1923, with *New Hampshire*).

1920 In February, resigns position at Amherst College over disagreements with President Meiklejohn, whom RF considers too morally permissive; hopes to devote more time to writing poetry (writes on February 2 to William Breed, chairman of the New York Amherst Alumni Association, which had invited the poet to speak: "I have decided to leave teaching and go back to farming and writing. Strangely enough, I was helped to this decision by your invitation. It was in turning over in my mind my subject chosen for the dinner that I came to the conclusion that I was too much out of sympathy with what the present administration seems bent on doing with this old New England college."). Holes up with his family in Franconia during the Great Winter Storm of 1920, which lasted from February 4 to 7: "I write this snowed in by the greatest snow-storm of all time with very little hope of ever mailing it," he says in a letter to Lesley, then at Barnard College. "We are running short of food fuel and water. How long we can last we are not experienced enough in rationing to calculate. (We could last longer of course if Marjorie would eat less.) Rescuing parties have been by with teams of six and eight horses, but these are merely local and neighborly: they are satisfied if they push the snow a little from our doors: they are not intended to establish communication with the outside world."

Acknowledgments

And feel a spirit kindred to my own;
So that henceforth I worked no more alone . . .
—"The Tuft of Flowers"

Many people, in many different places, have generously worked with us to bring *The Letters of Robert Frost* into existence. Kindred spirits in either a devoted admiration of Frost's poetry or an admirable devotion to the shared enterprise of primary scholarship—or both—they have allowed us to benefit from their time, effort, and expertise in collecting Frost's far-flung correspondence and preparing this scholarly edition. Listed below by the institutions with which they are affiliated are the many librarians, curators, archivists, executors, and technical support personnel whose invaluable assistance we wish with deep gratitude to acknowledge. Our work in locating and acquiring copies of the letters suitable for transcription would have been impossible without their help.

Our greatest debt, of course, is to the Estate of Robert Lee Frost for permission to publish the letters. To Peter A. Gilbert, Executor, we are additionally indebted for his unflagging enthusiasm, ready assistance, and expert advice. We are deeply grateful as well to the Frost family, in particular to Lesley Lee Francis and to John P. Cone, Jr., for their interest and encouragement. Patrick Alger not only granted us full access to his substantial Frost collection, but also provided welcome guidance in matters related to contemporary collectors and collecting. Jack Hagstrom generously shared his first-hand knowledge of the assembly and eventual disposition of early Frost collections. In locating materials and navigating the intricacies of catalogs and archives, we enjoyed the benefits of frequent consultation with John Lancaster and Daria D'Arienzo, librarian-archivists extraordinaire. Alex Gouttefangeas rendered an invaluable service in helping to voice-check final versions of all transcriptions. Among the special collections librarians listed below, we owe a special thanks for cordiality and patience to a few to whom we turned repeatedly, and often urgently, for help: Jay Satterfield at Dartmouth

College, Alice Staples at Plymouth State University, and Heather Riser at the University of Virginia.

Preparation of this edition of Frost's letters was supported by a National Endowment for the Humanities *We the People* grant (2006). Additional support was provided by the Japanese Ministry of Education (MEXT/JSPS) through two *kakenhi* grants (numbers 19520273 and 23520341). For this support, and for that of Edinboro University of Pennsylvania, Doshisha University, and Claremont McKenna College, we are grateful. In all matters related to the publication of this volume, we have depended upon the professionalism and patience of Lindsay Waters, Executive Editor for the Humanities at Harvard University Press, and Shanshan Wang, Editorial Assistant. We are thankful as well to Deborah Masi and Julie Erickson Hagen of Westchester Publishing Services for the efficient expertise with which our detailed and always evolving typescript was readied for publication.

Finally, we wish to acknowledge the personal as well as professional investment in the quality of this volume made by Robert Bernard Hass and Mark Scott. Scholar-poet and poet-scholar, each brought to a reading of the work as it developed a unique perspective, an extraordinary acuteness of perception, and a deep knowledge of Frost. Their contributions and corrections, small and great, have improved the quality of the annotations throughout and enhanced the arguments of the introductions such as they are. For their solicitous attention to the content of this volume, we thank them. For their solicitude in regard to the morale of the editors, we cannot thank them enough.

* * *

Estate of Edward Thomas
Richard Emeny, Executor; Rosemary Vellender

Estate of Laurence Binyon
Edmund Gray, Executor

Greenaway Family
David Greenaway III; Malcolm Greenaway

Makielski Family
Larry Elder, Elder Gallery

Agnes Scott College, McCain Library
Marianne Bradley, Library Administrative Coordinator

Amherst College Library
T. Michael Kelly, Head, Archives and Special Collections; Margaret R. Dakin, Archives & Special Collections Specialist

University of Arkansas Library
Tim Nutt, Head, Special Collections; Andrea Cantrell, Head, Research Services

Augustana College Library
Harry F. Thompson, Director of Research Collections and Publications, The Center for Western Studies

Bates College Library, Edmund Muskie Archives and Special Collections
Elaine Ardia, Archives Supervisor

Boston Athenaeum
Stanley Ellis Cushing, Curator of Rare Books and Manuscripts

Boston University Library, Howard Gotlieb Archival Research Center
Vita Paladino, Director; Ryan Hendrickson, Assistant Director for Manuscripts

Bowdoin College Library, George. J. Mitchell Depart of Special Collections and Archives
Richard Lindemann, Director; Daniel Hope, Assistant

Brandeis University Library, Robert D. Farber University Archives & Special Collections
Sarah Shoemaker, Special Collections Librarian

Brigham Young University Library
Russ Taylor, Supervisor of Reference Services

British Library (UK)
Rachel Foss, Curator of Modern Literary Manuscripts
Brown University, John Hay Library
Thomas Horrocks, Director of Special Collections; Timothy Engels, Senior Library Specialist

Bryn Mawr College Library
Marianne Hansen, Special Collections Librarian,

University of California at Berkeley, Bancroft Library
Elaine Tennant, Director; David Kessler, Archivist

University of California at Los Angeles Library
Thomas Hyry, Director, Library Special Collections; Robert D. Montoya, Operations Manager, Public Services Division

University of California at Santa Barbara Library
David Seubert, Head of Special Collections; Yolanda Blue, Special Collections Librarian

Cambridge University (UK), King's College Archives
Patricia McGuire, Archivist

Cardiff University (UK) Library
Peter Keelan, Head of Special Collections & Archives

University of Chicago Library, Special Collections Research Center
Daniel Meyer, Director, Special Collections Research Center, University Archivist, University of Chicago Library; Christine Colburn, Reader Services Manager

Coe College, Stewart Memorial Library
Jill Jack, Head of Reference; Sara Pitcher, Archives Assistant

Columbia University Library
Michael Ryan, Curator of Manuscripts, Rare Books and Manuscript Library, Columbia University; Tara C. Craig, Reference Services Supervisor

Connecticut College Library, Linda Lear Center for Special Collections and Archives
Benjamin Panciera, Director of Special Collections

Dartmouth College Library
Jay Satterfield, Special Collections Librarian

Derry (NH) Museum of History
Richard Holmes, Director and Town Historian

Duke University, David M. Rubenstein Rare Book & Manuscript Library
Naomi Nelson, Director; David Strader, Library Assistant

Emory University Library
Kathy Shoemaker, Research Services Associate Archivist

University of Florida, George A. Smathers Library
Carl Van Ness, Curator of Manuscripts and Archives

Franconia Heritage Museum
Barbara Holt

George Washington University Library
Christopher Walker, Archives and Manuscript Specialist

Georgetown University Library
Nicholas Scheetz, Manuscripts Librarian; Scott S. Taylor, Manuscripts Processor

University of Georgia, Hargrett Library
Mary Linnemann, Digital Imaging Coordinator

Gloucestershire (UK) Archives
Mick Heath, Archives Assistant, Gloucestershire Archives

Harvard University, Houghton Library
Leslie Morris, Curator of Modern Books and Manuscripts, Houghton Library, Harvard University; Heather G. Cole, Assistant Curator; Emilie L. Hardman, Public Services Assistant; Pamela Madsen, Curatorial Assistant, Harvard Theatre Collection

Harvard University, Schlesinger Library, Radcliffe Institute for Advanced Study
Sarah Hutcheon, Reference Librarian

Haverford College Library
Diana Franzusoff Peterson, Manuscripts Librarian and College Archivist

HistoryMiami Archives and Research Center
Dawn Hugh, Archives Manager

Hofstra University Library
Geri Solomon, Assistant Dean of Special Collections

Huntington Library
Sara S. (Sue) Hodson, Curator, Literary Manuscripts

University of Illinois Library
Chatham Ewing, Curator of Special Collections

Indiana University Library, Ruth Lilly Special Collections and Archives
Joel Silver, Director; Rebecca Cape, [former] Head of Reference and Public Services

Johns Hopkins University Library, Special Collections and Archives
Gabrielle Dean, Curator of Modern Literary Rare Books and Manuscripts; Kelly Betts, Assistant Curator of Manuscripts

Jones Library
Tevis Kimball, Curator, Special Collections; Kate Boyle, Assistant Curator

Library of Congress
Jeffrey M. Flannery, Head, Reference & Reader Services Section, Manuscript Division

Manchester (NH) Historic Association
Ben Baker, Library Assistant

University of Maryland Library
Beth (Ruth M.) Alvarez, Curator of Literary Manuscripts

Massachusetts Historical Society
Tracy Potter, Assistant Reference Librarian

Miami (OH) University Library, Walter Havighurst Special Collections
Elizabeth Brice, Assistant Dean for Technical Services & Head, Special Collections and Archives; Janet Stuckey, former Head, Special Collections

University of Miami, Otto G. Richter Library
Cristina Favretto, Head of Special Collections; Laura Capell, Research Services Assistant; Cory Czajkowski, Sr. Library Assistant

University of Michigan Library
Martha O'Hara Conway, Director, Special Collections; Nancy Bartlett, Head, University Archives and Records; Malgosia Myc, Assistant Reference Archivist

Middlebury College Library
Andrew Wentink, Curator, Special Collections & Archives

Milton Academy
Diane Pierce-Williams, Staff Assistant, Cox Library

University of Minnesota Archives, Elmer L. Andersen Library
Erin George, Assistant Archivist

University of Montana-Missoula, Mansfield Library
Donna McCrea, Head of Archives & Special Collections; Steve Bingo, Adjunct Archivist; Mark Fritch, Archives Photo Specialist

The Morgan Library and Museum
Declan Kiely, Curator and Department Head, Literary and Historical Manuscripts

The Newberry Library
Alison Hinderliter, Manuscripts and Archives Librarian

University of New Hampshire Library, Douglas and Helena Milne Special Collections and Archives
Roland Goodbody, Manuscripts Curator; Nancy Mason, Special Collections Assistant

New York Public Library
Isaac Gewirtz, Curator, Henry W. and Albert A. Berg Collection of English and American Literature; Laura Ruttum, Reference Archivist; Laura Slezak Karas, Archivist

New York University, The Fales Library and Special Collections
T. Michael Kelly, (former) Curator of Books; Kelsi Evans, Assistant

State University of New York at Buffalo
Michael Basinski, Curator, The Poetry Collection

University of North Carolina Library
Walter C. (Tim) West, Curator of Manuscripts/Director of the Southern Historical Collection; Robin Davies Chen, Assistant Manuscripts Reference Librarian

Northwestern University Library
Kevin B. Leonard, University Archivist; Janet C. Olson, Assistant Archivist

Ohio State University Library
Rebecca Jewett, Assistant Curator, Rare Books & Manuscripts

University of Pennsylvania, Rare Book and Manuscript Library
Nancy Shawcross, Curator of Manuscripts
Pennsylvania State University Library
Sandra Stelts, Curator of Rare Books and Manuscripts

Phillips Academy Andover
Ruth Quattlebaum, (former) Academy Archivist

Phillips Exeter Academy
Edouard L. Desrochers, Assistant Librarian & Academy Archivist

Pinkerton Academy
Anne Massa Parker, Director of Alumni Relations; Laura Burnham, Assistant Librarian

University of Pittsburgh Library System
Charles E. Aston, Jr., Curator, Rare Books, Prints, & Exhibits, Special Collections Department

Plymouth State University Library
Alice P. Staples, Archives/Special Collections Librarian; Susan Jarosz, Archives Assistant

Princeton University, Firestone Library
Don C. Skemer, Curator of Manuscripts; AnnaLee Pauls, Special Collections Assistant III

Rollins College, Olin Library
Wenxian Zhang, Head of Archives & Special Collections

St. Lawrence University
Mark McMurray, Curator of Special Collections & University Archivist; Darlene Leonard, (former) Archives Assistant

South Carolina Historical Society
Mary Jo Fairchild, Senior Archivist

University of Southern California, Doheny Memorial Library
Melinda Hayes, Head, Special Collections; Claude Zachary, University Archivist & Manuscript Librarian

Southern Illinois University at Edwardsville Library
Stephen Kerber, University Archivist and Special Collections Librarian

Stanford University Library
Polly Armstrong, [former] Public Services Manager, Special Collections and University Archives

Tennessee State Library and Archives
Jay Richiuso, Assistant Director for Manuscripts Services

University of Texas at Austin, Harry Ransom Center
Rick Watson, Head of Reference Services; Elspeth Healey, Public Services Intern

University of Toledo, Ward M. Canaday Center for Special Collections
Kimberly Brownlee, Manuscripts Librarian and Assistant University Archivist

Trinity College, Watkinson Library
Richard J. Ring, Head Curator

Tufts University Library
Laura Cutter, Archives and Research Assistant

University of Tulsa, McFarlin Library
Marc Carlson, Librarian of Special Collections and University Archives; Kristen Leatherwood Marangoni, [former] Assistant
University College Dublin (IE)
Seamus Helferty, Principal Archivist

University of Virginia, Albert and Shirley Small Special Collections Library
Molly Schwartzburg, Curator; Heather Riser, Head, Reference and Research Services; Christina Deane, Head, Digitization Services

Vassar College Library, Catherine Pelton Durrell Archives and Special Collections
Dean M. Rogers, Special Collections Assistant

Vermont Historical Society
Paul Carnahan, Librarian

Wellesley College, Margaret Clap Library
Ruth R. Rogers, Special Collections Librarian; Mariana S. Oller, Special Collections Research and Instruction Specialist

University of Wisconsin—La Crosse, Murphy Library
Laura M. Godden, Librarian; Megan Gosse, Library Assistant, Special Collections

Wisconsin Historical Society
Harry Miller, Reference Archivist

Yale University, Beinecke Library
Nancy Kuhl, Curator, Poetry, Yale Collection of American Literature

---

Eldred's Auction Gallery
Deborah Gaile Clemence

Quill & Brush
Beth Fisher

Index